Texts in Computer Science

Series Editors:
David Gries
Fred B. Schneider

For other titles published in this series, go to
http://www.springer.com/series/3191

Peter Revesz

Introduction to Databases

From Biological to Spatio-Temporal

 Springer

Prof. Peter Revesz
University of Nebraska-Lincoln
Dept. Computer Science & Engineering
358 Avery Hall
Lincoln NE 68588
USA
revesz@cse.unl.edu

Series Editors
David Gries
Department of Computer Science
Upson Hall
Cornell University
Ithaca, NY 14853-7501
USA

Fried. B. Schneider
Department of Computer Science
Upson Hall
Cornell University
Ithaca, NY 14853-7501
USA

ISSN 1868-0941   e-ISSN 1868-095X
ISBN 978-1-84996-094-6   ISBN 978-1-84996-095-3 (eBook)
DOI 10.1007/978-1-84996-095-3
Springer London Heidelberg Dordrecht New York

British Library Cataloguing in Publication Data
A catalogue record for this book is available from the British Library

Library of Congress Control Number: 2009942531

Cover design: SPi Publisher Services

Printed on acid-free paper

Springer is part of Springer Science+Business Media (www.springer.com)

In memory of
Paris C. Kanellakis
and
Alberto O. Mendelzon

I believe that there are a collection of planet-threatening problems, such as climate change and ozone depletion, that only scientists are in a position to solve. Hence, the sorry state of DBMS support...for this class of users is very troubling.

—Michael Stonebraker (2009), *CACM, 52(5):11.*

Preface

Introduced forty years ago, relational databases proved unusually successful and durable. However, relational database systems were not designed
for modern applications and computers. As a result, specialized database
systems now proliferate trying to capture various pieces of the database
market. Database research is pulled into different directions, and specialized database conferences are created. Yet the current chaos in databases
is likely only temporary because every technology, including databases,
becomes standardized over time.

The history of databases shows periods of chaos followed by periods of
dominant technologies. For example, in the early days of computing, users
stored their data in text files in any format and organization they wanted.
These early days were followed by information retrieval systems, which
required some structure for text documents, such as a title, authors, and
a publisher. The information retrieval systems were followed by database
systems, which added even more structure to the data and made querying
easier.

In the late 1990s, the emergence of the Internet brought a period of
relative chaos and interest in unstructured and "semistructured data" as it
was envisioned that every webpage would be like a page in a book. However,
with the growing maturity of the Internet, the interest in structured data
was regained because the most popular websites are, in fact, based on
databases. The question is not whether future data stores need structure
but what structure they need.

Today we see another period of relative chaos as specialized geographic,
moving objects, biological, and other types of databases are unable to communicate with each other in spite of the need of many advanced applications. Database interoperability and data integration become important
challenges in the current environment.

What are possible solutions to the above challenges? There are two observations that may be made. First, instead of expecting a radical movement away from relational data, future databases will probably provide various extensions of relational databases. Second, constraint databases, which are an extension of relational databases, appear to be suitable as a common standard for the various types of databases. In fact, geographic information systems sometimes convert internally their "vector data" into a constraint data to evaluate certain queries.

Purpose and Goals

This textbook provides comprehensive coverage of databases. The primary audience of the book is undergraduate computer science and non-computer science students with no or little prior exposure to databases. For them the extensive set of exercises at the end of each chapter will be useful. The text and the exercises assume as prerequisite only basic discrete mathematics, linear algebra, and programming knowledge. Many database experts will also find the bibliographic notes after each chapter a valuable reference for further reading. For both students and database experts the MLPQ constraint-relational database system is suggested for use. The MLPQ system, slides, solutions (for instructors), and other course aid is available free from the author's web page: `http://cse.unl.edu/~revesz`

Topics Coverage and Organization

This book has three parts:

- **Part I: Data and Queries:** The first part of the book defines databases in general (Chapter 1), describes eleven different types of databases (Chapters 2-12), and presents the MLPQ and the DISCO database systems (Chapters 13-14) that implement several different types of databases. The first part of the book is enough to start using a database system for simple applications.

- **Part II: Database Design and Applications:** The second part of the book describes database design (Chapter 15) and discusses the following advanced database application issues: database interoperability, which allows translating data from one database to another database (Chapter 16), data integration, which allows combining data from different sources (Chapter 17), interpolation and approximation, which allows a simple representation of complex data (Chapter 18), and prediction and data mining, which allows the discovery of new information (Chapter 19). The second part of the book enables the readers to develop more complex and rewarding database applications.

- **Part III: Query Evaluation, Safety, and Verification:** The third part of the book describes various issues related to the evaluation of database queries. The topics include indexing methods, which enable fast search in database tables (Chapter 20), data visualization, which is essential for a convenient interaction with the database system (Chapter 21), the safety of queries, that is, whether they are guaranteed to be evaluated precisely or approximately, or may enter an infinite loop and not terminate (Chapter 22), general evaluation algorithms (Chapter 23), the efficient implementation of the evaluation algorithms (Chapter 24), the complexity of the evaluation of different types of queries (Chapter 25). Computer software written in many programming languages can be translated into database queries. Software verification can be aided by translating the software to database queries, which are evaluated approximately by the above query evaluation algorithms (Chapter 26). The third part of the book gives students a deeper understanding and appreciation of the inside of database systems. It also enables students to read further scientific literature and begin research projects in database systems.

Figure 1 shows a dependency diagram of the chapters of the book. A special strength of the book is that it allows a flexible course design aided by the dependency diagram. We suggest the following courses.

- **Basic introductory course:** A basic introductory course, which is focused on a survey of various types of databases, would cover Chapters 1, 2, 3, and 4, any subset of Chapters 5-12, and the MLPQ system in Chapter 13. Such an introductory course would be suitable even for non-computer science majors. The topics could be easily fitted to the interest of the students. For example, geography majors may be interested in Chapters 5-8, while biology majors in Chapters 10-11. All of these students can be given a hands-on experience with a database system using the exercises in Chapter 13.

- **Enhanced introductory course:** An enhanced introductory course can add to the basic introductory course various applications-oriented chapters from the second part of the book (Chapters 15-19). These chapters enable more serious applications. For example, Chapter 18 discusses the triangulated irregular network (TIN) representation of surface data, which is important for geographic applications and enhances the material in Chapter 6. While Chapter 6 enables students to understand and use given geographic databases, Chapter 18 enables students to build geographic databases from measurement data. Many students may already have such measurement data from other projects outside of the database class.

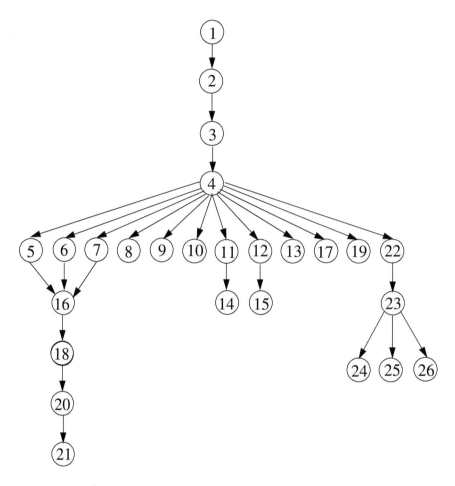

Figure 1: A dependency diagram of the chapters.

- **Advanced course:** The textbook also allows several types of advanced courses. An advanced course, focused on query evaluation, may cover interoperability (Chapter 16), indexing (Chapter 20), safety (Chapter 22), general evaluation algorithms (Chapter 23), and implementation methods (Chapter 24). These chapters already allow students to implement either individually or in group projects various simple query processors or propotype database systems. The coverage of the rest of the chapters depends on the interest of the students. Computer graphics students may study Chapter 21, theoretical computer science students may study Chapter 25, and software engineering students may study Chapter 26.

Acknowledgments

I'd like to thank for reviewing various parts of the book Berthe Choueiry, Manolis Koubarakis, Franz Mora, French Roy, and James Van Etten. I'd like to thank for introducing me to the database area the late Paris Kanellakis, my Ph.D. thesis advisor at Brown University, and the late Alberto Mendelzon, my postdoctoral advisor at the University of Toronto. I thank the following coauthors on books, journal articles or conference papers that contributed to the material in this book and from whom I learned much: András Benczur, Jan Chomicki, Floris Geerts, Sofie Haessevoets, Mark Griep, Gosta Grahne, Bart Kuijpers, Gabriel Kuper, Ram Narayanan, Agnes Novak, Robert Powers, James Pustejovsky, Raghu Ramakrishnan, Divesh Srivastava, Paolo Terenziani, and Jan Van den Bussche.

I would like to thank my former Ph.D. students for their comments on the text and other contributions to our database research group: Scot Anderson (Southern Adventist University), Mengchu Cai (IBM, DB2 Group), Rui Chen, Yi Chen, Ying Deng, Jun Gao (University of the Ozarks), Lixin Li (Georgia Southern University), Min Ouyang, Thomas Triplet (Concordia University), and Shasha Wu (Spring Arbor University). In addition, the following M.S. students also contributed significantly to the database research group: Brian Boon, Jo-Hag Byon, Vijay Eadala, Pradeep Gundavarapu, Pradip Kanjamala, Yiming Li, Yuguo Liu, Prashanth Nandavanam, Andrew Salamon, Yonghui Wang, and Lei Zhang.

The research, which forms several chapters of this book, was supported in part by the U.S. National Science Foundation under grants IRI-9625055, IRI-9632871, and EIA-0091530, by a NASA grant, by a Gallup Research Professorship, by an Alexander von Humboldt Research Fellowship, and by a J. William Fulbright Scholarship. The latter two awards enabled research leaves from the University of Nebraska-Lincoln to the Max Planck Institut für Informatik and the University of Athens, respectively. Andreas Podelski at the former and Manolis Koubarakis at the latter place served as great hosts during my visits.

I am grateful to the editors at Springer-Verlag, especially Wayne Wheeler, Senior Editor for Computer Science, and Simon Rees, Senior Editorial Assistant, for their careful editing and attention to several details in the production of the book.

Finally, I would like to thank Lilla, my wife, and our children, Sophie, Claire, and Gregory, for their enthusiasm and patience during the writing of this book.

Peter Revesz

Lincoln, Nebraska, USA

July 2009

Contents

Preface   vii

1 Data Models, Queries, Evaluation   **1**
   1.1   Data Models   1
   1.2   Queries   4
   1.3   Evaluation   5

2 Propositional Databases   **7**
   2.1   Propositional Data Model   7
   2.2   Implication Queries   10
   2.3   Evaluation   10
   2.4   Limitations   12

3 Relational Databases   **15**
   3.1   Relational Data Model   15
   3.2   Relational Algebra Queries   18
   3.3   SQL Queries   24
   3.4   Evaluation   34

4 Constraint Databases   **43**
   4.1   Infinite Relational Data Model   43
   4.2   Relational Algebra Queries   46
   4.3   SQL Queries   51
   4.4   Evaluation   55

5 Temporal Databases   **67**
    5.1   Allen's Relations   67
    5.2   Temporal Data Models   70
    5.3   Indefinite Temporal Data Model   71
    5.4   Temporal Database Queries   73

6 Geographic Databases   **81**
    6.1   Rectangles Data Model   82
    6.2   Vector Data Model   84
    6.3   Worboys' Data Model   86
    6.4   Constraint Data Model   87
    6.5   Topological Data Models   89
    6.6   Geographic Queries   91

7 Moving Objects Databases   **111**
    7.1   Moving Points Data Model   112
    7.2   Parametric Circles Data Model   112
    7.3   Parametric Rectangles Data Model   113
    7.4   Parametric Worboys Data Model   115
    7.5   Periodic Parametric Data Models   115
    7.6   Geometric Transformation Data Models   120
    7.7   Moving Objects Queries   122

8 Image Databases   **137**
    8.1   Affine Invariance   138
    8.2   Affine-Invariant Similarity Measures   140
    8.3   The Color Ratios Similarity Measure   141
    8.4   Similarity of Patterned Objects   143

9 Constraint Objects Databases   **153**
    9.1   The Constraint Objects Data Model   153
    9.2   Closed, Open, and Possible Worlds   154
    9.3   Syntax   156
    9.4   Semantics   161
    9.5   Projection Queries   167
    9.6   Evaluation of Refinement Queries   168
    9.7   Constraint XML   168

10 Genome Databases   **179**
    10.1 Biological Basics   179
    10.2 The Genome Map Assembly Problem   182
    10.3 Sequence Similarity   190
    10.4 Structure Similarity   198

11 Set Databases   **205**
   11.1 Syllogisms   205
   11.2 Boolean Algebras of Sets   219
   11.3 Relations with Sets   230

12 Constraint Deductive Databases   **235**
   12.1 Syntax   235
   12.2 Datalog with Sets   240
   12.3 Semantics   246
   12.4 Datalog with Aggregation and Negation   254

13 The MLPQ System   **261**
   13.1 The MLPQ System Architecture   262
   13.2 Relational Databases   264
   13.3 Geographic Databases   275
   13.4 Moving Objects Databases   286
   13.5 Topological Databases   302
   13.6 Recursive Queries   307
   13.7 Linear Programming   315
   13.8 Web Accessible Applications   316

14 The DISCO System   **335**
   14.1 DISCO Queries   335
   14.2 Implementation   339
   14.3 Using the DISCO System   346
   14.4 Extensibility of the DISCO System   348

15 Database Design   **351**
   15.1 Entity Relationship Diagrams   351
   15.2 Constraint Automata   361

16 Interoperability   **385**
   16.1 Data Interoperability   385
   16.2 Query Interoperability   402
   16.3 Other Types of Interoperability   410

17 Data Integration   **417**
   17.1 Decision Trees   417
   17.2 Support Vector Machines   421
   17.3 Classification Integration   421
   17.4 The Reclassification Problem   425
   17.5 Wrappers   426
   17.6 Data Fusion   430
   17.7 Security   430

18 Interpolation and Approximation   **435**
  18.1 Linear Interpolation   436
  18.2 Triangulated Irregular Networks   436
  18.3 Shape Functions   443
  18.4 Spatiotemporal Interpolation   449
  18.5 Inverse Distance Weighting   457
  18.6 Piecewise Linear Approximation   460

19 Prediction and Data Mining   **485**
  19.1 Prediction   485
  19.2 Data Mining   492
  19.3 Model-Based Diagnosis   495

20 Indexing   **501**
  20.1 Minimum Bounding Parametric Rectangles   502
  20.2 The Parametric R-Tree Index Structure   508
  20.3 Indexing Constraint Databases   515
  20.4 The MaxCount Operator   516

21 Data Visualization   **537**
  21.1 Isometric Color Bands   538
  21.2 Value-by-Area Cartogram   542
  21.3 Animation of Moving Objects   548

22 Safe Query Languages   **555**
  22.1 Safety Levels   555
  22.2 Restriction   558
  22.3 Safe Aggregation and Negation Queries   559
  22.4 Safe Refinement and Projection Queries   560
  22.5 Certification   560

23 Evaluation of Queries   **571**
  23.1 Quantifier Elimination and Satisfiability   572
  23.2 Evaluation of Relational Algebra Queries   590
  23.3 Evaluation of SQL Queries   594
  23.4 Evaluation of Datalog Queries   595
  23.5 Constraint Logic Programming   614

24 Implementation Methods   **621**
  24.1 Evaluation with Gap-Graphs   621
  24.2 Evaluation with Matrices   628
  24.3 Boolean Constraints   637
  24.4 Optimization of Relational Algebra   641

25 Computational Complexity   **655**
 25.1 Turing Machines 655
 25.2 Complexity Classes 659
 25.3 Complexity of Datalog 660
 25.4 Complexity of Relational Algebra 667

26 Software Verification   **685**
 26.1 Addition-Bound Matrices 685
 26.2 Abstract Interpretation 689
 26.3 Software Verification using MLPQ 695

Bibliography   **701**

Index   **739**

Colour Plate Section   **745**

1

Data Models, Queries, Evaluation

Storing data is not the main purpose of databases. The Internet is a data store but not a database. Library information systems are also data stores but not databases. Both Web browsers and library information systems can be queried using key words or phrases, but database queries are different. While Web browers always return only existing webpages, database queries can create new information that is not stored in the database, although it is logically implied by the stored data. Retrieving stored data is relatively easy. To dicover new knowledge is an enduring challenge. The main purpose of databases is to aid knowledge discovery. Even the simplest database system described in this book can aid in deriving new information that did not exist before.

Section 1.1 gives some example data that need to be stored in databases. Many details of the stored data are uninteresting for the users. Section 1.2 describes some essential features of database queries. Section 1.3 describes query evaluation within database systems.

1.1 Data Models

Many applications require the simultaneous use of several different types of data, such as the following:

Chart: Charts show continuous curves or discrete bars and are used to visually illustrate the relationship between two variables. For example, the chart in Figure 1.1 shows the relationship between total income on the x-axis and tax due on the y-axis.

P. Revesz, *Introduction to Databases: From Biological to Spatio-Temporal*,
Texts in Computer Science, DOI 10.1007/978-1-84996-095-3_1,
© Springer-Verlag London Limited 2010

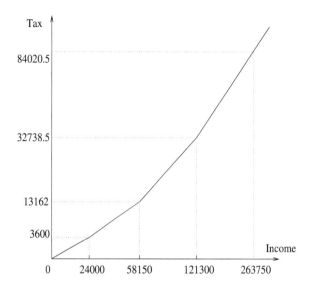

Figure 1.1: Income vs. tax chart.

Graph: Graphs are defined by nodes and edges between pairs of nodes. The nodes and the edges can be labeled or unlabeled. The edges can be directed or undirected. For example, the graph in Figure 6.6 represents the fastest possible travel times between pairs of cities in the midwest United States.

Map: The maps are commonly used to present geographic data, that is, data concerning phenomena occurring on the surface of the earth. Chapter 6 describes geographic databases.

Drawing: By drawings we mean simple black-and-white sketches of pictures. An example drawing of a bird is shown in Figure 1.1.

Video: For moving objects the best presentation is some form of video. This is especially important for *spatio-temporal* objects with a shape that is a spatial extent in either two or three dimensions and that keeps changing over time.

Sound: Sound is an important type of sensory information. Sound, such as human speech, frequently accompanies videos, but sound can be important in itself. For example, music is an especially sought after type of data.

The above list of different types of data can be continued without end. There are many specialized types of data that are important to particular

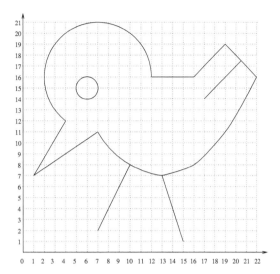

Figure 1.2: A bird.

organizations or scientific and engineering communities. Often many different types of data need to be used simultaneously.

Data Abstraction

All good products provide some abstraction for the users. For example, people can drive a car without knowing how its engine works. For the task of driving cars the details of the working of the engine are unimportant.

Every day and every way we receive millions of pieces of data in a bewildering range of forms. *Data abstraction* allows people to forget about some details of the data that may be unimportant to them. Good database systems provide an abstract view of the actual data stored in the computer. Data abstraction means a usable and attractive *data model*.

Data abstraction is actually a hierarchy of increasingly more abstract representations of the data because different groups of people need to view the data differently. For example, users who would like to receive some help in navigating from one location of a town to another location may want to see only a road map with a colored path connecting the two locations. Application programmers who write queries of the database may need to know more details about the database.

There are several principles of good data abstraction. First, a good data abstraction is functional. That is, a good data abstraction facilitates the tasks that need to be performed with the data. Different data abstractions may be needed for differrent tasks. A data abstraction that is good for one task may not be good for another task. Second, a good data abstraction is attractive, that is, it is pleasant and convenient to use. An attractive data abstraction takes into account users' preferences for color and layout, size of letters, readability, and so on. Both functionality and attractiveness are general goals in using computers and are studied in the areas of *human-computer interaction* and *computer visualization*. However, a good data abstraction is only partly a science; it remains partly an art, requiring creativity.

1.2 Queries

Database queries have the following special features.

Derive new information: What does it mean to derive something that is not in the database? As an example, try to find the most populous city in Nebraska. That can be done easily by typing into a Web browser the phrases "most populous city" and "Nebraska." The Web browser would retrieve webpages related to Omaha, which is the correct answer. If we try "second most populous city" or "third most populous city," then we still get some correct answers among an increasing number of irrelevant webpages. However, if we try "fourth most populous city," we get only junk. Apparently, nobody bothered to create a webpage for the fourth most populous city in Nebraska – at least not a webpage that says it is the fourth most populous city.

There are many other queries that would be difficult to answer by searching the Web. For example, in terms of population what is the rank of the town or city in the state or country that you live in? That is an even harder query because if you just type in the name of the city, then you could get many webpages that do not contain an asnwer to your query. You may guess that it is "fourth most populous" and type that into the Web browser together with the name of your town. You may be lucky and find a webpage that matches your key phrases, enabling you to verify that you live in the fourth most populous city. If you are unlucky, then you have to guess repeatedly until you succeed.

Many database queries in business are concerned with accounting. The queries summarize the data by adding up various numbers related to purchases, sales, payroll or prices for a particular customer or groups of customers and during a specified period of time. The answers to these queries do not exist, rather they are freshly calculated.

Ad hoc or unplanned: Most database users do know ahead the specific queries that will be asked. The queries depend on the circumstances like which customer is interested in what kind of product. Since they are not known ahead, these queries are called *ad hoc* queries.

High-level, declarative: If we knew ahead the queries, then we could write them in almost any programming language and provide them as menu options. That is the way people interact with, for instance, ATM machines. More sophisticated interaction requires a flexible yet high-level query language because the unplanned problems need to be expressed as ad-hoc database queries in a fast and easy way. Declarative database languages allow the database users to focus on specifying what is needed, not on how to calculate the information. These declarative languages are usually based on various kinds of mathematical logic.

1.3   Evaluation

Each database system contains a data store, both external storage and main memory storage, a user interface that allows interaction with users, such as entering queries and viewing answers, and a query processor. The query processor evaluates the queries and returns them to the users. Many of the query processors are greatly advanced software products written by database software developers. Query processors are essential for database systems. However, in general the users are not concerned with the exact operations of the query processor, like they are not concerned about the exact operations of a Web browser while surfing the Internet. Nevertheless, a serious study and appreciation of databases requires some understanding of the query evaluation algorithms. Therefore this book describes many query evaluation methods. For some evaluation methods, we give enough details that the readers could implement them, while for some other methods, we present only a high-level outline. It is possible for readers to skip these sections.

Bibliographic Notes

Data abstraction emerged as a major issue in database systems in the 1970s when relational databases were advocated by Edgar F. Codd and others largely on the ground that relational databases provide a more abstact view of the data than network databases provide. Initially, these arguments were countered by hierarchical and network database supporters by pointing out the higher computational requirements of relational database systems. To many respectable researchers it seemed unlikely that relational databases would ever become practical. Nevertheless, as explored in the following chapters, with the rapid advance of computer science, the initial computer memory and computational speed problems were mostly overcome. Relational database systems are challenged today only by truly huge relational data, and work on efficient query processing for huge relational databases is still an ongoing research. However, the more important future challenge is the development of database systems that are able to handle non-traditional data.

Exercises

1. Explain what you would expect from your dream database. What kind of data would you like to be able to store? What type of operations wou would like to have the database system provide for you? If you currently use a database system, explain how it may fall short of your expectations.

2

Propositional Databases

Most subjects try to teach a specific collection of things that are true, based primarily on observations. Logic is a very different subject. Logic is the branch of mathematics that is concerned with teaching not *what* facts are true but teaching *how* we can use the facts that we already know to be true, to deduce new ones by pure rational thinking. In fact, logic is a study of correct methods of thinking.

Several types of mathematical logic can be useful as a database because they have the two essential elements of databases. First, logic has a database, which is just the set of facts assumed to be true. Second, logic can derive new information by using the set of facts and axioms. A typical type of query from a logic database is to find out whether a statement is true or false. Only logics where such queries can be evaluated efficiently are interesting for database use. This chapter presents *propositional logic* from the perspective of databases.

Section 2.1 describes the propositional data model. Section 2.2 presents propositional queries. Section 2.3 outlines two different query evaluation methods. Section 2.4 discusses some of the limitations of propositional logic.

2.1 Propositional Data Model

Most readers have learned something about propositional logic. However, they probably did not learn propositional logic form a database perspective. Hence the following review may be refreshing for them too. First we give some basic definitions.

P. Revesz, *Introduction to Databases: From Biological to Spatio-Temporal*,
Texts in Computer Science, DOI 10.1007/978-1-84996-095-3_2,
© Springer-Verlag London Limited 2010

Definition 2.1.1 A *proposition* is a declarative sentence that is either true or false but not both. A proposition has *truth value* true, denoted T, if it is true, and false, denoted F, if it is false.

If p and q are existing propositions, then the following are also propositions:

1. The *negation* of p, denoted by $\bar{p}$, meaning that p is false.

2. The *conjunction* of p and q, denoted as $p \wedge q$, meaning that both p and q are true.

3. The *disjunction* of p and q, denoted as $p \vee q$, meaning that at least one of p and q is true. The *disjunction* is also called an *inclusive or*.

4. The *implication* of q by p, denoted as $p \rightarrow q$, meaning that if p is true, then q is true. The *implication* is also called a *conditional statement*.

5. The *biconditional* of p by q, denoted as $p \leftrightarrow q$, meaning that p and q have the same truth values. A biconditional is also called an *if and only if* statement.

We call ‾ the *negation operator* and $\wedge, \vee, \rightarrow$, and $\leftrightarrow$ the *connectives*. A proposition with the negation operator or a connective is called a *compound proposition*. A proposition that is not compound is a *simple proposition*.

Example 2.1.1 Let p and q be the propositions

  s : Tom studies.
  t : Tom passes the test.

Suppose that we learn the following facts

  (a) If Tom studies, then he will pass the test.
  (b) Tom does not pass the test.

The above can be written as the following compound propositions in terms of s and t:

  (a) $s \rightarrow t$.
  (b) $\bar{t}$.

Using parenthesis, to specify the order in which logical operators apply, we can write arbitrarily large compound propositions. When parenthesis are omitted, we assume that negation has the highest precedence, followed by conjunctions, disjunctions, implications, and biconditionals.

Definition 2.1.2 A *propositional database* is a proposition that is assumed to be true.

Example 2.1.2 Since both propositions (a) and (b) of Example 2.1.1 are true, their conjunction is also true. Hence we can describe our knowledge in the following propositional database:

$D: (s \rightarrow t) \wedge \overline{t}.$

A *truth table* lists all possible combinations of the truth values of the simple and compound propositions under discussion. Each possible combination of truth values of the simple propostions under discussion is a *truth assignment*.

For example, the following is a truth table for the simple propositions p and q and the compound propositions in Definition 2.1.1.

p	q	$\overline{p}$	$p \wedge q$	$p \vee q$	$p \rightarrow q$	$p \leftrightarrow q$
T	T	F	T	T	T	T
T	F	F	F	T	F	F
F	T	T	F	T	T	F
F	F	T	F	F	T	T

Similarly, below is a truth table for $(s \rightarrow t) \wedge \overline{t}$, where for convenience we added some extra columns for intermediate results.

s	t	$s \rightarrow t$	$\overline{t}$	$(s \rightarrow t) \wedge \overline{t}$
T	T	T	F	F
T	F	F	T	F
F	T	T	F	F
F	F	T	T	T

Definition 2.1.3 The *model* of a proposition p, denoted $M(p)$ is the set of all truth assignments that make p true.

For example, $M(p \vee q)$ is the following:

p	q
T	T
T	F
F	T

Similarly, $M((s \rightarrow t) \wedge (\overline{t}))$ is the following:

s	t
F	F

A *tautology* is a compound proposition that is true for each truth assignment of the simple propositions in it. Propositions p and q are *logically equivalent* if $p \leftrightarrow q$ is a tautology.

2.2   Implication Queries

Definition 2.2.1 A *propositional logic query q* is a proposition that needs to be tested whether it is true or false given a database D. That is, answering the propositional database query requires us to test whether $D \rightarrow q$ is a tautology.

Example 2.2.1 Let D be the database in Example 2.1.2. A possible query q may be to test whether the database implies that "Tom does not study." Note that q can be expressed as

q: $\bar{s}$.

Hence we need to test whether $((s \rightarrow t) \wedge \bar{t}) \rightarrow \bar{s}$ is a tautology.

2.3   Evaluation

Next we describe a query processor that can evaluate propositional logic queries. It will be based on the following theorem.

Theorem 2.3.1 For any compound proposition p, we can test whether p is a tautology.

Proof: The truth table method can be used to test whether any given compound proposition is a tautology. Suppose we have n simple propositions that occur in the compound propostion. Then the truth table method creates a table with 2^n rows, where in each row the single propositions are assigned a different combination of truth values. The table also has n columns for the single propositions, and a column for p. Then for each row, assuming the assignment in the row, we evaluate p. The proposition p is a tautology if and only if the value of p is true in each column.   ■

Example 2.3.1 Continuing Example 2.2.1, the following truth table shows that $((s \rightarrow t) \wedge \bar{t}) \rightarrow \bar{s}$ is a tautology.

s	t	$(s \rightarrow t) \wedge \bar{t}$	$\bar{s}$	$((s \rightarrow t) \wedge \bar{t}) \rightarrow \bar{s}$
T	T	F	F	T
T	F	F	F	T
F	T	F	T	T
F	F	T	T	T

Since $D \rightarrow q$ is a tautology, the database implies the query. Therefore, given our prior knowledge as represented in the database, "Tom does not study" is true.

It is easy to see that truth table method can be implemented in a computer program. However, if we already have found the models of D and q, then a simpler method would be to test whether $M(D)$ is included $M(q)$. This is spelled out in the following theorem.

Theorem 2.3.2 $D \to q$ is true if and only if $M(D) \subseteq M(q)$.

Axioms are basic facts that must always hold. The following are some well-known axioms of propositional logic.

Axiom 2.3.1 [contraposition]

For all propositions p and q $(p \to q) \leftrightarrow (\overline{q} \to \overline{p})$.

Axiom 2.3.2 [modus ponens]

For all propositions p and q $((p \to q) \wedge p) \to q$.

Axiom 2.3.3 [modus tollens]

For all propositions p and q $((p \to q) \wedge \overline{q}) \to \overline{p}$.

One can easily verify using truth tables that the above axioms are tautologies. Axioms can be useful to prove new propositions. There are some propositional logic query processors that take advantage of axioms to evaluate faster the queries.

For example, we can use from Example 2.1.1 fact (a) and Axiom 2.3.1 with the substitution of p by s and q by t to prove the following:

(c) $\overline{t} \to \overline{s}$.

Since (c) and (b) are both true, their conjunction is also true. Hence using the conjunction of (c) and(b) and Axiom 2.3.2 with the substitution of p by $\overline{t}$ and q by $\overline{s}$ we can prove that:

(d) $\overline{s}$.

Hence, if the facts are true, then it also must be true that Tom does not study. Although we proved using truth tables that the same fact, the above proof using the axioms is much simpler. An even simpler proof would have recognized that $((s \to t) \wedge (\overline{t})) \to \overline{s}$ is the same as Axiom 2.3.3, hence it is true. Perhaps parents use *modus tollens* when they have a sudden gut feeling that their child did not study for a test.

2.4　Limitations

Truth tables have certain limitations when we consider propositions about sets. For example, let p, q, and r be the propositions

> p : Alex is taller than Brad.
> q : Brad is taller than Carl.
> r : Alex is taller than Carl.

Now consider the problem of deciding whether the following compound proposition is true.

> If Alex is taller than Brad and Brad is taller than Carl, then Alex is taller than Carl.

This compound proposition can be written in the form

$(p \wedge q) \to r$.

We can analyze this proposition using truth tables as follows:

p	q	r	$p \wedge q$	$(p \wedge q) \to r$
T	T	T	T	T
T	**T**	**F**	**T**	**F**
T	F	T	F	T
T	F	F	F	T
F	T	T	F	T
F	T	F	F	T
F	F	T	F	T
F	F	F	F	T

The truth table shows that the compound proposition is not a tautology because it has a false value in the second row. However, it seems intuitive that whatever is the height of these three persons, even if they are all tall or all short, if Alex is taller than Brad and Brad is taller than Carl, then Alex must be taller than Carl. Hence the compound proposition is true, although it is not a propositional tautology. What went wrong? The problem lies in incorrectly equating propositional tautologies and true propositions. While all propositional tautologies are true propositions, not all true propositions are propositional tautologies.

Truth tables blindly look at all combinations of truth values of the propositions p, q, and r, whereas some combinations are impossible. Indeed, it is impossible that both p and q are true, but r is false.

Since all propositional axioms derive from truth tables, they also cannot show that the above compound proposition is true.

Bibliographic Notes

The study of logic is an ancient subject. Propositional logic was known by the ancient Greek Stoic philosophers, such as Chrysippus, who suggested a set of axioms for propositional logic. An early form of predicate logic with the existential and universal quantifiers was developed in the late 19th century by Gottlob Frege. Propositional and predicate logics are reviewed in many textbooks.

Exercises

1. Let p and q be the propositions

   p : The professors are good.
   q : John likes his classes.

   Write these propositions using p and q and logical connectives.

   (a) If the professors are not good, then John does not like his classes.

   (b) If John does not like his classes, then the professors are not good.

   (c) The professors are good, or the professors are not good.

2. Let p, q, and r be the propositions

   p : Alex is taller than Brad.
   q : Brad is taller than Carl.
   r : Alex is taller than Carl.

   Write the following compound propositions using p, q, r, and logical connectives.

   (a) Alex is taller than Brad, or Alex is not taller than Brad.

   (b) If Alex is taller than Brad, then Alex is not taller than Carl.

   (c) Alex is not taller than Brad or not taller than Carl if and only if it is not the case that Alex is taller than Brad and taller than Carl.

3. Let dm, ma, and da be the propositions

   dm : All dolphins are mammals.
   ma : All mammals are animals.
   da : All dolphins are animals.

   Write the following compound proposition using dm, ma, da, and logical connectives.

(a) If all dolphins are mammals and all mammals are animals, then all dolphins are animals.

Is the compound proposition true or

4. Determine using truth tables whether the propositions in Exercise 1 are tautologies.

5. Determine using truth tables whether the propositions in Exercise 2 are tautologies.

6. Determine whether the proposition in Exercise 3 is a tautology.

3

Relational Databases

Section 3.1 describes the *relational data model*, which is a particular data abstraction that uses *relations* or *tables* to represent the data in a database. Section 3.2 introduces the relational algebra query language, while Section 3.3 introduces the *Structured Query Language* (SQL) for relational databases. Finally, Section 3.4 discusses the evaluation of relational database queries.

3.1 Relational Data Model

The *relational data model* is a data abstraction that presents the data in a database as a set of tables, which are also called *relations*. Each table has a name and contains a special top row and a finite number of data rows. Each entry of the top row of a table is called an *attribute*. The number of attributes of a relation is called its *arity* or *dimension*, terms which we use interchangeably. The relation name together with its top row is called the *scheme*.

Taxrecord

SSN	Wages	Interest	Capital_Gain
111223333	10000	80	0
444556666	28000	400	0
777889999	75000	0	5000

For example, consider table *Taxrecord*, which lists for a set of persons their social-security numbers (SSNs), wages, interest incomes, and capital

P. Revesz, *Introduction to Databases: From Biological to Spatio-Temporal*,
Texts in Computer Science, DOI 10.1007/978-1-84996-095-3_3,
© Springer-Verlag London Limited 2010

gains. The *Taxrecord* table has three data rows and has four attributes, that is, it has arity 4. The scheme of this table is:

Taxrecord (SSN, Wages, Interest, Capital_Gain).

Each entry in a column beneath an attribute name is an attribute value. Each data row in a table, except the top row, describes a person, object, concept, or relationship identified by its list of attribute values. For example, the first data row of the relation *Taxrecord* describes that the person with the social security number (SSN) 111223333 earned $10,000 in wages, $80 in interest, and had no capital gains income.

Each row of a relation is called a *tuple* or *point*. We also use these two terms interchangeably with a preference for *point* in the case of spatial and spatiotemporal relations.

The set of table names together with their schemes is called a *database scheme*. In the above example, there is only one table, hence the database scheme is the same as the scheme of the *Taxrecord* table.

The set of data rows form an *instance* of the table scheme. We differentiate between schemes and instances because schemes are usually fixed while instances may change over time due to database updates.

Example 3.1.1 Mr. Johnson, who lives in Omaha, Nebraska, wants to send three packages to three clients who live in Atlanta, Boston, and Chicago. The weight of each package can be represented in the following relation.

Package

Number	Origin	Destination	Weight
101	Omaha	Chicago	12.6
102	Omaha	Atlanta	27.3
103	Omaha	Boston	37.5
104	Omaha	Atlanta	18.7
105	Omaha	Chicago	22.4

Example 3.1.2 The *Planet* relation records some information about the planets in the solar system, namely, the name, the mass relative to the mass of the earth, and the orbital period.

Planet

Name	Mass	Period
Mercury	0.06	0.24
Venus	0.82	0.62
Earth	1.00	1.00
Mars	0.11	1.88
Jupiter	317.80	11.86
Saturn	95.2	29.46
Uranus	14.6	84.01
Neptune	17.2	164.8

Example 3.1.3 For a hospital, the *Patient* relation records the name, identification number, height in centimeters, and weight in kilograms of the patients.

Patient

Name	ID	CM	KG
Anderson	100	200	130
Brown	111	150	50
Davis	222	190	90
Edwards	333	160	90
Ford	345	165	100
Hardy	454	175	70
Johnson	567	170	50
Smith	755	180	120

Similarly, the *Doctor* relation records the name, identification number, age, and specialty of the doctors.

Doctor

Name	ID	Age	Specialty
Cheney	987	50	pediatry
Hardy	454	53	osteopathology
McBride	377	36	radiology
Miller	300	60	neurology
Moss	244	30	neurology
Nelson	400	76	cardiology
Oltman	181	56	urology
Paine	266	45	cardiology
Pepper	555	42	cardiology
Snow	500	65	radiology

Finally, the *Visit* relation records the following information about each visit of a patient to a doctor in the hospital: the patient identification number (PID), the doctor identification number (DID), and the month, day, and year of the visit.

Visit

PID	DID	Month	Day	Year
100	181	5	20	2008
100	555	6	30	2009
111	987	8	20	2009
111	987	5	28	2010
222	266	9	12	2007
222	400	5	20	2008
222	555	5	20	2008
333	987	6	23	2009
345	300	5	16	2009
454	244	6	10	2010
567	377	2	20	2010
567	454	5	28	2010
755	987	6	23	2009

3.2 Relational Algebra Queries

Relational algebra is a query language composed of a number of operators described in Section 3.2.1. The operators can be composed to give relational algebra expressions or queries as shown in Section 3.2.2.

3.2.1 Operators

Relational algebra is a query language composed of a number of operators, each of which takes in relations as arguments and returns a single relation as result. Below we define the main operators in relational algebra and illustrate them using the *Planet* relation from Example 3.1.2.

Project: This operator is used to reorder the columns of a relation or to eliminate some columns of a relation. The project operator from a relation A is denoted $\Pi_L A$, where L is a list $[l_1, \ldots, l_k]$ that specifies an ordering of a subset of the attributes of A. The project operator creates a new relation that contains in its ith column the column of A corresponding to attribute l_i.

Example 3.2.1

$\Pi_{Mass,Period} \ Planet$

This query finds the mass and the period of each planet and returns:

Mass	Period
0.06	0.24
0.82	0.62
1.00	1.00
0.11	1.88
317.80	11.86
95.2	29.46
14.6	84.01
17.2	164.8

Select: The select operator is used to select from a relation A those tuples that satisfy a certain propositional logic formula F. The select operator has the form $\sigma_F A$.

Example 3.2.2

$\sigma_{Mass\ <\ 1}\ Planet$

This query finds the planets whose mass is less than one and return the following relation, which we call *Small_Planet*.

Small_Planet

Name	Mass	Period
Mercury	0.06	0.24
Venus	0.82	0.62
Mars	0.11	1.88

$\sigma_{Period\ >\ 1}\ Planet$

This query finds the planets whose period is greater than one and returns the following relation, which we call *Slow_Planet*.

Slow_Planet

Name	Mass	Period
Mars	0.11	1.88
Jupiter	317.80	11.86
Saturn	95.2	29.46
Uranus	14.6	84.01
Neptune	17.2	164.8

Rename: The rename operator, $\rho_{B(X_1/Y_1,...,X_n/Y_n)}A$ for any $n \geq 1$, changes the name of relation A to B and changes the attribute X_i to Y_i. If we only want to change the name of the relation, then the form $\rho_B A$ can be used.

Example 3.2.3

$$\rho_{Solar\_System(Mass/Weight)} \; Planet$$

This query changes the relation name *Planet* to *Solar_System* and the attribute name *Mass* to *Weight*. As a result, the query returns the following:

Solar_System

Name	Weight	Period
Mercury	0.06	0.24
Venus	0.82	0.62
Earth	1.00	1.00
Mars	0.11	1.88
Jupiter	317.80	11.86
Saturn	95.2	29.46
Uranus	14.6	84.01
Neptune	17.2	164.8

Intersection: The intersection of two relations A and B, denoted $A \cap B$, is the set of tuples that belong to both A and B. The intersection operator can be applied only to operands that have the same set and order of attributes.

Example 3.2.4

Small_Planet $\cap$ *Slow_Planet*

This query finds the planets which are small and slow and returns the following:

Name	Mass	Period
Mars	0.11	1.88

Union: The union of two relations A and B, denoted $A \cup B$, is the set of tuples that belong to A or B or both. The union operator can be applied only to operands that have the same set and order of attributes.

Example 3.2.5

Small_Planet $\cup$ *Slow_Planet*

This query finds the planets which are small or slow and returns the following:

Name	Mass	Period
Mercury	0.06	0.24
Venus	0.82	0.62
Mars	0.11	1.88
Jupiter	317.80	11.86
Saturn	95.2	29.46
Uranus	14.6	84.01
Neptune	17.2	164.8

Difference: The difference of two relations A and B, denoted $A \setminus B$ is the set of tuples that belong to A but do not belong to B. The difference operator can be applied only to operands that have the same set and order of attributes.

Example 3.2.6

$Planet \setminus Small\_Planet$

This query finds the planets which are not small and returns:

Name	Mass	Period
Earth	1.00	1.00
Jupiter	317.80	11.86
Saturn	95.2	29.46
Uranus	14.6	84.01
Neptune	17.2	164.8

Product: The product operator applied to an n-dimensional relation A and an m-dimensional relation B, denoted $A \times B$, returns a relation that contains all $(n + m)$-dimensional tuples whose first n components belong to A and last m components belong to B. The product operator can be applied only to operands that have no common attributes.

Example 3.2.7

$Small\_Planet \times Astronaut$

where $Austronaut$ is the following relation:

Austronaut

FirstName	Age
Claire	40
Gregory	38
Sophia	42

This query finds all combinations of small planets and candidate astronauts who may visit them. As a result, the query returns the following:

Name	Mass	Period	FirstName	Age
Mercury	0.06	0.24	Claire	40
Mercury	0.06	0.24	Gregory	38
Mercury	0.06	0.24	Sophia	42
Venus	0.82	0.62	Claire	40
Venus	0.82	0.62	Gregory	38
Venus	0.82	0.62	Sophia	42
Mars	0.11	1.88	Claire	40
Mars	0.11	1.88	Gregory	38
Mars	0.11	1.88	Sophia	42

Natural Join: The natural join operator applied to an n-dimensional relation A and an m-dimensional relation B that have k attributes in common is denoted $A \bowtie B$. The natural join operator returns a relation that contains all $(n+m-k)$-dimensional tuples whose projection onto the attributes of A belong to A and whose projection onto the attributes of B belong to B.

Example 3.2.8 Suppose the database has another relation called *Orbit*, which records for each planet the mean orbital radius from the sun relative to the mean orbital radius of the earth.

Orbit

Name	Radius
Mercury	0.39
Venus	0.72
Earth	1.00
Mars	1.52
Jupiter	5.20
Saturn	9.54
Uranus	19.22
Neptune	30.06

Then the query:

Planet $\bowtie$ *Orbit*

joins each tuple of *Planet* with the tuple of *Orbit* that has the same *Name* attribute value. As a result, the query returns the following:

Name	Mass	Period	Radius
Mercury	0.06	0.24	0.39
Venus	0.82	0.62	0.72
Earth	1.00	1.00	1.00
Mars	0.11	1.88	1.52
Jupiter	317.80	11.86	5.20
Saturn	95.2	29.46	9.54
Uranus	14.6	84.01	19.22
Neptune	17.2	164.8	30.06

3.2.2 Expressions

Since the result of each relational algebra operation is a relation, the operators can be composed to express queries. Relational algebra expressions or queries are defined as follows.

Definition 3.2.1 A relational algebra query is defined recursively as follows:

1. Each relation name R_i is a relational algebra expression. (This will just return the relation R_i as a result.)

2. If e_1 is a relational algebra expression, then $\Pi_L(e_1)$, where L is a subset of the attributes of the resulting relation, $\sigma_F(e_1)$, where F is a selection condition, and $\rho_C(e_1)$, where C is a renaming specification, are also relational algebra expressions.

3. If e_1 and e_2 are relational algebra expressions that result in relations that have the same set and order of attributes, then $(e_1 \cap e_2)$, $(e_1 \cup e_2)$, and $(e_1 \setminus e_2)$ are also relational algebra expressions.

4. If e_1 and e_2 are relational algebra expressions that result in relations with no common attributes, then $(e_1 \times e_2)$ is also a relational algebra expression.

5. If e_1 and e_2 are relational algebra expressions, then $(e_1 \bowtie e_2)$ is a relational algebra expression.

Next we consider some sample relational algebra queries.

Example 3.2.9 Find the name and the mass of the small planets.

$$\Pi_{Name,Mass}(\sigma_{Mass\ <\ 1}\ Planet)$$

This query is composed of a selection query within the parentheses and a projection query. The selection query within the parentheses is evaluated first yielding the *Small_Planet* relation that we saw earlier. Then the projection query is applied to the *Small_Planet* relation, yielding the following:

Name	Mass
Mercury	0.06
Venus	0.82
Mars	0.11

Example 3.2.10 Find the name of the planets that are small and slow.

$$\Pi_{Name} \ (Small\_Planet \ \cap \ Slow\_Planet)$$

This query at first finds the intersection of the small and the slow planets, which is the table that contained only the Mars tuple of the *Planet* relation. Then the projection operation returns the following:

Name
Mars

If we do not already have the *Small_Planet* and the *Slow_Planet* relations, then we have to express them as we did earlier in Section 3.2.1. That could be done by the following longer relational algebra query:

$$\Pi_{Name} \ ((\sigma_{Mass \ < \ 1} \ Planet) \ \cap \ (\sigma_{Period \ > \ 1} \ Planet))$$

3.3   SQL Queries

SQL is the standard query language for relational database systems. SQL was originally developed at IBM in the early 1970s, but it is a growing language with new features added to its standard every few years. The following sections give only a description of the most important concepts of SQL.

3.3.1   Basic Queries

The popularity of SQL is due to it being a high-level language that includes many English words as keywords, making simple SQL queries sound like English sentences. Below are some examples about the hospital database of Example 3.1.3.

Example 3.3.1 Find the height and weight of patient Anderson.

```
SELECT    CM, KG
FROM      Patient
WHERE     Name = "Anderson"
```

This query returns the answer:

CM	KG
200	130

Example 3.3.2 Find the specialty Dr. Snow.

```
SELECT    Specialty
FROM      Doctor
WHERE     Name = "Snow"
```

This query returns:

Specialty
radiology

Example 3.3.3 Find the dates when patient 111 visited doctor 987.

```
SELECT    Month, Day, Year
FROM      Visit
WHERE     PID = 111 AND DID = 987
```

This query returns:

Month	Day	Year
8	20	2009
5	28	2010

Example 3.3.4 Find the specialty of all the doctors in the hospital.

```
SELECT    Specialty
FROM      Doctor
```

This query returns:

Specialty
pediatry
osteopathology
radiology
neurology
neurology
cardiology
urology
cardiology
cardiology
radiology

Note that SQL allows repetitions in the rows of the relations. To avoid repetitions, we write the query using the DISTINCT keyword as follows:

SELECT   DISTINCT Specialty
FROM   Doctor

This query returns:

Specialty
pediatry
osteopathology
radiology
neurology
cardiology
urology

When $R(A_1, \ldots, A_n)$ is a relation, then SQL allows the use of the dot notation $R.A_i$ to refer to the ith attribute of R. This notation is especially helpful when the query contains two relations P and R with a common attribute A_i. Then the reference $R.A_i$ makes clear that we mean the attribute column A_i of relation R and not the attribute column A_i of relation P. Even when there are no common attributes, the dot notation is helpful to remind us which attribute comes from which relation. Hence, although the dot notation is not required by SQL in that case, we encourage using the dot notation whenever the query uses more than one relation.

Example 3.3.5 Find all the pairs of patient and doctor names.

SELECT   Patient.Name, Doctor.Name
FROM   Patient, Doctor

This query returns the product of the names in *Patient* and the names in *Doctor*.

Example 3.3.6 Find the pair of patient names and their visit dates.

> SELECT   Patient.Name, Visit.Month, Visit.Day, Visit.Year
> FROM   Patient, Visit
> WHERE   Patient.ID = Visit.PID

Without the last line, this query would return all the pairs of patient names in *Patient* and dates in *Visit*. However, the equality *Patient.ID = Visit.PID* restricts the answer to be only the pair of patient names and the dates they visited the hospital. In the output relation, each pair occurs the number of times the patient visited the hospital on that day.

Patient.Name	Visit.Month	Visit.Day	Visit.Year
Anderson	5	20	2008
Anderson	6	30	2009
Brown	8	20	2009
Brown	5	28	2010
Davis	9	12	2007
Davis	5	20	2008
Davis	5	20	2008
Edwards	6	23	2009
Ford	5	16	2009
Hardy	6	10	2010
Johnson	2	20	2010
Johnson	5	28	2010
Smith	6	23	2009

Example 3.3.7 Find the pair of patient and doctor names where the patient has visited the doctor in the hospital.

> SELECT   Patient.Name, Doctor.Name
> FROM   Patient, Doctor, Visit
> WHERE   Patient.ID = Visit.PID AND Doctor.ID = Visit.DID

This query returns:

Patient.Name	Doctor.Name
Anderson	Oltman
Anderson	Pepper
Brown	Cheney
Brown	Cheney
Davis	Paine
Davis	Nelson
Davis	Pepper
Edwards	Cheney
Ford	Miller
Hardy	Moss
Johnson	McBride
Johnson	Hardy
Smith	Cheney

General Form

After the above introduction, let us define the following general form for basic SQL queries:

$$
\begin{array}{ll}
\text{CREATE VIEW} & R(B_1, \ldots, B_m) \\
\text{SELECT} & A_1, \ldots, A_n \\
\text{FROM} & R_1, \ldots, R_l \\
\text{WHERE} & C_1 \text{ AND } \ldots \text{ AND } C_o
\end{array}
$$

where the As and Bs are attribute names, the Rs are relation names, and the Cs are selection conditions. The four lines of the basic SQL query are called the CREATE VIEW clause, the SELECT clause, the FROM clause, and the WHERE clause. The SELECT and FROM clauses are required, but the CREATE VIEW and WHERE clauses are optional.

The CREATE VIEW clause simply assigns the output relation to a new relation R and renames the ith column to the attribute B_i. When the attribute name $R.A$ (or simply an A that is intended to belong to R) appears in the SELECT clause, then the relation name R must appear in the FROM clause. In the WHERE clause instead of AND the conjunction OR may be also used. In some versions of SQL a comma may be used instead of an AND keyword.

In addition, in SQL the AS keyword can be used for renaming attribute names in the SELECT clause and relation names in the FROM clause of basic queries.

Example 3.3.8 Define the relation *Treats(DoctorName,PatientName)*. This is similar to the SQL query of Example 3.3.7 but we also need a

CREATE VIEW clause and have to make sure that the arguments are in the right order. The SQL query can be also expressed as follows:

CREATE VIEW	Treats(DoctorName, PatientName)
SELECT	D.Name, P.Name,
FROM	Patient AS P, Doctor AS D, Visit AS V
WHERE	P.ID = V.PID AND D.ID = V.DID

This query returns:

Treats

DoctorName	PatientName
Oltman	Anderson
Pepper	Anderson
Cheney	Brown
Cheney	Brown
Paine	Davis
Nelson	Davis
Pepper	Davis
Cheney	Edwards
Miller	Ford
Moss	Hardy
McBride	Johnson
Hardy	Johnson
Cheney	Smith

3.3.2 Aggregation Operators

Aggregate operators take in a set of values and return a single value. SQL allows aggregate operators in queries of the form:

SELECT	AGGREGATE_OPERATOR(A_i)
FROM	...
WHERE	...

where the AGGREGATE_OPERATOR is `AVG` for the average, `COUNT` for the number, `MAX` for the maximun, `MIN` for the minimum, and `SUM` for the sum of a set of values.

Example 3.3.9 Find the number of cardiologists.

```
SELECT    COUNT(ID)
FROM      Doctor
WHERE     Specialty = "cardiology"
```

This query returns:

Count(ID)
3

Suppose that instead of finding only the number of cardiologists, we need to find the number of doctors in each specialty. This requires the tuples within the *Doctor* relation to be grouped according to their specialty. Once the grouping is done, it is easy to apply any aggregate operator for each group. Sorted alphabetically on speciality, the groups look as follows:

Name	ID	Age	Specialty
Nelson	400	76	cardiology
Paine	266	45	cardiology
Pepper	555	42	cardiology
Miller	300	60	neurology
Moss	244	30	neurology
Hardy	454	53	osteopathology
Cheney	987	50	pediatry
McBride	377	36	radiology
Snow	500	65	radiology
Oltman	181	56	urology

There are six groups. Three groups contain more than one tuple. In particular, the cardiology group contains three, and the neurology and radiology groups contain two tuples. SQL allows aggregation within groups using queries of the following form:

```
SELECT      B_1, ..., B_n, AGGREGATE_OPERATOR(A_i)
FROM        ...
WHERE       ...
GROUP BY    B_1, ..., B_n
```

where the B_i for $1 \leq i \leq n$ are attribute names that belong to relations in the FROM clause. The GROUP BY clause partitions the relation that results from the execution of the basic SQL query (the top three lines without the aggregation operator) into groups such that within each group the tuples agree on the values of the attributes $B_1, \ldots, B_n$. The aggregation operator is applied to each group as the final step.

Example 3.3.10 Find the number of doctors in each specialty.

SELECT	Specialty, COUNT(ID)
FROM	Doctor
GROUP BY	Specialty

This query returns:

Specialty	Count(ID)
cardiology	3
neurology	2
osteopathology	1
pediatry	1
radiology	2
urology	1

3.3.3 Set Operators

SQL queries can be combined to form bigger queries using the set operators INTERSECT, UNION, and MINUS, which is set difference. In general, SQL queries with set operators have the form:

SQL Query 1
SET_OPERATOR
SQL Query 2

where the attribute names in the SELECT lines of Query 1 and Query 2 are the same and in the same order.

Example 3.3.11 Find those doctors who are also patients.

SELECT	Name
FROM	Doctor
INTERSECT	
SELECT	Name
FROM	Patient

This query returns:

Name
Hardy

3.3.4 Nested Queries

SQL queries can be combined by nesting one query inside another query. Nested SQL queries look as follows:

```
SELECT   ...
FROM     ...
WHERE    ... AND  A_i  NEST_OPERATOR  (SELECT  A_j
                                       FROM    ...
                                       WHERE   ...)
```

In a nested query, the outer query outside the parentheses has in the WHERE clause a special selection condition that says that in each selected tuple the attribute A_i must be in a NEST_OPERATOR relation with at least one tuple of the result of the inner query within the parentheses. The NEST_OPERATOR can be any one of the following: $>=$ ALL, $<=$ ALL, $>= SOME$, $<=$ SOME, IN, NOT IN.

Example 3.3.12 Find the oldest radiologist in the hospital.

```
SELECT   Name
FROM     Doctor
WHERE    Age >= ALL   (SELECT  Age
                       FROM    Doctors
                       WHERE   Specialty = "radiology")
```

This query returns:

Name
Snow

3.3.5 Recursive Queries

Suppose that patients with a flu may infect their doctors in the hospital during a visit that occurs after the infection. Suppose that Johnson catches a flu on 5/20/2010. Who else will be infected?

At first this may seem like a simple problem of finding Johnson's doctors. However, the dates have to be taken into consideration. Since Johnson visits McBride on 2/20/2010, which is earlier than when Johnson became sick, doctor McBride cannot catch the flu from Johnson. On the other hand, since Johnson visits Hardy on 5/28/2010, which is eight days after Johnson became sick, doctor Hardy may catch the flu.

Hence the right answer seems to be doctor Hardy. However, one should not forget that doctors can be also patients. In fact, Hardy is also a patient in the hospital. Since Hardy visits Moss on 6/10/2010, doctor Moss also may catch the flu. If doctor Moss were a patient in the hospital, he may also infect his doctors and so on. The entire chain of infection can be found using the following recursive SQL query.

CREATE VIEW	Infected(Name, Month, Day, Year)
SELECT	D.Name, V.Month, V.Day, V.Year
FROM	Patient AS P, Doctor AS D, Visit AS V
WHERE	P.Name = "Johnson" AND
	P.ID = V.PID AND
	D.ID = V.DID AND
	V.Month/V.Day/V.Year >= 5/20/2010
RECURSIVE	
SELECT	D.Name, V.Month, V.Day, V.Year
FROM	Infected AS I, Patient AS P, Doctor AS D, Visit AS V
WHERE	P.Name = I.Name AND
	P.ID = V.PID AND
	D.ID = V.DID AND
	V.Month/V.Day/V.Year >= I.Month/I.Day/I.Year

This query returns:

Infected

Name	Month	Day	Year
Hardy	5	28	2010
Moss	6	10	2010

The general form of SQL recursive queries, which we omit here, is similar to the form of SQL queries with set operators. However, the keyword RECURSIVE indicates that the second query needs to be executed repeatedly until no more infected person is found. Recursive queries are allowed to use in the FROM clause the output relation that is being computed, in this case the *Infected* relation.

3.3.6 Query Composition

Like relational algebra, SQL allows arbitrary degree of composition of queries. That is an extremely important feature because it satisfies the needs of both data vendors and application vendors.

Data Vendors: Data vendors buy raw data in the form of databases and produce refined data in the form of databases that they sell to other data vendors. In the information market, there is often a long chain of data vendors from raw data to the users. Each data vendor uses queries to transform raw data to the data product. These queries may be secret or patented.

Considering how data vendors work illustrates two important facts. First, queries to databases should yield other databases as the output. Second, because it is usually difficult to translate between different types of databases, for example, from network to relational databases, there is a tendency for one data model to become a common data communication standard. Currently the relational data model provides that standard. Data vendors using other types of databases have to translate their databases to relational databases and vice versa or be cut off from a large part of the information market. Fortunately, translating between constraint and relational databases is easy.

Application Vendors: Application vendors sell libraries of queries to users. Application vendors must guarantee the termination of the queries on each valid database input because no user will wait indefinitely for a query to complete execution. Termination is a minimum requirement; often vendors also need to guarantee the speed and space performance of their queries. The best way to fulfill these guarantees is by using query languages that allow only expression of queries that terminate fast. Query languages like relational algebra and SQL are such languages. Hence these would be preferable to use instead of a general-purpose programming language, where termination is not guaranteed.

3.4   Evaluation

Efficient query evaluation for relational database queries is an extensive subject. Chapter 24 discusses query evaluation techniques in more detail. We only describe below some of the key features of relational database query evaluation.

Translation to Relational Algebra: Each basic SQL query can be translated to a relational algebra query involving the project Π, select σ, and product $\times$ operators as follows:

$$\Pi_{A_1,\ldots,A_n}\left(\sigma_{C_1,\ldots,C_o}\left(R_1 \times \ldots \times R_l\right)\right)$$

This is fairly straightforward to understand except that for some historical reason the SQL SELECT clause is translated as the project operator of relational algebra. If one keeps that in mind, it is easy to translate basic SQL queries into relational algebra queries and vice versa. SQL queries with set operators are also straighforward to translate. SQL queries with aggregate operators, and nested and recursive queries can be translated into short C++ programs with loops that include calls to functions that evaluate relational algebra queries.

Algebraic Query Optimization: Relational algebra queries can be rewritten into logically equivalent but easier-to-evaluate, simpler relational algebra queries. The rewritings are based on relational algebra axioms. For example, one axiom states that the join operator is commutative, that is:

$$R_1 \bowtie R_2 \equiv R_2 \bowtie R_1$$

Table-Based Operations: Relational algebra provides table operators, which are more efficient to perform than working with individual tuples at a time. For example, joining two n-size relations on a common attribute can be done by a naive algorithm that has a nexted for-loop that requires $O(n^2)$ time. However, if we first sort both relations on the common attribute in $O(n \log n)$ time, then we can merge the two relations in $O(n)$ time.

Indexing: Indexing the relations on some attributes, which are unique in each tuple, for example the SSN in the *Taxrecord* relation, enables fast searching in $O(\log n)$ time for any tuple in the relation. Relational databases take advantage of indexing on unique attributes of sets of attributes called a *primary key*. In most relational database systems, the users have to declare a primary key for every relation. Hence the primary key is always readily identified to be indexed.

Today relations look like obvious data structures, and the above query evaluation features look like obvious techniques. Therefore, it is hard to appreciate the relational data model without putting it in a historical context. Some people are even surprised to learn that the relational data model was preceded by other data models. Many database textbooks do not even mention these older data models because they are considered obsolete. However, sometimes the knowledge of history and development of a subject is important to better foresee the future.

3.4.1   Network Data Model

The relational data model was preceded in the 1960s by two other closely related data models: the *hierarchical data model* and the *network data model*. Both the hierarchical and the network data models can represent tables. However, the tables are represented as a linked list of records. For example, the *Taxrecord* table is represented as follows:

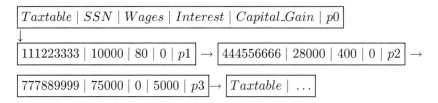

In the network data model the record with the table scheme is called an *owner record*. The owner record starts the linked list of data records by pointing using pointer $p0$ to the first data record, which points to the second data record by its pointer and so on until the last data record. The last data record points back to the owner record. The network data model allows the linking together in another list of those owner records that belong together, for example, all the owner records that are related to taxes. That linked list may have another owner declared for them. That higher-level owner record may be linked together with other owner records.

Although we omit many details of the network data model, it is clear from the already presented material that the network data model is a lower level data model than the relational data model. As a result, network database query languages were heavy on the use of pointers. The individual records became the focus of the query languages and not the tables. The network data model hindered thinking about tables as abstract entities and the development of abstract table operators for querying.

Many programmers in many places implemented in network database query languages a natural join operator on tables without realizing its significance. Natural join and many other table operators never became recognized units (either as symbols or as keywords) in the network database query languages. Hence the programming effort to implement the join operator had to be repeated needlessly and endlessly.

In the 1960s, most programming languages used pointers and linked data structures. Hence, instead of yearning for a greater simplicity, network database programmers took the database queries as natural and were even proud of their skills in navigating the pointer structures of their network databases.

The essential contribution of the relational data model was to introduce a higher level of data abstraction. Once the data was viewed as a table instead of a linked list of tuples, the definition of the relational algebra operators naturally followed. Then a few years later the relational algebra became a basis for the popular SQL language.

Bibliographic Notes

The relational data model and the relational algebra query language were proposed in 1970 by Edgar F. Codd while working at the IBM Almaden Research Center [94]. The SQL query language was developed in 1974 at IBM [26, 74].

The network data model was proposed in 1961 by Charles W. Bachman while working at the General Electric Company. He also built the Integrated Data Store (IDS) [27, 28], which was the first network database system.

Exercises

1. Consider the following relations where F means false and T means true.

Exam

Study	Pass
T	T
F	F

Life

Graduate	Rich	Famous
T	F	T
F	T	F

School

Pass	Graduate
T	T
F	F

Express the following in relational algebra and SQL.

   (a) Find whether those who are famous are also rich.
   (b) Find whether those who do not study graduate.
   (c) Find whether those who are rich study.

2. Express the following in relational algebra and SQL using the *Taxtable* relation.

(a) Find the wages earned by the employee with SSN = 777889999.

(b) Find the SSN of the employees who had no capital gain.

(c) Find the wages of the employee who had no interest income.

3. Express the following in SQL using the *Package* relation from Example 3.1.1.

(a) Find the total number of the packages sent to each destination.

(b) Find the total weight of the packages sent to each destination.

(c) Find the destination of the heaviest package.

(d) Find the serial number of the lighest package.

4. Express the following in SQL using the *Planet* relation from Example 3.1.2.

(a) Find the average mass of the planets.

(b) Find the planet which has the largest mass.

(c) Find the planet which has the longest orbital period.

(d) Find the planets which are heavier than Uranus.

5. Let *Size* be the following relation.

Size

Name	Diameter
Mercury	0.382
Venus	0.949
Earth	1.00
Mars	0.532
Jupiter	11.209
Saturn	9.449
Uranus	4.007
Neptune	3.883

Evaluate the following relational algebra queries.

(a) $Planet \bowtie Size$

(b) $(\Pi_{Name}(\sigma_{Mass<20} Planet)) \setminus (\Pi_{Name}(\sigma_{Diameter>3} Size))$

(c) $\Pi_{Name}((\sigma_{Mass<20} Planet) \bowtie (\sigma_{Diameter>3} Size))$

6. Express in relational algebra all the queries in Sections 3.3.1 and 3.3.3.

7. Express in SQL all the queries in Section 3.2.

8. Consider the *Weather* relation, which records the average precipitation in inches in various cities for each month of the year.

Weather

City	Month	Precipitation
Los Angeles	1	2.7
Los Angeles	2	3.1
Los Angeles	3	2.2
Los Angeles	4	1.3
Los Angeles	5	0.3
Los Angeles	6	0.1
Los Angeles	7	0
Los Angeles	8	0
Los Angeles	9	0.2
Los Angeles	10	0.4
Los Angeles	11	1.1
Los Angeles	12	2.5
New Orleans	1	4.9
New Orleans	2	5.3
New Orleans	3	4.8
New Orleans	4	4.7
New Orleans	5	4.5
New Orleans	6	5.8
New Orleans	7	6.7
New Orleans	8	6.6
New Orleans	9	5.7
New Orleans	10	3.0
New Orleans	11	4.3
New Orleans	12	5.2
New York	1	3.4
New York	2	3.3
New York	3	3.8
New York	4	3.6
New York	5	3.9
New York	6	3.5
New York	7	4.2
New York	8	4.4
New York	9	3.7
New York	10	3.5
New York	11	3.5
New York	12	3.6

Express in SQL the following queries:

(a) Find the months when the precipitation in Los Angeles is above one inch.

(b) Find the total yearly precipitation in New Orleans.

(c) Find the total precipitation in New York during the first six months of the year.

(d) For each city find the average monthly precipitation.

(e) Find the city that has the most precipitation in December.

9. Consider the *US_Census* relation, which is based on data provided by the U.S. Census Bureau in 2006 for U.S. states. In the relation *child* means under 18 years old, *middle* means between 18 and 64 years old, and *old* means 65 years old or over.

US_Census

State	Age_Group	Population
Kansas	child	696547
Kansas	middle	1710962
Kansas	old	356566
Nebraska	child	445619
Nebraska	middle	1070832
Nebraska	old	251880
Texas	child	6488148
Texas	middle	14692364
Texas	old	2327270

Express in SQL the following queries:

(a) Find the number of children in Nebraska.

(b) Find the states that have over 350,000 old people.

(c) Find the total population of Texas.

(d) Find the total number of children.

(e) Find the total population for each state.

(f) Find the total population for each age group.

(g) Find the state which has the most number of children.

(h) Find the state which has the fewest old people.

10. Consider the following relations that describe some information about languages.

SPEAKS

PERSON	LANGUAGE
Charles	English
Charles	French
Charles	German
Deb	Chinese
Deb	Greek
Joe	English
Joe	Spanish
Maggy	Italian
Maggy	Japanese
Maggy	Russian
Peter	Greek
Peter	Spanish
Peter	Italian
Susan	Chinese
Susan	Russian

OFFICIAL-LANGUAGE

COUNTRY	LANGUAGE
Canada	English
Canada	French
Mexico	Spanish
Switzerland	French
Switzerland	German
Switzerland	Italian
USA	English

Express in SQL the following queries:

(a) Find each person-country pair where the person can speak at least one official language of the country.

(b) Find each person who can speak all official languages of Canada.

(c) Find the most frequently spoken language.

(d) Find the person who speaks the most number of languages.

(e) Find the countries with more than one official language.

(f) Find the relation $Converse(x, y)$ which is true if and only if persons x and y can converse with each other directly.

(g) Find the relation $Interpreter(i, x, y)$ which is ture if and only if person i can serve as an interpreter between persons x and y.

(h) Find the relation $Message(x, y)$ which is true if and only if a verbal message can be passed between persons x and y.

11. Consider the following relations that describe an extended family.

$Father(Child, Parent)$
$Mother(Child, Parent)$
$Female(Name)$
$Male(Name)$

Express in SQL the following queries. (*Hint:* If a query is too difficult to express in one single SQL statement, then break it up into a series of smaller SQL queries.)

(a) Find the names of parents.

(b) Find the names of children who are not parents.

(c) Find the relation *Mom-or-Dad(Child,Parent)* where *Parent* is either the father or mother of *Child*.

(d) Find the relation *Grandparent(Child,Parent,Gparent)* where *Parent* is a parent and *Gparent* is a grandparent of *Child*.

(e) Find the relation *Cousin(A,B)* where *A* and *B* are cousins.

(f) Find the mother who has the most number of sons.

(g) Find the father who has the most number the daughters.

(h) Find the person who has the most number of cousins.

(i) Find the names of all pairs of persons where the second is an ancestor of the first.

4

Constraint Databases

Relational databases cannot represent many types of data reviewed in Chapter 1. Hence we need a more expressive data model. Section 4.1 describes the *infinite relational data model*, which is an extension of the relational data model to infinite tables. Section 4.2 describes relational algebra, and Section 4.3 describes SQL queries on infinite relations. Section 4.4 presents the key elements of query evaluation, including the finite representation of infinite relation using the *constraint data model*.

4.1 Infinite Relational Data Model

In the infinite relational data model a database instance could contain an infinite number of tuples. For example, one can represent the chart of Figure 1.1 by the *Taxtable* relation shown below. The *Taxtable* relation contains an infinite number of tuples because there are an infinite number of (*Income, Tax*) pairs in the chart when we allow arbitrarily long decimal number, that is, we do not assume that *Income* and *Tax* are always integers. In addition, we placed no limit on the maximum income and the chart can be expected to continue forever because the tax seems to be always some percentage of the income.

P. Revesz, *Introduction to Databases: From Biological to Spatio-Temporal*,
Texts in Computer Science, DOI 10.1007/978-1-84996-095-3_4,
© Springer-Verlag London Limited 2010

Taxtable

Income	Tax
0	0
⋮	
10080	1512
⋮	

Note that the preceding instance of *Taxtable* cannot be represented in the relational data model, where each table can contain only a finite number of tuples. Even if we use rounding and limit the maximum income, a finite representation can be very cumbersome. For example, the U.S. federal government currently provides a twelve-page tax table for taxpayers. This table only goes up to $100,000 and lists only incomes that are multiples of $50. To accommodate high-income people like Bill Gates, we would need to print an entire library.

The following are a few additional examples of using the infinite relational data model to model data.

Example 4.1.1 To all destinations within the U.S., the postage fee charged for packages can be computed based on the weight of the package and the postage rate associated with the weight. This association is described in the *Postage* relation.

Postage

Weight	Fee
0	0
⋮	⋮
5	2.65
⋮	⋮
50	16.65

Example 4.1.2 Kepler's law about the relationship between the period and the mean orbital radius from the sun for any object in the solar system is another infinite relation, which can be represented as follows:

Kepler

Period	Radius
⋮	⋮

Example 4.1.3 The following are also infinite relations related to the hospital example. Relation *Height* converts centimeters into inches, while *Weight* converts kilograms into pounds. These relations contain an infinite pair of tuples.

Height

CM	IN
⋮	⋮

Weight

KG	LB
⋮	⋮

One's physical fitness depends significantly on the combination of one's height and weight. Hence a heavy and tall person can be as fit as a light and short person. Suppose we consider only the following three different fitness types: "overweight," "normal," and "underweight." Then the following *Fit(Type, CM, KG)* relation is an infintie relation because it always contains in each tuple one of these three strings as the *Type* attribute but any pair of rational numbers as the *CM* and *KG* attributes:

Fit

Type	CM	KG
⋮	⋮	⋮

To get fitter, an overweight person may diet. Suppose some of the overweight hopital patients start a diet. As they diet, their weight gradually decreases over time, which we may measure in fractions of months elapsed since the beginning of their diet. This yields the following infinite relation:

Diet

ID	KG	Month
⋮	⋮	⋮

Example 4.1.4 Suppose a farmer can plant four types of crops, namely, corn, rye, sunflower, and wheat and can use for irrigation only 8000 units

of well water and 3000 units of fertilizer. Each acre of corn, rye, sunflower, and wheat needs 30, 25, 5, and 10 units of water, and 15, 8, 10, and 15 units of fertilizer.

The information here can be represented in relation *Crops* in which each tuple represents a possible combination of crops that the farmer could plant. This is also an infinite relation assuming that the farmer can plant any portion of the land with any crop.

Crops

Corn	Rye	Sunflower	Wheat
100	100	10	40
$\vdots$			
160	50	8	8
$\vdots$			
80	150	30	20

Here the farmer would likely want to maximize the profit after selling the crops. This problem is a simple instance of an optimization problem, commonly solved by mathematical programming techniques such as *linear programming*. Such problems are important in *operations research*, an area concerned with planning optimally the work done in companies.

4.2   Relational Algebra Queries

Section 3.2.1 introduced relational algebra queries for relational databases. The relational algebra query language can be also applied with the same ease to infinite relational databases.

Example 4.2.1 Consider the set of points $A(x, y)$ and $B(x, y)$ shown in Figure 4.1. Since both A and B have dimension two, the operators of intersection, union, and difference can be applied. Let us start with those operators.

- The intersection $A \cap B = C$, where C is shown in Figure 4.2.

- The union $A \cup B = D$, where D is shown in Figure 4.3.

- The difference $A \setminus B = E$, where E is shown in Figure 4.4.

- Let $F(z)$ be a relation that contains all points on the z-axis between $z = 5$ and $z = 15$. Then the product $A(x, y) \times F(z) = G(x, y, z)$, where G is the polyhedron shown in Figure 4.5.

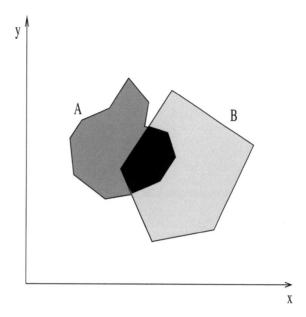

Figure 4.1: Two point sets.

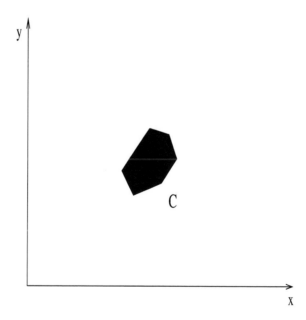

Figure 4.2: Intersection of A and B.

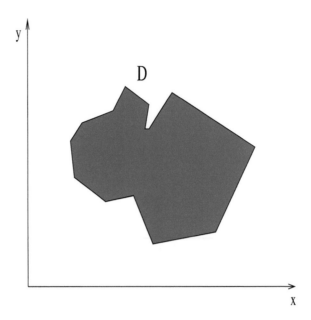

Figure 4.3: Union of A and B.

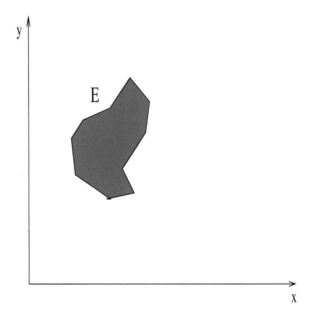

Figure 4.4: Difference of A and B.

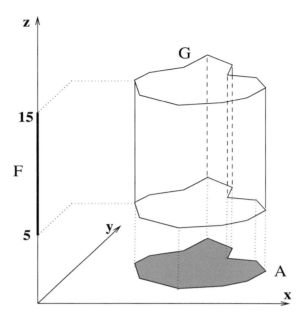

Figure 4.5: Product of A and F.

- Consider now $H(x, y, z)$, the polyhedron shown in Figure 4.6. The projection $\Pi_{x,y}H$ is the shaded rectangle in the (x, y) plane, while $\Pi_{y,z}H$ is the shaded rectangle in the (y, z) plane.

- Consider now the rectangular body $I(x, y, z)$ shown in Figure 4.7. The shaded rectangle that lies in the plane defined by the equation $2x + z = 0$ cuts I into two. The selection operation $\sigma_{2x+z \leq 0}I$ returns the part of I that lies below the shaded rectangle.

- Finally, in Figure 4.8 the natural join of the shaded rectangle $J(x, y)$ and the shaded circle $K(y, z)$ is the cylinder $L(x, y, z)$. This is written as $J(x, y) \bowtie K(y, z) = L(x, y, z)$.

As we saw in Section 3.2.2, the relational algebra operators can be composed to express relational algebra queries. Relational algebra queries also apply to infinite relational databases.

Example 4.2.2 Consider the *Planet* relation from Example 3.1.2 and the *Kepler* relation from Example 4.1.2. Find the name and the mean orbital radius of each planet in the solar system.

$$\Pi_{Name,Radius} \left(Planet \bowtie Kepler \right)$$

This query returns:

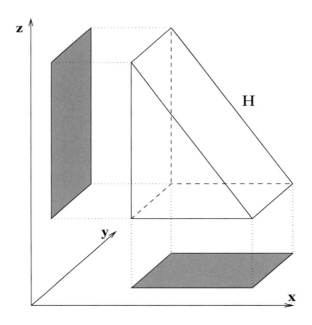

Figure 4.6: Projections from H.

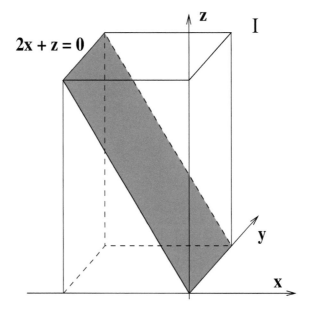

Figure 4.7: Select part of I below $2x + z = 0$.

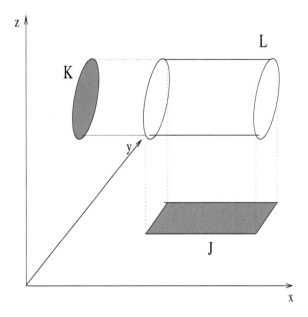

Figure 4.8: Natural join of J and K.

Name	Radius
Mercury	0.39
Venus	0.72
Earth	1.00
Mars	1.52
Jupiter	5.20
Saturn	9.54
Uranus	19.22
Neptune	30.06

The above is the *Orbit* relation of Example 3.2.8 except that it does not have a name. This shows that the *Orbit* relation is not necessary because it can be calculated from the information already available in the *Planet* relation using one of Kepler's laws, which is represented by the *Kepler* relation.

4.3 SQL Queries

Section 3.3 introduced the SQL query language for relational databases. The SQL query language allows a high-level view of relations as being composed of a scheme and an instance. Database queries need to work on all database instances, and SQL faciliates that by allowing the query writers to express the queries by considering only the relation schemes.

Since the schemes of finite and infinite relations are the same, writing queries for infinite relational databases is as easy as writing queries for finite relational databases. When writing queries, one should not worry about the fact that some relations are infinite. The user's task is only to specify using queries *what* is needed. The task of the database system is to evaluate the queries, that is, to figure out *how* the query can be answered in an efficient way.

4.3.1 Basic Queries

We give a few sample queries that use different infinite relations from Example 4.1.3. The first query uses the *Height* and *Weight* relations.

Example 4.3.1 Find the name, inches height, and pound weight of each patient.

```
SELECT   P.Name, H.IN, W.LB
FROM     Patient AS P, Height AS H, Weight AS W
WHERE    P.CM = H.CM AND
         P.KG = W.KG
```

The next query uses the *Fit* relation.

Example 4.3.2 Find the name of the patients who are underweight.

```
SELECT   P.Name
FROM     Patient AS P, Fit AS F
WHERE    P.CM = F.CM AND
         P.KG = F.KG AND
         F.Type = "underweight"
```

The last query uses the *Diet* relation.

Example 4.3.3 Suppose that patients Anderson and Smith participate in dieting program. Find the time when Anderson and Smith have equal weight.

```
SELECT   D1.Month
FROM     Patient AS P1, Patient AS P2, Diet as D1, Diet AS D2
WHERE    P1.Name = "Anderson" AND
         P1.ID = D1.ID AND
         P2.Name = "Smith" AND
         P2.ID = D2.ID AND
         D1.KG = D2.KG AND
         D1.Month = D2.Month
```

4.3.2 Aggregation Operators

Aggregation operators also can be applied with the same ease as in the case of finite relational databases.

Example 4.3.4 Find the number of cardiology patients who are overweight.

SELECT	COUNT(P.Name)
FROM	Patient AS P, Doctor AS D, Visit AS V, Fit AS F
WHERE	P.ID = V.PID AND
	D.ID = V.DID AND
	D.Specialty = "cardiology" AND
	P.CM = F.CM AND
	P.KG = F.KG AND
	F.Type = "overweight"

The next aggregation query also uses the GROUP BY clause.

Example 4.3.5 Find the number of overweight patients of each doctor.

SELECT	D.Name, COUNT(P.Name)
FROM	Patient AS P, Doctor AS D, Visit AS V, Fit AS F
WHERE	P.ID = V.PID AND
	D.ID = V.DID AND
	P.CM = F.CM AND
	P.KG = F.KG AND
	F.Type = "overweight"
GROUP BY	D.Name

There are some restrictions that apply to aggregation queries. The attributes in the GROUP BY clause must have a finite number of possible values, otherwise there would be an infinite number of groups. In the above query, this restriction is satisfied because the *D.Name* attribute can have only as many possible values as the number of doctors in the hospital.

Similarly, the attribute that is aggregated by AVG, COUNT, or SUM must also have a finite number of possible values. This restriction is also satisfied by the above query because the *P.Name* attribute can have only as many possible values as the number of patients in the hospital.

4.3.3 Set Operators

All the set operators also can be applied.

Example 4.3.6 Suppose the hospital wants to enroll new patients in its dieting program. To help the hospital, find the patients who are overweight but not currently dieting.

```
SELECT   P.Name
FROM     Patient AS P, Fit AS F
WHERE    P.CM = F.CM AND
         P.KG = F.KG AND
         F.Type = "overweight"
MINUS
SELECT   P.Name
FROM     Patient as P, Diet as D
WHERE    Patient.ID = Diet.ID
```

4.3.4 Nested Queries

Here is a nested query on infinite relations.

Example 4.3.7 Find the ID of the dieter who has the least weight at the end of 12 months.

```
SELECT   D.ID
FROM     Diet AS D
WHERE    D.Month = 12  AND
         D.KG  <=  ALL      (SELECT   D.KG
                             FROM     Diet AS D
                             WHERE    D.Month = 12)
```

4.3.5 Language Extensions

All the hospital examples used only standard SQL. However, there are some additional operators that are added to standard SQL to enhance its usability for infinite relational databases.

The first extension allows complex conditions, such as linear or polynomial equations, in the SELECT or the WHERE clauses.

Example 4.3.8 Suppose a tax accountant wants to find the Social Security Number (SSN) and the tax payable by each person in the *Taxrecord* relation. The tax can be found using the *Taxtable* relation and the following SQL query:

```
SELECT   SSN, Tax
FROM     Taxrecord, Taxtable
WHERE    Wages + Interest + Capital_Gain = Income
```

The second extension allows the argument of a MAX or MIN aggregate operator to be a linear function. The more general form of a basic SQL query with aggregation is the following:

```
SELECT      B_1, ..., B_m,  MAX(c_1 A_1 + ... + c_n A_n)
FROM        ...
WHERE       ...
GROUP BY    B_1, ..., B_m
```

where the A_i for $1 \leq i \leq n$ and B_j for $1 \leq j \leq m$ are attribute names and c_i for $1 \leq i \leq n$ are rational constants. The WHERE and the GROUP BY clauses are optional. Instead of MAX the MIN aggregate operator may be used. The linear function argument is called an *objective function*, a term that is borrowed from operations research.

Example 4.3.9 Suppose the farmer in Example 4.1.4 wants to find the maximum profit possible given that each acre of corn, rye, sunflower, and wheat yields a profit of 30, 25, 8, and 15, respectively. The following SQL query finds the maximum profit possible for any of the planting options:

```
SELECT    MAX(30 Corn +25 Rye + 8 Sunflower + 15 Wheat)
FROM      Crops
```

4.4 Evaluation

The infinite relational data model is a powerful generalization of the relational data model. However, the infinite relational data model is not suitable for direct computer representation because computers have only a finite memory. Hence in practice attention must be restricted to *finitely representable infinite relations*. Hence the first step of any query evaluation method is to give a finite representation.

The constraint data model provides a finite representation of the infinite relational data model. In the constraint data model each attribute is associated with an attribute variable, and the value of the attributes in a relation is specified implicitly using constraints. Section 4.4.1 reviews arithmetic constraints, Section 4.4.2 presents the constraint data model, and Section 4.4.3 discusses the place of the constraint data model in the data abstraction hierarchy. Finally, Section 4.4.4 compares the evaluation of relational and constraint database queries.

4.4.1 Constraints

In this section we review the most common types of arithmetic constraints that are used in constraint databases. Constraints apply to two or more variables. Each variable takes its value from a domain. Common domains are the set of nonnegative integer or natural numbers $\mathcal{N}$, the set of integer numbers $\mathcal{Z}$, the set of rational numbers $\mathcal{Q}$, and the set of real numbers $\mathcal{R}$.

Other domains include the set of English words in a dictionary, which we denote as $\mathcal{W}$.

In the following let u, v be either variables or constants and b and c_i be constant. Let $\pm$ denote $+$ or $-$ and p be a polynomial function over the variables $x_1, \ldots, x_n$ (any valid expression with constants, variables, addition, and multiplication symbols). Let θ be either $\geq$ or $>$. We define the most basic type of constraints, called the *atomic* constraints, over any of the domains $\mathcal{N}, \mathcal{Z}, \mathcal{Q}, \mathcal{R}$ as follows:

Equality :	u	$=$	v	
Inequality :	u	$\neq$	v	
Lower Bound :	u	θ	b	
Upper Bound :	$-u$	θ	b	
Order :	u	θ	v	
Gap-Order :	$u - v$	θ	b	where $b \geq 0$
Difference :	$u - v$	θ	b	
Half-Addition :	$\pm u \pm v$	θ	b	where $b \geq 0$
Addition :	$\pm u \pm v$	θ	b	
Linear :	$c_1 x_1 + \ldots + c_n x_n$	θ	b	
Polynomial :	$p(x_1, \ldots, x_n)$	θ	b	

We call b on the right-hand side of these constraints the *bound*. Note that the bound is restricted to be nonnegative in the case of gap-order and half-addition constraints. We will see the significance of this restriction in Chapter 22. We also call each c_i a *coefficient* in the linear constraint.

In general, if a constraint $\mathcal{C}$ is any of these types of constraints and the domain of the variables is Z or Q we talk of integer $\mathcal{C}$ constraints or rational $\mathcal{C}$ constraints, respectively.

Note that except for equality constraints we did not use the $=$ symbol. This is because we consider each $=$ constraint as the conjunction of two $\geq$ constraints. For example, the linear equation $5x + 7y = 8$ can be expressed as the conjunction of the linear inequality constraints $5x + 7y \geq 8$ and $5x + 7y \leq 8$. This is why we do not consider linear equations as *atomic* constraints. Atomic constraints are supposed to be constraints that cannot be expressed as conjunctions of other simpler constraints. Nevertheless, in this book we will often write constraints with $=$ signs. In each instance, however, the equality constraints should be understood to be conjunctions of two inequality constraints similarly to the preceding example.

We will not insist on always writing the constraints in this form. For example, an upper-bound constraint of the form $-u \geq b$ could be sometimes written as $-b \geq u$. As another example, the gap-order constraint $x - y \geq b$ could sometimes be written as $x \geq y + b$ or $b \leq x - y$ or some other equivalent form. Similarly, the linear equation mentioned earlier could be written as, for example, $y = (-5x + 8)/7$.

The form defined earlier should be considered a standard form for atomic constraints. It is only important to remember that each constraint we use can be expressed as the conjunction of one or more constraints in the standard forms.

The constraints defined earlier have several connections with each other. In general they are increasingly expressive. Hence we find, for example, that each gap-order constraint is also a half-addition constraint. Each half-addition constraint is also an addition constraint, which is a linear constraint. Each linear constraint is also a polynomial constraint.

Using the atomic constraints, we can define constraint formulas.

Definition 4.4.1 [Constraint Formula] Let $\mathcal{C}$ be any type of constraints discussed earlier. We define constraint formulas recursively as follows:

1. Each atomic constraint of $\mathcal{C}$ is a formula.

2. If F and G are formulas, then $(F \ \mathbf{and} \ G)$ and $(F \ \mathbf{or} \ G)$ are formulas.

3. If F is a formula, then $(\mathbf{not} \ F)$ is a formula.

A formula that contains only the "and" connective is called a *conjunction*. Similarly a formula that contains only the "or" connective is called a *disjunction*. A formula that contains only "and" and "or" connectives is called a *positive* formula.

Each of the atomic constraints is said to be *satisfiable*, if there is some instantiation of the variables by constants from the domain that makes it true. For example, the constraint $x - y \geq 5$ is satisfiable because the instantiation 9 for x and 3 for y makes the constraint true. A constraint is said to be *valid* if all instantiations make it true. The preceding constraint is not true because, for example, the instantiation 0 for x and 2 for y makes the constraint false.

Let F be a formula. Note that any instantiation of the variables of F makes each atomic constraint either true or false. Therefore, the formula can be evaluated to be true or false. We say that F is satisfiable if there is an instantiation that makes it true, and we say that it is valid if each possible instantiation makes it true.

Let $\mathcal{C}$ be any of the types of constraints and let $F(x_1, \ldots, x_n)$ be any $\mathcal{C}$ constraint formula with variables $x_1, \ldots, x_n$. If $t = (c_1, \ldots, c_n)$ is a tuple of constants and substituting each x_i by c_i makes F true, then we say that t satisfies F and we write $t \models F$.

Example 4.4.1 Let $F(x_1, x_2)$ be the formula $x_2 = x_1 \times 0.15$ and t be the pair of constants $(10080, 1512)$. Then $t \models F$ because $1512 = 10080 \times 0.15$ is true.

The *complement* of a formula F is the formula F'. We have that $t \models F$ is true if and only if $t \models F'$ is false.

Example 4.4.2 Let $F(x_1, x_2)$ be the formula $x_2 = x_1 \times 0.15$ and t be the pair of constants $(10080, 1512)$. Then F' is $x_2 \neq x_1 \times 0.15$ and $t \models F'$ is false because $1512 \neq 10080 \times 0.15$ is false.

Formulas are often put into *disjunctive normal form*, which means they are disjunctions of conjunctions. Any formula can be put into disjunctive normal form by using the Boolean algebra axioms and some useful identities, called *De Morgan's laws*, which can be derived from them. These laws are:

$$(F \ \textbf{and} \ G)' = F' \ \textbf{or} \ G'$$

$$(F \ \textbf{or} \ G)' = F' \ \textbf{and} \ G'$$

Example 4.4.3 Consider the formula $((a \ \textbf{or} \ b) \ \textbf{and} \ c)'$. Applying the first law we obtain $(a \ \textbf{or} \ b)' \ \textbf{or} \ c'$. Applying the second law we obtain $(a' \ \textbf{and} \ b') \ \textbf{or} \ c'$, which is already in disjunctive normal form.

In many cases the negation of a $\mathcal{C}$-type atomic constraint is also a $\mathcal{C}$ atomic constraint or a conjunction of $\mathcal{C}$-type atomic constraints. In this case we say that $\mathcal{C}$ is *closed under negation*. For example, addition, linear, and polynomial constraints are closed under negation. On the other hand, gap-order and positive linear constraints are not closed under negation.

4.4.2 Constraint Data Model

A *constraint database* is a finite set of constraint relations. A *constraint relation* is a finite set of constraint tuples, where each *constraint tuple* is a conjunction of atomic constraints using the same set of attribute variables. For simplicity, we abbreviate within constraint tuples the "and"s by commas.

Example 4.4.4 The U.S. federal tax rules for single-income taxpayers, assuming income means taxable income, state the following information.

- Up to $24,000 the tax is 15 percent of the income.

- Between $24,000 and $58,150 the tax is $3,600 plus 28 percent of the income above $24,000.

- Between $58,150 and $121,300 the tax is $12,162 plus 31 percent of the income above $58,150.

- Between \$121,300 and \$263,750 the tax is \$32,738.5 plus 36 percent of the income above \$121,300.

- Above \$263,750 the tax is \$84,020.5 plus 39.6 percent of the income above \$263,750.

This information can be represented by the following constraint relation:

Taxtable

Income	Tax	
i	t	$0 \leq i,\ i \leq 24000,\ t = 0.15i$
i	t	$24000 < i,\ i \leq 58150,\ t = 3600 + 0.28(i - 24000)$
i	t	$58150 < i,\ i \leq 121300,\ t = 13162 + 0.31(i - 58150)$
i	t	$121300 < i, i \leq 263750, t = 32738.5 + 0.36(i - 121300)$
i	t	$263750 < i,\ t = 84020.5 + 0.396(i - 263750)$

This constraint relation uses a variable i for the income and a variable t for the tax. Both variables range over the rational numbers. The first row of the *Taxrecord* relation means that a person with any income i such that the condition $0 \leq i, i \leq 24000, t = i \times 0.15$ is true should pay t amount in tax.

Note that the entire constraint relation consists of only five constraint tuples although it represents the infinite relation described earlier. The constraints in the table are order constraints and linear equations over the rational numbers.

Example 4.4.5 The *Kepler* relation of Example 4.1.2 can be represented by the following constraint database:

Kepler

Period	Radius	
t	r	$t^2 = r^3$

This constraint relation uses a variable t for the orbital period and r for the mean orbital radius around the sun relative to the orbital period of the earth. The only constraint in the table is a polynomial equation over the real numbers.

The entire constraint relation consists of only one constraint tuple, which is greatly surprising. In fact, Kepler derived his simple laws of planetary motion, out of which this is the most remarkable, from decades of careful observations and records by the Danish astronomer Tycho Brache. Although Brache's tables were not infinite, they were large and unwieldy to use.

Example 4.4.6 The *Height* relation of Example 4.1.3 can be represented by the following constraint relation:

Height

CM	IN	
c	i	$0.39c = i$

We can represent the *Weight* relation similarly to the *Height* relation.

Suppose that Anderson loses six kilograms per month during the first five months and two kilograms per months during the next seven months of the dieting program. Suppose also that Smith loses two kilograms per month during the entire twelve months of the dieting program. Then the *Diet* relation can be represented by the following constraint relation:

Diet

ID	KG	Month	
100	y	t	$y = -6t + 130, \ 0 \leq t, \ t \leq 5$
100	y	t	$y = -2t + 110, \ 5 \leq t, \ t \leq 12$
755	y	t	$y = -2t + 120, \ 0 \leq t, \ t \leq 12$

Example 4.4.7 The *Crops* relation of Example 4.1.4 can be represented by the following constraint relation:

Crops

Corn	Rye	Sunflower	Wheat	
x_1	x_2	x_3	x_4	$15x_1 + 8x_2 + 10x_3 + 15x_4 \leq 3000,$ $30x_1 + 25x_2 + 5x_3 + 10x_4 \leq 8000$

This constraint relation uses linear inequality constraints over the rational numbers.

4.4.3   Data Abstraction

Each data model provides some abstraction about the stored data. We distinguish four levels of data abstraction, namely, the view, logical, constraint, and physical levels. The various levels of data abstraction are linked by translation methods. Let us discuss these briefly.

View Level: This is how users can view their data. For different sets of users different views can be provided by a database. We saw several examples in Chapter 3. We'll see more examples of visualization used in the

MLPQ/PReSTO constraint database system in Chapter 13.

Logical Level: The second highest level of data abstraction is called the *logical* level. The logical level is the most important level for those who want to query the database. People who query the database write simple programs that are best written and understood when the data is thought of at the logical level.

In the constraint data abstraction hierachy, the logical level describes what data are stored in terms of sets of infinite relations. We saw examples of these in Section 4.1.

Constraint Level: This level describes the data stored using one or more constraint relations. We saw several examples of these in Section 4.4. There is a natural link between the logical and the constraint levels. Let r be the infinite relational model and R be the constraint model of a relation. Then a tuple t is in r if and only if there is a constraint tuple C in R such that after substitution of the constants in t into the variables of C we get a true formula, that is, t satisfies C. We can summarize:

$$t \in r \text{ iff } t \models C \text{ for some } C \in R$$

For example, $(10080, 1512)$ is in the infinite relational model of $Taxtable$ because it satisfies the first constraint tuple in the constraint data model, as we saw in Example 4.4.1.

Physical Level: This level corresponds to the way the data is actually stored in a computer system. We will see some examples of this in Chapter 20.

4.4.4   Query Processing

Although most of the key features of query evaluation described in Section 3.4 still apply to constraint databases, there are some significant differences. Below we highlight some of the interesting similarities and differences.

As described in Section 3.4, we still translate SQL queries into relational algebra queries, allowing a fast evaluation.

Example 4.4.8 The tax accountant query of Example 4.3.8 can be translated into the following relational algebra query:

$$\Pi_{SSN, Tax} \sigma_{Wages+Interest+Capital\_Gain=Income} \; Taxrecord \times Taxtable$$

Constraint database systems usually treat conditions like the linear equation in the above example as functions. That is, one of the variables is an unknown, while the others are known. The unknown value is computed during query processing. In the above example, *Income* is the unknown, which is computed from the known values of the *Wages*, the *Interest*, and the *Capital_Gain* attributes.

Although some relational database systems also allow linear equations, they cannot deal with them as functions. Relational database systems expect to find a finite number of values in the *Income* column of the *Taxtable* relation. During query evaluation, they substitute each of the finite values and test whether any of those values satisfy the linear equation. Obviously, this substitution is impossible for infinite relational databases. Hence relational databases cannot evaluate the above query. While constraint database systems can evaluate the above query, the details of the evaluation are postponed to Chapter 24.

Bibliographic Notes

Many branches of mathematics use tables and relations, both finite and infinite, as well as finite representations of infinite tables. For example, infinite semilinear sets are represented by conjunctions and disjunction of linear inequality constraints, which are expressible as a constraint table.

Kanellakis, Kuper, and Revesz [214, 215] initiated the area of constraint databases by combining finitely representable infinite relations and database queries. They presented a general framework for constraint databases that included a *closed form evaluation* requirement. Closed-form evaluation means that constraint database queries take as input and give as output constraint relations with the same type of constraints.

The closed-form evaluation requirement distinguishes constraint database queries from constraint logic programs [205] even when they are syntactically similar, such as, in the case of constraint deductive databases described in Chapter 12.

The closed-form evaluation enables the extension of SQL by the `MAX` and `MIN` operators using linear objective functions and rational linear constraint databases as input. The evaluation of these extended SQL queries is based on linear programming. The Management of Linear Programming Queries (MLPQ) system [351, 349] was the first constraint database system to extend SQL with linear programming.

Exercises

1. Express the following in SQL using the *Taxrecord* and the *Taxtable* relations.

   (a) Find the tax due from the taxpayer with SSN number 777889999.

(b) Find the total taxes due from each taxpayer.

(c) Find the SSN of the taxpayer who has to pay the most tax.

2. Express the following in SQL using the *Package* and the *Postage* relations.

   (a) Find how much Mr. Johnson should pay to send all the packages.

   (b) Find how much Mr. Johnson should pay for each destination city.

   (c) Find the name of the most expensive destination city for Mr. Johnson.

3. Express the following in SQL using the *Planet* and the *Kepler* relations.

   (a) Find the name and the mean orbital radius of each planet in the solar system.

   (b) Find the smallest mean orbital radius of any planet in the solar system.

   (c) Find the name of the planet which has the largest orbital radius.

4. Express the following in SQL using the hospital database.

   (a) Find the weight when Anderson and Smith have equal weight.

   (b) Find the number of kilograms by which Anderson is overweight after two months in the dieting program.

   (c) Find the period of time when Anderson is a normal weight person.

5. Find the constraint representation for the *Taxtable* relation using the current tax code in your country. (Hint: If needed, you may extend the *Taxtable* relation by adding an extra attribute for taxpayer category, for instance, single or married.)

6. Find the constraint representation for the *Postage* relation assuming the following information.

   • Up to 5 ounces, the fee is the weight of the package times 0.53.

   • Between 5 and 15 ounces the fee is $2.65 plus 0.45 times the weight over 5 ounces.

   • Between 15 and 30 ounces the fee is $7.15 plus 0.3 times the weight over 15 ounces

- For more than 30 ounces the fee is $11.65 plus 0.25 times the weight over 30 ounces.

7. Find the constraint representation for the *Weight* relation.

8. Find the constraint representation for the *Fit* relation assuming the following information:

   - Any person is overweight whose kilogram weight is more than his centimeter height minus 80.
   - Any person is underweight whose kilogram weight is less than 0.66 his centimeter height minus 53.33.
   - Any person who is not overweight or underweight is a normal weight person.

9. Suppose that Johnson, who is underweight, also enrolls in a dieting program in order to gain weight. Find the constraint representation for Johnson's progress by adding new constraint tuples to the *Diet* relation, assuming the following information:

   - Johnson gains 3 kilograms per month during the first three months of the program.
   - He gains 2 kilograms per month during the next five months of the program.
   - He gains 1 kilogram per month during the last four months of the program.

10. Find the constraint representations for the *BabyBoy(Type,Month,Inch)* and the *BabyGirl(Type,Month,Inch)* relations, which give some health statistics for babies, assuming the following information:

    During the first six months:

    - Any boy is tall whose inch height minus month age is more than 22.5.
    - Any girl is tall whose inch height minus month age is more than 21.5.
    - Any boy is short whose inch height minus month age is less than 18.5.
    - Any girl is short whose inch height minus month age is less than 18.
    - Any boy or girl who is neither tall nor short has an average height.

Between six and 18 months:

- Any boy is tall whose inch height minus half his month age is more than 25.5.
- Any girl is tall whose inch height minus half her month age is more than 24.5.
- Any boy is short whose inch height minus half his month age is more than 21.5.
- Any girl is short whose inch height minus half her month age is more than 21.
- Any boy or girl who is neither tall nor short has an average height.

11. Write SQL queries for the following.

    (a) Find those baby girls who are tall.
    (b) Find the minimum age of the boys who are at least 25 inches tall.
    (c) Find the number of baby boys who are average.
    (d) Find the union of the short baby boys and short baby girls.
    (e) Find how many inches is Alice below the lowest considered average for girls of her age if she is ten months old and 25 inches tall.
    (f) Find the height of the girls who are younger than Alice is.
    (g) Find the girls who are average but would be considered tall if they were boys.

5

Temporal Databases

Temporal databases represent events that occur in time. There is a long
tradition in computer science of dealing with temporal data, and many ways
of dealing with temporal data were discovered. Section 5.1 reviews Allen's
temporal relations, which had a great influence in artificial intelligence and
database systems. Section 5.2 discusses temporal data models. Section 5.3
discusses indefinite temporal data models. Section 5.4 considers temporal
queries.

5.1 Allen's Relations

An attractive and seminal proposal, made by James F. Allen, is to associate
with each event an interval of duration. This temporal data representation
leads naturally to a fixed number of possible relationships between pairs of
events I and J. The following are some of these relationships.

I Before J – when I is over before J starts.

I Contains J – when J occurs only when I occurs.

I Equals J – when I and J occur always simultaneously.

I Meets J – when I just finishes before J starts.

I Overlap J – when I and J overlap in time.

It is possible to develop a reasoning system for intervals. Such a reasoning system may include the following transitivity rules or axioms.

P. Revesz, *Introduction to Databases: From Biological to Spatio-Temporal*,
Texts in Computer Science, DOI 10.1007/978-1-84996-095-3_5,
© Springer-Verlag London Limited 2010

Axiom 5.1.1

If I_1 Before I_2 and I_2 Before I_3, then I_1 Before I_3.

If I_1 Contains I_2 and I_2 Contains I_3, then I_1 Contains I_3.

If I_1 Equals I_2 and I_2 Equals I_3, then I_1 Equals I_3.

One has to be careful because the transitivity does not hold for some of the other temporal relations, such as, the *Meets* relation. However, it is possible to define other valid rules using the *Meets* relations. For example, the following is another valid rule.

Axiom 5.1.2

If I_1 Meets I_2 and I_2 Meets I_3, then I_1 Before I_3.

It is an interesting exercise to find all the valid rules for Allen's interval relations. There are many reasoning systems for temporal intervals and these serve as the basis for temporal database systems.

Example 5.1.1 The Allen temporal relation

$I_{Guest}\ During\ I_{Database}$

describes that there will be a guest speaker during the database systems class.

5.1.1   Qualitative versus Metric Relations

Qualitative relations do not involve numerical values, while metric relations involve some numerical values that measure the degree of the relationship. For example, knowing that a guest speaker speaks during the database systems class does not tell us how long the speech will last. However, the statement that "there will be an at least 10 minutes long presentation by a guest speaker during the database systems class" is a metric temporal relationship. Most temporal databases are only considering qualitative temporal relationships.

5.1.2   Pointized Representation

For each temporal interval I, let I^- be the beginning of I, and let I^+ be the end of I. Then I can be represented by the set of time instances that are inclusively between I^- and I^+.

Definition 5.1.1 A temporal relation between two time intervals I and J is *pointisable* if it can be defined using conjunctions of $=$, $<$, and $>$ constraints between I^- and J^-, between I^- and J^+, between I^+ and J^-, and between I^+ and J^+.

It follows from Definition 5.1.1 that there are $4^4 = 256$ logically expressible pointizable temporal relations between two time intervals. However, out of those only 13 are enough to express every physically possible qualitative relationships between two time intervals. Those 13 are the following:

Relation of I and J	I^- J^-	I^- J^+	I^+ J^-	I^+ J^+
After :		$>$		
Before :			$<$	
Meets :			$=$	
Met by :		$=$		
During :	$>$			$<$
Contains :	$<$			$>$
Equal :	$=$			$=$
Finishes :	$>$			$=$
Finished by :	$<$			$=$
Starts :	$=$			$<$
Started by :	$=$			$>$
Overlaps :	$<$		$>$	$<$
Overlapped by :	$>$	$<$		$>$

Example 5.1.2 The Allen temporal relation between the guest speaker and the database systems class in Example 5.1.1 is pointizable because it can be represented as follows:

$$I^-_{Guest} > I^-_{Database} \quad \text{and} \quad I^+_{Guest} < I^+_{Database}.$$

Metric temporal relations can be also pointizable if we allow conjunctions of difference constraints between the end points of the intervals.

Example 5.1.3 The metric temporal relation expressed by the statement "there will be an at least 10 minutes long presentation by a guest speaker during the Database Systems class" can be represented as follows:

$$I^-_{Guest} > I^-_{Database} \quad \text{and} \quad I^+_{Guest} < I^+_{Database} \quad \text{and} \quad I^+_{Guest} - I^-_{Guest} \geq 10.$$

Some temporal constraints between time intervals are not pointizable. For example, *Inequal* can be expressed as the disjunction $(X^- \neq Y^-)$ or $(X^+ \neq Y^+)$ but cannot be expressed using only conjunctions.

5.2 Temporal Data Models

TQuel is a popular model for representing temporal data. In the TQuel data model each relation contains two special attributes called *From* and *To* to represent *valid time*. The value of these temporal attributes must be integers or the special constants $-\infty$ or $+\infty$. The *From* and *To* values represent the endpoints of a temporal interval. In TSQL the intervals in different tuples with identical nontemporal components have to be disjoint.

The abstract semantics of a TQuel database is a relational database which has the same scheme as the TQuel database except the temporal attributes *From* and *To* are replaced with a single temporal attribute.

Example 5.2.1 Relation *Employee* shown below describes where and when some employees worked.

Employee

Name	Company	From	To
Anderson	AT&T	1980	1993
Anderson	AT&T	1994	1997
Brown	IBM	1985	1996
Clark	Lotus	1990	1991

The above TQuel database is logically equivalent to the following relational database.

Employee

Name	Company	Year
Anderson	AT&T	1980
⋮	⋮	⋮
Anderson	AT&T	1997
Brown	IBM	1985
⋮	⋮	⋮
Brown	IBM	1996
Clark	Lotus	1990
Clark	Lotus	1991

Another time dimension, transaction time, can also be present and is represented similarly to valid time. For simplicity we do not consider it here.

Sometimes temporal events repeat themselves. These repetitions can be described by *linear repeating points* of the form $kn+c$ where n is an integer variable and k and c are constants.

Example 5.2.2 The Olympic games are held every four years since 1896 except the years 1916, 1940, and 1944 when they were cancelled due to the two World Wars. Hence the years of the Olympic games in modern times can be described by the following relation.

Olympics

Year
$4n + 1896$ $n \geq 0,\ n \neq 5,\ n \neq 11,\ n \neq 12$

5.3   Indefinite Temporal Data Model

Temporal databases can be extended with *marked null values*, which are represented by variables. We do not know the value of marked null values precisely, only imprecisely or *indefinitely*. Therefore, temporal databases with marked null values are called *indefinite temporal databases*.

Example 5.3.1 Consider the following indefinite temporal database where ω_1, ω_2 and ν are marked null values, where ω_1 and ω_2 denote time intervals whose duration is not known precisely, and ν denotes a time instance whose value is not known precisely.

On_Service

Vehicle	City	From	To
V1	Athens	ω_1^-	ω_1^+
V2	Athens	ω_2^-	ω_2^+

Trip

Vehicle	Origin	Destination	From	To
V3	Athens	Patra	5	8
V3	Patra	Athens	9	ν

The marked null values are constrained by a *global constraint*, which is applied to the whole relation. That is in constrast to the local constraints within constraint relations, where all local constraints apply to only one constraint tuple. For instance, consider the following global constraint G:

1. ω_1 starts at time 9 and ends at some time between 14 and 16,

2. ω_2 starts at some time between 10 and 10.5 and its duration is 2 to 4 time units, and

3. point ν is between 12 and 13.

The above global constraint can be expressed as follows:

$$\omega_1^- = 9,\ 14 \le \omega_1^+ \le 16,\ 10 \le \omega_2^- \le 10.5,\ 2 \le \omega_2^+ - \omega_2^- \le 4,\ 12 \le \nu \le 13.$$

This information is also presented graphically in the following picture, where the intervals are represented by line segments. Solid line segments depict the extent of an interval about which we have definite information. Dashed line segments depict the extent of an interval about which we have indefinite information. Similar conventions are followed for time points.

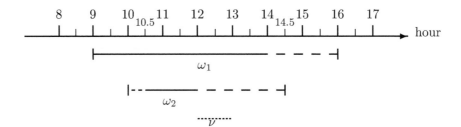

Indefinite temporal relations are semantically equivalent to a set of *possible worlds* which capture all the possible ways the domain of application could have been according to our indefinite information. Each possible world can be represented by a constraint relation. One can find all the possible worlds represented by a relation as follows:

- Find to the marked null values an assignment that satisfies the global constraint.

- Substitute these values for the marked nulls in the indefinite temporal relation.

Example 5.3.2 The assignment $\omega_1 = [9, 16]$, $\omega_2 = [10, 14.5]$ and $\nu = 13.25$, yields the following possible world.

On_Service

Vehicle	City	Hour
V1	Athens	9
⋮	⋮	⋮
V1	Athens	16
V2	Athens	10
⋮	⋮	⋮
V2	Athens	14.5

Trip

Vehicle	Origin	Destination	Hour
V3	Athens	Patra	5
⋮	⋮	⋮	⋮
V3	Athens	Patra	8
V3	Patra	Athens	9
⋮	⋮	⋮	⋮
V3	Patra	Athens	13.25

5.4 Temporal Database Queries

There area two main types of temporal database query languages. Section 5.4.1 describes interval-based query languages. Section 5.4.2 describes point-based query languages.

5.4.1 Interval-Based Queries

Interval-based query languages allow extra operations on the intervals, that is, the *From* and *To* attributes of relations. That is, these two attributes are considered a special abstract data type *interval*, and special operations are defined on these intervals. These operations may be Allen's temporal relations or some other operators. For example, the following are some operators that can be introduced.

before(I^-, I^+, J^-, J^+) → Boolean: This operator tests whether interval I occurs before interval J.

contains(I^-, I^+, J^-, J^+) → Boolean: This operator tests whether interval I contains interval J.

equals(I^-, I^+, J^-, J^+) → Boolean: This operator tests whether intervals I and J occur always simultaneously.

meets(I^-, I^+, J^-, J^+) → Boolean: This operator tests whether interval I just finishes before J starts.

overlap(I^-, I^+, J^-, J^+) → Boolean: This operator tests whether intervals I and J overlap.

Next we give some examples of using the above operators based on Allen's relations to express temporal database queries.

Example 5.4.1 Find the employee who worked at the same company during all the time that Clark worked at Lotus.

Using the Employee relation, the following query finds those employees who worked at a time interval that includes the time interval of Clark's work at Lotus.

CREATE VIEW	Contemporary_of_Clark(Name)
SELECT	DISTINCT E1.Name
FROM	Employee AS E1, Employee AS E2
WHERE	E1.Name $\neq$ "Clark" AND
	E2.Name = "Clark" AND
	contains(E1.From, E1.To, E2.From, E2.To)

The time interval associated with Clark working at Lotus is [1990, 1991]. The query returns "Anderson" because the first line of the *Employee* relation defined the time interval [1980, 1993] when Anderson worked at *AT&T*, and contains (1980,1993,1990,1991) is true. The query also returns "Brown" because the third line of the *Employee* relation defined the time interval [1985, 1996] when Brown worked at IBM, and contains (1985,1996,1990,1991) is true. Hence the above query returns as answer the following relation.

Contemporary_of_Clark

Name
Anderson
Brown

The following is a small variation of the abvoe query.

Example 5.4.2 Find the employee who worked at the same company during all the time that Brown worked at IBM.

At first we may be tempted to write the following query similarly to the previous query.

SELECT	DISTINCT E1.Name
FROM	Employee AS E1, Employee AS E2
WHERE	E1.Name $\neq$ "Brown" AND
	E2.Name = "Brown" AND
	contains(E1.From, E1.To, E2.From, E2.To)

Note that Anderson was working at AT&T during [1980, 1993] and [1994, 1997], and hence during [1980, 1997], which contains [1985, 1996], when Brown was working at IBM. Hence we would expect "Anderson" to be returned but the above query would not return "Anderson" because neither [1980, 1993] nor [1994, 1997] by itself contains [1985, 1996]. To correct this problem, we introduce another operator.

$coalesce(2^{[I^-,I^+]}) \rightarrow 2^{[J^-,J^+]}$: This operator takes as input a set of intervals and returns another logically equivalent set of intervals, such that in the returned set no interval meets or overlaps another interval.

Clearly, if we coalesce the time intervals associated with any distinct pair of employee names and companies, then we can avoid the previously described problem. The *coalesce* function is like an aggregate function in that it has to be applied to the entire temporal relation. Hence the *coalesce* operator can occur at the same places where aggregate operators can occur. For instance, we can coalesce the *Employee* relation as follows.

CREATE VIEW	Coalesce_Employee(Name, Company, From, To)
SELECT	Name, Company, Coalesce(From, To)
FROM	Employee
GROUP BY	Name, Company

Using the above relation, we can now correctly express the original query as follows.

CREATE VIEW	Contemporary_of_Brown(Name)
SELECT	DISTINCT E1.Name
FROM	Coalesce_Employee AS E1, Coalesce_Employee AS E2
WHERE	E1.Name $\neq$ "Brown" AND
	E2.Name = "Brown" AND
	contains(E1.From, E1.To, E2.From, E2.To)

The above query returns as answer the following relation.

Contemporary_of_Brown

Name
Anderson

There are still other operators that would be needed for other queries. For example, the following operator extends the overlap relation to three intervals.

$triple\_overlap(I^-, I^+, J^-, J^+, K^-, K^+) \rightarrow$ *Boolean:* This operator tests whether three intervals I, J, and K, overlap.

Example 5.4.3 Find all triplets of employees who worked at the same time.

SELECT	I.Name, J.Name, K.Name
FROM	Employee AS I, Employee AS J, Employee AS K
WHERE	I.Name $\neq$ J.Name AND
	I.Name $\neq$ K.Name AND
	J.Name $\neq$ K.Name AND
	triple_overlap(I.From,I.To,J.From,J.To,K.From,K.To)

The next example considers querying indefinite temporal databases.

Example 5.4.4 Find all vehicles that are on service in Athens throughout the first hour of the afternoon.

CREATE VIEW	Available(Vehicle)
SELECT	Vehicle
FROM	On_Service
WHERE	City = "Athens" AND
	From $\leq$ 12 AND
	To $\geq$ 13

Answering queries in indefinite temporal databases is more complex because some answers are valid only in a subset of the possible worlds represented by the indefinite temporal database. These possible worlds can be specified using *conditional constraints*.

Vehicle V1 is an anwer to the query that is valid in all possible worlds represented by the *On_Service* indefinite temporal relation. On the other hand, vehicle V2 is a valid answer to the query only in the possible worlds where the interval $\omega 2$ extends until time 13 or later. Therefore the answer to this query is the following.

Available

Vehicle	Condition
V1	*true*
V2	$\omega_2^+ \geq 13$

Queries do not alter the global constraint. Hence the global constraint associated with the output database is still G.

5.4.2   Point-Based Queries

Point-based temporal database queries query the finite or infinite relational database that is the semantics or logical-level data abstraction of temporal database. As a result, point-based queries look like standard SQL queries without extra operators.

Example 5.4.5 The query in Example 5.4.2, which required both operators based on Allen's relations and the *coalesce* operator, can be expressed in two steps. First, we find the complement of the *Contemporary_of_Brown* relation, that is, those persons who did not work each year when Brown worked.

CREATE VIEW	Not_Contemporary(Name)		
SELECT	E1.Name		
FROM	Employee AS E1, Employee AS E2		
WHERE	E1.Name ≠ "Brown" AND		
	E2.Name = "Brown" AND		
	E2.Year NOT IN	(SELECT	E3.Year
		FROM	Employee AS E3
		WHERE	E3.Name = E1.Name)

The second step of complementing the above relation is left as an exercise.

Example 5.4.6 The query of Example 5.4.3 can be expressed by the following point-based query that also finds the common years, which we could not do using the interval operators.

SELECT	I.Name, J.Name, K.Name, I.Year
FROM	Employee AS I, Employee AS J, Employee AS K
WHERE	I.Name ≠ J.Name AND
	I.Name ≠ K.Name AND
	J.Name ≠ K.Name AND
	I.Year = J.Year AND
	J.Year = K.Year

Example 5.4.7 Let relation *EarlyAfternoon(Hour)* contain the first hour in the afternoon. Then the complement of the query of Example 5.4.4 can be expressed using a point-based query as follows.

CREATE VIEW	Not_Available(Vehicle)		
SELECT	S1.Vehicle		
FROM	On_Service AS S1,		
	EarlyAfternoon AS T		
WHERE	T.Hour NOT IN	(SELECT	S2.Hour
		FROM	On_Service AS S2
		WHERE	S2.Vehicle = S1.Vehicle AND
			S2.City = "Athens")

Note that in the above the *Not_Available* means that a vehicle returned is not available in Athens at some time between noon and 1:00 pm. Finding the complement of this relation is again left as an exercise.

Bibliographic Notes

Özsu and Liu [295] is a comprehensive encyclopedia on database systems that contains also a wealth of information about temporal databases. Tansel et al. [393] is an older book that presents temporal data models, including the TQuel data model used in the TSQL database system. Snodgrass [380] reviews the TSQL temporal database language, and Frank et al. [137] review the Chorochronos research project on temporal and spatio-temporal databases. Example 5.2.1 is from Chomicki and Revesz [88].

There are various temporal data models that describe periodicly recurring events. A proposal using the modulus operator over the integers is described in [47, 402], linear repeating points, which are discussed in Section 5.2, are from [32, 213]. Another proposal using an extension of Datalog with the successor function in presented in [84]. Periodicity constraints are also considered in the case of moving objects databases in Chapter 7.

Temporal databases with indefinite information are considered in Koubarakis [236] and Koubarakis and Skiadopoulos [240]. Examples 5.3.1 and 5.4.4 are adopted with some modifications from Koubarakis [236]. Marked null values are also considered within relational databases by Imielinski and Lipski [203] and Abiteboul et al. [3].

A complete set of qualitative temporal interval relations was first proposed in Allen [12]. Efficient temporal constraint solving is considered in Dean and Boddy [105], Dechter et al. [107], and Vilain and Kautz [419].

Point-based and interval-based temporal database query languages are compared in Toman [399, 400, 401].

Exercises

1. Andrew and Barbara are two persons who have some free days next month as shown in the constraint relation *Free*, where d is an integer representing days of the month.

Free

PERSON	DAY	
Andrew	d	$3 \leq d,\ d \leq 6$
Andrew	d	$16 \leq d,\ d \leq 26$
Barbara	d	$6 \leq d,\ d \leq 18$
Barbara	d	$25 \leq d,\ d \leq 30$

(a) Convert the *Free* relation to the TQuel temporal data model.

(b) Convert the *Free* relation to the relational data model.

2. Answer the following queries using the *Free* relation converted to the TQuel temporal data model and interval-based temporal database queries.

(a) Find the days when Andrew and Barbara are both free.

(b) A common friend is visiting town from days 5 to 15. Find whether either Andrew or Barbara can be with the common friend on each of the days of the visit.

3. Answer the queries in the previous exercise using the *Free* relation converted to the relational data model.

4. Find whether 1976 was an Olympic year using the *Olympics* relation of Example 5.2.2.

5. Find a possible world that is different from the one given in Exercise 5.3.2 for the *On_Service* and the *Trip* relations. Indicate the assignment to the marked null values.

6. Suppose that relation *Torch*(*Athlete*, *From*, *To*) describes when athletes are expected to carry the Olympic torch in a relay. Find whether the assignment of athletes to carry the Olympic torch is a good assignment, that is, the time intervals meet each other in a chain. (*Hint:* Use a recursive SQL query.)

6

Geographic Databases

Geographic databases are concerned with the representation of objects and phenomena occurring on the surface of the earth. Geographic objects include countries, cities, roads, rivers, mountains, train and telephone line networks, weather patterns, etc. The geographic database representations take the form of various types of maps or different kinds of graphs that express some of the relationships among the geographic objects.

Spatial databases include geographic databases but are more general because they can be concerned with not strictly geographic phenomena. For example, spatial databases can store information about the astronomical information such as the galaxies and the stars of the universe or the layout of an integrated circuit. Despite this slight distinction, the terms geographic databases and spatial databases are often used interchangably. In addition, the term *geographic information system* (GISs) became popular instead of *geographic database systems*. Since our goal is to emphasize data models instead of systems, this chapter will talk about geographic databases and geographic data models.

Extreme points data models is the class of geographic data models that represent geographic objects via simple geometric shapes, such as, rectangles, lines, or polygons. Extreme point data models place a special emphasis on the endpoints of these geometric shapes. This chapter presents three extreme point data models. In particular, Section 6.1 describes the *rectangles* data model, which deals exclusively with rectangles, Section 6.2 introduces the *vector* data model, which deals with polylines and polygons, and Section 6.3 presents *Worboys'* data model, which deals with triangles.

Section 6.4 discusses the application of the constraint data model, which we saw in Chapter 4, to the representation of geographic data. The

P. Revesz, *Introduction to Databases: From Biological to Spatio-Temporal*,
Texts in Computer Science, DOI 10.1007/978-1-84996-095-3_6,
© Springer-Verlag London Limited 2010

constraint data model is an example of a *point set* geographic data model. This data model is compared with the previous geographic data models in terms of expressive power.

Section 6.5 describes an example of a topological data model. Topological data models aim not to describe the exact physical location of objects but only their relationships such as connectivity and distance. Topological data models often use some kind of graphs or closely related tables.

Section 6.6 considers geographic database queries. Section 6.6.1 describes relational database-based queries, and Section 6.6.2 presents constraint database-based queries. In addition, these two query approaches are compared via examples of common geographic problems.

6.1   Rectangles Data Model

The *rectangles data model* assumes that the spatial extent of each object is either a rectangle or the union of a set of rectangles. It also assumes that the sides of the rectangles are parallel to the x- or y-axes. In the rectangles data model the temporal extent of an object is a time interval or the union of a set of time intervals.

The rectangles data model represents the spatial extent of a d-dimensional rectangle as the cross product of d intervals, one for each dimension. The temporal extent of each object is represented as a set of time intervals. Each spatial and temporal interval is represented by its endpoints. The endpoints of the intervals are also called the *extreme points* of the intervals. We allow the special constants $-\infty$ or $+\infty$ as endpoints of temporal intervals.

Further, each tuple of the rectangle model represents just the combination of one rectangle and one time interval. Therefore, several tuples need to be used to describe objects whose spatial or temporal extents are composed of a set of intervals. An ID number unique to each object connects the different tuples representing the same object.

Example 6.1.1 Suppose an archaeologist excavating a settlement finds three houses built at different periods, as shown in Figure 6.1. The figure shows for each house its area and the time interval when it existed.

The first house was built in year 100 and lasted untill year 200. The second house was built in year 150 and lasted untill year 350. The third house was built in year 250 and lasted untill year 400. Note that by the time the third house was built the first house was demolished; hence the areas of the two houses did not overlap in any year.

Here the spatial extent of the first two houses are single rectangles, while the spatial extent of the third house is the union of two rectangles. The spatial extent of the third house can be described in several ways, depending on how we partition the house area into rectangular areas. One

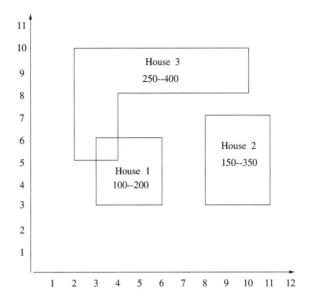

Figure 6.1: Archaeological site.

way to partition is to add in our imagination the line segment from $(2, 8)$ to $(4, 8)$ to the representation of the third house. We could choose other divisions of the area of the third house into rectangles, even a division in which the areas of the rectangles overlap. Any division leads to a good representation as long as the union of the points in the rectangles equals the points in the area of the third house.

Relation $House(Id, X, Y, T)$ is a rectangles data model representation of the archaeological site, where Id refers to the house ID number, the X and Y to the intervals in the x and y dimensions, respectively, and T to the time interval.

House

Id	X	Y	T
1	[3, 6]	[3, 6]	[100, 200]
2	[8, 11]	[3, 7]	[150, 350]
3	[2, 4]	[5, 10]	[250, 400]
3	[2, 10]	[8, 10]	[250, 400]

In the *House* relation the first house is represented by its ID, which is 1, the cross product of the interval $[3, 6]$ in the x and y dimensions, and the temporal interval $[100, 200]$. The second house is represented similarly to the first. The third house is more complicated by the use of two tuples, one for each rectangular piece of the area of the third house. The time dimension, of course, is the same interval $[250, 400]$ in each tuple representing the third house.

In the rectangles data model, as in other data models, the Id number is optional and usually used only if we are representing several objects. If we are only interested in representing one object then we do not use the Id fields. In the absence of an Id it is implicitly assumed that all the tuples represent just one object.

6.2 Vector Data Model

Although there are many problems where the objects are rectangular, the rectangles data model is clearly limited when the objects have a more complex shape or the sides of the rectangles are not parallel to either the x- or y-axis. The *vector data model*, which we introduce below can deal with more complex shapes.

The *vector data model* allows several types of spatial objects in the Euclidean plane. A *point* object is a pair of x and y coordinates. A *polyline* is a list of points. A *polygon* is a list of points where the last point is assumed to connect to the first point. Finally, a *region* is a set of polygons.

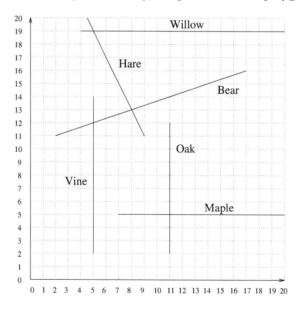

Figure 6.2: A street map.

Example 6.2.1 Figure 6.2 shows an outline of a city map with six streets. Since the roads are straight lines, they can be represented as polylines using their endpoints.

Street

Id	Type	List
Bear	polyline	[(2, 11), (17, 16)]
Hare	polyline	[(4.5, 20), (9, 11)]
Maple	polyline	[(7, 5), (20, 5)]
Oak	polyline	[(11, 2), (11, 12)]
Vine	polyline	[(5, 2), (5, 14)]
Willow	polyline	[(4, 19), (20, 19)]

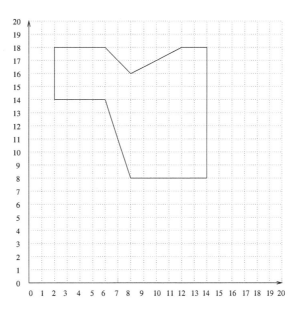

Figure 6.3: A town map.

Example 6.2.2 Figure 6.3 shows a map of Lincoln, Nebraska. The area of the town can be represented as follows.

Town

Id	Type	List
Lincoln	polygon	[(2, 18), (6, 18), (8, 16), (12, 18), (14, 18), (14, 8), (8, 8), (6, 14), (2, 14)]

The vector data model is better than the rectangles data model because the vector data model can represent precisely the shape of points, lines, and polygons. Hence the vector data model is a popular data model used within several geographic information systems to describe spatial data. Within geographic information systems the boundaries of geographic objects like islands and countries is approximated by a high-degree polygon.

6.3   Worboys' Data Model

An alternative solution to the problem of adding temporal data to the vector data model is to represent separately the two pieces of the road but without introducing arcs. *Worboys' data model*, named after its originator, M. Worboys, does exactly that.

In Worboys' data model the spatial extent of each spatial object is decomposed into a set of triangles (some are special triangles like points or lines) where each triangle is represented by its three corner vertices. The three corner points can be described using the special attributes Ax, Ay, Bx, By, Cx, and Cy in a relation, where the pairs (Ax, Ay), (Bx, By), and (Cx, Cy) represent the (x, y) coordinate values of the first, second, and third corner vertices, respectively.

In addition, the temporal extent is represented by two special attributes called *From* and *To*. The *From* and *To* values represent the endpoints of a time interval that belongs to the temporal extent of an object.

Example 6.3.1 Figure 6.4 shows a map of a rectangular-shaped park with a road, a fountain, a pond, and a tulip garden. The map shows the location of the objects in the park and indicates the time intervals of their existence. For example, the tulip garden ceased to exist in 1990, the year before the pond was created.

The park can be represented in Worboys' data model as follows. First, the fountain, which is a single point $(10, 4)$ is treated as the special rectangle with three corner vertices, each of which is $(10, 4)$. The road, which is composed of two separate line segments is treated as the union of two special cases of rectangles. For example, the first line segment between points $(5, 10)$ and $(6, 9)$ is represented as the triangle with one corner vertex $(5, 10)$ and the other two corner vertices being $(6, 9)$. The tulip is represented as one, the park as two, and the pond as the union of three triangles.

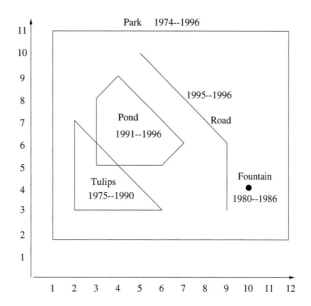

Figure 6.4: A park map.

Park

Id	Ax	Ay	Bx	By	Cx	Cy	From	To
Fountain	10	4	10	4	10	4	1980	1986
Road	5	10	9	6	9	6	1995	1996
Road	9	6	9	3	9	3	1995	1996
Tulip	2	3	2	7	6	3	1975	1990
Park	1	2	1	11	12	11	1974	1996
Park	12	11	12	2	1	2	1974	1996
Pond	3	5	3	8	4	9	1991	1996
Pond	4	9	7	6	3	5	1991	1996
Pond	3	5	7	6	6	5	1991	1996

6.4 Constraint Data Model

The constraint data model introduced in Chapter 4 can also represent geographic data. This approach starts by viewing geographic data as infinite relations with X and Y attributes that represent the x and y coordinate values of the points that belong to the object.

Example 6.4.1 Figure 6.5 is a radio broadcast map that shows the areas that can be reached by three different radio stations. The first radio station

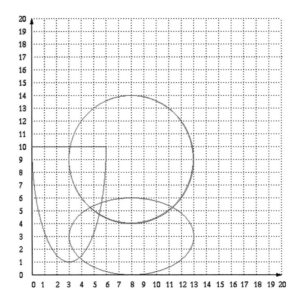

Figure 6.5: A radio broadcast map.

broadcasts within a circle, the second in an elliptic area, and the third in a parabolic area that is cut off by a line. The radio broadcast map can be represented by the following infinite relation.

Broadcast

Radio	X	Y
1	8	9
⋮	⋮	⋮
2	8	3
⋮	⋮	⋮
3	3	1
⋮	⋮	⋮

Constraint databases provide a finite representation of the infinite geographic relations. For example, the street map can be represented by linear and lower and upper bound constraints. Similarly, the town map can be decomposed into a set of convex polygons, and each convex polygon can be represented by a conjunction of linear inequalities. Hence the constraint data model can represent all the information that the previous geographic data models represent. The constraint data model can even represent the broadcast map, wich cannot be represented by the earlier data models.

Example 6.4.2 The *Broadcast* constraint relation shown below represents the broadcast map using quadratic polynomial constraints over the real numbers.

Broadcast

Radio	X	Y	
1	x	y	$(x-8)^2 + (y-9)^2 \leq 25$
2	x	y	$\frac{(x-8)^2}{5^2} + \frac{(y-3)^2}{3^2} \leq 1$
3	x	y	$(y-1) \geq (x-3)^2, y \leq 10$

6.5   Topological Data Models

In many geographic applications the important information is not a map but the relationship among the objects. For example, which objects are adjacent to other objects. Such adjacency information can be represented by graphs, where the nodes are spatial objects and the edges between pairs of nodes represent adjacency between objects. The simple adjacency graphs can be enhanced by extra information by adding labels or directions to the edges.

Example 6.5.1 The labels on the edges of the graph in Figure 6.6 are the miles distance on the highway between pairs of cities in the midwest United States. This can be represented as follows.

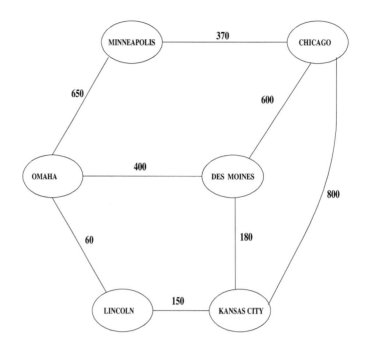

Figure 6.6: Fastest connections among cities.

Edge

City1	City2	Miles
Chicago	Des_Moines	600
Chicago	Kansas_City	800
Chicago	Minneapolis	370
Des_Moines	Chicago	600
Des_Moines	Kansas_City	180
Des_Moines	Omaha	400
Kansas_City	Chicago	800
Kansas_City	Des_Moines	180
Kansas_City	Lincoln	150
Lincoln	Kansas_City	150
Lincoln	Omaha	60
Minneapolis	Chicago	370
Minneapolis	Omaha	650
Omaha	Des_Moines	400
Omaha	Minneapolis	650
Omaha	Lincoln	60

Suppose I am traveling by car through these cities. I would like to know what milage the odometer of my car may show when I arrive at each city. Let relation *Travel(City1, Miles1, City2, Miles2)* contain tuples such that if I reach City1 when the odometer shows Miles1, then I can reach also City2 when the odometer shows Miles2.

My travel between a pair of cities may not be always the shortest possible. I may make detours because I wish to visit some nearby attractions, the road is under construction, or I lose my way. In fact, the only thing that seems sure as I travel along an edge from City1 to City2 is that if I arrive at City1 at d_1 miles, then I arrive to City2 at d_2 miles such that $d_2 - d_1 \geq m$, where m is the distance between the cities. This information can be represented by the following constraint relation.

Travel

City1	Miles1	City2	Miles2	
Chicago	d_1	Des_Moines	d_2	$d_2 - d_1 \geq 600$
Chicago	d_1	Kansas_City	d_2	$d_2 - d_1 \geq 800$
Chicago	d_1	Minneapolis	d_2	$d_2 - d_1 \geq 370$
Des_Moines	d_1	Chicago	d_2	$d_2 - d_1 \geq 600$
Des_Moines	d_1	Kansas_City	d_2	$d_2 - d_1 \geq 180$
Des_Moines	d_1	Omaha	d_2	$d_2 - d_1 \geq 400$
Kansas_City	d_1	Chicago	d_2	$d_2 - d_1 \geq 800$
Kansas_City	d_1	Des_Moines	d_2	$d_2 - d_1 \geq 180$
Kansas_City	d_1	Lincoln	d_2	$d_2 - d_1 \geq 150$
Lincoln	d_1	Kansas_City	d_2	$d_2 - d_1 \geq 150$
Lincoln	d_1	Omaha	d_2	$d_2 - d_1 \geq 60$
Minneapolis	d_1	Chicago	d_2	$d_2 - d_1 \geq 370$
Minneapolis	d_1	Omaha	d_2	$d_2 - d_1 \geq 650$
Omaha	d_1	Des_Moines	d_2	$d_2 - d_1 \geq 400$
Omaha	d_1	Minneapolis	d_2	$d_2 - d_1 \geq 650$
Omaha	d_1	Lincoln	d_2	$d_2 - d_1 \geq 60$

6.6   Geographic Queries

We review two different types of geographic database query languages. Section 6.6.1 describes geographic database query languages that are extensions of relational database query languages. Section 6.6.2 describes geographic database query languages that are extensions of constraint database query languages.

6.6.1 Relational Database Queries

One approach extends relational databases by adding to the relational data model some abstract data types. For example, the rectangles data model needs the *rectangle* abstract data type. The vector data model is more complex because it needs four abstract data types, namely the *point*, the *polyline*, the *polygon*, and the *region* abstract data types need to be defined. For Worboys' data model, the *triangle* data type is defined.

In addition, a set of geographic operators are defined on the new abstract data types. Without trying to be comprehensive, we list below a few examples of these operators using the "overlap" theme.

overlap_□□ (rectangle, rectangle) → Boolean: This operator tests whether two rectangle ADTs of the rectangles data model overlap.

overlap_◊◊ (region, region) → Boolean: This operator tests whether two region ADTs of the vector data model overlap.

overlap_□△ (rectangle, triangle) → Boolean: This operator tests whether a rectangle ADT of the rectangles data model overlaps a triangle ADT of the Worboys' data model.

These operators allow us to express many interesting geographic queries.

Example 6.6.1 Find which house remains overlap with the remains of House 1 at the archaeological site.

> SELECT DISTINCT H2.Id
> FROM House AS H1, House AS H2
> WHERE H1.Id = 1 AND
> H2.Id ≠ 1 AND
> overlap_□□(H1.X, H1.Y, H2.X, H2.Y)

Example 6.6.2 Suppose that the archaeological site lays under the park. If only House 1 is to excavated, which objects in the park are affected?

> SELECT DISTINCT P.Id
> FROM House AS H, Park AS P
> WHERE H.Id = 1 AND
> overlap_□△(H.X, H.Y, P.Ax, P.Ay, P.Bx, P.By, P.Cx, P.Cy)

Let us now turn our attention to the "in" theme. We list below some sample of operators on this theme too without being comprehensive.

in_$\Delta\Delta$(triangle, triangle) $\rightarrow$ Boolean: This operator tests whether a triangle of the Worboys' data model is located in another triangle of the Worboys' data model.

in_$\bullet\Diamond$(point, region) $\rightarrow$ Boolean: This operator tests whether a point of the vector data model is located in a region of the vector data model.

in_$\bullet\Box$(point, rectangle) $\rightarrow$ Boolean: This operator tests whether a point which is a degenerate triangle within the Worboys' data model is located in a rectangle of the rectangles data model.

Example 6.6.3 Find the objects of the park and the house remains that contain the fountain.

$$
\begin{array}{ll}
\text{SELECT} & \text{P.Id} \\
\text{FROM} & \text{Park AS F, Park AS P} \\
\text{WHERE} & \text{F.Id} = \text{``Fountain'' AND} \\
& in\_\Delta\Delta(\overline{F},\overline{P}) \\
\text{UNION} & \\
\text{SELECT} & \text{H.Id} \\
\text{FROM} & \text{Park AS F, House AS H} \\
\text{WHERE} & \text{F.Id} = \text{``Fountain'' AND} \\
& in\_\bullet\Box(\overline{F}, \text{H.X, H.Y})
\end{array}
$$

Next, again without pretending to be comprehensive, we list below some sample operators regarding the "intersection" theme.

intersect_$\Box\Box$(rectangle, rectangle) $\rightarrow$ rectangle: This operator returns the intersection of two rectangle ADTs of the rectangles data model.

intersect_$|\Diamond$(polyline, region) $\rightarrow$ $2^{polyline}$: This operator returns the intersection of a polyline and a region ADT of the vector data model. Note that the intersection is in general a set of polylines.

intersect_$\Delta\Delta$(triangle, triangle) $\rightarrow$ $2^{triangle}$: This operator returns the intersection of two triangle ADTs of the Worboys' data model. Note that the intersection of two triangles is in general not a single triangle but a set of triangles.

Example 6.6.4 Find the areas where at least three house remains intersect.

> SELECT   intersect$\_\square\square$(H1.X,H1.Y,intersect$\_\square\square$(H2.X,H2.Y,H3.X,H3.Y))
> FROM   House AS H1, House AS H2, House AS H3

This query evaluates first the intersect$\_\square\square$(H2.X,H2.Y,H3.X,H3.Y) operator, which returns a rectangle ADT of the rectangles data model. The result forms the third and the fourth arguments to the second intersection operator.

Example 6.6.5 Find the areas where at least three park objects intersect.

It is tempting to use a query similar to Example 6.6.4 but with intersect$\_\Delta\Delta$ instead of intersect$\_\square\square$ and three park objects instead of three houses. However, that query would not work because intersect$\_\Delta\Delta$ returns a set of triangles whereas the other intersect$\_\Delta\Delta$ operator expects a single triangle to be returned. This problem can be easily solved by defining the following additional operator:

$intersect\_\Delta 2^{\Delta} (triangle,\ 2^{triangle}) \rightarrow 2^{triangle}$: This operator returns the intersection of a triangle ADT of the Worboys' data model with a set of triangle ADTs of the Worboys' data model.

With this patch of the query language and the evaluation system, it is now convenient to express the above query as:

> SELECT   intersect$\_\Delta 2^{\Delta}(\overline{P1}$,intersect$\_\Delta\Delta(\overline{P2},\overline{P3}))$
> FROM   Park AS P1, Park AS P2, Park AS P3

where $\overline{Pi} = Pi.Ax, Pi.Ay, Pi.Bx, Pi.By, Pi.Cx, Pi.Cy$ for $1 \leq i \leq 3$.

Example 6.6.6 Find the parts of the streets of Figure 6.2 that are within the town of Figure 6.3.

It is tempting to answer this query as follows:

> SELECT   intersect$\_|\Diamond$(S.List, T.List)
> FROM   Street AS S, Town AS T

This query assumes that the street and the town maps have the same origin and use the same units on the x and the y-axes. Those assumptions may be incorrect. For example, one unit of the city map may be 100 meters, while one unit in the street map may be only 50 meters. Hence to find correctly the streets that are within the city, we have to be sure that the two maps have the same scales by enlarging or shrinking one of them. We also have to ensure that they have the same origin by shifting one of them up-down or left-right if necessary. To solve these problems we add to the query language and the evaluation system the following operators.

$scale\_|(polyline, c_1, c_2) \rightarrow polyline:$ This operator scales a polyline ADT of the vector data model by a factor of c_1 units in the x and c_2 units in the y direction.

$shift\_|(polyline, b_1, b_2) \rightarrow polyline:$ This operator shifts a polyline ADT of the vector data model by b_1 units in the x and b_2 units in the y direction.

Using these operators with the proper values of $c_1, c_2, b_1,$ and b_2, the query can be now correctly expressed as follows:

> SELECT   intersect_|◇(shift(scale(S.List,c_1,c_2),b_1,b_2), T.List)
> FROM   Street AS S, Town AS T

Another commonly used operator is the "buffer" operator, which also has some variations.

$buffer\_\square(rectangle, rational) \rightarrow rectangle:$ This operator takes in a rectangle in the rectangles data model and a rational number d and finds a rectangle in the rectangles data model such that the time dimension is unchanged and the spatial dimension contains the points (x, y) such that $|x' - x| \le d$ or $|y' - y| \le d$ from some point (x', y') of the rectangle.

$buffer(constraint, rational) \rightarrow constraint:$ This operator takes in the spatial dimensions of an object in the polynomial constraint data model and a rational number d and finds the points (x, y) such that they are d Eucledian distance from some point (x', y') of the object.

Example 6.6.7 Suppose that *Book* represents the shadow of a book on a table. Suppose that the book is raised up towards the lamp on the ceiling. This enlarges the shadow of the book by 10 centimeters on all sides. Write a query that finds the shadow of the book after it is raised up.

> SELECT   buffer_$\square$(X,Y,10)
> FROM   Book

It is possible to define many other geographic operators. However, the above set of operators are some of the most frequently used operators on geographic data. They also give a good flavor of the query languages based on abstract data types and operators defined on them.

6.6.2   Constraint Database Queries

Constraint database queries of geographic relations provide a great flexibility by allowing the users to access the x and y coordinates directly instead of accessing those only indirectly through abstract data types. As a result, there is no need for the extra overlap, intersection, or containment operators because those can be expressed with standard SQL queries.

Example 6.6.8 The problem of Example 6.6.5 can be expressed using constraint database queries as follows.

```
SELECT   P1.X, P1.Y
FROM     Park AS P1, Park AS P2, Park AS P3
WHERE    P1.X = P2.X  AND  P2.X = P3.X  AND
         P1.Y = P2.Y  AND  P2.Y = P3.Y
```

Example 6.6.9 Consider again the problem of Example 6.6.6. Assume that the two maps have different origins and scales such that point (x, y) in *Street* corresponds to point (x_2, y_2) in *Town* where the following holds:

$$x_2 = c_1 x + b_1$$
$$y_2 = c_2 y + b_2$$

Then the intersection query can be expressed as follows:

```
SELECT   T.X, T.Y
FROM     Street AS S, Town AS T
WHERE    S.X = c₁ T.X + b₁ AND
         S.Y = c₂ T.Y + b₂
```

A nice part of this solution is its uniform applicability. For example, one can just as easily intersect the street and the broadcast maps as we intersected the street and the town maps. In contrast, in Section 6.6.1 we did not even define any operator that can handle geographic relations that are composed of circles, ellipses, and parabolas. Those objects would require new abstract data types.

In some geometric problems, we use the following *Plane* relation that contains the entire Eucledian plane.

Plane

X	Y
x	y

Example 6.6.10 Suppose that *Book(Id,X,Y,T)* is an infinite relational database that represents the book considered in Example 6.6.7. Then instead of a buffer␣□ oeprator the shadow of the book can be found as follows.

```
SELECT   P.X, P.Y, B.T
FROM     Book AS B, Plane AS P
WHERE    ((B.X - P.X ≤ 10)  OR  (P.X - B.X ≤ 10))  AND
         ((B.Y - P.Y ≤ 10)  OR  (P.Y - B.Y ≤ 10))
```

Example 6.6.11 Find all the points within or at most 10 miles from the city of Lincoln, Nebraska.

```
SELECT   Plane.X, Plane.Y
FROM     Town Book AS B, Plane AS P
WHERE    (Town.X - Plane.X)² + (Town.Y - Plane.Y)² = 100
```

Another operator that constraint databases can express is the "envelop" operator that is defined as follows.

envelop(polygon) → *rectangle:* This operator finds the "envelop" or the minimum bounding box of a polygonal object. The minimum bounding box is the rectangular region whose sides are parallel to the x and y axes and which includes all the points in the object.

Example 6.6.12 Find the "envelop" of the town of Lincoln, Nebraska.

First, we find the corners of the envelop using the `Max` and `Min` operators.

```
CREATE VIEW   Corners(X1, Y1, X2, Y2)
SELECT        Min(X), Min(Y), Max(X), Max(Y)
FROM          Town
WHERE         Name = "Lincoln"
```

Then we define the envelop as a particular piece of the plane.

```
CREATE VIEW   Envelop(X,Y)
SELECT        X, Y
FROM          Corners, Plane
WHERE         X1 ≤ X  AND  X ≤ X2  AND
              Y1 ≤ Y  AND  Y ≤ Y2
```

Below we express a few more common geographic operators.

convex_hull(2^{point}) → *polygon:* This operator returns the minimum bounding convex polygon of a set of points.

The "convex hull" operator is similar to the envelop operator. In some versions of the convex hull problem, we need to return the convex hull of a concave polygon or a set of polygons, but these versions can be translated to the above problem by concentrating on the corner vertices of the given polygons.

For example, finding the convex hull of the town shown in Figure 6.3 is equivalent to finding the convex hull of the corner vertices, which are given by the following relation.

Point

X	Y
2	18
6	18
8	16
12	18
14	18
14	8
8	8
6	14
2	14

We say that a line divides a set of points P if the points in P that are not on the line are located on both sides of the line. For example, the line through points $(6, 14)$ and $(8, 8)$ divides *Points* because $(2, 14)$ is below and $(8, 16)$ is above the line.

To find the convex hull in the following example, we use the observation that the edges of the covex hull of P are those lines through pairs of points in P that do not divide P.

Example 6.6.13 Find the "convex hull" of the *Points* relation.

For convenience, at first we find all pairs of points.

CREATE VIEW   Pair(X1,Y1,X2,Y2)
SELECT   P1.X, P1.Y, P2.X, P2.Y
FROM   Point AS P1, Point AS P2

We find the pairs such that below the line through them, there is another point.

```
CREATE VIEW    Below(X1,Y1,X2,Y2)
SELECT         X1, Y1, X2, Y2
FROM           Pair, Point
WHERE          (X1 ≠ X2)  AND
               (Y-Y1)(X2-X1) < (Y2-Y1)(X-X1)
```

We find similarly the relations *Above*, *Left*, and *Right*. Next we find the pairs of points such that they do not divide *Points*.

```
CREATE VIEW    Only_Below(X1,Y1,X2,Y2)
SELECT         X1, Y1, X2, Y2
FROM           Below
MINUS
SELECT         X1, Y1, X2, Y2
FROM           Above
```

We can find similarly the relations *Only_Above*, *Only_Left*, and *Only_Right*. The lines through pairs of points in the last four relations are the edges of the convex hull. From these it is possible to calculate the point set that belongs to the convex hull. We leave that as an exercise.

The above algorithm has an $O(n^3)$ time complexity where n is the number of input points. There are more complex algorithms that have a running time of $O(n \log n)$. Here we were only interested in showing that it is possible to define the convex hull query using SQL and constraint databases.

shortest_distance(graph,vertex,vertex) → number: This operator takes in a distance graph with positive distances and two vertices and returns the shortest distance from the first vertex to the second vertex.

Example 6.6.14 Find the length of the shortest path from Lincoln to Chicago using the *Edge* relation.

First we calculate the possible distances from Lincoln to the other cities.

```
CREATE VIEW    Possible(City,Miles)
SELECT         City2, Miles2
FROM           Travel
WHERE          City1 = "Lincoln" AND
               Miles1 = 0
RECURSIVE
SELECT         City2, Miles2
FROM           Possible, Travel
WHERE          City = City1 AND
               Miles = Miles1
```

We can find now the length of the shortest path from Lincoln to any other city as follows.

CREATE VIEW	Distance(City,Miles)
SELECT	City, Min(Miles)
FROM	Possible
GROUP BY	City

If we only wanted the distance to Chicago we could add a WHERE clause which selects the city to be Chicago.

shortest_path(graph,vertex,vertex) → *number:* This operator takes in a distance graph with positive distances and two vertices and returns the shortest path from the first vertex to the second vertex.

Example 6.6.15 We can use the *Edge* relation as well as the *Distance* relation already found in Example 6.6.14. Note that an edge from City1 to City2 is on (one of) the shortest path(s) if City1 is Miles1 from Lincoln, City2 is Miles2 from Lincoln, and the length of the edge is exactly Miles2-Miles1 miles long. We can express this observation and find all the edges that are on any shortest path from Lincoln to any other city as follows.

CREATE VIEW	Shortest_DAG(City1,City2,Miles)
SELECT	E.City1, E.City2, L2.Miles
FROM	Distance AS D1, Distance AS D2, Edge AS E
WHERE	D1.City = E.City1 AND
	D2.City = E.City2 AND
	D2.Miles > D1.Miles AND
	D2.Miles - D1.Miles = E.Miles

Let us view the *Shortest_DAG* relation as a directed acyclic graph (DAG) where the edges are directed from City1 to City2 because a shortest path always goes from City1 to City2. Clearly, *Shortest_DAG* is acyclic because no shortest path can contain a cycle. There can be several incoming edges to a City2 only if all of the incoming edges are on equally short paths. Hence if $City1, City2, Miles)$ and $(City1', City2, Miles')$, then $Miles = Miles'$. The DAG can be made a tree by selecting for each City2 the alphabetically smallest parent node City1 in the DAG.

CREATE VIEW	Shortest_Tree(City1,City2,Miles)
SELECT	Min(City1), City2, Miles
FROM	Shortest_DAG
GROUP BY	City2, Miles

Now we can go from Chicago back to Lincoln, which is the root of this tree.

CREATE VIEW	Shortest_Path(City1,City2,Miles)
SELECT	City1, City2, Miles
FROM	Shortest_Tree
WHERE	City2 = "Chicago"
RECURSIVE	
SELECT	ST.City1, ST.City2, ST.Miles
FROM	Shortest_Tree as ST, Shortest_Path AS SP
WHERE	ST.City2 = SP.City1

Finally, we can sort on the Miles attribute the rows in the *Shortest_Path* relation to find the shortest path.

connected(street map) → *Boolean:* This operator takes in a street map and tests whether each pair of streets is connected by a path.

Example 6.6.16 Consider the *Street* relation and assume that it is represented as a constraint relation. If the streets are connected, then we can go from any arbitrary street point, for example $(5, 2)$, to any street.

At first we find each pair of streets that intersect, making it possible to cross from one to the other:

CREATE VIEW	Cross(From,To)
SELECT	S1.Name, S2.Name
FROM	Street AS S1, Street AS S2
WHERE	S1.X = S2.X AND
	S1.Y = S2.Y

Second, we use a recursive SQL to find all possible ways to turn,

CREATE VIEW	Reach(To)
SELECT	Name
FROM	Street
WHERE	X = 5 AND Y = 2,
RECURSIVE	
SELECT	C.To
FROM	Reach AS R, Cross AS C
WHERE	R.To = C.From

Finally, we find the number of different streets that we could reach.

> SELECT   Count(DISTINCT To)
> FROM   Reach

The streets are connected if and only if the count is six, the total number of streets.

We gave above examples of expressing in SQL and contraint databases some of the more difficult geographic operators. These examples dispell the notion that building a huge library of abstract data types with associated operators is the only way to define a geographic database query language. In fact, that is an undesirable approach because remembering the names of all these ADTs and their proper syntax and use can be a burden for the users. One advantage of constraint database-based query languages is that they greatly cut down on the number of new abstract data types that need to be provided in a library.

Another advantage of constraint database-based query languages is their immense flexibility. The elegant simplicity of relational algebra and basic SQL can mislead one into believing that they are primitive languages. The truth seems to be just the opposite. These languages achieve their flexibility and ease of use by their well-chosen operator set and keywords. Flexibility of a query language is best demonstrated not by textbook examples but by practice, where real ad hoc problems arise. Nevertheless, we give below two examples that hint at the flavor of these ad hoc problems.

Example 6.6.17 While going to an accident scene, an ambulance needs to minimize not the distance traveled but the number of turns made because an ambulance has to slow down while making turns and too frequent turns may also cause accidents. This is a slightly non-standard problem; hence *shortest_path* or other library functions cannot be applied to this problem.

To make the problem more concrete, suppose that in the streets map a hospital is located at $(5, 2)$ and an accident is on Willow Street. Find the minimum number of turns that an ambulance has to make to reach from the hospital to the accident scene.

We can modify the solution to Example 6.6.16 by extending the *Reach* relation to count the number of turns. To avoid infinite cycles, we count the turns only up to the total number of streets minus one, which in this case is five.

```
CREATE VIEW    Reach(To, Turn)
SELECT         Name, 0
FROM           Street
WHERE          X = 5  AND  Y = 2,
RECURSIVE
SELECT         C.To, R.Turn + 1
FROM           Reach AS R, Cross AS C
WHERE          R.To = C.From AND
               R.Turn <= 5
```

Finally, we find the minimum number of turns to Willow street.

```
SELECT    Min(Turn)
FROM      Reach
WHERE     To = "Willow"
```

Example 6.6.18 While making a furniture delivery, a truck cannot use wet streets with a slope greater than 27^0. The furniture store is at $(5, 2)$ on Vine street, just opposite the hospital. The delivery location is at $(19, 19)$ on Willow street. Suppose the entire town map is located on a hillside with the elevation $z = 0.5(x+y)$. If it rains now, can the truck make the delivery today?

First, find the slope of the streets. Consider any street with points (x_1, y_1) and (x_2, y_2) on it. Between these two points, the length of the street projected onto the (x, y) plane is:

$$length = \sqrt{(x_2 - x_1)^2 + (y_2 - y_1)^2}$$

The rise in elevation is:

$$rise = 0.5(x_2 + y_2) - 0.5(x_1 + y_1) = 0.5((x_2 - x_1) + (y_2 - y_1))$$

Hence we have the constraint: We also have:

$$\frac{rise}{length} \leq \tan(27^0) \approx 0.5$$

or

$$rise \leq 0.5 \; length$$

Since the truck has to go both up and down the street, we can assume that the rise is positive (otherwise interchange points (x_1, y_1) and (x_2, y_2)). Hence we can square both sides:

$$rise^2 \leq 0.25 \; length^2$$

Substituting, we get:

$$((x_2 - x_1) + (y_2 - y_1))^2 \le (x_2 - x_1)^2 + (y_2 - y_1)^2$$

Simplifying, we get:

$$(x_2 - x_1)(y_2 - y_1) \le 0$$

We can use the above observation to find the safe streets as follows.

CREATE VIEW	Safe(Name, X, Y)
SELECT	S1.Name, S1.X, S1.Y
FROM	Street AS S1, Street AS S2,
WHERE	S1.Name = S2.Name AND
	(S2.X - S1.X) (S2.Y - S1.Y) $\le$ 0

Finally, we can proceed as before but using relation *Safe* instead of *Street*.

Bibliographic Notes

Shekhar and Xiong [374] is a comprehensive encyclopedia on geographic information systems. Rigaux et al. [356] is a good introductory book on spatial databases.

Several temporal and spatial data models precede and in fact form the basis of the spatio-temporal data models presented in this chapter. Some of these temporal data models are reviewed in the bibliographic notes of Chapter 5.

The surveys by Bittner and Frank [50] and Kemper and Wallrath [225] and the book by Laurini and Thompson [260] review the area of spatial databases, including the 2-spaghetti data model often used in geographic information systems [5, 110, 383] such as the ARC/INFO system [283, 284, 307]. The 2-spaghetti data model is an extreme point data model that uses the corner vertices of polygons for the representation of polygonal-shaped areas. It can be extended to the 3-spaghetti data model for the representation of three-dimensional objects. The 3-spaghetti data model represents three-dimensional objects as a set of faces, and each face is a polygon and can be further extended as described in Paoluzzi et al. [296]. Egenhofer [119], Svensson and Zhexue [391], and Waugh and Healey [423] extend relational databases and SQL with spatial operators.

Helm et al. [195] describe a spatial data model based on Boolean constraints and range queries. Topological data models are considered in Egenhofer and Franzosa [120, 121], Egenhofer and Mark [122], Grigni et al. [164], Kuijpers [245], Kuijpers and Smits [248], Kuijpers and Van den

Bussche [246], Papadimitriou et al. [298], Paredaens et al. [302, 301, 299], and Segoufin and Vianu [367]. Geerts et al. [145] considers the efficient maintenance of topological properties. Fournier and Montuno [136] present algorithms for triangulating polygons. Ooi [290] discusses query processing in geographic information systems. Scholl and Voisard [365] present an object-oriented approach to building geographic information systems.

The point set view of geometric objects is from analytical geometry, which was pioneered by Descartes. Worboys' data model, which is simplified in the presentation in this chapter, is described in [431, 432]. The original model required simplices. Worboys [431] also describes a query language that contains more special spatio-temporal operators. Query languages for various other spatial and moving objects databases are described in [83].

Exercises

1. Represent in Worboys' data model the archaeological site of Example 6.1.1. (*Hint:* Divide along the diagonal each of the rectangles that were used to represent the houses.)

2. Represent using the vector data model the area of all the objects in the park shown in Figure 6.4. In the vector data model representation, ignore the temporal information.

3. Represent using a Worboys relation the town map shown in Figure 6.3, assuming that the town exists between times $t = 0$ and $t = 300$.

4. A continent approximately occupies a triangle with corner vertices $(50, 150)$, $(400, 600)$, and $(700, 100)$. Represent the area of this continent using a Worboys relation. (*Hint:* Use the time interval from $-\infty$ to $+\infty$.)

5. Represent using a Worboys relation the state of Florida as shown in Figure 6.8, using the fact that Florida became the 27th state of the United States in 1845.

6. Using a constraint relation represent the street map shown in Figure 6.2.

7. Using a constraint relation represent the area of the town shown in Figure 6.3. (*Hint:* Divide the town map into two convex polygons using the line $y = x + 8$ and represent each convex polygon by a separate constraint tuple with a conjunction of linear inequalities.)

8. Using a constraint relation represent the land areas shown in Figure 6.7.

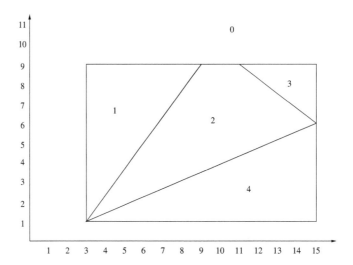

Figure 6.7: Land areas.

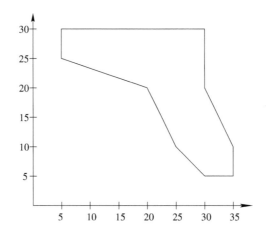

Figure 6.8: A map of Florida.

9. Assume that there are two water reservoirs $R1$ and $R2$ located at $(25, 20)$ and at $(30, 15)$, respectively. Represent using a linear constraint relation $R1\_Closer(x, y)$ those areas that are closer to $R1$ than to $R2$. Write a SQL query that finds the areas that are less than 3 units distance from the first reservoir and are also closer to the first reservoir than to the second reservoir.

10. Consider the map of Florida shown in Figure 6.8.

(a) Represent the map of Florida using Worboys' data model. (*Hint:* For the time period use the fact that Florida became part of the U.S. in 1845.)

(b) Represent the map of California using the constraint data model.

(c) Suppose Jacksonville is located at $(30, 30)$, Miami at $(35, 9)$, and Pensacola at $(10, 24)$. Represent using a linear constraint relation *Voronoi(id,x,y,name)*, which contains a Voronoi diagram, that is, the areas that are closest to each of these three cities.

(d) Betty wants to visit Orlando, which is located at $(30, 12)$, but she can fly only to one of the above three cities. Using an SQL query, help Betty to find the city that is closest to Orlando.

11. Using a constraint relation represent the heart shown in Figure 6.9.

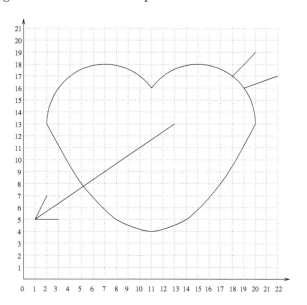

Figure 6.9: A heart.

12. Express in SQL the following query.

Find the parts of the town of Lincoln, Nebraska, that are reached by at least one radio station.

13. Complete the convex hull algorithm of Example 6.6.13 by writing the following.

(a) Define in SQL the *Above*, *Left*, and *Right* relations.

(b) Define in SQL the *Only_Above*, *Only_Left* and *Only_Right* relations.

(c) Define the complement of the convex hull as the union of the half-planes of the previous four sets of lines.

(d) Find the convex hull by taking the complement of the result of the previous query.

14. Suppose we know about a town the following information.

- *Contains(street,x,y)* –A street contains certain locations.

- *Emergency(type, number, street, t)* –An emergency of a specific type is detected at an address at time t.

- *Location(number, street, x, y)* –An address lies at a certain location.

- *Police(officer, vin, x, y, t)* –A police officer, who drives the car with vehicle identification number *vin* is at location (x, y) at time t.

- *Resident(name, number, street)* –A person resides at an address.

Express in SQL the following queries.

(a) Find the address where police officer Charles was at time 10.

(b) Find the address of all emergencies between times 0 and 50.

(c) Find the (x, y) location of Susan's home.

(d) Find the address of each police officer.

(e) Find which police officer was at which type of emergency.

(f) Find all pairs of persons who live on the same street.

(g) Find all pairs of police officers who responded to the same emergency.

(h) Find all streets that had two different types of emergencies at the same time.

(i) Find the residents who are not police officers.

(j) Find the residents who are also police officers.

(k) Find the residents and police officers of the town.

(l) Find the number of residents of the town.

(m) Find the number of residents on each street of the town.

(n) Find the number of emergencies of each type.

(o) Find the number of emergencies at each street.

(p) Find the street with the most number of residents.

(q) Find the most frequent type of emergency.

(r) Find the most frequent type of emergency on each street.

(s) Find the police officer who responded to the most number of emergencies.

(t) Find whether it is possible to go from $(5, 2)$ to $(20, 19)$.

(u) Find how many streets we need to cross to go from Vine to Willow street.

For the following problems assume that each street is a line segment.

(v) Find the slope of each street.

(w) Find the length of Vine street.

(x) Find the shortest distance for a car to go from $(5, 2)$ to $(20, 19)$.

(y) Find which is longer: the distance from $(5, 2)$ to $(20, 19)$ or the distance from $(20, 5)$ to $(11, 12)$.

(z) Suppose one police car drives from $(5, 2)$ to $(20, 19)$ while another police car drives from $(20, 5)$ to $(11, 12)$, starting at the same time and going with the same speed. Find when the two cars are within 6 units of each other as they are driving to their destinations.

7

Moving Objects Databases

Each moving objects database represents the trajectory and speed of moving objects. In all moving objects reprentations the spatial and the temporal extents of the objects depend on each other. This is in contrast to some earlier data models, such as, the rectangles and the Worboys data models, that had spatial and temporal extents that were independent of each other. Therefore, the earlier data models could only represent objects that appear and disappear suddenly. Hence they cannot represent continuously moving objects.

In this chapter we introduce several moving objects data models that generalize some of the earlier seen geographic data models by the use of an extra time parameter t allowing the expression of linear, polynomial, or periodic functions of time to extend a static space to a continously moving space.

Section 7.1 describes moving points, which are the simplest and most common of the moving objects data models. Unfortunately, moving points are limited because they cannot represent the shape of the objects.

Section 7.2 presents the parametric circles data model. This data model advanced the moving points data model by approximately representing the shape of the moving objects as circles that can change their sizes.

Section 7.3 describes *parametric rectangles*, while Section 7.4 describes the *parametric Worboys* data model. These generalize the rectangles and the Worboys data models, respectively, by representing the endpoints of rectangles or triangles using parametric functions of time. Section 7.5 further generalizes these two parametric extreme points data models by allowing periodic functions.

P. Revesz, *Introduction to Databases: From Biological to Spatio-Temporal*,
Texts in Computer Science, DOI 10.1007/978-1-84996-095-3_7,
© Springer-Verlag London Limited 2010

Section 7.6 describes *geometric transformation* data models. These data models generalize geometric transformations by using a time parameter. There are several types of geometric transformations that are considered, including affine, linear, scaling, and translation transformations, which are reviewed and defined in their traditional and parametric forms.

Section 7.7 describes query languages for moving objects databases. The query languages are based either on extensions of relational database query languages by abstract data types and special operators on them (Section 7.7.1) or on extensions of constraint databases (Section 7.7.2).

7.1   Moving Points Data Model

The *moving points* data model describes the x and the y locations of the moving points using two linear functions of the time parameter t. Hence the moving points data model can be also called the *parametric points* data model. In this model, the *From* and the *To* attributes are constants that describe the beginning and the end of the existence of the moving point. In addition, *Id* is an optional attribute that gives the identification number of each point.

Example 7.1.1 Suppose at time $t = 0$ three fishing boats are at locations $(3, 3)$, $(4, 4)$, and $(5, 3)$, respectively. The first boat goes south with a speed of one mile per hour, the second goes southeast with a speed of half mile per hour in both the south and the east directions, and the third goes east with a speed of one mile per hour for ten hours. The movement of three fishing boats can be represented in the moving points data model as follows.

Boat

Id	X	Y	From	To
1	3	$3 - t$	0	10
2	$4 + 0.5t$	$4 - 0.5t$	0	10
3	$5 + t$	3	0	10

7.2   Parametric Circles Data Model

A problem with the moving points data model is that it does not represent the shape of the objects. In many problems the shape of the objects can be approximated by a circle. This idea leads to the *parametric circles* data model in which the center of the circle is represented like a moving point, but a radius is added. To allow the size of the objects to change, the radius is also a parametric function of time.

Example 7.2.1 Suppose each of the fishing boats of Example 7.1.1 has a circular net with a radius of one mile at time $t = 0$. Suppose each of the fishing boats gradually draws in its fishing net between times $t = 0$ and $t = 10$. Represent the area of the nets at each time.

Boat

Id	X	Y	R	From	To
1	3	$3 - t$	$1 - 0.1t$	0	10
2	$4 + 0.5t$	$4 - 0.5t$	$1 - 0.1t$	0	10
3	$5 + t$	3	$1 - 0.1t$	0	10

7.3   Parametric Rectangles Data Model

In the *parametric rectangles* data model, a d-dimensional moving and growing or shrinking rectangle is represented as the cross product of d intervals, whose endpoints are functions of time, and a temporal interval, whose endpoints are constants.

Example 7.3.1 Suppose that a plankton-rich area of the ocean is located at time $t = 0$ in a rectangular area with left lower corner $(5, 5)$ and upper right corner $(10, 15)$ and it is moving with an ocean stream. Between $t = 0$ and $t = 20$, the right edge of the plankton-rich area is moving east with two and the left edge with one unit speed. At the same time, the top edge is moving north with three and the bottom edge with one unit speed. Relation *Plankton* represents the plankton-rich area using one parametric rectangle.

Plankton

X	Y	T
$[5 + t,\ 10 + 2t]$	$[5 + t,\ 15 + 3t]$	$[0,\ 20]$

The *Plankton* relation uses only linear functions of time. However, the parametric rectangles model also allows polynomial functions or even quotients of two polynomials as functions of time. The following is an example with quadratic parametric rectangles.

Example 7.3.2 Suppose a plane drops a bomb with one unit width, one unit length, and two units height at time $t = 0$ from a height of 100 meters to hit a target as shown in Figure 7.1. If we assume that the gravity constant is 9.8 meters per second and time is measured in seconds, then the movement of the bomb while it falls can be represented by the parametric rectangle relation *Bomb*, as shown here:

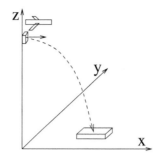

Figure 7.1: The trajectory of a bomb.

Bomb

X	Y	Z	T
$[t,\ t+1]$	$[t,\ t+1]$	$[100 - 9.8t^2,\ 102 - 9.8t^2]$	$[0, 3.19]$

Each of the previous two examples used only a single parametric rectangle. To represent moving objects that change their direction or speed due to additional forces not present initially, we may need to use several parametric rectangles.

Example 7.3.3 Suppose a sailboat, which at time $t = 0$ occupies the space $9 \leq x \leq 19$, $10 \leq y \leq 20$, first moves east with a speed of 5 feet per second until $t = 10$. Then it goes northeast until $t = 20$, with a speed of 10 feet per second in both the x- and y-axes. Finally, it goes north with a speed of 8 feet per second until $t = 25$. We can represent the sailboat in this data model as follows:

Sailboat

X	Y	T
$[5t + 9,\ 5t + 19]$	$[10,\ 20]$	$[0,\ 10]$
$[10t - 41,\ 10t - 31]$	$[10t - 90,\ 10t - 80]$	$[10,\ 20]$
$[159,\ 169]$	$[8t - 50,\ 8t - 40]$	$[20,\ 25]$

We can find the first parametric tuple that represents the movement between $t = 0$ and $t = 10$ as in the previous examples. Note that at $t = 10$, the boat is located in the rectangle with sides $[59, 69]$ and $[10, 20]$. Hence moving east 10 feet per second means to change the x dimension as $[59 + 10(t - 10),\ 69 + 10(t - 10)] = [10t - 41,\ 10t - 31]$. Similarly, to move north 10 feet per second means to change the y dimension as $[10 + 10(t - 10),\ 20 + 10(t - 10) = [10t - 90,\ 10t - 80]$.

Finally, at $t = 20$ the boat is located in the rectangle with sides $[159, 169]$ and $[110, 120]$. To go directly north 8 feet per second does not change the x dimension, but the y dimension changes as $[110+8(t-20), \ 120+8(t-20)] = [8t - 50, \ 8t - 40]$.

The next data model is a parametric generalization of Worboys' data model. For historical reasons it is called the parametric 2-spaghetti data model.

7.4 Parametric Worboys Data Model

The *parametric Worboys* data model generalizes Worboys' data model by allowing the vertex coordinates to be functions of time.

Example 7.4.1 Suppose each of the three fishing boats of Example 7.1.1 holds one corner of a fishing net. The shape of the fishing net can be represented in this data model as follows.

Net

Ax	Ay	Bx	By	Cx	Cy	From	To
3	$3-t$	$4+0.5t$	$4-0.5t$	$5+t$	3	0	10

7.5 Periodic Parametric Data Models

Periodic movements can be classified as either cyclic or acyclic. By a *cyclic periodic movement*, we mean that an object repeats its movement from the same position and with the same velocity every period. For example, a pendulum clock shows cyclic periodic movement.

An *acyclic periodic movement* is the composition of cyclic periodic movement and nonperiodic movement. For example, the movement of a light particle is a wave that is composed of an up-down movement and a linear movement.

In the previous section we considered only linear or polynomial functions of time. To represent periodic movements we need to consider more complicated functions. We use trigonometric functions like sines or cosines to represent periodic movement. However, trigonometric functions have not yet been implemented in any constraint database system. Therefore, we prefer to use periodic functions of time that use the modulus operator. The modulus operator is quite powerful, and as we will see in Example 7.5.1, it can be used to approximate trigonometric functions. The modulus operator is defined as follows:

$$x \bmod p = x - p \times \lfloor \frac{x}{p} \rfloor$$

where x is a real variable or constant and p is a positive rational constant. For example, $f(t) = (5t + 7) \bmod 8$ is a periodic function of time with $f(0) = 0$ and $f(0.2) = 1$. To use periodic functions we make some extensions to the parametric extreme point data models. First let us introduce some definition.

Let the temporal extent of the first period of a periodic object be the interval $[from, to]$. If the period is p and the periodic movement repeats until time end, then we write this as $[from, \ to]_{\mathrm{p,end}}$, which we call a *periodic interval*. Note that $[from, \ to]_{\mathrm{p,end}}$ is equal to the following:

$$\{[from + ip, \ \min(to + ip, end)] \ : \ 0 \le i \le \frac{end - from}{p}\}$$

where i is an integer variable. For example, $[80, 82]_{10,111}$ is equivalent to the union of the intervals $[80, 82]$, $[90, 92]$, $[100, 102]$, and $[110, 111]$. We also allow $end = +\infty$ for periodic movement that repeats without a time limit.

The Periodic Parametric Rectangles Data Model: We extend the parametric rectangles data model by allowing periodic functions of time in the spatial attributes and periodic intervals in the temporal attribute.

Example 7.5.1 Suppose a person A is swimming in a wavy sea. Figure 7.2 shows the position of A at four different time instances.

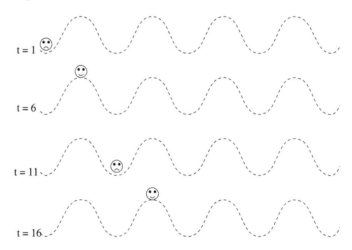

Figure 7.2: Periodic movements.

We represent the head of the person A as one foot in the swimming direction, along the x-axis, and one foot in height, along the z-axis. We also assume that A swims along the x-axis with a speed of one foot per second. Then we may approximate A's movement using a trigonometric function with a period of length 10 as shown in relation $Swimmer1$:

Swimmer1

X	Z	T
$[t,\ t+1]$	$[4.5\sin(\frac{\pi}{5}(t-1)-\frac{\pi}{2}),\ 4.5\sin(\frac{\pi}{5}(t-1)-\frac{\pi}{2})+1]$	$[0,+\infty]$

Alternatively, we may approximate A's movement using modulus functions. First we approximate the wave as shown in part (1) of Figure 7.3. We still assume that A swims along the x-axis with a speed of 1 feet per second. However, in every period A moves only horizontally at the bottom of the wave for two seconds, and at the top of the wave for another two seconds as shown in parts (2) and (4) of Figure 7.3. Between these, A moves either up with a speed of 3 feet per second in the z direction or down with the same speed for three seconds as shown in parts (3) and (5) of Figure 7.3. Hence the movement of A can be decomposed into four simple periodic functions.

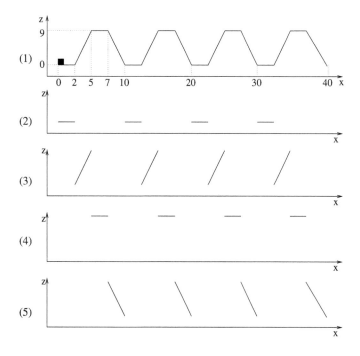

Figure 7.3: Approximate representation of the swimmer.

Each piece can be represented as a periodic parametric rectangle as shown in relation *Swimmer*. In each row, the x coordinate is defined as $[t, t+1]$ because the swimmer moves continuously with uniform speed in the x-axis and has width one. In the first and third periodic parametric rectangles, representing when the swimmer is at the bottom or top of the wave, respectively, there is no change in the height, hence the z-coordinate values will be defined by the intervals $[0, 1]$ and $[9, 10]$.

The second periodic parametric rectangle represents the upward movements displayed as part (3) in Figure 7.3. Note that $3t - 6$ is zero when $t = 2$ and nine when $t = 5$; hence it is the function that correctly describes the first upward movement. Because it is repeated every ten seconds, the periodic parametric rectangle contains the function $(3t - 6) \bmod 10$.

Similarly, the fourth periodic parametric rectangle represents the downward movements displayed as part (5) in Figure 7.3. Note that $-3t + 30$ is nine when $t = 7$ and zero when $t = 10$; hence it is the function that correctly describes the first downward movement. Because it is repeated every ten seconds, the periodic parametric rectangle contains the function $(-3t + 30) \bmod 10$.

Swimmer

X	Z	T
$[t,\ t+1]$	$[0,\ 1]$	$[0,\ 2]_{10,\infty}$
$[t,\ t+1]$	$[(3t-6) \bmod 10,\ ((3t-6) \bmod 10)+1]$	$[2,\ 5]_{10,\infty}$
$[t,\ t+1]$	$[9,\ 10]$	$[5,\ 7]_{10,\infty}$
$[t,\ t+1]$	$[(-3t+30) \bmod 10,\ ((-3t+30) \bmod 10)+1]$	$[7,\ 10]_{10,\infty}$

Next we see that the parametric 2-spaghetti data model can also be generalized with periodic functions.

The Periodic Parametric Worboys Data Model: This extends the parametric Worboys data model by allowing periodic parametric functions instead of only polynomial functions of time. Instead of using periodic intervals for time, we add two special columns for each relation. The first is P, which represents the period value, and the second is End, which represents the ending time of the periodic movement. Hence a periodic parametric 2-spaghetti tuple with $From, To, P, End$ values $from, to, p, end$ is applicable only at times in the periodic interval $[from, to]_{\mathrm{p,end}}$.

Example 7.5.2 Figure 7.4 shows a rectangular parking lot on a seashore. Suppose that a shoreline is changing continuously with the tide as shown by the set of parallel lines tagged by some of the time instances when the water level reaches them. The time instances shown are for the first period,

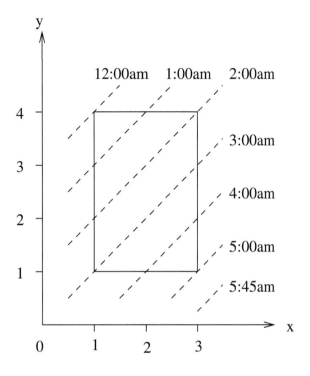

Figure 7.4: Tide and parking lot.

which starts at 12:00 midnight, then expands linearly until 5:45 a.m. and retreats in the opposite direction for the next 5 hours and 45 minutes, that is, until 11:30 a.m. The tide repeats its movement every 11 hours and 30 minutes.

For example, the shoreline will be at the same level at 2:00 a.m. (during expansion) and at 9:30 a.m. (during recession). Similarly, it will be at the same level at 3:00 a.m. and 8:30 a.m. and at 5:00 a.m. and 6:30 a.m. The tide can be represented in the parameric 2-spaghetti data model by noting that the shape of the area flooded by the tide will be a triangle, a quadrangle, or a pentagon in different time intervals. Hence each of these can be represented as areas are broken into triangles with each triangle having the proper time interval. In the following representation, time t is measured in hours from the first 12:00 midnight. Hence 5.75 represents 5:45 a.m., and 33 represents 9:00 a.m. the second day.

Tide

Ax	Ay	Bx	By	Cx	Cy	From	To	P	End
1	4	1	$4-t'$	$t'+1$	4	0	2	11.5	∞
1	4	1	2	3	4	2	9.5	11.5	∞
1	2	3	4	3	$6-t'$	2	3	11.5	∞
1	2	1	$4-t'$	3	$6-t'$	2	3	11.5	∞
1	2	3	4	3	3	3	8.5	11.5	∞
1	2	1	1	3	3	3	8.5	11.5	∞
1	1	3	3	3	$6-t'$	3	5	11.5	∞
1	1	$t'-2$	1	3	$6-t'$	3	5	11.5	∞
1	1	3	4	3	1	5	6.5	11.5	∞
1	1	3	4	1	4	5	6.5	11.5	∞
1	1	3	3	3	t'-5.5	6.5	8.5	11.5	∞
1	1	9.5-t'	1	3	t'-5.5	6.5	8.5	11.5	∞
1	1	3	4	3	t'-5.5	8.5	9.5	11.5	∞
1	2	1	t'-7.5	3	t'-5.5	8.5	9.5	11.5	∞
1	4	1	t'-7.5	12.5-t'	4	9.5	11.5	11.5	∞

where $t' = (t \bmod 11.5)$

7.6   Geometric Transformation Data Models

Before introducing the next data model, recall that a *geometric transformation* is a bijection of *d*-dimensional space into itself. Let A be a nonsingular $d \times d$ matrix and B be a d-vector of constants in $\mathcal{R}$. The following are some common geometric transformations that move the point $\overline{x} = (x_1, \ldots, x_d)$ to the point $\overline{x'} = (x'_1, \ldots, x'_d)$ according to *transformation functions* of the following form:

Affine Motion :	$\overline{x'}$	$=$	$A\overline{x} + B$
Linear Motion :	$\overline{x'}$	$=$	$A\overline{x}$
Scaling :	$\overline{x'}$	$=$	$A\overline{x}$ where A is diagonal
Translation :	$\overline{x'}$	$=$	$\overline{x} + B$
Identity :	$\overline{x'}$	$=$	$\overline{x}$

The restriction that A be nonsingular is required to assure that for every $\overline{x'}$ there exists a unique $\overline{x}$ that satisfies the system of linear equations. However, in special cases we allow A to be singular.

We can generalize affine, linear, scaling, and translation geometric transformations into parametric affine, parametric linear, parametric scaling, and parametric translations, respectively, by allowing within the matrix A and vector B functions of t wherever nonzero constants are allowed. Note that for each instance of t, the parametric geometric transformations give a corresponding geometric transformation.

The Geometric Transformation Data Model: This data model defines each spatio-temporal object as some spatial object together with a continuous transformation that produces an image of the spatial object for every time instant. More precisely, a *geometric transformation object G* of dimension d is a triple (V, I, f) where:

- $V \subseteq \mathcal{R}^d$ is a *representative spatial object*,

- $I \subseteq \mathcal{R}$ is a *time domain*, and

- f is a parametric geometric transformation function from $\mathcal{R}^{d+1}$ to $\mathcal{R}^d$.

Example 7.6.1 Suppose a group of whales is moving in the ocean. At time $t = 0$ they are located in the rectangular area with lower-left corner $(20, 20)$ and upper-right corner $(30, 30)$. The whales are moving until $t = 20$ directly west with a speed of one unit, and they do not go north or south. The whales can be represented by the geometric transformation $Whales(V, I, f)$ where V is the set of points $[20, 30] \times [20, 30]$, $I = [0, 20]$, and f is:

$$f(\overline{x}, t) = \overline{x} + \left[\begin{array}{c} -t \\ 0 \end{array} \right]$$

To express the *Whales* relation we needed only a transformation function that was a parametric translation. The following examples use parametric scalings.

Example 7.6.2 Suppose a water lily is growing on the surface of the water. At $t = 1$ its leaf is a unit circle. As the water lily grows, the radius of its leaf is expanding linearly with time until $t = 5$. The leaf of the water lily can be represented by the geometric transformation object $Lily = (x^2 + y^2 \leq 1, [1, 5], f)$ where f is the following parametric scaling from (x, y) points to (x', y') points:

$$\left[\begin{array}{cc} t & 0 \\ 0 & t \end{array} \right]$$

Suppose the water lily has some plant virus infection in area V. The virus is growing at an exponential rate in each direction at the same time the lily grows. The virus can be represented by $Virus = (V, [1, 5], g)$ where V is a subset of the unit circle at time 1 and g is:

$$\left[\begin{array}{cc} e^t & 0 \\ 0 & e^t \end{array} \right]$$

Example 7.6.3 Suppose a ball centered at the origin and having a radius of 0.1 meter is thrown at time $t = 0$ into the air with an initial velocity of 40 meters per second on the x- and 30 meters per second on the z-axis along the y-axis. We may represent the ball as the geometric transformation object $Ball = (x^2 + y^2 + z^2 \leq 0.1, [0, 6], f)$ where f is the parametric scaling

$$f(x, y, t) = \begin{bmatrix} x \\ y \\ z \end{bmatrix} + \begin{bmatrix} 40t \\ 0 \\ 30t - 0.5gt^2 \end{bmatrix}$$

and g is the gravitational force.

7.7   Moving Objects Queries

We review two different types of moving objects database query languages. Section 7.7.1 describes moving objects database query languages that are extensions of relational database query languages. Section 7.7.2 describes moving objects database query languages that are extensions of constraint database query languages.

7.7.1   Relational Database Queries

One approach to moving objects queries is to extend relational databases by adding to the relational data model some abstract data types. For example, the parametric rectangles data model needs the *parametric rectangle* abstract data type. The geometric transformation data model needs the *geometric transformation object* data type.

In addition, a set of moving objects operators are defined on the new abstract data types. Many of these operators are the necessary generalizations of the operators that we already saw in Section 6.6.1. Without trying to be comprehensive, we list below a few examples of these more general operators.

buffer_temporal(parametric rectangle,rational) → *parametric rectangle:* This operator takes in a (periodic) parametric rectangle A and a rational number d and finds a (periodic) parametric rectangle B that includes A and its surrounding moving points that are within d distance. Note that there are several variations of the buffer operator because there are several ways of measuring distance.

Example 7.7.1 Let relation *Swimmer(Id,X,Z,T)* describe the movement of several swimmers similar to Example 7.5.1. Suppose that there is a visibility of 75 feet. When can Andy and Betty see each other?

```
SELECT    T
FROM      Swimmer
WHERE     Id = "Andy" AND
          (X, Z, T)  IN     SELECT   buffer_temporal(X,Z,T,75)
                            FROM     Swimmer
                            WHERE    Id = "Betty"
```

area_temporal(Worboys relation) → time, area: This operator takes in a (periodic) parametric Worboys relation A and returns a parametric function for the area, which is represented as an infinite relation with tuples (t, a) where A has area a at time t.

Example 7.7.2 Consider again the tide and parking lot in Example 7.5.2. Find the area flooded at any time between 12:00 a.m. and 5:00 a.m. That can found by the following SQL query.

```
SELECT    area_temporal(X,Y,T)
FROM      Tide
WHERE     0 ≤ T  AND  T ≤ 5
```

Note that for SQL queries of (periodic) parametric rectangle databases in the WHERE clause all conditions must be of the form $X = c$, $X \leq c$, or $X \geq c$ where X is a spatiotemporal variable and c is a constant. For example, if X and Y are the spatial attributes, then $X \leq Y$ is not allowed as a WHERE clause condition. This is needed to guarantee that the output relation is representable by (periodic) parametric rectangles.

Querying Geometric Transformation Databases: Querying moving objects defined using geometric transformations often requires additional operators. We give below a few examples.

Compose(G_1, G_2): This is a function where the inputs $G_1 = (V_1, I_1, f_1)$ and $G_2 = (V_2, I_2, f_2)$ are two geometric transformation relations with $V_1 \subseteq V_2$ and $I_1 \subseteq I_2$ and f_1 and f_2 are geometric transformations with the same dimension. The output of compose is the geometric transformation $(V_1, I_1, f_1 f_2)$ where $f_1 f_2$ is the functional composition of f_1 and f_2, i.e., it takes each point $\overline{x}$ to $f_1(f_2(\overline{x}))$.

Example 7.7.3 Suppose we have the relations *Lily* and *Virus* as in Example 7.6.2. Which areas of the water lily will be infected at time 3?

Note that the operation *Compose$(Virus, Lily)$* yields the geometric transformation relation $A = (V, [1, 5], gf)$. The areas infected at time $t = 3$

must still be within the area of the leaf at that time. Hence we can express
the query as:

SELECT	X, Y
FROM	Compose(Virus,Lily)
WHERE	T = 3
INTERSECT	
SELECT	X, Y
FROM	Lily
WHERE	T = 3

Block: This operator considers the set of points in the spatial reference
object to be independent. Hence if some of the points are blocked by
the presence of another object, then the rest of the points just continue
moving along the trajectory determined by the transformation function.
Let $G_1(V, [from, to], f)$ and G_2 be two geometric transformation relations.
Then the meaning of $Block(G_1, G_2)$ is defined as follows.

$$\{(\overline{x}, t) : \exists \overline{x_0} \in V, \ f(\overline{x_0}) = \overline{x}, \ t \leq to, \ (\{\overline{x_0}\}, [from, t], f) \cap G_2 = \emptyset\}$$

This means the combination of a d-dimensional spatial point $\overline{x}$ and a
temporal instance t is in the output of the block operator, if there is a point
$\overline{x_0}$ in V from which the point $\overline{x}$ derives at time t, t is less than to, and as
the point $\overline{x_0}$ moves to $\overline{x}$, it is not intersected by any point in G_2.

Example 7.7.4 Let *Light* be a light source illuminating from behind a
screen in a shadow theater. Let *Ball* be the ball as in Example 7.6.3. What
will be the shadow of the ball on the screen?

In this case, *Block(Light,Ball)* gives what remains of the light when it
is blocked by the ball. Hence we can find the illuminated space by:

CREATE VIEW	Illuminated
SELECT	Block(Light,Ball)
FROM	Light, Ball

Let *Screen(X,Z,T)* be the screen area. Suppose the screen is parallel to
the plane $y = 10$. To find the shadow area we subtract from the screen area
the illuminated area of the screen. Hence the final query is:

```
SELECT   X, Z, T
FROM     Screen
MINUS
SELECT   X, Z, T
FROM     Illuminated
WHERE    Y = 10
```

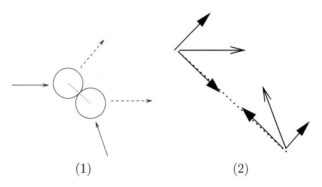

$$(1) \qquad\qquad\qquad\qquad (2)$$

Figure 7.5: (1) Dotted line joining centers (LC) at t_c; (2) collision along LC.

Collide: This operator assumes an extra attribute for moving objects, namely, *mass*. For simplicity we describe this operator in two dimensions. Suppose there are two objects that do not change their shape and that are traveling at uniform speeds defined by the transition functions:

$$\left[\begin{array}{cc} v_{1,x} & 0 \\ 0 & v_{1,y} \end{array} \right] \quad \text{and} \quad \left[\begin{array}{cc} v_{2,x} & 0 \\ 0 & v_{2,y} \end{array} \right]$$

Suppose both objects are valid in a time interval that includes time t_c when they collide with an angle of θ as shown in Figure 7.5. Depending on the degree of elasticity of the collision, we may calculate the transition functions of the two objects after the collision as

$$\left[\begin{array}{cc} v'_{1,x} & 0 \\ 0 & v'_{1,y} \end{array} \right] \quad \text{and} \quad \left[\begin{array}{cc} v'_{2,x} & 0 \\ 0 & v'_{2,y} \end{array} \right]$$

For example, if the x-axis is along the line connecting the centers of the objects and the collision is completely elastic, then the velocities in the y dimension do not change, i.e., $v'_{1,y} = v_{1,y}$ and $v'_{2,y} = v'_{2,y}$ and the other parameters may be calculated from the equations for the conservation of energy and momentum.

Example 7.7.5 Suppose the *Planet(Name,X,Y,T,Mass)* relation contains the all the planets of the solar system. They are represented by relations Suppose also that the motion of an asteroid is represented by the *Asteroid(Id,X,Y,T)* relation. What will happen if the asteroid collides with any of the planets?

    SELECT   Collide(A.X, A.Y, A.T, A.Mass, P.X, P.Y, P.T, P.Mass)
    FROM   Asteroid AS A, Planet AS P

The output describes the movement of the asteroids and the planets before and after a collision.

7.7.2   Constraint Database Queries

Each moving object database can be viewed more abstractly as an infinite relational database and translated into a finite constraint database representation. For a parametric rectangles relation $R(Id, X_1, \ldots, X_d, T)$, the corresponding infinite relational database contains all the tuples $(id, x_1, \ldots, x_d, t) \in \mathcal{R}^{d+2}$ such that $(x_1, \ldots, x_d)$ is a d-dimensional point within the rectangle with identification number id at time t.

A parametric Worboys relation $W(Id, Ax, Ay, Bx, By, Cx, Cy, From, To)$ similarly corresponds to an infinite relational database $W(Id, X, Y, T)$ that contains all the tuples $(id, x, y, t) \in \mathcal{R}^4$ such that (x, y) is a point in the triangle with identification number id at time t. Finally, the meaning of a geometric transformation object (V, I, f) is the following subset of $\mathcal{R}^{d+1}$:

$$\{(f(\overline{x}, t), t) \ : \ \overline{x} \in V, t \in I\}$$

In practice geometric or moving objects relations may contain other attributes that are regular relational database attributes that always have a constant value. Keeping in mind the above correspondences between the contraint data model and the other data model, enables one to write queries assuming the constraint data model.

Example 7.7.6 Suppose *Cloud(X,Y,T,Humidity)* is a relation where the attribute *Humidity* indicates the humidity of the cloud. Similarly, suppose that *Region(X,Y,T,Temperature)* is a relation where the attribute *Temperature* gives the temperature of each region in Fahrenheit degrees. Suppose it snows when a cloud with greater than 80 percent humidity moves into a region with less than 32 Fahrenheit degrees temperature. Where and when will it snow?

```
SELECT      X, Y, T
FROM        Clouds
WHERE       Humidity ≥ 80
INTERSECT
SELECT      X, Y, T
FROM        Region
WHERE       Temperature ≤ 32
```

Example 7.7.7 As in Example 7.7.1, let relation *Swimmer(Id,X,Z,T)* describe the movement of several swimmers, and let the horizontal visibility be 75 feet. In addition, suppose that a swimmer can see another swimmer only if the head of at least one of them is a minimum of 9 feet high. When can Andy and Betty see each other?

```
SELECT   A.T
FROM     Swimmer AS A, Swimmer AS B
WHERE    A.Id = "Andy"  AND
         B.Id = "Betty"  AND
         (A.X - B.X ≤ 75   OR   B.X - A.X ≤ 75)  AND
         (A.Z ≥ 9   OR   B.Z ≥ 9)  AND
         A.T = B.T
```

The next example uses periodic parametric Worboys relations.

Example 7.7.8 Consider again the tide and parking lot in Example 7.5.2. Let *Car* be the location of cars parked on the parking lot, with the *Id* attribute describing the license plate number of the cars. Find the license plates of the cars which will be flooded between 33 and 36 hours.

```
SELECT   Car.Id
FROM     Car, Tide
WHERE    Car.X = Tide.X  AND
         Car.Y = Tide.Y  AND
         Car.T = Tide.T  AND
         33 ≤ Tide.T  AND  Tide.T ≤ 36
```

Consider again the problem of Exercise 7.7.2. Using constraint databases and SQL, the problem can be solved as follows.

```
SELECT   T, 0.5T²
FROM     Tide
WHERE    0 ≤ T  AND  T ≤ 2
UNION
SELECT   T, 2 + 2(T − 2)
FROM     Tide
WHERE    2 ≤ T  AND  T ≤ 3
UNION
SELECT   T, 6 − 0.5(5 − T)(5 − T)
FROM     Tide
WHERE    3 ≤ T  AND  T ≤ 5
```

Example 7.7.9 Suppose $Window(Id, X, Y, T)$ is a relation that contains all windows that are open on a computer screen, where Id is the identification number of the window, X and Y are the locations that belong to the window, and T is the time instance when it was last active, that is, the cursor was in the window. Assume that more recently active windows cover less recently active windows. Which parts of which windows are at least partially hidden by other windows?

```
SELECT   W1.Id, W1.X, W2.Y
FROM     Window AS W1, Window AS W2
WHERE    W1.Id ≠ W2.ID  AND
         W1.X = W2.X  AND
         W1.Y = W2.Y  AND
         W1.T < W2.T
```

The next example uses the fishing net described in Example 7.1.1.

Example 7.7.10 Suppose the $Dolphin(ID, X, Y, T)$ relation describes dolphins swimming in the ocean. Suppose also that it is illegal to have dolphins caught or held captured in fishing nets north of the line $y = x + 10$. Will any dolphin be caught or held illegally in the fishing net?

```
SELECT      X, Y
FROM        Dolphin
INTERSECT
SELECT      X, Y
FROM        Net
WHERE       Y ≥ X + 10
```

Although we do not normally think of towns as moving areas, they are changing over time as urbanization gradually expands the boundaries of urban areas. The next example considers this urban sprawl.

Example 7.7.11 Suppose that relation *Urban_Sprawl(Name,X,Y,T)* represents the expanding areas of towns as they grow over time. The following query finds when the towns of Lincoln, Nebraska and Omaha, Nebraska will grow into each other.

SELECT	Min(Urban_Sprawl.T)
FROM	Urban_Sprawl AS L, Urban_Sprawl AS O
WHERE	L.Name = "Lincoln" AND
	O.Name = "Omaha" AND
	L.X = O.X AND
	L.Y = O.Y AND
	L.T = O.T

Finally, we give an example that uses a recursive query.

Example 7.7.12 Let us return to Example 6.1.1, but imagine that we have many more houses excavated at the archaeological site. Suppose a ghost haunts house number 1. The ghost remains in the area of a house even after it is demolished. However, if a new house is built whose area at least partially overlaps the old house that the ghost is haunting, then the ghost may move to the new house. This process may continue each time a house is demolished and a new house is built on top of it. Which houses and at what time may the ghost haunt?

CREATE VIEW	Ghost(Id, T)
SELECT	Id, T
FROM	House
WHERE	Id = 1
RECURSIVE	
SELECT	H2.Id, H2.T
FROM	Ghost AS G, House AS H1, House AS H2
WHERE	G.Id = H1.Id AND
	H1.X = H2.X AND
	H1.Y = H2.Y AND
	H1.T < H2.T

Bibliographic Notes

Güting and Schneider [178] is a good introductory book on moving objects.

Several temporal and spatial data models precede and in fact form the basis of the moving objects data models presented in this chapter. Tansel et al. [393] review temporal data models, including the TQuel data model, which is an extreme point data model that uses the endpoints of time intervals for the representation of time. Snodgrass [380] reviews the TSQL temporal database language, and Frank et al. [137] review the Chorochronos research project on temporal and spatio-temporal databases. Temporal data models that can represent periodicity constraints with the modulus operator over the integers are described in [47, 402], with linear repeating points in [32, 213] and an extension of Datalog with the successor function in [84]. These data models do not represent spatial dimensions or continuous movements of objects. Temporal databases with indefinite information are considered in Koubarakis [236] and Koubarakis and Skiadopoulos [240]. Efficient temporal constraint solving is considered in Dean and Boddy [105], Dechter et al. [107], and Vilain and Kautz [419].

The surveys by Bittner and Frank [50] and Kemper and Wallrath [225] and the book by Laurini and Thompson [260] review the area of spatial databases, including the 2-spaghetti data model often used in geographic information systems [5, 110, 383] such as the ARC/INFO system [283, 284, 307]. The 2-spaghetti data model is an extreme point data model that uses the corner vertices of polygons for the representation of polygonal-shaped areas. It can be extended to the 3-spaghetti data model for the representation of three-dimensional objects. The 3-spaghetti data model represents three-dimensional objects as a set of faces, and each face is a polygon and can be further extended as described in Paoluzzi et al. [296]. Egenhofer [119], Svensson and Zhexue [391], and Waugh and Healey [423] extend relational databases and SQL with spatial operators.

Helm et al. [195] describe a spatial data model based on Boolean constraints and range queries. Topological data models are considered in Egenhofer and Franzosa [120, 121], Egenhofer and Mark [122], Grigni et al. [164], Kuijpers [245], Kuijpers and Smits [248], Kuijpers and Van den Bussche [246], Papadimitriou et al. [298], Paredaens et al. [302, 301, 299], and Segoufin and Vianu [367]. Geerts et al. [145] consider the efficient maintenance of topological properties. Fournier and Montuno [136] present algorithms for triangulating polygons. Ooi [290] discusses query processing in geographic information systems. Scholl and Voisard [365] present an object-oriented approach to building geographic information systems.

Worboys' data model, which is simplified in the presentation in this chapter, is described in [431, 432]. Worboys [431] also describes a query language that contains more special spatio-temporal operators. Grumbach et al. [169] propose another spatio-temporal data model based on constraints in which, like in [431], only discrete change can be modeled. Frank and Wallace [139] use constraint databases for modeling orad design.

There are other temporal geographic information system data models, for example, the Raster Snapshot Model [24], the Temporal Map Set Model [36], the Event-Based Spatio-Temporal Model [306], the Space-Time Composite Model [256], and Yuan's data model that represent spatio-temporal information as a sequence of raster or vector snapshots. These also cannot represent continuous change.

Sistla et al. [378] and Wolfson et al. [428] present a model for moving objects along with a query language. This model represents the position of each object as a continuous function of time $f(t)$ and updates the database when the parameters of the motion, like speed or direction, change. However, the model captures just the *current* part of motions that are composed of several parts described by different functions. It does not describe complete trajectories and the spatial extents of moving objects. Some other object-relational models for spatio-temporal data are also available in Oracle8i [373] and PostgreSQL [282].

Data models based on moving points and regions are described by Erwig et al. [125] and Forlizzi et al. [134] but in these data models the moving objects do not change their shapes over time and periodic movements are not considered. These spatio-temporal models are used within the Chorochronos project [140].

The parametric 2-spaghetti data model with linear constraints is from Chomicki and Revesz [87, 88]. Example 6.3.1 is modified from [87, 88]. The extension of the parametric 2-spaghetti data model to polynomial and periodic constraints is new to this chapter. Chomicki et al. [86] describe an application of the parametric 2-spaghetti data model in the animation of linear constraint databases (see Chapter 21).

The parametric rectangle model is from Cai et al. [64]. This data model also considered polynomial and periodic constraints. Examples 7.3.3 and 7.3.2 are modified from [64]. An extension to noncyclic periodic constraints and the computational complexity of query evaluation is considered in [347, 348]. The block and collide operators are presented in a simpler form in [64].

The geometric transformation model is by Chomicki and Revesz [89]. The closure properties of geometric object transformation relations are studied in [83, 181]. We postpone review of other issues in moving object databases until later chapters on interoperability (Chapter 16) and indexing (Chapter 20). Moving objects are also used in many advanced applications, for example, in epidemiology [354]. Example 7.7.11 is from [345].

Exercises

1. Represent using a parametric rectangle a unit square, which at time $t = 0$ starts at the first square of the first quadrant of the plane and moves to the northeast with a speed of one unit to the north and one unit to the east per second.

2. (a) Suppose that at time $t = 0$ a person stands at a rectangular location with lower-left corner $(20, 20)$ and upper-right corner $(21, 21)$ measured in meters and starts walking toward the east with a speed of 1 meter per second until $t = 100$. For simplicity assume the x and y dimensions of this person are one meter each. Represent the person as (i) a parametric rectangle and (ii) a geometric transformation relation.

   (b) The ozone hole above a certain area of the earth is growing. Assume that it is modeled at year 2007 as an area that is approximately a rectangle with lower left corner $(100, 200)$ and upper right corner $(300, 400)$. According to the model in the next 10 years the ozone hole grows with uniform speed until it occupies a rectangular area with lower left corner $(0, 0)$ and upper right corner $(500, 800)$. Represent the area of the ozone hole as (i) a parametric rectangle and (ii) a geometric transformation relation.

   (c) Suppose a ship is located at time $t = 0$ in a rectangular area with lower-left corner $(20, 20)$ and upper-right corner $(130, 30)$ and is moving east with a speed of 5 meters per second until time $t = 100$ seconds. Represent the ship as (i) a parametric rectangle and (ii) a geometric transformation relation.

   (d) Suppose an iceberg at time $t = 0$ is in a rectangular location with lower-left corner $(690, 80)$ and upper-right corner $(700, 100)$ and is floating southwest with a speed of 2 meters per second in the west and 1 meter per second south. Represent the iceberg as (i) a parametric rectangle and (ii) a geometric transformation relation.

3. Continuing the previous example, write queries to find out the following:

   (a) Will the iceberg hit the ship?

   (b) Suppose the person stands on the ship. What is the combined movement of the person and the ship?

   (c) Suppose there is a visibility of 50 meters. Will the person on the ship see the iceberg?

4. Suppose an eagle nest sits at location $(0,0)$. At time $t = 0$ an eagle leaves the nest and flies northeast with a speed of 15 feet per second north and 10 feet per second east for 10 seconds. Another eagle leaves the same nest at time $t = 0$ and flies west with a speed of 8 feet per second for 5 seconds and then flies south with the same speed for 5 more seconds. Represent by a parametric Worboys relation the triangular area of the nest and the two birds between times $t = 0$ and $t = 10$.

5. There are three airplanes A, B, and C flying at the same altitude, each starting at time $t = 0$. Airplane A starts at location $(0,0)$ and flies straight north with a speed of 500 miles per hour. Airplane B starts at location $(150, 280)$ and flies southeast with a speed of 400 miles to the south and 300 miles to the east per hour. Finally, airplane C starts at location $(390, 410)$ and flies southwest with a speed of 200 miles to the south and 600 miles to the west. Represent by a parametric Worboys relation the triangular area formed by the three airplanes between times $t = 0$ and $t = 10$.

6. Three whales swim in the ocean. At time $t = 0$ whale A is at location $(20, 30)$ and swims north with a speed of 20 miles per hour for 10 hours. At time $t = 0$ whale B is at location $(150, 210)$ and swims northeast at an angle 45^0 and with a speed of $10\sqrt{2}$ miles per hour for 10 hours.

   (a) Express as a parametric rectangle the rectangle whose lower-left corner vertex is whale A and upper-right corner vertex is whale B.

   (b) Suppose whale C is at always remains at location $(230, 300)$. Is whale C in the parametric rectangle at time $t = 10$?

   (c) Represent by a parametric Worboys relation the triangular area formed by the three whales between times $t = 0$ and $t = 10$.

7. In this example you have to supply some of the specific data values. Represent using periodic parametric rectangle relations the following:

   (a) Any shuttle bus running periodically around a route. First draw the route of the bus as a polygon, then specify the speed on each piece of the route, and finally give the periodic parametric rectangle relation that represents the movement of the shuttle bus. Assume that the shuttle bus has a width and length of one unit distance.

   (b) The bus stops along the route of the shuttle bus.

(c) A passenger walking toward some bus stop during some part of the day.

8. Suppose that relations $Shuttle(id, x, y, t)$ and $Bus\_Stop(x, y)$ represent a number of shuttle buses and bus stops. Write a Datalog query that finds the ID number of the shuttle buses one can transfer to from shuttle bus number 1 either directly or indirectly.

9. Consider a bicycle wheel with an air-pump valve. Represent the motion of the air-pump valve assuming that the wheel moves with a constant speed on a flat road (a) using trigonometric functions and (b) using modulus functions. (*Hint:* Use a linear approximation for one complete rotation of the wheel, then extend the representation with a period.)

10. Represent the *Plankton* relation of Example 7.3.1 using the geometric transformation data model.

11. Represent the *Whales* relation of Example 7.6.1 using the parametric rectangles data model.

12. Assuming we have geometric transformation relations that represent the plankton-rich area and the whales of Examples 7.3.1 and 7.6.1, write a query to find the plankton-rich area at time $t = 10$ assuming that the whales are eating the plankton as they swim.

13. Using the given spatio-temporal input relations, express the following using SQL queries.

    (a) Relations *Snow*, which describes the snow cover on the top of a mountain, and *Rock*, which describes a rocky area on its side.

    Query: What part of the rock will be free from snow at time 10?

    (b) Relation *Lake*, which describes the changing shape of a lake.

    Query: What is the total area of the lake at time 20?

    (c) Relation *Mall*, which describes the shops in a mall, and *Customer*, which describes customers that visit the mall.

    Query: Which pairs of customers are one or more floors at least partially directly above or below each other at any time?

    Query: Which pairs of customers visit the same shop at the same time?

14. A set of birds at $t = 0$ minutes are in an area that is approximately a rectangle with lower left corner $(10, 20)$ and upper right corner $(20, 40)$. After the birds move with a uniform speed for ten minutes they occupy the rectangular area with lower left corner $(110, 320)$ and upper right corner $(120, 440)$.

    (a) Represent the area occupied by the birds using the parametric rectangle data model.

    (b) Represent the area occupied by the birds using the Worboys' data model.

    (c) Represent the area occupied by the birds using the geometric transformation data model.

15. A set of bees at $t = 0$ minutes are in an area that is approximately a rectangle with lower left corner $(0, 0)$ and upper right corner $(5, 10)$. After the bees move with a uniform speed for ten minutes they occupy the rectangular area with lower left corner $(40, 60)$ and upper right corner $(55, 70)$.

    (a) Represent the area occupied by the bees using the parametric rectangle data model.

    (b) Represent the area occupied by the bees using the geometric transformation data model.

16. Suppose that relation *Town(Name,X,Y)* represents towns and *Airplane_Shadow(Id,X,)* represents the shadow of the airplanes on the earth as they fly. Write an SQL query that finds when the shadow of airplane 123 will leave the town of Chicago.

8

Image Databases

Many applications, such as medical diagnosis and military target identification, require the retrieval from a large image database of those images that are similar to a new camera image. This requires the following tasks:

- **Affine-Invariant Similarity Measure:** When a flat object is photographed from different camera angles the photographic images are *affine transformations* of each other. Hence if one image is stored in the image database and another image is seen by the camera, to recognize that both images are showing the same object, there has to be an *affine-invariant similarity measure* between pairs of images.

- **Efficient Indexing:** Efficient indexing is essential when the image database contains a large number of images.

The combination of these two tasks is difficult. In general, computer vision research focuses on the first and neglects the second, while database research focuses on the second and neglects the first.

Computer vision researchers proposed several affine-invariant similarity measures between pairs of pictures, for example, the *minimum Hausdorff distance measure*, the *geometric hashing* technique, and similarity measures based on least squares distance. None of these measures leads to efficient indexing.

Database researchers proposed efficient indexing methods based on the following properties: *shape or contour, color* and *color histograms, attributed relational graphs*, which represent the spatial relationship between objects by a labeled graph, and various *image compression coefficients*. None of these properties is affine-invariant.

P. Revesz, *Introduction to Databases: From Biological to Spatio-Temporal*,
Texts in Computer Science, DOI 10.1007/978-1-84996-095-3_8,
© Springer-Verlag London Limited 2010

Section 8.1 defines affine invariance using constraint databases. Section 8.2 defines affine-invariant similarity measures and gives several examples that do not lead to efficient indexing. Section 8.3 describes a similarity measure based on *color ratios*. This similarity measure is shown to be affine-invariant and efficiently indexable. Finally, Section 8.4 considers similarity measures when the surface of the objects contains various patterns.

8.1 Affine Invariance

We assume that each image is represented by a set of black points on a white background in the (x, y) plane. The representation can contain all the points in an image or only a special subset of its points. For example, a polygon can be represented by all the points within it or by only its corner vertices.

In either way, we can assume that each picture is described using a constraint relation. Let $A(x, y)$ and $B(x, y)$ be two real constraint relations describing two images. The two are *affine transformations* of each other, denoted $A \sim B$, if and only if the following is true:

$$\exists a, b, c, d, e, f \ ad \neq bc \ \forall x, y \ A(x, y) \leftrightarrow B(ax + by + e, cx + dy + f)$$

This is a first-order logical formula with real polynomial constraints and is equivalent to the definition of affine transformation given in Section 7.6. This formula can be evaluated in several different ways. For any fixed real number constants a, b, c, d, e, f such that $ad \neq bc$, we can simplify it and express it as an MLPQ query, which we leave as an exercise.

Example 8.1.1 The two images of a bird shown in Figures 8.1 are affine transformations of each other because we can choose the following values in the formula:

$$a = \frac{1}{4}, \ b = \frac{3}{4}, \ c = \frac{6}{7}, \ d = \frac{-5}{14}, \ e = 0, \ f = 5$$

A key property of affine transformations is the following.

Lemma 8.1.1 Let A and B be areas that are affine transformations of each other. Then the following holds:

$$Area(B) = |ad - bc| \ Area(A)$$

Proof: We partition the area A into a disjoint set of triangles. Then each triangle in that set is transformed into another triangle that belongs to B.

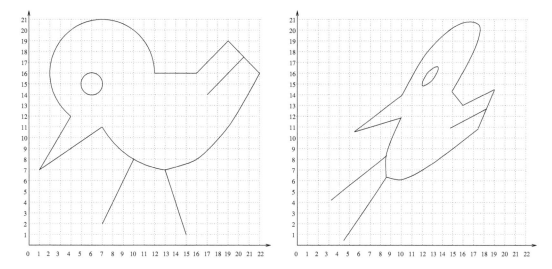

Figure 8.1: Two images of a bird.

Clearly, if the lemma holds for each pair of triangles, then it holds for A and B. Hence it is enough to prove that the lemma holds for triangles.

Without loss of generality we can assume that the vertices of A are (x_1, y_1), (x_2, y_2), and (x_3, y_3). If these points are collinear then their transformation is also collinear, hence both areas will be zero and the lemma holds. If they are not collinear, then we can calculate the area of A as follows:

$$Area(A) = \frac{(x_1 - x_3)(y_2 - y_3) - (x_2 - x_3)(y_1 - y_3)}{2}$$

For the transformed triangle we can calculate that $Area(B)$ is:

$$\frac{1}{2} \quad [[(ax_1 + by_1) - (ax_3 + by_3)][(cx_2 + dy_2) - (cx_3 + dy_3)]$$
$$-[(ax_2 + by_2) - (ax_3 + by_3)][(cx_1 + dy_1) - (cx_3 + dy_3)]]$$

Simplifying and taking the ratios we get:

$$\frac{Area(B)}{Area(A)} = \frac{(ad - bc)[(x_1 - x_3)(y_2 - y_3) - (x_2 - x_3)(y_1 - y_3)]}{(x_1 - x_3)(y_2 - y_3) - (x_2 - x_3)(y_1 - y_3)}$$
$$= ad - bc$$

from which the condition of the lemma follows.   ∎

In many applications some noise is present, hence the two images are not precise affine transformations of each other. We make the assumption that the noise is at most δ in both the x and y directions. That means that each point (x, y) of A may, due to noise, become some other point (x', y') where $|x' - (ax + by + e)| \leq \delta$ and $|y' - (cx + dy + f)| \leq \delta$. Another type of noise would simply delete the (x, y) point. To account for these possibilities we modify the previous formula as follows:

$$\exists a, b, c, d, e, f \ ad \neq bc \forall x, y \ A(x, y) \ \rightarrow \ \exists x', y' (B(x', y') \ and$$
$$|x' - (ax + by + e)| \leq \delta \ and$$
$$|y' - (cx + dy + f)| \leq \delta)$$

8.2 Affine-Invariant Similarity Measures

Let $dist(A, B)$ be any distance measure between pairs of images A and B. Then $dist$ is *affine-invariant* if

$$\forall_{A' \sim A, \ B' \sim B} \ dist(A, B) = dist(A', B')$$

Next we give some examples of affine-invariant similarity measures.

Minimum Hausdorff Distance Measure: Let $Euclid(I, J)$ be the Euclidean distance function between two points $I, J \in \mathcal{R}^2$. We define the *directed Hausdorff* distance between A and B as follows:

$$hausdorff(A, B) = \max_{I \in A} \min_{J \in B} Euclid(I, J)$$

The *Hausdorff* distance is defined as:

$$Hausdorff(A, B) = \max(hausdorff(A, B), hausdorff(B, A))$$

The Hausdorff distance measures the mismatch between two sets that are at fixed positions and is not affine-invariant. However, we can define the *minimum Hausdorff* distance between the two sets as follows:

$$m \ Hausdorff(A, B) = \min_{A' \sim A, \ B' \sim B} Hausdorff(A', B')$$

The minimum Hausdorff distance is affine-invariant. However, there is no efficient algorithm to compute the minimum Hausdorff distance. Therefore, the minimum Hausdorff distance cannot be used for efficient indexing.

Geometric Hashing: Geometric hashing stores not the coordinates of the points but their affine-invariant coordinates in a *geometric hash table*. The affine-invariant coordinates can be explained as follows.

Given a triplet of noncollinear points $P_1, P_2, P_3 \in \mathcal{R}^2$ any other point P_4 in an image can be represented as the combination:

$$P_4 = \alpha(P_2 - P_1) + \beta(P_3 - P_1) + P_1$$

After an affine transformation that takes the four points to P_1', P_2', P_3', and P_4', respectively, the condition

$$P_4' = \alpha(P_2' - P_1') + \beta(P_3' - P_1') + P_1'$$

also holds. Therefore, this gives for the point P_4 the affine-invariant representation $(\alpha.\beta)$, which is stored in the geometric hash table.

Suppose that we have made a geometric hash table corresponding to each noncollinear triple of points in the image A. When a new image B is presented, in it some triple (P_1', P_2', P_3') of noncollinear points is chosen and for all the other points in B an affine-invariant representation (α, β) is found using the preceding equation. If B is an affine transformation of A, then there must be a triple of points (P_1, P_2, P_3) in A such that the affine transformation takes that triple to (P_1', P_2', P_3'). Therefore, there must be a geometric hash table associated with (P_1, P_2, P_3) and A such that it contains all the affine-invariant point representations (α, β).

Therefore, we need to test only whether the affine-invariant representations of the points in B are all in one of the geometric hash tables associated with A. If they are, then B and A are affine transformations of each other.

Suppose that there are $O(n)$ points in A and in B. Then there are $O(n)$ affine-invariant representations derived from B. Because there are $O(n^3)$ geometric hash tables associated with A, a naive check of matching the affine-invariant representations with the geometric hash tables would take $O(n^4)$ time. However, a randomized algorithm would just check a constant number of points among the affine-invariant representations against the geometric hash tables. This would give an $O(n^3)$ time randomized algorithm for checking whether A and B are affine transformations of each other. If we have in the database m different images, then the total time would be $O(mn^3)$.

Therefore, the geometric hashing technique does not lead to efficient retrieval when there are a large number of stored images. Moreover, this method is not very robust under noise.

8.3   The Color Ratios Similarity Measure

In this section we assume that each image is represented as a set of colored points. Most pixel-based image representations allow 256 different shades of green, red, and blue. From these a large set of colors can be defined. Suppose we classify each part of an image as having one of n different colors. The following lemma shows that the ratio of the total areas of any pair of colors is *affine-invariant*.

Lemma 8.3.1 Let A_i and A_j be the total areas colored with colors c_i and c_j, respectively, within image A. Let B_i and B_j be the same within an affine transformation B of A. Then

$$\frac{A_i}{A_j} = \frac{B_i}{B_j} \quad \text{if} \quad A_j \neq 0$$

Proof: By Lemma 8.1.1 we have:

$$B_i = |ad - bc|\ A_i$$

and

$$B_j = |ad - bc|\ A_j$$

Hence, by taking the ratio of the first and the second we get the required condition. ∎

Example 8.3.1 Assume that the bird in Figure 8.1 is red except for the eyes which are black. Then the ratio of black to red areas in both images of Figures 8.1 is the same constant.

Suppose that we have a number of different colors and m possible ratios that are independent of each other. For example, with only the colors *blue, green,* and *red,* we can have only two independent ratios. For example, we may select *blue/red* and *green/red.* Then the *blue/green* ratio can be calculated from those two; hence it is not independent from them.

Given the m independent color ratios, we can describe each image as a vector of m values, where the ith entry corresponds to the value of the ith color ratio. Then the m-dimensional vectors can be indexed using several efficient multidimensional point indexing techniques.

We can define a color-ratio similarity measure that is robust under noise. Let V_A and V_B be the vectors of the color ratios in images A and B, respectively. Then the distance between A and B is defined as the Eucledian distance between A and B.

Finally, we can distinguish between two variations of affine-invariant color measures: the *primary color ratio measure* and the *rainbow color ratio measure.* The primary color ratio measure finds the ratios $\frac{R}{G}$ and $\frac{B}{G}$ for the total amount of R, G, and B in the triangles, that is, even for composite colors, only the ratios of redness, greeness, and blueness are counted.

The rainbow color ratio measure uses a range of different colors, for example, it can use *red, green, blue, yellow, turquoise, purple, white, gray and black.* These colors can be defined precisely, in the sense that for any object of the picture, it can be decided which of these nine colors it belongs to. These colored nine colors can be denoted by R, G, B, Y, T, P, W, Gr and Bl, respectively. For each image, we take out the background. Let I be the total area of the picture without its background. The rainbow color ratio vector of each image consists of the ratios $\frac{R}{I}, \frac{G}{I}, \frac{B}{I}, \frac{Y}{I}, \frac{T}{I}, \frac{P}{I}, \frac{Gr}{I}$ and $\frac{Bl}{I}$.

Although it may seem intuitive that the rainbow color ratio measure is better than the primary color ratio measure because it uses more statistics, in the computer experiments performed so far to compare these two measures, the primary color ratio measure was clearly better. However, there is some arbitrariness in the definition of the nine colors. Future experiments may redefine the values of these nine colors or use a completely different set of colors. Therefore, at this time it is primature to claim either method to be superior to the other method.

8.4   Similarity of Patterned Objects

In many applications, we have to consider not only the shape and the color but also the patterns that may be present on the surface of the objects. Barcodes provide an inspiration for robust affine-invariant similarity measures between pairs of patterned objects. Barcodes encode information in a robust machine-readable way using sequences of dark and light bars with different widths. The optical scanners which read barcodes are quite robust and already allow the presentation of barcodes from slightly different angles.

Although natural objects do not have barcodes, they have rich patterned and textured surfaces with a variety of colors. For example, the feathers of many birds have interesting patterns, such as the feathers of a parrot.

The surface of objects can be broken into a set of triangles that each contain some interesting pattern. Let us concentrate on just one triangular area ABC with some unique pattern as shown on the left side of Figure 8.2. Triangle ABC is transformed by the affine motion:

$$f(x, y) = \begin{bmatrix} \frac{5}{4} & \frac{1}{3} \\ \frac{1}{2} & 2 \end{bmatrix} \begin{bmatrix} x \\ y \end{bmatrix}$$

into another triangle $A'B'C'$ shown on the right side of Figure 8.2. The shape of triangle ABC becomes highly distorted. However, in triangle ABC one can identify the point D as the midpoint on the edge CD. Similarly, one can identify also the corresponding midpoint D' on the edge $C'D'$.

Now let us consider scanning the line segment AD from point A to point D. During the scan one sees a series of lighter and darker areas. In

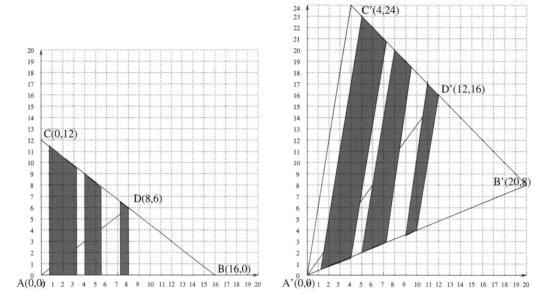

Figure 8.2: A striped triangle ABC (left) and its affine-transformation $A'B'C'$ (right).

particular, one sees in sequence 1 unit light area, 3 units dark area, 1 unit light area, 2 units dark area, 2 units light area, and 1 unit dark area. Hence the barcode of the AD segment can be represented as $(1, \mathbf{3}, 1, \mathbf{2}, 2, \mathbf{1})$, with the boldface numbers representing the dark areas.

Interestingly, when one scans the line segment $A'D'$, one finds also a similar sequence of light and dark areas. In particular, one sees 2 units light area, 6 units dark area, 2 unit light area, 4 units dark area, 4 units light area, and 2 units dark area. Hence the barcode of $A'D'$ can be represented as $(2, \mathbf{6}, 2, \mathbf{4}, 4, \mathbf{2})$.

The two barcodes are similar because they have the same number of light and dark areas and those have the same length ratios, which are equal to the ratio of the lengths of the two line segments.

Let the length of a line segment l be denoted as $length(l)$. The similarity of barcodes is a general feature of affine transformations as expressed in Theorem 8.4.1.

Theorem 8.4.1 Let $(a_1, \ldots, a_n)$ and $(b_1, \ldots, b_m)$ be the barcodes of two corresponding line segments l_1 and l_2 in two affine transformations of a patterned triangle. Then $n = m$, and the following hold for each $1 \le i \le n$:

$$\frac{a_i}{b_i} = \frac{length(l_1)}{length(l_2)}$$

Example 8.4.1 Consider again the barcodes of AD and $A'D'$ of the two affine transformations shows in Figure 8.2. In this case the barcode of AD is:

$$(a_1, a_2, a_3, a_4, a_5, a_6) = (1, \mathbf{3}, 1, \mathbf{2}, 2, \mathbf{1})$$

and the barcode of $A'D'$ is:

$$(b_1, b_2, b_3, b_4, b_5, b_6) = (2, \mathbf{6}, 2, \mathbf{4}, 4, \mathbf{2})$$

We have that $length(AD) = 10$ and $length(A'D') = 20$. Further, as expected by Theorem 8.4.1,

$$\frac{a_i}{b_i} = \frac{10}{20} = 0.5 \qquad \forall \ 1 \le i \le 6$$

8.4.1   Similarity Measures for Barcodes

Let us now consider a similarity measure for two barcodes. Let $\overline{a} = (a_1, \ldots, a_n)$ and $\overline{b} = (b_1, \ldots, b_m)$ be the barcodes of two corresponding line segments l_1 and l_2 in two affine transformations of a patterned triangle. If $n \neq m$, then we simply say that the two barcodes are not similar. Otherwise, let

$$d = \frac{length(l_1)}{length(l_2)}$$

Equalize the total length of the two line segments by scaling l_2 by the factor d. After scaling we obtain a barcode $\overline{c} = (c_1, \ldots, c_n)$ where each $c_i = b_i \times d$ for $1 \le i \le n$.

Next compare $\overline{a}$ and $\overline{c}$. If one is an affine transformation of the other, then by Theorem 8.4.1 and the choice of the scaling factor d, the following holds:

$$\frac{a_i}{c_i} = \frac{a_i}{b_i \times d} = \frac{length(l_1)}{length(l_2) \times d} = 1 \qquad \forall \ 1 \le i \le n$$

In general, one cannot expect two barcodes to be perfect affine transformations of each other, that is to have $a_i = c_i$ for each $1 \le i \le n$. Hence one needs to consider how much a_i and c_i deviate from each other. One can use a root mean square error measurement as follows:

$$E(\overline{a}, \overline{c}) = \sqrt{\frac{\sum_{k=1}^{N}(a_i - c_i)^2}{n}}$$

Example 8.4.2 Let $\bar{a} = (1, \mathbf{2.5}, 1, \mathbf{2}, 2.5, \mathbf{1})$ and $\bar{b} = (2, \mathbf{5.5}, 2, \mathbf{4.5}, 4, \mathbf{2})$. Then

$$length(\bar{a}) = 1 + 2.5 + 1 + 2 + 2.5 + 1 = 10$$

and

$$length(\bar{b}) = 2 + 5.5 + 2 + 4.5 + 4 + 2 = 20.$$

Hence

$$d = \frac{length(a)}{length(b)} = \frac{10}{20} = 0.5$$

and

$$\bar{c} = (1, \mathbf{2.75}, 1, \mathbf{2.25}, 2, \mathbf{1}).$$

Further,

$$E(\bar{a}, \bar{c}) = \sqrt{\frac{0^2 + (-.25)^2 + 0^2 + (-.25)^2 + .5^2 + 0^2}{6}} = 0.375$$

Since the root mean square error is small, the two barcodes are quite similar.

8.4.2   Different Patterns

The barcode-based similarity measure can accommodate other patterns beside striped patterns. For example, Figure 8.3 shows that if the triangles are spotted with ovals instead of having stripes, then the barcodes are still similar after the same affine transformation.

Note that the barcodes in Figures 8.2 and 8.3 are the same. That means that a single barcode for a triangle is incapable of distinguishing between the striped and the spotted patterns within the triangle. However, one can improve the situation by considering not one but two or three barcodes for a single triangle. Each barcode is scanned along the line segment whose endpoints are a corner vertex of the triangle and the midpoint vertex on the opposite side of the triangle. Figure 8.4 shows the three line segments $A'D'$, $B'E'$ and $C'F'$ in the striped and the spotted triangles.

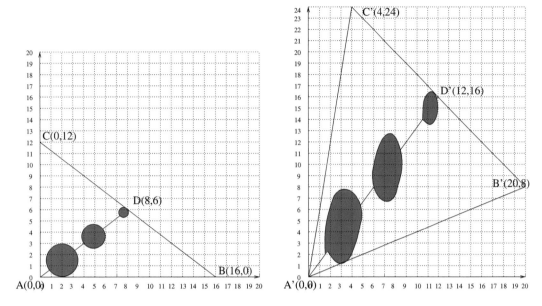

Figure 8.3: A spotted triangle ABC (left) and its affine-transformation $A'B'C'$ (right).

8.4.3   Colored Patterns

There are several ways to add color to the barcode-based similarity measure. For example, the barcode can be enhanced with a sensor of the color (or average color) in each "bar" instead of sensing only white and black. Assume that in Figure 8.2 non-white stripes (shown as black) are from left to right red, blue, and red. Then a barcode representation of the striped triangle would be $(1-white, 3-red, 1-white, 2-blue, 2-white, 1-red)$. Such a colored barcode representation would be distinguishable from another colored barcode representation such as $(1-white, 3-blue, 1-white, 2-red, 2-white, 1-blue)$ based purely on the color differences.

8.4.4   Complex Objects

The above discussion focused on the handling of triangles. Of course, many objects are more complex than triangles. However, the more complex objects can be decomposed into a set of triangles. In fact, a particular triangulation, or subdivision into non-overlapping triangles, can be found that can be shown to be affine-invariant. That is, the same object, no matter what particular affine invariant image is given, can be triangulated into the same set of triangles, such that, the set of triangles are also affine-invariant to each other.

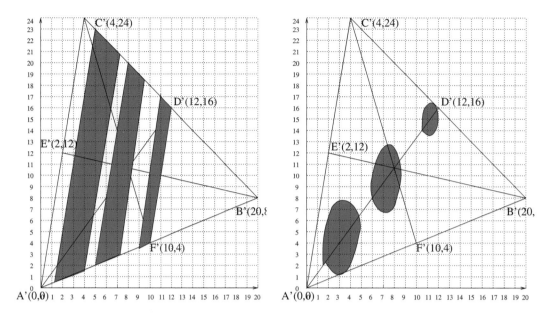

Figure 8.4: Midpoints of a striped triangle ABC (left) and a spotted triangle $A'B'C'$ (right).

Applying the above affine-invariant triangulation method should be the first step in handling complex objects, once they are identified and separated from the background and other objects. Since each complex object is triangulated also into a set of affine-invariant triangles, to find whether two images are similar, we need to find the best mapping from triangles to triangles in the two sets, then we need to sum the similarity scores.

Example 8.4.3 Suppose that a complex object I_1 consists of the following three affine-invariant triangles:

$$\Delta_{1,1}, \Delta_{1,2}, \Delta_{1,3}.$$

Similarly, suppose that another complex object I_2 consists of the following three affine-invariant triangles:

$$\Delta_{2,1}, \Delta_{2,2}, \Delta_{2,3}.$$

Further suppose that the best mapping (the mapping that yields the lowest sum of the triangle-triangle similarity scores) is the following:

$$\Delta_{1,1} \leftrightarrow \Delta_{2,3}, \quad \Delta_{1,2} \leftrightarrow \Delta_{2,1}, \quad \Delta_{1,3} \leftrightarrow \Delta_{2,2}.$$

Then the similarity score $\mathcal{S}\rangle\updownarrow$ between the two complex objects is the following.

$$\mathcal{S}\rangle\updownarrow(I_1, I_2) = \mathcal{S}\rangle\updownarrow(\Delta_{1,1}, \Delta_{2,3}) + \mathcal{S}\rangle\updownarrow(\Delta_{1,2}, \Delta_{2,1}) + \mathcal{S}\rangle\updownarrow(\Delta_{1,3}, \Delta_{2,2}).$$

As a practical matter, when the complex objects that occur in an application are composed of a large number of triangles, then we cannot expect the affine-invariant triangulation to find for two different images of an object two different triangulations that are perfectly mappable into each other. It could well happen, for instance, that one triangluation yields 90 triangles and another triangulation yields 100. Obviously, in this case at last five triangles in the first triangulation cannot be mapped into the other.

However, notice that the triangles in any given triangulation tend to vary greatly in size. Hence, even in the above case, one can expect the largest triangles to be correctly identified by each triangulation. Hence, they should be mappable into each other. Therefore, it may be possible to find in general a reasonably small number k, such that the k largest triangles in each of the two triangulations are always mappable into each other.

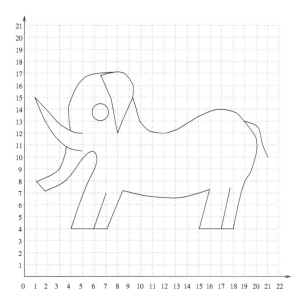

Figure 8.5: An elephant.

A further practical issue is the complication that arises when one object occludes another object, that is, the first object partially hides from view the second object. Occlusions can occur through the triangulation of track, making the above method problematic. However, sometimes the obvious original contour of the occluded object can be restored. For example, consider the image of the elephant in Figure 8.5. No person would have a difficulty identifying the elephant if it tried to hide behind a tree. Even though the tree would occlude the elephant, the contour of the elephant is so obvious that it can be instantly recognized. There are computer vision algorithms that can handle well the occlusion problem. These need to be used to restore the original object before any triangulations or other calculations.

Bibliographic Notes

For indexing image databases, *shape or contour* is used, for example, by Jagadish [208] and Mehrotra and Grosky [274]; *color* and *color histograms* are used, for example, by Stricker and Orengo [387] and Swain and Ballard [392]. A combination of color and shape is used by the QBIC system [132] and in Smoliar and Zhang [379]. *Attributed relational graphs*, which represent the spatial relationship between objects by a labeled graph, are used by Petrakis and Faloutsos [305]. *Image compression coefficients*, derived from different methods, are used by the Photobook system [303], and Ravela [317]. In general, these papers hardly even raise the issue of invariance under geometric transformations, except for Ravela [317].

The *minimum Hausdorff distance measure* was proposed by Huttenlocher et al. [200], and the *geometric hashing* technique by Lamdan et al. [254]. An affine-invariant similarity measure based on least squares distance was proposed by Werman and Weinshall [425]. A slight extension of the point representation together with an *absolute difference measure*, which is also affine-invariant, is given by Hagedoorn and Veltkamp [184].

Several other similarity measures require a good knowledge of the shape of the object in the image. These include *Fourier descriptors* used by Arbter et al. [23], *moment invariants* of Wang [420], *curvature scale space* of Mokhtarian et al. [1, 280, 281], and the decomposition approaches of Tsai [404] and Cyganski and Vaz [102]. Ben-Arie and Wang [37] use similar decompositions for small areas of patches identifiable in the picture. The common problem with these approaches is that they are not robust under noise. For example, some of these methods try to identify when the first or second derivative of a contour line is zero. These are difficult to distinguish with any confidence from a noisy image. Another problem is that the contour of objects used in several of these methods may not be the most important information. For example, the curvature scale space representation [1, 280] is applied to marine creatures, but it cannot be applied to human faces.

Lemma 8.1.1 about the ratio of areas is well known, but Lemma 8.3.1 about affine-invariance of the ratio of colors within an image and its use for efficient indexing are new. Other similarity measures that are not affine-invariant are presented for point sets by Eiter and Mannila [124], for constraint databases by Deng [109] and Revesz [328], and for time series data by Goldin and Kanellakis [154].

The affine-invariant triangulation method was first described in [182]. The color similarity measure was described in the first edition of this textbook [339]. Computer experiments in [183] combined the affine-invariant traingulation on complex objects with the primary color measure and the rainbow color measure. The computer experiments were performed on a set of colorful bird images. The computer experiments showed that the primary color ratio measure performs better than the rainbow color ratio measure under the same lightning conditions. Affine-invariant similarity measures for patterned objects were considered in [346].

Exercises

1. When all the stored images are photographed at a certain angle and we know the current camera angle, then we may calculate the values of a, b, c, d, e, f of the affine transformation between the stored and the new images. For example, a database may contain images of people photographed directly from the front, while the camera may face a door through which people enter at a slight angle.

   Write an MLPQ query (see Chapter 13) that tests whether two images are affine transformations of each other, assuming that we know the values of the constants a, b, c, d, e, f and $ab \neq cd$.

2. Show, using a counterexample, that the Hausdorff distance is not affine-invariant.

3. Calculate the black and red areas as specified in Example 8.3.1 for the original and the distorted images of the bird. How close are the ratios of the black and red areas in the two images?

4. Apply the same affine transformation as in Example 8.1.1 to the image of the elephant in Figure 8.5.

9

Constraint Objects Databases

In many applications, our information about the world is incomplete. For example, we may know about a group of persons some information about their ages, such as that one person's age is greater or less than forty or one person is older than another, without knowing their precise ages. Section 9.1 describes how our incomplete information about the whole world or universe can be represented as a single *universal constraint object relation*, or UCOR.

The UCOR requires different assumptions about the database than the assumptions made in earlier chapters. Section 9.2 describes the closed, open, and possible world assumptions. The UCOR satisfies the possible world assumption.

Refinement queries add (conjoin) new constraints to the UCOR. Each constraint added eliminates some of the possibilities or ambiguities from the UCOR. For example, as we add more constraints about the ages of the group of persons, we may get more precise knowledge about their ages. In the limit, this will approach the state where there is only one solution of the UCOR, and then we obtain the exact age of each person. Sections 9.3 and 9.4 describe the syntax and the semantics of refinement queries. Section 9.5 describes projection queries from the UCOR. Section 9.6 describes the evaluation of refinement queries. Finally, Section 9.7 considers the related notion of constraint XML objects.

9.1 The Constraint Objects Data Model

Our incomplete information can be described using constraint objects and a special relation called the *universal constraint object relation*, or UCOR.

P. Revesz, *Introduction to Databases: From Biological to Spatio-Temporal*,
Texts in Computer Science, DOI 10.1007/978-1-84996-095-3_9,
© Springer-Verlag London Limited 2010

Each *constraint object* is composed of a unique object identifier (oid) and a set of attributes. For example, each person in a set of persons with different names can be represented by an object, with oid equal to the name of the person and an age attribute variable. The UCOR contains all known constraints about all objects and their attribute variables.

For example, suppose we represent the persons Alice, Brian, and Tom as constraint objects with oids equal to their names and the constraint attribute y representing their ages. If we know that Alice is three years older than Brian, the total age of the three persons is less than 60, and Tom is the youngest, then this information can be represented by the following UCOR:

UCOR

Alice_Age	Brian_Age	Tom_Age	
Alice.y	Brian.y	Tom.y	$Alice.y = Brian.y + 3$ $Alice.y + Brian.y + Tom.y \leq 60$ $Tom.y \leq Alice.y$ $Tom.y \leq Brian.y$

The UCOR is a constraint relation like the ones we saw earlier, except that instead of regular variables it contains attribute variables of constraint objects. All substitutions of nonnegative integer constants for the three attribute variables that satisfy the constraint are possible age combinations for the three persons.

9.2   Closed, Open, and Possible Worlds

There are three types of assumptions that are commonly made about the validity of the data stored in a database relation:

- **Closed world assumption:** This means that every tuple in the relation is true, and every tuple outside the relation is false. For example, the *Crops* relation satisfies the closed world assumption because every possible combination of planting is within the relation, and what is not a possible combination is left out.

- **Open world assumption:** This means that every tuple in the relation is true, and every tuple outside the relation is either true or false. For example, the *Go* relation satisfies the open world assumption. Every tuple within this relation is a possible travel between two cities, but there are travel possibilities that are not in the relation. Another example, comprises the following relations *Firesource* and *Flammable*:

Firesource

Object
Cigarette
Fireplace

Flammable

Object
Gasoline
Spray can
Wood

The open world assumption holds for these relations because the objects they contain are indeed normally fire sources and flammable, respectively. However, the closed world assumption fails because there are other fire sources, for example, a stove top or a match, which are not in the first relation, and other flammable objects, such as coal and gas, which are not in the second object.

- **Possible world assumption:** This means that every tuple in the relation is possibly true, and every tuple outside the relation is false. This is meaningful, for example, for the UCOR relation of Section 9.1. For example, the UCOR in Section 9.1 contains many solutions including $Alice.y = 23$, $Brian.y = 20$, $Tom.y = 15$ and $Alice.y = 28$, $Brian.y = 25$, $Tom.y = 5$. That means that both of these are possible at this time. None of the possible solutions can be excluded until more information is learned that contradicts them.

It is important to know exactly what assumptions we can make about the input database relations.

For example, it would not make sense to try to write a query to find the maximum profit the farmer could earn without the closed world assumption in the *Crops* relation. If the closed world assumption does not hold, then any query may fail when the planting combination that yields the maximum profit is not in the *Crops* relation. The closed world assumption in this case is warranted and helpful.

On the other hand, it would be unwarranted to assume the closed world assumption in the case of the *Firesource* and *Flammable* relations. One may write a query that says "x won't burn y if x is not a fire source or y is not flammable." Under the closed world assumption, everything not listed in *Firesource* is not a fire source, and everything not listed in *Flammable* is not flammable. Hence this query would derive wrong conclusions, for example, that a stove top will not burn a spray can.

Most useful queries preserve the condition of the database. Sometimes a query fails to do that. Suppose we list enough objects in the *Firesource* and *Flammable* relations and they satisfy the closed world assumption. Then the query "x won't burn y if x is not a fire source" will not derive the true tuple that a cigarette will not burn a steel knife. Hence the output relation *Won't_Burn* will not satisfy the closed world assumption.

In every query, the assumptions that we can make about the output relations depend on the assumptions that hold about the input relations. Also some queries are meaningful to apply only under some assumptions and not under others. Therefore, it is important to know what assumptions we can make about the input database relations.

9.3   Syntax

Each refinement query consists of a finite set of rules of the form

$$\phi(y_1, \ldots, y_k) :\!- R_1(x_{1,1}, \ldots, x_{1,k_1}), \ldots, R_n(x_{n,1}, \ldots, x_{n,k_n}).$$

where ϕ is a constraint formula of attribute variables, each R_i is an input relation, and the xs are either oids or variables ranging over oids and the ys are attribute variables. The formula may contain conjunction, disjunction, implication ($\rightarrow$), and atomic constraints that may be any type we saw in Chapter 12. The R_is contain only a finite number of tuples of oids. They do not contain constraints. We call ϕ the *rule head* and the R_is together the *rule body*.

We refer to the value of attribute A of an object with oid O by the syntax $O.A$. We give a few examples.

Example 9.3.1 Suppose that Alfred, Alice, Bernard, Bernice, Carl, Donald, Denise, Edward, Elise, Fred, Felice, Gerald, and Harold are persons in an extended family. We know that Alfred is not yet 70, and Harold is already in school (i.e., 5 years or older). Gerald was born just last month. Elise is more than 4 years older than Fred, and Bernard is more than 25 years older than Edward.

This incomplete information can be represented by one object for each person with the oid equal to the name of the person and an attribute variable y representing the person's age. The UCOR in this case would be the following (where comma means logical and):

$$
\begin{aligned}
Alfred.y &< 70, \\
Gerald.y &= 0, \\
Harold.y &\geq 5, \\
Bernard.y - Edward.y &> 25, \\
Elise.y - Fred.y &> 4
\end{aligned}
$$

Finally, suppose we learn that no siblings are twins or were born in the same year and that between parents and their children there is at least 18 years difference. We also know that each person's age is nonnegative. This information can be expressed by the following refinement rules:

$$x.y < z.y \quad :\!- \quad Sibling(x, z).$$

$$z.y - x.y \geq 18 \quad :\!- \quad Parent(x, z).$$

$$x.y \geq 0 \quad :\!- \quad Person(x).$$

where we assume that relations $Parent(x, y)$, $Person(w)$, and $Sibling(z, u)$ contain object oids such that x is a child of y, z is a younger sibling of u, and w is a person.

Example 9.3.2 Suppose that Customer, Employee, Manager, and Person are classes in a class hierarchy shown in Figure 9.1. We know about each class that it is a subset or superset of other classes. We also know the elements of some lower and upper bounds of these classes. The lower bound tells which persons must be in the class, while the upper bound tells which persons may be in the class. Any set in between the two is a possible solution. For example, the given constraint for the Employee class allows two possible solutions, one is $\{Al, Bob, Carl\}$ the other is $\{Al, Bob, Carl, Dave\}$.

We can represent all this information by creating four objects with oids Person, Employee, Manager, and Customer. Each of these objects has one attribute variable S representing the set of members of the class with the same name as the oid. The UCOR will be the conjunction of the following:

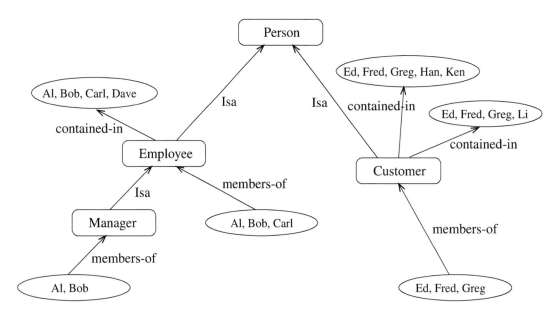

Figure 9.1: The inheritance hierarchy.

$$
\begin{aligned}
\{Al, Bob, Carl\} &\subseteq Employee.S \\
Employee.S &\subseteq \{Al, Bob, Carl, Dave\} \\
\{Al, Bob\} &\subseteq Manager.S \\
\{Ed, Fred, Greg\} &\subseteq Customer.S \\
Customer.S &\subseteq \{Ed, Fred, Greg, Li\} \\
Customer.S &\subseteq \{Ed, Fred, Greg, Han, Ken\}
\end{aligned}
$$

It is intuitive that the upper bound of a superclass is also an upper bound of its subclasses, and the lower bound of a subclass is also a lower bound of its superclass. This can be expressed using the following refinement rule:

$$x.S \subseteq y.S \quad :- \quad Isa(x, y).$$

where relation $Isa(x, y)$ records which object x is a subclass of which other object y.

Example 9.3.3 A classical syllogism is a valid deductive rule involving the binary relations *All*, *No*, *Some*, and *Somenot* whose arguments are oids of objects that represent sets. We assume that each object has an attribute S ranging over sets of strings representing possible members of these sets. Then the following refinement rules define the implications of the four relations:

$$x.S \subseteq y.S \quad :- \quad All(x, y).$$

$$x.S \cap y.S = \emptyset \quad :- \quad No(x, y).$$

$$x.S \cap y.S \neq \emptyset \quad :- \quad Some(x, y).$$

$$x.S \not\subseteq y.S \quad :- \quad Somenot(x, y).$$

Sometimes our initial UCOR is empty and the information needs to be represented by rules whose rule bodies may also be empty. This means that the left-hand side of these rules should be added to the UCOR. The following is an example.

Example 9.3.4 In many numerical cryptographic problems, we have to find out which digit value each letter represents in a summation or multiplication. For example, in the *send + more = money* problem we need to find for each letter a different digit value from 0 to 9 such that the resulting numbers satisfy the summation. Here we show the summation, including the carry-in and carry-out variables:

```
c1 c2 c3 c4 c5
    s  e  n  d
 +  m  o  r  e
 --------------
 m  o  n  e  y
    c1 c2 c3 c4
```

Let each letter digit be represented by a constraint object with an oid, which we take to be equal to the letter itself, and an attribute n denoting its digit value. Similarly, let each carry-in and carry-out be represented by a constraint object with an oid, equal to character string ci, and an attribute n denoting its digit value. Let relations $Letter$ and $Carry$ contain the oids of these two objects. The following refinement rules express that each letter has a different digit value:

$$0 \leq x.n \leq 9 \quad :- \quad Letter(x).$$

$$x.n \neq y.n \quad :- \quad Letter(x), Letter(y), x \neq y.$$

Implicit in this problem is that no number starts with a 0 digit, hence m, which is the carry-out in the leftmost column, must be 1. We also have to note that in the rightmost column the carry-in c_5 must be 0. This can be expressed by the following refinement rules:

$$c1.n = m.n \quad :- \quad .$$

$$c5.n = 0 \qquad :- \quad .$$

In this problem there are some constraints among the variables in each column of the summation. In particular, let relation $Column(i, x, y, z, o)$ contain all quintets of carry-in i, input digits x and y, output digit z, and carry-out o. The following refinement query expresses the constraint that holds among these objects:

$$i.n + x.n + y.n = z.n + 10 \times o.n :- Column(i, x, y, z, o).$$

Example 9.3.5 A department needs to select a team of students to participate in a programming contest. The selection must satisfy a number of requirements on a team object with oid T and attribute variable S representing the members of the team. We state each requirement separately and express it by a refinement rule.

The students eligible to participate are Jenny, David, Pat, Mark, Tom, Lilly, and Bob. This is expressed as:

$$T.S \subseteq \{\text{``Jenny''}, \text{``David''}, \text{``Pat''}, \text{``Mark''}, \text{``Tom''}, \text{``Lilly''}, \text{``Bob''}\} :- .$$

If Bob is selected, then David must be selected:

$$\text{``Bob''} \in T.S \rightarrow \text{``David''} \in T.S :- .$$

If both David and Pat are selected, then Mark cannot be selected:

$$\{\text{``David''}, \text{``Pat''}\} \subseteq T.S \rightarrow \text{``Mark''} \notin T.S :- .$$

If both Jenny and Tom are selected, then Bob cannot be selected:

$$\{\text{``Jenny''}, \text{``Tom''}\} \subseteq T.S \rightarrow \text{``Bob''} \notin T.S :- .$$

If Pat is selected, then either Lilly or Tom must be selected:

$$\text{``Pat''} \in T.S \rightarrow (\text{``Lilly''} \in T.S \lor \text{``Tom''} \in T.S) :- .$$

Either Jenny or Lilly must be selected, but Jenny and Lilly cannot be both selected:

$$(\text{``Jenny''} \in T.S, \text{``Lilly''} \notin T.S) \lor (\text{``Jenny''} \notin T.S, \text{``Lilly''} \in T.S) :- .$$

It makes sense to associate certain attributes with a set of objects instead of a single object. For example, the distance between a pair of cities is associated with a composition of the two cities. In general, if a and b are object oids, then $a \times b$ is an object oid for a composite object. The following is an example of the use of this feature.

Example 9.3.6 Suppose that each city is represented by an object with attribute variables x for the longitude and y for the latitude of its location. Pairs of cities are composite objects with attribute variable d for the distance between them. We also define input relations $city(c)$, which is true if c is the oid of a city object, and $road(a, b)$, which is true if a and b are oids of city objects connected by a direct road. We can assume that the road between two cities follows a straight line. Then the following refinement query finds the distance between pairs of cities:

$$(a \times b).d = \sqrt{(a.x - b.x)^2 + (a.y - b.y)^2} \quad :\!\!- \quad road(a, b).$$

$$(a \times b).d \leq (a \times c).d + (c \times b).d \quad :\!\!- \quad city(a), \; city(b), \; city(c).$$

The first rule states that the distance is equal to the Eucledian distance between two cities with a direct road connection. The second rule is useful for pairs of cities between which there is no direct road connection, but only connections that go through other cities. For all cities $a, b,$ and c the distance between a and b is defined to be always smaller than or equal to the sum of the distances between a and c and between c and b.

9.4   Semantics

The semantics of refinement rules is that for any instantiation, if the body is true, then the head is added (i.e., conjoined with a logical **and**) to the UCOR.

Evaluation of Example 9.3.1: Suppose we learn that Alfred and Alice have children Bernard, Carl, and Donald in this order. Bernard and Bernice have child Edward. Donald and Denise have children Elise and Fred. Edward and Elise have child Gerald. Fred and Felice have child Harold (see Figure 9.4 where husband-wife pairs are connected by the symbol ∞).

In this case the *Sibling* relation is:

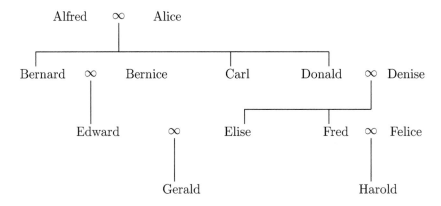

Figure 9.2: Alfred and Alice's family.

Sibling

Younger	Older
Carl	Bernard
Donald	Carl
Fred	Elise

The evaluation of the first rule adds to the UCOR the following constraints:

$$
\begin{aligned}
Carl.y &< Bernard.y \\
Donald.y &< Carl.y \\
Fred.y &< Elise.y
\end{aligned}
$$

The *Parent* relation is:

Parent

Child	Parent
Bernard	Alfred
Bernard	Alice
Carl	Alfred
Carl	Alice
Donald	Alfred
Donald	Alice
Edward	Bernard
Edward	Bernice
Elise	Donald
Elise	Denise
Fred	Donald
Fred	Denise
Gerald	Edward
Gerald	Elise
Harold	Fred
Harold	Felice

The evaluation of the second refinement rule adds to the UCOR the following constraints:

$$Alfred.y - Bernard.y \geq 18$$
$$Alice.y - Bernard.y \geq 18$$
$$Alfred.y - Carl.y \geq 18$$
$$Alice.y - Carl.y \geq 18$$
$$Alfred.y - Donald.y \geq 18$$
$$Alice.y - Donald.y \geq 18$$
$$Bernard.y - Edward.y \geq 18$$
$$Bernice.y - Edward.y \geq 18$$
$$Donald.y - Elise.y \geq 18$$
$$Denise.y - Elise.y \geq 18$$
$$Donald.y - Fred.y \geq 18$$
$$Denise.y - Fred.y \geq 18$$
$$Edward.y - Gerald.y \geq 18$$
$$Elise.y - Gerald.y \geq 18$$
$$Fred.y - Harold.y \geq 18$$
$$Felice.y - Harold.y \geq 18$$

Finally, the *Person* relation contains the oids of all the family members. The evaluation of the third rule will add to the UCOR the following constraints:

$$
\begin{aligned}
Alfred.y &\geq 0 \\
Alice.y &\geq 0 \\
Bernard.y &\geq 0 \\
Bernice.y &\geq 0 \\
Carl.y &\geq 0 \\
Donald.y &\geq 0 \\
Denise.y &\geq 0 \\
Edward.y &\geq 0 \\
Elise.y &\geq 0 \\
Fred.y &\geq 0 \\
Felice.y &\geq 0 \\
Gerald.y &\geq 0 \\
Harold.y &\geq 0
\end{aligned}
$$

The final UCOR will be the conjunction of the original UCOR and all of the preceding constraints. The UCOR may be simplified by rewriting it into logically equivalent but simpler forms. For example, the constraint $Fred.y < Elise.y$ generated during the evaluation of the second rule can be dropped because of the presence of the stronger constraint $Elise.y - Fred.y > 4$ in the original UCOR.

Evaluation of Example 9.3.2: The information about which class is a subclass of another class can be represented by the following relation:

Isa

Subclass	Class
Employee	Person
Customer	Person
Manager	Employee

There is only one refinement rule in Example 9.3.2. The body of this rule can be satisfied by the instantiation of x by *Employee* and z by *Person*. Therefore, the constraint $Employee.S \subseteq Person.S$ will be added to the UCOR. The instantiation *Customer* and *Person* for x and z also makes the body true. Hence $Customer.S \subseteq Person.S$ will also be added. Finally, the instantiation $Manager.S \subseteq Employee.S$ also makes the body true. Hence

Manager.S ⊆ *Employee.S* will also be added to the UCOR. Because only these three instantiations make the body of the refinement rule true, the final UCOR will be:

$$
\begin{aligned}
\{Al, Bob, Carl\} &\subseteq Employee.S \\
Employee.S &\subseteq \{Al, Bob, Carl, Dave\} \\
\{Al, Bob\} &\subseteq Manager.S \\
\{Ed, Fred, Greg\} &\subseteq Customer.S \\
Customer.S &\subseteq \{Ed, Fred, Greg, Li\} \\
Customer.S &\subseteq \{Ed, Fred, Greg, Han, Ken\} \\
Employee.S &\subseteq Person.S \\
Customer.S &\subseteq Person.S \\
Manager.S &\subseteq Employee.S
\end{aligned}
$$

Evaluation of Example 9.3.3: Suppose we represent the class of people who are allowed to drive, drive sometimes, drink alcoholic beverages sometimes, have a license, and have passed a driver's license test by five objects with oids *A, D, I, L,* and *P*. Suppose also that we learn the following facts about these objects (see Figure 9.3):

1. All persons must pass a test before getting a driver's license.

2. All persons allowed to drive must have a license.

3. No one drives without having passed the test.

4. No one who drinks has a license.

5. Some person *X* both drives and drinks.

We can represent these constraints as an input database that contains the tuples $All(L, P)$, $All(A, L)$, $All(D, P)$, $No(L, I)$, and $Some(D, I)$. After the evaluation of the refinement rules with this input database we obtain the following UCOR:

$$
\begin{aligned}
L.S &\subseteq P.S \\
A.S &\subseteq L.S \\
D.S &\subseteq P.S \\
I.S \cap L.S &= \emptyset \\
D.S \cap I.S &\neq \emptyset
\end{aligned}
$$

Evaluation of Example 9.3.5: The UCOR in this case will be the conjunction of the refinement rule heads. The UCOR will define all possible

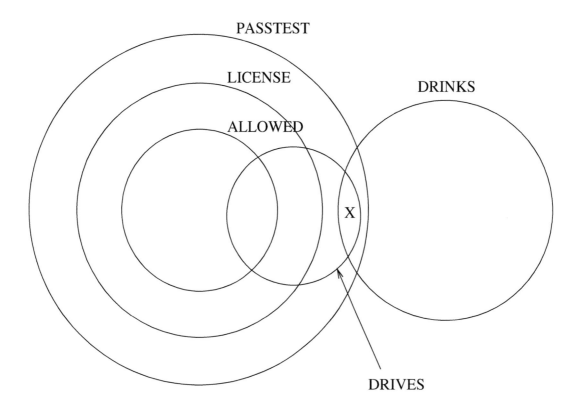

Figure 9.3: Drivers and drinkers.

teams that may be sent to the programming contest.

Evaluation of Example 9.3.6: Suppose we are given as objects the cities in the map shown in Figure 6.6 with the x and y coordinates of the cities defined such that the distance between cities with a direct connection is exactly the distance shown in the labels of the connecting edges. Then the evaluation of the first refinement rule will generate 16 constraints to be added to the UCOR, including the following:

$$(Omaha \times Lincoln).d = 60$$
$$(Lincoln \times KansasCity).d = 150$$

The evaluation of the second refinement rule will generate $6^3 = 216$ constraints to be added to the UCOR, including:

$$(Omaha \times KansasCity).d \leq 210$$

where the variable a is substituted by $Omaha$, variable b by $KansasCity$, and c by $Lincoln$.

9.5   Projection Queries

Refinement queries yield a UCOR that may contain a huge formula with one variable $O.A$ for each object O having an attribute A. Most users will not want to read the entire UCOR and try to understand it. Instead, to obtain a meaningful result, a user may want to concentrate on a small subset of the variables and ask a refinement query system to display only the known or implied relationships among them and eliminate any other variables.

For this, a user may use *projection* queries of the following form:

SELECT $y_1, \ldots, y_k$
FROM UCOR

where the ys are attribute variables. Next we give some examples.

Projection from the UCOR in Example 9.3.1: In this example a user may want to know only the age of Donald. Our best information based on the UCOR can be found by the projection query:

SELECT *Donald.y*
FROM UCOR

A refinement query system in this case would return the following formula as the answer:

$$47 \leq Donald.y, \ Donald.y \leq 49$$

This would mean that according to our current knowledge Donald's age is somewhere between 47 and 49, inclusively.

Projection from the UCOR in Example 9.3.3: A user may wish to know in Example 9.3.3 the relationship between people who have passed a driver's license test and those who have been caught driving drunk. The information needed can be found by the projection query:

SELECT *I.S*, *P.S*
FROM UCOR

A refinement query system in this case would return the answer:

$$I.S \cap P.S \neq \emptyset$$

which means that there is someone caught driving drunk who has passed the driver's license test.

Projection from the UCOR in Example 9.3.6: A user may wish to know in Example 9.3.6 the distance between Omaha and Chicago. The information can be found by the following:

SELECT $(Omaha \times Chicago).d$
FROM UCOR

A refinement query system in this case would return the answer:

$(Omaha \times Chicago).d \leq 990$

which means that currently the shortest known distance between the two cities is 990 miles.

9.6 Evaluation of Refinement Queries

Refinement queries are evaluated similarly to Datalog rules, except that whenever the rule body is true, instead of adding a tuple in the head to the database, we add a constraint in the head to the UCOR. The refinement query evaluation algorithm can be described as follows:

Algorithm Eval Refinement Query(Q,D,C)

input: Refinement query Q, input database D and UCOR C
output: The refined UCOR

for each refinement rule of Q **do**
    for each instantiation that makes the body true **do**
        add instantiated head to C
    end-for
end-for

if C is satisfiable **then**
    return(C)
else
    return(''False'')

9.7 Constraint XML

XML is a standard data model for data representation and exchange on the Internet. In XML, the type of each node is defined as an "element".

We regard nodes as the counterpart of tuples in relational databases. The difference is that the data type of the field in a certain element could be another element. All of the nodes of the same element type belong to a *layer*, which is the counterpart of a relation in relational databases. The layer name is the same as the element name defined for these nodes. We say layer A is the *parent layer* of layer B if the element B is the sub-element of element A in the XML document.

We define *inferred layers* of a layer L as the set of layers, which are child layers of L. Similarly, the *inferred layer of a node* is the subtree that is rooted from this node. Thus, the inferred nodes of a certain node n and the edges between these nodes form an XML tree with root n. We assume that each node has a virtual attribute *nid* as the identifier of the node and a hidden attribute *pid* as a pointer to the parent node. We may use the *nid* to access a node, from which we may access its child nodes. In DataFoX, we also use this *nid* to identify the subtree that is rooted at the current node.

We also assume *nid* is ordered, to maintain the order information of the XML tree model. For those elements defined as primitive data types, we assign an internal attribute named *data*. The value of this attribute is the content of the element. For example, the node in the XML document `<author>Maggie</author>` can be represented by the schema `author(nid, data)` such that the value of "data" is "Maggie" in this case.

We apply the same notation used to represent relational schema to represent the layer schema. However, the domain of variables for the layer schema is "tree". For example, the layer schema `LAYERNAME`$(L_1, \ldots, L_n)$ means that there is an element named "LAYERNAME" defined in the XML document, which has n child elements, with the layer names L_1, L_2, ..., L_n respectively. The data type of the child layers can be atomic (e.g., string, integer etc.) or a tree type defined by another layer schema. An instance of a layer and all of its inferred layers is a tree, whose root is an instance of the root layer.

The layer definition can be generated from the element definition of the XML document. We assume that every XML document comes with a Data Type Definition (DTD). XML Schema is a stronger schema definition of XML, but DTD is adequate (note: we can always generate DTD from the XML schema to create the layer data model.) With the layer data model, an XML document is treated as a collection of layers, and the traversal of the XML document is actually the traversal between the layers.

Example 9.7.1 Consider the following XML document regarding a library.

```
<!ELEMENT library (book*)>
<!ELEMENT book     (title, year, author+)>
<!ELEMENT title    #PCDATA>
<!ELEMENT year     #PCDATA>
<!ELEMENT author   #PCDATA>

<library>
    <book>
        <title>Landscape</title>
        <year>1997</year>
        <author> Steve </author>
    </book>
    <book>
        <title>Portrait</title>
        <year>2000</year>
        <author>John</author>
        <author>Maggie</author>
    </book>
</library>
```

The above XML document can be modeled in the layer model shown in Figure 9.4. Every layer corresponds to an "element" definition in DTD. The *book* layer and *author* layer are called the *inferred layers* of the *library* layer. The layers with primitive data types like "PCDATA" are merged into their parent layer for simplicity.

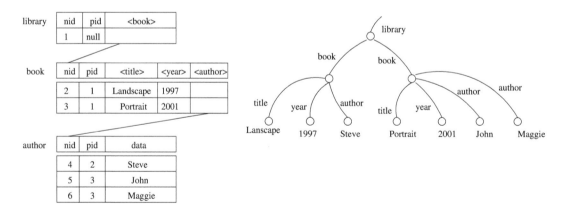

Figure 9.4: The layer model for a library document.

9.7.1 XML for Geographic and Moving Objects Data

With the self-descriptive style of XML, it is easy to extend XML to languages that encode geographic or moving objects data, as we saw in Chapters 6 and 7. For example, the Vector Markup Language (VML) can represent vector data objects, the Geography Markup Language (GML) can represent coordinates of OpenGIS features, and the Parametric Rectangle Markup Language (PRML) can represent parametric rectangles.

Example 9.7.2 Figure 9.5 shows a university campus map.

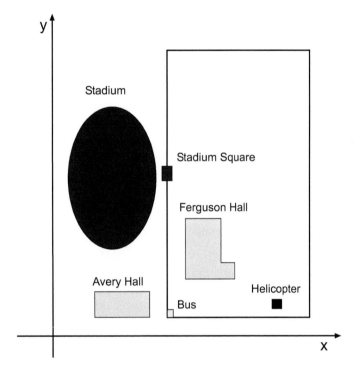

Figure 9.5: A university campus map.

The university campus map is composed of three different data sources. Figure 9.6 shows the first data source, which is in GML and describes the classroom buildings. Here rectangles are described by their lower-left and upper-right corner vertices.

Figure 9.7 shows the second data source, which is in VML and describes the stadium and the square in front of it. Note that the stadium is an ellipse and is described using a center points and height and a width.

```
<buildings>
  <lecture_hall>
    <name> Ferguson Hall </name>
    <dept> Computer Science </dept>
    <boundedby>
      <rectangle>
        <coord> <x> 35 </x> <y> 15 </y> </coord>
        <coord> <x> 45 </x> <y> 30 </y> </coord>
      </rectangle>
      <rectangle>
        <coord> <x> 45 </x> <y> 15 </y> </coord>
        <coord> <x> 50 </x> <y> 20 </y> </coord>
      </rectangle>
    </boundedby>
  </lecture_hall>
    .
    .
    .
</buildings>
```

Figure 9.6: GML description of lecture halls.

Figure 9.8 shows the third data source, which is in PRML and describes a moving bus and a helicopter. The description of parametric rectangles follows the one in Chapter 7.

The GML, VML, and PRML data models share a common characteristic, namely, the structures of the spatial and spatiotemporal attributes are well-formatted and also form a well-formatted subtree in the document, although the entire structure could be very complex. Applying the layer data model, we may transform any of the three specialized XML data models to a *constraint XML* data model that use aggregates the geographic and moving objects data into a constraint database. This transformation is performed by a *wrapper* function. Figure 9.9 shows an example of this transformation of from a PRML that describes a bus schedule into a constraint XML.

Bibliographic Notes

The constraint objects data model of Section 9.1 is from Srivastava et al. [382]. The definition of refinement queries is an improvement of the query language in [382] and is from Revesz [339]. Saraswat [362] uses a constraint store, which is similar to the UCOR, but a different query language that is suitable for concurrent programming. Other types of constraint objects

```
<sport_facilities>
  <stadium>
    <name> Husker Stadium </name>
    <shape>
      <ellipse>
        <x> 15 </x>
        <y> 40 </y>
        <w> 10 </w>
        <h> 15 </h>
      </ellipse>
    </shape>
  </stadium>
  <square>
    <name> Stadium Square </name>
    <shape>
      <rectangle>
        <x> 30 </x>
        <y> 40 </y>
        <w> 5 </w>
        <h> 5 </h>
      </rectangle>
    </shape>
  </square>
</sport_facilities>
```

Figure 9.7: VML description of the stadium and the square.

and query languages were considered by Brodsky and Kornatzky [55] and by Warmer and Kleppe [422].

Closed, open, and possible world relational databases are considered by Reiter [321], by Imielinski and Lipski [203, 202], by Abiteboul et al. [2, 3], and by Grahne [161].

Examples 9.3.1, 9.3.2, and 9.3.5 are modified from Revesz [325, 326, 335]. A refinement query system was implemented in Gundavarapu [175]. Di Deo and Boulanger [114] present an object-oriented approach to implementing constraint objects.

The constraint objects data model is only one way of representing incomplete information, which has a long history in relational databases, in deductive database [319, 320], and knowledge representation [261]. Incomplete information is usually represented in relational databases by null values. Imielinski and Lipski [203, 202] study marked null values with equality

```
<transportation>
  <vehicle>
    <name> Bus </name>
    <schedule>
      <prectangle>
        <x>
          <from> <a> 0 </a> <b> 32 </b> </from>
          <to> <a> 0 </a> <b> 33 </b> </to>
        </x>
        <y>
          <from> <a> 1 </a> <b> 5 </b> </from>
          <to> <a> 1 </a> <b> 6 </b> </to>
        </y>
        <t>
          <from> 0 </from>
          <to> 55 </to>
        </t>
      </prectangle>
          .
          .
          .

    </schedule>
  </vehicle>
      .
      .
      .
</transportation>
```

Figure 9.8: PRML description of a bus and a helicopter.

and inequality constraints. The computational complexity of queries and updates in the framework of Imielinski and Lipski is investigated by Abiteboul et al. [3] and Grahne [161].

Koubarakis [234, 237, 236, 238] presents a framework of indefinite constraint databases that unifies the constraint data model of Chapter 4 and the work on marked nulls by Imielinski and Lipski [203]. This is the most expressive framework based on the relational model that is able to represent infinite and indefinite information using constraints. Another interesting recent paper on indefinite information with order constraints over the rational numbers is by van der Meyden [412, 413].

Constraint XML objects and the PRML language are described in Revesz [78] as a part of the DataFoX project. The description in Section 9.7 is based on [78]. The DataFoX project used its own query language based on Datalog. Other XML query languages, include XQuery[73], Quilt[75],

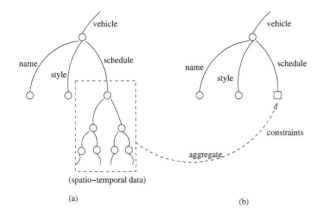

vehicle			
nid	\<name>	\<style>	\<schedule>
...	...	...	...
1	Bus	...	x=10, y=2t, 0<=t<=10
2	shuttle	...	...

(a)   (b)   (c)

Figure 9.9: Transformation from PRML to a constraint XML.

Lorel[4], XML-QL[111], and XPathLog[270], do not fully support query-ing geographic and spatiotemporal XML documents. Querying based on relational database systems[70, 127, 112, 372, 371] also does not support spatiotemporal queries. Constraint objects and constraint XML objects are related to several other object-oriented and object-relational database pro-posals by their common focus on objects.

Exercises

1. Using a UCOR represent the latitude and longitude locations of the towns of Chicago, Lincoln, and Omaha when we know only that Lincoln is 60 miles to the west of Omaha and Chicago is at least 200 miles north of both Lincoln and Omaha.

2. Each constraint object represents a person with an appointment with Mr. Brown. Each object has an oid and attributes b and e for the beginning and ending times of the person's appointment. Relation $Duration(x, t)$ is true if x has an appointment that lasts at least t minutes. Relations $After(x, t)$ or $Before(x, t)$ are true if x's ap-pointment takes place entirely after or before time t, respectively. Relations $Follow(x, y)$ or $Precede(x, y)$ are true if x's appointment is after or before y's appointment, respectively. We know that each person's appointment lasts at least one hour and that no two persons meet at the same time. Write a refinement query for the appointment schedule of Mr. Brown.

3. Each constraint object represents one of a set of cars parking next to each other in some unknown order on one side of a street with an oid and an attribute for its location. Relation $Next(x, y)$ or $Next(y, x)$

is true if x is parking next to y. Relation $Gap(x, y, z)$ or $Gap(y, x, z)$ is true if there are at least z number of cars parking between x and y. Write a refinement query for the parking locations of the cars.

4. Each constraint object represents a person with oid and attributes for height and weight. Relation $Taller(x, y)$ is true if x is taller than y. Relation $Heavier(x, y)$ is true if x is heavier than y. Write a refinement query for the height and weight of the persons.

5. Each constraint object represents a person sitting in a movie theater with an oid and attributes for the row and column locations. Relation $Behind(x, y, z)$ is true if x is sitting behind y with z seats between them. Relation $Right(x, y, z)$ is true if x is sitting to the right of y with z seats between them. Relation $Same\_Row(x, y)$ is true if x and y are sitting in the same row. Relation $Same\_Column(x, y)$ is true if x and y are sitting in the same column. Write a refinement query for the row and column locations of the persons.

6. Each constraint object represents a city on a map with an oid and attributes for the longitude and latitude of its location. Relation $East(x, y, z)$ is true if x is to the east of y with z miles between them. Relation $South(x, y, z)$ is true if x is to the south of y with z miles between them. Relation $Same\_Latitude(x, y)$ is true if x and y are located at the same latitude. Relation $Same\_Longitude(x, y)$ is true if x and y are located at the same longitude. Write a refinement query for the row and column locations of the cities. (*Hint:* Use Eucledian distance measure for measuring distance between cities on a map.)

7. We know about a set of events some information recorded in the relations:

   - $Before(x, y)$, which is true if event x ended before event y
   - $Overlap(x, y)$, which is true if events x and y overlap in time
   - $Not\_Overlap(x, y)$, which is true if events x and y do not overlap in time.

   Write a refinement query for the duration of the events. (*Hint:* Consider objects defining events with an oid and attributes for the beginning and ending instances.)

8. A computer science department consists of six professors: Anderson, Brown, Clark, Davis, Edmonds, and Fagin. The professors' offices are located in a row of rooms, which are numbered consequtively 101, 102, 103, 104, 105, and 106, with each professor having a different office. Each professor is teaching exactly one course this semester. The

courses offered are artificial intelligence, databases, graphics, hardware, software, and theory. We know the following information:

(a) Anderson's office is room 102 and Fagin's is room 105.

(b) Brown has the office in room 103 and teaches databases.

(c) Clark teaches software and his office is not room 101.

(d) Davis teaches theory and his only neighbor teaches graphics.

(e) The professor who teaches hardware has the office in room 104.

Write a refinement query for the office room numbers and the subjects taught by each professor.

9. Write refinement rules that reflect the following information about a certain group of musicians:

(a) Lilla plays the piano.

(b) Bob and Peter play the flute.

(c) Only Bob, Jenny, Peter, and Tom could possibly play the trumpet.

(d) All organ players are also piano players.

(e) All trumpet players are also flute players.

(f) All piano players are also drummers.

(g) All violin players are also guitar and piano players.

(h) Some person can play both the flute and the guitar.

(i) Some person can play both the drum and the piano.

(j) Some person can play the trumpet and either the violin or the organ.

10. Suppose that the objects in a problem are the departments at a university, and that each object has a single attribute *offers* that describes the courses that it offers. Assume that the database also contains the unary relations *Object* and *Course*. Express the following using refinement rules:

(a) The computer science department offers some course other than the courses 410, 413, 428, and 479.

(b) Not all database and information retrieval courses, i.e., courses 410, 412, and 413, are offered by the computer science department.

(c) The business management department teaches 412.

(d) Each course is offered by only one department. (*Hint:* Assume that the $\neq$ between oids is an input relation.)

11. A number of pigeons are sitting on a telephone line between two poles. The pigeons are numbered according to the order of their location from left to right. We know that the third pigeon is located more than 29 inches from the pole on the left. The fifth pigeon is located between 47 and 54 inches and the seventh pigeon is located more than 72 inches from the same pole. We also know that between any two pigeons there is exactly 10 inches:

    (a) Write a refinement query for the location of the pigeons.

    (b) Write a projection query to find the location of the fourth pigeon.

    (c) Evaluate the projection query.

12. After the refinement rules are applied, find the set of possible ages for each member of the family in Figure 9.4.

13. After the refinement rules are applied, find the set of possible members for each class of the inheritance hierarchy in Figure 9.1.

14. Solve the *send + more = money* cryptographic problem.

15. Solve the *fall + wind = cools* cryptographic problem.

16. Solve the *gale + neal = elsa* cryptographic problem.

17. Express and then evaluate the following projection query for Example 9.3.2: Find the set of managers.

18. Complete the evaluation of the possible team members for Example 9.3.5.

19. Write Datalog queries for the following examples and compare them with the refinement queries presented in this chapter:

    (a) Example 9.3.1.

    (b) Example 9.3.2.

    (c) Example 9.3.3.

    (d) Example 9.3.5.

    (*Hint:* For your queries you may define additional input relations that help order the children, classes, and conditions to be satisfied.)

10

Genome Databases

This chapter describes an application of constraint automata to the *genome map assembly* problem, which is one of the most important problems in bioinformatics.

Section 10.1 gives a brief review of the genome biology. Section 10.2 presents the *genome map assembly* problem and several approaches to solving that problem.

10.1 Biological Basics

Deoxyribonucleic acid, or DNA, is the genetic material that encodes the blueprint of all living organisms. Each DNA is composed of four nucleotides that are adenine (A),thymine (T), cytosine (C), and guanine (G). These nucleotides can form long chains or strands, called the sugar-phosphate backbone, using peptide bonds. Each strand has a $5'$ and a $3'$ end, which are chemically distinguishable. DNA is a double-stranded and helical structure where the chain of nucleotides on the first strand, called the *forward strand* that runs from the $5'$ to the $3'$ end, complement the chain of nucleotides on the second strand, called the *reverse strand* that runs from the $3'$ to the $5'$ end. Due to their different chemical structures, an A and a T can complement each other, and a C and a G can also complement each other forming hydrogen bonds.

Only the forward strand of the DNA contains directly useful information, which is always read from the $5'$ to the $3'$ end. The reverse strand is useful for reproduction. During reproduction, the two DNA strands are separated and new complementing nucleotides are added to both strands, forming two copies of the original DNA. Genome libraries contain only the

P. Revesz, *Introduction to Databases: From Biological to Spatio-Temporal*,
Texts in Computer Science, DOI 10.1007/978-1-84996-095-3_10,
© Springer-Verlag London Limited 2010

CATCGATCTCGGGAGGGATCCATTATCGATTCCCGGGCTC
GGGGGATCCTTCCATCGATGGGCCCGAGGCGGATCCCTAC
TATCGATCCCGGGGGGATCCTTAATTCTCGAGAAGGCCTA
TCGATCAAGGATCCTATCGATCCCGAGTCCCGGGAT

Figure 10.1: A genome sequence part of the Lambda bacterium.

forward strand data for each DNA. For example, Figure 10.1 shows a part of one strand of the Lambda bacterium DNA. Its length is 156 nucleotides.
The DNA contains coding regions, which store information about building proteins. Proteins are composed of a sequence amino acids. There are twenty amino acids that are commonly found in living organisms. These amino acids and their three letter and one letter abbreviations are shown in the table below.

Alanine	Ala	A
Arginine	Arg	R
Asparagine	Asn	N
Aspartic acid	Asp	D
Cysteine	Cys	C
Glutamic acid	Glu	E
Glutamine	Gln	Q
Glycine	Gly	G
Histidine	His	H
Isoleucine	Ile	I
Leucine	Leu	L
Lysine	Lys	K
Methionine	Met	M
Phenylalanine	Phe	F
Proline	Pro	P
Serine	Ser	S
Threonine	Thr	T
Tryptophan	Trp	W
Tyrosine	Tyr	Y
Valine	Val	V

The sequence of nucleotides is translated into a sequence of amino acids using a *genetic code* shown in Figure 10.2. The translation uses triplets of nucleotides called *codons*. There are 64 different codons. Each codon is either translated to one of the amino acids or is a terminal codon, indicated with an asterisk. The translation stops when a terminal codon is reached.

For example, the forward strand DNA of the Lambda bacterium DNA from Figure 10.1 can be translated as follows.

TTT	F	Phe	TCT	S	Ser	TAT	Y	Tyr	TGT	C	Cys
TTC	F	Phe	TCC	S	Ser	TAC	Y	Tyr	TGC	C	Cys
TTA	L	Leu	TCA	S	Ser	TAA	*	Ter	TGA	*	Ter
TTG	L	Leu	TCG	S	Ser	TAG	*	Ter	TGG	W	Trp
CTT	L	Leu	CCT	P	Pro	CAT	H	His	CGT	R	Arg
CTC	L	Leu	CCC	P	Pro	CAC	H	His	CGC	R	Arg
CTA	L	Leu	CCA	P	Pro	CAA	Q	Gln	CGA	R	Arg
CTG	L	Leu	CCG	P	Pro	CAG	Q	Gln	CGG	R	Arg
ATT	I	Ile	ACT	T	Thr	AAT	N	Asn	AGT	S	Ser
ATC	I	Ile	ACC	T	Thr	AAC	N	Asn	AGC	S	Ser
ATA	I	Ile	ACA	T	Thr	AAA	K	Lys	AGA	R	Arg
ATG	M	Met	ACG	T	Thr	AAG	K	Lys	AGG	R	Arg
GTT	V	Val	GCT	A	Ala	GAT	D	Asp	GGT	G	Gly
GTC	V	Val	GCC	A	Ala	GAC	D	Asp	GGC	G	Gly
GTA	V	Val	GCA	A	Ala	GAA	E	Glu	GGA	G	Gly
GTG	V	Val	GCG	A	Ala	GAG	E	Glu	GGG	G	Gly

Figure 10.2: The standard genetic code.

HRSREGSIIDSRARGILPSMGPRRIPTIDPGGILNSREELSIKDPIDPESRD

Genome biologists use *restriction enzymes* to cut DNA into smaller fragments at specific sites. For example, one restriction enzyme may cut the DNA at each occurrence of the substring GTTAAC (from left to right or right to left; it does not matter for the enzyme) into GTT and AAC. Each different restriction enzyme cuts the nucleotide string at different sites.

We can apply the restriction enzyme ClaI, which always cuts the genome at each site where AT^CGAT appears with the wedge symbol showing where the cut will take place. Then we obtain the subsequence shown in Figure 10.3.

Alternatively, if we use another restriction enzyme BamHI, which cuts at sites G^GATCC, then we obtain the subsequences shown in Figure 10.4.

Restriction enzymes can be applied together. For example, if a and b are two restriction enzymes, then their union $a \cup b$ can also be used. Their union cuts the DNA at all sites where either a or b cuts it.

Genome biologists can use *electrophoresis* or other techniques to measure the lengths of the small DNA fragments. The length of the fragments is measured in the number of nucleotides they contain. Genome biologists can also *sequence* small fragments, that is, they can identify using some

A1: CAT
A2: CGATCTCGGGAGGGATCCATTAT
A3: CGATTCCCGGGCTCGGGGGATCCTTCCAT
A4: CGATGGGCCCGAGGCGGATCCCTACTAT
A5: CGATCCCGGGGGGATCCTTAATTCTCGAGAAGGCCTAT
A6: CGATCAAGGATCCTAT
A7: CGATCCCGAGTCCCGGGAT

Figure 10.3: Subsequences of the Lambda bacterium sequence after `ClaI`.

B1: CATCGATCTCGGGAGG
B2: GATCCATTATCGATTCCCGGGCTCGGGG
B3: GATCCTTCCATCGATGGGCCCGAGGCG
B4: GATCCCTACTATCGATCCCGGGGG
B5: GATCCTTAATTCTCGAGAAGGCCTATCGATCAAG
B6: GATCCTATCGATCCCGAGTCCCGGGAT

Figure 10.4: Subsequences of the Lambda bacterium sequence after `BamHI`.

sequencing machine the chain of nucleotides that the fragments contain. Further, genome biologists can make multiple copies of the entire DNA or any fragment.

10.2   The Genome Map Assembly Problem

After cutting a large DNA strand with restriction enzymes, all information about the original order of the fragments is lost because the small fragments just float randomly in the solution. The *genome map assembly problem* is the task of finding the original order of the fragments after they are cut by a restriction enzyme. Since the small fragments can be sequenced, knowing the original order allows genome biologists to recover the sequence of the entire original DNA strand. Below we review several methods that solve the genome map assembly problem.

10.2.1   Overlap Multigraph

The *overlap multigraph* method relies on sequencing each end of each subsequence. Then the ends are analyzed for overlaps among them. The result of such an analysis is usually illustrated by an overlap multigraph in which each node is one of the subsequences and each directed edge from node A to node B has a label $k \geq 0$ if and only if the last k nucleotides of A and the first k nucleotides of B are the same.

For example, let F be the union of the As and Bs in Figures 10.3 and 10.4. Then part of the overlap multigraph of F is shown in Figure 10.5. We only show the edges that have positive labels and are incident on both an A and a B node. In general, there are many edges possible between two nodes; hence it is called a multigraph. For example, we have two directed edges, one labeled by 2 the other by 16, from $B3$ to $A4$.

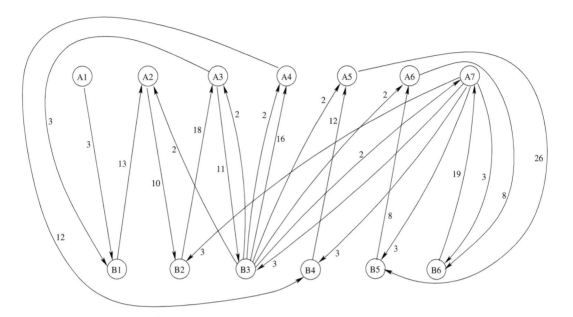

Figure 10.5: The overlap multigraph for F.

In the overlap multigraph, the Hamiltonian path whose total sum of the labels is the largest corresponds to a *shortest common superstring* of the sequences in F. Therefore, it is the preferred solution to the genome sequencing problem.

For example, a Hamiltonian path is shown in Figure 10.6. This Hamiltonian path matches the original genome sequence in Figure 10.1, and incidentally also gives a genome map in terms of As on the top and in terms of Bs on the bottom.

Unfortunately, such a Hamiltonian path is hard to find. A typical greedy search of the graph would always choose to explore the edges with the highest label. The greedy search would start at node $A5$ because it has the highest label, namely 26, on one of its edges. However, $A5$ is a failure node. Then the greedy search would explore $B6$ because it has the edge with the next highest label, namely 19. Continuing this way, the last node that the greedy search will explore is $A1$ or $A7$. Out of these only $A1$ is a success

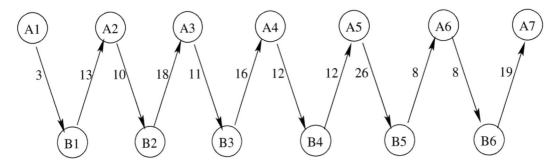

Figure 10.6: A Hamiltonian path in the overlap multigraph.

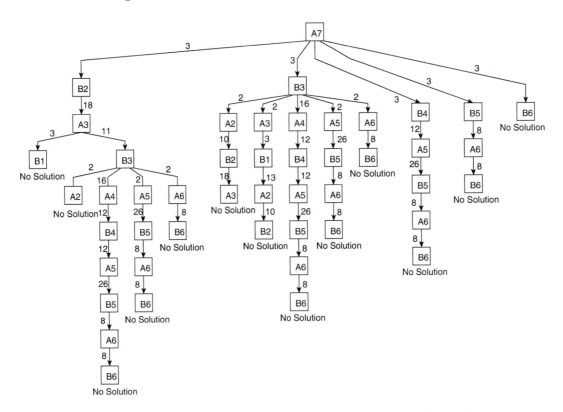

Figure 10.7: Greedy search from node $A7$ of the overlap multigraph.

node. Figure 10.7 shows that $A7$ is a failure node. It is clear that the greedy search on the overlap multigraph is doing a huge amount of work.

The overlap multigraph method requires that the set of fragments provide a good coverage of the original DNA string. Clearly F provides a uniform coverage of two because each nucleotide basis of the original DNA string appears in exactly one of the A and one of the B fragments. However, in many instances of using the overlap multigraph method, the fragments are randomly selected from the original DNA string but overlap with enough frequency to provide a coverage of at least two on average. When a random set of fragments is used, then there is a chance that there will be gaps in the genome map. Hence the above method of choosing the fragments is advantageous because it ensures that there are no gaps in the coverage.

10.2.2 Offset String

The offset string method relies on sequencing all the subsequences shown in Figures 10.3 and 10.4. The offset method starts by $A1$ and tries to find a matching B subsequence. Since $A1$ is CAT, and only $B1$ starts with CAT, they can be aligned as follows:

    A1:   CAT
    B1:   CATCGATCTCGGGAGG

Clearly, $B1$ is longer than $A1$. The substring CGATCTCGGGAGG by which $B1$ is longer than $A1$ is called the *offset*. The offset string method now looks for an A subsequence that starts with this offset. It finds that $A2$ is one such string. Therefore, now $A2$ can be alligned with $B1$ as follows:

    A1A2:   CATCGATCTCGGGAGGGATCCATTAT
    B1:   CATCGATCTCGGGAGG

Since $A1A2$ is now longer than $B1$, the new offset will be GATCCATTAT. The offset string method now looks for a B subsequence that starts with this offet. Now $B2$ can be alligned as follows:

A1A2:   CATCGATCTCGGGAGGGATCCATTAT
B1B2:   CATCGATCTCGGGAGGGATCCATTATCGATTCCCGGGCTCGGGG

It is clear that this process can be continued until the A subsequences on the top and the B subsequences on the bottom are completely alligned, giving a solution to the genome map assembly problem.

10.2.3 Offset Fingerprint

Before the development of fast and reliable sequencing methods, biologists would run the DNA fragments through a large polycrylamide gel using an electrophoresis process. During electrophoresis the DNA fragments that are smaller can move faster through the gel. In fact, the distance traveled by each fragment is proportional to its size measured by the num-

A1: CAT   {3}
A2: CGATCTCGGGAGG GATCCATTAT   {10,13}
A3: CGATTCCCGGGCTCGGGG GATCCTTCCAT   {11,18}
A4: CGATGGGCCCGAGGCG GATCCCTACTAT   {12,16}
A5: CGATCCCGGGGG GATCCTTAATTCTCGAGAAGGCCTAT   {12,26}
A6: CGATCAAG GATCCTAT   {8,8}
A7: CGATCCCGAGTCCCGGGAT   {19}

Figure 10.8: Fragments obtained by `ClaI` and then `BamHI`.

ber of nucleotides it contains. The polycrylamide gel can be dried and exposed to an X-ray film. The resulting visualization can distinguish fragments whose length differ by only one nucleotide. Interestingly, the set of fragment lengths alone is almost unique for each genome and restriction enzyme pair. Therefore, the set of fragment lengths is called a *fingerprint*.

The *2-dimensional electrophoresis* method is an extension of the simple electrophoresis fingerprinting method. The 2-dimensional electrophoresis at first cuts the DNA by one restriction enzyme. Then using an electrophoresis the fragments are run through the polycrylamide gel in one direction, which we can call the x-axis. Then after some time, we apply to the gel a second enzyme, which cuts the fragments into smaller fragments. Then using another electrophoresis, the smaller fragments are run in the y-axis. As a result of the 2-dimensional electrophoresis, there will be a DNA fragment in the (x, y) location of the gel if there was a DNA fragment in the x location after the first phase and cutting that DNA fragment by the second restriction enzyme yielded a smaller fragment of size y.

For example, a 2-dimensional electrophoresis method could apply first the `ClaI` restriction enzyme on the Lambda bacterium genome in Figure 10.1. That would yield the set of fragments in Figure 10.3, which will be separated along the x-axis. Then in the second phase the 2-dimensional electrophoresis method could apply the `BamHI` restriction enzyme, cutting the subsequences in Figure 10.3 into smaller fragments as shown in Figure 10.8. For each A subsequence, we get the bag of the lengths of the small fragments shown on the right side of Figure 10.8. Here by *bag* we mean a multiset, i.e., a generalization of a set in which each element can occur multiple times.

Alternatively, the 2-dimensional electrophoresis method could apply first the restriction enzyme `BamHI` and then `ClaI`. This would cut the B subsequences in Figure 10.4 into the smaller fragments shown in Figure 10.9. Again, the bag of the lengths of the smaller fragments are shown on the right side the figure.

The 2-dimensional electrophoresis method uses the two sets of bags instead of the actual sequences to allign the A and the B subsequences.

B1: CAT CGATCTCGGGAGG $\{3,13\}$
B2: GATCCATTAT CGATTCCCGGGCTCGGGG $\{10,18\}$
B3: GATCCTTCCAT CGATGGGCCCGAGGCG $\{11,16\}$
B4: GATCCCTACTAT CGATCCCGGGGG $\{12,12\}$
B5: GATCCTTAATTCTCGAGAAGGCCTAT CGATCAAG $\{8,26\}$
B6: GATCCTAT CGATCCCGAGTCCCGGGAT $\{8,19\}$

Figure 10.9: Fragments obtained by `BamHI` and then `ClaI`.

The important observation is that the cutting regions of `ClaI` and `BamHI` do not overlap. Hence no matter which order we apply these two restriction enzymes, we obtain the same set of small fragments.

In the allignment, we again start with $A1$, whose bag of fragment lengths is $\{3\}$. That bag implies a fragment whose length is three nucleotides. Clearly, this can be alligned only by the bag of $B1$, which alone contains the number 3. Therefore, our first allignment will be:

A1: $\{3\}$
B1: $\{3,13\}$

Like in the offset string method, we also have here an offset, but it is not a string but the set difference $\{3,13\} - \{3\} = \{13\}$. Therefore, we need to look now for an A subsequence, whose bag contains this offset. Clearly, the bag of $A2$ is $\{10,13\}$ contains $\{13\}$. Hence we can continue the allignment as follows:

A1A2: $\{3,10,13\}$
B1: $\{3,13\}$

In the offset string method, the allignment took the concatenation of the strings, while here we take the bag union of the bags. Now the new offset is $\{3,10,13\} - \{3,13\} = \{10\}$. Since this new offset is contained in $\{10,18\}$, the bag of $B2$, we can continue the allignment as follows:

A1A2: $\{3,10,13\}$
B1B2: $\{3,10,13,18\}$

Clearly, this method can allign all the A and the B fragments similarly to the offset string method. The only drawback of the offset fingerprint method with respect to the offset string method is that the offset fingerprint method has a larger chance of ambiguity because occasionally two or more choices can be made, because all those match the offset fingerprint. To alleviate this problem, one can refine the fingerprints by adding a third restriction enzyme.

A1: CAT   {3}
A2: CGATC TCGGGAGG GATCCATTAT   {5,8,10}
A3: CGATTC CCGGGC TCGGGG GATCCTTCCAT   {6,6,6,11}
A4: CGATGGGC CCGAGGCG GATCCCTACTAT   {8,8,12}
A5: CGATC CCGGGGG GATCCTTAATTC TCGAGAAGGCCTAT   {5,7,12,14}
A6: CGATCAAG GATCCTAT   {8,8}
A7: CGATC CCGAGTC CCGGGAT   {5,7,7}

Figure 10.10: Fingerprints of the A subsequences.

B1: CAT CGATC TCGGGAGG   {3,5,8}
B2: GATCCATTAT CGATTC CCGGGC TCGGGG   {10,6,6,6}
B3: GATCCTTCCAT CGATGGGC CCGAGGCG   {11,8,8}
B4: GATCCCTACTAT CGATC CCGGGGG   {12,5,7}
B5: GATCCTTAATTC TCGAGAAGGCCTAT CGATCAAG   {12,14,8}
B6: GATCCTAT CGATC CCGAGTC CCGGGAT   {8,5,7,7}

Figure 10.11: Fingerprints of the B subsequences.

For example, we could add the restriction enzyme AvaI, which cuts at the C^YCGRG, where Y means either C or T and R means either A or G. This would result in the fragments and the bag of their lengths shown in Figure 10.10.

Similarly, further cutting the B fragments by the restriction enzyme AvaI, we get the fragments and the bag of their lengths shown in Figure 10.11.

In general, the offset fingerprint method with three restriction enzymes a, b, and c uses the following procedure to obtain the input fingerprint data for the genome map assembly problem:

1. Take a copy of the DNA.

2. Apply restriction enzyme a to the copy.

3. Separate the fragments.

4. For each fragment apply restriction enzymes $b \cup c$, cutting the fragment into subfragments.

5. Find the lengths of the subfragments.

6. Repeat steps 1–5 applying b instead of a and $a \cup c$ instead of $b \cup c$.

Example 10.2.1 Applying to a certain DNA string steps 1–5 we could obtain Figure 10.12. Applying to the same DNA string step 6, we could obtain Figure 10.13.

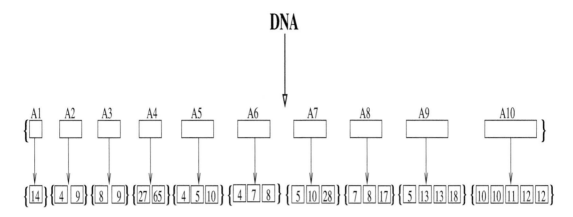

Figure 10.12: Cutting by a and then by $b \cup c$.

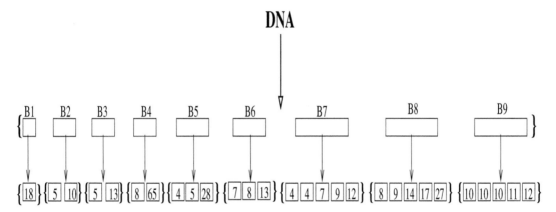

Figure 10.13: Cutting by b and then by $a \cup c$.

Finally, we present an abstraction of the genome map assembly problem. A *big-bag* is a multiset whose elements are bags that can occur multiple times. We call each permutation of the bags and permutation of the elements of each bag within a big-bag a *presentation*. A big-bag can have several different presentations.

For example, $a_1 = [[1, 3], [2, 4], [5, 7, 8]]$ is one presentation of a big-bag A. Similarly, $b_1 = [[1, 2, 4, 8], [3], [5, 7]]$ is a presentation of another big-bag B.

We say that the ith element of a presentation a, written as $a[i]$, is the ith Σ symbol seen when the presentation is read from left to right. For example, in a_1 the third element is 2 and the sixth element is 7, i.e., $a_1[3] = 2$ and $a_1[6] = 7$. The total number of elements, which is independent of any presentation, in A is 7. We say that two big-bags A and B, both of which have n elements, *match* if there are presentations a for A and b for B such that $a[i] = b[i]$ for $1 \leq i \leq n$. For example, A and B match because A can be presented as

$$a_2 = [[3, 1], [2, 4], [8, 5, 7]]$$

and B can be presented as

$$b_2 = [[3], [1, 2, 4, 8], [5, 7]].$$

The *big-bag matching decision* problem is the problem of deciding whether two big-bags match. The *big-bag matching* problem is the problem of finding matching presentations for two given big-bags if they match. Both the big-bag matching decision and the big-bag matching problems can be easily solved using constraint automata that are described in Chapter 15.

10.3 Sequence Similarity

Suppose we would like to find the similarity between two proteins. Since proteins are sequences of amino acids, as a first approach this requires comparing two protein strings. This may look simple, but this comparison requires some special considerations and holds some surprises. For example, suppose, that the two proteins that we would like to compare are described by the amino acid sequences CATTLE and WAFFLE. The first step in the comparison is to align them by putting the second below the first. This yields the following:

CATTLE

WAFFLE

After this alignment, it is clear that the two strings agree on the second, fifth, and the sixth amino acids. Therefore, we suspect that the two proteins are quite similar. However, in protein comparisons we are interested in a special kind of similarity that reveals biological relatedness. That is, we need to measure whether the two proteins derive from DNAs that have a common evolutionary ancestor. Because each amino acid is translated from a different set of codons, the closeness of those codons determines how easy it is to change from one codon to another codon so that the amino acid encoding changes too.

For example, C and W mean the amino acids cysteine and tryptophan, respectively. Since C is encoded by the codons TGT and TGC and W is encoded by the codon TGG, it would require the last nucleotide of one of the cysteine codons to change from T or C to G. As another example, T, that is, threonine, is encoded by ACT, ACC, ACA, ACG while F, that is, phenylalanine, is encoded by TTT and TTC. Hence at the minimum the

AC beginning nucleotide pair of either threonine codon needs to change to the TT beginning of a phenylalanine codon.

Hence we may suspect that a C and W alignment shows a closer similarity than a T and F alignment for two proteins. However, that is also incorrect because evolution has two main parts. The first part of evolution is random mutations. According to this part of the theory, one single nucleotide or point mutation is more likely to occur that two nucleotide mutations. However, the second part of evolution is selection, which we forgot to consider. Some of the mutations are less viable than others. By a statistical analysis, it can be shown that the change from a C to a W is much rarer than a change from a T to a F. This statistic indicates that the organisms whose DNA mutates from C to W have less viable offsprings than organisms whose DNA mutates from T to F.

In general, evolutionarily accepted mutations occur between two amino acids that have similar chemical properties. For example, a pair of amino acids that are both hydrophobic, that is repel water, or both hydrophilic, that is attract water, can be more easily exchanged with each other than a pair of amino acids that are mismatched, that is, one of them is hydrophobic while the other is hydrophilic. However, even this general rule has certain exceptions. For example, both cysteine and tryptophan are hydrophobic, yet there are few mutations from cysteine to tryptophan or vice verse. A possible reason for this is that some other chemical properties of cysteine and tryptophan may be still significantly mismatched.

Although we do not understand perfectly all the reasons why some mutations are more favored by evolution than others, a careful statistical observation can be made about the frequences of the various types of pairwise mutations. The pairwise values can be presented in a 20 × 20 matrix. One statistical matrix is called the *point accepted mutation* or PAM matrix. The basic PAM matrix, numbered as PAM1, shows the amount of divergence that occurs when 1 percent of the amino acids change during evolution. This statistic is gathered from proteins that are obviously similar to each other. For large evolutionary times of hundreds of millions of years another matrix needs to be used that reflects closer what can be expected to happen over that larger period of time.

The matrix that is commonly used for investigating evolutionary relationships is numbered PAM250. The PAM250 matrix is derived from the PAM1 matrix by taking its 250th power. Intuitively, if it takes some amount of evolutionary time, say one million years, to cause a mutation of 1 percent of the amino acids and that is what PAM1 measures, then PAM250 would describe what can be expected to happen in about 250 million years. During this time, each amino acid may change into each other with certain probability.

Figure 10.14 shows a normalized version of the PAM250 matrix. In this normalized version a positive matrix entry at location (i, j) indicates a possible evolutionary relationship between the ith and j^{th} amino acids, while a negative entry indicates no evolutionary relationship. The matrix is symmetric, hence only the lower diagonal entries are shown. Some features of the PAM250 include the following. Cysteine or C has no positive relationship with any other amino acid, while W and Y both have a positive relationship with only one other amino acid. This shows that the C, W, and Y amino acids are the most conserved amino acids in any protein. Hence the alignment of these is the most significant proof of an evolutionary relationship. Another observation is the existance of two groups of amino acids that are positively related. In the VILM group each of the four hydrophobic amino acids have a relationship of two or more. In the DENHQ group each of the five hydrophilic amino acids have a relationship of one or more.

	A	C	D	E	F	G	H	I	K	L	M	N	P	Q	R	S	T	V	W	Y
A	2																			
C	-2	12																		
D	0	-5	4																	
E	0	-5	3	4																
F	-4	-4	-6	-5	9															
G	1	-3	1	0	-5	5														
H	-1	-3	1	1	-2	-2	6													
I	-1	-2	-2	-2	1	-3	-2	5												
K	-1	-5	0	0	-5	-2	0	-2	5											
L	-2	-6	-4	-3	2	-4	-2	2	-3	6										
M	-1	-5	-3	-2	0	-3	-2	2	0	4	6									
N	0	-4	2	1	-4	0	2	-2	1	-3	-2	2								
P	1	-3	-1	-1	-5	-1	0	-2	-1	-3	-2	-1	6							
Q	0	-5	2	2	-5	-1	3	-2	1	-2	-1	1	0	4						
R	-2	-4	-1	-1	-4	-3	2	-2	3	-3	0	0	0	1	6					
S	1	0	0	0	-3	1	-1	-1	0	-3	-2	1	1	-1	0	2				
T	1	-2	0	0	-3	0	-1	0	0	-2	-1	0	0	-1	-1	1	3			
V	0	-2	-2	-2	-1	-1	-2	4	-2	2	2	-2	-1	-2	-2	-1	0	4		
W	-6	-8	-7	-7	0	-7	-3	-5	-3	-2	-4	-4	-6	-5	2	-2	-5	-6	17	
Y	-3	0	-4	-4	7	-5	0	-1	-4	-1	-2	-2	-5	-4	-4	-3	-3	-2	0	10

Figure 10.14: The PAM250 matrix model of protein evolution.

The evolutionary relationship of two amino acid sequences can be estimated by finding between each pair of aligned amino acids the similarity score from the normalized PAM250 matrix in Figure 10.14. This changes our example to the following.

```
CATTLE
-+--++
823364
WAFFLE
```

We inserted two rows between the pair of aligned amino acid chains. In the first row a minus sign – indicates that the evolutionary relationship is negative, and a plus sign + indicates that the evolutionary relationship is non-negative. The second row indicates the strength of the connection. The normalized PAM250 matrix has three entries where the strength value has two digits. Since all of these two digit values are positive, for space efficiency we describe these by replacing + by 1 instead of introducing a third row.

Next we add up the similarity scores for each aligned amino acid pair. This gives a total sequence similarity score of $-8 + 2 - 3 - 3 + 6 + 4 = -2$. This indictes that the proteins CATTLE and WAFFLE have no evolutionary relationship. Only a large positive score on a long aligned chain of amino acids would be generally recognized as a proof of an evolutionary relationship.

Another problem in similarity testing is the that the two amino acid chains may have different lengths. For example, one may try to align CASTLE and APPLE in the following way.

```
CATTLE
-++--
21123
APPLE-
```

where the dash after APPLE indicates a gap, that is, we have no amino acid paired together. There are are various ways to score such a pair. For now, let us assign to these gaps a score of zero. Hence this alignment gives a total score of $-2 + 1 + 1 - 2 - 3 = -5$. This indicates no similarity. However, another possible alignment of the two proteins is the following.

```
CATTLE
+++++
20064
-APPLE
```

This alignment gives a total score of 12, which is high enough to suggest an evolutionary relationship between APPLE and CATTLE. In general, it is always the alignment with the highest score that is the most important for establishing an evolutionary relationship.

In most alignments the gaps are allowed to occur not only at the end but also in the middle. For example, the proteins CATTLE and CALF can be aligned as follows.

```
CATTLE
1+  +-
22  65
CA--LF
```

This alignment gives a total score of $12 + 2 + 6 - 5 = 15$, indicating an even stonger relationship. Alignments may allow gaps in both amino acid chains. For example, `CATTLES` and `CALVES` could be alligned as follows.

```
CATTL-ES
1+  + ++
22  6 42
CA--LVES
```

This increases the alignment score to 26. In general, every pair of proteins could be aligned with 0 score if we allow indiscriminate use of gaps. Therefore, in many alignment algorithms the gaps receive some penalty score. These penalties are somewhat arbitrary because the PAM1 matrix did not establish statistics for the frequency of gaps. In addition, the lengths of gaps should be also considered. For example, should the length one gap in `CATTLES` and the length two gap in `CALVES` receive the same penalty score or should the latter be penalized twice as heavily? Against our intuition, some studies indicate that evolution favors more a single long gap than many small gaps whose total length is the same. Considering this, let us allow for a moment a penalty of -1 for each gap regardless of length. Then the similarity score between `CATTLES` and `CALVES` drops to 24.

10.3.1 Similarity by Composition from the Same Substrings

The Worlwide Protein Data Bank (PDB), with the website `www.rcsb.org/pdb`, contains both the sequence and the structure of a large number of proteins. One of the proteins is the alanine racemase protein (PDB ID: 1RCQ), which has the following sequence.

`1RCQ` protein sequence:

```
  1 MRPARALIDLQALRHNYRLAREATGARALAVIKADAYGHGAVRCAEALAAEADGFAVACI
 61 EEGLELREAGIRQPILLLEGFFEASELELIVAHDFWCVVHCAWQLEAIERASLARPLNVW
121 LKMDSGMHRVGFFPEDFRAAHERLRASGKVAKIVMMSHFSRADELDCPRTEEQLAAFSAA
181 SQGLEGEISLRNSPAVLGWPKVPSDWVRPGILLYGATPFERAHPLADRLRPVMTLESKVI
241 SVRDLPAGEPVGYGARYSTERRQRIGVVAMGYADGYPRHAADGTLVFIDGKPGRLVGRVS
301 MDMLTVDLTDHPQAGLGSRVELWGPNVPVGALAAQFGSIPYQLLCNLKRVPRVYSGA
```

In the above the numbers at the beginning of each row indicate the sequnce number of the first amino acid in that row. For example, the first amino acid is M, the beginning of the first row, and the 61st amino acid is E, the beginning of the second row. There are a total of 357 amino acids in this protein. Let us cut the 1RCQ protein into smaller pieces as shown below and eliminate the pieces indicated by small case letters.

```
mrpara LIDLQAL rhnyrlareatgaral AVIKADA YGHGAVR CAEA LAAEADGFAV
ACIEE glelreag IRQP ILLL egffeaselelivahdf WCVVH CAWQL EAIE RASL
arplnvwlkmdsgmhr VGFF PEDFRAA he RLRA SGKVAK IVMMSH F SRADELDC pr
TEE QLAA fsaa SQGLEGE ISL RNSPAVLGWPKV pswd VRPGILLYGATP ferahp
LADRLRP VMTLES KVISVRD LPAG epv GYGARYSTE RRQ rigvvamgyadgy
PRHAADGT lvf IDGKPG RLVG RVSMDM ltvd LTDH pqaglgsrvelwgpnvpvgalaa
QFGSIP YQLLCNL KRVPRVYSG a
```

We obtain a set of fragments similar to the genome fragments obtained by cutting a strand of DNA by restriction enzymes. Now let us consider another protein, namely the yeast hypothetical protein YBL036C (PDB ID: 1B54), which has the following amino acid sequence.

1B54 protein sequence:

```
  1 MSTGITYDEDRKTQLIAQYESVREVVNAEAKNVHVNENASKILLLVVSKLKPASDIQILY
 61 DHGVREFGENYVQELIEKAKLLPDDIKWHFIGGLQTNKCKDLAKVPNLYSVETIDSLKKA
121 KKLNESRAKFQPDCNPILCNVQINTSHEDQKSGLNNEAEIFEVIDFFLSEECKYIKLNGL
181 MTIGSWNVSHEDSKENRDFATLVEWKKKIDAKFGTSLKLSMGMSADFREAIRQGTAEVRI
241 GTDIFGARPPKNEARII
```

At first glance, 1B54 looks to be a completely different and unrelated protein to 1RCQ. However, it is possible to reconstruct the entire 1B54 protein with only a few gaps from the above capital letter fragments of the 1RCQ protein as shown in Figure 10.15.

How good is such a reconstruction or tiling of one string by the fragments of another? We can develop some measure of the goodness of the tiling, called the *tiling similarity*, as follows. First, note that the more tile fragments that are cut out from the first string, the easier the tiling becomes. Hence the number of tiles used, counting each tile as many times as it is used, seems to be inversely proportional to the tiling similarity. Therefore, we define the tiling similarity TS between two strings a and b as:

$$TS(a,b) = \frac{\text{sum of the similarities in the alignments}}{\text{number of tiles in the tiling}}$$

We can further refine the tiling similarity measure for two proteins by ignoring the initial Ms because they represent only the starts of the two proteins and are probably added to each protein regardless of the order of the tiles that follow them.

```
  2 STGITYDEDRKTQLIAQYESVREVVNAEAKNVHVNENASKILLLVVSKLKPASDIQIL
    +-+--1+-+++-++-+++++++++++++++-+-++++++-+++++++++++--+++-+
    1351100336314612470240044123252414030223566620036362142416
    GYGARYSTERRQ   QFGSIP      KVISVRD    ILLL        LIDLQAL
            QLAA       AVIKADA       RASL    LADRLRP

 60 YDHG-VREFGENYVQELIEKAKLLPDDIKWHFIGGLQTNKCKDLAKVPNLYSVETIDSLKKAK
    1+++ +++++++1--++++-+-+++++--1++--+++++-1-+--+++++1+-+++++-+-++
    0165 4607500011465330166601217321156201122331346020214153245225
    YGHGAVR       LIDLQAL   CAWQL      ACIEE        EAIE
            GYGARYSTE      LPAG    SQGLEGE    KRVPRVYSG   SGKVAK

122 KLNESRAKFQPDCNPILCNVQINTSHEDQKSGLNNEAEIFEVIDFFLSEECKYIKLNG
    ++++++++ +-+1-+++1++-+--++-+-+++++++++-+++++++++++1---++-+
    36002620 2342202622224212624151560042339044199613121413625
    RLRA       YQLLCNL    IDGKPG       VGFF    CAEA
        SRAD-ELDC      IVMMSH    LAAEADGFAV    LTDH    RLVG

180 LMTIGSWNVSHEDSKENRDFATLVEWKKKIDAKFGTSLKLSMGMSADFREAIRQGTAE
    ++++++1-+-+-+++-+++-+++++1-+-++++-+++++++++++++++++-+++
    2632027441624151062311220715254155502632261610496025641304
    VMTLES     IDGKPG       IDGKPG   RVSMDM      IRQP
        WCVVH      RNSPAVLGWPKV      ISL    PEDFRAA    TEE

238 VRIGTDIFGARPPKNEARII
    ++-++-++++-++++++--+
    46250427521663202130
    VRPGILLYGATP
            PRHAADGT
```

Figure 10.15: Tiling of the 1B54 protein by pieces of the 1RCQ protein.

The above tiling used 41 tiles, where GYGARYSTERRQ is counted as a single tile instead of two tiles because it occurs within 1RCQ as one string, although we cut it into GYGARYSTE RRQ. Counting as zero the two gaps, the total of the alignment similarities in the five rows is $131 + 169 + 153 + 158 + 39 = 650$. Therefore, the above tiling has the tiling similarity:

$$TS(1B54, 1RCQ) = \frac{650}{41} = 15.85$$

Actually, for each pair of strings, we need to choose the tiling that yields the highest tiling similarity. That requires considering an exponential number of possibilities. We do not know whether the above tiling is the best possible between 1B54 and 1RCQ. It seems worthwhile to compare the above tiling with a primitive tiling that cuts out each single amino acid from 1RCQ and then tiles the 1B54 with the songle amino acids. That primitive tiling would give the highest possible values in both the numerator and the denominator in the *TS* equation. The denominator would be 256, that is, one less than the number of amino acids in 1B54. The numerator would be about doubled, but that would still give only the value $\frac{1300}{257} = 5.06$. Such a primitive tiling is possible between any pair of proteins that both contain all 20 amino acids.

It seems clear that the above tiling of 1B54 by the pieces of 1RCQ is not accidental because its TS value is over three times higher than the TS value of the primitive tiling of the same pair of proteins. Therefore, it indicates some evolutionary relationship. In particular, it suggests that originally 1B54 and 1RCQ were composed of the same set of pieces but in different orders.

The existence of pairs of proteins with high tiling similarities and the above putative evolutionary relationships seems puzzling. However, the HIV virus may provide a hint at the solution to this puzzle. The HIV virus can insert its genetic code into the host DNA. Then based on this insertion, the infected host cell produces a large protein, which the HIV virus cuts into several smaller coat proteins using the HIV protease enzyme. The coat proteins are needed for the virus to build a coat and infect other cells. Apparently, the various HIV virus genes are inserted adjacent to each other, but their order can be arbitrary if the HIV protease can still identify their boundaries.

It is possible that 1B54 and 1RCQ were built from insertions of the same set of viral genes from some virus. If that is the case, then the boundaries of the genes should show some pattern. Indeed the boundaries seem non-random because when cutting the 1RCQ protein, the tiles used only a small subset of the possible $20 \times 20 = 400$ boundaries. Moreover, some of the cut sites are repeated. For example, the pairs `EAIE RASL`, `he RLRA`, and `GYGARYSTE RRQ` are all cut between E and R. The pairs `LIDLQAL rhnyrlareatgaral` and `ISL RNSPAVLGWPKV` are both cut between L and R. The triplet `IDGKPG RLVG RVSMDM` is cut twice between G and R. Interestingly, when we tile the 1B54 protein, then the L and R cut reappears as `ISL RVSMDM`, and the G and R cut reappears as `IDGKPG RNSPAVLGWPKV`. Although many amino acids may have changed due to random genetic point mutations of the genomes that encode them, the above repetitive features look like conserved patterns that suggest a permutable set of viral genes with a preference to start with R and end with E, G, or L. There are many other tiles that follow the same starting or ending pattern.

10.4   Structure Similarity

The main reason for searching for proteins with similar sequences is that proteins with a high sequence similarity have usually similar functions. Two proteins with similar functions can bind the same or closely related ligands in the same cellular environments. Suppose, for example, that a patient cannot naturally produce a certain protein because of a genetic deficiency. Then a similarity search can be important in discovering some drug, which is an artificially producable protein that has a similar function to the missing protein.

The function of a protein depends more on its structure than on its sequence. In a protein many amino acids may be substituted by other amino acids with similar chemical properties without changing either the structure or the function of the protein. In fact, such substitutions may occur during evolution without harmful effects. As a result, the structure of the proteins may be more evolutionarily stable than the sequence of the proteins. Therefore, to do a more complete search for similar proteins, it is better to look for proteins that have a similar structure.

The structure of a protein can be described by a sequence of points in $\mathcal{R}^3$. These points are the centers of the amino acids in sequence. The similarity of two protein structures requires finding an optimal structural alignment of the two proteins by rotation and translation of at least one of the two proteins. The optimal structural alignment minimizes some distance function. A commonly used distance function is the *root mean square difference* of the two proteins. In a structural alignment, like in a sequence alignment, some gaps may occur. These also may be assigned some penalty scores.

10.4.1   Comparison of Protein Active Site Structures

Sometimes even the common structural similarity algorithms fail to detect that two proteins have similar functions. For example, both 1B54 and 1RCQ can bind the pyridoxal-5′-phosphate ligand; hence they share some common function. However, DALI and VAST, the most widely-used structural alignment algorithms, give only a poor alignment of these two proteins.

A way to improve the structural alignment algorithms is to take one step further the idea of focusing on the more evolutionarily stable parts of the protein structure. The function of a protein depends more on the structure of its binding or active sites than on its overall structure. Hence in a protein much of the non-active-site structure may also change during evolution without harmful effects on the protein in maintaining its original function.

CPASS, which is an acromyn for *Comparison of Protein Active Site Structures*, is a structural alignment program that focuses on comparing the binding sites of two proteins. The CPASS scoring function S between a protein active sites a with n amino acid residues and protein active site b with m amino acid residues is:

$$S(a,b) = \sum_{i,j=1}^{i=n,j=m} \frac{d_{\min}}{d_i}(e^{-\Delta\text{rmsd}_{i,j}})^2 \, p_{i,j}$$

where $d_{\min}$ is the shortest distance to the ligand among all amino acids of a, d_i is the shortest distance to the ligand of the ith amino acid of a, $\Delta\text{rmsd}_{i,j}$ is the corrected root mean square difference between the ith amino acid of a and the jth amino acid of b, and $p_{i,j}$ is the probability of replacing the ith amino acid of a with the jth amino acid of b. The $p_{i,j}$ values may be based on either the PAM1 matrix discussed earlier or the more modern BLOSUM62 matrix, which is considered to be more accurate.

$S(a,b)$ is only summed over the optimal alignment for the ith amino acid of a and the jth amino acid of b. It is not summed over all possible combinations. If the number of residues are not identical between active sites a and b, that is, $n \neq m$, then the additional amino acids will not have a corresponding match. Each residue can be used only once in the alignment. If the active site contains unmatched amino acids, then no contribution is made to $S(a,b)$, which effectively reduces the maximal possible score that can be achieved. As an example, if active site a contains an unmatched A, a score of 0 is added instead of a possible maximum score of 4 that would be added if active site b contained an appropriately aligned A.

The calculated $\text{rmsd}_{i,j}$ is corrected by 1 A° to account for structural variations less than 1 A° that are within the experimental accuracy of the two aligned structures without letting the value to drop below zero. That is,

$$\Delta\text{rmsd}_{i,j} = \max(\text{rmsd}_{i,j} - 1, \ 0)$$

According to this correction any $\text{rmsd}_{i,j} < 1.0A^\circ$ would result in a $\Delta\text{rmsd}_{i,j}$ of $0A^\circ$, hence the weight $(e^{-\Delta\text{rmsd}_{i,j}})^2$ will be 1.0.

To further normalize the score between 0 and 100 percent similarity, the CPASS program generates the following normalized similarity score:

$$\mathcal{S} = \frac{S(a,b)}{S(a,a)} \times 100$$

In addition, CPASS generates a file containing the sequence alignment of the two active sites. The active sites were defined as those amino acids that are within $6A^\circ$ from the ligand. For example, the CPASS program generated the following alignment for the pyridoxal-5'-phosphate ligand active sites of 1B54 and 1RCQ:

| 1B54 | V47 | K49 | I91 | T113 | M181 | S224 | R239 | I240 | G241 |
| 1RCQ | V31 | K33 | L78 | S157 | M156 | S193 | R208 | I211 | G210 |

This output aligns, for example, the 47th amino acid of 1B54 with the 31st amino acid of 1RCQ. Both happen to be valine amino acids. It is interesting to compare the tiling similarity measure of Section 10.3.1 with the CPASS similarity program. A high tiling similarity was found using an alignment that included:

```
1B54 238   VRIGTDIFGARP
           ++-++-++++-+
           462504275216
1RCQ 207   VRPGILLYGATP
```

In this alignment the second and the fourth amino acids are aligned the same way as in CPASS. That agreement between the tiling similarity measure and the CPASS program suggests that the R239 and the G241 amino acids in the 1B54 protein are crucial for the pyridoxal-5'-phosphate binding function. However, the tiling similarity measure and the CPASS program makes different alignments of the other active site amino acids, which suggests that those alignments may be spurious. That is, not all active site amino acids contribute to the actual binding of the ligand. Some amino acids just happen to be in the vicinity of the ligand without participating in its binding.

Bibliographic Notes

The abstraction of the genome assembly problem as a big-bag matching problem is new. The big-bag matching problem is studied and shown to be NP-complete in Revesz [337]. Several other variations of the genome map assembly problem are shown to be NP-complete in Karp [220].

A common alternative abstraction to obtain the genome data is to pick random substrings from the DNA as, for example, in Gillett et al. [151], Olson et al. [288], Revesz [331], and Wong et al. [430] (which use restriction enzymes) or in Green and Green [163] and Harley et al. [191] (which use a technique called *hybridization* to test whether two substrings overlap). The random-substrings approach is discussed in Lander and Waterman [255], which gives some estimates about the number of substrings of certain average size required to get good coverage for a DNA of a given size. Unfortunately, the random-substrings approach has the limitation that there could be some gaps in the DNA, that is, regions that are not covered by any randomly picked substring.

In addition, Dix and Yee [115] and Yap [434] considered the following version of the map assembly problem using two restriction-enzymes a and

b. For three copies of the same genome the following information is obtained: the set of fragment lengths after complete digestion by enzyme a, the set of fragment lengths after complete digestion by enzyme b, and the set of fragment lengths after complete digestion by both enzymes a and b. Yap [434] shows that this leads to a formulation of the map assembly problem, which is also NP-complete but can be solved in some cases using the CLP(R) system of Jaffar et al. [207]. This method uses only three bags as data, whereas our method uses a separate bag for each substring obtained after step 2. The method in Section 21.11 has more structure and is less likely to lead to a combinatorial explosion during the search.

One other abstraction of the genome map assembly problem, called the probed partial digestion problem, is considered in Tsur et al. [405]. Partial digestion occurs when a restriction enzyme fails to cut all the sites specific to it. The probed partial digestion problem is solved using the LDL deductive database system [406].

The *overlap multigraph* method is described in [370]. Although the fingerprinting-based methods are older than the sequencing-based methods, even today we cannot sequence reliably DNA strings that are more than 500 nucleotides in length. Therefore, fingerprinting-based method can be still useful for large genomes.

Exercises

1. While studying the mechanisms of biological evolution, a genome biologist discovers a new species of bacteria that has a genome with the following DNA.

   AGTGAACTGGAGTGTACTACCCATGAATTCATAACA

   Can you help the genome biologist? (*Hint:* Translate the DNA strand into a protein using the genetic code in Figure 10.2.)

2. A biology professor discovers a new species of bacteria that has a genome with the following DNA.

   AGAGAAGGGATTTCCACGGAGCGATGTCTACGTTCGTCA

   Can you help the biology professor? (*Hint:* Translate the DNA strand into a protein using the genetic code in Figure 10.2.)

3. Show the greedy search tree of the overlap multigraph in Figure 10.5 when the search starts with node $B3$.

4. Consider the fingerprint data shown in Figures 10.12 and 10.13. Using the offset fingerprint method find all possible solutions of matching between the As and the Bs.

5. Suppose that 2-dimensional electrophoresis yields the fingerprint data shown in the table below. Using the offset fingerprint method find all possible solutions of matching between the As and the Bs.

A_Fragments

Fragment	Bag
A1	{ 10, 45 }
A2	{ 10, 17, 25, 50 }
A3	{ 15, 17, 45, 60 }
A4	{ 8, 12, 30, 40, 50 }
A5	{ 8, 10, 12, 20, 25, 40 }
A6	{ 5, 8, 10, 15, 25, 30, 35, 45, 50, 60 }

B_Fragments

Fragment	Bag
B1	{ 15, 17 }
B2	{ 8, 25, 45 }
B3	{ 8, 10, 25 }
B4	{ 15, 30, 60 }
B5	{ 10, 12, 40, 50 }
B6	{ 5, 10, 12, 20, 40 }
B7	{ 8, 30, 45, 50, 60 }
B8	{ 10, 17, 25, 35, 45, 50 }

6. In practice the measurements taken in by the 2-dimensional electrophoresis are subject to error. That is, each fragment length measured can be off by some nucleotides from its actual length:

(a) Modify the offset fingerprint method to allow a measurement error of at most d nucleotides.

(b) Write a computer program that implements the offset fingerprint method.

(c) Assume that $d = 1$. Modify the input data in the previous exercise by changing half of the values in A and B by either adding one or subtracting one. Apply your program to the changed data. How well does your program work on the noisy data?

7. Suppose that you have a set of $2n$ dominos where each domino has a left and a right side with a number of dots between 0 and c, where c is some constant. We divide the dominos into two sets with n dominos each. We give the first set of dominos to one player and the other

set to a second player. The two players are trying to build together two parallel rows of dominos with the first player always putting the dominos in the first row and the second player always in the second row such that:

(i) the two rows are shifted by one-half domino length with respect to each other,

(ii) in each column the dots match, i.e., the two half-dominos have the same number of dots, and

(iii) the leftmost and rightmost columns have the same number of dots.

Find an efficient polynomial time algorithm to find a solution to this domino matching problem. Note that the domino matching problem is a special case of the big-bags matching problem in which each little bag contains exactly two elements. (*Hint:* Reduce this to the Euler circle problem.)

11

Set Databases

Sets form a natural data type in many applications. Several database systems are based on sets. Section 11.1 reviews *syllogisms* which are binary set relations. Section 11.2 reviews *Boolean Algebras*, including Boolean Algebras of sets.

11.1 Syllogisms

Syllogisms are simple axioms using binary relations to reason about sets. Section 11.1.2 describes some basic set relations and some axioms that characterize those relations. It also gives examples of using the axioms to prove theorems.

11.1.1 Relations

Let U be the *universe* of objects, which is some countably finite or infinite set of objects. Let C be a finite number of classes. Each class contains some possibly empty subset of U. We denote the empty set by $\emptyset$. Consider the following four binary relations between classes.

All(x,y):	All x are y.
Some(x,y):	Some x are y.
No(x,y):	No x is y.
SomeNot(x,y):	Some x are not y.

It is important to keep in mind that these relations are only either true or false for any given pair of set names. They are not functions that return

P. Revesz, *Introduction to Databases: From Biological to Spatio-Temporal*,
Texts in Computer Science, DOI 10.1007/978-1-84996-095-3_11,
© Springer-Verlag London Limited 2010

an actual set as output. They are *propositional functions* that return true or false, depending on whether the given pair of set names is in the relation.

Example 11.1.1 We abbreviate the names of sets by their first letters, for example, d means dolphins, c means carnivores, and p means plants. Then the following are some propositions using the above binary relations.

$Some(c,d)$: Some carnivores are dolphins.
$Some(p,c)$: Some plants are carnivores.

The next example is adopted from *Symbolic Logic* by Charles L. Dodgson, who used the pseudonym of Lewis Carroll.

Example 11.1.2 Consider the following propositions.

(a) All hummingbirds are richly colored.
(b) No large bird lives on honey.
(c) Birds that are richly colored live on honey.

In this problem we use the following classes:

h : Hummingbirds.
r : Richly colored birds.
la : Large birds.
l : Birds that live on honey.

We can express the three propositions as follows.

(a) $All(h,r)$
(b) $No(la,l)$
(c) $All(r,l)$

Here is another problem by Lewis Carroll.

Example 11.1.3 Consider the following propositions.

(a) Babies are illogical.
(b) Nobody is despised who is able to manage a crocodile.
(c) Illogical persons are despised.

Let us define the following classes.

b : Babies.
i : Illogical persons.
d : Despised persons.
c : Those who are able to manage a crocodile.

We can write the propositions as follows.

   (a) $All(b, i)$
   (b) $No(d, c)$
   (c) $All(i, d)$

One of the cases where the *Some* relation is natural to use is when a proposition mentions one or more specific elements of a set.

Example 11.1.4 Consider the following propositions.

   (a) All coffee drinkers wake up early.
   (b) Mary drinks coffee.

We can represent "coffee drinkers" by c and "persons who wake up early" by e. Hence proposition (a) can be expressed by $All(c, e)$.

Proposition (b) can be written as "Mary is someone who drinks coffee." This shows that (b) is a *Some* relation between a set m, which contains only Mary, and c. Hence it can be expressed as $Some(m, c)$. Therefore we obtain the following.

   (a) $All(c, e)$
   (b) $Some(m, c)$

The next example uses the same idea.

Example 11.1.5 Express the following propositions.

   (a) Mary or Michael Johnson walks their dog.
   (b) All those who walk dogs wake up early.

We can represent "those who walk dogs" by d and "persons who wake up early" by e. Proposition (a) can be rewritten as "Someone of the Johnsons walks their dog." This shows that (a) is a *Some* relation between a set j that contains both Mary and Michael Johnson and d. Hence it can be expressed as $Some(j, d)$.

Proposition (b) can be expressed by $All(d, e)$. Hence we obtain the following.

   (a) $Some(j, d)$
   (b) $All(d, e)$

The next example summarizes some facts about logic.

Example 11.1.6 Express the following propositions using *All* and *Some*.

   (a) All tautologies are true propositions.
   (b) Some true propositions are not tautologies.
   (c) Some tautologies are boring.
   (d) All true propositions are useful.
   (e) Some true propositions are proven using syllogistic axioms.

Let us define the following sets.

> *tau* : Tautologies.
> *tp* : True propositions.
> *bp* : Boring propositions.
> *up* : Useful propositions.
> *syl* : Propositions proven using syllogistic axioms.

The propositions can now be expressed as follows.

> (a) *All(tau, tp)*
> (b) *SomeNot(tp, tau)*
> (c) *Some(tau, bp)*
> (d) *All(tp, up)*
> (e) *Some(tp, syl)*

11.1.2   Axioms

The four class relations have some basic properties that can be expressed by axioms, which use $\forall x$ to denote the expression "for all x" where x ranges over the possible classes. The first axiom says that *All* is a *reflexive* relation.

Axiom 11.1.1

$\forall x \quad All(x, x)$.

Some is not reflexive because $Some(x, x)$ means that some element of x is an element of x, which is not the case if $x = \emptyset$. The second axiom says that *Some* and *No* are *symmetric* relations.

Axiom 11.1.2

$\forall x, y \quad Some(x, y) \rightarrow Some(y, x)$.

$\forall x, y \quad No(x, y) \rightarrow No(y, x)$.

Hence, if $Some(c, d)$ is true, then $Some(d, c)$, that is, some dolphins are carnivores, is also true. The third axiom says that *All* is a *transitive* relation.

Axiom 11.1.3

$\forall x, y, z \quad All(x, y) \wedge All(y, z) \rightarrow All(x, z)$.

Some is not transitive. That is easy to see, for otherwise, $Some(d, c)$ and $Some(c, p)$ would imply that $Some(d, p)$, that is, some dolphins are plants, which is false. Axiom 11.1.3 is usually written in the form:

Minor premise:	$All(x, y)$
Major premise:	$All(y, z)$
Conclusion:	$All(x, z)$

The order of the minor and the major premises can be reversed without affecting the meaning of the syllogism. The minor and the major premises are distinguished according to the following rule: The first argument of the conclusion appears in the minor premise, and the second argument of the conclusion appears in the major premise. The third class, in this case y, appears as an argument in both the minor and the major premises.

Axioms that follow these rules are called *syllogisms*. People have discovered many syllogisms since they were first studied by Aristotle. However, not all the traditional syllogisms are valid if we allow classes to be empty. Today we find natural the notion of an empty set, but in ancient times people were apparently unfamiliar or uncomfortable with the notion of empty sets, just as they were unfamiliar with the concept of zero in arithmetic. Hence people implicitly assumed that the classes are nonempty. As a result, they would find the following a perfectly valid syllogism.

Minor premise:	$All(unicorns, horses)$
Major premise:	$All(horses, eatgrass)$
Conclusion:	$Some(unicorns, eatgrass)$

Suppose the universe U is composed of real objects, including some horses. Then the class *unicorns* is an empty set because unicorns are not real objects. In modern logic, we accept the minor premise as *vacuously true* and the major premise as true based on observations. However, modern logic does not accept `Some(unicorns, eat grass)` because it means that there exists within U at least one object, which belongs to both the class of unicorns and the class of grass eaters. Hence below we restrict attention to those 15 syllogisms that do not require the classes to be nonempty. Figure 11.1 shows those 15 syllogisms.

In Figure 11.1, we can apply the three abbreviated relation names in any circle to any variables scheme within a box if they are connected. For example, connect the leftmost circle in the second row to the box at its right to get the following syllogism.

Axiom 11.1.4

$$Some(x, y)$$
$$All(y, z)$$
$$\overline{Some(x, z)}$$

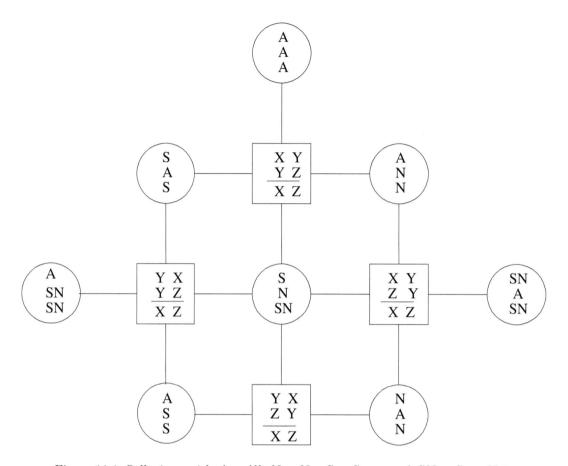

Figure 11.1: Syllogisms with $A = All$, $N = No$, $S = Some$, and $SN = SomeNot$.

For example, $Some(c, d)$ and $All(d, a)$ imply $Some(c, a)$, that is, some carnivores are animals.

A *deduction* is a sequence of applications of axioms to prove a new proposition from a given set of propositions. Let $p_1, \ldots, p_n$ be propositions assumed to be true. We call each p_i a *premise* and the set of premises D a *database*. Let q be also a proposition that we would like to test for whether it is true or false with respect to the database, that is, we want to answer the query:

If $p_1, \ldots, p_n$ are true, is q also true?

Alternatively, is $D \to q$ true? If it is true, then we will call it a *theorem* and the whole chain of steps in the deduction a *proof*. The following are a few examples.

Example 11.1.7 Show that the premises "All dolphins are mammals" and "All mammals are animals" lead to the conclusion "All dolphins are mammals." Here the premises can be expressed as $All(d, m)$ and $All(m, a)$.

Step	Reason
1. $All(d, m)$.	First premise
2. $All(m, a)$	Second premise
3. $All(d, a)$	Axiom 11.1.3 using Steps 1 and 2

Example 11.1.8 Show that the premises of Example 11.1.4 lead to the conclusion "Mary wakes up early." Since this can be rewritten as "Mary is someone who wakes up early," the needed conclusion is $Some(m, e)$.

Step	Reason
1. $Some(m, c)$	Premise (b)
2. $All(c, e)$	Premise (a)
3. $Some(m, e)$	Axiom 11.1.4 using Steps 1 and 2

The next example is similar to the above.

Example 11.1.9 Show that the premises of Example 11.1.5 lead to the conclusion "Someone of the Johnsons wakes up early." This conclusion can be expressed as $Some(j, e)$.

Step	Reason
1. $Some(j, d)$	Premise (a)
2. $All(d, e)$	Premise (b)
3. $Some(j, e)$	Axiom 11.1.4 using Steps 1 and 2

Example 11.1.10 Show that the premises of Example 11.1.2 lead to the conclusion "Hummingbirds are not large." Note that this conclusion can be rephrased as "No hummingbird is a large bird" and can be expressed as $No(h, la)$.

Step	Reason
1. $All(h, r)$	Premise (a)
2. $All(r, l)$	Premise (c)
3. $All(h, l)$	Axiom 11.1.3 using Steps 1 and 2
4. $No(la, l)$	Premise (b)
5. $No(h, la)$	Syllogism using Steps 3 and 4

Example 11.1.11 Show that the premises of Example 11.1.3 lead to the conclusion "Babies are unable to manage crocodiles," which can be expressed as $No(b, c)$.

Step	Reason
1. $All(b, i)$	Premise (a)
2. $All(i, d)$	Premise (c)
3. $All(b, d)$	Axiom 11.1.3 using Steps 1 and 2
4. $No(d, c)$	Premise (b)
5. $No(b, c)$	Syllogism using Steps 3 and 4

Here is an example deduction when q is a compound proposition.

Example 11.1.12 Show that the premises of Example 11.1.6 lead to the conclusion "Some boring proposition are true, some useful propositions are not tautologies, and some useful propositions are proven using syllogistic axioms." This conclusion can be expressed as

$$q = Some(bp, tp) \land SomeNot(up, tau) \land Some(up, syl).$$

Step	Reason
1. $Some(tau, bp)$	Premise (c)
2. $All(tau, tp)$	Premise (a)
3. $Some(bp, tp)$	Syllogism using Steps 1 and 2
4. $All(tp, up)$	Premise (d)
5. $SomeNot(tp, tau)$	Premise (b)
6. $SomeNot(up, tau)$	Syllogism using Steps 4 and 5
7. $Some(tp, syl)$	Premise (e)
8. $Some(up, syl)$	Syllogism using Steps 5 and 7
9. q	Conjunction of Steps 3, 6, and 8

11.1.3   Incompleteness

Let S denote the syllogistic axiom system, that is, Axioms 11.1.1 and 11.1.2 and the 15 syllogisms shown in Figure 11.1. In the following let U be the universe, C the set of classes, D a database, and q a syllogistic proposition.

Definition 11.1.1 $D \vdash q$ if it is possible to prove q from D using the axiom system S.

Definition 11.1.2 A *model* of D is any assignment of a subset of U to each class in C such that all the propositions in D are satisfied.

Example 11.1.13 Suppose that $U = \{1, 2, 3, \ldots\}$, $C = \{a, b, c\}$, and D contains the following propositions.

(a) $All(b, c)$
(b) $All(c, a)$
(c) $No(c, b)$
(d) $Some(a, a)$

Then $a = \{1, 2\}$, $b = \emptyset$, and $c = \{1\}$ is a model of D.

Definition 11.1.3 $D \models q$ if q holds in every model of D.

Intuitively, we would like to have an axiom system that allows proving from D exactly those propositions that hold in all models of D. Such a system is called *sound* and *complete*. More formally, we define these as follows.

Definition 11.1.4 An axiom system is *sound* when for all q if $D \vdash q$ then $D \models q$.
An axiom system is *complete* when for all q if $D \models q$ then $D \vdash q$.
An axiom system that is not complete is called *incomplete*.

Since the axioms of S are valid, as can be verified by Venn diagrams, we have the following.

Lemma 11.1.1 S is sound.   ∎

An important question is whether S is complete. We can answer that negatively.

Theorem 11.1.1 S is incomplete.

Proof: Let $C = \{a, b\}$. Let q be $SomeNot(a, b)$ and D be the database:

(a) $All(a, a)$
(b) $All(b, b)$
(c) $No(b, b)$
(d) $Some(a, a)$

To show that S is incomplete, we prove below that $D \not\vdash q$ and $D \models q$.

(*Proof of $D \not\vdash q$:*) First note that q is not already in D. Hence if $D \vdash q$, then q must be derived using a proof. However, we show that in fact nothing new can be proven using S and D.

Axiom 11.1.1: This cannot be used to prove anything new because propositions (a) and (b) are already in D.

Axiom 11.1.2: This cannot be used to prove anything new because propositions (c) and (d) are symmetric.

Syllogisms: The matrix below considers all the possibilities. Clearly, the syllogisms also cannot prove anything new.

	$All(a,a)$	$All(b,b)$	$No(b,b)$	$Some(a,a)$
$All(a,a)$	$All(a,a)$			$Some(a,a)$
$All(b,b)$		$All(b,b)$	$No(b,b)$	
$No(b,b)$		$No(b,b)$		
$Some(a,a)$	$Some(a,a)$			

(*Proof of $D \models q$:*) Premise $No(b,b)$ implies $b = \emptyset$. Premise $S(a,a)$ implies $a \neq \emptyset$. Hence $SomeNot(a,b)$ must hold in all models of D.   ∎

It seems that the axiom system S misses the following axioms.

Axiom 11.1.5

$$\frac{\begin{array}{c} Some(x,y) \\ No(z,z) \end{array}}{SomeNot(x,z)} \qquad \frac{\begin{array}{c} Some(y,x) \\ No(z,z) \end{array}}{SomeNot(x,z)}$$

11.1.4   Negation

The axioms we have seen so far do not contain the negation operator. In fact, we avoided the negation operator because propositions with negations can be confusing. Fortunately, in many cases the negation operators can be eliminated. Consider the following example, where an overline means negation.

$\overline{All(a,d)}$: Not all animals are dolphins.

This can be rewritten as the following simpler proposition:

$SomeNot(a,d)$: Some animals are not dolphins.

The above can be generalized as follows.

Axiom 11.1.6

$\forall\, x, y \quad \overline{All(x,y)} \rightarrow SomeNot(x,y).$

$\forall\, x, y \quad \overline{SomeNot(x,y)} \rightarrow All(x,y).$

Consider now another proposition that is a negation of a *Some* proposition.

$\overline{Some(a,p)}$: It is not true that some animal is a plant.

This too can be written in a simpler way as follows.

$No(a,p)$: No animal is a plant.

This rewriting can be generalized as follows.

Axiom 11.1.7

$\forall\, x, y \quad \overline{Some(x,y)} \rightarrow No(x,y).$

$\forall\, x, y \quad \overline{No(x,y)} \rightarrow Some(x,y).$

It follows from Axioms 11.1.6 and 11.1.7 that negation of an entire single proposition can be always eliminated. Sometimes the negation occurs in either the first or the second argument of a single proposition.

Axiom 11.1.8

$\forall\, x, y \quad All(x,\overline{y}) \rightarrow No(x,y).$

$\forall\, x, y \quad No(\overline{x},y) \rightarrow All(y,x).$

$\forall\, x, y \quad No(x,\overline{y}) \rightarrow All(x,y).$

$\forall\, x, y \quad Some(\overline{x},y) \rightarrow SomeNot(y,x).$

$\forall\, x, y \quad Some(x,\overline{y}) \rightarrow SomeNot(x,y).$

$\forall\, x, y \quad SomeNot(x,\overline{y}) \rightarrow Some(x,y).$

There are two cases that we have not considered yet. Let us consider now $SomeNot(\overline{x},y)$, which means that some non-x is non-y. This is true if and only if there is a $z \neq \emptyset$ that is neither x nor y. Hence this can be expressed as follows.

Axiom 11.1.9

$\forall\, x, y \quad SomeNot(\overline{x},y) \rightarrow \exists z\, Some(z,z) \wedge No(x,z) \wedge No(y,z).$

Finally, let us consider $All(\overline{x}, y)$, which means that all non-x is y. By Axiom 11.1.6, this is equivalent to $\overline{SomeNot(\overline{x}, y)}$. Therefore this is just the negation of the previous case. Hence we get:

Axiom 11.1.10

$$\forall\, x, y \quad All(\overline{x}, y) \rightarrow \forall z\, No(z, z) \vee Some(x, z) \vee Some(y, z).$$

Although the negation can be eliminated from the four binary connectives, the elimination introduced existential and universal quantifiers. Besides incompleteness, that is another limitation of syllogistic logic.

Example 11.1.14 Given the propositions

(a) $All(\overline{a}, b)$
(b) $No(a, c)$
(c) $No(b, c)$

Prove that $No(c, c)$.

Step	Reason
1. $No(a, c)$	Premise (b)
2. $All(c, \overline{a})$	Axiom 11.1.8 using Step 1
3. $All(\overline{a}, b)$	Premise (a)
4. $All(c, b)$	Axiom 11.1.3 using Steps 2 and 3
5. $No(b, c)$	Premise (c)
6. $No(c, c)$	Syllogism using Steps 4 and 5

Some complicated propositions have both of their arguments negated. These we can rewrite in two steps by eliminating the negation from the first and then the second argument. However, it is sometimes simpler to use a new axiom as a shortcut. The following is such an example.

$All(\overline{a}, \overline{d})$: All non-animals are not dolphins.

This proposition can be rewritten into the following simpler one.

$All(d, a)$: All dolphins are animals.

The above observation can be generalized as follows.

Axiom 11.1.11

$$\forall\, x, y \quad All(\overline{x}, \overline{y}) \rightarrow All(y, x).$$

11.1.5   Nor and Or

Let us define two new binary set relations.

Nor(x,y):   Something is neither x nor y.

Or(x,y):   Everything is either an x or a y.

The following are some examples of these new relations.

Nor(animals, plants) : Some things are neither animals nor plants.
Or(movie-lovers, music-lovers) : Everyone likes movies or music.

The Venn diagram in Figure 11.2 shows that the functions *Nor* and *Or* are complements of each other.

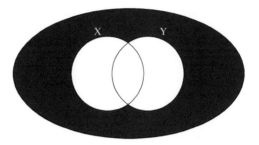

Figure 11.2: The oval region repesents the entire universe. $Nor(x, y) = True$ and $Or(x, y) = False$ if and only if the shaded region is nonempty.

The *Nor* and *Or* relations are symmetric.

Axiom 11.1.12

$\forall x, y \quad Nor(y, x) \ \rightarrow \ Nor(x, y).$

$\forall x, y \quad Or(y, x) \ \rightarrow \ Or(x, y).$

The new relations enable us to eliminate negation from the two difficult cases omitted in Axiom 11.1.8.

Axiom 11.1.13

$\forall x, y \quad All(\overline{x}, y) \ \rightarrow \ Or(x, y)$

$\forall x, y \quad SomeNot(\overline{x}, y) \ \rightarrow \ Nor(x, y)$

Consider now the six binary set relations. The old and the new relations together form a complete set in the sense that any common English language statement about pairs of sets can be expressed by them without the use of the negation operator. First, the negation of these new relations can be eliminated as follows.

Axiom 11.1.14

$$\forall x, y \quad \overline{Nor(x,y)} \;\rightarrow\; Or(x,y)$$

$$\forall x, y \quad \overline{Or(x,y)} \;\rightarrow\; Nor(x,y)$$

Second, any negation operator in the arguments of the *Nor* and *Or* relations can be also eliminated.

Axiom 11.1.15

$$\forall x, y \quad Nor(\overline{x}, y) \;\rightarrow\; SomeNot(x,y).$$

$$\forall x, y \quad Nor(x, \overline{y}) \;\rightarrow\; Some(x,y).$$

$$\forall x, y \quad Or(\overline{x}, y) \;\rightarrow\; All(x,y).$$

$$\forall x, y \quad Or(x, \overline{y}) \;\rightarrow\; All(y,x).$$

Since negation often leads to ambiguity, it is almost always preferable to express propositions without negation by using the above axioms. The following theorem shows that it is always possible to eliminate negation.

Theorem 11.1.2 Let p be any compound proposition using the set relations $All, No, Nor, Or, Some$, and $SomeNot$. Then p can be written in the form:

$$p_1 \vee \ldots \vee p_n$$

where p_i for $1 \leq i \leq n$ contains only conjunctions of simple propositions without negation.

With the new relations, it is possible to define new valid syllogisms, such as the following.

Axiom 11.1.16

$$\forall x, y, z \quad Or(x,y) \wedge All(y,z) \;\rightarrow\; Or(x,z).$$

$$\forall x, y, z \quad No(x,y) \wedge Or(y,z) \;\rightarrow\; All(x,z).$$

$$\forall x, y, z \quad Or(x,y) \wedge Nor(y,z) \;\rightarrow\; SomeNot(x,z).$$

The new relations and syllogisms work similarly to the old ones, although they allow a greater variety and flavor of problems.

Example 11.1.15 Express the following propositions using the eight relations without negation.

(a) No teaching assistant is an undergraduate student.
(b) Every student is either an undergraduate or a graduate student.
(c) Some honors students are not graduate students.

Let us define the following sets.

grad : Graduate students.
honors : Honors students.
ugrad : Undergraduate students.
ta : Teaching assistants.

The three premises can be represented by $No(ta, ugrad)$, $Or(ugrad, grad)$, and $SomeNot(honors, grad)$, respectively. Then we can show that "Some honors students are not teaching assistants" as follows.

Step	Reason
1. $No(ta, ugrad)$	First premise
2. $Or(ugrad, grad)$	Second premise
3. $All(ta, grad)$	Axiom 11.1.16 using Steps 1 and 2
4. $SomeNot(honors, grad)$	Third premise
5. $SomeNot(honors, ta)$	Old syllogism using Steps 4 and 3

11.2   Boolean Algebras of Sets

Syllogisms have a long and distinguished history in mathematical logic stretching back to the times of Aristotle, who introduced them in the fifth century BCE. The limitations of syllogisms became apparent only in the 19th century when George Boole proposed what has come to be called Boolean algebras, which are defined as follows.

Definition 11.2.1 A *Boolean algebra* is a tuple $\langle \delta, \cap, \cup, ^{-}, \emptyset, 1 \rangle$, where δ is a set called the *domain*; $\cap$ and $\cup$ are functions from $\delta \times \delta$ to δ; $^{-}$ is a function from δ to δ; and $\emptyset$, 1 are two specific elements of δ (called the *zero* and the *identity* element, respectively) such that for any elements x, y, and

z in δ the following axioms hold:

$$
\begin{aligned}
x \cup y &= y \cup x & x \cap y &= y \cap x \\
x \cup (y \cap z) &= (x \cup y) \cap (x \cup z) & x \cap (y \cup z) &= (x \cap y) \cup (x \cap z) \\
x \cup \overline{x} &= 1 & x \cap \overline{x} &= \emptyset \\
x \cup \emptyset &= x & x \cap 1 &= x \\
\emptyset &\neq 1
\end{aligned}
$$

Definition 11.2.1 describes some properties of Boolean algerbas without specifying exactly the Boolean algerba elements and operators. This vagueness is intentional and has the purpose of grouping together a large number of specific structures under the general term of "Boolean algebra."

The advantage of dealing with the abstract term "Boolean algebra" is that many properties that follow from the Boolean algebra axioms can be stated for the entire class of Boolean algebras. Hence those properties do not need to be proven repeatedly for each specific instance of Boolean algebras.

The axioms in Definition 11.2.1 are minimal requirements. In many other applications the specific Boolean algebra satisfies additional conditions. In these cases, of course, more properties may be derivable that hold for the Boolean algebra under consideration but not for all Boolean algebras.

Specific instances of Boolean algebras are given by *interpretations* for the elements and the operators. In the following, we will be interested in a specific subclass of Boolean algebras called *Boolean algebras of sets*. These are defined as follows.

Definition 11.2.2 A *Boolean algebra of sets* is a Boolean algebra in which the $\cap$ operator is interpreted as set intersection, $\cup$ is interpreted as set union, $^{-}$ is interpreted as set complement with respect to the identity element, and $\emptyset$ is interpreted as the empty set.

Definition 11.2.2 leaves open only the interpretation of δ and the identity element. Hence it may appear that Boolean algebras of sets form only a small subset of Boolean algebras. However, that is not the case because logically two Boolean algebras are essentially the same if they are *isomorphic*, that is, there is between them a bijection which preserves their respective Boolean operations.

To explain what this means, suppose that B_1 and B_2 are two Boolean algebras, and the B_1 has elements $a_1, \ldots, a_n$ and B_2 has elements $b_1, \ldots, b_n$, and there is a bijection that maps each a_i to b_i. Then if $a_i \cap a_j = a_k$ in B_1, then $b_i \cap b_j = b_k$ in B_2. Similarly, if $a_i \cup a_j = a_k$ in B_1, then $b_i \cup b_j = b_k$ in B_2. Finally, if $\overline{a_i} = a_j$, then $\overline{b_i} = b_j$.

Surprisingly, by Stone's representation theorem, which we omit here, any Boolean algebra is isomorphic to a Boolean algebra of sets. Hence essentially every Boolean algebra is the same as some Boolean algebra of sets. By Stone's representation theorem, when we restrict attention only to Boolean algebras of sets, we do so without any loss of generality.

The following are some examples of specific Boolean algebras of sets.

Example 11.2.1 Let H be the set of all finite unions of half-open intervals of the form $[a, b)$ over the rational numbers, where $[a, b)$ means all rational numbers that are greater than or equal to a and less than b, where a is a rational number or $-\infty$ and b is a rational number. Then:

$$B_H = \langle H, \cap, \cup, ^-, \emptyset, \mathcal{Q} \rangle$$

is a Boolean algebra of sets.

In many Boolean algebras of sets, the domain is the set of subsets of some set $\mathcal{S}$, called the *powerset* of $\mathcal{S}$, and denoted as $\mathcal{P}(\mathcal{S})$. Often $\mathcal{S}$ is $\mathcal{N}$, the set of non-negative integers, $\mathcal{Z}$, the set of integers, $\mathcal{Q}$, the set of rational numbers, or $\mathcal{R}$, the set of real numbers.

Example 11.2.2 The specific Boolean algebra of sets B_Z interprets the domain to be $\mathcal{P}(\mathcal{Z})$ and the identity element as $\mathcal{Z}$. We can write B_Z as follows:

$$B_Z = \langle \mathcal{P}(\mathcal{Z}), \cap, \cup, ^-, \emptyset, \mathcal{Z} \rangle$$

Example 11.2.3 Let $\mathcal{W}$ the set of English words in a dictionary. The Boolean algebra of sets B_W is the following:

$$B_W = \langle \mathcal{P}(\mathcal{W}), \cap, \cup, ^-, \emptyset, \mathcal{W} \rangle$$

Example 11.2.4 Many applications deal with a set of points in $\mathcal{R}^2$, the real plane. A Boolean algebra of sets of points in the real plane is the following:

$$B_{Euclid} = \langle \mathcal{P}(\mathcal{R}^2), \cap, \cup, ^-, \emptyset, \mathcal{R}^2 \rangle$$

Definition 11.2.3 For Boolean algebras we define the *precedence* relation, denoted as $\subseteq_B$, by the following identity:

$$x \quad \subseteq_B \quad y \quad \text{means} \quad x \cap \overline{y} = \emptyset$$

where x and y are elements of the Boolean algebra B. For Boolean algebras with sets the precedence relation is interpreted as the *subset or equal* relation between sets and is written as $x \subseteq y$, that is, without any subscript.

The following are some useful facts about the precedence relation.

Lemma 11.2.1 For any elements x, y, z, w in any Boolean algebra of sets,

$$x \subseteq x \qquad \text{(Reflexivity)}$$
$$x \subseteq y \text{ and } y \subseteq x \text{ imply } x = y \qquad \text{(Antisymmetry)}$$
$$x \subseteq y \text{ and } y \subseteq z \text{ imply } x \subseteq z \qquad \text{(Transitivity)}$$
$$\emptyset \subseteq x \qquad \text{(Zero element)}$$
$$(x \cap y) \subseteq x \qquad \text{(Augment)}$$
$$x \subseteq y \text{ and } w \subseteq z \text{ imply } (x \cap w) \subseteq (y \cap z) \qquad \text{(Merge)}$$

The precedence relation allows us to distinguish between two different types of Boolean algebras.

Definition 11.2.4 An *atom* of a Boolean algebra B is an element $x \neq \emptyset$ such that there is no other element $y \neq \emptyset$ with $y \subseteq_B x$. A Boolean algebra is *atomless* if it has no atoms; otherwise, it is called *atomic*.

Example 11.2.5 B_H is an atomless Boolean algebra. On the other hand, B_Z is an atomic Boolean algebra. In B_Z each $\{i\}$ is an atom, where $i \in \mathcal{Z}$.

Atomic Boolean algebras of sets are further subdivided according to the number of atoms that they contain. For example, the Boolean algebra B_Z has a countably infinite number of atoms. There are many finite subsets of B_Z, for example, the Boolean algebra B_n where $n \geq 2$ is any integer. In B_n the domain $\delta = \{-n, \ldots, 0, \ldots, n\}$.

For atomic Boolean algebras of sets with a countably infinite number of atoms, we assume that we can take the union or the intersection of an infinite number of the elements of the Boolean algebra, i.e., the Boolean algebras are *complete*. For complete Boolean algebras, we can define the *cardinality* operator as follows.

Definition 11.2.5 Let x be any element of an atomic Boolean algebra of sets with a finite or countably infinite number of atoms. If x can be written as the finite union of $n \in \mathcal{N}$ number of distinct atoms, then the *cardinality* of x, denoted $|x|$, is n. Otherwise the cardinality of x is infinite, which is denoted as $+\infty$.

The following lemma shows that the cardinality is a well-defined function from elements of an atomic Boolean algebra to $N \cup \{+\infty\}$.

Lemma 11.2.2 Let x be any element of an atomic Boolean algebra of sets with a finite or countably infinite number of atoms. Then x can be written as the union of some $n \in \mathcal{N}$ or $+\infty$ number of distinct atoms in the Boolean algebra. Moreover, there is no other set of atoms whose union is equivalent to x.

Example 11.2.6 The element $\{1, 2\}$ of the Boolean algebra B_Z is equivalent to $\{1\} \cup \{2\}$ or $\{2\} \cup \{1\}$. Both expressions use the same two distinct atoms, i.e., $\{1\}$ and $\{2\}$. Hence $|\{1, 2\}| = 2$.

11.2.1 Boolean Algebra Constraints

When writing Boolean algebra constraints, it is convenient to use *constant symbols* besides $\emptyset$ and 1 to refer to specific elements of the Boolean algebra. These constant symbols, as we will see, also need to be interpreted. For any Boolean algebra, we define *Boolean terms* recursively as follows:

1. $\emptyset$ and 1 are terms.

2. Each element of δ, specified explicitly or by a constant symbol, is a term.

3. Each variable is a term.

4. If S and T are terms, then $(S \cap T)$ and $(S \cup T)$ are terms.

5. If S is a term, then $\overline{S}$ is a term.

We sometimes omit the parentheses when they are not necessary within a term. We assume that $^{-}$ has a higher precedence than $\cup$ and $\cap$.

A *ground Boolean term* is a Boolean term that does not contain variables. A *monotone Boolean term* is a Boolean term that does not contain the complement operator, except for elements of δ. For example, if x, y, and z are Boolean variables, then $\overline{(x \cap y)} \cup \overline{z}$ is a term, but it is not a monotone Boolean term. On the other hand, $(x \cup y) \cap (z \cup \overline{0})$ is a monotone Boolean term. Neither of these is a ground term. The following is an interesting connection between monotone terms and the precedence relation.

Lemma 11.2.3 If $g(x_1, \ldots, x_n)$ is a monotone Boolean algebra term, then $g(x_1, \ldots, x_n) \subseteq_B g(y_1, \ldots, y_n)$ whenever $x_i \subseteq_B y_i$ for each $1 \leq i \leq n$.

Definition 11.2.6 Boolean atomic constraints are expressions of the form:

Equality :	$T \ =_B \ \emptyset$
Inequality :	$T \ \neq_B \ \emptyset$
Monotone Equality :	$T_{mon} \ =_B \ \emptyset$
Monotone Inequality :	$T_{mon} \ \neq_B \ \emptyset$
Order :	$x \subseteq_B T_{mon} \ \text{ or } \ T_{mon} \ \neq_B \ \emptyset$
Linear Cardinality :	$c_1|T_1| + \ldots + c_k|T_k| \quad \theta \quad b$

where T and each T_i for $1 \leq i \leq k$ is a Boolean term, T_{mon} is a monotone Boolean term, x is a Boolean variable, each c_i for $1 \leq i \leq k$ and b is an integer constant, and θ is:
   $=$, the equality relation,
   $\geq$, the greater than or equal comparison operator,
   $\leq$, the less than or equal comparison operator, or
   $\equiv_n$, the congruence relation modulus some positive integer constant n.

Example 11.2.7 The following is a Boolean linear cardinality constraint in the Boolean algebra B_Z of Example 11.2.2:

$3|x \cap y| - 2|z| = 4$

Boolean constraint formulas can be built similarly to propositional formulas using the same logical connectives.

Example 11.2.8 Suppose that we know the following facts about a company:

1. The number of salespersons is a multiple of 6.

2. The number of engineers is a multiple of 9.

3. There are seven employees who are both salespersons and engineers but not managers.

4. There are twice as many managers who are salespersons than managers who are engineers.

5. Each manager is either a salesperson or an engineer but not both.

Using variables x for managers, y for salespersons, and z for engineers, we express the above using the following Boolean linear cardinality formula S:

$$
\begin{aligned}
|y| &\equiv_6 & 0 \;\wedge \\
|z| &\equiv_9 & 0 \;\wedge \\
|\overline{x} \cap y \cap z| &= & 7 \;\wedge \\
|x \cap y| - 2|x \cap z| &= & 0 \;\wedge \\
|x \cap y \cap z| + |x \cap \overline{y} \cap \overline{z}| &= & 0
\end{aligned}
$$

Example 11.2.9 Suppose that we know the following additional fact about the company in Example 11.2.8:

6. Person a is both a manager and an engineer but not a salesperson.

Here a is a constant symbol that denotes a particular atom of the Boolean algebra. We can express this by the following linear cardinality constraint:

$$
|x \cap \overline{y} \cap z \cap a| \;=\; 1
$$

The following lemma shows in the case of atomic Boolean algebras of sets a simple translation from formulas with only equality and inequality constraints into formulas with only linear cardinality constraints.

Lemma 11.2.4 In any atomic Boolean algebra of sets B, for every term T we have the following:

$$
\begin{aligned}
T &=_B \emptyset \quad \text{if and only if} \quad |T| = 0 \\
T &\neq_B \emptyset \quad \text{if and only if} \quad |T| \geq 1
\end{aligned}
$$

Moreover, using the above identities, any formula with only equality and inequality constraints can be written as a formula with only linear cardinality constraints.

Some Boolean constraints occur with great frequency and have their own names and symbolic abbreviations. We give some examples. For any terms S, T, and V in any Boolean algebra B:

Exclusive-Or : $\quad T \oplus S =_B \emptyset \quad$ means $\quad (T \cap \overline{S}) \cup (\overline{T} \cap S) =_B \emptyset$

Difference : $\quad\;\; T \setminus S =_B V \quad$ means $\quad (\overline{T} \cap V) \cup (S \cap V) \cup (T \cap \overline{S} \cap \overline{V}) =_B \emptyset$

In the following we may use the abbreviation $T =_B S$ for the constraint $T \oplus S =_B \emptyset$. We may also omit the subscript B when it is clear which Boolean algebra we are talking about.

11.2.2   Minterms Normal Form

Next we look at a standard representation of Boolean constraint formulas. Each Boolean formula can be rewritten into an equivalent Boolean formula in *disjunctive normal form*, that is, as a disjunction of conjunctions. Disjunctive normal forms are important for many reasons. For example, we can use disjunctive normal forms to show that there is a finite number of possible distinct terms that can be expressed in Boolean algebras with a fixed number of constants and variables.

Lemma 11.2.5 There are only $2^{2^{m+k}}$ different disjunctive normal forms of Boolean terms with the m constant symbols and k variables that refer to the elements of a Boolean algebra.

Proof: Let $t(z_1, z_2, \ldots, z_n)$ be any term where the zs are the distinct variable or constant symbols occurring in it. Then the following equation is true:

$$t(z_1, z_2, \ldots, z_n) = (t(\emptyset, z_2, \ldots, z_n) \cap \overline{z_1}) \cup (t(1, z_2, \ldots, z_n) \cap z_1)$$

Let us use the convention that $z^\emptyset$ means $\overline{z}$ and z^1 means z, and that the zs are ordered from z_1 to z_n. Then we also may write the previous equation as

$$t(z_1, z_2, \ldots, z_n) = \bigcup_{a_1 \in \{\emptyset, 1\}} (t(a_1, z_2, \ldots, z_n) \cap z_1^{a_1}).$$

By repeatedly using the above equation and the Boolean algebra axioms, it is possible to transform each term into the following *minterms normal form*:

$$t(z_1, \ldots, z_n) = \bigcup_{(a_1, \ldots, a_n) \in \{\emptyset, 1\}^n} (t(a_1, \ldots, a_n) \cap z_1^{a_1} \cap z_2^{a_2} \cap \ldots \cap z_n^{a_n}).$$

The function determined by $t(z_1, \ldots, z_n)$ depends only on the values of the 2^n expressions $t(a_1, \ldots, a_n)$, where each a_i is either $\emptyset$ or 1. One can see that each of these 2^n expressions has value either $\emptyset$ or 1. Hence, it is possible to see that there are 2^{2^n} disjunctive normal forms with n variable and constant symbols. ∎

Definition 11.2.7 Suppose a Boolean constraint formula uses m constant symbols and k variables that refer to the elements of a Boolean algebra B_m. We call all possible conjunctions of the constants and the variables the *minterms* of the formula. We call all possible conjunctions of the constants the *ground minterms* of the algebra.

In a *free Boolean algebra of sets* B_m with m constant symbols, the constant symbols are uninterpreted. The constant symbols are said to generate B_m because the elements of a free Boolean algebra can be represented by disjunctions of the ground minterms. By Lemma 11.2.5, there are 2^{2^m} different elements of B_m. However, when the constants are interpreted, then a Boolean algebra with m constants may have fewer than 2^{2^m} different elements.

Example 11.2.10 Consider the free Boolean algebra B_3 of sets generated by the constant symbols a, b, c. B_3 has 2^3 minterms. These minterms, in descending order of binary superscript values, are:

$$a \cap b \cap c,$$
$$a \cap b \cap \overline{c},$$
$$a \cap \overline{b} \cap c,$$
$$a \cap \overline{b} \cap \overline{c},$$
$$\overline{a} \cap b \cap c,$$
$$\overline{a} \cap b \cap \overline{c},$$
$$\overline{a} \cap \overline{b} \cap c,$$
$$\overline{a} \cap \overline{b} \cap \overline{c}$$

By Lemma 11.2.5 each element of B_3 can be written in a disjunctive normal form in which each minterm either occurs as a disjunct or does not. Hence there are 2^{2^3} elements of the free Boolean algebra B_3.

The interpretation function σ assigns specific values to the constant symbols of a Boolean algebra. For example, if a is constant symbol, then its specific value is denoted by $\sigma(a)$.

Two terms that are equal in a free Boolean algebra are also equal in an interpreted Boolean algebra with the same set of constant symbols, but in the interpreted Boolean algebra some terms may be equal that are not equal in the free Boolean algebra. We denote by $=_{B,\sigma}$ the equality relation in the interpreted Boolean algebra B when it uses the interpretation function σ.

Example 11.2.11 Consider the following specific interpretation of the free Boolean of sets in Example 11.2.10. Element 1 is interpreted as the set $\{1, 2, 3, 4, 5, 6, 7, 8\}$ and δ as the powerset of 1. Also, the constants are interpreted as:

$$\sigma(a) = \{1,2,3,4\}$$
$$\sigma(b) = \{1,2,5,6\}$$
$$\sigma(c) = \{1,3,5,7\}$$

Under this interpretation, the minterms in B_3 are all different elements:

$$a \cap b \cap c =_{B,\sigma} \{1\}$$
$$a \cap b \cap \bar{c} =_{B,\sigma} \{2\}$$
$$a \cap \bar{b} \cap c =_{B,\sigma} \{3\}$$
$$a \cap \bar{b} \cap \bar{c} =_{B,\sigma} \{4\}$$
$$\bar{a} \cap b \cap c =_{B,\sigma} \{5\}$$
$$\bar{a} \cap b \cap \bar{c} =_{B,\sigma} \{6\}$$
$$\bar{a} \cap \bar{b} \cap c =_{B,\sigma} \{7\}$$
$$\bar{a} \cap \bar{b} \cap \bar{c} =_{B,\sigma} \{8\}$$

The free Boolean algebra of sets B_3 under the interpretation (B, σ) became a specific Boolean algebra of sets with eight different minterms that are not equal to $\emptyset$. Hence the algebra has a total of 2^8 elements.

Example 11.2.12 Now let us look at a different interpretation (B, σ_2) for the free Boolean algebra of sets B_3. In this interpretation assume again that 1 is interpreted as the set $\{1,2,3,4,5,6,7,8\}$ and δ as the powerset of 1. However, now assume that σ_2 interprets the constants as follows:

$$\sigma_2(a) = \{1\}$$
$$\sigma_2(b) = \{2\}$$
$$\sigma_2(c) = \{3\}$$

In this case some of the minterms are equivalent. In fact,

$$a \cap b \cap c \quad =_{B,\sigma_2} \quad \emptyset$$
$$a \cap b \cap \overline{c} \quad =_{B,\sigma_2} \quad \emptyset$$
$$a \cap \overline{b} \cap c \quad =_{B,\sigma_2} \quad \emptyset$$
$$a \cap \overline{b} \cap \overline{c} \quad =_{B,\sigma_2} \quad \{1\}$$
$$\overline{a} \cap b \cap c \quad =_{B,\sigma_2} \quad \emptyset$$
$$\overline{a} \cap b \cap \overline{c} \quad =_{B,\sigma_2} \quad \{2\}$$
$$\overline{a} \cap \overline{b} \cap c \quad =_{B,\sigma_2} \quad \{3\}$$
$$\overline{a} \cap \overline{b} \cap \overline{c} \quad =_{B,\sigma_2} \quad \{4,5,6,7,8\}$$

Under this interpretation of the constants, only a subalgebra of the Boolean algebra in Example 11.2.11 is generated. This subalgebra has only four different minterms that are not equal to $\emptyset$. Hence, now the algebra has only 2^4 elements.

Example 11.2.13 Recall from Example 11.2.1 B_H, the Boolean algebra whose elements are finite unions of half-open intervals over the rational numbers. Let a, b, c be three constants used within the terms, and let their interpretations be defined by σ_3 as follows:

$$\sigma_3(a) \quad = \quad [2, 10)$$
$$\sigma_3(b) \quad = \quad [3, 35)$$
$$\sigma_3(c) \quad = \quad [4, 21)$$

The minterms of the free Boolean algebra B_3 under the interpretation (B_H, σ_3) are various elements of B_H. For example, the minterm $a \cap b \cap c$ would be the half-open interval $[4, 10)$. It is not an atom because it contains the half-open interval $[5, 8)$, which is also an element of B_H.

Next we give some examples where the minterms contain some variables.

Example 11.2.14 Suppose that we use only the following variables and no constant symbols in a formula: x, y, z. Then we can form from these variables the following eight minterms in order:

$$x \cap y \cap z, \quad x \cap y \cap \overline{z}, \quad x \cap \overline{y} \cap z, \quad x \cap \overline{y} \cap \overline{z},$$
$$\overline{x} \cap y \cap z, \quad \overline{x} \cap y \cap \overline{z}, \quad \overline{x} \cap \overline{y} \cap z, \quad \overline{x} \cap \overline{y} \cap \overline{z}$$

If we also use the constant symbol a, then we can form the following minterms:

$$
\begin{array}{llll}
x \cap y \cap z \cap a, & x \cap y \cap z \cap \overline{a}, & x \cap y \cap \overline{z} \cap a, & x \cap y \cap \overline{z} \cap \overline{a}, \\
x \cap \overline{y} \cap z \cap a, & x \cap \overline{y} \cap z \cap \overline{a}, & x \cap \overline{y} \cap \overline{z} \cap a, & x \cap \overline{y} \cap \overline{z} \cap \overline{a}, \\
\overline{x} \cap y \cap z \cap a, & \overline{x} \cap y \cap z \cap \overline{a}, & \overline{x} \cap y \cap \overline{z} \cap a, & \overline{x} \cap y \cap \overline{z} \cap \overline{a}, \\
\overline{x} \cap \overline{y} \cap z \cap a, & \overline{x} \cap \overline{y} \cap z \cap \overline{a}, & \overline{x} \cap \overline{y} \cap \overline{z} \cap a & \overline{x} \cap \overline{y} \cap \overline{z} \cap \overline{a}
\end{array}
$$

Each Boolean linear cardinality constraint with n variables and constants can be put into the *normal form*:

$$
c_1 |m_1| + \ldots + c_{2^n} |m_{2^n}| \ \ \theta \ \ b \tag{11.1}
$$

where b and each c_i is an integer constant and each m_i is a minterm of the Boolean algebra for $1 \leq i \leq 2^n$, and θ is as in Definition 11.2.6.

Example 11.2.15 We rewrite S of Example 11.2.8 into the following normal form (omitting minterms with zero coefficients and the $\wedge$ symbol at the end of lines):

$$
\begin{array}{lcl}
|x \cap y \cap z| + |x \cap y \cap \overline{z}| + |\overline{x} \cap y \cap z| + |\overline{x} \cap y \cap \overline{z}| & \equiv_6 & 0 \\
|x \cap y \cap z| + |x \cap \overline{y} \cap z| + |\overline{x} \cap y \cap z| + |\overline{x} \cap \overline{y} \cap z| & \equiv_9 & 0 \\
|\overline{x} \cap y \cap z| & = & 7 \\
|x \cap y \cap z| - |x \cap y \cap \overline{z}| + 2|x \cap \overline{y} \cap z| & = & 0 \\
|x \cap y \cap z| + |x \cap \overline{y} \cap \overline{z}| & = & 0
\end{array}
$$

The interpretation function also inteprets the variables that occur in a Boolean constraint formula. Under each interpretation a formula can be evaluated to be true or false. A true interpretation is a solution to the formula.

Example 11.2.16 The linear cardinality constraint of Example 11.2.7 has many solutions. For example, $x = \{3, 6, 9\}$ and $y = \{3, 4, 5, 6\}$ and $z = \{1\}$ is a solution. The Boolean linear cardinality constraint:

$$
|x \cup \{1\} \cup \{2\}| \geq 2
$$

is true for any interpretation of x.

11.3   Relations with Sets

In the preceding chapters, we assumed that the domain of the attributes is a scalar value, that is, string or integer, rational or real number. It is possible to define as the domain of the attributes sets of these scalar data types, that is, elements of the Boolean algebras of sets.

Example 11.3.1 Elements of the Boolean algebra B_W described in Example 11.2.3 can be the domain of the *Cities* attribute of the *Vertices* relation shown below.

Vertices

Cities
$\{Chicago, Des\_Moines, Kansas\_City, Lincoln, Minneapolis, Omaha\}$

The *Vertices* relation represents all the cities shown in Figure 6.6 in just one tuple.

Example 11.3.2 Elements of the Boolean algebra B_H described in Example 11.2.1 can be the domain of the spatial and temporal attributes of the *House* relation shown below.

House

Id	X	Y	T
1	[3, 6)	[3, 6)	[100, 200)
2	[8, 11)	[3, 7)	[150, 350)
3	[2, 4)	[5, 10)	[250, 400)
3	[2, 10)	[8, 10)	[250, 400)

The *House* relation represents the archaeological site shown in Figure 6.1.

Example 11.3.3 Elements of the Boolean algebra B_{Euclid} described in Example 11.2.4 can be the domain of the *Extent* attribute of the *Street* relation shown below.

Street

Name	Extent
Bear	$\{(2, 11), \ldots, (5, 12), \ldots, (8, 13), \ldots\}$
⋮	⋮
Willow	$\{(4, 19), \ldots, (5, 19), \ldots, (20, 19)\}$

Since the set of points is infinite on any street, the above representation is an abstract, logical-level representation of the street map shown in Figure 6.2. This representation is not suitable for computers but is useful for writing queries, especially ones where we need to apply special operators for the *Extent* attribute. For example, one opertor would be to find the length of a set of points.

Bibliographic Notes

Aristotle was the first to describe binary set relations and syllogistic axioms using those relations. The set of syllogistic axioms was developed further in the middle ages by scholastic philosophers. Boolean algebras were invented by George Boole, who also presented the first equation of Lemma 11.2.5.

Stone's representation theorem is from [385]. Boolean algebras are discussed in several textbooks, including Burris and Sankappanavar [60] and Halmos [188]. Marriott and Odersky [266] give an interesting discussion and a quantifier elimination result for atomless Boolean algebras. Helm et al. [195] describe the approximation of database queries using Booleas algebras.

There are many uses of cardinality constraints in computer science. Calvanese and Lenzerini [69, 68] study a form of cardinality constraints that occur in ER-diagrams and ISA hierarchies. Ohlbach and Koehler [286, 287] consider a description logic with cardinality constraints. Seipel and Geske [368] use constraint logic programming to solve conjunctions of cardinality constraints. Boolean algebras of sets with linear cardinality constraints was studied in Revesz [341] and Kuncak et al. [249]. More discussion of specific results related to quantifier elimination and computational complexity is given at the end of Chapter 23.

Exercises

1. Express the following propositions as syllogisms.

   > All mothers are parents.
   > All flowers are plants.
   > Some dolphins are mothers.
   > Some plants are flowers.
   > Plants are not animals.
   > Some parents are not mothers.

2. Express the following propositions as syllogisms.

   > dm : All dolphins are mammals.
   > ma : All mammals are animals.
   > da : All dolphins are animals.

   Write the following compound proposition using dm, ma, da, and logical connectives.

   (a) If all dolphins are mammals and all mammals are animals, then all dolphins are animals.

3. Express the following propositions as syllogisms.

p : All computer science majors take discrete mathematics.
q : All discrete mathematics students are smart.
r : All computer science majors are smart.

Write the following compound propositions using p, q, r, and logical connectives.

(a) If not all computer science majors are smart, then not all computer science majors take discrete mathematics.

(b) If some computer science majors are not smart, then some computer science majors do not take discrete mathematics.

(c) If all computer science majors take discrete mathematics, and not all computer science majors are smart, then not all discrete mathematics students are smart.

(d) If all computer science majors take discrete mathematics, and some discrete mathematics students are not smart, then some computer science majors are not smart.

(e) If all computer science majors take discrete mathematics, and all discrete mathematics students are smart, then all computer science majors are smart.

4. Determine using axioms whether the propositions in Exercise 3 are true.

5. Consider the following propositions.

> (a) It is not true that some student who studies fails the test.
> (b) It is not true that some student who passes the test drops out.
> (c) It is not true that some student who graduates will be unemployed.

where "fails" means "does not pass," and "drops out" means "does not graduate."

(a) Express the propositions using the following classes:

> s : Students who study.
> p : Students who pass the test.
> g : Students who graduate.
> e : Students who will be employed.

(b) Simplify the propositions by eliminating negation.

(c) Prove using syllogisms that "All students who study will be employed."

6. Find all syllogisms that use *Nor* or *Or* in addition to the four basic set relations.

7. Find all the minterms of the Boolean algebra B_H using only the constant symbols a, b and c and the interpretation function σ_3 of Example 11.2.13.

8. The following are some facts about students in a computer class.

   - There are ten honors students.
   - There are four graduate students.
   - The number of students from Lincoln is a multiple of three.
   - There are five honors students who are from Lincoln.
   - No graduate student is from Lincoln.

   Represent the above information using a conjunction of Boolean algebras with cardinality constraints. Find one solution to the set of constraints.

12

Constraint Deductive Databases

Datalog is a rule-based language that is related to Prolog, which is a popular language for implementing expert systems. Each rule is a statement saying that if some points belong to some relations, then other points must also belong to a defined relation. Each Datalog query contains a Datalog program and an input database.

12.1 Syntax

We divide the set of relation names $\mathcal{R}$ into defined relation names $\mathcal{D}$ and input relation names $\mathcal{I}$. Each Datalog query consists of a finite set of rules of the form:

$$R_0(x_1, \ldots, x_k) \quad :- \quad R_1(x_{1,1}, \ldots, x_{1,k_1}), \ldots, R_n(x_{n,1}, \ldots, x_{n,k_n}).$$

where each R_i is either an input relation name or a defined relation name, and the xs are either variables or constants.

The relation names $R_0, \ldots, R_n$ are not necessarily distinct. They could also be built-in relation names, such as $\leq, +, \times$, which we will write using the usual infix notation. For example, we will write $x + y = z$ instead of $+(x, y, z)$ for the ternary input relation $+$ that contains all tuples (a, b, c) such that a plus b equals c.

The preceding rule is read "R_0 is true if R_1 and ... and R_n are all true." R_0 is called the *head* and $R_1, \ldots, R_n$ is called the *body* of the rule.

Example 12.1.1 The tax accountant from Chapter 1 may use the following query Q_{tax} to find the Social Security number and taxes due for each

P. Revesz, *Introduction to Databases: From Biological to Spatio-Temporal*,
Texts in Computer Science, DOI 10.1007/978-1-84996-095-3_12,
© Springer-Verlag London Limited 2010

person:

$$Tax\_Due(s, t) \quad :\!\!- \quad Taxrecord(s, w, i, c), \ Taxtable(inc, t),$$
$$w + i + c = inc.$$

Here $Taxrecord, Taxable \in \mathcal{I}$ are input database relations and $Tax\_Due \in \mathcal{D}$ is the only defined relation.

Example 12.1.2 Suppose that relation $Street(n, x, y)$ contains all combinations of street name n and locations (x, y) such that a location belongs to the street. Find the set of streets that are reachable from point (x_0, y_0).

$$Reach(n) \quad :\!\!- \quad Street(n, x_0, y_0).$$
$$Reach(n) \quad :\!\!- \quad Reach(m), \ Street(m, x, y), \ Street(n, x, y).$$

Here $Street \in \mathcal{I}$ and $Reach \in \mathcal{D}$. The first rule says that street n is reachable if it contains the initial point. The second rule says that if m is reachable and m and n intersect on some point, then n is also reachable.

Next we give several more examples of Datalog queries where the domain of the attributes is scalar values, i.e., $\mathcal{Z}$, $\mathcal{Q}$, $\mathcal{R}$, or $\mathcal{W}$ as defined in Section 4.4.1.

Example 12.1.3 The following query Q_{travel} defines the $Travel(x, y, t)$ relation, which is true if it is possible to travel from city x to city y in time t:

$$Travel(x, y, t) \quad :\!\!- \quad Go(x, 0, y, t).$$
$$Travel(x, y, t) \quad :\!\!- \quad Travel(x, z, t_2), \ Go(z, t_2, y, t).$$

Example 12.1.4 Let relation $Go2(x, y, c)$ represent the fact that we can go from city x to city y by a direct route in c units of time. The following query Q_{travel2} defines the travel relation, which is true if it is possible to travel from city x to city y in time t:

$$Travel2(x, y, t) \quad :\!\!- \quad Go2(x, y, c), \ t \geq c.$$
$$Travel2(x, y, t) \quad :\!\!- \quad Travel2(x, z, t_2), \ Go2(z, y, c), \ t \geq t_2 + c.$$

The main difference between this query and that in Example 12.1.3 is that this query puts the constraint in the query while the other puts the constraint in the database.

Example 12.1.5 Suppose a river and its tributaries are subdivided into a set of river segments such that the river flows through each segment in c hours, where c is some constant. Let the input relation $River(r, x, y)$

represent the area of segment r and $Flows(r_1, r_2)$ that segment r_1 flows into segment r_2. Suppose some pollution spills into the river at location (x_0, y_0) at time t_0. Find which river segments will be affected by the pollution at what times:

$$Polluted(r, t) \quad :- \quad River(r, x_0, y_0),\ t \geq t_0.$$
$$Polluted(r_2, t_2) \quad :- \quad Polluted(r_1, t_1),\ Flows(r_1, r_2),\ t_2 \geq t_1 + c.$$

Suppose relation $Town(name, x, y)$ describes the areas of towns. Find which town areas will be endangered and at what times:

$$Crosses(r, n) \quad :- \quad River(r, x, y),\ Town(n, x, y).$$
$$Endangered(x, y, t) \quad :- \quad Polluted(r, t),\ Crosses(r, n),$$
$$Town(n, x, y).$$

Example 12.1.6 Suppose there is a number of dams on a river and its tributaries. The river is subdivided into segments delimited by either a dam or a merge point, i.e., a point where two segments flow into each other. Let relation $Flows(r_1, r_2)$ represent that r_1 flows into r_2 and let relation $Merge(r_1, r_2, r_3)$ represent that river segments r_1 and r_2 merge and flow into river segment r_3. Let $Dam(r, c)$ represent that at the end of river segment r there is a dam with a capacity to hold up to c units of water. Suppose relation $Source(r, a)$ records that the beginning of river segment r is a source point of the river and receives a units of water. Find the amount of water flowing in each river segment if the dams are holding water at the maximum of their capacities. For simplicity, we neglect all losses due to evaporation, irrigation, and other uses of water.

$$Amount(r, a) \quad :- \quad Source(r, a).$$
$$Amount(r_2, a_2) \quad :- \quad Amount(r_1, a_1),\ Dam(r_1, c),$$
$$Flows(r_1, r_2),\ a_2 = a_1 - c.$$
$$Amount(r_3, a_3) \quad :- \quad Amount(r_1, a_1),\ Amount(r_2, a_2),$$
$$Merge(r_1, r_2, r_3),\ a_3 = a_1 + a_2.$$

In this query, the first rule says that the amount of water flowing in a river segment whose beginning is a source point is the same as the amount of water at the source. The second rule says that the amount of water flowing from one river segment to another is c units less in the second segment than in the first, if the dam has capacity c. Finally, the third rule says that the amount of water after a merge is the sum of the amounts of water in the two branches before the merge.

Example 12.1.7 Three bank accounts initially have the same balance. Only deposits are made to the first account and only withdrawals are taken from the second account, while neither withdrawals nor deposits are made to the third account. Transactions always come in pairs, namely, each time a deposit is made to the first account, a withdrawal is made from the second account. Each deposit is at most \$200, and each withdrawal is at least \$300. What are the possible values of the three accounts?

Let x, y, z denote the amount in the three accounts respectively:

$$
\begin{aligned}
Balance(x, y, z) \quad &:- \quad x = y, \; y = z. \\
Balance(x', y', z) \quad &:- \quad Balance(x, y, z), \; x' - x \geq 0, \\
& \qquad x - x' \geq -200, \; y - y' \geq 300.
\end{aligned}
$$

Here the first rule declares the initial balance of the three accounts to be the same. The second rule says that if at some time the current values of the three accounts are x', y', and z, then after a sequence of transactions the new account balances are x, which is less than $x' + 200$ because at most \$200 is deposited; y, which is less than $y' - 300$ because at least \$300 is withdrawn; and z, which does not change.

Example 12.1.8 For the broadcasting example of Chapter 3 a possible query may be to find every place in the town that can be reached by at least one broadcast station. Problems of this kind are called *map overlay* problems. It is usual in this kind of problem that the scales and the points of origin of the maps to be overlayed are not the same. Suppose that a relation $Parameters(ID, Scale, X_0, Y_0)$ records for each map its scale and point of origin.

For example, let us suppose that in the town map each unit corresponds to a half kilometer, in the broadcast map each unit corresponds to one kilometer, and the point of origins are the same for the two maps. Then $(1, 1, 0, 0)$, $(2, 1, 0, 0)$, $(3, 1, 0, 0)$, and $(Lincoln, 0.5, 0, 0)$ would be in the *Parameters* relation, as mentioned earlier.

We can find the points in the town that are covered using the following query Q_{cover}:

$$
\begin{aligned}
Covered(x_2, y_2) \quad :- \quad & Broadcast(n, x, y), \; Town(t, x_2, y_2), \\
& Parameters(n, s, blat, blong), \\
& Parameters(t, s_2, tlat, tlong), \\
& x_2 = \tfrac{s}{s_2} x + (tlat - blat), \\
& y_2 = \tfrac{s}{s_2} y + (tlong - blong).
\end{aligned}
$$

This query at first scales up and shifts every point (x, y) in the broadcast map n to match the scale and point of origin of the town map. Finally, if it corresponds to a point (x_2, y_2) in the town map, then it is added to relation *Covered*.

Example 12.1.9 Suppose that each tuple of relation $Forest(r, x, y)$ denotes the area of a wooded region r. Suppose also that nonforest areas are lakes, rocks, and sand. Suppose a fire starts in a region described by relation $Fire(x, y)$ and the wind is blowing east. Fire could spread from a wooded region to another wooded region that is d distance to the east of the first. Once a wooded region catches fire it will burn down entirely. Find the areas that could burn down:

$$Burn(x, y) \quad :— \quad Fire(x, y).$$
$$Burn(x_2, y) \quad :— \quad Burn(x, y), Forest(r, x_2, y), x_2 \geq x, x_2 - x \leq d.$$
$$Burn(x_2, y_2) \quad :— \quad Burn(x, y), Forest(r, x, y), Forest(r, x_2, y_2).$$

Here the first rule simply says that the area where the fire starts will burn down. The second rule says that if some forest location (x_2, y_2) is less than d distance to the east from a burning location (x, y), then (x_2, y_2) will also burn down. The third rule expresses the fact that forests burn down entirely once any part of them catches fire.

Example 12.1.10 In the *subset sum* problem we are given a set of n items with weights $w_0, \ldots, w_{n-1}$ and we have to find whether the items can be partitioned into two disjoint sets such that the sum of the weights in both sets are equal.

Let *Item* be the input relation that contains the tuple (i, w) when the $(i + 1)$th element has weight w. The following Datalog query, $Q_{\text{subsetsum}}$ defines the relation $Sum(i, x, y)$, which is true when it is possible to add the elements from 0 to $i - 1$ to either the first or the second set such that as a result x is the total weight of the first and y is the total weight of the second set:

$$Same\_Sum(x) \quad :— \quad Sum(n, x, x).$$
$$Sum(i', x', y) \quad :— \quad Sum(i, x, y), Item(i, w), \ i' = i + 1, \ x' = x + w.$$
$$Sum(i', x, y') \quad :— \quad Sum(i, x, y), Item(i, w), \ i' = i + 1, \ y' = y + w.$$
$$Sum(0, 0, 0).$$

The last line of the query defines the case when no item has yet been added to either set. The second and third lines define recursively the addition of a new item to either the first or the second set, and the top line expresses that if all items can be added to one of the two sets and the total weight of the two sets is the same, then an equal partition is possible.

In the preceding queries we assumed that each variable is ranging over the same domain. That does not need to always be true, as the following example shows.

Example 12.1.11 Suppose a piece of land has a right triangle shape with width a and height b. Divide the land into n pieces.

Let the input relation $Divide(a, b, n)$ represent the parameters of the problem. Imagine the triangle to be located such that its corner vertices are at locations $(0, 0)$, $(a, 0)$, and (a, b). If we cut the land parallel to the

y-axis the first cut should be at a location that cuts off $1/n$ of the area. Similarly, the ith cut should be at a location that would cut off i/n of the area. The following query finds where to cut the land:

$$Cut(x) \quad :\!\!- \quad Divide(a, b, n),\ 1 \leq i,\ i \leq n,\ \tfrac{i}{n}a^2 = x^2.$$

Here the total area of the triangle is $(ab)/2$. If we cut at location x, then the area cut off will be $(x^2 b)/2a$. Hence the ith cut is taking away i/x of the land. For Cut to contain only the x locations where to divide the land we need i and n to be integers and the other variables to be real numbers.

Example 12.1.12 Express the relations $Sum(x, y, z)$, that is true if the sum of x and y is z, and $Mult(x, y, z)$, that is true if x times y is z, where x, y, and z are integers, using addition constraints:

$$Inc(x1, x) \qquad :\!\!- \quad x1 - x \geq 1,\ x - x1 \geq -1.$$

$$
\begin{aligned}
Sum(x1, y, z1) \quad &:\!\!- \quad Sum(x, y, z),\ Inc(x1, x),\ Inc(z1, z).\\
Sum(x, y1, z1) \quad &:\!\!- \quad Sum(x, y, z),\ Inc(y1, y),\ Inc(z1, z).\\
Sum(0, 0, 0).\\
Sum(x, y, z) \quad &:\!\!- \quad Sum(x1, y, z1),\ Inc(x1, x),\ Inc(z1, z).\\
Sum(x, y, z) \quad &:\!\!- \quad Sum(x, y1, z1),\ Inc(y1, y),\ Inc(z1, z).
\end{aligned}
$$

$$
\begin{aligned}
Mult(x1, y, z2) \quad &:\!\!- \quad Mult(x, y, z),\ Sum(y, z, z2),\ Inc(x1, x).\\
Mult(x, y1, z2) \quad &:\!\!- \quad Mult(x, y, z),\ Sum(x, z, z2),\ Inc(y1, y).\\
Mult(0, 0, 0).\\
Mult(x, y, z) \quad &:\!\!- \quad Mult(x1, y, z2),\ Sum(y, z, z2),\ Inc(x1, x).\\
Mult(x, y, z) \quad &:\!\!- \quad Mult(x, y1, z2),\ Sum(x, z, z2),\ Inc(y1, y).
\end{aligned}
$$

12.2   Datalog with Sets

Section 11.1 dicussed the use of syllogisms as one way to reason about sets. As the next example shows, syllogisms are easily expressible by Datalog rules.

Example 12.2.1 The following Datalog rules implement the syllogisms shown in Figure 11.1.

$$
\begin{aligned}
All(x,z) \quad &:\!\!- \quad All(x,y), \quad All(y,z).\\
Some(x,z) \quad &:\!\!- \quad Some(x,y), \quad All(y,z).\\
No(x,z) \quad &:\!\!- \quad All(x,y), \quad No(y,z).\\
SomeNot(x,z) \quad &:\!\!- \quad Some(x,y), \quad No(y,z).
\end{aligned}
$$

$$
\begin{aligned}
Some(x,z) \quad &:\!\!- \quad Some(y,x), \quad All(y,z).\\
SomeNot(x,z) \quad &:\!\!- \quad All(y,x), \quad SomeNot(y,z).\\
SomeNot(x,z) \quad &:\!\!- \quad Some(y,x), \quad No(y,z).\\
Some(x,z) \quad &:\!\!- \quad All(y,x), \quad Some(y,z).
\end{aligned}
$$

$$
\begin{aligned}
No(x,z) \quad &:\!\!- \quad All(x,y), \quad No(z,y).\\
SomeNot(x,z) \quad &:\!\!- \quad Some(x,y), \quad No(z,y).\\
SomeNot(x,z) \quad &:\!\!- \quad SomeNot(x,y), \quad All(z,y).\\
No(x,z) \quad &:\!\!- \quad No(x,y), \quad All(z,y).
\end{aligned}
$$

$$
\begin{aligned}
SomeNot(x,z) \quad &:\!\!- \quad Some(y,x), \quad No(z,y).\\
Some(x,z) \quad &:\!\!- \quad All(y,x), \quad Some(z,y).\\
No(x,z) \quad &:\!\!- \quad No(y,x), \quad All(z,y).
\end{aligned}
$$

Instead of working with strings, we give an identification number to each set using an input relation *Set*. For instance, for Example 11.1.2 we write:

$$
\begin{aligned}
Set(x,name) \quad &:\!\!- \quad x = 1, \quad name = \text{``hummingbird''}.\\
Set(x,name) \quad &:\!\!- \quad x = 2, \quad name = \text{``richlycolored''}.\\
Set(x,name) \quad &:\!\!- \quad x = 3, \quad name = \text{``large''}.\\
Set(x,name) \quad &:\!\!- \quad x = 4, \quad name = \text{``livesonhoney''}.
\end{aligned}
$$

We express the complement of any set using a "minus" sign for integers. Hence, for instance, $x = -3$ would be "small," which is the complement of "large." This convention leads to the following implementation of Axiom 11.1.8

$$
\begin{aligned}
No(x,y) \quad &:\!\!- \quad All(x,y1), \quad y1 = -y.\\
All(y,x) \quad &:\!\!- \quad No(x1,y), \quad x1 = -x.\\
All(x,y) \quad &:\!\!- \quad No(x,y1), \quad y1 = -y.\\
SomeNot(y,x) \quad &:\!\!- \quad Some(x1,y), \quad x1 = -x.\\
SomeNot(x,y) \quad &:\!\!- \quad Some(x,y1), \quad y1 = -y.\\
Some(x,y) \quad &:\!\!- \quad SomeNot(x,y1), \quad y1 = -y.
\end{aligned}
$$

We can similarly express any other axiom that requires set complement of the arguments. Premises can be represented as follows.

$$
\begin{aligned}
AllPremise(n,m) \quad &:\!\!- \quad n = \text{``hummingbird''}, \quad m = \text{``richlycolored''}.\\
NoPremise(n,m) \quad &:\!\!- \quad n = \text{``large''}, \quad m = \text{``livesonhoney''}.\\
AllPremise(n,m) \quad &:\!\!- \quad n = \text{``richlycolored''}, \quad m = \text{``livesonhoney''}.
\end{aligned}
$$

Finally, to get a complete syllogistic deductive system, we turn the premises into syllogistic propositions using the following Datalog rules.

$$
\begin{array}{lll}
All(x,y) & :\!- & AllPremise(n,m), \ Set(x,n), \ Set(y,m). \\
No(x,y) & :\!- & NoPremise(n,m), \ Set(x,n), \ Set(y,m). \\
Some(x,y) & :\!- & SomePremise(n,m), \ Set(x,n), \ Set(y,m). \\
SomeNot(x,y) & :\!- & SomeNotPremise(n,m), \ Set(x,n), \ Set(y,m).
\end{array}
$$

Next we assume that the domain of each attribute is an element of some Boolean algebra of sets. With this assumption, we can represent an undirected graph like the one in Figure 6.6 as relation $Vertices$, containing the set of vertices, and a relation $Edge(X_1, X_2)$, which contains a pair of singleton sets of city names if and only if there is an edge between them. For example, $Edge(\{Lincoln\}, \{Omaha\})$ would be one tuple in the second relation.

A Hamiltonian cycle in an undirected graph is a path that starts and ends with the same vertex and goes through each vertex exactly once. The next example shows that the Hamiltonian cycle problem can be expressed using Datalog with Boolean algerbas of sets.

Example 12.2.2 Assume that $Start(X)$ is an input relation where X is a singleton set containing the name of the starting vertex of the cycle. To find a Hamiltonian cycle, we try to find a path always going from the last vertex seen to an unvisited vertex. We always stay in set A, the set of vertices not yet visited:

$$
Path(X_1, B) \quad :\!- \quad Vertices(A), \ Start(X_1), \ X_1 \subseteq A, \ A \setminus X_1 = B.
$$

$$
Path(X_1, B) \quad :\!- \quad Path(X_2, A), \ Edge(X_2, X_1), \ X_1 \subseteq A, \ A \setminus X_1 = B.
$$

$$
Hamiltonian(X_1) \quad :\!- \quad Path(X_2, \emptyset), \ Edge(X_2, X_1), \ Start(X_1).
$$

Let us see how the query $Q_{\text{hamiltonian}}$ works. The relation $Path(X_1, A)$ is true if and only if between the start vertex and vertex X_1 there is a path that traverses all vertices except those that are in A. The first rule is the initialization, saying that when we start from some start vertex X_1, then all vertices except X_1 will still be unvisited.

The second rule says that if there is a path from the start vertex to some vertex X_2 and there is an edge from vertex X_2 to X_1 and X_1 was not yet visited, then $Path(X_1, B)$ will be true where $A \setminus X_1 = B$. Finally, the third rule says that if there is a path from the start vertex X_1 to some vertex X_2 such that all vertices were visited and there is an edge from X_2 to X_1, then there is a Hamiltonian cycle in the graph. The relation $Hamiltonian$ will contain the start vertex if there is a Hamiltonian cycle in the input graph.

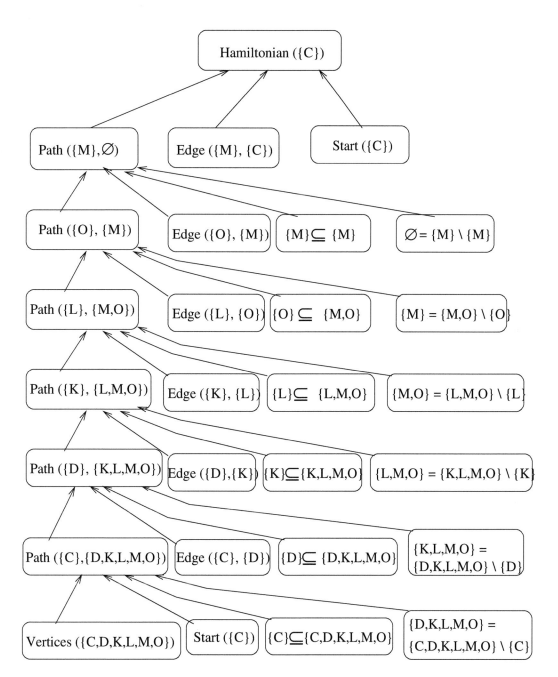

Figure 12.1: A proof tree for a Hamiltonian cycle.

Next we consider a case when the Boolean of algebra of sets contains constants.

Example 12.2.3 Let the constant c describe the set of computer science majors, m mathematics majors, and a, d, s the students who took an abstract algebra, database systems, or software engineering class at a university. We assume that B is any Boolean algebra of sets that includes the constants $\{a, c, d, e, s\}$.

Suppose that those eligible for a mathematics minor must be non-mathematics majors and have taken an abstract algebra class, among other requirements. Similarly, those eligible for a computer science minor must be noncomputer science students and have taken either a database systems or software engineering class, among other requirements. These can be expressed using the following constraint tuples:

$$Math\_Minor(x) \quad :- \quad x \subseteq \overline{m} \cap a.$$

$$CS\_Minor(x) \quad :- \quad x \subseteq \overline{c} \cap (d \cup s).$$

Suppose further that those who can apply to the computer science master's program must be either computer science majors or eligible for a computer science minor, among other requirements. Note that if x are the students eligible for a computer science minor, then y, the students who can apply, is expressible as $y \subseteq c \cup x$. This constraint can be rewritten as $\overline{x} \cap y \subseteq c$. Hence this information can be expressed by the rule:

$$Can\_Apply\_CS\_MS(y) \quad :- \quad CS\_Minor(x), \ \overline{x} \cap y \subseteq c.$$

The two preceding constraint tuples form an input database, and the above rule is a Datalog program.

The next example considers B_{Euclid}, which is another Boolean algebra of sets and was introduced in Example 11.2.4.

Example 12.2.4 In Example 11.3.3 the *Extent* attribute of the *Street* relation ranged over the elements of B_{Euclid}. The query in Example 12.1.2 can be rewritten using the *Extent* attribute as follows:

$$Reach(n) \quad :- \quad Street(n, Extent), \ \{(x_0, y_0)\} \subseteq Extent.$$
$$Reach(n) \quad :- \quad Reach(m), \ Street(m, S1), \ Street(n, S2), \ S1 \cap S2 \neq \emptyset.$$

In this case the first rule declares that any street is reachable that contains the point (x_0, y_0). The second rule asserts that if street m is reachable and intersects street n, then street n is also reachable.

It is worthwhile to compare Example 12.1.2 and Example 12.2.4. These two examples express the same query in different ways. The first query uses more attributes, but it avoids using set constraints.

Example 12.2.5 Suppose the input relation $Mobile\_Phone(u, A)$ describes which person can use a mobile phone to call anyone within area A, where A is an area of the plane. Let's also suppose that the constant NE describes the land area of the state of Nebraska. We can find the set of mobile phone users who call only within Nebraska by the following query:

$$NE\_Mobile\_Phone\_User(u) \quad :- \quad Mobile\_Phone(u, A), \ A \subseteq NE.$$

We could have used $Mobile\_Phone\_Area(Name, x, y)$ as a relation to describe each person's mobile phone area and $State(Name, x, y)$ to describe each state's area similarly to the $Town$ relation in Example 6.2.2. However, then we would not be able to express the query as a simple one-line rule. We could express it using Datalog with negation (see Section 12.4), although it would not be simple. Hence in this case the use of Boolean algebras of sets shows a clear improvement in simplicity of expression.

Example 12.2.6 As another example, we can find all pairs of persons who can talk with each other and who can send a message to each other with the following Datalog program:

$$Can\_Send\_Message(u, v) \quad :- \quad Can\_Send\_Message(u, w),$$
$$Can\_Talk(w, v).$$

$$Can\_Send\_Message(u, v) \quad :- \quad Can\_Talk(u, v).$$

$$Can\_Talk(u, v) \quad :- \quad Mobile\_Phone(u, A),$$
$$Mobile\_Phone(v, B),$$
$$A \cap B \neq \emptyset.$$

The following is another example of Datalog where some attributes range over the integers and some other attributes range over elements of B_{Euclid}.

Example 12.2.7 Consider the relation $Range(x, R)$ stating that animal x can be found within range R in a national park. Suppose that each x is a string and each R is a set of points in the Euclidean plane.

Suppose that animal $deer12$ is infected with a virus that spreads by contact with other animals. The following Datalog program defines the set of animals that are in danger of being infected by the first infected animal:

$$Infection\_Area(R) \quad :\!- \quad Range(`deer12', R).$$

$$Infection\_Area(R) \quad :\!- \quad Infection\_Area(R1), \; Range(x, R2),$$
$$R1 \cap R2 \neq \emptyset, \; R1 \cup R2 = R.$$

$$In\_Danger(A) \quad :\!- \quad Infection\_Area(R1), \; Range(A, R2),$$
$$R1 \cap R2 \neq \emptyset.$$

12.3 Semantics

The proof-based semantics of Datalog queries views the input database as a set of axioms and the rules of the query as a set of inference rules to prove that specific tuples are in some defined relation. We will define this more precisely shortly.

We call an *instantiation* of a rule, the substitution of each variable in it by constants from the proper domain. (For example, the domain may be the set of character strings, the set of integers, or the set of rational numbers.)

Let Q be a query, I an input database, $a_1, \ldots, a_k$ constants, and R a relation name. We say that $R(a_1, \ldots, a_k)$ has a proof using Q and I, written as $\vdash_{Q,I} R(a_1, \ldots, a_k)$, if

$R \in \mathcal{I}$ represents the relation r and $(a_1, \ldots, a_k) \in r$ or

$R \in \mathcal{D}$ and for some rule in Q there is an instantiation

$$R(a_1, \ldots, a_k) :\!- R_1(a_{1,1}, \ldots, a_{1,k_1}), \ldots, R_n(a_{n,1}, \ldots, a_{n,k_n}).$$

where $\vdash_{Q,I} R_i(a_{i,1}, \ldots, a_{i,k_i})$ for each $1 \leq i \leq n$.

The *proof-based* semantics of Datalog queries is the following. Each Datalog query Q is a function that, on any input database I, returns for each relation name R the relation $\{(a_1, \ldots, a_k) \; : \; \vdash_{Q,I} R(a_1, \ldots, a_k)\}$.

When the query and the input database are obvious, we will write $\vdash$ without any subscript.

Example 12.3.1 Let us prove using the query in Example 12.1.2 that from point $(5, 2)$ we can reach Willow Street.

We apply the first rule with the instantiation $n/Vine$, $x_0/5$, $y_0/2$ to get:

$$Reach(Vine) :\!- Street(Vine, 5, 2).$$

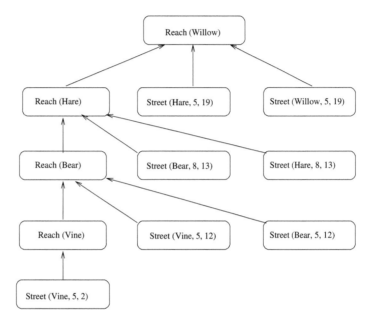

Figure 12.2: A proof tree for reaching Willow Street.

Because point $(5, 2)$ is the south end of Vine Street, the rule body is true. Hence we have:

$$\vdash Reach(Vine)$$

We apply the second rule with $n/Bear$, $m/Vine$, $x/5$, $y/12$ to get:

$$Reach(Bear) :\!\!-\ Reach(Vine), Street(Vine, 5, 12), Street(Bear, 5, 12).$$

Because point $(5, 12)$ is the intersection point of Bear and Vine Streets, the rule body is true. Hence:

$$\vdash Reach(Bear)$$

We apply the second rule with $n/Hare$, $m/Bear$, $x/8$, $y/13$ to get:

$$Reach(Hare)\ :\!\!-\quad Reach(Bear), Street(Bear, 8, 13),$$
$$Street(Hare, 8, 13).$$

Because point $(8, 13)$ is the intersection point of Bear and Hare Streets, the rule body is true. Hence:

$$\vdash Reach(Hare)$$

We apply the second rule with $n/Willow$, $m/Hare$, $x/5$, $y/19$ to get:

$$Reach(Willow)\ :\!\!-\quad Reach(Hare), Street(Hare, 5, 19),$$
$$Street(Willow, 5, 19).$$

Because point $(5, 19)$ is the intersection point of Hare and Willow Streets, the rule body is true. Hence:

$$\vdash Reach(Willow)$$

Example 12.3.2 Let us prove using the query in Example 12.1.3 and the input instance of *Go* from Chapter 3 that one can travel from Omaha to Chicago in 990 minutes. We show only the derived tuples without mentioning the instantiations used:

$\vdash Go(Omaha, 0, Lincoln, 60)$	by the first displayed tuple
$\vdash Go(Lincoln, 60, Kansas\_City, 210)$	by the seventh tuple
$\vdash Go(Kansas\_City, 210, Des\_Moines, 390)$	by the eighth tuple
$\vdash Go(Des\_Moines, 390, Chicago, 990)$	by the ninth tuple
$\vdash Travel(Omaha, Lincoln, 60)$	by the first rule
$\vdash Travel(Omaha, Kansas\_City, 210)$	by the second rule
$\vdash Travel(Omaha, Des\_Moines, 390)$	by the second rule
$\vdash Travel(Omaha, Chicago, 990)$	by the second rule

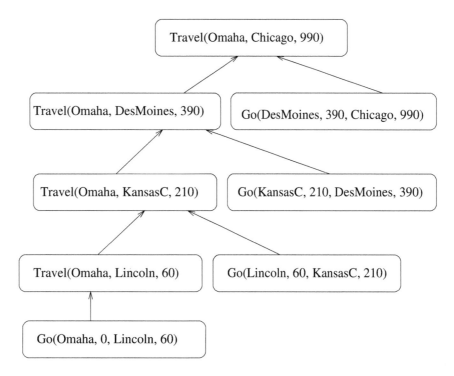

Figure 12.3: A proof tree for traveling from Omaha to Chicago.

12.3.1 Proof Trees

It is easy to draw any proof as a tree in which each internal node is the head of an instantiated rule, and its children are the instantiated relations in the body of the rule. For example, the proof that one can reach Willow Street from the original location $(5, 2)$ can be visualized by the proof tree in Figure 12.2.

In many applications, a user will be interested not only in the set of provable tuples, but also in the reason why they are true. Such users may want to have a proof tree displayed for specific tuples in the output database.

Fortunately, it is easy to add more meaning to Datalog queries. We can require that when adding to the current database a new derived tuple, it should be affixed with the rule number and the instantiation of the rule that was used in the last step of its derivation. (Note that if a derived tuple is not new but already exists in the database, then the affix stays the same and the later derivation is ignored.) This way we can reconstruct a proof tree for any tuple in the output.

A proof tree is convenient if one would like to find the actual path to be taken from location $(5, 2)$ to Willow Street and not just to know that there exists some path. For this purpose, it is sufficient to look at the leftmost branch of the proof tree in Figure 12.2. As we read this branch from the leaf to the root node, the instantiated attribute of relation *Reach* is always the next street to reach.

Another example of a proof tree is shown in Figure 12.3. This proof tree summarizes the proof given in Example 12.3.2. A user looking for a path from Omaha to Chicago that takes only 990 minutes needs to look only at the leftmost branch. There, the second instantiated attribute of relation *Travel* is always the next city to go to.

Finally, let us prove using the query in Example 12.2.2 that there is a Hamiltonian cycle in the graph of Figure 6.6 using as the input database the relation *Vertices* with a set of cities and *Chicago* as the start vertex. This can be done using the proof tree in Figure 12.1. The proof tree uses only the first letters of the cities instead of their full names. The Hamiltonian cycle can be read off from the leftmost branch of the proof tree from the leaf to the root node as the first argument of the *Path* relation in sequence.

Example 12.3.3 Between continents A and B lies an ocean with several islands as shown in Figure 12.4.

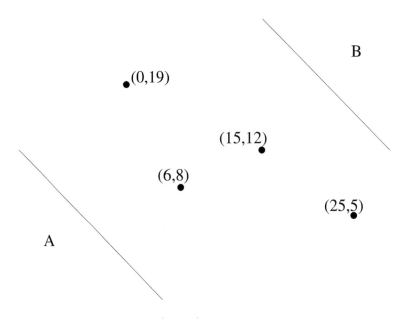

Figure 12.4: An ocean with some islands.

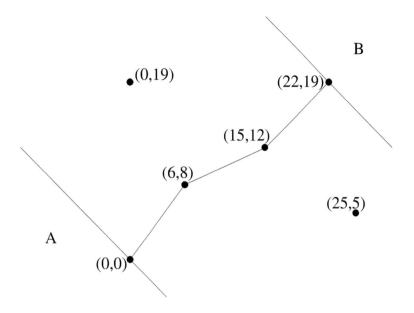

Figure 12.5: One possible path for the ship to cross the ocean.

The islands and the continents can be represented by:

$$
\begin{array}{lll}
Island(x,y) & :\!-\!\!- & x = 0, \quad\; y = 19. \\
Island(x,y) & :\!-\!\!- & x = 6, \quad\; y = 8. \\
Island(x,y) & :\!-\!\!- & x = 15, \quad y = 12. \\
Island(x,y) & :\!-\!\!- & x = 25, \quad y = 5. \\
\\
Cont(n,x,y) & :\!-\!\!- & n = \text{"}A\text{"}, \quad -x - y \geq 0. \\
Cont(n,x,y) & :\!-\!\!- & n = \text{"}B\text{"}, \quad +x + y \geq 41.
\end{array}
$$

While crossing the ocean, a ship can cruise at most 10 units of distance before getting some resupplies at one of the islands. How can the ship cross the ocean? One possible path for the ship to cross the ocean, as shown in Figure 12.5, is to start from location $(0, 0)$ of continent A and cruise first to the island at locations $(6, 8)$, then to the island at location $(15, 12)$, and finally from there cruise to location $(22, 19)$ of continent B.

The above process requires defining the relation $Close$ relation, which contains pairs of points within 10 units of each other according to a Euclidean distance function. The $Close$ relation is expressed using the difference D, the absolute difference AD, and the multiplication M operators.

$$
\begin{array}{lll}
D(x,y,z) & :\!\!- & x = y,\ z = 0. \\
D(x,y,z) & :\!\!- & D(x',y,z'),\ x = x' + 1,\ z = z' + 1.
\end{array}
$$

$$
\begin{array}{lll}
AD(x,y,z) & :\!\!- & D(x,y,z),\ x \geq y. \\
AD(x,y,z) & :\!\!- & D(y,x,z),\ y \geq x.
\end{array}
$$

$$
\begin{array}{lll}
M(x,y,z) & :\!\!- & x = 0,\ y = 0,\ z = 0. \\
M(x,y,z) & :\!\!- & M(x',y,z'),\ D(z,z',y),\ x = x' + 1. \\
M(x,y,z) & :\!\!- & M(x,y',z'),\ D(z,z',x),\ y = y' + 1.
\end{array}
$$

$$
\begin{array}{lll}
Close(x',y',x,y) & :\!\!- & AD(x,x',dx),\ AD(y,y',dy), \\
& & M(dx,dx,dx2),\ M(dy,dy,dy2), \\
& & -dx2 - dy2 \geq -100.
\end{array}
$$

We find whether we can get from a location on continent A to a location on continent B via a sequence of the islands as follows:

$$
\begin{array}{lll}
Ship(x,y) & :\!\!- & Cont(n,x,y),\ n = \text{``A''}. \\
Ship(x,y) & :\!\!- & Ship(x',y'),\ Island(x,y),\ Close(x',y',x,y). \\
Reach(x,y) & :\!\!- & Ship(x',y'),\ Cont(n,x,y),\ n = \text{``B''},\ Close(x',y',x,y).
\end{array}
$$

Figure 12.6 is a partial proof tree, without an expansion for *Close*.

12.3.2   Least Fixpoint

There is an alternative description of the semantics of Datalog queries that can be explained as follows.

Let Q be any Datalog query. We call an *interpretation* of Q any assignment r_i of a finite or infinite number of tuples over $\delta^{\alpha(R_i)}$ to each R_i that occurs in Q, where δ is the domain of the attribute variables and $\alpha(R_i)$ is the arity of relation R_i.

The *immediate consequence operator* of a Datalog query Q, denoted T_Q, is a mapping from interpretations to interpretations as follows. For each interpretation db that assigns to $R, R_1, R_2, \ldots$ the relations $r, r_1, r_2, \ldots$ we say that $R(a_1, \ldots, a_k) \in T_Q(db)$, if

$R \in \mathcal{I}$ and $(a_1, \ldots, a_k) \in r$ or

$R \in \mathcal{D}$ and for some rule in Q there is an instantiation

$$
R(a_1, \ldots, a_k) :\!\!- R_1(a_{1,1}, \ldots, a_{1,k_1}), \ldots, R_n(a_{n,1}, \ldots, a_{n,k_n}).
$$

where $R_i(a_{i,1}, \ldots, a_{i,k_i}) \in r_i$ for each $1 \leq i \leq n$.

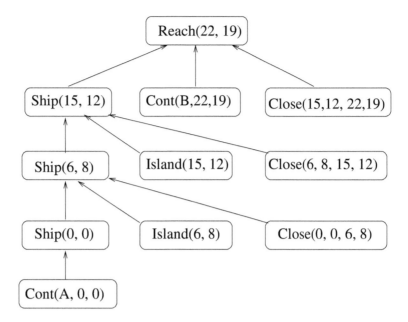

Figure 12.6: A proof tree showing one solution to the ocean crossing problem.

Each input database I is an interpretation that assigns a finite or infinite relation to each $R \in \mathcal{I}$ and the empty set to each $R \in \mathcal{D}$. Let

$$T_Q^0(I) = T_Q(I)$$

Also let

$$T_Q^{i+1}(I) = T_Q^i(I) \cup T_Q(T_Q^i(I))$$

We call the *least fixpoint semantics* of Q on I, denoted $lfp(Q(I))$, the interpretation $\bigcup_i T_Q^i(I)$.

Note: Any interpretation J is called a *fixpoint* of a query Q if $J = T_Q(J)$. There could be many fixpoints of a query. The interpretation $\bigcup_i T_Q^i(I)$ is a fixpoint that is distinguished from other fixpoints in that it is a subset of any other fixpoint that the query may have. That is why it is called the least fixpoint.

The proof-based and the least fixpoint semantics are equivalent, as shown in the following theorem.

Theorem 12.3.1

$$\{(a_1, \ldots, a_k) \;:\; \vdash_{Q,I} R(a_1, \ldots, a_k)\} = \{(a_1, \ldots, a_k) \;:\; R(a_1, \ldots, a_k) \in \bigcup_i T_Q^i(I)\}$$

We define a binary relation *depends_on* on $\mathcal{R}$ as follows: *depends_on* (H, B) is true if for $H, B \in \mathcal{R}$ there is a rule such that H occurs in the head and B occurs in the body of the rule. For each query the *depends_on* relation can be easily illustrated by a directed graph.

Definition 12.3.1 A Datalog query is *recursive* if the graph of the *depends_on* relation contains a cycle. Otherwise the Datalog query is *non-recursive*.

For example, Q_{travel} is a recursive and Q_{tax} is a non-recursive Datalog query.

12.4 Datalog with Aggregation and Negation

Aggregate operators are operators that take in a set of values and return a single value. Negation of a relation with arity k returns a constraint representation of the complement of the relation. That is, if δ is the domain, then those tuples in δ^k that do not belong to the relation should be returned.

Both aggregation and negation require that the entire relation be completely known. Therefore we apply these only to input relations, although the input relations to these operators could be relations that were defined earlier in Datalog queries and already completely computed in some way. This is called the *stratified composition* of queries.

First we describe some common aggregate operators and negation in constraint databases, then we will discuss the composition of Datalog queries.

12.4.1 Set Grouping

The set grouping operator has the syntax:

$$R_0(y_1, \ldots, y_m) \quad :\!\!- \quad R(x_1, \ldots, x_n).$$

where each y_i is either x_j or $\langle x_j \rangle$ for $1 \leq i \leq m$ and $1 \leq j \leq n$.

This operator is restricted to cases where at least the (column of) attributes referred to by the regular variables in the head are constants. This operator first groups all the tuples in R into groups where these variables have the same values. Then for each group it takes the union of the column of attributes referred to by $\langle \rangle$ bracketed variables in the head.

For example, let $Can\_Send\_Message(x, y)$ be true if person x can send a message to person y using mobile phones as in Example 12.2.6. Suppose we want to find for each person x the set of persons that x can reach. We can do that using a set grouping operator as follows:

$$Reach(x, \langle y \rangle) \quad :\!\!- \quad Can\_Send\_Message(x, y).$$

To find the set of mobile phone users, we can use:

$$Mobile\_Phone\_Users(\langle x \rangle) \quad :- \quad Mobile\_Phone(x, A).$$

Set grouping operators can be also applied to a column of intentional set constants. For example, to find the areas with at least one mobile phone user we can use:

$$Areas\_with\_Mobile\_Phones(\langle A \rangle) \quad :- \quad Mobile\_Phone(x, A).$$

12.4.2   Average, Count, Sum

These aggregate operators are like the set grouping operators. In fact, the syntax is similar to the set grouping operator, with each $\langle \rangle$ bracketed variable in the head preceded by one key word: $avg, count,$ or sum. For these aggregate operators, the column of attributes referred to by bracketed variables in the head must also be constants.

For example, the following query finds for each person x the number of persons that x can reach:

$$Reach(x, count\langle y \rangle) \quad :- \quad Can\_Send\_Message(x, y).$$

As another example, let's consider $NE\_Mobile\_Phone\_User(x)$, which describes the mobile phone users in the state of Nebraska, as in Example 12.2.5, as an input relation. Then the following query $Q_{number\_NE\_Users}$ finds the number of mobile phone users in Nebraska:

$$Number\_NE\_Users(count\langle x \rangle) \quad :- \quad NE\_Mobile\_Phone\_User(x).$$

12.4.3   Area and Volume

The *area* aggregate operator works on relations that represent maps. In each such relation we assume that the two distinguished attributes, called the *spatial attributes*, are rational variables x, y on which we place linear constraints. The other attributes, called the *nonspatial attributes*, are constants. The relation describes which attributes hold for regions of the plane.

For example, the *Town* relation in Chapter 3 represents maps as we described earlier. In the *Town* relation the second and third attributes are the spatial attributes and the first attribute is the only nonspatial attribute.

The syntax of the area operator is similar to the other aggregate operators, but we will have $area\langle x, y \rangle$ in the head because area is a two-argument operator unlike average, count, and sum. For example, to find the total area of each town, we can write the following:

$$Town\_Area(t, area\langle x, y \rangle) \quad :- \quad Town(t, x, y).$$

The *volume* aggregate operator is like the area aggregate operator except that it takes three variables as arguments.

In many geographic applications it is useful to find total area statistics for each band region of a map. Therefore in the area aggregate operator we allow the following constant parameters as an optional argument: x_0, d, and n. With these parameters present, the area operator will find the total area now in each band. That is, it will return two more attributes following the area attribute. Namely, it will return $x_0 + id$ and $x_0 + (i+1)d$ for each $0 \leq i \leq n$, and the total area value will be only the total area where $x_0 + id \leq x \leq x_0 + (i+1)d$. For example, the following query returns for each 1-unit-wide x band the total area of each town, where the left side of the first band will be 2 and there are 12 bands:

$$Town\_Area(t, area\langle x, 2, 1, 12, y\rangle) \quad :\!- \quad Town(t, x, y).$$

We also allow similar optional constant parameters after the y argument. In this case, the total area statistics will be returned for each little square or rectangular region of the map.

12.4.4   Minimum and Maximum

The *minimum* and *maximum* aggregate operators work on relations within which all attributes occurring in the head outside of the $\langle\rangle$ brackets are constants while attributes occurring within the brackets can be variables constrained by linear constraints.

The syntax of the minimum and maximum operators differs from the syntax of the average, count, and sum operators only in that the argument of max can be a linear function, called the *objective* function. That is, the argument list will be $\langle c_1 x_1 + \ldots + c_n x_n\rangle$ where $x_1, \ldots, x_n$ occur in the input relation.

Example 12.4.1 Suppose the farmer in Chapter 3 wants to find the maximum profit possible given that each acre of corn, rye, sunflower, and wheat yields a profit of 30, 25, 8, and 15, respectively.

The following query Q_{profit} can calculate the maximum profit possible for any of the planting options:

$$Profit(\max\langle 30x_1 + 25x_2 + 8x_3 + 15x_3\rangle) \quad :\!- \quad Crops(x_1, x_2, x_3, x_4).$$

As another example, the following query Q_{edge} finds the minimum time between each pair of towns connected by a single edge:

$$Edge(x, y, \min\langle t\rangle) \quad :\!- \quad Go(x, 0, y, t).$$

12.4.5 Negation

The negation operator has the following syntax:

$$R_0(x_1, \ldots, x_k) \quad :\!- \quad not\ R(x_1, \ldots, x_k).$$

R could be a relation with linear constraints over the rationals or polynomial constraints over the reals. R could also be a relation with $=, \neq, <$, and $\leq$ constraints over the integers. In all of these cases it is possible to find a constraint representation of the complement of R. The constraint representation will contain the same type of constraints as the input relation. (For example, if R is a relation with polynomial constraints over the reals, then R_0 will also be a relation with polynomial constraints over the reals.) This is called a *closed-form* representation.

As an example, suppose that relation $Covered(x, y)$ describes the areas reached by at least one radio station as in Example 12.1.8. Then the areas that are not reached by any radio station or that are not within the town can be found by the following query $Q_{\text{not\_cover}}$:

$$Not\_Covered(x, y) \quad :\!- \quad not\ Covered(x, y).$$

12.4.6 Stratified Datalog Queries

Let us suppose that we want to find the fastest possible travel time between any pair of cities. This can be done by first evaluating Q_{travel} and then finding the minimum travel times by the following query Q_{fastest}, which assumes $Travel$ as an input relation:

$$Fastest(x, y, \min\langle t \rangle) \quad :\!- \quad Travel(x, y, t).$$

The composition of the Q_{fastest} and Q_{travel} queries is a new query that we write as $Q_{\text{fastest}}(Q_{\text{travel}}())$. The composite query takes as input the relation $Could\_Go$ and returns relations $Could\_Go, Travel$, and $Fastest$.

Each part of a composite query is called one level, or *stratum*. A composite query is called a *stratified Datalog* query. Here Q_{travel} is the first and Q_{fastest} is the second stratum of the composite query.

As another example, the Q_{cover} query in Example 12.1.8 took as input relations $Town$ and $Broadcast$, while query $Q_{\text{not\_cover}}$ took as input the relation Q_{cover}. We write the composition of these two queries as $Q_{\text{not\_cover}}(Q_{\text{cover}}())$.

We call a stratified Datalog query nonrecursive if each of its component queries is nonrecursive. Otherwise, we call it a recursive query. For example, the composite query $Q_{\text{fastest}}(Q_{\text{travel}}())$ is recursive because Q_{travel} is itself recursive. However, $Q_{\text{not\_cover}}(Q_{\text{cover}}())$ is nonrecursive, because neither Q_{cover} nor $Q_{\text{not\_cover}}$ is a recursive query.

Finally, let us see a stratified Datalog query that uses set constants.

Example 12.4.2 Let's call $Q_{\text{mobile\_phone\_users}}$ and Q_{reach}, respectively, the queries that define relations $Mobile\_Phone\_Users$ and $Reach$ as shown in Section 12.4.1. Let's call the following query Q_{Alice}:

$$
\begin{aligned}
Alice\_Cannot\_Reach(Z) \quad :- \quad & Mobile\_Phone\_Users(X), \\
& Reach(\text{``Alice''}, Y), \\
& X \setminus Y = Z.
\end{aligned}
$$

The stratified Datalog query $Q_{\text{Alice}}(Q_{\text{mobile\_phone\_users}}(Q_{\text{reach}}()))$ finds the set of people to whom Alice cannot send a message.

Bibliographic Notes

Constraint deductive databases were proposed in 1990 by Kanellakis, Kuper, and Revesz [214, 215] by taking simplified cases of constraint logic programming proposed in 1987 by Jaffar and Lassez [205] but evaluating them efficiently in a "database-style." The Prolog-style evaluation of Jaffar and Lassez [205] and the database-style evaluation of Kanellakis et al. [214, 215] are compared in Section 23.5.

Constraint deductive databases are decribed in Kuper et al. [251] and Revesz [339]. Constraint logic programs are discussed in the books by Benhamou and Colmerauer [44], Marriott and Stuckey [267], and Van Hentenryck [415].

The earlier history of deductive databases and logic programming (both without constraints) is reviewed in several textbooks, including the ones by Abiteboul et al. [2], O'Neil [289], Ramakrishnan [313], Silberschatz et al. [377], and Ullman [408]. Stratified Datalog queries are reviewed in the above books. Stratified constraint Datalog queries are studied in Revesz [332]. Datalog can be extended with other types of negation and aggregation, for example, well-founded negation and aggregation [389, 148, 414] and inflationary negation [229].

Datalog with nested sets is discussed by Vadaparty [410]. The Hamiltonian cycle example is from [330] and the travel example is from [335].

Exercises

1. Find every city within 500 minutes of Omaha. Assume that we know the minimum traveling time on each direct route connection between cities.

2. A sales agency has offices in 30 major cities in the continental United States. Find all cities where the agency can ship goods within 500 minutes. Assume that we know the minimum traveling time on each direct route connection between cities and the cities where the agency is located.

3. Assume that you want to design a database of flight schedules where flights are represented by numbers 1,2,3, etc. Relation *Flights* lists for each flight an origin and a destination city and information on the time of arrival and the time of departure measured in minutes past 12 midnight. Relation *Airport* lists the minimum delay in transit at airports in various cities. Find all pairs of cities between which travel is possible.

Flights

No	Orig	Dest	Depart	Arrive
1	Atlanta	Chicago	870	925
2	Atlanta	Denver	830	940
3	Boston	Atlanta	690	800
4	Boston	Chicago	545	645
5	Chicago	Atlanta	710	765
6	Chicago	Denver	660	780

Airport

Name	Arrive	Depart	
Atlanta	t_1	t_2	$t_2 - t_1 \geq 60$
Boston	t_1	t_2	$t_2 - t_1 \geq 50$
Chicago	t_1	t_2	$t_2 - t_1 \geq 45$
Denver	t_1	t_2	$t_2 - t_1 \geq 70$

4. In a garden there are two types of flowers: tulips and daffodils. We know the location of these flowers with respect to the southwest corner of the garden. In the garden there are several hives of bees and wasps' nests. We know the area where each hive of bees and colony of wasps collects pollen from flowers. For example, the first hive of bees visits flowers in the rectangular area 50 to 200 meters east and 100 to 350 meters north from the southwest corner of the garden. Bees visit both tulips and daffodils, while wasps visit only daffodils. Both insects may carry pollen from one flower to another. Suppose there is a special strain of daffodils at location 2 meters east and 3 meters north from the southwest corner. Find all daffodils that may be pollinated by this flower.

5. Write a query that tests whether propositional formulas are true. (In this exercise you have to define a representation for the input database propositional formulas.)

6. Using MLPQ, implement the syllogistic rules of Example 12.2.1, and test whether they can automatically prove the result of Example 11.1.10.

7. Translate Axiom 11.1.15 into Datalog.

8. Write a query that finds all parts of the town that are reached by two broadcast stations but not by three.

9. Suppose relation $Postage(w, f)$ describes the postage fee f required for a package with weight w. Mr. Johnson, who lives in Omaha, Nebraska, wants to send three packages to three clients who live in Atlanta, Boston, and Chicago. He wants to know the total amount he should pay for his packages. The weight of each package can be represented in the following relational database table.

Package

No.	From	To	Weight
101	Omaha	Chicago	12.6
102	Omaha	Atlanta	27.3
103	Omaha	Boston	37.5

Write a Datalog query with linear constraints that finds the total postage fee required.

10. Suppose a farmer can harvest 1125, 500, and 250 pounds of asparagus from locations 1, 2, and 3, respectively. The asparagus can be shipped to two cool rooms, which can store 1250 and 950 pounds, respectively.

The average cost of transporting asparagus from location 1 to cool rooms 1 and 2 is 0.03 and 0.07 dollars per pound, respectively. The average cost of transporting asparagus from location 2 to cool rooms 1 and 2 is 0.05 and 0.03 dollars per pound, respectively. The average cost of transporting asparagus from location 3 to cool rooms 1 and 2 is 0.08 and 0.10 dollars per pound.

The farmer would like to buy some extra land adjacent to one of the three locations that will yield an extra 325 pounds of asparagus.

Write a Datalog query that finds where the farmer should buy extra land and how many pounds of asparagus should be shipped from which location to which cool room for the maximum profit.

13

The MLPQ System

MLPQ, short for *Management of Linear Programming Queries*, is a constraint-relational database system that is continuously built and updated at the University of Nebraska-Lincoln since 1995. The initial goal of the MLPQ system was to seamlessly extend traditional relational database systems. For example, MLPQ extends the minimum and maximum aggregation operators, which relational database systems apply only to a finite set of constant values, to operators that find the minimum or the maximum of a linear function over k attribute variables, which range over a k-dimensional polyhedral space represented by rational linear inequality constraints in the database. Of course, that is exactly *linear programming*, something that goes way beyond the normal capabilities of relational databases and was thought before to be a "separate issue." This separation was unfortunate because raw operations research data needs to be often reformulated before it becomes suitable as input to a linear program solver. MLPQ allows such reformulations to be done by simple database queries.

The MLPQ system was later found to be also excellent as an extension of geographic information systems (GISs). Although GISs normally use the vector representation of geographic data, the vector representation is easily translated into a linear constraint representation. The vector representation becomes increasingly hard to maintain for higher-dimensional data. For instance, a k-dimensional hypercube can be represented only by 2^n vertices in the vector data model. However, they can be represented by only $2n$ linear constraints. This example only hints at the difficulties that GISs encounter when they try to provide more than 2-dimensional cartographic data management. In fact, to make advances GISs are increasingly forced to translate internally the vector representation into a constraint representation to effi-

P. Revesz, *Introduction to Databases: From Biological to Spatio-Temporal*,
Texts in Computer Science, DOI 10.1007/978-1-84996-095-3_13,
© Springer-Verlag London Limited 2010

ciently evaluate the queries. After the query evaluation is completed, GISs routinely translate back the result into the "normal" vector representation. The MLPQ system can be viewed simply as an advanced GIS that omits this "normal" vector representation and keeps instead internally the constraint representation at all times. The greater generality of the constraint representation provides MLPQ the flexibility to handle three dimensional spatial data and three or four-dimensional spatio-temporal data.

Another application area where MLPQ proves advantageous is the management of moving objects databases. It is becoming increasingly accepted to represent the trajectory of moving objects by linear constraint approximations. These approximation also can be conveniently represented in constraint databases, which are then easily queried by the MLPQ constraint-relational system.

Although MLPQ has wide-ranging capabilities, it integrates all of its parts in a natural manner, using the same graphical user interface and query languages. Even a user who is only familiar with standard SQL can solve some difficult problems as shown by the examples in this chapter.

Section 13.1 gives a brief overview of the MLPQ system architecture and describes the functions of its six main modules. Section 13.2 describes how the MLPQ system can be used as a relational database system. Section 13.3 describes how the MLPQ system can be used as a geographic information system. Section 13.4 describes how the MLPQ system can be used as a moving objects database system. Section 13.5 discusses some topological queries in MLPQ. Section 13.7 considers linear programming. Section 13.6 discusses some applications of recursive SQL and Datalog queries in MLPQ. Finally, Section 13.8 describes how to make MLPQ databases webaccessible.

13.1   The MLPQ System Architecture

An overview of the architecture of the MLPQ system is shown in Figure 13.1. The architecture consists of six main modules, which can be described as follows:

Representation: The *representation module* is responsible for the internal representation of constraint databases and queries. This module communicates with the external constraint database storage structures. If it cannot find some needed constraint relation in the constraint database store, then it calls the approximation module that searches its relational database store and provides a converted constraint relation. The representation module provides output to the query evaluation module. The constraint relations of the input files are like those described in Chapter 4.

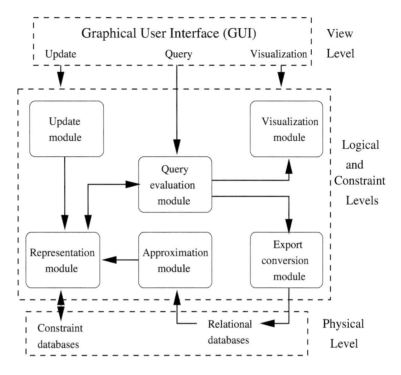

Figure 13.1: The MLPQ database system architecture.

Query Evaluation: The *query evaluation module* is used to evaluate the queries provided by the user via an input file or graphical userinterface (GUI). This module can evaluate several kinds of query languages, such as, SQL, Datalog, relational algebra, and their extensions. In addition, there are special operators available from the graphical user interface tool bar. These additional operators are especially useful for data visualization.

The output of this module is another constraint relation, which may be added to the database; therefore it may be passed to the data representation module. Alternatively, it may be a relation that is passed to the visualization module, if the query involves query visualization operators. Finally, it could pass the data to the export conversion module, if the query asks for exporting to a relational database. The query evaluation module uses some of the algorithms described in Chapter 24.

Visualization: The *visualization module* shows on the GUI the data that the user asks to see. The visualization module provides many options. One of the interesting options special to spatio-temporal applications is animation of three-dimensional spatio-temporal data. The input of this module is from the query evaluation module and the output is to the GUI. The visualization module uses some of the algorithms described in Chapter 21.

Approximation: The *approximation module* can be used to convert from relational databases to constraint databases. Typically, the conversion involves a significant data reduction and interpolation of the original relational data. The input is from relational database storage, and the output is to the representation module. The approximation module uses some of the algorithms described in Chapter 18.

Update: The *update module* is responsible for updating the constraint relations as requested by the user. There are several update languages that the user may use to express updates or use the GIS tool bar operators. There are several algorithms to implement the update requests. One update algorithm is described in Section 18.6.1.

Export Conversion: The *export conversion module* provides conversion from constraint databases to relational databases. The conversion may not always be available because constraint databases are sometimes equivalent to infinite relational databases, as described in Chapter 3.

The above outline of the MLPQ system architecture hints at the immense amount of work that was necessary to build this system. However, MLPQ users do not need to be concerned about the complexity of the software any more than they need to be concerned about the complexity of other database software while they use them. In fact, MLPQ users do not even need to learn a new query language. If they have used before any relational database, then they can use the MLPQ system with the same ease, continuing to use standard SQL with only minor modifications. As this architecture overview shows, MLPQ provides many extra features for its users. The more advantage the users take as those extra features, the more satisfied they will be.

13.2   Relational Databases

The MLPQ system can be used as a relational database system. This section explains how to represent relational database files and query them.

13.2.1 Non-Recursive SQL Queries

Input files intended for non-recursive queries have the following structure:

```
begin %MLPQ%
    r_1
    ⋮
    r_n
end %MLPQ%
```

where each r_i is a row of some relation. A row $(c1, \ldots, cn)$ of relation `R(a1,...,an)` is represented as follows.

```
R(a1, ..., an) :- a1 = c1, ..., an = cn.
```

Example 13.2.1 Supppose that a gallery database is composed of three relations. The *Painter(Id,Name,Phone)* relation records the identification number, the name, and the phone number of some famous painters.

Painter

Id	Name	Phone
123	Ross	888-4567
126	Pollock	345-1122
234	Picasso	456-3345
335	O'Keefe	567-8999
456	Wharhol	777-7777

The *Painting(Pnum, Title, Price, Id)* relation records for each painting its identification number, the name of its painter, its price, and the identification number of its painter.

Painting

Pnum	Title	Price	Id
2345	Wild Waters	245.00	126
4536	Sea Storm	8359.00	335
6666	Wild Waters	6799.00	234
6789	Paradise	590,000.00	234
7878	High Tide	98,000.00	456
7896	Faded Rose	145.00	123
9889	Sunset	975,000.00	234

The *Gallery(Pnum, Owner)* relation records for each painting its identification number and the owner of the gallery where the painting is stored.

Gallery

Pnum	Owner
2345	Johnson
6666	Johnson
4536	McCloud
7878	McCloud
6789	Palmer
7896	Palmer
9889	Palmer

The following `gallery.txt` file stores the entire gallery database.

```
begin %MLPQ%
painter(id, name, phone) :- id=123, name="Ross",    phone="888-4567".
painter(id, name, phone) :- id=126, name="Pollock", phone="345-1122".
painter(id, name, phone) :- id=234, name="Picasso", phone="456-3345".
painter(id, name, phone) :- id=335, name="OKeefe",  phone="567-8999".
painter(id, name, phone) :- id=456, name="Warhol",  phone="777-7777".

painting(pnum, title, price, id) :- pnum=2345, title="Wild Waters", price=245, id=126.
painting(pnum, title, price, id) :- pnum=4536, title="Sea Storm",   price=8359, id=335.
painting(pnum, title, price, id) :- pnum=6666, title="Wild Waters", price=6799, id=234.
painting(pnum, title, price, id) :- pnum=6789, title="Paradise",    price=590000, id=234.
painting(pnum, title, price, id) :- pnum=7878, title="High Tide",   price=98000, id=456.
painting(pnum, title, price, id) :- pnum=7896, title="Faded Rose",  price=145, id=123.
painting(pnum, title, price, id) :- pnum=9889, title="Sunset",      price=975000, id=234.

gallery(pnum, owner) :- pnum=2345, owner="Johnson".
gallery(pnum, owner) :- pnum=6666, owner="Johnson".
gallery(pnum, owner) :- pnum=4536, owner="McCloud".
gallery(pnum, owner) :- pnum=7878, owner="McCloud".
gallery(pnum, owner) :- pnum=6789, owner="Palmer".
gallery(pnum, owner) :- pnum=7896, owner="Palmer".
gallery(pnum, owner) :- pnum=9889, owner="Palmer".
end %MLPQ%
```

When one starts the MLPQ system, a window is created. In the top of the window there is a tool bar with several buttons as shown below.

The following are some of the frequently used buttons.

OpenFile – This is used to open a file. After clicking this button, the input file can be opened by going to the proper directory and selecting a file to be opened. The file has to be a textfile in the above described format and with a ".txt" ending.

Disk – This is used to save the file.

Del – This is used to delete files. First select the relations to be deleted by clicking on their names. Then click this button. A popup message box will ask you to verify that the relations are to be deleted. Check carefully the relation names and if everything is correct, then click "OK" to execute the delete operation.

When MLPQ loads the file, it lists in the upper left hand corner the names of all the active relations as well as the number of rows currently stored in each active relation. The MLPQ system also opens a geometry side window in which it tries to visualize the relations if they are two dimensional spatial relationships. This side window is empty if there is nothing to visualize.

Example 13.2.2 After opening the `gallery.txt` file, the relations painter, painting, and gallery relations are displayed in the upper left corner of a new window as shown below.

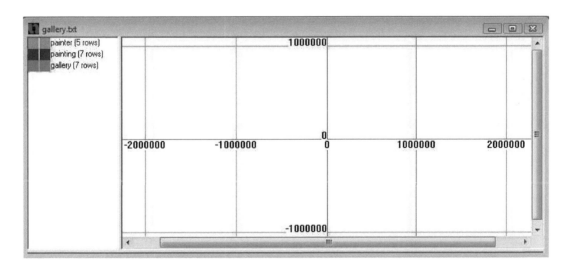

The window also tells us that there are five rows in the painter and seven rows in the both of the painting and the owner relations.

To view the data stored in any of the active relations, the mouse needs to be moved until it points to the relation and then it has to be clicked by the right button.

Example 13.2.3 The number of rows already gives some indication that the `gallery.txt` file was loaded correctly. However, we can right click the gallery relation to see exactly the seven rows that it contains. This results in the following new window.

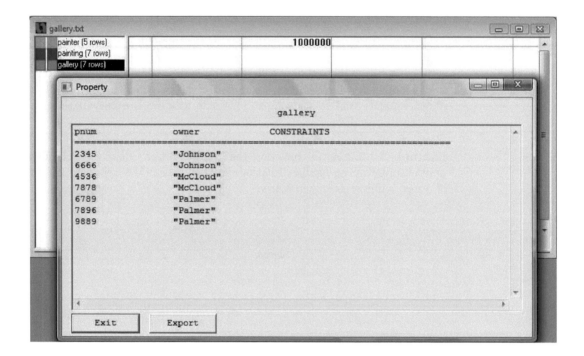

When we are satisfied with the result, we can save it to another file by clicking $\boxed{\text{Export}}$, or we can click $\boxed{\text{Exit}}$ and return to the earlier window.

In MLPQ the syntax of the SQL queries follows the SQL standard with some restrictions that are explained below. The database users can start SQL queries by clicking in the upper leftmost part of the tool bar the $\boxed{\text{SQL}}$ button, which pops up the following dialog box:

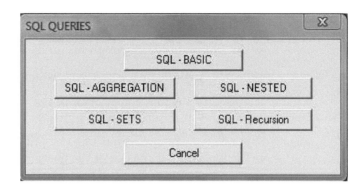

The first five menu options correspond to the types of SQL queries that we saw in Chapter 3. We can start any of these types of SQL queries by clicking on the corresponding button.

If we click on the $\boxed{\text{SQL-Basic}}$ button, then we get a new dialog box that we can fill in with a basic SQL query. For example, we may fill in the fields as shown below to find the titles of the paintings in Palmer's gallery.

The dialog box provides a reminder of all the components of a basic SQL query and saves typing the routine keywords. Note the following special features of the MLPQ SQL syntax:

- The <u>relation.attribute</u> dot notation is <u>required</u> for attributes.

- The <u>AS</u> keyword is <u>required</u> when declaring tuple variables.

- <u>Double quotation</u> marks are <u>required</u> for string constants.

- A <u>comma</u> is <u>required</u> instead of an AND for conjunctions.

- The <u>OR</u> keyword is <u>not allowed</u>.

- The <u>semicolon</u> at the end of the query is <u>not allowed</u>.

- Only the =, >, <, >=, and <= relational operators are allowed.

Using the above requirements enables one to write clearer queries. For example, it is quite frequent to have the same attribute name occur in several relations that are used in an SQL query. That situation causes many ambiguities. In the long term, the habit of always using the dot notation when first writing down a query is better than trying to save some typing by omitting the relation name. Similarly, using the AS keyword makes the queries more readable.

The bottom of the dialog box shows several buttons, which are used as follows.

- The $\boxed{\text{OK}}$ button executes the query. The execution creates a new relation, which is added to the list of active relations in the upper right corner of the window that was created when the original file was loaded.

- The $\boxed{\text{Cancel}}$ button cancels the query.

- The $\boxed{\text{Save}}$ button saves the query into a new textfile.

- The $\boxed{\text{Load}}$ button allows loading an already saved query.

- The $\boxed{\text{Clear}}$ button clears all the fields and allows the writing of the query to start again from the beginning.

For example, the execution of the above query creates the *titles_in_Palmer* relation. We can immediately see that it contains three rows. By clicking on the relation name, we can see a display of the whole relation. By clicking the $\boxed{\text{Export}}$ button at the bottom of the display window, the *titles_in_Palmer* relation is saved to a new textfile.

Note that exporting the new relation is different from saving it by clicking the disk button of the tool bar. The latter saves the *titles_in_Palmer* relation by modifying the original `gallery.txt` file. Hence the next time the `gallery.txt` file is opened, the *titles_in_Palmer* relation will be also uploaded together with the original *Painter*, *Painting*, and *Gallery* relations.

Next, let us see an example of an SQL aggregation query in MLPQ.

Example 13.2.4 The following SQL aggregation query finds the highest price for any paintings of Picasso.

MLPQ allows the `avg`, `count`, `max`, `min` and `sum` aggregate operators. The `avg` and the `sum` operators require numeric values. The `count` operator can work on both string and numeric values. The `max` and the `min` are the most flexible because they can work on string values, numeric values or, as we will see later, on variables defined by linear constraints. These operators work on multi-sets, that is, they allow repetitions of the inputs and handle those repetitions as expected. For the VIEW line, the view name must be followed in parentheses by the new attribute names.

Example 13.2.5 The following SQL aggregation query with both a GROUP BY and a HAVING clause finds the painters with an average painting price higher than 8000 dollars.

MLPQ allows only the intersection and the union set operators. The intersection operator is illustrated by the next example.

Example 13.2.6 Find the painting titles that are commonly used by both Picasso and Pollock.

At first we use the $\boxed{\text{SQL}}$ button to start again the SQL menu window, then we select the $\boxed{\text{SQL-SETS}}$ button, which brings up a new dialog box into which the query can be entered. This box is like two basic SQL dialog boxes, but it contains a drop down menu, which allows the selection of either INTERSECT or UNION as the keyword that connects the two parts of the query. We select the latter operator and fill in the rest of the dialog box as shown below.

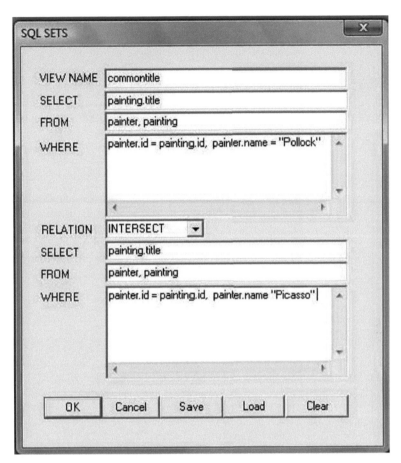

This query returns a relation that contains only one row because "Wild Waters" is the only title that is used by both painters.

The MLPQ nested SQL queries can be done only through one attribute. Nested SQL queries also have a composite dialog box that is connected by another drop down menu. The drop down menu allows the selection of the following keywords: `in`, `not in`, $>=$ `some`, $<=$ `some`, $>=$ `all`, and $<=$ `all`. The $>=$ `all` and the $<=$ `all` keywords cannot be used for string comparisons.

Example 13.2.7 Find the title and the price of the most expensive painting.

After selecting the SQL-NESTED button, we get a dialog box, which we fill in as shown below. While filling in the details, we select from the drop down menu the $>=$ `all` keyword. The $>=$ `all` operator can be used in MLPQ within this query because we compare with it only prices, which are numeric values.

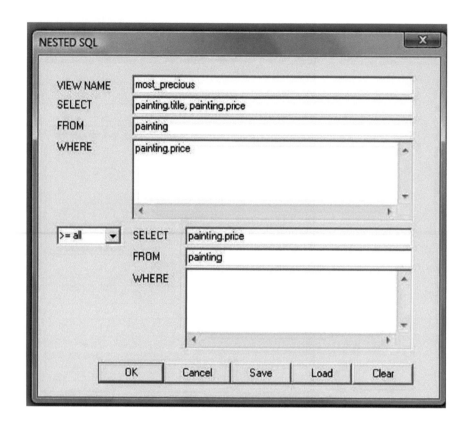

13.2.2 Recursive SQL and Datalog Queries

MLPQ provides an option for recursive SQL and Datalog queries. Input files intended for recursive queries have the following structure:

```
begin %RECURSIVE%
    ⋮
end %RECURSIVE%
```

that is, the keyword `MLPQ` is replaced by `RECURSIVE`. To use recursive SQL queries, select the ⎡SQL-Recursion⎤ button from the SQL queries menu.

Example 13.2.8 Suppose that relation *Go(city1, t1, city2, t2)* records for pairs of cities the minimum time required to go from *city1* to *city2*. The *Go* relation is similar to the *Travel* relation of Section 6.5, which discussed topological queries. Using the *Go* relation, we can find the possible traveling times between pairs of cities as follows.

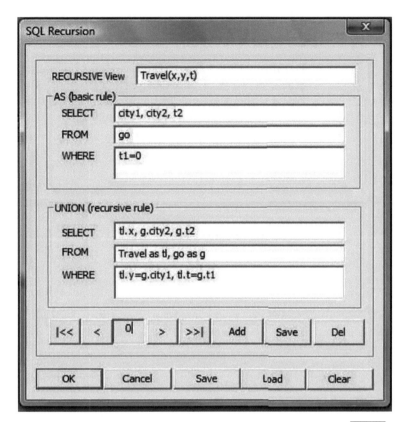

Instead of SQL, we can use Datalog queries by clicking the $\boxed{\text{Dlog}}$ button, which is next to the $\boxed{\text{SQL}}$ button on the tool bar.

13.3 Geographic Databases

Input files intended for geographic queries have the following structure:
```
begin %MLPQ%
    r_1
    .
    .
    .
    r_n
end %MLPQ%
```

where each r_i is a constraint tuple where the right hand side of the ":-" symbol is always a conjunction of linear constraints of the form:

$$a_1 x_1 + a_2 x_2 + \cdots + a_n x_n \ \theta \ b$$

where each a_i is a constant and each x_i is a rational variable, and θ is a relational operator of the form =, <, >, <=, or >=.

Example 13.3.1 The file `usmap.txt` represents a map of the United States as a set of polygonal regions, whose sides are linear constraints. Below is the beginning of the file where the letters `AL` stand for Alabama, AK for Alaska, and AZ for Arizona.

```
begin%MLPQ%
AL(id, x, y) :- id = 1,                         y <  297,
                                               -y < -217,
                          x + 0.137500y <  682.837524,
                         -x + 0.087500y < -578.012512.


AL(id, x, y) :- id = 1,                         y <  217,
                                               -y < -203,
                         x              <  614,
                        -x              < -597.


AK(id, x, y) :- id = 2,   x + 8.375000y < 1832,
                          x + 0.253333y <  207.666672,
                          x -         y <   51,
                          x - 1.075472y <   44.056602,
                         -x + 1.444444y <  210.444443,
                         -x - 0.728814y < -114.423729,
                         -x + 0.096386y <  -33.554218.


AK(id, x, y) :- id = 2,   x + 0.321429y <  216.178574,
                          x - 8.400000y < -629.799988,
                         -x +         y <  -51.


AK(id, x, y) :- id = 2,   x + 2.352941y <  413.235291,
                          x - 0.812500y <  213.812500,
                         -x - 1.634146y < -328.804871,
                         -x            <  -185.


AZ(id, x, y) :- id = 3,                         y <  339,
                                               -y < -223,
                         x              <  268,
                        -x              < -178,
                         -x - 1.928571y < -662.071411,
                         -x + 0.230769y < -108.769234.
```

Each object may be composed of several convex polygons. Usually a row with k number of linear constraints defines a convex polygon with k sides.

For example, the second constraint row contains four linear constraints that define a rectangular piece of Alabama.

There are cases when one or more of the input linear constraints are redundant. When reading in the data, the MLPQ system simplifies the representation by eliminating the redundant linear constraints. After loading the `usmap.txt` file, we need to click on each state that we want to display. The following is the result of displaying the entire map.

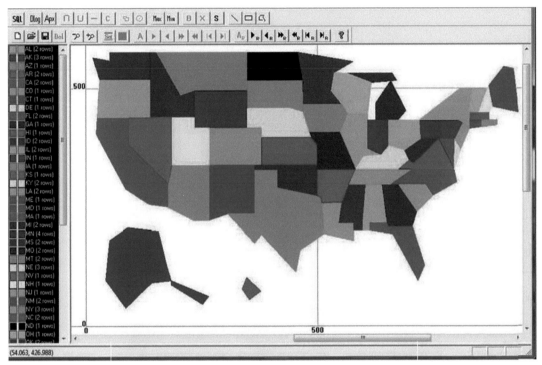

In this display the colors are assigned automatically according to a predetermined sequence. The colors are indicated by the two boxes before each relation name as follows.

To change the color of any state, right click the leftmost box before the corresponding relation name. After this, a color menu will appear. After choosing the selected color from the menu, the leftmost box before the relation name as well as the display of the state on the right side of the window changes to the new color. For example, if we change the color of Alaska to white, then the following will appear on the left.

AL
AK
AZ

A frequent problem in geographic databases is the overlay of different maps. Map overlays are easy in the MLPQ system. Consider the following time zones map of the United States.

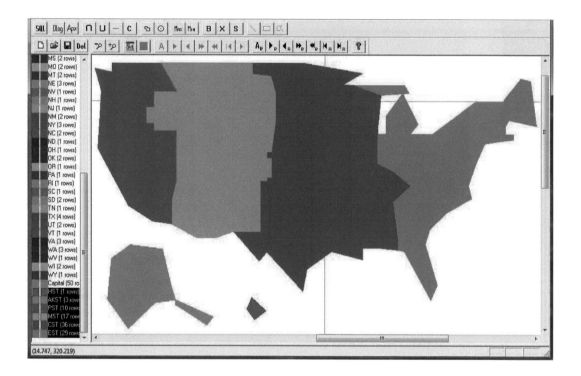

Overlaying the two maps helps us to answer the question of what time zones are used in each state. The following MLPQ SQL query finds the area of Nebraska (NE) that is within the Central Standard Time (CST) zone.

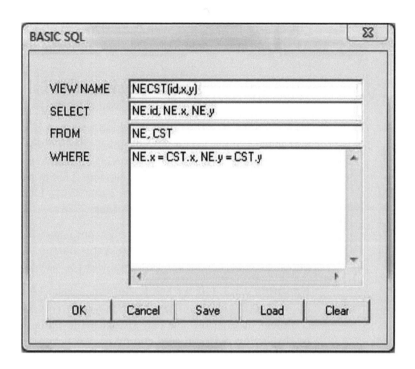

Note that the first three attributes have to be *id, x,* and *y* for the MLPQ system to visualize the relation. Omitting the *id* would still find the correct area, but the visualization procedure would skip this relation because it does not have all the required attributes.

Tool Bar Menu (2D): The MLPQ system provides several operators available from the tool bar. The following may be appropriate for 2-dimensional geographic data.

$\boxed{^-\rho}$ – Click this button to shrink the display of the objects.

$\boxed{^+\rho}$ – To enlarge the displayed object, click this button, then left click the mouse, drag a rectangle to include the area to be enlarged, then release the mouse button.

$\boxed{\cap}$ – This button allows taking the intersection of relations. Select two or more relations (by clicking on them) and press this button. The MLPQ system computes the intersection relation and asks the user to assign a name to it. **Note:** Two relations intersect only if they have the same attribute values for *id, x,* and *y*.

Example 13.3.2 In the `usmap.txt` file the time zones are numbered such that the id of the Alaska Standard Time zone (AKST) is two, which is the same as the id of the state of Alaska (AK). Hence clicking on both AK and AKST and then applying ⊓ returns the entire state of Alaska.

∪ – This button allows taking the union of relations. Select two or more relations (by clicking on them) and press this button. The MLPQ system computes the union relation and asks the user to assign a name to it.

Example 13.3.3 If we are interested in seeing the whole United States as one colored object, then we can union the individual states together. This can be done by first selecting the relation names corresponding to the fifty states and then applying the ∪ button. This pops up a dialog box asking for a relation name, where we can enter *USA*. This new relation will store all the rows of the fifty input relations.

C – This button allows taking the complement of a relation. Select the relation (by clicking on it) and press this button. The MLPQ system computes the complement relation and asks the user to assign a name to it.

Example 13.3.4 If we select state of Alaska (AK) from the `usmap.txt` file and click C, then the MLPQ system returns a relation that is the complement relation. We can give this the name of *compAK*. Afterwards by displaying both AK and compAK, it can be seen that the two relations indeed are complements of each other and together fill in the plane.

▢▫ – This button finds the area of a selected object. Click on the relation name that describes the object, and then click on this button. A dialog box will ask to enter the x-axis range in which the area is to be measured. This is done by specifying the values of *MinX* and *MaxX*. The MLPQ system will crop the object and measure only the area of the object that lies between *MinX* and *MaxX*. The dialog box also asks for the step size, which is the size of the longitude bands that the area needs to be measured in. Normally, *Step = MaxX - MinX*.

Example 13.3.5 In the `usmap.txt` file select the relation AK for Alaska. Then call the area button and specify *MinX = 0*, *MaxX = 500*, and *Step = 500*. The system will compute the total area of Alaska and ask for an output relation name. One can find the computed value by clicking on the name of this new relation.

Example 13.3.6 Find which part of the continental United States is bigger: the part west or the east of $x = 500$. To answer this, we first use create the relation `continental_US.txt` by selecting the four continental time zones in `usmap.txt` and unioning them by clicking ∪. Then we click ▢▫ and specify *MinX = 0*, *MaxX = 1000*, and *Step = 500*. In this case, the output relation contains two tuples that measure separately the areas east and west of the line $x = 500$.

⊙ – This "buffer" button allows extending by a specified distance in each direction the area of a selected object. Click on the relation name that describes the object, and then click on this button. A dialog box will ask the user to enter the name of the new relation and the distance value. Then a new relation is computed, which contains the surrounding region of the selected relation, up to the given distance. In MLPQ the surrounding region of the objects is approximated by a high-degree polygon.

Example 13.3.7 To find the territorial waters of Hawaii, select the HI relation in the `usmap.txt` file and then click the ⊙ button. In the dialog box specify the distance 50. After another prompt specify the new relation name `HIbuffer`. It is possible to display the `HIbuffer` relation first and then on top of it the original `HI` relation to see the expansion in size.

S – This "similarity" button allows the users to search for similar image files. For this operation, the user must first open a new database by going to the *File* menu and selecting *New*. Then go to the *File* menu again, and select *Import File*, followed by *Import Line*. This will allow the user to load an image database (extension `.lin`) into the system. Select a relation from the image database and press the similarity button. The MLPQ system computes and displays the similarity of each relation in the database with respect to the selected relation, which is labeled as the *Prototype*. The similarity values are displayed in the relation list.

The last three buttons on the top of the tool bar are used for drawing lines, rectangles, and polygons, respectively.

Polygon – The "draw polygon" button is the last in the first row of the tool bar. Open a nonempty database (i.e., a database that already contains at least one relation). Click on the display grid on the right and press this button. The MLPQ system allows the user to draw a polygon in the display grid, with the left mouse button held down. Double-click to complete the drawing. After drawing a polygon, pressing the right button the user will be asked to enter a new relation name. The MLPQ system converts each drawing to a linear constraint database representation.

□ – This buttom draws a rectangle similar to the above button.

\ – This buttom draws a line similar to the two earlier buttons.

Example 13.3.8 The "draw polygon" button is easpecially useful for curvy figures. For instance, an oval can be drawn on the screen, and it would be approximated by MLPQ by a large number of high-degree convex polygons. This approximation would be practical for most applications that need to represent 2-dimensional curvy objects like circles, ovals, and parabolas.

Spatio-Temporal Data (Non-Moving): It is easy to extend the 2-dimensional geographic relations to simple spatio-temporal relations where the objects have an existence only during specific time intervals.

Example 13.3.9 The following describes a modified version of the park relation from Example 16.1.2. We assume that objects continue to exist unchanged unless it is explicitly stated that their temporal existence has expired at a certain time.

```
begin%MLPQ%
park(id,x,y,t):- id=1, x=10, y=4,                              t>=1980, t<=1986.
park(id,x,y,t):- id=2, x>=5, x<=9, x+y=15,                     t>=1995.
park(id,x,y,t):- id=2, x=9,  y>=3, y<=6,                       t>=1995.
park(id,x,y,t):- id=3, x>=2, x<=6, x+y<=9, y>=3, y<=7,         t>=1975, t<=1990.
park(id,x,y,t):- id=4, x=1,  y>=2, y<=11,                      t>=1974.
park(id,x,y,t):- id=4, x=12, y>=2, y<=11,                      t>=1974.
park(id,x,y,t):- id=4, y=2,  x>=1, x<=12,                      t>=1974.
park(id,x,y,t):- id=4, y=11, x>=1, x<=12,                      t>=1974.
park(id,x,y,t):- id=5, x>=3, y>=5, x-y<=1, x-y>=-5, x+y<=13, t>=1991.
end%MLPQ%
```

Suppose we would like to see how the park looked in 1986. For this we can enter the following SQL query.

VIEW NAME	park1986
SELECT	park.id, park.x, park.y
FROM	park
WHERE	park.t = 1986

This creates a new relation called `park1986`, which we can visualize by clicking on its name as usual. However, it is hard to see clearly all the objects because the fountain is shown as only a tiny dot on the screen. The road is also only a thin line, which may be hard to see on some computer screens. One way to solve this problem is to use from the tool bar the buffer operator, which we saw earlier.

Using the buffer operator with a distance of 0.2 units, we can create a new relation called `park1986b`. By clicking on this relation, we can visualize the park as it was in 1986 as shown below.

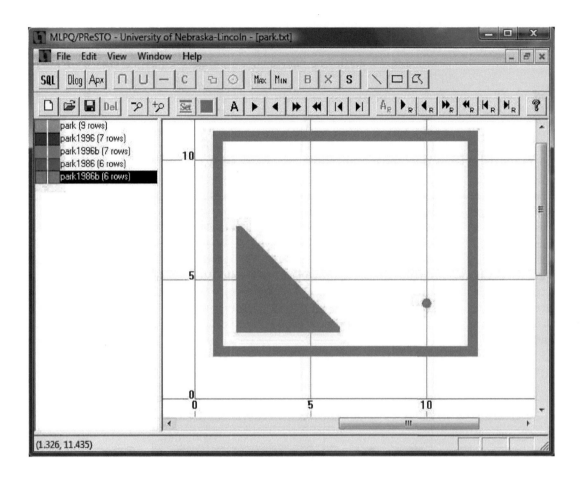

13.3.1 3D Geography

Turning now from 2-dimensional to 3-dimensional geography, let us consider the surface of the earth. One way of representing the surface of the earth is to approximate it by a sheet that is composed of triangles. This is called a *triangulated irregular network* or TIN. Figure 18.2 shows a triangulated irregular network of a mountain range. Chapter 18 describes ways of obtaining a triangulated irregular network from more basic data. In this chapter, we are only interested in representing TINs in MLPQ and querying them using simple database queries.

Each triangle has a flat surface in 3-dimensional space and can be represented by a linear equation of the latitude, the longitude, and the elevation variables. Let these be x, y, and z, respectively.

The projection of each TIN triangle onto the (x, y)-plane can be described by three linear constraints in only x and y. The complete specification of each TIN triangle requires only the linear equation of the plane the triangle lies in and the projection of the TIN triangle onto the (x, y)-plane.

Example 13.3.10 The following is an MLPQ input file that describes a TIN with thirteen triangles that represent a lake and the neighboring land area. In this example the elevation z is measured in millimeters.

```
begin%MLPQ%
tin(id,x,y,z) :- id=1, y>=0, -3x-y>=-15, 2x-y>=0,        600x-307.5y-z= -9915.
tin(id,x,y,z) :- id=2, -y>=-6, 3x+y>=15, -6x+5y>=-30,    390x-377.5y-z=-10965.
tin(id,x,y,z) :- id=3, y>=0, -3x-5y>=-60, 6x-5y>=30,       51x-95y-z=-12660.
tin(id,x,y,z) :- id=4, x>=0, -2x+y>=0, -4x-3y>=-30,      -132x+58y-z=- 9915.
tin(id,x,y,z) :- id=5, y>=6, -2x-5y>=-50, 4x+3y>=30,     390x+450y-z= -6000.
tin(id,x,y,z) :- id=6, 3x+5y>=60, -3x-y>=-60, x-y>=4,     45x-105y-z=-12780.
tin(id,x,y,z) :- id=7, 2x+5y>=50, 7x+5y<=100, 3x-5y>=-50, 378x+420y-z= -6300.
tin(id,x,y,z) :- id=8, 7x+5y>=100, -7x+y>=-64, x-y>=-8,  -259x-35y-z=-15400.
tin(id,x,y,z) :- id=9, -x+y>=-4, -2x-y>=-44, 7x-y>=64,     14x-74y-z=-12904.
tin(id,x,y,z) :- id=10, x>=0, -3x+5y>=50, -7x-5y>=-100,  567x+105y-z= -9450.
tin(id,x,y,z) :- id=11, -y>=-20, 7x+5y>=100, -x+y>=8,    3.5x-297.5y-z=-17500.
tin(id,x,y,z) :- id=12, -y>=-20, -2x+y>=-20, 2x+y>=44,     6x-78y-z=-13080.
tin(id,x,y,z) :- id=13, x>=-20,  2x-y>=20, 3x+y>=60,      54x-102y-z=-12600.
end%MLPQ%
```

Suppose we would like to find a contour map, that is, a map that shows which areas are at the same elevation range using a set of color bands. We can assign colors in the contour map as follows.

blue	$9000 - 10000$ mm
yellow	$10000 - 11000$ mm
green	$11000 - 12000$ mm
brown	$12000 - 13000$ mm
gray	$13000 - 14000$ mm

To find the contour map, we use a separate basic SQL query for each elevation range. For instance, the following SQL query finds the areas where the elevation is between 9000 and 10000 mm.

VIEW NAME	from9000to10000
SELECT	tin.id, tin.x, tin.y
FROM	tin
WHERE	tin.z $>=$ 9000, tin.z $<=$ 10000

When all the five SQL queries are computed, we adjust the colors of the ranges as shown in the above legend. Then we display the ranges by clicking on them, resulting in the following contour map.

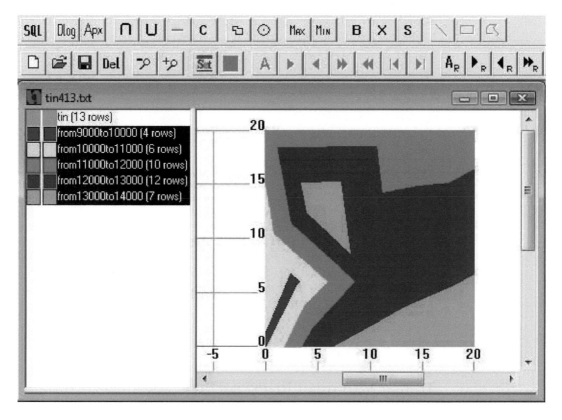

The MLPQ system provides two colorful buttons on the tool bar as a shortcut in generating contour maps. Since these buttons are rarely used, the MLPQ system needs the following type of input file to activate these functions:

```
begin %GIS%
    ⋮
end %GIS%
```

Note that the keyword `GIS`, in the first and last lines, and an identification number called *id*, as the first argument of each tuple, are required by the MLPQ system. Some of the visualization algorithms expect to see these keywords and do not work properly without them. The following two coloring buttons also need the above "GIS flag."

$\boxed{Set}$ – We can use this button to set the color ranges. After pressing this button a color set dialog box appears. We can add new ranges by pressing the $\boxed{Add}$ button on the right side of the color set dialog box. That brings up a new dialog box that allows the specification of the begining and the ending of a single range and the selection of a color from a color menu. Users can add, delete, or modify the color ranges.

$\boxed{\diamond}$ – After setting the color ranges of the relation and selecting the relation to be colored, pressing this button displays the relation according to the prescribed color bands.

Example 13.3.11 Figure 21.3 shows a color band map for the total precipitation in the continental United States in 1997.

We can similarly display in MLPQ as maps with color bands other data where the z stands not for elevation but for other spatially distributed measures, such as, precipitation or temperature.

13.4 Moving Objects Databases

Moving objects databases are increasingly important and frequent in many application areas. These applications often record or predict a piecewise linear approximation of the movement of objects. In this section we give some examples of handling moving objects using the MLPQ system.

The most natural extension of the geographic data to a constraint data is to have moving objects, whose shape is one or more moving polygons. We needed only linear inequalities in x and y to describe the shape of static polygonal objects. However, to describe moving polygonal objects, we now need linear inequalities in x, y, and t. The half-plane defined by such a linear inequality changes gradually as t changes.

Example 13.4.1 The habitat area of California gulls, a bird species usually found in the western United States, is a moving object described by a constraint table with 96 linear constraint tuples. Below we give as a sample the first three rows that define a triangular area whose lower side changes linearly over time from $t = 0$ to $t = 60$.

```
Gull(i,x,y,t):- i=0,      -85x              <= -28900,
                          -15x -18y -13t <= -10770,
                         +100x +18y       <=  41200,
                                        t >=      0,
                                        t <=     20.


Gull(i,x,y,t):- i=0,      -85x              <= -28900,
                          -15x -18y +19t <= -10130,
                         +100x +18y       <=  41200,
                                        t >=     21,
                                        t <=     40.


Gull(i,x,y,t):- i=0,      -85x              <= -28900,
                          -15x -18y -48t <= -12810,
                         +100x +18y       <=  41200,
                                        t >=     41,
                                        t <=     60.
```

Three-dimensional spatio-temporal relations are visualized in MLPQ using animations. For animating 3D spatio-temporal relations, MLPQ provides some the following operator from the tool bar.

$\boxed{\text{A}}$ – This is the **animation** button on the lower row of the tool bar. Clicking the animation button brings up a dialog box that allows the user to choose between either linear animation, which is the typical execution mode chosen by most users, or an exponential animation, which is used in special cases as explained later. Then another dialog box appears that asks the user to set up the animation parameters such as:

- *Start* – This is the start time (t_{begin}) of the animation.

- *Step* – This is the "step size" δ, which is the time granularity of the animation. In general, the smaller the step size, the smoother the movement of the objects will appear.

- *No. of steps* – From the number of steps, the system computes the end time (t_{end}) of the animation.

- *Speed* – The speed of the animation with 100 being a maximum and default speed. Most applications run best with this maximum speed. However, lowering the speed may be needed occasionally if the precise sequence of events needs to be observed and cannot be using the faster speed.

Next to the $\boxed{\text{A}}$ button are the following auxiliary animation buttons.

$\boxed{\triangleright}$ – The **play** button. The system will automatically animate from the start time to the end time, using the animation parameters for the selected relation(s).

$\boxed{\triangleright}$ – The **play back** button. The system will automatically animate from the end time to the start time, using the animation parameters for the selected relation(s).

$\boxed{\gg}$ – The **next step** button. The system will show the snapshot of the next time point in the animation.

$\boxed{\ll}$ – The **previous step** button. The system will show the snapshot of the previous time point in the animation.

$\boxed{\triangleleft}$ – The **goto start** button. The system will reset the animation back to the start time, that is, the first snapshot.

$\boxed{\triangleright|}$ – The **goto end** button. The system will set the animation to the end time, that is, the last snapshot.

Example 13.4.2 We used the MLPQ animation button to visualize the changes in the habitat areas of the California gull. We selected the linear animation mode and the parameters zero for start, which represented the beginning of 1970, one for step size, which represented four months, and sixty for the number of steps, making the ending time correspond to the end of 1990. Figure 21.12 shows two instances of the animation display of the habitat areas of the California Gull bird species. The left area corresponds to the beginning and the right area to the ending of the animation.

As expected, for the linear animation, the MLPQ system displays the moving object at times $t_{\text{begin}} + i\delta$ for $i \geq 0$ until $t_{\text{begin}} + i\delta > t_{\text{end}}$. For the exponential animation, MLPQ displays the moving object at times t_{begin} and $t_{\text{begin}} + 2^i\delta$ until $t_{\text{begin}} + 2^i\delta > t_{\text{end}}$. We give next an example where the exponential animation is the preferred option.

Example 13.4.3 Suppose several bacterial colonies grow in a Petri dish medium. We approximate the shape of the colonies with polygons. The growth of each bacterial colony can be approximated by the sides of the polygons growing outward. For a good approximation we would need exponential outward growth of the sides, but in MLPQ we have only linear constraints. However, when choosing an exponential animation mode, the bacterial colonies appear to grow exponentially during the animation. Two snapshots of the animation are shown on the next page.

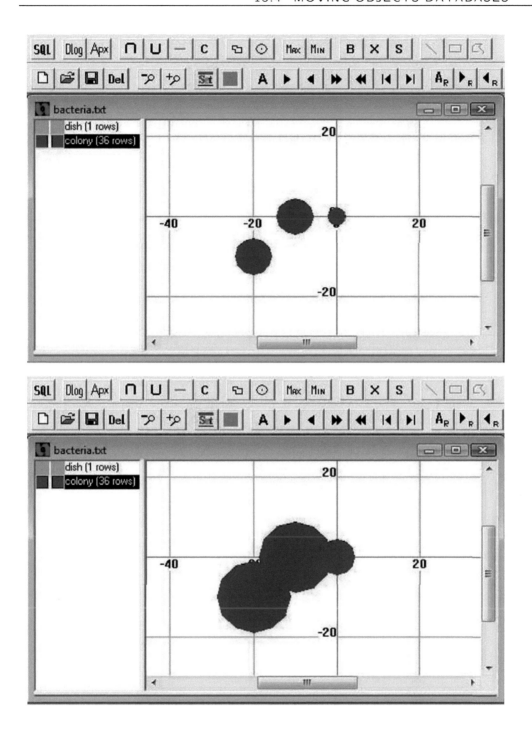

Example 13.4.4 Suppose that the lake in Example 13.3.10 is normally at 10 meters, that is, at 10,000 millimeters. Suppose also that during a flood the water level of the lake rises a total of two meters with the rate of one millimeter per minute. Which areas of the land will be flooded and at what time?

Let us assume for convenience that the flood starts at $t = 10000$ minutes. Then at $t = 10000$ the lake covers only the blue area in the contour map of Example 13.3.10, but at $t = 12000$, the lake also covers the yellow and the green areas too.

We would like to animate the flood as it rises gradually over the yellow and green regions. Such an animation conveys more information than a contour map. For example, it may reveal the order in which the water may flood some houses, which are hence in immediate danger and need to be evacuated in that order.

It is easy to modify the *tin* relation of Example 13.3.10 as shown on the next page. The modification consists in the following. First, we record the entire area in a *land* relation. Second we modify the *tin* relation into a *lake* relation by changing the variable z to t and changing the linear equality constraint into a $<=$ constraint. The latter modification is warranted because any tin elment becomes a part of the lake if its height is less than or equal to t. For example, in the first tin element, the original constraint was $600x - 307.5y - z = -9915$, which is equivalent to:

$$600x - 307.5y - 9915 = z$$

Being at or below z means

$$600x - 307.5y - 9915 <= z$$

which by changing variables becomes

$$600x - 307.5y - 9915 <= t.$$

The last inequality can be rewritten as

$$600x - 307.5y - t <= -9915$$

which is one we used in the first *lake* constraint tuple. We also bounded the time variable t to be between $10,000$ and $12,000$. Finally, weadded a couple of houses as an additional detail.

We used the MLPQ animation function $\boxed{A}$ and ran it in a non-exponential animation mode with the following parameters: the start was 10000, the step size was 1, and the number of steps was 2000.

```
begin%MLPQ%
land(id,x,y)  :-id=0, x>=0, x<=20, y>=0, y<=20.

lake(id,x,y,t):-id=1, y>=0, -3x-y>=-15, 2x-y>=0,      600x-307.5y-t<= -9915,
                                                       t>=10000, t<= 12000.

lake(id,x,y,t):-id=2, -y>=-6, 3x+y>=15, -6x+5y>=-30,  390x-377.5y-t<=-10965,
                                                       t>=10000, t<= 12000.

lake(id,x,y,t):-id=3, y>=0, -3x-5y>=-60, 6x-5y>=30,    51x-95y-t<=-12660,
                                                       t>=10000, t<= 12000.

lake(id,x,y,t):-id=4, x>=0, -2x+y>=0, -4x-3y>=-30,    -132x+58y-t<=- 9915,
                                                       t>=10000, t<= 12000.

lake(id,x,y,t):-id=5, y>=6, -2x-5y>=-50, 4x+3y>=30,   390x+450y-t<= -6000,
                                                       t>=10000, t<= 12000.

lake(id,x,y,t):-id=6, 3x+5y>=60, -3x-y>=-60, x-y>=4,   45x-105y-t<=-12780,
                                                       t>=10000, t<= 12000.

lake(id,x,y,t):-id=7, 2x+5y>=50, 7x+5y<=100, 3x-5y>=-50, 378x+420y-t<= -6300,
                                                       t>=10000, t<= 12000.

lake(id,x,y,t):-id=8, 7x+5y>=100, -7x+y>=-64, x-y>=-8, -259x-35y-t<=-15400,
                                                       t>=10000, t<= 12000.

lake(id,x,y,t):-id=9, -x+y>=-4, -2x-y>=-44, 7x-y>=64,   14x-74y-t<=-12904,
                                                       t>=10000, t<= 12000.

lake(id,x,y,t):-id=10, x>=0, -3x+5y>=50, -7x-5y>=-100, 567x+105y-t<= -9450,
                                                       t>=10000, t<= 12000.

lake(id,x,y,t):-id=11, -y>=-20, 7x+5y>=100, -x+y>=8, 3.5x-297.5y-t<=-17500,
                                                       t>=10000, t<= 12000.

lake(id,x,y,t):-id=12, -y>=-20, -2x+y>=-20, 2x+y>=44,    6x-78y-t<=-13080,
                                                       t>=10000, t<= 12000.

lake(id,x,y,t):-id=13, x>=-20,  2x-y>=20, 3x+y>=60,     54x-102y-t<=-12600,
                                                       t>=10000, t<= 12000.

house(id,x,y) :-id=1, x>=17, x<=18, y>=17, y<=18.
house(id,x,y) :-id=2, x>= 5, x<= 6, y>=13, y<=14.
end%MLPQ%
```

The flood is shown below at $t = 11500$ (top) and at $t = 12000$ (bottom).

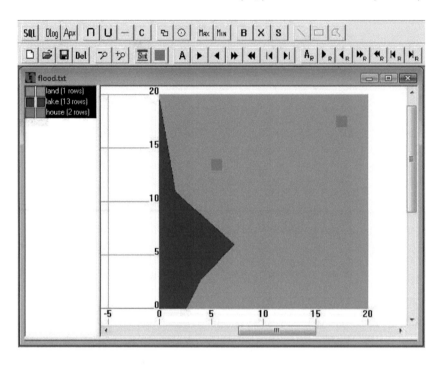

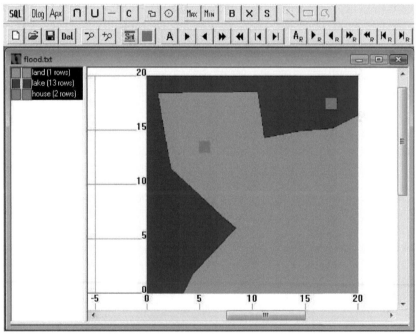

The animation shows that the house which is initially farther from the lake is going to be flooded, while the house that is closer to the lake is not affected by the flood. The animation also reveals that for a long time there is only a gradual expansion of the lake and then the expansion of the lake suddenly speeds up in the last quater time of the flood. The animation suggests that the owner of the house which is farther from the lake may have a false sense of security during most of the flood and then may have too little time to escape. That is an interesting additional information that the contour map does not show.

We often have only incomplete information about the initial location and the trajectory of moving objects. As the next example shows, we can represent and reason about incomplete information using MLPQ.

Example 13.4.5 Consider an airspace that ranges from -3000 to 3000 miles along both the x-axis and the y-axis. The first plane departs from some location between 100 and 200 miles east and between 50 and 150 miles south of location $(0,0)$, and the second plane departs from some location between 900 and 1000 miles west and between 690 and 750 miles north of $(0,0)$.

The first plane flies east between 490 and 580 miles and north between 400 and 440 miles per hour for four hours. The second plane flies west between 900 and 1000 miles and north between 0 and 20 miles per hour for four hours. The airspace, the departure locations, and the speed of the two planes can be represented by the following MLPQ input file:

```
begin%MLPQ%
Air(id,x,y)   :- id=0, x >= -3000, x <=  3000, y >= -3000, y <= 3000.
Depart(id,x,y):- id=1, x >=   100, x <=   200, y >=  -150, y <=  -50.
Depart(id,x,y):- id=2, x >= -1000, x <=  -900, y >=   690, y <=  750.

Speed(id,x,y,t):-id=1, x-490t>=0, x-580t<=0, y-400t>=0, y-440t<=0, t>=0, t<=4.
Speed(id,x,y,t):-id=2, x-900t>=0, x-1000t<=0, y>=0,      y- 20t<=0, t>=0, t<=4.
end%MLPQ%
```

The following SQL query finds the possible flight trajectories of the two planes.

VIEW NAME	Fly(id,x,y,t)
SELECT	S.id, S2.x, S2.y, S.t
FROM	Depart AS D, Speed AS S, Air AS S2
WHERE	D.id = S.id,
	D.x + S.x - S2.x = 0,
	D.y + S.y - S2.y = 0

The next SQL query finds when the two planes could meet at the same location:

VIEW NAME	Meet(id1,id2,t)
SELECT	F1.id, F2.id, F1.t
FROM	Fly AS F1, Fly AS F2
WHERE	F1.id = 1, F2.id =2,
	F1.x = F2.x,
	F1.y = F2.y,
	F1.t = F2.t

The existence of an intersection can be also identified by an animation of the flights of the two planes. That is left as an exercise.

13.4.1   Color Change during Animation

MLPQ allows the color of the objects to change during an animation. Note that the relation list has two color boxes to the left of each relation. The left color is the color of the relation at the start of the animation, and the right color is the color at the end of the animation. These colors can be changed by right-clicking on the color boxes. The color changes gradually during the animation from the start color to the end color. For example, in the `usmap.txt` file, the following changes the color of Alaska from green to white.

 AK

For the color representation, MLPQ uses the RGB format. In that format each color is represented with three basic colors: red, green, and blue. Each color is composed of a shade of these three colors, where the shade ranges from 0 to 255. For example, a pure red color would be represented as $(255, 0, 0)$. A pure green color would be $(0, 255, 0)$. A black color is $(0, 0, 0)$, and a medium gray color would be $(128, 128, 128)$.

Suppose the start color is represented as (r_0, g_0, b_0) and the end color after n time steps is represented as (r_n, g_n, b_n). MLPQ implements a linear change in time for each basic color. That is, for the ith time step the display color will be

$$(r_0 + \frac{i(r_n - r_0)}{n}, g_0 + \frac{i(g_n - g_0)}{n}, b_0 + \frac{i(b_n - b_0)}{n})$$

Example 13.4.6 Shape and color change can be combined in an animation that shows a person laughing. The initial and the final face of the laughing person is shown in the pictures below.

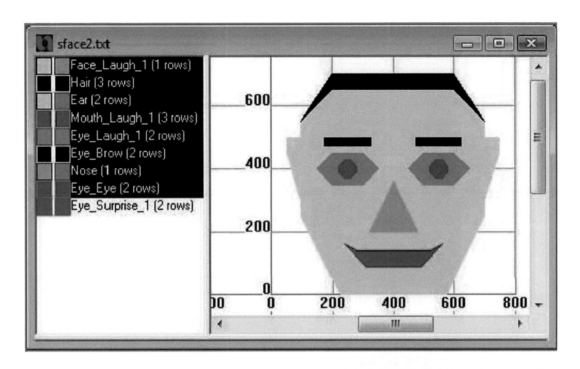

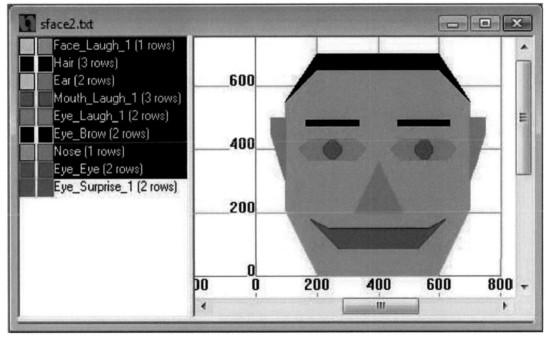

13.4.2   Periodic Parametric Rectangles

MLPQ/PReSTO is an extension of the MLPQ system specially designed for periodic parametric rectangles. The name PReSTO, is short for *parametric rectangle spatio-temporal objects*. The MLPQ/PReSTO system allows relational algebra queries and several special tool bar functions that we have not seen before. In the MLPQ/PReSTO system the input files have the following structure:

> begin %STDB%
> $\quad r_1$
> $\quad r_2$
> $\quad \vdots$
> $\quad r_n$
> end %STDB%

where each r_i is a rule or a 2-dimensional periodic parametric rectangle. In particular, MLPQ/PReSTO allows 2-dimensional periodic parametric rectangles with the general form:

$$R = (id,\ [a_1t + b_1,\ c_1t + d_1],\ [a_2t + b_2,\ c_2t + d_2],\ [from,\ to]_{m,n})$$

where $id, a_1, b_1, c_1, d_1, a_2, b_2, c_2, d_2, from, to, m$, and n are constants as described in Chapter 7, to be augmented with regular relational attributes $z_1, \ldots, z_k$. The combined tuple can be expressed in an MLPQ/PReSTO input file with the following syntax:

$$
\begin{aligned}
R(z_1, \ldots, z_k) \quad :\!-\quad & i = id, \\
& x1 - a_1t = b_1, \\
& x2 - c_1t = d_1, \\
& y1 - a_2t = b_2, \\
& y2 - c_2t = d_2, \\
& t >= from, \\
& t <= to, \\
& p = m, \\
& s = n, \\
& z_1 = e_1, \\
& \quad \vdots \\
& z_k = e_k.
\end{aligned}
$$

where the period p and the end time s are both -1 for nonperiodic parametric rectangles. Note that the attributes i, $x1$, $y1$, $x2$, $y2$, t, p, and s are *default attributes* and must always occur in an MLPQ/PReSTO relation. The default attributes are not listed all the time in the argument list of MLPQ/PReSTO relations, but they are assumed to belong there. This convention saves much unnecessary typing. Each z_i can be any variable string. The nondefault attributes must always be listed in the argument list of MLPQ/PReSTO relations. There may also be no nondefault attributes. In that case the argument list is empty.

Example 13.4.7 Suppose that the parametric rectangles

$$Ship = (1, \ [t+20, \ t+30], \ [20, \ 30], \ [0, \ 25])$$

and

$$Torpedo = (1, \ [45, \ 48], \ [-t+45, \ -t+51], \ [0, \ 25])$$

represent a ship and a torpedo that is fired toward the ship. These can be represented in MLPQ/PReSTO as follows:

```
Ship() :-      i=1,
               x1 - t = 20,
               x2 - t = 30,
               y1 = 20,
               y2 = 30,
               t >= 0,
               t <= 25,
               p = -1,
               s = -1.

Torpedo() :-   i=1,
               x1 = 45,
               x2 = 48,
               y1 + t = 45,
               y2 + t = 51,
               t >= 0,
               t <= 25,
               p = -1,
               s = -1.
```

The next example uses a nondefault attribute.

Example 13.4.8 In Example 7.7.6, the $Clouds(X, Y, T, humidity)$ relation used *humidity* as a nondefault attribute. The following could be a valid parametric rectangle of this relation in MLPQ/PReSTO:

```
Clouds(h) :- i=1,
              x1 - t = 105,
              x2 - t = 111,
              y1 - 0.5t = 200,
              y2 - 0.6t = 205,
              t >= 0,
              t <= 300,
              p = -1,
              s = -1,
              h = 90.

Clouds(h) :- i=1,
              x1 - t = 230,
              x2 - t = 420,
              y1 - 2t = 10,
              y2 - 3t = 50,
              t >= 100,
              t <= 500,
              p = -1,
              s = -1,
              h = 80.
```

This would mean that the humidity is always 90, respectively 80, percent in the area of the 2-dimensional parametric rectangle defined by the default attributes in the first and second tuples.

In the input file queries can also be defined. Currently, MLPQ/PReSTO implements a subset of relational algebra queries that are written in a rule style. The projection operation is allowed on any set of the nondefault attributes. The syntax of the projection operation is a Datalog rule, where the attributes in the defined relation list only the projected regular attributes.

Example 13.4.9 We can find the area of the $Clouds(X, Y, T, humidity)$ relation by the following MLPQ/PReSTO query:

```
Clouds_Area() :- Clouds(h).
```

The selection operation is allowed on the regular attributes and the logical level attributes x, y, and t with some minor restrictions discussed below. The selection operation is indicated by a $ symbol followed by a parenthesized list of conditions.

Example 13.4.10 We can find the cloud areas with a humidity above 75 percent between times 0 and 200 by the following MLPQ/PReSTO query:

```
Clouds75(h) :- $(h >= 75, t >= 0, t <= 200) Clouds(h).
```

The intersection operation has the symbol * in PReSTO input files. The operand relations must both be 2-dimensional parametric rectangles.

Example 13.4.11 Let us find using the relations in Example 13.4.7 whether the torpedo hits the ship:

```
Hit() :- Ship() * Torpedo().
```

Example 13.4.12 Let *Clouds* be a set of moving and changing cloud areas, and for each of the continental United States let there be a separate relation, that is, *California*, *Oregon*, *Washington*, etc. We can use the **Animation** icon to display the movement of the clouds over the states. First we select all the states by clicking on them. Then we select *Clouds* and press the **Animate** icon. Figure 13.2 shows two snapshots of the animation.

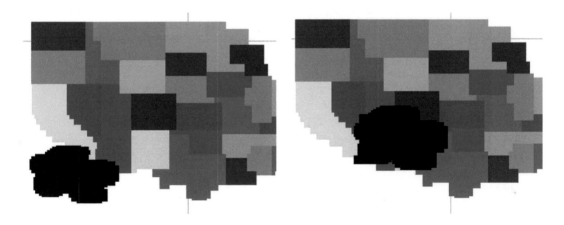

Figure 13.2: Clouds at $t = 25$ (left) and $t = 182$ (right).

Next we consider an example with periodic motion.

Example 13.4.13 The file `comet3.txt` describes all the planets in the solar system and three different comets. The elliptical movement of the planets is approximated by linear motions along a set of line segments. On each line segment the speed of the planets may change. For example, the movement of Mercury is represented as follows.

```
begin%STDB%
Mercury() :- i = 1,  x1 + 0.4775 t = 8.0000,   y1 - 1.4695 t = -2.0000,
                     x2 + 0.4775 t = 12.0000,  y2 - 1.4695 t = 2.0000,
                     t>= 0, t < 4, p = 40, s=-1.
Mercury() :- i = 2,  x1 + 1.2500 t = 11.0902,  y1 - 0.9082 t = 0.2451,
                     x2 + 1.2500 t = 15.0902,  y2 - 0.9082 t = 4.2451,
                     t>= 4, t < 8, p = 40, s=-1.
Mercury() :- i = 3,  x1 + 1.5451 t = 13.4508,  y1 - 0.0000 t = 7.5106,
                     x2 + 1.5451 t = 17.4508,  y2 - 0.0000 t = 11.5106,
                     t>= 8, t < 12, p = 40, s=-1.
Mercury() :- i = 4,  x1 + 1.2500 t = 9.9098,   y1 + 0.9082 t = 18.4087,
                     x2 + 1.2500 t = 13.9098,  y2 + 0.9082 t = 22.4087,
                     t>= 12, t < 16, p = 40, s=-1.
Mercury() :- i = 5,  x1 + 0.4775 t = -2.4508,  y1 + 1.4695 t = 27.3893,
                     x2 + 0.4775 t = 1.5492,   y2 + 1.4695 t = 31.3893,
                     t>= 16, t < 20, p = 40, s=-1.
Mercury() :- i = 6,  x1 - 0.4775 t = -21.5491, y1 + 1.4695 t = 27.3893,
                     x2 - 0.4775 t = -17.5491, y2 + 1.4695 t = 31.3893,
                     t>= 20, t < 24, p = 40, s=-1.
Mercury() :- i = 7,  x1 - 1.2500 t = -40.0902, y1 + 0.9082 t = 13.9184,
                     x2 - 1.2500 t = -36.0902, y2 + 0.9082 t = 17.9184,
                     t>= 24, t < 28, p = 40, s=-1.
Mercury() :- i = 8,  x1 - 1.5451 t = -48.3525, y1 - 0.0000 t = -11.5106,
                     x2 - 1.5451 t = -44.3525, y2 - 0.0000 t = -7.5106,
                     t>= 28, t < 32, p = 40, s=-1.
Mercury() :- i = 9,  x1 - 1.2500 t = -38.9098, y1 - 0.9082 t = -40.5723,
                     x2 - 1.2500 t = -34.9098, y2 - 0.9082 t = -36.5723,
                     t>= 32, t < 36, p = 40, s=-1.
Mercury() :- i =10,  x1 - 0.4775 t = -11.0983, y1 - 1.4695 t = -60.7785,
                     x2 - 0.4775 t =  -7.0983, y2 - 1.4695 t = -56.7785,
                     t>= 36, t < 40, p = 40, s=-1.
end%STDB%
```

The MLPQ/PReSTO subsystem allows some extra tool bar operators that are not available in the plain MLPQ system. These operators include the following.

$\boxed{\backslash}$ – This operator takes the set **difference** of two parametric rectangles. Select two relations (by clicking on them) and press the difference button. The MLPQ/PReSTO system returns a parametric rectangles relation that is equivalent to the relation clicked first minus the relation clicked second.

Example 13.4.14 The `cloudmap.txt` file describes the cloud cover and the western United States. We can find the sunny parts of California by selecting first the *California* and then the *Clouds* relations. The new relation, which we may name *Sunny_CA*, is a relation that is also composed of a set of parametric rectanges. Animating this relation shows the changing parts of California that are currently sunny.

$\boxed{\text{X}}$ – This button is the **collide** operator. The collide operator requires that the objects have masses. Select two nonperiodic relations (by clicking on them) and press the collide button. The two relations need to have an extra attibute called mass, which has to follow t in the order of the attributes. The MLPQ/PReSTO system returns a parametric rectangles relation that expresses the motion of the objects before and after collision.

Example 13.4.15 The following MLPQ/PReSTO database describes a passenger car with mass 5 and a van with mass 10.

```
begin%STDB%
Car(m):-i=1, x1-t=10, x2-t=15, y1=33, y2=38, t>=0, t<=40, p=-1, s=-1, m=5.
Van(m):-i=1, x1-t=6, x2-t=13, y1-t=10, y2-t=17, t>=0, t<=40, p=-1, s=-1, m=10.
end%STDB%
```

If we animate the car and the van, the van seems to fly over the car, which is impossible. Using the $\boxed{\text{X}}$ button, we can create a new relation called *Collide*, which stores the trajectory of the car and the van before and after the collision. Animating simultaneously all of the three relations shows the difference between the trajectory of the car and the van with and without the collision.

$\boxed{\text{B}}$ – This button is the **block** operator. Select two nonperiodic relations (by clicking on them) and press the $\boxed{\text{B}}$ button. A dialog box pops up that asks for a time instance t_k the name of the relation to be created. The MLPQ/PReSTO block operator returns the points of the first relation at time instance t_k that are not blocked by the second relation at any time before t_k.

Example 13.4.16 Suppose that relation *Tornado* represents the movement of a tornado and relation *Mountain* represents the location of a tall mountain range that can stop the tornado. Find the trajectory of the tornado at time $t = 20$.

This can be answered by clicking on *Tornado* and then *Mountain*. A dialog box pops up and asks for a time instance. We enter **20** and the name of the new relation. The result of the query, evaluated in the MLPQ/PReSTO system, is shown in Figure 13.3 superimposed on the map of the continental United States, which covers the *Mountain* relation. We give further examples of the use of PReSTO and the block operator in Chapter 19.

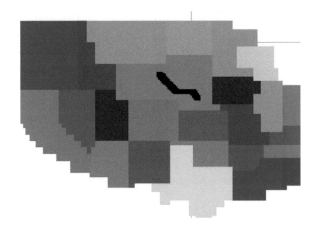

Figure 13.3: Trajectory of a tornado.

13.5   Topological Databases

Topological information is a high-level view of the spatial data. For instance, recognizing that two land areas are neighbors is a higher-level view than merely giving the exact shape and location of the two land areas. The MLPQ system can also derive some topological information from the input constraint database as shown in the next example.

Example 13.5.1 Consider the land areas in the following figure.

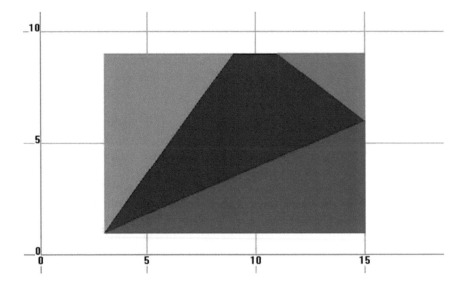

These land areas can be represented by the following input file.

```
begin%MLPQ%
land(id,x,y) :- id = 1, x >=  3, y <= 9, 4x-3y <= 9.
land(id,x,y) :- id = 2,          y <= 9, 4x-3y >= 9, 3x+4y <= 69, 5x-12y <= 3.
land(id,x,y) :- id = 3, x <= 15, y <= 9,             3x+4y >= 69.
land(id,x,y) :- id = 4, x <= 15, y >= 1,                          5x-12y >= 3.
end%MLPQ%
```

To find the identification numbers of each pair of land areas that touch each other on at least one point, we can use the following SQL query.

VIEW NAME	Touch(A,B)
SELECT	l1.id, l2.id
FROM	land AS l1, land AS l2
WHERE	l1.x = l2.x, l1.y = l2.y, l1.id < l2.id

This query returns five pairs of land areas that touch each other, namely the following.

Touch

A	B
1	2
1	4
2	3
2	4
3	4

The first and the fourth land areas, and similarly the third and the fourth land areas, touch on a single point. Some readers would say these land areas are not neighbors because they do not share a line boundary. Note that land areas that share two points also share a line boundary normally. Hence to find the neighbors we can modify the above query to return those pairs of land areas that share at least two points as follows.

VIEW NAME	Neighbor(A,B)
SELECT	l1.id, l2.id
FROM	land AS l1, land AS l2, land AS l3, land AS l4
WHERE	l1.x = l2.x, l1.y = l2.y, l1.id < l2.id,
	l1.id = l3.id, l2.id = l4.id,
	l3.x = l4.x, l3.y = l4.y, l1.y < l3.y

Now the above modified query returns the following answer.

Neighbor

A	B
1	2
2	3
2	4

Instead of finding too many pairs, the above queries may return too few pairs for some input databases because of the imprecise representation of the land areas and the possible round off errors during some computations. A practical solution in these cases is to extend with some small distance the size of each land area using the buffer operator. This modification guarantees that the queries find all the needed pairs, although they may find some extra pairs too. However, such an over-approximation is still useful in many applications.

Example 13.5.2 Suppose that the owner of land area 4 applies for a building permit. Suppose also that the law requires a notification of all the "neighbors" of land area 4, in order that they may register any objections to the building plan. In this case, even if notifications are sent to the owners of land areas 1 and 3, there is no harm done. In fact, the owners of land areas 1 and 3 may have some reasonable concerns about the building plans of 4. Hence their concerns should be considered as the law likely intended.

In the next example the topological concept of connectivity plays an important role.

Example 13.5.3 In the screen shot below, a person is traveling in a car (brown square) eastward on an east-west highway (blue line) looking for some hotel (small red rectangles) to stay for the night. Being tired and sleepy, the person would like to find the "nearest hotel."

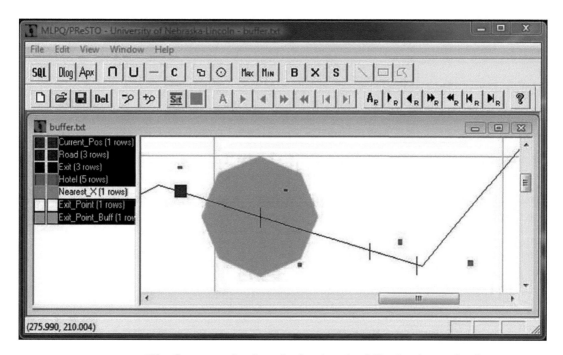

The figure can be described using the following input database:

```
begin%MLPQ%
/* The current position of the car. */
Current_Pos(id,x,y) :- id=1, x>= 172, x<=180, y>=172, y <= 180.

/* Three road segments of Highway 80 */
Road(id, x, y) :- id = 80, x >=  29, x <= 161,  -65x + 132y =  13295.
Road(id, x, y) :- id = 80, x >= 161, x <= 344,   54x + 183y =  41634.
Road(id, x, y) :- id = 80, x >= 344, x <= 484, -164x + 140y = -38776.


/* Three exits from the highway */
Exit(id, x, y) :- id = 409, x = 231, y >= 152.344, y <= 165.344.
Exit(id, x, y) :- id = 410, x = 307, y >= 130.918, y <= 140.918.
Exit(id, x, y) :- id = 411, x = 340, y >= 120.18,  y <= 132.18.

/* Five hotels near the highway */
Hotel(id, x, y):- id = 1, x >= 174,   x <= 177,   y >= 191.5, y <= 192.5.
Hotel(id, x, y):- id = 1, x >= 248.2, x <= 250.2, y >= 176.3, y <= 177.3.
Hotel(id, x, y):- id = 1, x >= 258,   x <= 260,   y >= 126.1, y <= 128.1.
Hotel(id, x, y):- id = 1, x >= 327.5, x <= 329.5, y >= 140.7, y <= 143.7.
Hotel(id, x, y):- id = 1, x >= 376.5, x <= 379.5, y >= 126.7, y <= 129.7.
end%MLPQ%
```

At first, this looks like a simple problem of finding the hotel with the smallest Euclidean distance. The hotel with the smallest Euclidean distance is just a short distance north of the current position of the car. However, it not topologically feasible because the car cannot just fly over the westbound lane of the highway and into the hotel. The car has to find first one of the exits (vertical line segments). Obviously, the driver would like to find the nearst exit and look for something around there. The nearest exit has the smallest x value, which can be found by the following query.

VIEW NAME	Nearest_X(x)
SELECT	min(E.x)
FROM	Current_Pos AS C, Road AS R, Exit AS E
WHERE	E.x = R2.x, E.y = R2.y,
	C.x - E.x <= 0

Hence the nearest exit point is the following.

VIEW NAME	Exit_Point(id,x,y)
SELECT	R.id, R.x, R.y
FROM	Road AS R, Nearest_X AS N
WHERE	N.x = R.x

It is from this exit point that we have to search for the nearest hotel. Hence we enlarge the exit point using the $\boxed{\odot}$ operator with a distance of 40 to find the relation *Exit_Point_Buffer*, which is shown in the screen shot as the green octagon. The octagon approximates a circle with radius 40 around the exit point. It requires only linear constraints, whereas a circle would require a quadratic polynomial constraint to represent. Finally, we click on relations *Hotel* and *Exit_Point_Buffer* and call the tool bar operator $\boxed{\cap}$ to find the hotels that are within the buffer area. Since we find exactly one hotel, we can assume that it is the hotel that is the shortest driving distance away from the current position of the car. In those cases where several hotels area found, the buffer operation may be repeated with a smaller distance value until only one hotel is left.

The above solution used practical observations (on an east-west highway the exits can be ordered according to their x-axis values), approximations (an octagon instead of a circle), and reasonable assumptions (in general, it does not lead to a better solution to go to the next exit and search for a hotel there). Hence this problem has the flavor of many real applications. Amazingly, a linear constraint database system found a solution that would satisfy most pragmatic travelers, even though the problem seemed to require quadratic polynomial constraints for the Euclidean distance and the representation of a circular buffer area.

13.6 Recursive Queries

This section looks at the recursive queries that are available in the MLPQ system. Since many textbooks simply skip the discussion of recursive algorithms, the use of recursion may need some extra explanation and motivation. Hence Section 13.6.1 first describes in general recursively defined concepts that are related to geographic data. Then Section 13.6.2 applies recursive SQL queries to process the recursively defiend concepts. For those who may prefer Datalog queries to recursive SQL queries, Section 13.6.3 gives a brief introduction of MLPQ Datalog queries and their applications.

13.6.1 Recursively Defined Concepts

Many advanced applications need to deal with recursively defined concepts. Below we mention only a few application areas.

Drought: Droughts cause billions of dollars damage each year world wide. Predicting where droughts may arise is one step in their prevention or mitigation. How can we find the areas that are under a drought condition? Obviously, the amount of precipitation and the drought in an area are closely tied together. However, one cannot say that anywhere is a drought where there is currently, for at least one week, low or no precipitation because even if there is currently low or no precipitation, the area may have stored enough groundwater to avoid a drought. Therefore, any definition of drought has to consider the amount of ground water at an area.

The problem is that it is not feasible to measure the ground water level at every location. Since we have only the precipitation measurements, we have to estimate the ground water level indirectly from the earlier precipitation. Hence we have to look at the data from the previous week. If there was plenty of precipitation, then the ground was soaked with water, and we can assume that some of it is still preserved as groundwater for the current week.

But what happens if last week was just a week where the precipitation was about the same that we would expect the area to lose due to evaporation? In that case, we can expect the ground water level to have remained unchanged last week. Hence the data from last week did not help us to decide whether there is enough ground water this week to avoid a drought condition in spite of a low or no precipitation this week.

Therefore, it becomes necessary to look at what happened two weeks ago. For if it was a drought two weeks ago, and last week the precipitation only equaled the evaporation, then there is clearly a drought now too. Conversely, if there was plenty of precipitation two weeks ago, then enough ground water was stored at that time to avoid a drought this week, although this week there is little or no precipitation and last week the amount of precipitation only equaled the evaporation.

Now what happens if two weeks ago too, the precipitation only equaled the evaporation. Then, clearly, we have to consider also the amount of precipitation that the area received three weeks ago. Obviously, this process of looking increasingly further back in time is a recursive process. The good news is that we need to keep this recursive process going back in time only on those areas that repeatedly receive only an amount of precipitation that is equal to the evaporation. Clearly, it is unlikely that in an area week after week, and month after month, the precipitation and the evaporation will exactly be in balance. Therefore, after looking back in time for a reasonable number of weeks, the drought status of only a few small spots of land may remain uncertain.

Epidemics: With the modern travel and transportation methods, epidemics may spread fast over the whole world. Hence the early identification and containment of epidemics close to their source is an important and well-researched topic. Epidemics behave similarly to droughts. While for drought low precipitation was an idicator of occurrence, for epidemics the number of already known disease carriers serves as an indicator. The disease carriers may be either human or various animals. For example, for the West Nile Virus disease, which infects both animals and humans, the carriers that are usually considered are: wild birds, chickens, horses, and mosquitos. Each of these indicators is useful to some extent, but the best predictions are achieved when they are considered together. However, when they are considered together, they need to be given appropriate relative weights. For example, an infection of a dozen horses is more serious than the infection of a dozen mosquitos.

Now suppose that we arrive at some aggregate indicator value. Then an area may be said to have an epidemic if the aggregate indicator for the current week is a high value above some threshold. If it is a medium value, then it is in itself not enough to declare an epidemic emergency. However, if there was an epidemic last week, then there may be still be a latent epidemic in the area warranting caution, and it is officially considered to be still an epidemic. The reason is that many infected humans and animals only transmit the disease with a time delay.

It is easy to see that if last week there was only a medium value of the aggregate indicator, then we need to consider the situation two weeks ago. Again this process leads to a recursion. However, we need to look further and further back in time only in those areas where the number of new infections (given by the aggregate indicator value) is about the same as the number of expected cured persons. Therefore, like in the case of the drought, the recursive process of searching back in time can end after a reasonable number of weeks.

Pollution: There are many dangerous substances that cause serious environmental pollution and endanger human health and life. Fortunately, many of the environmental pollutants naturally degrade over time, enabling the return of the normal animal and plant life. Obviously, the current amount of accumulated pollution determines whether an area is safe or polluted and dangerous for humans.

To predict where pollution may arise or persist in the future, we can take as an indicator some measure or estimate of the amount of new pollutants released each year into the environment. We consider yearly data instead of weekly data because pollution conditions change slower than drought conditions.

Like in the previous cases, if the indicator for the current year is above a threshold, then there is a pollution. For example, that may happen if there is an oil spill this year. However, if an area receives no significant pollution this year, then it may still be polluted if it was considered polluted, that is, above the threshold, last year, and it received about the same amount of new pollution that it was able to degrade. Hence we only have to decide whether it was polluted last year. However, that requires in this case one to look back at the indicator values from two years ago. Obviously, like in the case of drought and epidemics, this leads to a recursive process. This recursive process can again stop at some point because no area can be expected to always receive just enough pollution that it can degrade or eliminate.

It is possible to generalize from the above examples as follows.

Definition 13.6.1 Let relation $M(x, y, t, m)$ represent that for property P some indicator at location (x, y) at time unit t measured m. The relation $P(x, y, t)$ is recursively defined as follows:

1. $P(x, y, t)$ if $M(x, y, t, m)$ and $m \geq k$ or

2. $P(x, y, t)$ if $P(x, y, t-1)$ and $M(x, y, t-1, m)$ and $k_1 \leq m < k$.

Intuitively, relation $P(x, y, t)$ represents that property P is present according to the indicator at location (x, y) at time unit t. The k is the threshold value above which property P is present because of events during the current time unit. The threshold k_1 represents the amount of property P that can be naturally degraded within one time unit.

Both the time unit and the threshold values have to be chosen carefully by the scientists who study the property in question. However, once the proper values are established, all of the various scientists can take advantage of a general algorithmic solution to the above problem. In fact, we develop below such an algorithmic solution based on the MLPQ system.

First, let us define the following relations.

$$A(x, y, t) \quad \text{if} \quad M(x, y, t, m) \text{ and } m \geq k.$$

$$B(x, y, t) \quad \text{if} \quad M(x, y, t-1, m) \text{ and } k_1 \leq m < k.$$

Here $A(x, y, t)$ represents the areas for which we can immediately see the conclusion that they have property P at time t without any further look back in time. On the other hand, $B(x, y, t)$ represents the areas for which we cannot say anything definite at time t but we need to look further back in time to decide whether at time t they had property t.

Now let us further define the following relation.

Definition 13.6.2 The relation $C(x, y, t, n)$, where n is a recursion variable, is recursively defined as follows:

1. $C(x, y, t, n)$ if $B(x, y, t)$ and $n = 0$ or

2. $C(x, y, t, n)$ if $C(x, y, t, n-1)$ and $B(x, y, t-n)$ and $n \geq 1$.

Relation $C(x, y, t, n)$ represents those locations (x, y) where at time t, we need to look back at least $n + 1$ time units. Note that C is monotone decreasing in areas, that is,

$$\text{for all } t \quad \pi_{x,y} C(x, y, t, n_1) \subseteq \pi_{x,y} C(x, y, t, n_2) \text{ if } n_1 > n_2.$$

where π is the relational algebra projection operator.

13.6.2   Recursive SQL Queries

As explained earlier in Section 13.2.2 regarding simple relational queries, the MLPQ system has a recursive SQL query option that is available by clicking on the $\boxed{\text{SQL-Recursion}}$ button in the query selection menu. This section applies recursive SQL queries to recursively defined concepts, which is new because the resursively defined concepts use constraint data instead of simple relational data.

Since in Definition 13.6.2 C is monotone decreasing, it is natural to place a constant N as a limit on the number of recursion steps. Presumably, after N recursion steps, we are left with only small patches of areas, which are not worth further pursuit and computational time. Hence in practice, we can compute relation C approximately as follows.

```
CREATE VIEW   C(x,y,t,n)
SELECT        B.x, B.y, B.t, n
FROM          B
WHERE         n = 0
RECURSIVE
SELECT        C.x, C.y, C.t, n
FROM          B, C
WHERE         n = C.n + 1  AND
              n <= N  AND
              B.x = C.x  AND
              B.y = C.y  AND
              B.t = C.t - C.n - 1
```

It is possible to prove the following theorem.

Theorem 13.6.1 Let relations A, B, C, M, and P be as described above. Then the following equality holds.

$$P = \left\{ (x, y, t) \mid A(x, y, t) \lor \left(\bigvee_{n=1}^{+\infty} (C(x, y, t, n-1) \land A(x, y, t-n)) \right) \right\}$$

Theorem 13.6.1 allows computing relation P using the following SQL query.

```
CREATE VIEW   P(x,y,t)
SELECT        A.x, A.y, A.t
FROM          A
UNION
SELECT        C.x, C.y, C.t
FROM          A, C
WHERE         A.x = C.x  AND
              A.y = C.y  AND
              A.t = C.t - C.n - 1
```

Example 13.6.1 The above general evaluation scheme was used within the West Nile Virus epidemics tracking systems called *WeNiVIS.*. The WeNiVIS system considered input data like the one shown below for week 139 for the state of Pennsylvania, where blue and red regions were areas with a high number of new reported cases of the West Nile Virus infections.

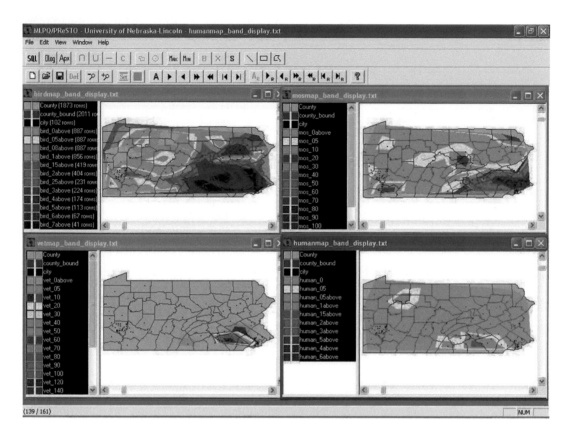

The four smaller maps show the data for wild birds (upper-left), mosquitoes (upper-right), horses (lower-left), and humans (lower-right). The WeNiVIS system combined such data and gave good predictions for West Nile Virus outbreaks three or more weeks in advance. The WeNiVIS system is only a sample system. Instead of the West Nile Virus, other types of epidemics may be also trackable and predictable in a similar way.

13.6.3   Constraint Deductive Databases

Recursive Datalog queries are entered the same way as nonrecursive queries except that we use %RECURSIVE% instead of %MLPQ%. That keyword activates some special evaluation routines that are applicable only for recursive queries.

The syntax of Datalog queries follows exactly the syntax described in Chapter 12. When MLPQ opens an input file, all the Datalog rules in it are evaluated, and the defined relations and input relations are all listed on the left-hand side of the graphical user interface, just below the tool bar.

As with the input relations, the user can right-click on any defined relation in the list to view the rows in that relation.

Example 13.6.2 In Example 13.5.3, instead of using an SQL with aggregation query to find the *Nearest_X* relation, it is possible to insert into the input file `buffer.txt` the following Datalog rule that has the same effect as the SQL query has.

```
/* Datalog rules inserted after the Hotel relation.  */

Nearest_Exit(id, MIN(x)):- Current_Pos(id2, x0, y0),
                           Exit(id, x, y),
                           x - x0 >= 0.
```

Instead of putting a Datalog query in a file, one can also use the Dlog tool bar button for initiating a Datalog query. This brings up a dialog box, in which the user can type in a Datalog rule to add to the database at run time. One can even combine different types of queries. For instance, one may use a Datalog query in the input file, then a buffer query to find the areas close to the nearest exit point. Then finally another query that is entered via the Dlog command.

Example 13.6.3 As an alternative in Example 13.5.3, after the buffer operator from the tool bar, we may enter into the Datalog dialog box the following.

```
Convenient_Hotel(id,x,y) :-  Hotel(id, x, y),
                             Buf_Nearest_Exit(id1, x, y).
```

The above example used only non-recursive Datalog queries. However, Datalog is mostly used for recursive queries. In fact, Datalog recursive queries are more general and flexible than recursive SQL queries. For example, recursive SQL queries may have only one recursive rule in most database systems, while Datalog queries may have any number of recursive rules. The MLPQ system is unique in that it allows the entry of multiple recursive rules in SQL. The user has to add each rule by clicking the Add button on the higher of the two rows of buttons at the bottom of the query entering dialog box.

Example 13.6.4 The two recursive SQL queries can be expressed in Datalog as follows.

```
%RECURSIVE%
C(x,y,t,n) :- B(x,y,t), n= 0.
C(x,y,t,n) :- C(x,y,t,cn), B(x,y,bt), bt=t-cn-1, n=cn+1, n<=N.

P(x,y,t) :-  A(x,y,t).
P(x,y,t) :-  C(x,y,t,cn), A(x,y,at), at=t-cn-1.
%RECURSIVE%
```

As is apparent, Datalog provides a denser style of writing, which is preferred in some applications.

A potential problem with recursive queries, either recursive SQL or recursive Datalog, is that the queries may not terminate on some inputs. This is due simply to the nature of computations in general, leading us all the way to the famous halting problem in computer science, as explained in Chapter 22. The beginner user only needs to know that such non-terminating queries are possible but they can be avoided by using an approximate evaluation. For this we have yet another tool bar button.

$\boxed{\text{Apx}}$ – This is the **approximation** button, which is located right of the Datalog button. Clicking the $\boxed{\text{Apx}}$ button will allow the user to specify whether they want an over-approximation or an under-approximation of the ideal query results. Then a parameter can be entered. A higher parameter value results in a tighter approximation of the result.

Example 13.6.5 Consider the following recursive Datalog query that defines the difference relation $D = \{(x,y,z) \mid x - y = z\}$ for integers x, y, and z.

```
D(x,y,z):- x-y >= 0, -x+y >= 0, z >= 0, -z >= 0.
D(x,y,z):- D(x1,y,z1), x-x1>=1, -x+x1>=-1, z-z1>=1, -z+z1>=-1.
```

This query runs forever without approximation. However, if we ask for only an approximate evaluation with a parameter ℓ, then the recursion stops after only ℓ number of iterations. Since most applications need the difference relation for only relatively small integer values, the approximation is satisfactory for those applications.

Approximate evaluations are strongly recommended for recursive Datalog queries.

13.7   Linear Programming

Linear programming is a widely used optimization algorithm. Linear programming asks to maximize or minimize a linear objective function subject to a set of linear inequality constraints. Example 4.4.7 gave a set of constraints that a farmer may face while trying to decide the combination of crops to plant to achieve the maximum profit. Example 4.3.9 gave the objective function to be maximized. These are easy to express in MLPQ as follows.

```
begin%MLPQ%
Crops(corn,rye,sunflower,wheat):- 15corn+ 8rye+10sunflower+15wheat<=3000,
                                   30corn+25rye+ 5sunflower+10wheat<=8000.

Profit(max(300corn+250rye+100sunflower+150wheat)):-
                                   Crops(corn,rye,sunflower,wheat).
end%MLPQ%
```

The MLPQ system can evaluate the above query and return the maximum possible profit for the farmer. However, the MLPQ system can do much more than simply evaluate one linear programming problem. As a database system, MLPQ provides a flexibility that linear programming does not provide. For instance, MLPQ allows *choice-based linear programming*, that is, linear programming where the composition of constraints is chosen from a menu of options.

Example 13.7.1 As water is increasingly expensive, the farmer wants to cut down on the usage of water. A subsurface drip irrigation (SDI) system cuts the water usage by an estimated 50 percent. After calculating the water savings and the estimated amortized cost of the SDI, the farmer would lose about 10 units of profit per acre.

Fertilizers are also getting expensive. A special iron supplement cuts down on the traditional fertilizers by about one third. After calculating the fertilizer savings and the estimated amortized cost of the iron supplement, the farmer would lose about 5 units of profit per acre.

Now the farmer has not one but four choices, which are four separate linear programming problems. We can express these in MLPQ as follows.

```
begin%MLPQ%
Fertilizer(iron,corn,rye,sunflower,wheat):-
          iron=0, 15corn+8rye+10sunflower+15wheat<=3000.

Fertilizer(iron,corn,rye,sunflower,wheat):-
          iron=1, 10corn+5.33rye+6.67sunflower+10wheat<=2000.

Water(sdi,corn,rye,sunflower,wheat):-
          sdi=0,  30corn+25rye+5sunflower+10wheat<=8000.

Water(sdi,corn,rye,sunflower,wheat):-
          sdi=1,  15corn+12.5rye+2.5sunflower+5wheat<=4000.

Profit(max(300corn+250rye+100sunflower+150wheat-10sid-5iron),iron,sdi):-
          Fertilizer(iron,corn,rye,sunflower,wheat),
          Water(sdi,corn,rye,sunflower,wheat).
end%MLPQ%
```

In the above MLPQ Datalog program, the *Fertilizer* and the *Water* relations express some options that the farmer may choose regarding fertilizer and water usage. The last line of the Datalog program expresses a join of the *Fertilizer* and the *Water* relations. In general, it can be a join of any number of options, that is, with n two-way options, we express in a single line 2^n number of linear programming problems.

MLPQ returns four values as the answer to the above Datalog query. These values are the optimized profits in the four cases of choices. If we want to find the global maximum, that is the best of each of the four linear programming problems, the MLPQ system requires the use of MAX instead of max. Similarly, min returns all the minimums of the objective function for each of the constraint tuples, while MIN returns a global minimum. The MLPQ system also provides a sum_max and a sum_min function to find the sum of the local maximums or the sum of the local minimums, respectively.

13.8 Web Accessible Applications

This section describes how to develop a web accessible MLPQ application. The three-tier browser/server architecture of the MLPQ web access system is shown in the figure below.

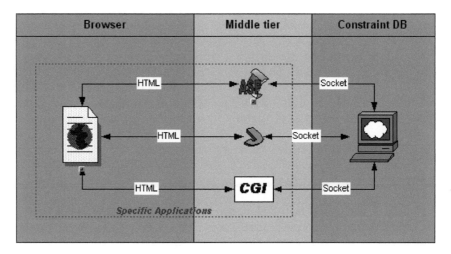

Each of the three tiers has its own responsibilities.

Browser: – The browser sends the user's requests to the web server, accepts the results from the *middle tier*, and displays the results on the user interfaces.

Middle Tier: – The middle tier, which is based on ASP, accepts requests from the browser, parses the request to a database system server acceptable command and arguments, sends commands to the *constraint database server*, and accepts the results from the constraint database server and returns those to the browser.

Constraint DB Server: – The database system server accepts commands and arguments from the web server, activates related operations according to the command and arguments, and returns the results to the middle tier.

The MLPQ web accessible server uses sockets to communicate with other programs. To make MLPQ work for web access, select "listen" from the drop down "Help" menu on the top of the main MLPQ window. That selection makes the MLPQ server listen to a predefined socket port ready to act according to the messages received from that port.

The default environment settings are saved in the `mlpq_nt.cfg` file. The following three elements need to be specified: the *WorkDir*, which defines the directory into which the server will load the constraint database files, the *OutPut*, which defines the directory for the server to output its result file, and the *Port*, which defines the socket port value. The system administrator can modify these three settings to configure the server.

The table below lists all the commands recognized by the MLPQ web accessible server.

MLPQ Web Commands

Command	Arguments	Actions on CDB
Clear	`<user> <filename>$`	Deselect all relations in the view.
Close	`<user> <filename>$`	Close user's view.
ColorRelation	`<user> <filename>` `<relation name>$`	Color selected relation.
GetAnimation	`<user> <filename>` `<start time> <end time>` `<interval time>$`	Generate animation images to the output directory.
Include	`<user> <filename>` `<relation name> <color>$`	Highlight relation name and assign a color for it in the view.
Open	`<user> <filename>$`	Create user's view, open data file.
Zoom	`<user> <filename>` `<x> <y> <w> <h>$`	Zoom the image.
GetImage	`<user> <filename>$`	Copy screen image, save to disk.
SQLAggregate	`<user> <filename>` `<relation name>` `#<select>#<from>#<where>` `#<group>#<having>$`	Execute SQL on user's view.
SQLBasic	`<user> <filename>` `<relation name>` `#<select>#<from>#<where>$`	Execute SQL on user's view.
SQLNested	`<user> <filename>` `<relation name>` `#<select1>#<from1>#<where1>` `#<nest_op>` `#<select2>#<from2>#<where2>$`	Execute SQL on user's view.
SQLSet	`<user> <filename>` `<relation name>` `#<select1>#<from1>#<where1>` `#<set_op>` `#<select2>#<from2>#<where2>$`	Execute SQL on user's view.
Datalog	`<user> <filename>` `<datalog string>$`	Execute Datalog on user's view.

In the table, the `<user>` records the login user name. The `<filename>` is the name of the constraint database file opened in the server. The `<relation name>` provides the name of the new relation that will be created on the MLPQ web accessible server. The `<color>` is used to assign a color for the selected relation.

The execution of each command may return 0, 1, or a file name. A "1" always means that there are some errors within the execution. For the first seven commands, a "0" result indicates that the command is executed successfully. For the other commands, returning a file name (a `.bmp` file in case of *GetImage* and a `.txt` textfile in the case of SQL and Datalog queries) indicates that the command is executed successfully. The value of `<color>` is a numerical value that should be assigned according to the following table.

MLPQ Color Assignment

Color	`<color>` value
black	0
red	1
green	2
blue	3
RGB color	4-16777216

In the above table the RGB value refers to the standard encoding of colors that are composites of red, green, and blue, the computer primary colors.

13.8.1 The Police Emergency Database

The *Police Emergency Database* is an example of an MLPQ web accessible database application. This database contains the following input relatins.

Contains(Street, X, Y) – describes which *Street* contains which locations *(X, Y)*.

Emergency(Type, No, Street, T) – describes what type of emergency occurs at address *(Number, Street)* at time *T*.

Location(No, Street, X, Y) – describes which house *(Number, Street)* is at which location *(X, Y)*.

Police(Name, VIN, X, Y, T) – describes which police officer *(Name)* drives a car with vehicle identification number *VIN* at location *(X, Y)* and time *T*.

Resident(Name, No, Street) – describes which person *(Name)* resides at which address *(Number, Street)*.

For the Police Emergency Database, we define the following login and logout functions for the Middle Tier using ASP and VB code.

Login:

```
Session.Contents("SERVER") = Request.ServerVariables("SERVER_NAME")
Session.Contents("USR") = Request("STR_USR") Session.Contents("VIEW_NM") = 0
Response.Redirect "a1.htm"
```

Create a Socket.TCP object and connect to the server:

```
asObj = Server.CreateObject( "Socket.TCP" )
asObj.Host = Session.Contents("SERVER") & ":2222"
asObj.Open
asObj.Wait
```

Open a database file:

```
str = "Open" & Session.Contents("USR") & "police.txt$"
asObj.SendText str
asObj.Wait
```

Select a relation:

```
str = "Include" & Session.Contents("USR")
      & "police.txt Townmap 0$"
asObj.SendText str
asObj.Wait
```

Return the image:

```
str = "GetImage " & Session.Contents("USR") &" police.txt$"
asObj.SendText str
asObj.Wait
```

Using the above basic functions, it is now possible to add a few sample queries that are callable by clicking on one of the buttons on the lower half of the Police Emergency Database login page. When the queries require some input parameters, then some dialog boxes with the appropriate prompt messages appear on the top half of the login page.

Example 13.8.1 The login page of the Police Emergency Database is shown in the figure below. Initially the top half of the login page is empty. The figure shows the result after clicking *Emergency as the menu option. This menu option finds the location of the emergencies during a given time interval. The prompt message asks the user to enter the start time and the end time and then click the Find button below the dialog boxes.

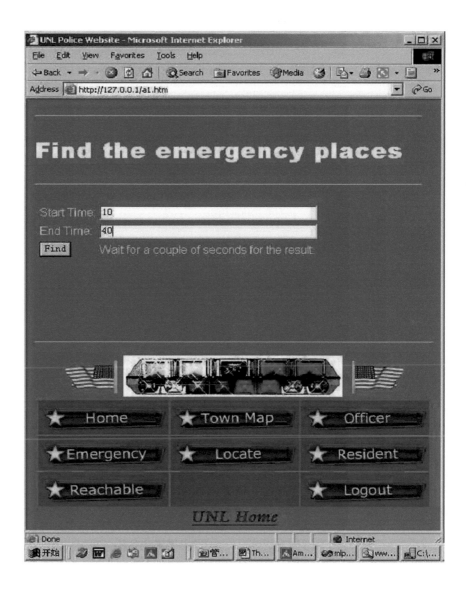

Ignoring for the moment the display issues, we can find using MLPQ SQL the emergency places, assuming that *starttime* and *endtime* are some constants, as follows:

VIEW NAME	ViewNM_1
SELECT	Emergency.Type, Location.x, Location.y
FROM	Emergency, Location
WHERE	Emergency.No = Location.No,
	Emergency.Street = Location.Street,
	Emergency.T $>=$ *starttime*,
	Emergency.T $<=$ *endtime*

Hence in the Middle Tier the ASP and VB code to find the emergency places is the following:

```
Session.Contents("VIEW_NM") = Session.Contents("VIEW_NM") + 1
str = "SQLBasic " & Session.Contents("USR") & " police.txt " &
Session.Contents("USR") & Session.Contents("VIEW_NM")
str = str & "# Emergency.Type, Location.x, Location.y"
str = str & "# Emergency, Location"
str = str & "# Emergency.No=Location.No, Emergency.Street=Location.Street"
str = str & ", Emergency.T>= " & Request("STR_TIME1")
str = str & ", Emergency.T<="& Request("STR_TIME2")
str = str & "$"
asObj.SendText
str asObj.Wait
```

After evaluating the query, the MLPQ web server returns the following figure, which displays in red four places where some emergency took place between times 10 and 40. The figure also displays in black the other streets and significant locations of the town.

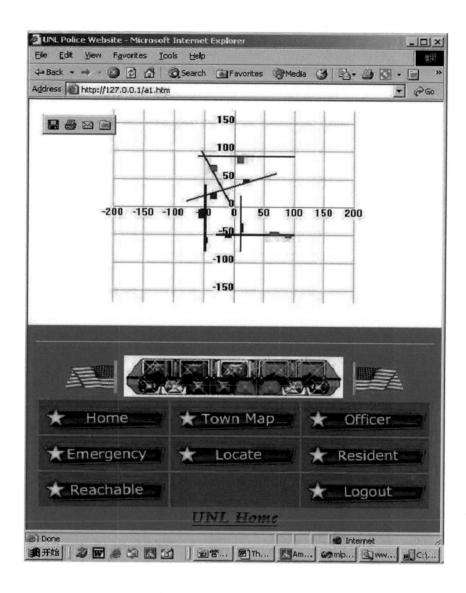

The MLPQ web server can handle Datalog queries too, as shown in the next example.

Example 13.8.2 The next menu option on the login page of the Police Emergency Database is $\boxed{\text{*Reachable}}$. This menu option finds the streets to which a given police officer can go with his car starting at a given time. Let *pname* be the name of the police officer, and *time* be the starting time.

Then this query can be expressed in Datalog as follows.

$$Reach(n) \quad :- \quad Contains(n,x,y), Police(Name, VIN, x, y, T),$$
$$Name = pname, T = time.$$
$$Reach(n) \quad :- \quad Reach(m), Contains(m,x,y), Contains(n,x,y).$$
$$Reachable(n,x,y) \quad :- \quad Reach(n), Contains(n,x,y).$$

Hence the ASP and VB code in the Middle Tier to find the reachable streets is the following:

```
Session.Contents("VIEW_NM") = Session.Contents("VIEW_NM") + 1
prefix = Session.Contents("USR") & Session.Contents("VIEW_NM")
str = "Datalog " & Session.Contents("USR") & " police.txt " & prefix
str = str & "Reach(n) :- Contains(n,x,y), Police(Name,VIN,x,y,T),
     Name=" & Chr(34) & Request("STR_NAME") & Chr(34) & ", T=" &
     Request("STR_TIME") & ".$"
asObj.SendText str
asObj.Wait
str = "Datalog " & Session.Contents("USR") & " police.txt " & prefix
str = str & "Reach(n) :- "& prefix &
     "Reach(m), Contains(m,x,y), Contains(n,x,y).$"
asObj.SendText str
asObj.Wait
str = "Datalog " & Session.Contents("USR") & " police.txt " & prefix
str = str & "Reachable(n,x,y) :- " & prefix & "Reach(n), Contains(n,x,y).$"
asObj.SendText
str asObj.Wait
```

Suppose that the user enters into the dialog boxes "Charles" as the name of the police officer and 12 as the initial time. After evaluating the query, the MLPQ web server returns the following figure, which displays in red four streets that are connected with each other. Charles is on one of these streets at time 12. The other streets, which are shown in black, are not connected with the red streets. Hence, if there is an emergency on one of the black streets, then another police officer has to be sent there.

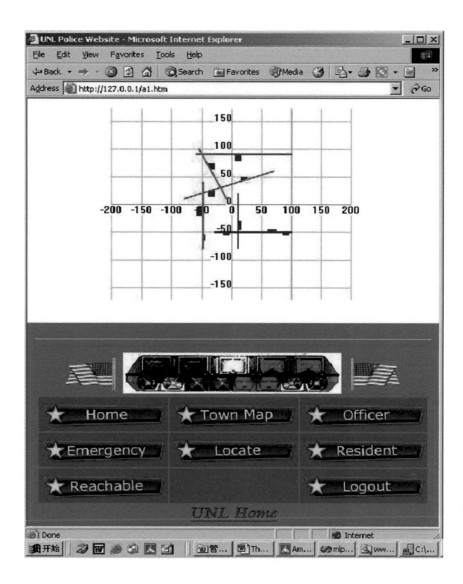

The other login menu options similarly execute either SQL or Datalog queries and display their results.

Bibliographic Notes

The MLPQ system was built at the University of Nebraska-Lincoln over several years. The first version of the MLPQ system was presented in Revesz and Li [351]. This version included linear programming as a basic function to implement minimum and maximum aggregate operators. The MLPQ/GIS system was presented in Kanjamala et al. [218]. This version included a graphical user interface with most of the 2D spatial operators geared towards geographic applications. The MLPQ/PReSTO system was presented in Revesz et al. [349]. This version included 3D spatial operators, animation of moving objects, and the PReSTO subsystem. The latest version of the MLPQ system is available from the web page `http://cse.unl.edu/~revesz/MLPQ`.

MLPQ is only one of a growing number of linear constraint database systems that includes the CCUBE system by Brodsky et al. [57, 58] and the DEDALE system by Grumbach et al. [168].

All of these systems use several ideas for query optimization, including efficient implementation of linear constraint database versions of selection, projection, join, union, and intersection operators [54, 155, 167, 168, 334]. Chapter 24 gives more related references on implementation of SQL and Datalog queries.

In MLPQ the 3D spatial operators are based on the color band display algorithms in Chapter 21. The MLPQ system animation algorithms are based on the description given in Chomicki and Revesz [89] and Chomicki et al. [86], which also contains Example 13.4.2. Example 13.4.3 is by Vijay Eadala.

Exercises

1. Find the times when the two planes in Example 13.4.5 can meet by implementing in MLPQ the database queries described in the example. Visualize the movements of the two airplanes using the animation button of the MLPQ system.

2. Add to the `usmap.txt` file a relation *Route(id,x,y,t,name,type)*, which describes the movements of vehicles on the interstate highway. Let *id* be the vehicle identification number, x and y the location of the vehicle, t the time instance when the vehicle is at location (x, y), *name* be the driver's name, and *type* be "car," "motorcycle," or "truck." Let time be measured in hours from 0 (Saturday midnight) to 168 (Saturday midnight). Express the following queries in the MLPQ system.

   (a) Find the type of vehicle that Jim drives.

   (b) Find the number of cars that are in Nebraska at any time on Monday.

   (c) Find the state which has the most number of trucks at time $t = 10$.

   (d) Find each pair of vehicles that are in the same state at the same time.

3. A cadastral survey is a land ownership database. Suppose that such a database is represented by the relationship *C(id,x,y,t,n)*, where for each piece of land we have its identification number *id*, its exact location in the (x, y) plane, and the time period t during which the a person with name *n* owned the land. For instance, extending data in Example 13.5.1, we can build the following land ownership database.

```
begin%MLPQ%
C(id,x,y,t,n):-id=1, x>=3, y<= 9,    4x- 3y<=9, t>=1980, t<1995, n="Adam".
C(id,x,y,t,n):-id=2, y<=9,           4x- 3y>=9,
                         3x+4y<=69, 5x-12y<=3, t>=1980, t<1990, n="Barb".
C(id,x,y,t,n):-id=3, x<=15, y<= 9,   3x+4y>=69, t>=1970, t<1995, n="Carl".
C(id,x,y,t,n):-id=4, x<=15, y>= 1,   5x-12y>=3, t>=1980, t<1995, n="Deb".
C(id,x,y,t,n):-id=5, x>=3,   x<=10, y>=1, y<=9, t>=1995, t<2010, n="Eve".
C(id,x,y,t,n):-id=6, x>=10, x<=15, y>=1, y<=9, t>=1995, t<2009, n="Fred".
end%MLPQ%
```

Enter the above data into the MLPQ system and write queries for the following.

(a) Find the names of the persons who owned some land in 1992.

(b) Find the total area of land owned by Fred in 2000.

(c) Find which parts of the land belonged to Adam and later to Eve.

4. Suppose relation *Herbicide(id,x,y,t,h)* records which land areas were sprayed at time *t* with which herbicide *h*. Define an instance of the *Herbicide* relation as an MLPQ input file, focusing on the land areas within the region $0 \leq x \leq 15, 0 \leq y \leq 15$. Express the following queries on your MLPQ database.

(a) Find the areas that were sprayed by herbicide *atrazine*.

(b) Find the areas that were sprayed by either herbicide *atrazine* or *dicamba*.

(c) Find the areas that were sprayed first by herbicide *atranize* and later by *dicamba*.

(d) Find the areas that were sprayed by some herbicide in the past five years.

(e) Find the total area that were sprayed by some herbicide in the past five years.

(f) Find the areas that were not sprayed by any herbicide in the past five years.

5. Combine the cadastral database and the herbicide database of the previous two exercises and express the following queries in the MLPQ system.

    (a) Find the herbicides that Adam used while he owned land.

    (b) Find the herbicides that Eve used or a previous owner used on her land.

    (c) Find the land areas which are suitable for organic farming. Assume that an organic farm requires that there were no herbicides used in the past five years.

    (d) Find the owners who may have an organic garden on at least part of their land.

6. Implement the *park* relation of Example 13.3.9, and use the MLPQ system to do the following.

    (a) Use the buffer operator to enlarge the objects in the park.

    (b) Browse through the history of the park. In particular find and print the outline of the park in 1975, 1985, and 1995.

    (c) Find the pair of object identification numbers such that the two objects overlapped in space.

    (d) Find the (x, y) locations that belonged to two or more different objects during the history of the park.

    (e) Find the total area of the overlapping regions in the previous question.

7. Instead of using SQL queries use the MLPQ coloring functions to generate a contour or isomorphic color band map using the database of Example 13.3.10. Find the total area of each band. Check that sum of all the color band areas add up to 400, which is the total area of the map.

8. Use the MLPQ system with the `sgull.txt` relation, which describes the California gull input data, to do the following.

    (a) Find the total area of the habitat range of the California gull in 1970 and 1990 and the amount of change between these two dates.

    (b) Find the amount of change in the habitat ara of the California gull in the state of California.

9. Implement the flood database of Example 13.4.4. Find the total area of the flooded region at time $t = 10000$, $t = 10500$, $t = 11000$, $t = 11500$, and $t = 12000$. During which 500 minutes is the flood growing the fastest?

10. Implement in MLPQ the wilderness relation of Example 21.3.1. Show the animation. Using SQL, create new relations for the grass, the oak tree, and the pine forest areas at times $t = 0$, $t = 5$, and $t = 10$. Find the total area of the various types of vegetation at these times. How much area has the grass land lost between $t = 0$ and $t = 10$? When out of these three times is the pine forest area the largest?

11. Implement in MLPQ the query in Example 13.4.5 and display on the computer screen the area where the two planes may meet.

12. Suppose we model a red-hot iron as it cools from $t = 0$, when it has a pure red color of $(255, 0, 0)$, to $t = 10$, when its color is black $(0, 0, 0)$. What colors will be displayed by an MLPQ animation if we go from time 0 to time 10 with one-unit time steps?

13. Using the MLPQ/PReSTO system and input relations in Example 13.4.7, evaluate the query in Example 13.4.11.

14. Using the MLPQ/PReSTO system do the following:

    (a) Define a parametric rectangles relation $Clouds(X, Y, T, h)$ as in Example 13.4.8 but with more tuples.

    (b) Define a parametric rectangles relation $Temperature(X, Y, T, f)$ with moving warm and cold regions.

    (c) Write a query that finds those areas that are colder than 32 degrees Fahrenheit.

    (d) Write a query that finds the areas where it is likely to snow. Assume that it is likely to snow when a cloud area with 80 percent or greater humidity meets an area colder than 32 degrees Fahrenheit.

15. Using the MLPQ/PReSTO system do the following:

    (a) Define relations $Weather(X, Y, T, climate)$, which describes the climatic conditions of regions, and $Soil(X, Y, T, quality)$, which describes the type of soil in each region. For climate, the values could be *dry, humid*, and *wet* and for soil the values could be *sand, clay*, and *rock*, for example.

    (b) Write a query that finds those areas that are not suitable for cultivation due to too dry climate or bad soil.

(c) Display the areas that are not suitable for cultivation.

16. Using the MLPQ/PReSTO system do the following:

    (a) There is a city located in an area with length $[530, 560]$ and width $[410, 420]$ miles. Represent this by the relation *City*.

    (b) Suppose that the shape of a desert at time $t = 0$ is approximately a rectangle with length $[0, 500]$ and width $[0, 400]$ miles. The desert expands 1 mile to the east and 3 miles to the north per year. Represent this by the relation *Desert*.

    (c) At time $t = 0$ there is a forest with length $[520, 560]$ and width $[405, 410]$ miles. To protect the city from the desert, people start to expand the forest at the rate of 5 miles per year to the south. Represent this by the relation *Forest*.

    (d) Write a query that finds the area of the desert as blocked by the forest 10 and 20 years later. Display the desert at these times.

    (e) Write a query that finds the area of the city still free from the desert 10 and 20 years later. Display the remaining areas of the city.

17. Implement in MLPQ the `regions.txt` input file shown below and write SQL queries to find the following.

    (a) Find a buffer of radius 30 for each city.

    (b) Find the area that belonged to country 3 at 1900.

    (c) Find the pairs of city and coutry identification numbers such that the city belongs to the country in 1800 and 2000.

    (d) Find the areas that changed from one coutry to another country any time from 1800 to 2000.

    (e) Find the cities that changed from one coutry to another country from 1800 to 2000.

    (f) Find the population of each city in 1800 and 2000.

    (g) Find the population of each city in 2000.

    (h) Find the cities which grew at least 50,000 in population from 1800 to 2000.

    (i) Find the pair of countries that were neighbors of each other in 1800.

    (j) Find the pair of countries that were neighbors of each other in 2000.

```
begin%MLPQ%
city(id,x,y):- id = 101, x =  300, y =  200.
city(id,x,y):- id = 102, x =  700, y =  300.
city(id,x,y):- id = 103, x =  500, y =  600.
city(id,x,y):- id = 104, x =  700, y = 1300.
city(id,x,y):- id = 105, x = 1200, y =  800.


country(id,x,y,t):- id = 1, x >=    0, x <=  800,
                            y >=  500, y <= 1500, t >= 1800, t <= 1950.
country(id,x,y,t):- id = 1, x >=    0, x <=  400,
                            y >=  500, y <= 1500, t >= 1950, t <= 2000.
country(id,x,y,t):- id = 2, x >=  800, x <= 1200,
                            y >=  500, y <= 1500, t >= 1800, t <= 1950.
country(id,x,y,t):- id = 2, x >=  400, x <= 1200,
                            y >=  500, y <= 1500, t >= 1950, t <= 2000.
country(id,x,y,t):- id = 3, x >=    0, x <=  600,
                            y >=    0, y <=  500, t >= 1800, t <= 2000.
country(id,x,y,t):- id = 4, x >= 1200, x <= 1500,
                            y >=    0, y <= 1500, t >= 1800, t <= 2000.
country(id,x,y,t):- id = 4, x >=  600, x <= 1200,
                            y >=    0, y <=  500, t >= 1800, t <= 2000.


/* Population is measured in thousands */
growth(id,p,t):- id = 101, p-0.7t = 900,  t >= 1800, t <= 2000.
growth(id,p,t):- id = 102, p+0.1t = 700,  t >= 1800, t <= 2000.
growth(id,p,t):- id = 103, p      = 500,  t >= 1800, t <= 2000.
growth(id,p,t):- id = 104, p-0.1t = 300,  t >= 1800, t <= 2000.
growth(id,p,t):- id = 105, p-0.3t =  40,  t >= 1800, t <= 2000.
end%MLPQ%
```

18. Consider again the urban sprawl described in Example 7.7.11. Suppose that Figure 6.3 shows the map of Lincoln, Nebraska in year 2000, and since then the town expanded to the east continuously at the rate of one unit per year. Find the constraint representation of the growing town area between the years 2000 and 2007 and visualize it using MLPQ.

19. Implement in MLPQ a triangulated irregular network which has the following five points with (x, y, w) values.

$P1(0, 0, 125)$
$P2(1, 0, 120)$
$P3(0, 1, 100)$
$P4(-1, 0, 150)$

$P5(0, -1, 130)$

20. A manufacturer produces three types of soft drink. Each bottle of the first type needs 6 units of sugar, 4 units of coloring, and 3 units of flavoring. Each bottle of the second type needs 5 units of sugar, 3 units of coloring, and 4 units of flavoring. Finally, each bottle of the third type needs 10 units of sugar, 7 units of coloring, and 2 units of flavoring. The manufacturer can use each day at most only 1000 units of sugar, 800 units of coloring, and 500 units of flavoring. Represent as a constraint relation with scheme $Produce(x, y, z)$ all production possibilities where x, y, and z are, respectively, the amount of type one, two, and three soft drinks produced. Write a Datalog query that finds the maximum profit for the manufacturer if the profit made on each bottle of the first, second, and third type of soft drink is 50, 40, and 65 cents, respectively.

21. A software company contracts with other companies for the following types of projects: (a) designing and building basic web-pages, (b) developing a web-enabled database, and (c) building multimedia applications.

    Building a basic web-page takes on average 5 hours of design time, and 10 hours of HTML programming. Building a web-enabled database takes on average 10 hours of design, 5 hours of HTML, and 10 hours of JAVA programming. Building a multimedia application takes on average 12 hours of design, and 25 hours of JAVA programming.

    The company has three groups of employees: interface designers, HTML and JAVA programmers. The three groups of employees can work a total of 2000, 4000, and 3500 hours, respectively, per month.

    (a) Define using linear constraints the database relation
    `contracts(x1,x2,x3)` which contains all the possible number $x1$ of webpage, $x2$ of web database, and $x3$ of multimedia application contracts that the company could do in a month.

    (b) Suppose that on average building a basic web-page, web-enabled database, and multimedia application yields a profit of $120, $500, and $750, respectively. Write a query that finds the maximum profit that the company would earn by contracting the best possible way. (We assume that there is more demand for each type of jobs than the company could accept.)

22. A housing developer wants to build three types of houses: luxury, family, and town houses. There are two options for the number of bedrooms and garages.

- The first option is to have the luxury, family, and town houses 4, 3, and 1 bedroom, and 3, 3, and 1 garage, respectively.

- The second option is to have the luxury, family, and town houses 3, 2, and 1 bedroom and 2, 2, and 1 garage, respectively.

There are also two options for the number of fire places and swimming pools.

- The first option is to have the luxury, family, and town houses 2, 1, and 0 fire places, and 1, 0, and 0 swimming pools, respectively.

- The second option is to have the luxury, family, and town houses 1, 0, and 0 fire places, and 1, 1, and 0 swimming pools, respectively.

Assuming that the developer has permission to build only a total of 43 bedrooms, 36 garages, 25 fire places, and 17 swimming pools, and that the profit on the luxury, family, and town houses are 100, 70, and 30, respectively, find the following.

(a) The four possible choices of the developer.

(b) The maximum profit on each of the four choices.

(c) The maximum profit of the developer with the best choice.

14

The DISCO System

DISCO, short for *Datalog with integer set constraints*, is a constraint database system that implements Datalog with *Boolean constraints* on set variables that range over the finite and infinite sets of integers.

Although some deductive database systems allow both Datalog queries and set data types, they do not allow constraints in the input database. This is a problem because often the data that we have is incomplete data that cannot be described precisely but only by using constraints.

Section 14.1 describes the syntax of DISCO queries and gives a few examples. Section 14.2 describes the implementation of the DISCO system, including conversion to relational algebra, and naive and semi-naive evaluation. Section 14.3 describes how the DISCO system can be used and gives some performance results on the sample queries. Section 14.4 talks about extending the DISCO system to other Boolean algebras.

14.1 DISCO Queries

The input file starts with a line that contains "`begin`" and ends with a line that contains "`end.`" Between these lines is a set of Datalog rules and facts with Boolean constraints as defined in Chapter 12.

The domain of every variable in DISCO is an element of the Boolean algebra $B_Z = \langle \mathcal{P}(\mathcal{Z}), \cap, \cup, ^-, \emptyset, \mathcal{Z} \rangle$, which is described in Example 11.2.2.

Since the keyboard does not contain the symbols $\cap$, $\cup$, and $\emptyset$, the DISCO system uses instead of those the symbols $/\backslash$, $\backslash/$, and @, respectively. In addition, DISCO uses `<=` instead of the precedence relation $\subseteq$, and ! $=$ instead of the inequality relation $\neq$.

P. Revesz, *Introduction to Databases: From Biological to Spatio-Temporal*,
Texts in Computer Science, DOI 10.1007/978-1-84996-095-3_14,
© Springer-Verlag London Limited 2010

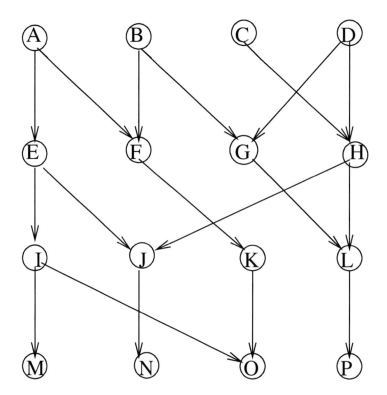

Figure 14.1: A packet switching network.

Example 14.1.1 Consider the packet switching network in Figure 14.1. In this hierarchical network there are four layers, each with four nodes. Each node represents a router and the directed edges represent connections across which packets can be sent. A set of packets arrives at the top layer and needs to be dynamically routed to given nodes of the bottom layer, with some restrictions on the routing in the middle layers.

The connections of the network imply some restrictions, which can be represented by the relation *connect*:

```
/* connections between 1st and 2nd layers */

connect({1},A,B,C,D,E,F,G,H) :- E <= A,
                                 F <= A \/ B,
                                 G <= B \/ D,
                                 H <= C \/ D.


/* connections between 2nd and 3rd layers */

connect({2},E,F,G,H,I,J,K,L) :- I <= E,
                                 J <= E \/ H,
                                 K <= F,
                                 L <= G \/ H.


/* connections between 3rd and 4th layers */

connect({3},I,J,K,L,M,N,O,P) :- M <= I,
                                 N <= J,
                                 O <= I \/ K,
                                 P <= L.
```

Now suppose that some packets are to be sent from the nodes in the top layer to the nodes in the bottom layer. For example, we may have the following set of packets to be routed from and to:

```
from(A,B,C,D) :- A == {1,2,3},
                 B == {4,5},
                 C == {6,7},
                 D == {8,9}.

to(M,N,O,P) :- M == {1},
               N == {2,6,8},
               O == {3,4},
               P == {5,7,9}.
```

To count the number of layers in the network, we define the *next* relation with the following facts:

```
next({1},{2}).
next({2},{3}).
next({3},{4}).
```

The following DISCO query finds to where each packet may be sent:

```
path({1},A,B,C,D) :- from(A,B,C,D).

path(Z,V,W,X,Y) :- path(Z1,Q,R,S,T),
                   connect(Z1,Q,R,S,T,V,W,X,Y),
                   next(Z1,Z).
```

Example 14.1.2 The following query finds which packets should be sent to which nodes in each layer. The query defines the set of packets routed to a layer to be such that each node receives a subset of the packets that can be sent to that layer (hence the *path* relation is used) with the additional constraint that each packet is sent only to one node in each layer, and in particular only the requested packets are to be sent to the bottom layer.

```
route({4},M,N,O,P) :- path({4},M,N,O,P),
                      to(M,N,O,P).

route(Z,Q,R,S,T) :- path(Z,Q,R,S,T),
                    connect(Z,Q,R,S,T,V,W,X,Y),
                    route(Z1,V,W,X,Y),
                    next(Z,Z1),
                    Q /\ R == @,
                    Q /\ S == @,
                    Q /\ T == @,
                    R /\ S == @,
                    R /\ T == @,
                    S /\ T == @.
```

Example 14.1.3 Now suppose that instead of the requirement that each packet be sent to only one successor, we have the rule that each packet is broadcast, that is, sent to all successors. Then the connections can be represented as follows:

```
/* broadcast connections between 1st and 2nd layers */

connect({1},A,B,C,D,E,F,G,H) :- A <= E, A <= F,
                                 B <= F, B <= G,
                                 C <= H,
                                 D <= G, D <= H.

/* connections between 2nd and 3rd layers */

connect({2},E,F,G,H,I,J,K,L) :- E <= I, E <= J,
                                 F <= K,
                                 G <= L,
                                 H <= J, H <= L.

/* connections between 3rd and 4th layers */

connect({3},I,J,K,L,M,N,O,P) :- I <= M, I <= O,
                                 J <= N,
                                 K <= O,
                                 L <= P.
```

Suppose we know that in the top layer some packet occurs in both nodes B and C:

```
from(A,B,C,D) :- B /\ C != @.
```

What can be said about the nodes in the bottom layer? The same DISCO query for *path* as in Example 14.1.1 can be used.

14.2   Implementation

Section 24.2.4 describes a basic Datalog evaluation algorithm. In this section we review some of the concepts and refine them for the case of DISCO queries. In particular, Section 14.2.1 describes the conversion from DISCO Datalog rules to relational algebra formulas, and Section 14.2.2 describes a *naive* and *semi-naive* evaluation of DISCO Datalog queries.

14.2.1   Converting Datalog Rules to Relational Algebra Formulas

DISCO converts each Datalog rule into a relational algebra representation. In the internal relational algebra the following operators are used: join ($\bowtie$), project (π), union ($\cup$), and select (σ). In DISCO the normal cross-product

($\times$) operator is treated as a special case of join. Also, the join and union operators can have more than two arguments.

There are two slightly different functions used for converting Datalog rules to relational algebra rules:

- *EVAL function*—The translation of Datalog to relational algebra is standard, except for the slightly different syntax of the selection operations. Basically, each Datalog rule body is translated as a relational algebra expression that is a join of the relations occurring in the body followed by a sequence of selections, one for each constraint in the body, followed by a projection to the variables that occur in the rule head. If there are several rules for the same relation, then the relational algebra formulas for the individual rules are connected with a union operator.

- *EVAL_INCR function*—This function is similar to the *EVAL* function. The difference is that before conversion each rule is copied as many times as the number of defined relation symbols in its body. In the ith copy a Δ symbol is put before the ith defined relation.

Example 14.2.1 The query in Example 14.1.1 is changed by *EVAL_INCR* into:

```
path({1},A,B,C,D) :- from(A,B,C,D).

path(Z,V,W,X,Y) :- Δpath(Z1,Q,R,S,T),
                   connect(Z1,Q,R,S,T,V,W,X,Y),
                   next(Z1,Z).
```

Next this will be translated to relational algebra formulas as follows. The first rule is translated to:

$$\pi_{Z,A,B,C,D}\ (\sigma_{Z=\{1\}}\ From(A,B,C,D) \bowtie Z(Z)$$

where $Z(Z)$ is the relation that contains just the single variable Z without any constraints. The second rule is translated to:

$$\pi_{Z,V,W,X,Y} \quad (\Delta Path(Z1,Q,R,S,T)$$
$$\bowtie Connect(Z1,Q,R,S,T,V,W,X,Y)$$
$$\bowtie Next(Z1,Z))$$

The union of the first two expressions will be a relational algebra expression for *Path*.

14.2.2   Naive and Semi-Naive Evaluation Methods

DISCO uses the naive and semi-naive methods for evaluating queries. The naive method repeatedly evaluates the relational algebra formulas that are obtained using the *EVAL* function until the size of the output relations keeps growing. The pseudo code of the naive method is the following:

Naive Method

```
for i := 1 to m do
     P_i := ∅
repeat
     for i:= 1 to m do
          Q_i := P_i
     for i:= 1 to m do
          P_i := EVAL(i,Q_1, ..., Q_m)
until P_i = Q_i for all i ( 1 ≤ i ≤ m)
```

---

where P_i is the tuples of the ith relation and Q_i is the tuples of the ith relation in the previous step. At the beginning we erase all tuples. Then we repeat the steps of the algorithm until the results of the last two steps are identical. During one step we store the tuples first ($Q_i := P_i$), then calculate the new tuples using the tuples calculated in the previous steps. The calculation is done by the *EVAL* function. In the function, i denotes the index of the current relation and $Q_1, \ldots, Q_m$ denote the tuples of the relations, which can be used by *EVAL*.

Semi-Naive Method

The main disadvantage of the naive method is that it recalculates the same tuples in every iteration. In the previous example during the first step the algorithm calculates the parents; during the second step the parents and the grandparents; during the third and fourth steps the parents, grandparents, and great-grandparents. Therefore the algorithm calculated the parents four times. If the number of the steps is greater—and in a real application it is several times greater—then this disadvantage is also greater. The main idea of the semi-naive method is to omit these recalculations.

If during the calculation we use only old tuples (tuples that were calculated before the previous step), then we only recalculate some older tuples.

Therefore if we want to calculate new tuples we should use at least one new tuple that was calculated during the previous step.

Naturally the first step is an exception, because there are no new tuples before the first step; hence the first steps of the semi-naive and naive methods are identical.

The pseudo code of the semi-naive evaluation is the following:

Semi-Naive Method

```
for i := 1 to m do
      ΔP_i := EVAL(p_i, ∅, ..., ∅)
      P_i := ΔP_i
repeat
      for i:= 1 to m do
            ΔQ_i := ΔP_i
      for i:= 1 to m do
      begin
            ΔP_i := EVAL_INCR(i, P_1, ..., P_m ΔQ_1, ..., ΔQ_m)
            ΔP_i := ΔP_i - P_i
      end
      for i:=1 to m do
            P_i := P_i ∪ ΔP_i
until ΔP_i = ∅ for all i ( 1 ≤ i ≤ m)
```

---

where P_i denotes the tuples of the ith relation, ΔP_i the new tuples in the current relation, and ΔQ_i the new tuples in the previous iteration of the relations. At the first iteration we use the $EVAL$ function to calculate the tuples. Then we iterate the algorithm until there are no new tuples derived. In each iteration we first store the new tuples ($\Delta Q_i = \Delta P_i$) and then calculate the new tuples using the $EVAL\_INCR$ function. After this we check whether the new tuples are really new tuples ($\Delta P_i = \Delta P_i - P_i$). At the end of the iteration we should update the value of P_i ($P_i = P_i + \Delta P_i$). The $EVAL\_INCR$ function has more parameters than the $EVAL$ function, because the $EVAL\_INCR$ function needs not only all the tuples, but the new tuples as well.

Example 14.2.2 Let's see how Example 14.2.1 is evaluated using DISCO. In the first iteration the algebra expression for the first rule is the only one that will give a tuple:

```
path({1},A,B,C,D) :- A == {1,2,3},
                     B == {4,5},
                     C == {6,7},
                     D == {8,9}.
```

In the second iteration, the algebra expression for the second rule will give us the tuple, where we use some renamings for greater readability:

```
/* E,F,G,H are renamings for V,W,X,Y */

path({2},E,F,G,H) :- E <= {1,2,3},
                     F <= {1,2,3,4,5},
                     G <= {4,5,8,9},
                     H <= {6,7,8,9}.
```

Similarly, in the third and fourth iterations, we obtain:

```
/*  I,J,K,L are renamings for V,W,X,Y */

path({3},I,J,K,L) :- I <= {1,2,3},
                     J <= {1,2,3,6,7,8,9},
                     K <= {1,2,3,4,5},
                     L <= {4,5,6,7,8,9}.
```

```
/* M,N,O,P are renamings for V,W,X,Y */

path({4},M,N,O,P) :- M <= {1,2,3},
                     N <= {1,2,3,6,7,8,9},
                     O <= {1,2,3,4,5},
                     P <= {4,5,6,7,8,9}.
```

For constraint databases and queries that contain only subset or equal to and monotone inequality constraints, DISCO implements the projection operator based on part (2) of the existential quantifier elimination method in Theorem 23.4.5.

Example 14.2.3 It is easy to check that the constraint database in Example 14.1.3 contains only set-order and monotone inequality constraints. When the same *path* query as in Example 14.1.1 is run on this input database, DISCO finds the following tuples:

```
path({1},A,B,C,D) :- B /\ C != @.


/*  E,F,G,H are renamings for V,W,X,Y */

path({2},E,F,G,H) :- F /\ G != @,
                     F /\ H != @,
                     G /\ H != @.


/*  I,J,K,L are renamings for V,W,X,Y */

path({3},I,J,K,L) :- J /\ K != @,
                     J /\ L != @,
                     K /\ L != @.


/*  M,N,O,P are renamings for V,W,X,Y */

path({4},M,N,O,P) :- N /\ O != @,
                     N /\ P != @,
                     O /\ P != @.
```

This is a correct answer because these are the only conclusions that can be drawn from the input fact that B /\ C != @ because O and P are reachable from B, and N and P are reachable from C, and as far as we know the other nodes in the top layer may be empty.

Interactive Semi-Naive Method

The interactive semi-naive evaluation method is like the semi-naive evaluation method except that after each iteration, the user can investigate the new tuples and decide whether to add them to the constraint database. The following is an example of the interactive semi-naive evaluation.

Example 14.2.4 Consider the evaluation of the *route* relation in Example 14.1.2 after the *path* relation of Example 14.1.1 is calculated and added to the constraint database. In interactive mode the first iteration would yield:

```
> route({4},M,N,O,P) :- M == {1},
                        N == {2,6,8},
                        O == {3,4},
                        P == {5,7,9}.
> accept tuple (Y/N)?
```

Suppose the tuple is accepted. Then the next iteration will give (here variables Q, R, S, T mean I, J, K, L):

```
> route({3},Q,R,S,T) :- {1} <= Q, Q <= {1,3},
                        {2,6,8} <= R, R <= {2,3,6,8},
                        {4} <= S, S <= {3,4},
                        T == {5,7,9},
                        Q /\ R = @, Q /\ S = @, R /\ S = @.
```

This tuple shows that while most of the packets have a determined place, packets 3 can be sent to three different places. Suppose the user decides to send packet 3 to I by entering:

```
> accept tuple (Y/N)? N
> replace tuple (Y/N)? Y
> replace tuple with:

  route({3},Q,R,S,T) :- Q == {1,3},
                        R == {2,6,8},
                        S == {4},
                        T == {5,7,9}.
```

Now the interactive evaluation continues, and the following tuple (where variables Q, R, S, T mean E, F, G, H) is returned:

```
> route({2},Q,R,S,T) :- Q == {1,2,3},
                        R == {3,4},
                        {5} <= S, S <= {5,9},
                        {6,7,8} <= T, T <= {6,7,8,9},
                        S /\ T = @.
```

There is still some ambiguity about the place of packet 9. The user may choose to send it to G by typing:

```
> accept tuple (Y/N)? N
> replace tuple (Y/N)? Y
> replace tuple with:

  route({2},Q,R,S,T) :- Q == {1,2,3},
                        R == {3,4},
                        S == {5,9},
                        T == {6,7,8}.
```

Finally, the fourth iteration will return the final tuple, where variables Q, R, S, T mean A, B, C, D, which is accepted:

```
> route({1},Q,R,S,T) :-  Q == {1,2,3},
                         R == {4,5},
                         S == {6,7},
                         T == {8,9}.
> accept tuple (Y/N)? Y
```

The *route* relation calculated with the interactive semi-naive evaluation shows which packages should be sent to which node in each layer.

Although it is not implemented in DISCO, we remark that the interactive method of evaluation can be replaced by a method where the choices are made by some program. For example, a C program may interact with the DISCO system and always make the following choices for each *route*(Z, Q, R, S, T) tuple:

$$
\begin{aligned}
Z &= Z \\
Q &= Q_{\text{max}} \\
R &= R_{\text{max}} - Q_{\text{max}} \\
S &= S_{\text{max}} - Q_{\text{max}} - R_{\text{max}} \\
T &= T_{\text{max}} - Q_{\text{max}} - R_{\text{max}} - S_{\text{max}}
\end{aligned}
$$

where subscripts min and max denote the lower and upper bounds of the variable.

14.3   Using the DISCO System

The DISCO system has been implemented in the Java programming language. Hence it can be run on both UNIX and Windows. The program is started by typing in the executable DISCO file name at the operating system prompt. After starting the program a new prompt will appear and the system waits for a user command. After the user enters the command, the system waits for the next command. This process is finished if the user exits from the system.

The most important commands provided in the DISCO system are the following:

- `consult filename` —This command loads an the input file "filename" that should be in the format described in Section 14.1.

- `display [R] [onto filename]` —When a relation name "R" is given DISCO prints out the rules of the relation. If no "R" is given, then DISCO prints out the names and arities of all the relations. If a file name is specified, then the formula will be printed out to the file, otherwise it will be printed out to the screen.

- `displaydf [onto filename]`—This command prints out all the derived facts in the database to the screen or the specified file.

- `memory`—This command displays the total and free memory used by the system.

- `clear`—This command erases all the relations and rules from the database.

- `R(`$E_1, \ldots, E_n$`)?`—In this command each E_i can be either a variable or a set of constants. Variables need not be distinct. DISCO will return any derived fact of the relation "R" that can match the input.

- `bye`—This command exits the program.

The DISCO system also provides several switches that control the evaluation of the system. These on-off switches include `time`, to display the time used during the evaluation; `trace`, to display the inner representation of rules; `optimize`, to use the relational algebra optimization routines; `seminaive`, to use semi-naive instead of naive evaluation; and `interactive`, to use interactive (semi)-naive evaluation. To set a switch, one has to type any of the switch names at the command mode `switchname on` or `switchname off`. The default for `time`, `trace`, and `interactive` is off and for `optimize` and `seminaive` is on.

14.3.1 Experimental Results

We tested the running times of the *path* query in Example 14.1.1, the *route* query in Example 14.1.2, and the *path* query again in Example 14.1.3 with the broadcast network connections. We ran all three queries in non-interactive mode. We measured the results on a Pentium II 267 MHz computer running Windows. The running times are displayed in Figure 14.2, measured in real seconds, not CPU seconds.

Problem	Naive		Semi-Naive	
	Without optimization	With optimization	Without optimization	With optimization
Path	3.746	1.472	2.383	1.261
Broadcast	1.392	0.921	1.131	0.921
Route	35.872	17.966	40.819	18.036

Figure 14.2: Test results (Pentium II 267 MHz).

14.4   Extensibility of the DISCO System

Although the DISCO system implements a specific Boolean algebra, that is, B_Z, the Boolean algebra of sets of integers, it is possible to extend the system to deal with other Boolean algebras. Implementing new Boolean algebras enables us to express many more interesting queries.

In changing to a new Boolean algebra, we need to replace only a few of the basic DISCO routines. First, we need to redefine the operators $\cap$, $\cup$, and $^-$. We also have to change some of the data storage structures and modify the naive and semi-naive evaluation methods with a new subsumption test. Some of these require some work, but in principle much of the software written for the DISCO system could be reused.

Bibliographic Notes

The DISCO system was developed over several years at the University of Nebraska. The first version of the system implemented only *set-order* and positive *gap-order* constraints and was presented in Byon and Revesz [62]. The quantifier elimination technique of this system was described in Srivastava et al. [382], and the naive evaluation of Datalog queries was considered in Revesz [326, 335]. More details of the evaluation and example queries were given in [330]. This first version was also used to solve some genome assembly problems (see Chapter 10) in Revesz [331]. A shortened earlier version of this chapter appears in Kuper et al. [251].

The second version of DISCO, which we described in this chapter, added to set-order constraints monotone Boolean inequality constraints and Boolean equality constraints over sets of integers [358]. However, general Boolean equality and inequality constraints cannot be used together. For the projection operator two quantifier elimination methods are implemented for the two different additions to set-order constraints. If equality and inequality constraints are found together in a formula before quantifier elimination, then an error message is generated.

The quantifier elimination method for Boolean equality constraints is due to G. Boole, while the one for set-order and monotone Boolean inequality constraints is described in Revesz [333]. More on methods for quantifier elimination in the case of Boolean equality and inequality constraints can be found in Helm et al. [195] and Marriott and Odersky [266].

Examples 14.1.1, 14.1.2, and 14.1.3 are new. The discussion about the relational algebra identities and the naive and semi-naive evaluation are adopted with necessary modifications to include constraints from Ullman [408].

Conjuncto by Gervet [149] is a constraint logic programming system that uses set constraints. The evaluation method is different and its termination is not guaranteed in general for Conjuncto queries.

Exercises

1. Implement in DISCO the street reachability problem in Example 12.2.4.

2. Implement in DISCO the Hamiltonian cycle problem in Example 12.2.2.

3. Implement in DISCO the propositional satisfiability problem in Exercise 12.5.

4. Write a DISCO query that solves the SEND + MORE = MONEY puzzle in Example 9.3.4.

15

Database Design

Database design methods, like many other design methods, rely on visualizations of an abstraction of the database. We already discussed data abstraction in the context of the constraint data model in Section 4.4.3. The visualization produced by database design methods may be considered to be at the view-level of the abstraction hierarchy.

One database design method that captured wide attention in databases is the *entity relationship diagram* method, which is discussed in Section 15.1. Entity relationship diagrams describe many aspects of the database but say little about how the database is going to be queried. However, databases and software engineering may increasingly merge in the future because more and more data processing is expected to be performed by the database before comminicating the query result to the rest of the computer software that uses the database. Hence it seems likely that the analysis of more powerful databases, such as constraint databases, needs to be done similarly to the analysis of programs done in software engineering. *Constraint automata*, which are related to *transition systems* in software engineering, form an attractive design method for constraint databases. Section 15.2 describes constraint automata.

15.1 Entity Relationship Diagrams

An entity relationship diagram contains the following parts.

Entity sets: Each *entity set* is a set of persons, objects, or concepts that form a major focus of the database. In the entity relationship diagram, entity sets are represented by rectangles.

P. Revesz, *Introduction to Databases: From Biological to Spatio-Temporal*,
Texts in Computer Science, DOI 10.1007/978-1-84996-095-3_15,
© Springer-Verlag London Limited 2010

Relationships: Each *relationship* is some interaction or other connection between two entity sets or among more entity sets. In the entity relationship diagram, relationships are represented by diamonds and line connections to all the entity sets involved in the relationship. A relationship between only two entity sets is called a *binary relationship*, while among three entity sets it is called a *ternary relationship*, an so on. Binary relationships play an especially important role in database design and are further divided into three categories, which are as follows.

One-to-one: A binary relationship between two entity sets A and B is *one-to-one* if each entity in A participates in the relationship with at most one entity in B and vice versa. One-to-one relationships are represented by a pair of arrows. Both arrows run from the relationship to the entity sets. Hence the arrow heads touch the rectangles representing the entity sets.

One-to-many: A binary relationship between two entity sets A and B is *one-to-many* if each entity in A may participate in the relationship with several entities in B, but each entity in B participates in the relationship with at most one entity in A. A one-to-many relationship between A and B is represented by an arrow from the relationship R to A with the arrowhead touching the rectangle representing A, and a plain line, that is, a line without arrowheads between the relationship and B.

Many-to-many: A binary relationship between two entity sets A and B is *many-to-many* if each entity in A may participate in the relationship with several entities in B, and vice versa. Many-to-many relationships are represented by a pair of plain lines. One plain line connects entity set A and the relationship R, and the second plan line connects entity set B and relationship R.

Attributes: Both entity sets and relationships can have *attributes*, which describe specific features or characteristics of the entities or the relationships. In the entity relationship diagram, attributes are represented by ovals.

Next we look at an insurance company example.

Example 15.1.1 Suppose that we need to design a database system for an insurance company that insures against natural disaster, such as a flood or a tornado. We need to represent in the insurance company database at least the following.

Person: This is an entity set that represents all the persons who are clients and were insured by the insurance company.

Disaster: This is an entity set that represents all floods, tornados and other natural disasters that have occurred in the areas insures and may have affected some of the clients.

Hit: This is a relationship between the entity sets *Person* and *Disaster*. The *Hit* relationship means that the particular persons in *Person* were hit by particular disaster events in *Disaster*. Note that *Hit* is a many-to-many relationship because each person can be hit by several disasters, and each disaster can hit several persons.

Name: This is an obvious attribute of the *Person* entity set.

Type: This is an obvious attribute of the *Disaster* entity set.

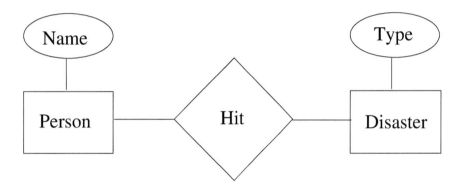

Figure 15.1: Entity relationship diagram.

Figure 15.1 shows an entity relationship diagram with all of the above described elements. Usually, entity relationship diagrams are extended and revised in many iterations until they are considered a good design for the database. After looking at Figure 15.1, we may realize that we forgot some important attributes. For instance, a person should have an address. Likewise, a disaster should have a date of occurrence. Hence we may add to the diagram new ovals into which we write "address" and "date," and then we may connect the ovals with the enity sets *Person* and *Disaster*, respectively.

However, even with the additions, the design would not be considered in genreal to be correct because "address" and "date" are *composite attributes*. One of the goals of good design is to arrive at a final entity relationship diagram in which there are no composite attributes. In the insurance company example, the composite attributes can be easily broken up into simpler attributes. For simplicity, let us suppose that we break "address" into "house number" and "street name" attributes. Similarly, assume that we split "date" into "month," "day," and "year."

The completed entity relationship diagram is easy to translate into several types of databases.

Example 15.1.2 Suppose that the *Person* entity set contains the following five clients of the insurance company: Anderson, Brown, Clark, David, and Edwards, who live at 98 Maple, 21 Oak, 35 Bear, 79 Hare, and 64 Willow streets, respectively. Further suppose that the *Disaster* entity set contains one flood on 3/15/2002, and two tornados on 6/18/2001 and 7/20/2003. Finally suppose that the *Hit* relationship records that Anderson, Brown, and Clark were hit by the flood, Clark and Davis were hit by the first tornado, and David and Edwards were hit by the second tornado.

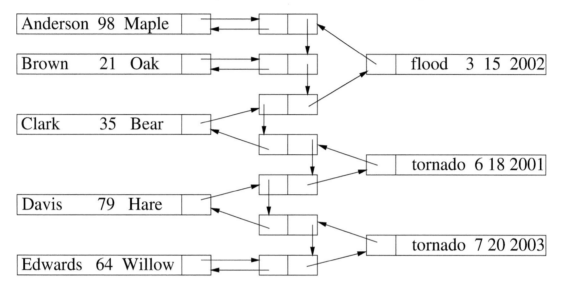

Figure 15.2: Network data model.

Figure 15.2 shows the translation of the entity relationship diagram into the network data model. Note that the hit relation is nicely implemented by a linked data structure using pointers. A clever idea in the network data model for the implementation of many-to-many relationships is to create a record with two pointers for each element of the relationship. The first pointer is used in circular lists connecting all the persons, and the second pointer is used in other circular lists connecting all the disasters. As a result, in the network data model each entity is linked in a circular list with all of the relationship elements with which it is involved. The circular list enables an easy cycling through of all the records related to any chosen entity.

Although the network data model was a major advance over the hierarchical data model, which could not implement many-to-many relationships, even the network data model became cumbersome when databases started to have a large number of entity sets and relationships.

Entity relationship diagrams form a flexible, high-level design method. Hence they are translatable also into other data models. The next example considers relational databases.

Example 15.1.3 As we saw in Chapter 3, relational databases were the next great advance in the database area. Entity relationship diagrams can be even more easily translated into relational databases because each entity set and each relationship in the diagram simply becomes a table in the relational database. However, before doing the translation one small step is necessary because the relational data model requires that each tuple has a *primary key*, which is one or more attributes whose values uniquely identify each record in the table. Therefore, we also need to find a primary key for the *Person* and the *Disaster* entity sets.

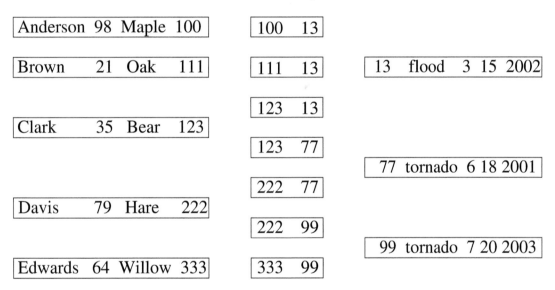

Figure 15.3: Relational data model.

It is possible to consider all the attributes of *Person*, that is, name, house number, and street as the primary key. Similarly, it possible to consider all the attributes of *Disaster*, that is, type, month, day, and year, as the primary key of *Disaster*. However, since primary keys are routinely used for indexing, they work best if they are single attributes. Therein lies the need for relational databases to introduce a new "identication number" attribute for both the persons and the disasters. Let us assume, we introduce such id numbers. Then it becomes possible to represent the *Hit* relationship simply by a table of pairs of person id numers and disaster id numbers. Figure 15.3 shows the result.

The relational data model is more convenient to use than the network model is. For example, when testing which disaster types Clark was hit by, the network data model has to cycle through all the pointers for the flood and find Anderson and Brown first before getting to Clark. Then it has to start again with the first pointer of tornado, cycle through them all unsucessfully, and then it has to do the same for the second tornado. Expressing the required pointer manipulation in any network database query language is not trivial.

In contrast, in the relational data model, assuming we have the relations:

- *Person(Name,HouseNo,Street,Pid)*

- *Hit(Pid,Did)*

- *Disaster(Did,Type,Month,Day,Year)*

we can write the following basic SQL query, which almost feels trivial compared to the earlier alternative.

CREATE VIEW	Clark_Disaster(Ctype)
SELECT	Type
FROM	Person, Disaster
WHERE	Name = "Clark"

Databases do not exist in a vacuum but are influenced by larger currents in computer science. Hierarchical databases in their time took a good use of sequential storage devices like magnetic tapes. Network databases with their heavy use of pointers were made possible by the development of random access storage devices. Relational databases came at a time when the idea of what is convenient for the programmer was beginning to be taken seriously. Prior to that time the cost of the computer dominated the cost of software engineers. Hence software engineers were expected to program in a way that saved machine time and computer memory.

Object-oriented programming was another great computer science advance that inlfuenced the databases. The next example describes *object-oriented databases*, or *object-databsases*.

Example 15.1.4 Object-oriented databases turn all the entity sets and relationships into objects. Communication with the objects is accomplished via methods or functions written for the objects. For example, the entity relationship diagram could be translated into an object-oriented database

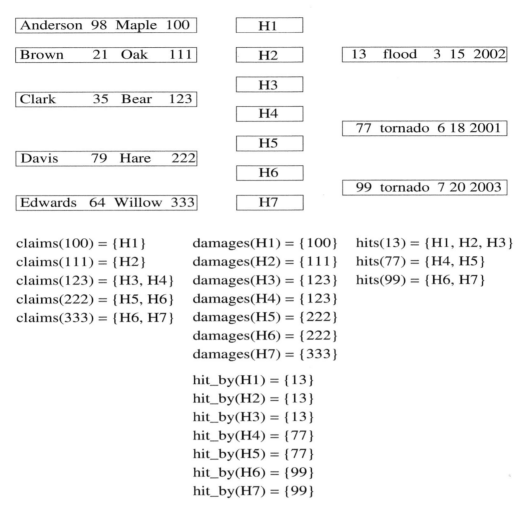

Figure 15.4: Object-oriented data model.

by creating the objects *Person_Obj*, *Hit_Obj*, and *Disaster_Obj* as shown in Figure 15.4.

In addition to the identification numbers already created by the relaional database, the object-oriented database creates an identifier for each hit record. Finally, it would also create the following four functions with both domains and ranges over the object identifiers.

- claims: Person_Obj → Hit_Obj

- damages: Hit_Obj → Person_Obj

- hit_by: Hit_Obj → Disaster_Obj

- hits: Disaster_Obj → Hit_Obj

- get_person_obj_id: Name → Person_Obj

The last function returns the object identification number of the *Person_Obj* where the name field matches a given name. Using the above functions, the type of disasters that Clark was involved in can now be found by the following simple one line query.

$$Clark\_Disaster = hit\_by(claims(get\_person\_obj\_id("Clark"))).type$$

Databases today are further influenced by the spread of geographic data and their applications. It seems that future databases need to incorporate more geographic and spatial data or lose their commercial lead to geographic information systems.

Example 15.1.5 Database design sometimes yields surprises. Just when we thought that we can no longer improve the entity relationship diagram and its implementation, a new idea may still lead to further improvements. Indeed, let us consider the insurance company database from a geographic database perpective. Surprisingly, we do not need in the entity relationship diagram a *Hit* relationship if we know the disaster areas and the house locations of each person because then we can simply compute whether any particular house was within a disaster area. This gives the idea of redesigning the entity relationship diagram as shown in Figure 15.5.

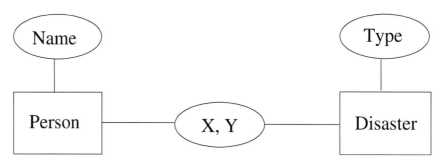

Figure 15.5: Revised entity relationship diagram.

The new entity relationship diagram can be translated into the constraint-geographic relations:

- *Person2(Name,HouseNo,Street,X,Y)*

- *Disaster2(Type,Month,Day,Year,X,Y)*

The new design not only eliminates the *Hit* relation, but it offers further advantages. First, we can test whether a claim is valid.

CREATE VIEW	Valid_Claim(Name,No,Str,Type,M,D,Y)
SELECT	Name, HouseNo, Street,
	Type, Month, Day, Year
FROM	Person2 AS P, Disaster2 AS D
WHERE	P.X = D.X AND
	P.Y = D.Y

Second, suppose the insurance company suspects that some clients made fraudulent insurance claims in the past. That is, some clients claimed damages for a house that was never in a disaster area. For instance, Figure 15.6 shows the town with streets as straight lines and disaster areas as small ovals. It is clear that Bear street, which is the street with slope $\frac{1}{3}$, was never hit by either a flood or a tornado. Therefore, Clark's claims to have been hit by the flood and by the tornado on 6/18/2001 are clearly fraudulent.

Luckily for the insurance company, but not so luckily for Clark, by looking at their earlier records, the insurance company can catch the cheating clients using the following query.

CREATE VIEW	Fraudulent_Claim(Name,No,Str,Type,M,D,Y)
SELECT	Name, HouseNo, Street,
	Type, Month, Day, Year
FROM	Person AS P, Disaster AS D, Hit AS H
WHERE	P.Pid = H.PID AND
	D.Did = H.Did
MINUS	
SELECT	Name, HouseNo, Street,
	Type, Month, Day, Year
FROM	Valid_Claim

It is interesting to compare the above solution with the earlier approaches. The above solution uses the (x, y) location of the person's house as a unique identifier. Hence it is like a primary key in the relational and the object-oriented data models. However, it is a meaningful primary key instead of a randomly assigned number. The meaningfulness of that primary key enabled the natural connection to the disaster areas. The constraint-geographic database design did no extra work in deliberately creating relationships in the diagram and in assigning a host of primary keys or object access methods. Instead it got the link between houses and disaster areas basically for free because the (x, y) locations were only attributes of the entity sets.

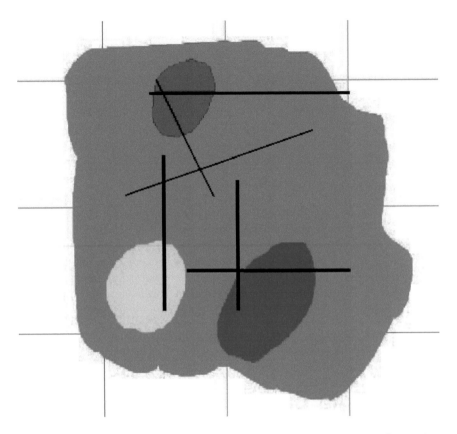

Figure 15.6: A town map with the areas hit by flood (blue oval area at lower right) and by tornados (red and yellow ovals on left side).

Once the insurance company knows that a claim is not completely fraudulent, the next step is to represent the exact damage amount. That can be done by adding "Amount" as an attribute to the *Disaster2* entity set in the entity relationship diagram of Figure 15.5. Note that the name of the client claiming that amount can be always found by a join on (x, y) of the *Person2* and the *Disaster2* relations.

As the above examples reveal, although the entity relationship diagrams provide a high-level view of the entire database, the exact diagram may need to be designed slightly differently depending on the type of database system that will implement it after the design phase. Moreover, sometimes an upgrade from one type of database to another type may require a reconsideration of some aspects of the entity relationship diagram.

15.2   Constraint Automata

Constraint automata are used to control the operation of systems based on conditions that are described using constraints on variables. Section 15.2.1 presents a concrete definition and gives several examples of constraint automata.

A constraint automaton can be simplified using *reduction rules* that redraw constraint automata into equivalent constraint automata. Section 15.2.2 presents some reduction rules.

An important problem for constraint automata is to find the set of *reachable configurations*, which is the set of states and state values that a constraint automaton can enter. Section 15.2.3 presents a method of analyzing the reachable configurations of constraint automata by expressing the constraint automata in Datalog with constraints.

15.2.1   Definition of Constraint Automata

A constraint automaton consists of a set of states, a set of state variables, transitions between states, an initial state, and the domain and initial values of the state variables. Each transition consists of a set of constraints, called the *guard* constraints, followed by a set of assignment statements. The guard constraints of a constraint automaton can contain relations. In constraint automata the guards are followed by question marks, and the assignment statements are shown using the symbol :=.

A constraint automaton can move from one state to another if there is a transition whose guard constraints are satisfied by the current values of the state variables. The transitions of a constraint automaton may contain variables in addition to the state variables. These variables are said to be *existentially quantified* variables. Their meaning is that some values for these variables can be found such that the guard constraints are satisfied.

A constraint automaton can interact with its environment by sensing the current value of a variable. This is expressed by a $read(x)$ command on a transition between states, where x is any variable. This command updates the value of x to a new value. The read command can appear either before or after the guard constraints.

The following is an example of a constraint automaton with a single state.

Example 15.2.1 While visiting some countries, a tourist who has dollars, euros, and yen always exchanges these at the rate of one dollar equals two euros, which equals three hundred yen. Each exchange is a multiple of 100 dollars, 200 euros, or 30,000 yen and has a commission charge of 1 percent.

Let d be the total amount of dollars the tourist has spent on anything except commissions plus the amount that remains in his wallet. Let e and

y be defined similarly. We are interested in the possible values of d, e, and y at any time during the trip. The constraint automaton that defines the possible values of d, e, and y is shown in Figure 15.7.

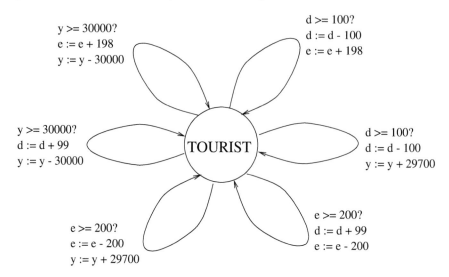

Figure 15.7: The tourist's currency constraint automaton.

Each constraint automaton can be drawn as a graph in which each vertex represents a state and each directed edge represents a transition. There is only one state and three state variables, d, e, and y.

The following two examples show the use of read commands.

Example 15.2.2 A hotel elevator can move from the lobby up to the restaurant or down to the underground parking garage. The elevator can sense the number of people waiting in front of the elevator on each floor, the up and down signals pushed in the lobby, and the floor request signals pushed within the elevator. (There are no up and down signals in the restaurant or the parking garage.)

The elevator does not always go all the way up and down. Instead it operates as follows. If while going from the parking garage to the lobby it senses no request for the restaurant either within the elevator or in the lobby and there are more people in the lobby than in the restaurant, then it will go down again after reaching the lobby. Otherwise, it will go up to the restaurant.

Similarly, if while going from the restaurant to the lobby it senses no request for the parking garage either within the elevator or in the lobby and there are more people in the lobby than in the parking garage, then it will go up again after reaching the lobby. Otherwise, it will go down to the parking garage.

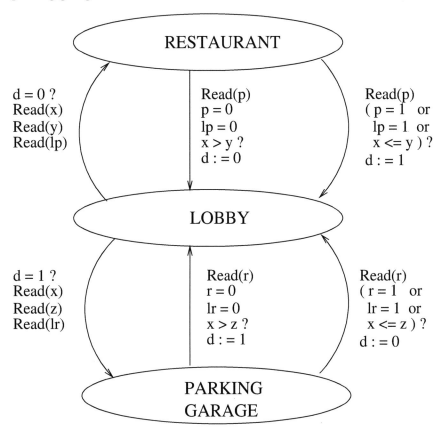

Figure 15.8: The hotel elevator system.

This hotel elevator system can be described by the constraint automaton shown in Figure 15.8. The constraint automaton has three states, each corresponding to and named after a possible position of the elevator. Each state has the following variables:

- $x, y,$ and z, which describe the number of people sensed to be waiting for the elevator in the lobby, in the parking garage, and in the restaurant, respectively;

- d, which shows whether the next move of the elevator will be down;

- p and r, which show whether anyone in the elevator requested the parking garage or the restaurant, respectively; and

- lp and lr, which show whether anyone in the lobby pushed the down or the up button.

Each of the last five variables is 1 when the answer is yes and 0 when it is no.

Example 15.2.3 A ferry takes passengers across a river between shores A and B. The ferry also stops occasionally at an island C, which is visited by few passengers. The ferry visits the island according to the following rules. (1) If there is any passenger waiting to stop at C, then visit C on the third crossing since the last visit. (2) If there are at least ten passengers who are waiting to stop at C, then the ferry may visit C earlier, but never on two subsequent crossings.

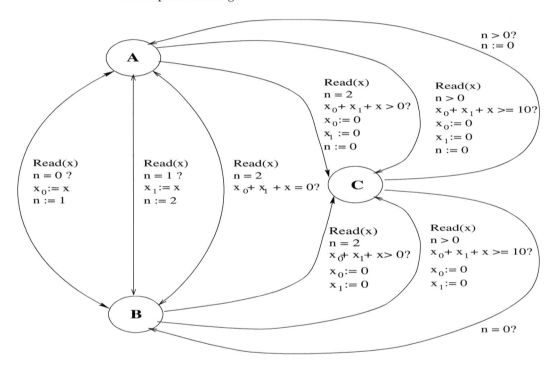

Figure 15.9: The ferry system.

Assume that we know how many new passengers who want to go to island C board the ferry in each hour. Find all possible combinations of location and number of passengers waiting in the ferry for one or two crossings.

The constraint automaton is shown in Figure 15.9. There are three states for the three possible locations of the ferry. The state variables are

n, the number of crossings since the last visit to C; variables x_0 and x_1, the number of passengers waiting to visit C since $t = 0$ and $t = 1$, respectively; and x, the number of passengers freshly boarding with tickets to the island.

Drawing a constraint automata can be a good way to design a control system. The next is a real-life example of a complex design.

Example 15.2.4 A subway train speed regulation system is defined as follows. Each train detects beacons that are placed along the track and receives a "second" signal from a central clock.

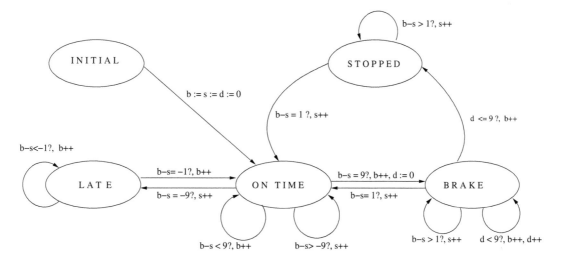

Figure 15.10: The subway train control system.

Let b and s be counter variables for the number of beacons and second signals received. Further, let d be a counter variable that describes for how long the train is applying its brake. The goal of the speed regulation system is to keep $\mid b - s \mid$ small while the train is running.

The speed of the train is adjusted as follows. When $s + 10 \leq b$, then the train notices it is early and applies the brake as long as $b > s$. Continuously braking causes the train to stop before encountering 10 beacons.

When $b + 10 \leq s$ the train is late and will be considered late as long as $b < s$. As long as any train is late, the central clock will not emit the second signal.

The subway speed regulation system can be drawn as a constraint automaton shown in Figure 15.10, where $x + +$ and $x - -$ are abbreviations for $x := x + 1$ and $x := x - 1$, respectively, for any variable x.

The following is an example constraint automaton with existentially quantified variables.

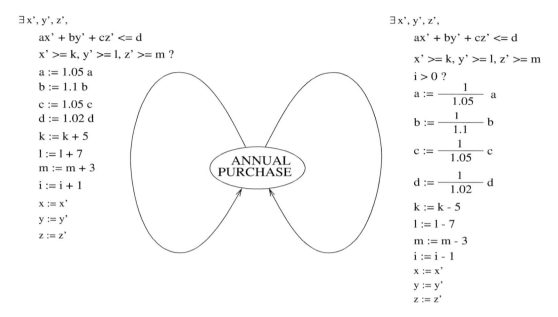

$\exists x', y', z',$

$\quad ax' + by' + cz' <= d$

$\quad x' >= k, y' >= l, z' >= m$?

$\quad a := 1.05\, a$

$\quad b := 1.1\, b$

$\quad c := 1.05\, c$

$\quad d := 1.02\, d$

$\quad k := k + 5$

$\quad l := l + 7$

$\quad m := m + 3$

$\quad i := i + 1$

$\quad x := x'$

$\quad y := y'$

$\quad z := z'$

$\exists x', y', z',$

$\quad ax' + by' + cz' <= d$

$\quad x' >= k, y' >= l, z' >= m$

$\quad i > 0$?

$\quad a := \dfrac{1}{1.05}\, a$

$\quad b := \dfrac{1}{1.1}\, b$

$\quad c := \dfrac{1}{1.05}\, c$

$\quad d := \dfrac{1}{1.02}\, d$

$\quad k := k - 5$

$\quad l := l - 7$

$\quad m := m - 3$

$\quad i := i - 1$

$\quad x := x'$

$\quad y := y'$

$\quad z := z'$

Figure 15.11: The annual purchase constraint automaton.

Example 15.2.5 A business needs to annually purchase three resources x, y, and z. Currently the price of these resources are a, b, and c, respectively, and the purchase budget is d. The business needs at least k, l, and m of these items, respectively.

Each year we have either an inflation or a deflation. During an inflationary year, a and c increase 5 per cent, b increases 10 per cent, and d increases 2 per cent, while k, m, and l increase 5 per cent, 7 per cent, and 3 per cent, respectively. Each deflationary year cancels the effect of a previous inflationary year, and the prices and limits decrease to regain their previous values. Assume that the number of inflationary years is always more than the number of deflationary years.

This problem can be represented using the constraint automaton shown in Figure 15.11.

The following is an example of a constraint automaton in which the guards contain relations.

Example 15.2.6 A cafeteria has three queues where choices for salad, main dishes, and drinks can be made. A customer has a coupon for $10. He first picks a selection. His selection must include a main dish and a salad, but drink may be skipped if the salad costs more than $3. If the total cost of the selection is less than $8 then he may go back to make a new choice for salad or drink.

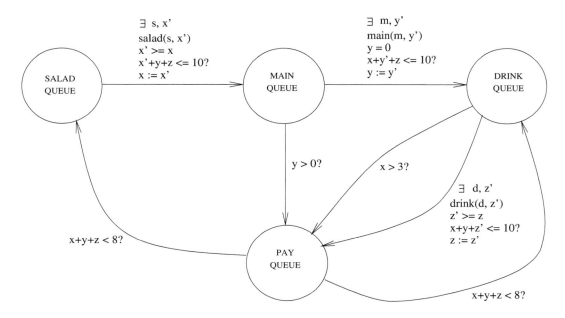

Figure 15.12: The cafeteria constraint automaton.

Let *salad*, *main*, and *drink* be three binary relations in which the first argument is the name of a salad, main dish, or drink and the second argument is its price. The constraint automaton in Figure 15.12 expresses this problem.

An interesting special case of constraint automata has only one state and one transition, which updates the values of the state variables such that each variable is a linear combination of the others. The following is an example.

Example 15.2.7 On a certain planet water can occur in the form of clouds, rain, streams, and ocean. We know that each year one-sixtieth of the ocean becomes clouds, one-half of the clouds become rain, one-third of the rain becomes clouds, one-third of the rain becomes streams, and one-third of the rain becomes ocean. One-sixth of the streams become clouds and one-sixth become ocean.

The water cycle on this planet can be represented by the constraint automaton shown in Figure 15.13, where c, r, s, and o represent the amount of water in the four forms before and c', r', s', and o' represent them after a transition. Given an initial amount of water in the four forms, an interesting problem would be to find whether the proportion of water in the different forms ever stabilizes.

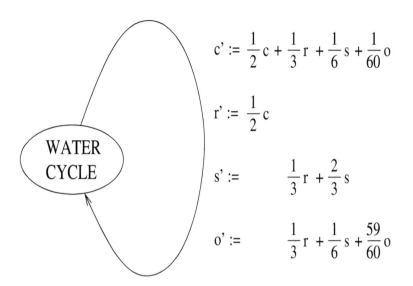

$$c' := \frac{1}{2}c + \frac{1}{3}r + \frac{1}{6}s + \frac{1}{60}o$$

$$r' := \frac{1}{2}c$$

$$s' := \frac{1}{3}r + \frac{2}{3}s$$

$$o' := \frac{1}{3}r + \frac{1}{6}s + \frac{59}{60}o$$

Figure 15.13: The water cycle constraint automaton.

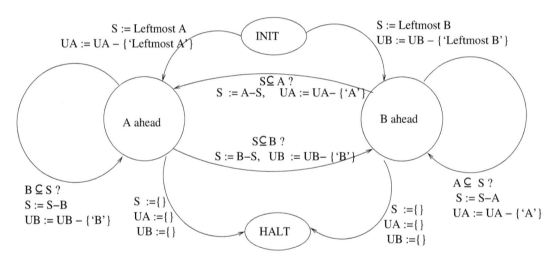

Figure 15.14: The automaton.

Example 15.2.8 Figure 15.14 shows a constraint automaton for solving the big-bag matching problem using the offset fingerprint method described in Section 10.2.3. The automaton uses the constraints $\subseteq$ and difference over multisets. The automaton starts in the INIT state and tries to reach the

HALT state. From the INIT state, we start building a figure like the one shown in Figure 15.15, going from left to right by adding either an A or a B bag. Each bag represents a contiguity constraint for the elements it contains. That is, any valid presentation must contain the elements within a bag next to each other. Therefore, adding a new bag really adds a new contiguity constraint to a set of other such constraints. Only if the set of constraints is solvable (and there could be several solutions) is the automaton allowed to continue with the next transition.

At any point either the list of A bags will be ahead of the list of B bags (and the automaton will be in state "A ahead") or vice versa (and it will be in the state "B ahead") or neither will be ahead, in which case it goes back to the INIT state and starts the matching algorithm again using only the unused A and B bags.

The automaton keeps for each state the following state variables: UA and UB indicating the ID numbers of the unused A and B bags, and S the bag of elements by which either the A list or the B list is currently ahead.

Whenever there are possible alternatives the automaton makes a guess. If the automaton cannot reach the HALT state after a series of guesses, then it will backtrack and try a new guess. We will explain the run of the automaton without backtracking, assuming only correct guesses.

First the automaton guesses the first bag and moves from the INIT state to either the "A ahead" or the "B ahead" state.

If the automaton is in the "A ahead" state then it can guess the next B bag. If the next B bag contains S, which is the set of elements by which A is currently ahead, then the automaton will move to the "B ahead" state and set the value of S to be the value of the new bag minus the current value of S. Otherwise, if the next B bag is contained in S, then the automaton stays in the "A ahead" state but subtracts from S the value of the new bag. In both cases, the elements of S and the new bag are matched as far as possible and the new bag is taken out from UB. The automaton behaves similarly when it is in the "B ahead" state, except that A and B are reversed.

When all the bags are used and UA, UB, and S are empty, then the automaton enters the HALT state and stops.

Now we give an example execution of the automaton using the input data shown in Figures 10.12 and 10.13. The first five steps of the constraint automaton are shown in Figure 15.15.

First, the automaton moves from the INIT state to the "B ahead" state after choosing $B3$ as the first bag. We have $S = B3$.

Second, the automaton chooses $A9$ because $S \subseteq A9$, sets $S = A9 - S = \{13, 18\}$ and moves to the "A ahead" state.

Third, the automaton chooses $B1$ because $B1 \subseteq S$, sets $S = S - B1$ and remains in the "A ahead" state.

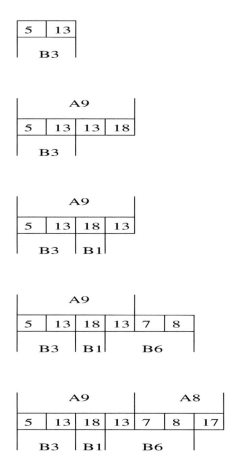

Figure 15.15: The first five steps of the constraint automaton.

Fourth, the automaton chooses $B6$ because $S \subseteq B6$, sets $S = B6 - S = \{7, 8\}$ and moves to the "B ahead" state.

Fifth, the automaton chooses $A8$ because $S \subseteq A8$, sets $S = A8 - S = \{17\}$ and moves to the "A ahead" state.

We can continue in this way until we reach a solution like the one shown in Figure 15.16.

Figure 15.17 summarizes each move of the automaton and gives for each transition the name of the new bag added to the figure, the update operation on S, and the values of S, UA, and UB.

The correctness of the automaton will be proved in the next theorem.

A9					A8		A3	A1	A4		A6		A2		A10			A7		A5	
5	13	18	13	7	8	17	8	9	14	27	65	8	7	4	9	4	12	11	12	10	10	10	28	5	4	5	10
B3	B1	B6		B8			B4		B7			B9			B5		B2				

Figure 15.16: A solution for the big-bags matching problem.

New	S=	S	Unused As	Unused Bs
—	—	—	1, 2, 3, 4, 5, 6, 7, 8, 9, 10	1, 2, 3, 4, 5, 6, 7, 8, 9
B3	B3	5, 13	1, 2, 3, 4, 5, 6, 7, 8, 9, 10	1, 2, 4, 5, 6, 7, 8, 9
A9	A9 - S	13, 18	1, 2, 3, 4, 5, 6, 7, 8, 10	1, 2, 4, 5, 6, 7, 8, 9
B1	S - B1	13	1, 2, 3, 4, 5, 6, 7, 8, 10	2, 4, 5, 6, 7, 8, 9
B6	B6 - S	7, 8	1, 2, 3, 4, 5, 6, 7, 8, 10	2, 4, 5, 7, 8, 9
A8	A8 - S	17	1, 2, 3, 4, 5, 6, 7, 10	2, 4, 5, 7, 8, 9
B8	B8 - S	8, 9, 14, 27	1, 2, 3, 4, 5, 6, 7, 10	2, 4, 5, 7, 9
A3	S - A3	14, 27	1, 2, 4, 5, 6, 7, 10	2, 4, 5, 7, 9
A1	S - A1	27	2, 4, 5, 6, 7, 10	2, 4, 5, 7, 9
A4	A4 - S	65	2, 5, 6, 7, 10	2, 4, 5, 7, 9
B4	B4 - S	8	2, 5, 6, 7, 10	2, 5, 7, 9
A6	A6 - S	4, 7	2, 5, 7, 10	2, 5, 7, 9
B7	B7 - S	4, 9, 12	2, 5, 7, 10	2, 5, 9
A2	S - A2	12	5, 7, 10	2, 5, 9
A10	A10 - S	10, 10, 11, 12	5, 7	2, 5, 9
B9	B9 - S	10	5, 7	2, 5
A7	A7 - S	5, 28	5	2, 5
B5	B5 - S	4	5	2
A5	A5 - S	5, 10	—	2
B2	B2 - S	—	—	—
—	—	—	—	—

Figure 15.17: A run of the automaton.

Theorem 15.2.1 The nondeterministic constraint automaton reaches the HALT state if and only if the two big-bags match.

Proof: We prove by induction on the number of transitions of the automaton the following: After the ith transition, i number of bags in A and B match, and S is a bag that contains those elements of the rightmost bag in A (respectively B) that do not match any of the B (or A) bags if the automaton is in the state "A ahead" (or "B ahead"). (Here the rightmost bag is that bag among those the automaton used that *ends* at the rightmost position. Similarly, the leftmost bag *ends* at the leftmost position.)

Initially, we are given for the value of S the leftmost bag in A and B. The leftmost bag is taken away from one of the big-bags, but nothing is taken from the other big-bag. Hence no bags match yet and the claim is true for $i = 0$.

Now assume that the claim is true for i transitions and prove it for $i+1$. Because the automaton is symmetric in A and B, we can assume without loss of generality that the automaton is in state "A ahead" after the ith transition. By the induction hypothesis S is the bag of those elements in the current rightmost A bag that were not yet matched to any elements in B bags. During the $i + 1$st transition the automaton either stays in "A ahead" or moves to "B ahead."

If the automaton stays in "A ahead," then it must find a new B bag whose elements are in S. Hence B can be matched. The transition also updates S by subtracting the elements of B from S. This preserves the condition that S contains the yet unmatched elements of the rightmost A bag. Also, the rightmost bag will remain the same bag in A because S had only a subset of the elements in it and B cannot end later than A because while all of its elements are matched, there may be unmatched elements remaining in S.

If the automaton moves to state "B ahead," then it must find a new B bag that contains S. Therefore all the yet unmatched elements can be matched by the new B bag. Therefore, the rightmost bag will now be the new B bag. Further, the elements in B that are not matched are exactly $B \setminus S$, which is the new value of S. Hence the condition is preserved.

When S is empty and all A and B bags are used, then the automaton moves to the HALT state. Because each transition uses exactly one A or B bag, the only time the automaton could move to the HALT state is on the nth transition, where n is the total number of bags in A and B. Because of the condition, which we proved to be preserved after each transition, all n bags must match. Hence if the automaton reaches the HALT state, then the two big-bags must match. On the other hand, if the two big-bags match, then the automaton can guess correctly the order of the big-bags according to their ending points and use the transition that uses up the next B bag if it is in state "A ahead" or the next B bag if it is in state "B ahead." ∎

15.2.2 Simplifications of Constraint Automata

Drawing a constraint automaton can be a good start in solving a problem. However, the first drawing may be more complex than necessary and may need to be simplified. The following example illustrates the simplification process.

A correct design of the constraint automaton in Figure 15.10 would mean that $b - s$ is at least some constant c_1 and at most some constant c_2.

The value of $b - s$ may be unbounded in case of an incorrect design. To test the correctness of the constraint automaton, let's rewrite it using variable x instead of the value $(b - s) - 20$ and variable y instead of d. This change of variables yields the automaton shown in Figure 15.18.

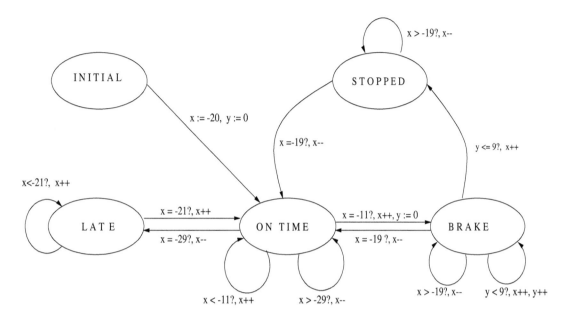

Figure 15.18: The subway system after changing variables.

Now we can make some observations of equivalences between automata. We call these equivalences *reduction rules*. Reduction rules allow us to either rewrite complex constraints into simpler ones (like rules 1 and 2 in the following) or eliminate some transitions from the constraint automaton (like rule 3 in the following).

1. Moving increment after self-loop: This reduction rule is shown in Figure 15.19. This rule can be applied when no other arcs are ending at state S. This rule says that if there is only one self-loop at S and it can decrement repeatedly a variable while it is greater than c, then the $x + +$ before it can be brought after it, if we replace c by $c - 1$ in the guard condition of the self-loop. It is easy to see that in state S for each possible configuration before this reduction there will be a corresponding configuration with the same values except that x is one smaller. The set of possible configurations in the other states is not changed by this reduction rule. We give an example of the use of this reduction rule later.

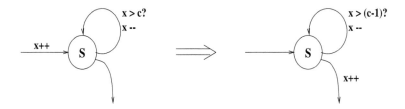

Figure 15.19: Moving increment after self-loop.

2. Elimination of increment/decrement from self-loops: This reduction rule is shown in Figure 15.20. There are two variations of this rule shown on the top and bottom, depending on whether the variable is incremented or decremented. The top variation says that if a variable is decremented one or more times using a self-loop until a guard condition $x > c$ is satisfied, then the repetition is equivalent to a self-loop, which just picks some value x' greater than or equal to c and less than the initial value of x and assigns x' to x. The bottom variation is explained similarly. Note that both reduction rules eliminate the need to repeatedly execute the transition. That is, any repetition of the transitions on the left-hand side is equivalent to a single execution of the transition on the right-hand side.

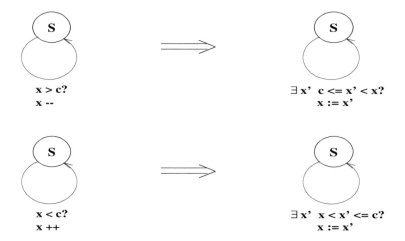

Figure 15.20: Elimination of increment/decrement from self-loops.

3. Elimination of increment/decrement from a pair of self-loops: This reduction rule is shown in Figure 15.21. This rule can be applied when $c_1 < a$ and $b < c_2$ and no other arcs end at S. Clearly, the repetitions of the double increment loop alone will keep $y - x = (b - a)$ because both y and x are incremented by the same amount. The incrementing applies between $c_2 \geq y \geq b$. However, the double increment loop may be interleaved with one or more single decrement rules that can decrease x to c_1. The net effect will be that the condition $x' \geq c_1, c_2 \geq y' \geq b, y' - x' \geq (b - a)$ must be true after any sequence of the two self-loop transitions.

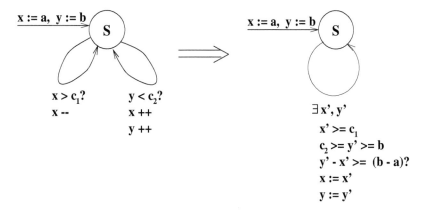

Figure 15.21: Elimination of increment/decrement from pairs of self-loops.

Now let's see how these reduction rules can be applied to the constraint automaton in Figure 15.18. Applying the first rule brings $x + +$ after the self-loop over state *Stopped*. Then it is trivial to note that "increment x, test whether it is -19 and if yes decrement x" is the same as "test whether $x = -20$." Hence we can further simplify the constraint automaton as shown in the top of Figure 15.22.

After applying the second rule with the self-loops over the states *Late, Ontime,* and *Stopped* and the third rule over the state *Brake* we obtain the constraint automaton shown in the bottom of Figure 15.22.

15.2.3 Analysis of Reachable Configurations

Each combination of a state name with values for the state variables is a *configuration*. It is often important to know the set of configurations to which a constraint automaton may move. This set is called the set of *reachable* configurations.

The set of reachable configurations can be found by translating the constraint automaton into a Datalog query. The Datalog query will use a separate relation to represent each state. Each relation will have the set of state variables as its attributes. Each transition of the constraint automaton

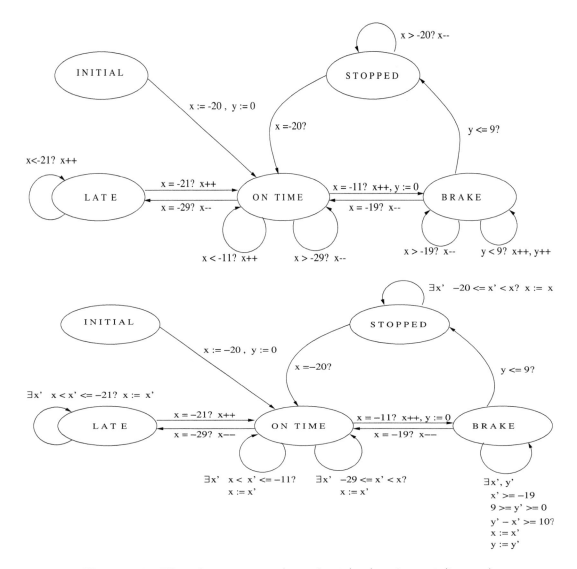

Figure 15.22: The subway system after rules 1 (top) and 1 to 3 (bottom).

will be translated to a Datalog rule. We give a few examples of translations.

Analysis of Example 15.2.1 We can translate the constraint automaton of Example 15.2.1 into Datalog as follows. Note that the assignment statements are expressed in Datalog by introducing new variables (d', e', y') and using these within the arguments of the defined relation:

$$
\begin{aligned}
T(d',e',y) &\;:\!-\; T(d,e,y),\; d \geq 100,\; d' = d - 100,\; e' = e + 198.\\
T(d',e,y') &\;:\!-\; T(d,e,y),\; d \geq 100,\; d' = d - 100,\; y' = y + 29700.\\
T(d',e',y) &\;:\!-\; T(d,e,y),\; e \geq 200,\; d' = d + 99,\; e' = e - 200.\\
T(d,e',y') &\;:\!-\; T(d,e,y),\; e \geq 200,\; e' = e - 200,\; y' = y + 29700.\\
T(d',e,y') &\;:\!-\; T(d,e,y),\; y \geq 30000,\; d' = d + 99,\; y' = y - 30000.\\
T(d,e',y') &\;:\!-\; T(d,e,y),\; y \geq 30000,\; e' = e + 198,\; y' = y - 30000.
\end{aligned}
$$

Analysis of Example 15.2.2 Let us assume that in Example 15.2.2 the number of people waiting in the parking garage grows by at least one between each reading until the elevator goes down to the parking garage. Similarly, the number of people waiting in the restaurant grows by at least two between each reading.

We also assume that the elevator is initially empty and at the lobby. Initially, the elevator will go down if there are more people waiting at the parking garage than at the restaurant. Otherwise it will go up. We can express the set of possible configurations of the constraint automaton using Datalog as follows:

$$
\begin{aligned}
R(x',y',z,p,r,lp',lr,d) &\;:\!-\; L(x,y,z,p,r,lp,lr,d), d = 0,\\
&\qquad y' - y \geq 1.\\[1em]
L(x,y,z,p',r,lp,lr,0) &\;:\!-\; R(x,y,z,p,r,lp,lr,d), p' = 0,\\
&\qquad lp = 0, x > y.\\
L(x,y,z,p',r,lp,lr,1) &\;:\!-\; R(x,y,z,p,r,lp,lr,d), p' = 1.\\
L(x,y,z,p',r,lp,lr,1) &\;:\!-\; R(x,y,z,p,r,lp,lr,d), lp = 1.\\
L(x,y,z,p',r,lp,lr,1) &\;:\!-\; R(x,y,z,p,r,lp,lr,d), x \leq y.\\[1em]
L(x,y,z,0,0,lp,lr,1) &\;:\!-\; 0 \leq lp \leq 1, 0 \leq lr \leq 1, y > z.\\
L(x,y,z,0,0,lp,lr,0) &\;:\!-\; 0 \leq lp \leq 1, 0 \leq lr \leq 1, y \leq z.\\[1em]
L(x,y,z,p,r',lp,lr,1) &\;:\!-\; P(x,y,z,p,r,lp,lr,d), r' = 0,\\
&\qquad lr = 0, x > z.\\
L(x,y,z,p,r',lp,lr,0) &\;:\!-\; P(x,y,z,p,r,lp,lr,d), r' = 1.\\
L(x,y,z,p,r',lp,lr,0) &\;:\!-\; P(x,y,z,p,r,lp,lr,d), lr = 1.\\
L(x,y,z,p,r',lp,lr,0) &\;:\!-\; P(x,y,z,p,r,lp,lr,d), x \leq z.\\[1em]
P(x',y,z',p,r,lp,lr',d) &\;:\!-\; L(x,y,z,p,r,lp,lr,d), d = 1,\\
&\qquad z' - z \geq 2.
\end{aligned}
$$

In this Datalog program the two middle rules express the initial state when the automaton starts from the lobby. Because the elevator is empty, there is no one to push the buttons inside. Hence p and r must be 0 initially.

Analysis of Example 15.2.3 Let us assume that the number of newly boarding passengers to the island is always between 0 and 5 inclusive. Then we can express the set of possible configurations of the constraint automaton of Example 15.2.3 using Datalog as follows:

$$A(0, x_0, x_1, x).$$

$$
\begin{aligned}
A(1, x', x_1, x') &\;:\!\!-\; B(0, x_0, x_1, x), 0 \le x' \le 5. \\
A(2, x_0, x', x') &\;:\!\!-\; B(1, x_0, x_1, x), 0 \le x' \le 5. \\
A(2, 0, 0, x') &\;:\!\!-\; B(2, 0, 0, 0), 0 \le x' \le 5. \\
A(0, x_0, x_1, x) &\;:\!\!-\; C(n, x_0, x_1, x), n > 0.
\end{aligned}
$$

$$
\begin{aligned}
B(1, x', x_1, x') &\;:\!\!-\; A(0, x_0, x_1, x), 0 \le x' \le 5. \\
B(2, x_0, x', x') &\;:\!\!-\; A(1, x_0, x_1, x), 0 \le x' \le 5. \\
B(2, 0, 0, x') &\;:\!\!-\; A(2, 0, 0, 0), 0 \le x' \le 5. \\
B(0, x_0, x_1, x) &\;:\!\!-\; C(0, x_0, x_1, x).
\end{aligned}
$$

$$
\begin{aligned}
C(0, 0, 0, x') &\;:\!\!-\; A(2, x_0, x_1, x), 0 \le x' \le 5,\ x_0 + x_1 + x' > 0. \\
C(0, 0, 0, x') &\;:\!\!-\; A(n, x_0, x_1, x), 0 \le x' \le 5,\ n > 0, \\
&\qquad\quad x_0 + x_1 + x' \ge 10. \\
C(2, 0, 0, x') &\;:\!\!-\; B(2, x_0, x_1, x), 0 \le x' \le 5,\ x_0 + x_1 + x' > 0. \\
C(n, 0, 0, x') &\;:\!\!-\; B(n, x_0, x_1, x), 0 \le x' \le 5,\ n > 0, \\
&\qquad\quad x_0 + x_1 + x' \ge 10.
\end{aligned}
$$

Analysis of Example 15.2.4 We saw in Section 15.2.2 that the constraint automaton of Example 15.2.4 can be simplified to the one shown in Figure 15.22. The set of reachable configurations of the constraint automaton shown in Figure 15.22 can be expressed in Datalog as follows:

$$Initial(-20, 0).$$

$$
\begin{aligned}
Ontime(x, y) &\;:\!\!-\; Initial(x, y). \\
Ontime(-20, y) &\;:\!\!-\; Late(-21, y). \\
Ontime(-20, y) &\;:\!\!-\; Brake(-20, y). \\
Ontime(-20, y) &\;:\!\!-\; Stopped(-20, y). \\
Ontime(x', y) &\;:\!\!-\; Ontime(x, y),\ x < x' \le -11. \\
Ontime(x', y) &\;:\!\!-\; Ontime(x, y),\ -29 \le x' < x.
\end{aligned}
$$

$$
\begin{aligned}
Stopped(x', y) &\;:\!\!-\; Stopped(x, y),\ -20 \le x' < x. \\
Stopped(x, y) &\;:\!\!-\; Brake(x, y),\ y \le 9.
\end{aligned}
$$

$$
\begin{aligned}
Brake(-10, 0) &\;:\!\!-\; Ontime(-11, y). \\
Brake(x', y') &\;:\!\!-\; Brake(x, y),\ x' \ge -19,\ 9 \ge y' \ge 0, \\
&\qquad\quad y' - x' \ge 10.
\end{aligned}
$$

$$
\begin{aligned}
Late(-30, y) &\;:\!\!-\; Ontime(-29, y). \\
Late(x', y) &\;:\!\!-\; Late(x, y),\ x < x' \le -21.
\end{aligned}
$$

Analysis of Example 15.2.5 The set of reachable configurations of the constraint automaton shown in Figure 15.11 can be expressed in Datalog as follows. The first rule represents the inflationary years; the second rule represents the deflationary years:

$$Purchase(i', x',\ y', z', a', b', c', d', k', l', m') :\!-$$
$$Purchase(i, x, y, z, a, b, c, d, k, l, m),$$
$$ax' + by' + cz' \le d,\ x' \ge k,\ y' \ge l,\ z' \ge m,$$
$$a' = 1.05a,\ b' = 1.1b,\ c' = 1.05c,\ d' = 1.02d,$$
$$k' = k + 5,\ l' = l + 7,\ m' = m + 3,\ i' = i + 1.$$

$$Purchase(i', x',\ y', z', a', b', c', d', k', l', m') :\!-$$
$$Purchase(i, x, y, z, a, b, c, d, k, l, m),$$
$$ax' + by' + cz' \le d,\ x' \ge k,\ y' \ge l,\ z' \ge m,\ i > 0$$
$$a' = \tfrac{1}{1.05}a,\ b' = \tfrac{1}{1.1}b,\ c' = \tfrac{1}{1.05}c,\ d' = \tfrac{1}{1.02}d,$$
$$k' = k - 5,\ l' = l - 7,\ m' = m - 3,\ i' = i - 1.$$

Analysis of Example 15.2.6 Assume that in Example 15.2.6 each main dish costs between five and nine dollars, and each salad and drink costs between two and four dollars. The set of reachable configurations of the constraint automaton shown in Figure 15.12 can be expressed in Datalog as follows:

$$Drink\_Queue(x, y', z) \quad :\!- \quad Main\_Queue(x, y, z),\ 5 \le y' \le 9,$$
$$y = 0,\ x + y' + z \le 10.$$
$$Drink\_Queue(x, y, z) \quad :\!- \quad Pay\_Queue(x, y, z),\ x + y + z < 8.$$

$$Main\_Queue(x', y, z) \quad :\!- \quad Salad\_Queue(x, y, z),\ 2 \le x' \le 4,$$
$$x' \ge x,\ x' + y + z \le 10.$$

$$Pay\_Queue(x, y, z') \quad :\!- \quad Drink\_Queue(x, y, z),\ 2 \le z' \le 4,$$
$$z' \ge z,\ x + y + z' \le 10.$$
$$Pay\_Queue(x, y, z) \quad :\!- \quad Drink\_Queue(x, y, z),\ x > 3.$$

$$Pay\_Queue(x, y, z) \quad :\!- \quad Main\_Queue(x, y, z),\ y > 0.$$

$$Salad\_Queue(x, y, z) \quad :\!- \quad Pay\_Queue(x, y, z),\ x + y + z < 8.$$
$$Salad\_Queue(0, 0, 0).$$

Analysis of Example 15.2.7 Let the initial proportion of cloud, rain, stream, and ocean be 20, 20, 30, and 30 per cent. Then all possible end-of-year proportions of the four forms of water can be expressed by the following Datalog query:

$$Water(0.2, 0.2, 0.3, 0.3).$$

$$
\begin{aligned}
Water(c', r', s', o') \quad :- \quad & Water(c, r, s, o), \\
& c' = \tfrac{1}{2}c + \tfrac{1}{3}r + \tfrac{1}{6}s + \tfrac{1}{60}o, \\
& r' = \tfrac{1}{2}c, \\
& s' = \tfrac{1}{3}r + \tfrac{2}{3}s, \\
& o' = \tfrac{1}{3}r + \tfrac{1}{6}s + \tfrac{59}{60}o.
\end{aligned}
$$

As these examples illustrate, Datalog with constraints can be used to define the set of reachable configurations of constraint automata. In some cases this is helpful because the Datalog with constraints program can be evaluated. In some cases the evaluation may not terminate. Chapter 22 discusses when and Chapter 23 how Datalog with constraints can be evaluated.

Bibliographic Notes

Hernandez [197] is a gentle introduction to database design. Batini et al. [30], Teorey [396], and Thalheim [397] are textbooks devoted to database design.

Many cases of constraint automata have been studied by various authors. Constraint automata with increment and decrement by one operators and comparison operators as guard constraints have been called *counter machines* and were studied by Minsky [278, 279], who showed that they have the same expressive power as Turing machines. Floyd and Beigel [133] is an introduction to automata theory that covers counter machines.

More complex guard constraints have been allowed in later extensions of counter machines and applied to the design of control systems in Boigelot and Wolper [52], Fribourg and Olson [142], Fribourg and Richardson [143], Halbwachs [186], and Kerbrat [226]. Boigelot et al. [51], Cobham [93], and Wolper and Boigelot [429] study automata and Presburger definability. Alur and Dill [15] consider timed automata, which is subsumed by constraint automata.

The problem description of the subway train control system in Example 15.2.4 is from [186]. The reduction rules and simplifications applied to this constraint automaton, Example 15.2.6, and Exercise 9 are from Revesz [338].

Fribourg and Richardson [143] presented another simplification method that gives an approximation of the reachable configurations for Example 15.2.4. Another approximation method in analyzing automata with linear constraints is presented in Kerbrat [226].

Translations of constraint automata into constraint logic programming or constraint Datalog queries are presented by Fribourg and Richardson [143], Delzanno and Podelski [108], and Revesz [331, 338].

Constraint automata with comparison guard constraints and the update of state variables by addition of constants to them are called *Petri nets* or *vector addition systems*. Example 15.2.1 is an example of a Petri net. The reachable configuration problem has been studied extensively in Petri nets and vector addition systems. More details about these are given in the bibliographic notes of Chapter 22.5.

The problem of verifying the correctness of counter machines and related systems without a full constraint evaluation of the set of possible states is called *symbolic model checking*. McMillan [272] and Clarke et al. [92] are books on symbolic model checking, and Alur et al. [14] is a survey. Other works on model checking include Alur et al. [13, 16], Cimatti et al. [91], Comuzzi and Hart [97], Graf and Saidi [160], and Havelund et al. [193]. A model checking system called HyTech is presented in Henzinger et al. [196].

Exercises

1. Design an entity relationship diagram for a hospital ambulance that operates in the town shown in Figure 15.6.

2. Design an entity relationship diagram for a tourist who wants to visit certain sites in a city.

3. Can you find any potential problems with the hotel elevator system? If yes, can you correct it?

4. Suppose that in Example 15.2.3 the ferry can carry both cars and people. Suppose each car takes up as much space as three people. Modify the constraint automaton in Figure 15.9 to reflect this change.

5. Suppose that in Example 15.2.6 instead of replacing the salad or drink with one of a higher value, one can choose a second salad or drink of the same type, provided the total cost is at most ten dollars. Modify the constraint automaton in Figure 15.12 to reflect this change.

6. A thermostat operates the following way. It can sense m, the measured temperature in the room; r, the requested temperature; and s, a switch that can be set to heat, off, or cool (assume that these are indicated by the values one, zero, and minus one, respectively). If r is more than three degrees above m and s is on "heat," then the system starts heating and will continue to heat until m is greater than or equal to r. If r is more than two degrees below m and s is on "cool," then the system starts cooling and will continue to cool until m is less

than or equal to r. When the system is neither heating nor cooling, it will rest in a wait state.

(a) Draw a constraint automaton for the thermostat.

(b) Assume that while the thermostat is heating, the temperature rises at least two degrees between each pair of readings. While the thermostat is cooling, the temperature decreases at least one degree between each pair of readings. Also assume that initially the thermostat is in the wait state, s is zero, and r and m could be anything. Using Datalog, express the set of reachable configurations of the constraint automaton you drew.

7. Draw a constraint automaton for the subset-sum problem discussed in Example 12.1.10.

8. Find a variation of the reduction rule shown in Figure 15.21, for example, when x is incremented in the single-variable self-loop and x and y are both decremented in the double-variable self-loop.

9. A person with $500 cash, a checking account with balance $3000, and a credit card with balance minus $100 can make the following transactions: pay cash, write a check, or make charges on the credit card to buy something, deposit cash into the checking account, write a check to pay the credit card, withdraw money from the checking account using an ATM machine, or get a cash advance from the credit card. On all these transactions the checking account balance must remain positive and the credit card balance must stay above the credit limit of minus $1000. Each month this person gets $1000 in cash, pays from the checking account mortgage of $600, and charges on the credit card at least $500.

(a) Draw a constraint automaton that describes the possible values for the cash x, the checking account balance y, and the credit card balance z of this person, for each month m.

(b) Simplify the constraint automaton as much as possible.

(c) Express the set of reachable configurations using Datalog.

10. There are people who are employed (by others), unemployed, and self-employed. Each year one-eighth of the employed become unemployed and the same number become self-employed. Also, one-third of the unemployed are hired as new employees and the same number become self-employed by opening a business. One-fourth of the self-employed are hired, and become employed and one-eighth become unemployed. Draw a constraint automaton that counts the number of employed, unemployed, and self-employed persons.

11. Persons in a country are rich, middle class, or poor. Each year one in 30 middle-class and one in 50 poor persons become rich. Also one in ten rich and one in 20 poor become middle class. Further, 1 percent of the rich and one in 60 middle-class persons become poor. Draw a constraint automaton that counts the number of rich, middle-class, and poor persons.

12. Translate the constraint automaton in Figure 15.14 into Datalog with Boolean set constraints. (*Hint:* You may assume that the bags contain no repetitions of fragment lengths.)

16

Interoperability

Database interoperability is the problem of making the data and queries of one database system usable to the users of another database system. Obviously, interoperability involves many issues, such as networking, and security. However, interoperability between databases that are written in different data models poses an especially challenging task. We focus here on the issues arising from data model incompatibility.

Section 16.1 describes the problem of *data interoperability*, which occurs when the data of one database system needs to be made available for users of another database system. For each of the spatio-temporal data models in Chapter 7 we give an equivalent constraint data model with some type of constraints. We also describe data interoperability between parametric extreme point and geometric transformation databases.

Section 16.2 describes the problem of *query interoperability*, in which case the queries of one database system need to be made available for users of another system. This section describes three ways of accomplishing query interoperability, namely, the approaches via *query translation*, *data translation*, and the use of a *common basis*.

Section 16.3 looks at other issues of database interoperability that are not limited to spatio-temporal databases.

16.1 Data Interoperability

Data interoperability between two database systems Δ_1 and Δ_2 requires that the data models used in them have the same *data expressiveness*. That means that each database written in the data model used in Δ_1 can be translated into an equivalent database in the data model of Δ_2. This

P. Revesz, *Introduction to Databases: From Biological to Spatio-Temporal*,
Texts in Computer Science, DOI 10.1007/978-1-84996-095-3_16,
© Springer-Verlag London Limited 2010

section describes several pairs of spatio-temporal data models that have the same data expressiveness and between which translation is possible in either direction.

Section 16.1.1 describes equivalences between cases of constraint and extreme point data models, Section 16.1.2 between constraint and parametric extreme point data models, Section 16.1.3 between parametric and geometric transformation data models, and Section 16.1.4 between constraint and geometric transformation data models.

16.1.1 Constraint and Extreme Point Data Models

In this section we show that each database in the rectangles data model and Worboys' data model is equivalent to a constraint database with some suitable types of constraints. We start with rectangles databases.

Theorem 16.1.1 Any rectangle relation R is equivalent to a constraint relation C with only inequality constraints between constants and variables.

Proof: $R \rightarrow C$: Let $T = ([a_1, b_1], \ldots, [a_d, b_d], [from, to])$ be any tuple in a rectangle relation. This can be represented by the constraint tuple $a_1 \leq x_1$, $x_1 \leq b_1, \ldots, a_d \leq x_d, x_d \leq b_d, from \leq t, t \leq to$. If $from = -\infty$ or $to = +\infty$, then the constraints with the last two constraints are omitted.

$C \rightarrow R$: Let T be any constraint tuple. Find the highest lower bound a_i and lowest upper bound b_i for each x_i. Also find the highest lower bound $from$ and lowest upper bound to for t. The rectangle relation will be $([a_1, b_1], \ldots, [a_d, b_d], [from, to])$. $\blacksquare$

Example 16.1.1 Using Theorem 16.1.1 the *House* relation in Example 6.1.1 can be translated to relation *House*2 shown here:

House2

ID	X	Y	T	
1	x	y	t	$3 \leq x$, $x \leq 6$, $3 \leq y$, $y \leq 6$, $100 \leq t$, $t \leq 200$
2	x	y	t	$8 \leq x$, $x \leq 11$, $3 \leq y$, $y \leq 7$, $150 \leq t$, $t \leq 300$
3	x	y	t	$2 \leq x$, $x \leq 4$, $5 \leq y$, $y \leq 10$, $250 \leq t$, $t \leq 400$
3	x	y	t	$2 \leq x$, $x \leq 10$, $8 \leq y$, $y \leq 10$, $250 \leq t$, $t \leq 400$

Theorem 16.1.2 Any Worboys relation W is equivalent to a constraint relation C with two spatial variables with linear constraints and one temporal variable with inequality constraints.

Proof: $W \rightarrow C$: Let $T = (a_x, a_y, b_x, b_y, c_x, c_y, from, to)$ be any tuple in a Worboys relation where $a_x, a_y, b_x, b_y, c_x, c_y$ are rational constants and $from, to$ are rational constants or $-\infty$ or $+\infty$. We translate T into a linear constraint tuple with variables (x, y, t). The tuple will be the conjunction of the linear inequalities in (x, y) that define the area of the triangle with corner vertices (a_x, a_y), (b_x, b_y), and (c_x, c_y) and the constraints $t \geq from$ if $from \neq -\infty$ and $t \leq to$ except if $to \neq +\infty$.

We obtain the equivalent linear constraint relation by repeating for each tuple in the Worboys relation the preceding translation.

$C \rightarrow W$: Let T be any conjunction of a set of linear inequality constraints over the variables x and y. By replacing each $\leq, \geq$ with an $=$ we get a corresponding set of linear equations L.

Let S be the set of intersection points of each pair of lines in L. Let $H \subseteq S$ be the set of points in S that satisfy all of the constraints in T. The convex hull of the points in H is an ordered list of points $P_1, \ldots, P_n$ that are the corner vertices of the convex polygon that encloses precisely the points that are the solutions of T.

We find the convex hull and then divide it into the set of triangles (P_1, P_{1+i}, P_{2+i}) for $1 \leq i \leq n-2$. Finally, we represent each of these triangles by a single Worboys tuple. $\blacksquare$

Example 16.1.2 We represented the park in a Worboys relation in Example 6.3.1. Using the algorithm described in Theorem 16.1.2 that relation can be translated to the linear constraint relation $Park2$ shown here:

Park2

ID	X	Y	T	
fountain	x	y	t	$x = 10, y = 4, 1980 \leq t, t \leq 1986$
road	x	y	t	$5 \leq x, x \leq 9, y = -x + 15, 1995 \leq t, t \leq 1996$
road	x	y	t	$x = 9, 3 \leq y, y \leq 6, 1995 \leq t, t \leq 1996$
tulip	x	y	t	$2 \leq x, x \leq 6, y \leq 9 - x, 3 \leq y, y \leq 7,$ $1975 \leq t, t \leq 1990$
park	x	y	t	$1 \leq x, x \leq 12, 2 \leq y, y \leq 11, 1974 \leq t, t \leq 1996$
pond	x	y	t	$x \geq 3, y \geq 5, y \geq x - 1, y \leq x + 5, y \leq -x + 13,$ $1991 \leq t, t \leq 1996$

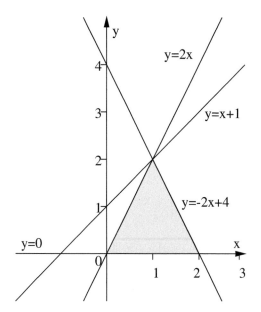

Figure 16.1: A set of lines.

Example 16.1.3 Suppose that T is the following set of linear inequality constraints:

$$
\begin{aligned}
y &\geq 0 \\
y &\leq x + 1 \\
y &\leq 2x \\
y &\leq -2x + 4
\end{aligned}
$$

By changing it into a set of equations we get L:

$$
\begin{aligned}
y &= 0 \\
y &= x + 1 \\
y &= 2x \\
y &= -2x + 4
\end{aligned}
$$

Figure 16.1 shows the set of lines. Here the first line intersects the second line at $(-1, 0)$, the third line at $(0, 0)$, and the fourth line at $(2, 0)$. The other three lines intersect each other only at point $(1, 2)$. Hence S is these four points. Because $(-1, 0)$ does not satisfy the third linear inequality, i.e., $y \leq 2x$, it is eliminated. The other three points satisfy all four inequalities; hence they will be H. The convex hull is therefore the triangle with corner vertices $(0, 0)$, $(2, 0)$, and $(1, 2)$. This can be represented by the Worboys tuple $(0, 0, 2, 0, 1, 2, -\infty, +\infty)$.

16.1.2 Constraint and Parametric Extreme Point Data Models

Next we look at the translation from parametric relations into constraint relations.

Theorem 16.1.3 Any parametric rectangle relation R with m-degree polynomial parametric functions of t is equivalent to a constraint relation C with inequality constraints in which the spatial variables are bounded from above or below by m-degree polynomial functions of t and t is bounded from above and below by constants.

Proof: $R \rightarrow C$: Let $T = ([X_1^{[}, X_1^{]}], \ldots, [X_d^{[}, X_d^{]}], [from, to])$ be any tuple in a R where each $X_i^{[}$ and $X_i^{]}$ are m-degree polynomial functions of t and $from, to$ are real constants or $-\infty$ or $+\infty$. We translate T into the constraint tuple with variables $(x_1, \ldots, x_d, t)$ and the constraints:

$$X_1^{[} \leq x_1, \ x_1 \leq X_1^{]}, \ldots, X_d^{[} \leq x_d, \ x_d \leq X_d^{]}, from \leq t, \ t \leq to$$

except for the special cases when either $from = -\infty$ or $to = +\infty$, when we omit from the preceding the constraint involving $from$ or to, respectively.

$C \rightarrow R$: The translation is similar to Theorem 16.1.1 except we have functions of t instead of constants. Therefore, the highest lower bound and the lowest higher bound will be different functions of t in different time intervals. The endpoints of the time intervals will be the time instances when two functions will be equivalent, or their difference is zero. Therefore, this translation requires finding the roots of polynomials. That can be done precisely for $m \leq 5$ and for higher degree to any desired precision using numerical analysis techniques.   ∎

Example 16.1.4 The parametric rectangle relation of Example 7.3.2 can be translated to the following constraint relation:

Bomb2

X	Y	Z	T	
x	y	z	t	$t \leq x, x \leq t+1, t \leq y, y \leq t+1,$
				$100 - 9.8t^2 \leq z, z \leq 102 - 9.8t^2, 0 \leq t, t \leq 3.19$

Theorem 16.1.4 Any parametric 2-spaghetti relation W with quotient of polynomial functions of t is equivalent to a constraint relation C with polynomial constraints over the variables x, y, t such that for each instance of t all the constraints are linear.

Proof: $W \to C$: Let $T = (a_x, a_y, b_x, b_y, c_x, c_y, from, to)$ be any tuple in W. We translate T into a constraint tuple with variables (x, y, t) as in Theorem 16.1.2, except that all the constraints will be parametric functions of t.

For example, the parametric line between (a_x, a_y) and (b_x, b_y) can be represented for instances of t when $b_x - a_x = 0$ as $x = a_x$ and otherwise as:

$$y = (x - a_x)\frac{b_y - a_y}{b_x - a_x} + a_y$$

or by first subtracting a_y and then multiplying by $b_x - a_x$ as:

$$(y - a_y)(b_x - a_x) = (x - a_x)(b_y - a_y) \tag{16.1}$$

The other sides of the parametric triangle can be represented similarly. We can represent the points within T by turning the $=$ signs into $\leq$ or $\geq$ signs as appropriate. Note that each inequality contains only polynomial constraints and for each instance of t only linear constraints. The translation of *from* and *to* to constraints are like in Theorem 16.1.2, and they only introduce inequality constraints.

$C \to W$: Do the following:

1. For each pair of parametric lines find a parametric intersection point and find out when it is valid, i.e., satisfies all the constraints.

2. Find which set of parametric points are valid in which time interval. Order the time intervals $I_1, \ldots, I_k$.

3. For each time interval the valid parametric points define a parametric convex polygon, i.e., for each instance of t in the interval define a convex polygon. Triangulate that parametric polygon and represent each triangle as a parametric 2-spaghetti tuple.

∎

Example 16.1.5 We translate the *Net* relation of Example 7.1.1 to a constraint relation. After substituting into Equation (16.1) we obtain:

$$(y - (3 - t))((4 + 0.5t) - 3) = (x - 3)((4 - 0.5t) - (3 - t))$$

This simplifies to:

$$y = x - t$$

Similarly, substituting into Equation (16.1) with B replaced by C we get:

$$(y - (3 - t))((5 + t) - 3) = (x - 3)(3 - (3 - t))$$

Simplifying we get:

$$y(t + 2) = xt - t^2 - 2t + 6$$

Substituting into Equation (16.1) with A replaced by C we get:

$$(y - 3)((4 + 0.5t) - (5 + t)) = (x - (5 + t))((4 - 0.5t) - 3)$$

Simplifying we get:

$$y(t + 2) = x(t - 2) - t^2 + 16$$

Finally we find whether the equality symbols should be replaced by $\leq$ or $\geq$ symbols by checking which of these the third point satisfies. The translation will yield the following constraint relation:

Net2

X	Y	T	
x	y	t	$y \leq x - t$
			$y(t + 2) \geq xt - t^2 - 2t + 6,$
			$y(t + 2) \geq x(t - 2) - t^2 + 16$

Example 16.1.6 Consider the conjunction of constraints C:

$$
\begin{array}{rcl}
y & \geq & 0 \\
y & \leq & (2t + 1)x \\
y & \leq & (t + 1)(1 - x)
\end{array}
$$

From these we create the system of equations:

$$
\begin{array}{rcl}
y & = & 0 \\
y & = & (2t + 1)x \\
y & = & (t + 1)(1 - x)
\end{array}
$$

Now we can calculate that the intersection of the first two lines is $(0, 0)$ except for $t = -0.5$ when the two lines overlap, the intersection of the first and third lines is $(1, 0)$ except for $t = -1$ when these lines overlap, and the intersection of the last two lines is $((t+1)/(3t+2), ((t+1)(2t+1))/(3t+2))$.

These three points define the corner vertices of a triangle. The substitution of $(0, 0)$ makes the three inequalities true simultaneously only when $t \geq -1$. The substitution of $(1, 0)$ makes the three inequalities true simultaneously only when $t \geq -0.5$. The substitution of $((t + 1)/(3t + 2), ((t + 1)(2t + 1))/(3t + 2))$ makes the three inequalities true simultaneously only when t is in the interval $[-1, -2/3)$ or $[-1/2, +\infty]$. Hence the parametric 2-spaghetti relation that contains the single tuple:

$$(0, 0, 1, 0, \frac{t+1}{3t+2}, \frac{(t+1)(2t+1)}{3t+2}, -0.5, +\infty)$$

is equivalent to C.

Example 16.1.7 Consider the moving region P represented by the following conjunction of linear constraints:

$$
\begin{array}{llcl}
l_1 : & y & \geq & x \\
l_2 : & y & \leq & 26 - x \\
l_3 : & y & \leq & x + 10 \\
l_4 : & y & \geq & 16 - x \\
l_5 : & x & \geq & 5 + t \\
& t & \geq & 0 \\
& t & \leq & 4
\end{array}
$$

This moving object is a polygon with one side moving linearly with t, that is, the side represented by the linear constraint $x \geq 5 + t$. At times $0, 2, 3$, and 4 this moving region looks as shown in Figure 16.2. At time 0 the region is a pentagon. Between 0 and 3 the front side of the pentagon moves backward until at time 3 it becomes a triangle. Between 3 and 4 the moving object remains a triangle as the front side of the triangle moves backward. Note that the object only exists between times 0 and 4.

We translate P using the algorithm described in Theorem 16.1.4.

Step 1: First we calculate the parametric intersection points and when they are valid. Each row of the following table shows a pair of parametric lines, their intersection and when it is valid. We only list those intersections that are valid at some time:

$$
\begin{array}{lll}
l_1, l_2 & (13, 13) & [0, 4] \\
l_1, l_4 & (8, 8) & [0, 3] \\
l_1, l_5 & (5 + t, 5 + t) & [3, 4] \\
l_2, l_3 & (8, 18) & [0, 3] \\
l_2, l_5 & (5 + t, 21 - t) & [3, 4] \\
l_3, l_5 & (5 + t, 15 + t) & [0, 3] \\
l_4, l_5 & (5 + t, 11 - t) & [0, 3]
\end{array}
$$

Step 2: We see that during $[0, 3]$ the following points are valid:

$$(8, 18), (13, 13), (8, 8), (5 + t, 11 - t), (5 + t, 15 + t)$$

During the interval $[3, 4]$ the following points are valid:

$$(5 + t, 21 - t), (13, 13), (5 + t, 5 + t)$$

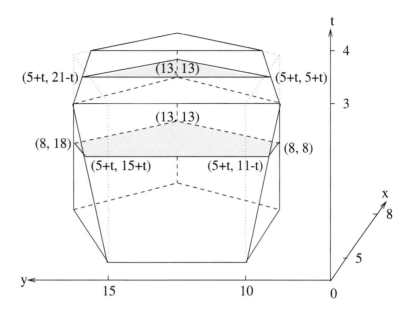

Figure 16.2: A polygon with one side moving.

Step 3: By triangulating these parametric pentagons for $[0, 3]$ and using directly the parametric triangle for $[3, 4]$ we get the following parametric 2-spaghetti representation of P:

Ax	Ay	Bx	By	Cx	Cy	From	To
8	18	13	13	8	8	0	3
8	18	8	8	$5+t$	$11-t$	0	3
8	18	$5+t$	$11-t$	$5+t$	$15+t$	0	3
$5+t$	$21-t$	13	13	$5+t$	$5+t$	3	4

Now we look at the translation of periodic parametric relations. The following can be proven similarly to the previous theorem.

Theorem 16.1.5 Any periodic parametric 2-spaghetti relation with periodic parametric functions of t is equivalent to a constraint database relation with periodic constraints over the variables x, y, t such that for each instance of t all the constraints are linear. ∎

Example 16.1.8 The *Tide* relation of Example 7.5.2 is a periodic parametric 2-spaghetti relation. We can simplify the translation by noting that

Tide2

X	Y	T	
x	y	t	$1 \leq x,\, x \leq 3,\, 1 \leq y,\, y \leq 4,\, 0 \leq t',\, t' \leq 5.75,\, y \geq x - t' + 3.$
x	y	t	$1 \leq x,\, x \leq 3,\, 1 \leq y,\, y \leq 4,\, 5.75 \leq t',\, t' \leq 11.5,$ $y \geq x + t' - 8.5.$

where $t' = (t \bmod 11.5)$.

the edge of the tide water is always described by the constraint $y = x - (t \bmod 11.5) + 3$ during the expansion and by $y = x + (t \bmod 11.5) - 8.5$ during the recession phase.

16.1.3   Parametric and Geometric Transformation Models

In this section we investigate the relationship between the parametric and geometric transformation models. First we show an equivalence between parametric rectangles and a restricted type of geometric transformation objects. We start with some definitions.

A parametric rectangle $R = (\Pi_{i=1}^{d}[X_i^{[},X_i^{]}], [from, to])$ is in *normal form* if $X_i^{[}(t) \leq X_i^{]}(t)$ for each $1 \leq i \leq d$ and $t \in [from, to]$.

Example 16.1.9 Consider the two-dimensional parametric rectangle $R = ([2t - 10, t], [t + 12, 3t], [6, 10])$. Note that $2t - 10 \leq t$ for any $t \leq 10$ and $t + 12 \leq 3t$ for any $t \geq 6$. Hence $2t - 10 \leq t$ and $t + 12 \leq 3t$ are both true for each $t \in [6, 10]$. Therefore, R is a normal form parametric rectangle.

It is always possible to represent a parametric rectangle as a set of normal form parametric rectangles.

Example 16.1.10 Consider the one-dimensional parametric rectangle $R = ([0, t^2 - 3t + 2], [0, 3])$. Note that $0 \leq t^2 - 3t + 2$ only if $t \leq 1$ or $t \geq 2$. Hence R can be expressed as the union of the normal form parametric rectangles $R_1 = ([0, t^2 - 3t + 2], [0, 1])$ and $R_2 = ([0, t^2 - 3t + 2], [2, 3])$.

A geometric transformation object $G = (\Pi_{i=1}^{d}[a_i, b_i], [from, to], f)$ where f is definable as the system of equations $x_i' = g_i\, x_i + h_i$ where g_i and h_i are functions of t for $1 \leq i \leq d$ is in *normal form* if $g_i(t) \geq 0$ for all $t \in [from, to]$ or $g_i(t) \leq 0$ for all $t \in [from, to]$ and $a_i < b_i$ for all $1 \leq i \leq d$.

It is always possible to represent a geometric transformation object as a set of normal form geometric transformation objects.

Example 16.1.11 Consider the one-dimensional geometric transformation object $G = ([10, 20], [0, 3], (t^2 - 4t + 3)x)$. This is not in normal form because $t^2 - 4t + 3 \geq 0$ for $t \in [0, 1]$ and $t^2 - 4t + 3 \leq 0$ for $t \in [1, 3]$. We can represent G as the union of two normal form geometric transformation objects $G_1 = ([10, 20], [0, 1], (t^2 - 4t + 3)x)$ and $G_2 = ([10, 20], [1, 3], (t^2 - 4t + 3)x)$.

Theorem 16.1.6 Let $[a_i, b_i]$ for $1 \leq i \leq d$ be any set of d intervals with $a_i < b_i$. Let

$$R = (\Pi_{i=1}^{d}[X_i^{[}, X_i^{]}], [from, to])$$

be any normal form parametric rectangle. Let

$$G = (\Pi_{i=1}^{d}[a_i, b_i], [from, to], f)$$

be any normal form geometric transformation object where f is definable as the system of equations $x_i' = g_i x_i + h_i$ where g_i and h_i are functions of t for $1 \leq i \leq d$. Then R and G are equivalent if:

$$\left\{ \quad g_i = \frac{X_i^{]} - X_i^{[}}{b_i - a_i} \quad \text{and} \quad h_i = -\frac{X_i^{]} - X_i^{[}}{b_i - a_i} a_i + X_i^{[} \right.$$

or alternatively if:

$$\left\{ \begin{array}{ll} X_i^{[} = g_i \, a_i + h_i \quad \text{and} \quad X_i^{]} = g_i \, b_i + h_i & \text{if} \quad g_i(t) \geq 0 \;\; \forall t \in [from, to] \\ X_i^{[} = g_i \, b_i + h_i \quad \text{and} \quad X_i^{]} = g_i \, a_i + h_i & \text{if} \quad g_i(t) \leq 0 \;\; \forall t \in [from, to] \end{array} \right.$$

Proof: $R \rightarrow G$: We can choose f such that it maps each point $(x_1, \ldots, x_d)$ in $\Pi_{i=1}^{d}[a_i, b_i]$ to another point $(x_1', \ldots, x_d')$ at time $t \in [from, to]$ such that if $X_i^{[} \neq X_i^{]}$ then x_i' is always located at a fixed ratio of the distance between the endpoints of the ith interval, or else $x_i' = X_i^{[}$. Therefore,

$$\frac{x_i' - X_i^{[}}{X_i^{]} - X_i^{[}} = \frac{x_i - a_i}{b_i - a_i}$$

We can rewrite this as:

$$x_i' = \frac{X_i^{]} - X_i^{[}}{b_i - a_i}(x_i - a_i) + X_i^{[}$$

Further simplifying we get:

$$x_i' = \frac{X_i^{]} - X_i^{[}}{b_i - a_i}x_i - \frac{X_i^{]} - X_i^{[}}{b_i - a_i}a_i + X_i^{[}$$

Hence we can take

$$g_i = \frac{X_i^{]} - X_i^{[}}{b_i - a_i} \quad \text{and} \quad h_i = -\frac{X_i^{]} - X_i^{[}}{b_i - a_i}a_i + X_i^{[}$$

Note that when $X_i^[= X_i^]$, the preceding gives $x_i' = X_i^[$ and $g_i = 0$ and $h_i = X_i^[$.

$G \to R$: For each i and $t \in [from, to]$ the interval $[a_i, b_i]$ is mapped by f to a set of points in $[X_i^[, X_i^]]$.   ∎

Next we look at some applications of Theorem 16.1.6.

Example 16.1.12 Consider the parametric rectangle $R = ([2t - 10, t], [t + 12, 3t], [6, 10])$, which we know by Example 16.1.9 to be normal. Suppose that $a_1 = 6$, $b_1 = 8$, $a_2 = 20$, and $b_2 = 24$. We can calculate for the first dimension that:

$$g_1 = \frac{t - (2t - 10)}{8 - 6} = -0.5t + 5$$

$$h_1 = -6\frac{t - (2t - 10)}{8 - 6} + (2t - 10) = 5t - 40$$

Similarly, for the second dimension, we have:

$$g_2 = \frac{3t - (t + 12)}{24 - 20} = 0.5t - 3$$

$$h_2 = -20\frac{3t - (t + 12)}{24 - 20} + (t + 12) = -9t + 72$$

By Theorem 16.1.6, R is equivalent to the geometric transformation object $G = (V, [6, 10], f)$ where V is the set of points in the rectangle $[6, 8] \times [20, 24]$ and f is:

$$f(\bar{x}, t) = \begin{bmatrix} -0.5t + 5 & 0 \\ 0 & 0.5t - 3 \end{bmatrix} \bar{x} + \begin{bmatrix} 5t - 40 \\ -9t + 72 \end{bmatrix}$$

Example 16.1.13 Consider the parametric rectangle $R = ([5t, 5t], [0, 2t - t^2], [0, 2])$. Suppose that $a_1 = 0$, $b_1 = 1$, $a_2 = 0$, and $b_2 = 1$. By Theorem 16.1.6 we have for the first dimension:

$$g_1 = \frac{5t - 5t}{1 - 0} = 0$$

$$h_1 = -0\frac{5t - 5t}{1 - 0} + (5t) = 5t$$

For the second dimension, we have:

$$g_2 = \frac{(2t - t^2) - (0)}{1 - 0} = 2t - t^2$$

$$h_2 = -0\frac{(2t - t^2) - (0)}{1 - 0} + 0 = 0$$

By Theorem 16.1.6, R is equivalent to the geometric transformation object $G = (V, [0, 2], f)$ where V is the set of points in the rectangle $[0, 1] \times [0, 1]$ and f is:

$$f(\overline{x}, t) = \begin{bmatrix} 0 & 0 \\ 0 & 2t - t^2 \end{bmatrix} \overline{x} + \begin{bmatrix} 5t \\ 0 \end{bmatrix}$$

The preceding example shows that nonsingularity cannot be guaranteed if the parametric rectangle has a dimension in which the lower bound and upper bound functions are equivalent. In this case, like for the first dimension in the preceding example, all the points in the interval will be mapped to one point.

The following is an example of translation from a geometric transformation to a parametric rectangle object.

Example 16.1.14 Consider the geometric transformation objects G_1 and G_2 of Example 16.1.11. By Theorem 16.1.6 the parametric rectangle $R_1 = ([t^2 - 4t + 3)10,\ (t^2 - 4t + 3)20], [0, 1])$ is equivalent to G_1 and $R_2 = ([t^2 - 4t + 3)20,\ (t^2 - 4t + 3)10], [1, 3])$ is equivalent to G_2.

Now we look at parametric 2-spaghetti relations.

Theorem 16.1.7 Any parametric 2-spaghetti relation W with m-degree polynomial functions of t is equivalent to a two-dimensional parametric affine transformation object relation G with m-degree polynomial functions of t and a polygonal reference object.

Proof: $W \rightarrow G$: We represent separately each parametric 2-spaghetti tuple as a geometric transformation object. Let S be any parametric 2-spaghetti tuple with the attributes Ax, Ay, Bx, By, Cx, Cy, which are functions of time, and $from$ and to, which are constants.

We choose any $t_0 \in [from, to]$ such that the parametric 2-spaghetti tuple is a nonempty triangle T at time t_0. If there is no such t_0, then the parametric 2-spaghetti tuple only represents the empty relation and need not be translated.

We translate the parametric 2-spaghetti tuple into the geometric transformation tuple $(T, [from, to], f)$ where f is a parametric affine transformation of the form:

$$f(x, y, t) = \begin{bmatrix} a & b \\ c & d \end{bmatrix} \begin{bmatrix} x \\ y \end{bmatrix} + \begin{bmatrix} e \\ f \end{bmatrix}$$

where a, b, c, d, e, f are functions of t. Because an affine transformation in the plane is uniquely defined by the transformation of three points, we can find the parametric affine transformation by substituting the values of the corner vertices of T for (x, y) and then solving the system of equations using Gaussian elimination.

During Gaussian elimination we only multiply by constants or add together the right-hand sides, which are the only ones to contain functions of t. Therefore, if initially the right-hand sides are at most m-degree polynomials of t, then in the solution we also get at most m-degree polynomials of t.

$G \to W$: Let $G = (S, I, f)$ be a parametric affine transformation object relation with m-degree polynomial functions of t. If S is not a triangle, i.e., it is a general n-degree polygon, then we break S into a set of triangles $T_1, \ldots, T_{n-2}$ and create new geometric transformation objects $G_i = (T_i, I, f)$ for $1 \leq i \leq (n - 2)$.

Similarly, if I is not describable as a single interval of time, then we break I into a set of intervals $I_1, \ldots, I_m$. We also further break each G_i into m smaller pieces $G_{i,j}$ by replacing I with I_j for $1 \leq j \leq m$.

We have now created $(n - 2)m$ geometric transformations. By the definition of geometric transformations, the union of the $G_{i,j}$s has the same meaning as G has. Therefore, it is enough to show that each $G_{i,j}$ can be transformed into an equivalent parametric 2-spaghetti relation. Hence without loss of generality for the rest of the proof we assume that S is a triangle and I is a single time interval of the form $[from, to]$ where $from, to$ are real constants.

Let $(a_x, a_y), (b_x, b_y)$, and (c_x, c_y) be the vertices of S at time $t = 0$. Let $(Ax, Ay) = f(a_x, a_y, t)$, $(Bx, By) = f(b_x, b_y, t)$, and $(Cx, Cy) = f(c_x, c_y, t)$. Then the vertices $(Ax, Ay), (Bx, By)$, and (Cx, Cy) describe a triangle for each instance of t. Therefore, it can be represented as the parametric 2-spaghetti relation

$$T = (Ax, Ay, Bx, By, Cx, Cy, from, to)$$

Finally, note that if f contains only m-degree polynomial functions, then T will also contain only m-degree polynomial functions.   ∎

Example 16.1.15 Let us translate the *Net* parametric 2-spaghetti relation of Example 7.1.1 into a geometric transformation object. This relation has only one tuple. The spatial extent of the fishing net at time $t = 0$ is a triangle T with corner vertices $(3, 3)$, $(4, 4)$, and $(5, 3)$. We choose T as the spatial reference object. We now substitute as described in Theorem 16.1.7 to obtain a parametric affine transformation function f. The vertex $(3, 3)$ is always mapped to $(3, 3 - t)$, hence the transformation must satisfy:

$$\begin{bmatrix} a & b \\ c & d \end{bmatrix} \begin{bmatrix} 3 \\ 3 \end{bmatrix} + \begin{bmatrix} e \\ f \end{bmatrix} = \begin{bmatrix} 3 \\ 3 - t \end{bmatrix}$$

Similarly, vertex $(4, 4)$ is always mapped to $(4 + 0.5t, \ 4 - 0.5t)$; hence the transformation must also satisfy:

$$\begin{bmatrix} a & b \\ c & d \end{bmatrix} \begin{bmatrix} 4 \\ 4 \end{bmatrix} + \begin{bmatrix} e \\ f \end{bmatrix} = \begin{bmatrix} 4 + 0.5t \\ 4 - 0.5t \end{bmatrix}$$

Finally, $(5, 3)$ is mapped to $(5 + t, 3)$, hence:

$$\begin{bmatrix} a & b \\ c & d \end{bmatrix} \begin{bmatrix} 5 \\ 3 \end{bmatrix} + \begin{bmatrix} e \\ f \end{bmatrix} = \begin{bmatrix} 5 + t \\ 3 \end{bmatrix}$$

The preceding yields the following system of equations:

$$\begin{aligned} 3a + 3b + e &= 3 \\ 3c + 3d + f &= 3 - t \\ 4a + 4b + e &= 4 + 0.5t \\ 4c + 4d + f &= 4 - 0.5t \\ 5a + 3b + e &= 5 + t \\ 5c + 3d + f &= 3 \end{aligned}$$

By solving this system, we can find that the affine parametric transformation f is:

$$\begin{bmatrix} 1 + 0.5t & 0 \\ 0.5t & 1 \end{bmatrix} \begin{bmatrix} x \\ y \end{bmatrix} + \begin{bmatrix} -1.5t \\ -2.5t \end{bmatrix}$$

Therefore, $(T, [0, 10], f)$ is a geometric transformation object that is equivalent to the Net relation. Note that in this example both the Net and the parametric affine transformation contain only linear functions of t.

As a check, let us now translate back G to a parametric 2-spaghetti relation. Because T is a triangle and the time domain is a single interval, we do not need to break up G. By substituting the coordinate values of the first vertex for x and y we get that:

$$\begin{bmatrix} 1 + 0.5t & 0 \\ 0.5t & 1 \end{bmatrix} \begin{bmatrix} 3 \\ 3 \end{bmatrix} + \begin{bmatrix} -1.5t \\ -2.5t \end{bmatrix} = \begin{bmatrix} 3 \\ 3 - t \end{bmatrix}$$

For the second vertex we find:

$$\begin{bmatrix} 1 + 0.5t & 0 \\ 0.5t & 1 \end{bmatrix} \begin{bmatrix} 4 \\ 4 \end{bmatrix} + \begin{bmatrix} -1.5t \\ -2.5t \end{bmatrix} = \begin{bmatrix} 4 + 0.5t \\ 4 - 0.5t \end{bmatrix}$$

Finally, for the third vertex we obtain:

$$\begin{bmatrix} 1 + 0.5t & 0 \\ 0.5t & 1 \end{bmatrix} \begin{bmatrix} 5 \\ 3 \end{bmatrix} + \begin{bmatrix} -1.5t \\ -2.5t \end{bmatrix} = \begin{bmatrix} 5 + t \\ 3 \end{bmatrix}$$

Therefore, we can say that G is equivalent to the parametric 2-spaghetti tuple $(3, 3 - t, 4 + 0.5t, 4 - 0.5t, 5 + t, 3, 0, 10)$, which is exactly the original definition of the *Net* relation.

Note that the restriction in Theorem 16.1.7, that the reference object is a polygon, is important. For example, a geometric transformation object may be a circle that is growing with a circle reference object. It is easy to see that this geometric transformation object cannot be represented as a parametric 2-spaghetti, because at any instance of time it is a circle, while any instance of the parametric 2-spaghetti relation is a 2-spaghetti relation, which is a union of triangles.

Figure 16.3 gives a summary of the equivalences among spatio-temporal data models. All the parts of the table follow from the theorems given earlier except the equivalence between rectangles relations and identity transformations with rectangular reference objects, and the equivalence between Worboys relations and identity transformations with polygonal reference objects. These two follow directly from the definition of these models and the fact that each polygon reference object can be broken into triangles and represented separately as a tuple in a Worboys relation.

Constraint	(Parametric) Extreme Point	(Parametric) Geometric Transformation
Inequality	Rectangles	Identity transformation Rectangle reference object
x, y linear t inequality	Worboys	Identity transformation Polygon reference object
Each x_i bounded by functions of t	Parametric Rectangles	Parametric scaling+translation Rectangle reference object
x, y linear for each t	Parametric 2-spaghetti	Parametric affine motion Polygon reference object

Figure 16.3: Equivalences among spatio-temporal data models.

16.1.4   Constraint and Geometric Transformation Models

If the reference spatial object is not a polygon or set of polygons, but, for example, a circle, then we cannot use Theorem 16.1.7 to achieve a two-step transformation from a geometric relation to a constraint relation. However, we can still say the following.

Theorem 16.1.8 Any d-dimensional parametric affine transformation object relation with m-degree polynomial functions of t can be represented as a $(d+1)$-dimensional constraint relation with polynomial constraints.

Proof: Let $G = (S, I, f)$ be any parametric affine transformation object as stated. At first create a $(2d+1)$-dimensional constraint relation $C = (x_1, \ldots, x_d, t, x'_1, \ldots, x'_d)$ with the d equality constraints that describe the system of equations implied by:

$$f(x_1, \ldots, x_d, t) = (x'_1, \ldots, x'_d)$$

as its conjunction of constraints. Then find $\pi_{x'_1, \ldots, x'_d, t} C$. Because projection is doable from conjunctions of real polynomial constraints in closed form, the result is a constraint relation with real polynomial constraints that represents the meaning of G. ∎

Example 16.1.16 Let $G = (x^2 + y^2 = 1, [1, 5], f)$ where f is the following parametric scaling from (x, y) points to (x', y') points:

$$\begin{bmatrix} t & 0 \\ 0 & t \end{bmatrix} \begin{bmatrix} x \\ y \end{bmatrix} = \begin{bmatrix} x' \\ y' \end{bmatrix}$$

This defines a unit circle centered at the origin with radius 1 at time $t = 1$. The circle is expanding linearly with time until $t = 5$. At each time its radius will be equal to t. Here f is also expressible as the following system of equations:

$$\begin{aligned} tx &= x' \\ ty &= y' \end{aligned}$$

Hence the geometric transformation object is equivalent to the following conjunction of constraints:

$$tx = x', \ ty = y', \ x^2 + y^2 = 1, \ 1 \le t, \ t \le 5$$

We can rewrite this as:

$$x = \frac{x'}{t}, \ y = \frac{y'}{t}, \ x = \sqrt{1 - y^2}, \ 1 \le t, \ t \le 5$$

Eliminating x yields:

$$\frac{x'}{t} = \sqrt{1 - y^2}, \ y = \frac{y'}{t}, \ 1 \le t, \ t \le 5$$

This we rewrite as:

$$y^2 = 1 - \left(\frac{x'}{t}\right)^2, \ y = \frac{y'}{t}, \ 1 \le t, \ t \le 5$$

Eliminating y yields:

$$\left(\frac{x'}{t}\right)^2 + \left(\frac{y'}{t}\right)^2 = 1, \ 1 \leq t, \ t \leq 5$$

It is easy to see that the last conjunction of constraints defines a circle with radius t as expected.

16.2 Query Interoperability

Query interoperability between two database systems Δ_1 and Δ_2 requires that the queries of Δ_2 be usable by the users of Δ_1. Typically, a user wants to find the result of running Q_2 on D_1 where D_1 is a local Δ_1 database and Q_2 is a distant site Δ_2 query. Here we assume that the user is unaware of the issue of different data models and knows only what Q_2 is supposed to do normally if run on Δ_2 databases. There are three different approaches to query interoperability.

Section 16.2.1 describes the approach of query translation, Section 16.2.2 data translation, and Section 16.2.3 the use of a common basis to solve the query interoperability problem. Several of the query interoperability examples will solve the problem of intersection in spatio-temporal data models via the use of constraint databases. Section 16.2.4, which discusses the difficulties of defining intersection of linear parametric rectangles directly without the use of query interoperability.

16.2.1 Query Interoperability via Query Translation

One approach to solving the problem mentioned earlier is to translate query Q_2 to a logically equivalent Δ_1 query Q_1 before the execution. This process requires *query translation* and is illustrated in Figure 16.4.

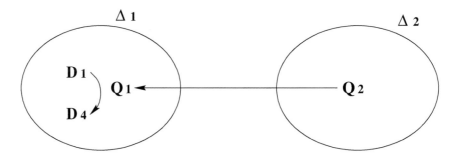

Figure 16.4: Query interoperability via query translation.

By insisting that the query languages use the logical level of data in any spatio-temporal and constraint data model, the queries written for different databases are very similar. Hence query translation is not a major problem in the case of queries that use only relational algebra, SQL, or Datalog and the database systems allow all these languages. However, we may still need query translation when one database system allows only one of these query languages and the other allows another. For example, we may still need to translate from Datalog to SQL. In addition, we learned about some special spatio-temporal operators that may not be available in all database systems.

Example 16.2.1 Suppose that Δ_2 is a rectangles database system that contains the *Book* relation of Example 6.6.7, where we used the buffer_$\square$ operator and SQL to find the shadow of the book. Suppose Δ_1 is a constraint database system that contains a translation of the *Book* relation but uses only Datalog queries. Hence we have to translate the SQL query to Datalog, which we can do as follows:

$$Buffer(x,y) \quad :— \quad Book(x_2, y_2),\ 0 \le x - x_2 \le 10,\ 0 \le y - y_2 \le 10.$$

$$Buffer(x,y) \quad :— \quad Book(x_2, y_2),\ 0 \le x - x_2 \le 10,\ 0 \le y_2 - y \le 10.$$

$$Buffer(x,y) \quad :— \quad Book(x_2, y_2),\ 0 \le x_2 - x \le 10,\ 0 \le y - y_2 \le 10.$$

$$Buffer(x,y) \quad :— \quad Book(x_2, y_2),\ 0 \le x_2 - x \le 10,\ 0 \le y_2 - y \le 10.$$

Note that we may expect the *Buffer* operator in Δ_2 to be closed, i.e., to give a rectangles relation if the input is a rectangles relation. Analogously, the *Buffer* operator always gives an inequality constraint database output if the input is an inequality constraint database.

16.2.2   Query Interoperability via Data Translation

Another approach to solving the query interoperability problem is to translate D_1 (or at least its part relevant to Q_2) into a logically equivalent Δ_2 database D_2, then execute Q_2 on D_2 to obtain a new Δ_2 database D_3, and finally translate it to a Δ_1 database D_4. This approach is shown in Figure 16.5. Clearly, D_4 is logically equivalent to the database we obtained using the previous approach with query translation. However, in this alternative process we used only *data translation*. In other words we reduced the problem to data interoperability.

Example 16.2.2 Consider again Example 16.2.1 and suppose that the definition of the *Book* relation contains only inequality constraints. Then by Theorem 16.1.1 the *Book* relation can be translated into a rectangles

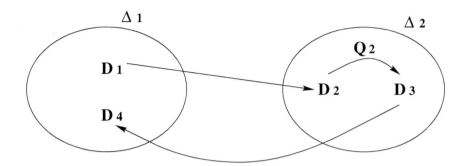

Figure 16.5: Query interoperability via data translation.

relation D_2. Then the query $\textit{Buffer}(D_2, 10)$ can be executed in Δ_2, resulting in a rectangles database D_3. Finally, D_3 can be translated back to an inequality constraint relation that is equivalent to D_4 of Example 16.2.1.

In theory all the query languages of relational algebra, SQL, and Datalog can be made available in any spatio-temporal database system because of the closure of the data models mentioned in Figure 16.3, as shown by the following theorem.

Theorem 16.2.1 All the spatio-temporal models appearing in Figure 16.3 are closed under intersection, complement, union, join, projection, and selection with inequality constraints that contain spatio-temporal variables and constants.

Proof: All the operators are easily seen to be closed in the four cases of constraint data models shown in Figure 16.3. Because the other data models are equivalent to one of the four constraint data models, they are also closed. ∎

In practice, some spatio-temporal database systems do not even implement the full relational algebra. In these cases, query interoperability via data translation to a constraint database can be used to enhance the query capabilities of other spatio-temporal databases. We illustrate that in the following examples.

Example 16.2.3 Suppose Δ_1 is a parametric 2-spaghetti database system that does not allow the intersection operator. Suppose also that Δ_2 is a constraint database system that allows intersection. Let D_1 contain the parametric 2-spaghetti relations

$$R_1 = (0, 0, 1, 0, 0, t+1, -\infty, +\infty)$$

and

$$R_2 = (0, 0, 1, 0, 1, 2t + 1, -\infty, +\infty)$$

We can use query interoperability to find the intersection of R_1 and R_2. First, we translate R_1 to the constraint relation:

$$C_1 = \{y \geq 0, \ x \geq 0, \ y \leq (t+1)(1-x)\}$$

and R_2 to the constraint relation

$$C_2 = \{y \geq 0, \ x \leq 1, \ y \leq (2t+1)x\}$$

Then the intersection of C_1 and C_2 is:

$$C = \{y \geq 0, \ y \leq (t+1)(1-x), \ y \leq (2t+1)x, \ x \geq 0, \ x \leq 1\}$$

Because the first three constraints imply the last two, the preceding simplifies to:

$$C = \{y \geq 0, \ y \leq (t+1)(1-x), \ y \leq (2t+1)x\}$$

Finally, as in Example 16.1.6, we translate C back to the parametric 2-spaghetti relation

$$R = (0, 0, 1, 0, \frac{t+1}{3t+2}, \frac{(t+1)(2t+1)}{3t+2}, -0.5, +\infty)$$

This example shows that parametric 2-spaghetti relations with linear functions of time are not closed under intersection, because R_1 and R_2 both contain only linear functions, but their intersection R contains a rational of polynomial functions of t.

Example 16.2.4 Suppose Δ_1 is a geometric transformation database system that does not allow the intersection operator. Suppose also that Δ_2 is a constraint database system that allows intersection. Let D_1 contain $G_1 = ([0,1] \times [0,1], (1, +\infty), f_1)$ where f is the identity transformation and $G_2 = ([0,1] \times [0,1], (1, +\infty), f_2)$ where f_2 is:

$$f_2(x, y, t) = \begin{bmatrix} 1 & t \\ -1 & 1 \end{bmatrix} \begin{bmatrix} x \\ y \end{bmatrix}$$

We can use query interoperability to find the intersection of G_1 and G_2. First, we translate G_1 to:

$$C_1 = \{0 \leq x, \ x \leq 1, \ 0 \leq y, \ y \leq 1, \ t \geq 1\}$$

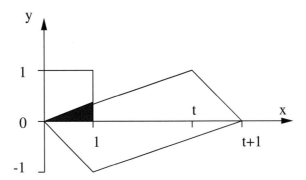

Figure 16.6: Unit square mapped to a parallelogram.

Note that G_2 maps the unit square at each time $t \geq 0$ into a parallelogram with corner vertices $(0,0)$, $(1,-1)$, $(t+1,0)$, and $(t,1)$ as shown in Figure 16.6.

Hence we can translate G_2 to:

$$C_2 = \{y \geq -x, \ y \leq -x + t + 1, \ y \leq \frac{x}{t}, \ y \geq \frac{x-1}{t} - 1\}$$

Therefore, after simplifying the intersection of C_1 and C_2 is:

$$C = \{y \leq \frac{x}{t}, \ x \geq 0, \ y \geq 0, \ t \geq 1\}$$

Finally, we translate C to the geometric transformation $G(T, [1, +\infty], f)$ where T is the triangle with corner vertices $(0,0)$, $(1,0)$, and $(1,1)$, and f is:

$$f(x, y, t) = \begin{bmatrix} 1 & 0 \\ 0 & 1/t \end{bmatrix} \begin{bmatrix} x \\ y \end{bmatrix}$$

This example shows that parametric affine transformation objects with rectangle spatial reference objects are not closed under intersection even if the rectangles have sides parallel to the x- and y-axes.

16.2.3 Query Interoperability via a Common Basis

We would need to write a total of $2n(n-1)$ data and query translation algorithms to interoperate directly between each pair of n data models. Instead, we simplify the interoperability problem by finding a *common basis* database system into which the data and queries of every other data model are translated. The common basis approach requires only $4n$ data and query translations.

Let us see how the query interoperability problem, as discussed earlier, can be solved using a common basis. Let Δ_0 be the common basis. Then in this approach, D_1 is translated into a logically equivalent database D_0 in Δ_0 and query Q_2 is translated into a logically equivalent Δ_0 query Q_0. Then Q_0 is executed and the resulting relation D_5 is translated into a Δ_1 relation D_4. This approach is shown in Figure 16.7.

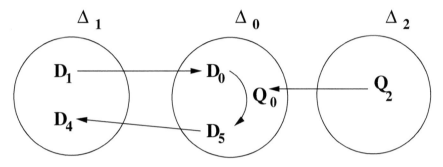

Figure 16.7: Query interoperability via a common basis.

Example 16.2.5 Suppose Δ_0 is a parametric 2-spaghetti and Δ_1 is a geometric transformations database system and that they do not allow the intersection operator. Suppose also that Δ_2 is a constraint database system that allows intersection. Let D_1 contain $G_1 = (T_1, (-\infty, +\infty), f_1)$ where T_1 is a triangle with vertices $(0,0)$, $(0,1)$, and $(1,0)$, and f_1 is:

$$f_1(x, y, t) = \begin{bmatrix} 1 & 0 \\ 0 & 1+t \end{bmatrix} \begin{bmatrix} x \\ y \end{bmatrix}$$

and $G_2 = (T_2, (-\infty, +\infty), f_2)$ where T_2 is a triangle with vertices $(0,0)$, $(0,1)$, and $(1,1)$, and f_2 is:

$$f_2(x, y, t) = \begin{bmatrix} 1 & 0 \\ 0 & 2+t \end{bmatrix} \begin{bmatrix} x \\ y \end{bmatrix}$$

We can use query interoperability via a common basis to find the intersection of G_1 and G_2. First, we translate G_1 and G_2 to the parametric 2-spaghetti relations R_1 and R_2, respectively. These happen to be the same as those of Example 16.2.3. We also translate the intersection operator from Δ_2 to Δ_0. Then we evaluate in Δ_0 the intersection of R_1 and R_2 to be the parametric 2-spaghetti relation R of Example 16.2.3. Finally, we translate R to the geometric transformation $G(T_1, [-0.5, +\infty], f)$ where T_1 is as in Example 16.2.3 and f is:

$$f(x, y, t) = \begin{bmatrix} 1 & \frac{-t}{3t+2} \\ 0 & \frac{2(t+1)(2t+1)}{3t+2} \end{bmatrix} \begin{bmatrix} x \\ y \end{bmatrix}$$

This example shows that parametric scaling transformation objects with triangle spatial reference objects are not closed under intersection, because G is a parametric affine transformation that is not a parametric scaling transformation.

The common basis also facilitates the addition of new data models. For example, suppose one would like to use a new data model Δ_n that is not already available in some database system. One needs only to define data and query translations between the common basis Δ_0 and Δ_n. Then any Q_n query on D_n database in Δ_n can be executed by translating the query and the database to the common basis, executing the query in the common basis and translating the result back into Δ_n. Hence the common basis could also save writing separate query processors for data models that are used only infrequently.

Constraint databases are a good common basis for many types of databases for the following reasons:

1. *Precise data translation:* We can translate each of the spatio-temporal data models of Chapter 7 into a syntactically restricted type of constraint database. We can also easily compare the expressive power of several different data models by translating them to restricted types of constraint databases.

2. *Easy query translation:* Many spatio-temporal query languages contain numerous special operators and other special language features. In general, it is difficult to translate directly from a query language with a set of special operators to another query language with a different set of special operators. It is usually easier to translate between constraint queries and specialized languages. Many query processors also work better and more robustly if the query language contains only a few or no special operators.

3. *Safety and complexity:* By knowing the allowed syntax of the constraints in the common basis, we can gain valuable information about

the safety and computational complexity of queries following the results of Chapters 22 and 25.

16.2.4 Intersection of Linear Parametric Rectangles

Query interoperability via data translation to a constraint database is not the only way to evaluate the intersection of parametric extreme point relations or geometric transformation relations. It is possible but cumbersome to define directly the intersection of relations in those spatio-temporal data models. To hint at some of the difficulties, let us consider the simple question of just finding out whether two linear parametric rectangles intersect. For added simplicity, the following lemma is stated only for one spatial dimension.

Lemma 16.2.1 The parametric rectangles

$$R_1 = ([a_1 t + b_1, \ c_1 t + d_1], \ I_1)$$

and

$$R_2 = ([a_2 t + b_2, \ c_2 t + d_2], \ I_2)$$

where $a_1, b_1, c_1, d_1, a_2, b_2, c_2, d_2$ are constants and I_1 and I_2 are time intervals intersect if and only if

$$I_1 \cap I_2 \cap I_3 \cap I_4 \cap I_5 \cap I_6$$

is nonempty, where:

I_3 is the time interval when $a_1 t + b_1 \leq c_1 t + d_1$ is true;
I_4 is the time interval when $a_2 t + b_2 \leq c_2 t + d_2$ is true;
I_5 is the time interval when $a_1 t + b_1 \leq c_2 t + d_2$ is true; and
I_6 is the time interval when $a_2 t + b_2 \leq c_1 t + d_1$ is true.

Proof: It is obvious that R_1 and R_2 can intersect only at times t, which are within both I_1 and I_2. Also, R_1 must have a lower bound that is less than its upper bound, which occurs exactly when I_3 is true. Similarly, R_2 must have a lower bound that is less than its upper bound, which occurs exactly when I_4 is true.

In addition, at any time t when R_1 and R_2 intersect the lower bound of R_1 must be less than the upper bound of R_2 and the lower bound of R_2 must be before the upper bound of R_1, which are true in the intervals I_5 and I_6, respectively. ∎

We can use Lemma 16.2.1 to prove the following theorem for d dimensions.

Theorem 16.2.2 Whether two d-dimensional linear parametric rectangles intersect can be checked in $O(d)$ time.

Proof: For each ith dimension we can easily calculate the values of all the intervals in Lemma 16.2.1 and express those intervals in terms of constraints on the permissible values of t. For example, we have the following cases of intervals for I_3:

$$I_3 = \begin{cases} \emptyset & \text{if } a_1 = c_1 \text{ and } b_1 > d_1 \\ t & \text{if } a_1 = c_1 \text{ and } b_1 \leq d_1 \\ t \leq (d_1 - b_1)/(a_1 - c_1) & \text{if } a_1 > c_1 \\ t \geq (d_1 - b_1)/(a_1 - c_1) & \text{if } a_1 < c_1 \end{cases}$$

We can similarly express the other intervals as constraints on t. The conjunctions of these constraints is either satisfiable or not and can be easily checked. Furthermore, we can take the conjunction of all the constraints in all the dimensions. The two linear parametric rectangles intersect if and only if the resulting constraint is satisfiable. Note that picking for each ith dimension for each of the intervals $I_1, \ldots, I_6$ one of the four cases takes a constant time. Therefore, for the d dimensions together it takes $O(d)$ time to build the large constraint that needs to be checked for satisfiability.

Checking satisfiability also takes $O(d)$ time because as we scan the constraint from left to right we can keep track of the highest lower bound c_1 constraint and lowest upper bound c_2 constraint on t and whether any $\emptyset$ was seen. If $\emptyset$ occurs anywhere or $c_1 > c_2$ then the constraint is not satisfiable; otherwise it is satisfiable. ∎

Theorem 16.2.2 can be extended to yield a theorem that actually states the precise intersection for any two d-dimensional linear parametric rectangles.

16.3   Other Types of Interoperability

There are many possible sources of mismatches between different databases that are not due to the use of different data models. For example, the schemas of the relations may not match even in the case of two relational databases.

For example, in one database Δ_1 the attribute name "cars" is used while in the other database Δ_2 the attribute name "vehicles" is used. Then before executing a query Q_2 that was written originally for Δ_2 on some Δ_1 database instance, we have to change Q_2 by replacing "vehicles" with "cars" before execution, along with other changes that may be necessary.

There is also a potential for mismatch when some data are missing or inconsistent. For example, suppose that in Δ_2 we can assume that each employee works in only one company. Suppose further that some query Q_2 is written for that database to find the total salary of each employee. Therefore Q_2 could be easily expressed using only select, project, and join operations. However, if each employee in Δ_1 may work in several companies, then Q_2 has to be modified, for example, by inserting into it the maximum aggregate function where appropriate, before running it in Δ_1.

Another type of mismatch occurs when the same attribute, for example, weight, is measured in different units, for example, in pounds in one database relation and kilograms in another database relation.

These issues are sometimes called *application-dependent* interoperability issues. In this chapter we limited our attention to the differences in the data models and were concerned only with *application-independent* interoperability, because that is the part where constraint databases could be most useful. Obviously, for practical applications the two types of interoperability should be considered together.

Bibliographic Notes

Interoperability is traditionally motivated by several possible sources of mismatches between different relational databases [228]. Interoperability between a GIS database and application programs was studied in Scheck and Wolf [363]. Interoperability in the sense of combining spatial and attribute data managers for the implementation of GIS systems was studied in Kolovson et al. [232]. A functional specification facilitating interoperability of GIS systems was studied by Frank and Kuhn [138]. Application-dependent interoperability issues of resolving semantic and representational mismatches and conflict detection and resolution have found a very elegant formulation using the language of first-order logic by Qian and Lunt [311].

Data interoperability of a number of temporal databases via a common basis, that is, a unifying temporal database, was studied in Jensen et al. [211]. More recent work on the interoperability of temporal databases, e.g., Wang et al. [421, 49], also considers interoperability among different temporal data models.

Chomicki and Revesz [87, 88] initiated a study of the interoperability of constraint and spatio-temporal databases, emphasizing the interoperability problem that derives from differences in data models. Theorem 16.1.2 is from that paper, and it gave a translation from linear constraint databases to parametric 2-spaghetti databases with linear functions of time, which is a subcase of Theorem 16.1.4. Chomicki et al. [86] provide a use of the one-way translation, and the paper contains Exercise 3. The other data interoperability results are new.

Theorem 16.2.1 is a culmination of previous work on the closure of spatio-temporal data models under relational algebra. The previous approaches did not have the benefit of the data translation results and were based on direct arguments on the structure of various spatio-temporal data models. Such direct arguments are more complicated but desirable for potentially more efficient implementations of the operators. Examples of direct arguments include Theorem 16.2.2, which checks whether two linear parametric rectangles intersect, and a definition of the intersection of two parametric scaling+translation objects with rectangle reference objects in [89].

The nonclosure of parametric 2-spaghetti relations with linear functions of time, which is illustrated in Example 16.2.3, was noticed by Chomicki and Revesz [87, 88]. The closure of parametric rectangles even with periodic and polynomial constraints is from Cai et al. [64]. A generalization of the periodic functions in [64] and the computational complexity of query evaluation is considered in [347, 348]. The closure of parametric scaling and translation transformations with rectangle spatial reference objects is from Chomicki and Revesz [89]. An earlier version of Example 16.2.5 also appeared in Chomicki and Revesz [89] but was solved incorrectly.

As mentioned earlier, Example 16.2.5 illustrates that parametric scaling transformations with polygonal spatial reference objects are not closed under intersection. This result was also proven by Haesevoets and Kuijpers [181] as well as some other results on the closure properties of geometric transformation objects.

The result that parametric affine transformations with rectangle spatial reference objects (with sides parallel to the x- and y-axes) are not closed under intersection is new. This follows from Example 16.2.4 and the fact that the intersection is a parametric triangle and parametric affine transformations cannot map any rectangle to parametric triangles

Exercises

1. Translate the following instance of the *Window* relation of Example 7.7.9 into an inequality constraint relation:

Window

Id	X	Y	T
1	[60, 90]	[10, 60]	[0, 3]
1	[60, 90]	[10, 60]	[17, 20]
2	[0, 100]	[0, 80]	[3, 8]
3	[50, 80]	[40, 50]	[8, 12]
4	[20, 60]	[30, 70]	[12, 17]

2. Translate the parametric 2-spaghetti relation of Exercise 7.6 into a constraint relation.

3. Translate the following constraint relation *Desert*, which describes a changing desert area, into a parametric 2-spaghetti relation:

$$Desert(x, y, t) \quad :- \quad \begin{aligned} &x \geq 0 \\ &y \geq 0 \\ &x - t \leq 10 \\ &x + y \leq 20 \\ &t \geq 0 \\ &t \leq 10 \end{aligned}$$

$$Desert(x, y, t) \quad :- \quad \begin{aligned} &x \geq 0 \\ &y \geq 0 \\ &x + y + t \leq 30 \\ &t \geq 10 \\ &t \leq 20 \end{aligned}$$

4. Translate the following constraint relation into a parametric 2-spaghetti relation:

$$\begin{aligned} x &\geq 5 \\ x &\leq 10 \\ y &\leq xt^2 \\ y &\geq -xt^3 \\ t &\geq -20 \\ t &\leq 20 \end{aligned}$$

5. For each of the following parametric rectangles (i) test whether it is normal, and if it is not normal, then rewrite it into a set of normal parametric rectangles and (ii) translate them into geometric transformation relations, assuming the spatial reference object is $[0, 1] \times [0, 1]$:

   (a) $R_1 = ([0, \ t + 1], \ [2t, \ t], \ [-1, \ 0])$

   (b) $R_2 = ([2t + 5, \ 3t], \ [8t^3, \ 8t^3 + t], \ [0, \ 10])$

   (c) $R_3 = ([2t, \ 50 - 3t], \ [t^2, \ 4t - 77], \ [-20, \ 20])$

6. Find the intersection of the following pairs of parametric rectangles.

   (a) $R_1 = ([5, 15], [3t, 3t + 8], [0, 24])$ and

   $R_2 = ([3, 7], [2t + 8, 2t + 24], [0, 30])$

   (b) $R_3 = ([3 + t, 8 + t], [2 - t, 6 - t], [0, 10])$ and

   $R_4 = ([2t, 12 + 3t], [t, 10 - 2t], [0, 20])$

   (c) $R_5 = ([20 + t, 30 + t], [20, 25], [0, 25])$ and

   $R_6 = ([45, 48], [45 - t, 51 - t], [0, 25])$

   (d) $R_7 = ([2t, 6t - 12], [12, 24], [5, 10])$ and

   $R_8 = ([4t - 10, 3t + 6], [12, 12 + 2t], [0, 6])$

   (e) $R_9 = ([t^2 + 40, t^2 + 45], [11, 22], [0, 20])$ and

   $R_{10} = ([t^2 + 33, 14t], [17, 34], [3, 10])$

7. Suppose you use a rectangles database system Δ_1 that allows only SQL queries. Suppose you have the instance of relation *Window* given in Exercise 1 and would like to execute the Datalog query of Example 7.7.9 that finds the windows that are completely hidden on a computer screen. However, Datalog queries are available only in some constraint database system Δ_2:

   (a) Use query interoperability via query translation to solve the problem. (*Hint:* Translate the Datalog query to a SQL query.)

   (b) Use query interoperability via data translation to solve the problem.

   (c) Compare these two approaches for query interoperability.

8. A car is traveling on a highway near a tornado.

   (a) The car is going with uniform speed from location $(50, 10)$ to location $(20, 10)$ between time $t = 0$ and $t = 6$. Represent the car by a parametric rectangle.

   (b) The tornado starts at $t = 2$ from an area that is approximately a square with lower left corner $(0, 0)$ and upper right corner $(1, 1)$. After moving with a uniform speed for ten hours it occupies the square area with lower left corner $(50, 25)$ and upper right corner $(51, 26)$. Represent the tornado by a parametric rectangle.

(c) Convert the parametric rectangles relation for the car into a constraint relation $Car(x, y, t)$ and the parametric rectangles relation for the tornado into a constraint relation $Tornado(x, y, t)$.

(d) Write an SQL query that finds the space and time when the tornado hits the car.

9. An oil spill occurs in the ocean near an archipelago of islands that is the habitat area of several endangered animals.

   (a) At time $t = 0$, the oil spill is in an area that is approximately a rectangle with lower left corner $(2, 6)$ and upper right corner $(8, 16)$. In the next 24 hours the ocean currents move the oil spill with a uniform speed until it occupies a rectangular area with lower left corner $(50, 30)$ and upper right corner $(80, 40)$. Represent the area of the oil spill using the parametric rectangles data model.

   (b) The archipelago of islands approximately occupies a triangle with corner vertices $(25, 25)$, $(30, 45)$, and $(45, 15)$. Represent the area of the archipelago using the Worboys data model. (*Hint:* Use the time interval from $t = 0$ to $t = 24$.)

   (c) Convert the parametric relation for the oil spill into a constraint relation $Oil(x, y, t)$ and the Worboys relation for the archipelago into a constraint relation $Archipelago(x, y, t)$.

   (d) Will the oil spill reach the archipelago? Write an SQL query that finds the part of the archipelago that is affected by the oil spill at time $t = 10$.

10. A computer screen projector is shining a rectangle on the wall of a classroom when it is turned on at time $t = 0$. As it is moved slowly backward the rectangle is enlarged until time $t = 10$. In particular, the lower-left corner moves with uniform speed from $(2, 1)$ to $(0, 0)$, and the upper-right corner moves with uniform speed from $(8, 4)$ to $(10, 5)$.

   (a) Represent the rectangle between times $t = 0$ and $t = 10$ using a parametric rectangles relation.

   (b) Represent the rectangle using parametric Worboys data model.

   (c) Translate the above parametric rectangle relation into a geometric transformation relation.

11. A triangular soap film whose corner vertices are three fingers is created at time $t = 0$. The three fingers move with uniform speed from time $t = 0$ minutes to time $t = 10$ minutes as follows. The first finger

moves from $(10, 10)$ to $(0, 0)$, the second finger moves from $(30, 30)$ to $(40, 40)$, and the third finger moves from $(10, 50)$ to $(10, 100)$. At time $t = 10$ the soap film pops.

(a) Represent the soap film using a parametric Worboys relation.

(b) Translate the above parametric Worboys relation into a constraint database relation.

17

Data Integration

In many problems, we need to classify items, that is, we need to predict some characteristic of an item based on several parameters of the item. Classifications are usually done by classifiers. After being trained on some sample data, these *classifiers* can be used to classify new data. Section 17.1 describes *decision trees*, which were frequently used in the nineties by artificial intelligence experts to classify data because they can be easily implemented, and they provide an explanation of the classification. Section 17.2 describes *support vector machines*, which are increasingly popular classification tools because of the high accuracy of their classifications.

Many challenging applications also require the reuse of the old classifiers to derive a new classifier. Section 17.3 describes the classification integration problem, while Section 17.4 describes the reclassification problem. Section 17.5 discusses data integration via wrappers. Section 17.6 summarizes data fusion. Finally, Section 17.7 discusses the trust management approach to computer security. Constraint databases are helpful in solving all of these problems.

17.1 Decision Trees

Consider a set of items, with each item described by a set of parameters. Each parameter is represented by a variable which can take a numerical value. Each variable is called a *feature* and the set of variables is called a *feature space*. The number of features is the *dimension* of the feature space. The actual characteristic of the item we want to predict is called the *label* or *class* of the item.

P. Revesz, *Introduction to Databases: From Biological to Spatio-Temporal*,
Texts in Computer Science, DOI 10.1007/978-1-84996-095-3_17,
© Springer-Verlag London Limited 2010

To make the predictions, we use *classifiers*, which map the feature space X to a set of labels Y. The classifiers are found by various methods using a set of *training examples*, which are items where both the set of features and the set of labels are known. A well-known example of classifiers are *decision trees*. Each decision tree is a tree with the following properties:

- Each internal node is a feature,

- Each arc from an internal node to a child node tests a condition.

- Each leaf node is a label.

Example 17.1.1 A set of *primary biliary cirrhosis* or liver cancer patients were classified by two decision trees. Figure 17.1 shows a decision tree that classifies the patients according to the drug they took during the treatment. The feature space $X_1 = \{Bilirubin, Cholesterol, Gender, Hepatomegaly\}$ and the set of labels is $Y_1 = \{Penicillamine, Placebo\}$. The feature *Bilirubin* is the serum bilirubin measured in mg/dl, *Cholesterol* is the serum cholesterol in mg/dl, *Gender* is "0" for female and "1" for male, and *Hepatomegaly* is "1" if the liver is enlarged and "0" otherwise. The label *Penicillamine* means that the patient was prescribed penicillamine, and the label *Placebo* means that the patient was given only a sugar pill. Figure 17.1 shows the features in ovals and the labels in diamonds.

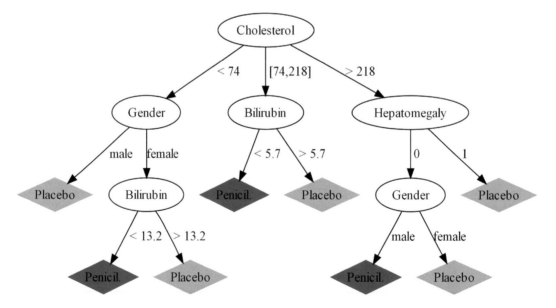

Figure 17.1: Decision tree predicting the prescribed drug using *primary biliary cirrhosis* data.

Figure 17.2 shows another decision tree that uses the feature space $X_2 = \{Cholesterol, Gender, Hepatomegaly, Triglicerides\}$ and the set of labels is $Y_2 = \{Alive, Dead, Transplanted\}$. The feature *Triglicerides* is the triglicerides level measured in mg/dl. The label *Alive* means that the patient is alive with no spread of the cancer, *Transplanted* means the patient is alive but the cancer spread to other organs, and *Dead* means that the patient died by the end of the study period.

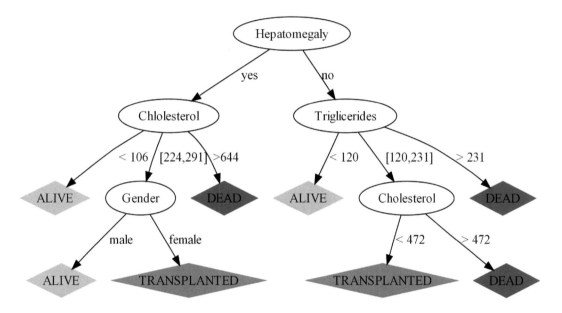

Figure 17.2: Decision tree predicting the patient status using *primary biliary cirrhosis* data.

To find the label of any particular item whose features are known, the decision tree is read from the root node down to one of the leaf nodes. At each internal node, one of the child nodes is selected where the test condition holds. For the sake of unique classifications, the test conditions are mutually exclusive. For example, suppose that a patient is described by the following features: bilirubin is 9.3 mg/dl, cholesterol is 67 mg/dl, gender is 0, and hepatomegaly is 1. To find the patient's label, we start searching at the root node of the decision tree shown in Figure 17.1. The root node tests the cholesterol level. We choose the first child because $67 < 74$. The first child tests the gender. We choose next the second child because gender is 0, that is, female. The second child tests the bilirubin serum level. Finally, we choose the first child because $9.3 < 13.2$. Now we arrived at a leaf node, which shows that the label of the patient is *Pennicillamine*.

There are a number of algorithms to build decision trees, which are discussed in detail in many other books. For constraint databases, the important fact is that the resulting decision trees can be always described by constraint relations.

Example 17.1.2 Assume the following abbreviations for the various features and labels discussed in Example 17.1.1:

- B, the bilirubin serum,
- C, the cholesterol rate,
- D, the drug prescribed.
- G, the gender of the patients,
- H, the hepatomegaly,
- S, the patient's status at the end of the study.
- T, the triglicerides rate,

The decision tree in Figure 17.1 can be translated to the following constraint relation.

Drug

B	C	G	H	D	
b	c	g	h	d	$c < 74,\ g = 1,\ d =$ 'Placebo'
b	c	g	h	d	$c < 74,\ g = 0,\ b < 13.2,\ d =$ 'Penicil.'
b	c	g	h	d	$c < 74,\ g = 0,\ b > 13.2,\ d =$ 'Placebo'
b	c	g	h	d	$c \geq 74,\ c \leq 218,\ b < 5.7,\ d =$ 'Penicil.'
b	c	g	h	d	$c \geq 74,\ c \leq 218,\ b > 5.7,\ d =$ 'Placebo'
b	c	g	h	d	$c > 218,\ h = 0,\ g = 1,\ d =$ 'Penicil.'
b	c	g	h	d	$c > 218,\ h = 0,\ g = 0,\ d =$ 'Placebo'
b	c	g	h	d	$c > 218,\ h = 1,\ d =$ 'Placebo'

Similarly, the decision tree in Figure 17.2 can be translated as follows.

Status

C	G	H	T	S	
c	g	h	t	s	$h = 1,\ c < 224,\ s =$'Alive'
c	g	h	t	s	$h = 1,\ c \geq 224,\ c \leq 291,\ g = 1,\ s =$'Alive'
c	g	h	t	s	$h = 1,\ c \geq 224,\ c \leq 291,\ g = 0,\ s =$'Transplanted'
c	g	h	t	s	$h = 1,\ c > 291,\ s =$'Dead'
c	g	h	t	s	$h = 0,\ t < 120,\ s =$'Alive'
c	g	h	t	s	$h = 0,\ t \geq 120,\ t \leq 231,\ c < 472,\ s =$'Transplanted'
c	g	h	t	s	$h = 0,\ t \geq 120,\ t \leq 231,\ c > 472,\ s =$'Dead'
c	g	h	t	s	$h = 0,\ t > 231,\ s =$'Alive'

17.2 Support Vector Machines

Suppose that numerical values can be assigned to each of the n features in the feature space. Let $\vec{x_i} \in \mathbb{R}^n$ with $i \in [1..l]$ be a set of l training examples. Each training example $\vec{x_i}$ can be represented as a point in the n-dimensional feature space.

Suppose further that the data is linearly separable, that is, there is a hyperplane of dimension $n - 1$ that separates the items into two sets of classes $+1$ and -1. *Support Vector Machines* (SVMs) classify the items by constructing a separating hyperplane. Since several separating hyperplanes may be suitable to split a set of training examples, an SVM selects the *maximum-margin hyperplane*, that is, the hyperplane which maximizes the distance to the closest training examples.

If the data is not linearly separable, then the SVM tries to find a hyperplane that is the best possible separator, that is, a hyperplane that missclassifies the fewest number of items. Since SVMs find hyperplane separators, they are linear classifiers that map X to Y by linear functions. That makes it possible to express the SVM classifiers in constraint databases.

Example 17.2.1 Suppose that businesses are classified as either *Bankrupt* or *Solvent* based on the features *Assets* and *Liabilities*, which are measured in dollars. That is, $X_3 = \{Assets, Liabilities\}$ and $Y_3 = \{Bankrupt, Solvent\}$. Then every business can be envisioned as a point in the plane with the x-axis representing the total liabilities and the x-axis representing the total assets of the business as shown in Figure 17.3. This set is linearly separable because the black line in the middle separates correctly all the training examples. Parallel to the black line are two gray lines that are *support vectors* that cross the training examples that are closest to the classifier line. The distance between the two support vector lines and the classifier line is called the *margin*.

Suppose that after training on shown training examples, an SVM finds that bankrupt businesses are those that are below the line $y = x + 1$. That can be represented by the following constraint relation.

Finance

Assets	Liabilities	Status	
y	x	s	$y < x + 1$, $s = $ "Bankrupt"
y	x	s	$y \geq x + 1$, $s = $ "Solvent"

17.3 Classification Integration

A common problem in classification arises when we have several different data sources.

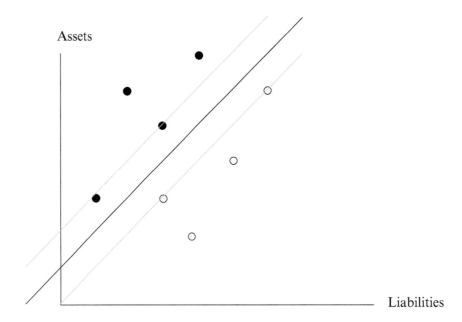

Assets

Liabilities

Figure 17.3: Training examples with labels ● for solvent and ○ for bankrupt businesses.

Example 17.3.1 Suppose that Cottonwood Hospital has six patients with the following recorded features: chest pain P, cholesterol C, gender G, and resting blood pressure B, and with the recorded label disease D, which is "Yes" or "No" according to whether a patient has a heart disease.

Cottonwood

P	C	G	B	D
1	233	1	145	No
3	250	1	130	Yes
3	275	0	110	No
4	230	1	117	Yes
2	198	0	105	No
4	266	1	124	Yes

Similarly, Pineridge Hospital records the following set of data for seven patients.

Pineridge

P	C	G	B	D
1	237	0	170	No
2	219	0	100	No
4	270	1	120	Yes
2	198	0	105	No
4	246	0	100	Yes
1	156	1	140	Yes
2	257	1	110	Yes

Suppose the two hospitals are interested in classifying patients in order to predict the outcome of heart disease treatments for new patients. Intuitively, the two hospitals could get a potentially better classification if they could combine their databases. Combining these two databases seems like a trivial problem of *data integration*, which in this case simply takes the union of the two data sets, yielding the following integrated data set with thirteen patients:

Cottonwood-Pineridge

P	C	G	B	D
1	233	1	145	No
3	250	1	130	Yes
3	275	0	110	No
4	230	1	117	Yes
2	198	0	105	No
4	266	1	124	Yes
1	237	0	170	No
2	219	0	100	No
4	270	1	120	Yes
2	198	0	105	No
4	246	0	100	Yes
1	156	1	140	Yes
2	257	1	110	Yes

Using the above integrated data as a training set, the two hospitals could run any algorithm that gives either a decision tree or an SVM classifier.

The above simplistic approach often fails for several reasons. First, it is possible that the hospitals tested different variables on their own patients. This would yield many null values in the integrated data set. Most classification algorithms perform poorly when there are many null values in the data. Second, even in the absence of null values, the hospitals may be restricted in sharing their data due to privacy and legal concerns.

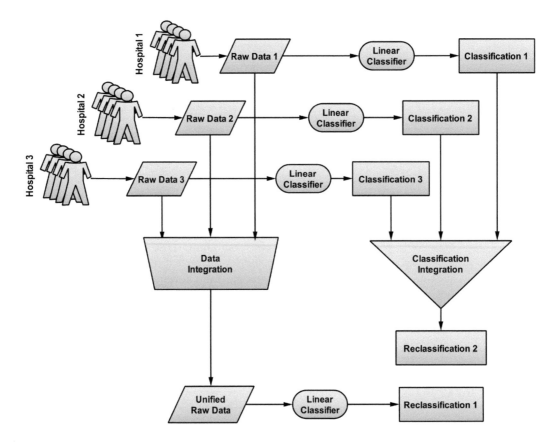

Figure 17.4: Comparison of data integration and classification integration methods.

Classification integration is an alternative approach that avoids privacy problems of data integration. The concept of classification integration is illustrated in Figure 17.4, which shows three hospitals. Whereas with the data integration approach, the hospitals share their raw data and then run the classifier building algorithms, in classification integration, they first analyze their patients and build separate classifiers for them. Then these classifiers are represented as constraint relations, which are then joined together by a constraint database natural join operator.

Example 17.3.2 Suppose that Cottonwood Hospital builds an SVM that can be represented by the following constraint relation:

Cottonwood Classification

$PCGBD_1$
$p\,c\,g\,b\,d_1$ $1.1568p - 0.0172c + 0.4278g + 0.0333b - 3.404 = d_1$

Similarly, Pineridge Hospital may build, based on its data set, another SVM linear classification that can be represented as follows:

Pineridge Classification

P C G B D_2
p c g b d_2 $1.0213p - 0.0016c + 1.9091g + 0.015b - 4.2018 = d_2$

We take the natural join of the two linear constraint relations and then selec the value $d = 0.5d_1 + 0.5d_2$ as a weighted average classification value. That yields the following:

Cottonwood-Pineridge Classification

P C G B D
$d = 0.5d_1 + 0.5d_2,$
p c g b d $1.1568p - 0.0172c + 0.4278g + 0.0333b - 3.404 = d_1,$
$1.0213p - 0.0016c + 1.9091g + 0.015b - 4.2018 = d_2$

Simplifying the above, we get:

Cottonwood-Pineridge Classification

P C G B D
p c g b d $1.0891p - 0.0094c + 1.1685g + 0.0242b - 3.8029 = d$

Since the integrated classification is based on two data sets, it can be expected to be better than either the Cottonwood classification or the Pineridge classification in itself.

17.4 The Reclassification Problem

Classification integration only considered the same label. The problem may be further complicated if the two classifiers use a different set of labels.

Example 17.4.1 Example 17.1.1 presented a decison tree for the status of the patients in Figure 17.2 and another decision tree for the drug prescribed in Figure 17.1. Analysis of such decision trees is difficult. For instance, just by looking at these decision trees, it is hard to tell whether any patient died after taking a placebo, or whether any patient who used the drug is still alive. The problem with the above simple-looking queries is that no decision tree contains both *patient status* and *drug efficiency*. Finding a single decision tree that contains both *patient status* and *drug efficiency* would provide a convenient solution to the above queries. That is, we need to find a classifier with the combined feature space

$$X = X_1 \cup X_2 = \{Bilirubin, Cholesterol, Gender, Hepatomegaly, Triglicerides\}$$

and the combined set of labels

$$
Y = Y_1 \times Y_2 \quad = \quad \{Alive\_Penicillamine, \; Alive\_Placebo,
$$
$$
Dead\_Penicillamine, \; Dead\_Placebo,
$$
$$
Transplanted\_Penicillamine, \; Transplanted\_Placebo\}
$$

This is a reclassification problem because the set of labels change. The reclassification problem also can be solved by a constraint database natural join of the *Drug* and *Status* relations. We can express this natural join in SQL as follows.

```
CREATE VIEW    Reclass(B,C,G,H,T,D,S)
SELECT         Dr.B, Dr.C, Dr.G, Dr.H, St.T, Dr.D, St.S
FROM           Drug AS Dr, Status as St
WHERE          Dr.C = St.C  AND
               Dr.G = St.G  AND
               Dr.H = St.H
```

Further, assume that relation *Patients(id,b,c,g,h,t)* records the identification number and the features of each patient. Then the following SQL query can be used to predict the drug and the status for each patient:

```
CREATE VIEW    Predict(D,S)
SELECT         R.D, R.S
FROM           Patients AS P, Reclass AS R
WHERE          P.B = R.B  AND
               P.C = R.C  AND
               P.G = R.G  AND
               P.H = R.H  AND
               P.T = R.T
```

17.5 Wrappers

In several other approaches to data integration, *wrappers*, which are virtual relations computed based on the source data, play a critical role. A program may use as many different *wrapper functions*, which create the virtual relations, as many diffferent types of data sources it needs to integrate during an application. As we have seen in Chapter 16, it is possible to translate most types of databases into constraint databases. Hence in many applications the wrapper functions may be based on programs that translate the other types of databases into contraint databases. In addition to the difference in database types, the wrappers need to take care of more mundane issues, such as, synonyms in the attribute names among the different sources. We illustrate the wrapper approach to the problem of data integration using an example.

Example 17.5.1 A university has four residence halls, which keep different records about their members. Each uses a single database relation but with different schemes. In particular, they use the following schemes:

$Fraternity(Name, \ Major)$
$Freshman\_Dorm(Name, \ Advisor)$
$Honors\_Hall(Name, \ Sex, \ CHR)$
$Sorority(Name, \ CHR, \ GPA)$

where CHR is an abbreviation for credit hours earned, and GPA is an abbreviation for grade point average. Many queries may require integration of the data from these sources. For example:

Find the names of all female senior students who live in a residence hall and have a 3.5 or better grade point average.

In answering the above query, we need to take a closer look at the data sources, including many implicit assumptions about the data. One possible wrapper is a constraint tuple over the set of attributes that occur in the database in any of these relations. For example, the following is a wrapper for the first relation:

$wrapper(Freshman\_Dorm) \ \equiv \ (CHR < 30)$

This expresses that every student in the $Freshman\_Dorm$ has less than thirty total earned credit hours. Similarly, the following is a wrapper for the second relation:

$wrapper(Honors\_Hall) \ \equiv \ (GPA \geq 3.7)$

This expresses that every student in the honors hall has at least a 3.7 GPA. For the last two relations the wrappers may be:

$wrapper(Fraternity) \ \equiv \ (Sex = \text{``}male\text{''})$

and

$wrapper(Sorority) \ \equiv \ (Sex = \text{``}female\text{''})$

which express, respectively, that only men live in the fraternity, and only women live in the sorority. The wrappers help us to identify which relations we need to use to answer the query. Let us assume that seniors are those who earned more than 90 credit hours. Then the selection condition C_1 of the above query can be expressed as follows:

$$C_1 \equiv (Sex = \text{``}female\text{''} \text{ and } CHR > 90 \text{ and } GPA \geq 3.5)$$

A source relation is needed to answer the query only if its wrapper is consistent with C_1. Hence we can identify the relevant source relations as follows:

> Relevant_Sources $\leftarrow \emptyset$
> **for** each relation symbol R_i in the database **do**
>   **if** (wrapper(R_i) **and** C_1) is satisfiable **then**
>   Relevant_Sources $\leftarrow$ Relevant_Sources $\cup \{R_i\}$
>   **end-if**
> **end-for**
> **return**(relevant)

Using the above we can find that *Freshman_Dorm* is not relevant because in its wrapper the constraint $CHR < 30$ conflicts with the constraint $CHR > 90$ in the selection condition. Similarly, *Fraternity* is not relevant because in its wrapper the constraint $Sex = \text{``}male\text{''}$ conflicts with the constraint $Sex = \text{``}female\text{''}$ in the selection condition. Only the other two relations are relevant.

Each wrapper is a constraint relation. Hence the cross product or natural join of any wrapper with another constraint relation is also a constraint relation. For example, the cross product of the *Honors_Hall* relation and its wrapper is a constraint relation to which we can apply C_1 as a selection condition. We can do the same with *Sorority* and its wrapper. Therefore, we can express Query 1 in SQL as follows:

CREATE VIEW	Smart_Women(Name)
SELECT	Name
FROM	Honors_Hall, wrapper(Honors_Hall)
WHERE	Sex = "female" AND
	CHR > 90 AND
	GPA ≥ 3.5
UNION	
SELECT	Name
FROM	Sorority, wrapper(Sorority)
WHERE	Sex = "female" AND
	CHR > 90 AND
	GPA ≥ 3.5

This example shows that constraint relations are useful in several ways. They are used within the wrappers to express the implicit information about the given relations. They are used also to identify those relations that may contain records that are relevant to a query. Finally, they are used to express queries using a simple SQL language.

17.5.1 The DataFoX System

The *Datalog For XML*, or *DataFoX*, system integrates XML, GML, VML, and PRML documents into a layered constraint XML data, which queried using a Datalog language or *layer algebra*, which is an extension of relational algebra for XML and provides the basis of query evaluation and optimization in DataFoX. Since XML and the related data models were already described in Section 9.7, here we decribe their integration.

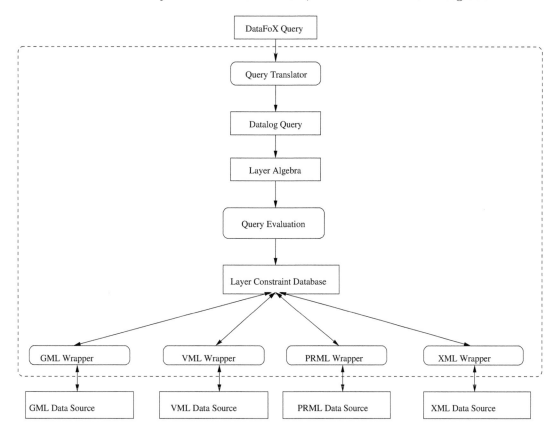

Figure 17.5: The DataFoX system architecture.

The architecture of the DataFoX system is outlined in Figure 17.5. The XML and other data sources in different formats are wrapped into a uniform representation called the *constraint XML*. The DataFoX query language is translated into a Datalog query, which is further translated into the layer algebra. Then the query is evaluated and the result may be translated back to XML using reverse wrappers.

17.6 Data Fusion

Data may be fused if we are certain that different information from multiple sensors refer to the same object. In other words, while data integration collects related tuples in an output relation, data fusion collects related constraints in a single constraint tuple. Constraint databases are useful for the data fusion problem because each small piece of data is considered a constraint tuple and those are naturally conjoined together to form a new constraint tuple during the data fusion process.

Example 17.6.1 Two sensors S_1 and S_2 sense the positions of some airplanes. If the positions of S_1 and S_2 are very close, that is, their distance is within some error tolerance value, then the information may be merged from the two sensors. For example, if S_1 senses the speed and S_2 the direction of the airplane, then data fusion allows us to know all of the following: current location, speed, and direction. Although data fusion is a well-known problem, constraint database queries can express many of the typical data fusion problems in a easy and natural way.

17.7 Security

Data integration is related to computer security in several ways. First, our computer needs to decide whether the data sources are trustworthy. Second, the computers which provide the source data need to decide whether our computer is trustworthy to gain access to their data.

For the problem of authorization and access control in distributed systems, *trust management* is a flexible and powerful approach based on policy statements that are expressed in some policy language. For example, Datalog with new types of constraints can make a good policy language.

In the new types of constraints, the variables may range over *hierarchical domains*. The elements of a hierarchical domain are path names that start from the root of a given tree, such as, machine domain names. For any hierarchical domain H and $g, h \in H$, the constraint $h \prec g$ means that the path name h is an expansion of the path name g. For example, $nsf.gov \prec gov$. An alternative notation for machine names is to reverse the order and to put them in brackets. For example, $nsf.gov$ is written as $\langle gov, nsf \rangle$.

Example 17.7.1 An entity A grants to an entity B the permission to connect to machines in the domain "stanford.edu" at port number 1, and allows B to further delegate any part of the permission from time 0 to 8. In addition, assume that B grants to another entity D the permission to connect to the host "cs.stanford.edu" and any machine in the domain "cs.stanford.edu" at any port number with validity period from time 5 to 12.

Let us introduce a relation $Grant(x, y, h, p, v)$ which is true when entity x grants to entity B the permission to connect to machines in the domain h at port number p during time v. Here the domains of x and y are strings, the domain of h is hierarchical, the domain of p is the integers, and the domain of v is the real numbers. Then the above policies can be represented as follows:

$$Grant(\text{"}A\text{"}, \text{"}B\text{"}, h, p, v) \quad :- \quad h \prec \langle edu, stanford \rangle, \; p = 1, \; 0 \leq v \leq 8.$$
$$Grant(\text{"}A\text{"}, x, h, p, v) \quad :- \quad Grant(\text{"}B\text{"}, x, h, p, v), h \prec \langle edu, stanford \rangle, p = 1, 0 \leq v \leq 8.$$
$$Grant(\text{"}B\text{"}, \text{"}D\text{"}, h, p, v) \quad :- \quad h \prec \langle edu, stanford, cs \rangle, \; p = 1, \; 5 \leq v \leq 12.$$

From the above, we can conclude the following:

$$Grant(\text{"}A\text{"}, \text{"}D\text{"}, h, p, v) \quad :- \quad h \prec \langle edu, stanford, cs \rangle, \; p = 1, \; 5 \leq v \leq 8.$$

Hierarchical domains are easy to add to the framework of constraint databases because conjunctions of hierarchical constraints admit variable elimination. In fact, we can show that directed acyclic graph (DAG) domains also admit variable elimination. We say that the hierarchical constraint $g = h$ holds if $g \prec h$ and $h \prec g$ both hold, that is, g and h are identical names or aliases for the same entity.

With aliases it could happen that two different domain names refer to the same entity. For example, the aliases `nsf.gov` and `USAnsf.gov` may refer to the same entity. This is permissible. Abbreviations are also permissible. For example, $a.b.c.d$ and $a.d$ could also refer to the same entities. However, cycles are not permissible with DAG domains. For example, $a.b.c.d$ and $a.b$ should refer to different machines otherwise there would be a cycle. That means the hierarchical constraints $a.b = a.b.c.d$ and $a.b \prec a.b.c.d$ are not allowed.

Theorem 17.7.1 Conjunctions of directed acyclic graph domains admit variable elimination.

Proof: Suppose we would like to eliminate the hierarchical variable x from a conjunction of hierarchical constraints S. First we rewrite S into S' by changing any hierarchical constraint of the form $g = h$ into a conjunction of $g \prec h$ and $h \prec g$. Now we need to eliminate x only from S'. After elimination, we will have a new set of constraints S'' that will consist of all the constraints in S' that do not contain the variable x, plus constraints of the form $y \prec z$ whenever there are constraints $y \prec x$ and $x \prec z$ in S'. If the y and z are constants, then we have to check that no cycle is created, that is y is not a string that is a substring of z. If it is, then we return *false*, else we return S''.   ∎

Bibliographic Notes

Quinlan [312] proposed ID3, which is one of the best known decision trees. Since then Quilan gave the improved decision tree algorithms C4.5 and C5. Vapnik [416] introduced support vector machines. A good library of support vector machines is C. C. Chang and C. J. Lin's SVMLib, which is available from `www.csie.ntu.edu.tw/~cjlin/libsvm`. Example 17.3.1 used *data integration* [67, 187, 265, 409], which has many other interesting aspects.

Geist [147] and Johnson et al. [212] discussed the representation of decision trees by constraint databases. Revesz and Triplet [352] applied constraint databases to reclassification. Revesz and Triplet [353] extended the results to classification integration and demonstrated by experiements its improved accuracy over data integration. The experiments used the Mayo Clinic data set [131], which contains the medical records of 314 primary biliary cirrhosis patients, and a heart disease diagnosis data set, which is available from the website: `http://www.ics.uci.edu/~mlearn/MLRepository.html`. The experiments also used the representation of support vector machines by constraint databases. The decision tree and the classification integration method figures and some of the discussion related to these figures are from [353].

Data integration is related to federated databases, mediator-based systems and data warehouses, which are covered in other database textbooks. Cheng et al. [80] and Goh et al. [153] consider data integration using the constraint databases approach. In particular, Cheng et al. [80] show that constraint relations provide a significant speed-up in query evaluation. The DataFoX system and Figure 17.5 is described in Revesz [78].

Aschenbrenner et al. [25] consider the problem of data fusion of multiple sensor data using constraint databases. Example 17.6.1 is a summary of a nice example from their work.

Becker and Sewell [33, 34] and Li and Mitchell [264] develop policy languages that use Datalog and constraint databases with hierarchical domains. Example 17.7.1 is simplified from Li and Mitchell [264], who show that variable elimination is possible for hierarchical constraints. Theorem 17.7.1 is based on their ideas.

Exercises

1. A patient has the following record: $id = 1, b = 6.5, c = 326, g = 1, h = 0$ and $t = 130$.

   (a) Find the drug of the patient using the decision tree in Figure 17.1.

   (b) Find the status of the patient using the decision tree in Figure 17.2.

2. Explain the problems that may arise when one tries to use the data in Example 17.2.1 to build a decision tree.

3. Explain the problems that may arise when one tries to use the SVM classification found in Example 17.2.1.

4. Consider again the training examples of Example 17.2.1. Find another separator line and show that it is not optimal by proving that it has a smaller margin than the one shown in Figure 17.3.

5. A study investigates the relationship between the features $X = \{Age, Children, Education, Wealth\}$ and the set of labels $Y = \{Happy, Sad\}$, which are abbreviated by the capital letters $X = \{A, C, E, W\}$ and $Y = \{H, S\}$. The study finds the following linear classification using an SVM.

Mood1

A	C	E	W	Y_1	
a	c	e	w	y_1	$-0.07a + 0.18c + 0.25e - 0.29w = y_1$

where $y_1 > 0$ means that a person is predicted to be happy. Similarly, another study investigating the same relationship found the following linear classification using an SVM.

Mood2

A	C	E	W	Y_2	
a	c	e	w	y_2	$-0.13a + 0.22c + 0.15e - 0.11w = y_2$

Sadly, the investigators of neither study are willing to share the raw data with you citing privacy and legal concerns. Fortunately, they are willing to share the classifications that they found. Using classification integration find a potentially even better classification than either one of the study groups have obtained separately.

6. A study investigates the relationship between the features $X_1 = \{Age, Children, Education, Gender\}$ and the set of labels $Looks = \{Pretty, Ugly\}$, which are abbreviated by the capital letters $X_1 = \{A, C, E, G\}$ and $L = \{P, U\}$. Further, suppose that the study finds the following linear classification using an SVM.

Looks

A	C	E	G	L	
a	c	e	g	l	$-32a - 14c + 17e + 29g \geq 100,\ l =$'P'
a	c	e	g	l	$-32a - 14c + 17e + 29g < 100,\ l =$'U'

Another study investigates the relationship between the features $X_2 = \{Age, Children, Education, Race\}$ and the set of labels $Jobs = \{Success, Failure\}$, indicating performance achievement in the work environment. Abbreviating by the capital letters $X_2 = \{A, C, E, R\}$ and $J = \{S, F\}$, the second study finds the following linear classification using an SVM.

Jobs

A	C	E	R	J	
a	c	e	r	j	$11a + 37c + 23e - 15r \geq 100,\ j =$'S'
a	c	e	r	j	$11a + 37c + 23e - 15r < 100,\ j =$'F'

The investigators of neither study are willing to share the raw data with you citing privacy and legal concerns. Fortunately, they are willing to share the classifications that they found. Using reclassification find a more refined classification than either one of the study groups have obtained separately.

7. Find using reclassification whether there could be any patient who is *Transplanted* and had the *Penicillamine* drug. (*Hint*: Implement the SQL queries in Example 17.4.1 with an extra WHERE clause that corresponds to the specified condition.)

18

Interpolation and Approximation

Most engineering and scientific phenomena, such as the surface of a landscape or the continuously changing temperature at a location are inherently infinite in space or time or both. We cannot measure all the data. Generally it is possible to record surface elevation values or the temperature only at some specific locations and times.

However, it is possible to estimate the values at the unmeasured locations and times from the measured ones. This estimation can be done by *interpolation* or *approximation*. Both interpolation and approximation methods develop for the entire studied phenomena some interpolation functions, such as for temperature a temperature function and for the landscape elevation a surface function. Interpolation functions preserve the measured values, while approximation functions are more general, and they may not preserve the individual measured values. The interpolation and approximation functions are usually expressed by constraints, hence they can be conveniently represented in constraint databases.

Section 18.1 describes *linear interpolation*, which is used frequently to estimate the missing values of a partially known function.

Section 18.2 describes *triangulated irregular networks*, or TINs, which are used in several geographic information systems to interpolate the surface of a landscape.

Section 18.3 describes *shape functions*, which are popular interpolation functions used in engineering applications..

Section 18.4 describes *spatiotemporal interpolation* algorithms, which are useful to interpolate spatiotemporal data such as house prices or climate data.

P. Revesz, *Introduction to Databases: From Biological to Spatio-Temporal*,
Texts in Computer Science, DOI 10.1007/978-1-84996-095-3_18,
© Springer-Verlag London Limited 2010

Section 18.5 describes the *inverse distance weighting* interpolation method, which is applicable in any dimension. Section 18.5 points out also some problems with the inverse distance weighting method.

Finally, Section 18.6 describes *piecewise linear approximations* and an approximation of movies by *parametric rectangles*, which were introduced in Chapter 7. For example, a time series data, such as the temperature data recorded at a finite number of time instances can be approximated by a piecewise linear approximation. An advantage of approximate representation is *data compression*. In general, the constraint representation requires fewer tuples and less computer memory than the original representation. As a result, queries can be evaluated much faster on the constraint approximation with a high *precision* and *recall*.

18.1   Linear Interpolation

Consider a sequence of data points $(t_1, y_1), \cdots, (t_n, y_n)$ of a function f where t_i are monotone increasing real numbers and y_i are real numbers for $1 \leq i \leq n$. When t_i are time instances, then the sequence of data points is called a *time series*. Databases often record time series data.

For example, consider four weather stations at different locations. A database may record the daily high temperature for the first weather station on Mondays and Fridays, for the second on Tuesdays and Thursdays, for the third on Saturdays, and for the fourth on Sundays. These measurements yield a separate time series for each of the four weather stations, and assuming that day 1 is a Monday, the first month of these four time series may be represented as shown in relation *Temperature*.

Suppose we want to find the location where the daily high temperature was the highest on the second Wednesday, i.e., day ten. Since none of the four weather stations measures the temperature on Wednesdays, we cannot know the answer precisely. However, we may use *linear interpolation* to estimate the missing temperature values. Linear interpolation estimates $f(t)$ where $t_i < t < t_{i+1}$ for some $1 \leq i < n$ as follows:

$$f(t) = \frac{t_{i+1} - t}{t_{i+1} - t_i} \, y_i \; + \; \frac{t - t_i}{t_{i+1} - t_i} \, y_{i+1} \tag{18.1}$$

For example, the interpolated temperature for the fourth station is represented in relation *Interpolated_Temperature*.

18.2   Triangulated Irregular Networks

Triangulated irregular networks (TINs) are used in geographic information systems to interpolate the unknown surface elevation values at arbitrary

Temperature

SN	T	Temp
1	1	68
1	5	71
1	8	76
1	12	73
1	15	71
1	19	68
1	22	70
1	26	74
1	29	73
2	2	71
2	4	69
2	9	68
2	11	66
2	16	70
2	18	68
2	23	71
2	25	75
2	30	77
3	6	75
3	13	78
3	20	72
3	27	68
4	7	72
4	14	75
4	21	72
4	28	74

Interpolated_Temperature

SN	T	Temp			
4	t	y	$t \geq 7,$	$t \leq 14,$	$y = \frac{3}{7}t + 69$
4	t	y	$t \geq 14,$	$t \leq 21,$	$y = \frac{-3}{7}t + 81$
4	t	y	$t \geq 21,$	$t \leq 28,$	$y = \frac{2}{7}t + 66$

locations based on the known elevation values at locations where measurements are recorded.

Figure 18.2 shows a natural landscape surface with a mountain range. Such a landscape is hard to represent in a database system because it would require an infinite number of tuples. One way to estimate this representa-

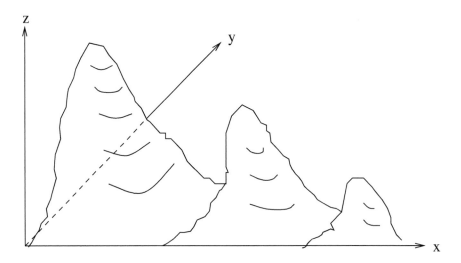

Figure 18.1: The mountain range.

tion is to first take a *sample* of points on the surface. For example, for the mountain range surface we may select the points shown in Figure 18.2. The solid black points are on the visible and the gray points are on the hidden part of the surface of the mountains.

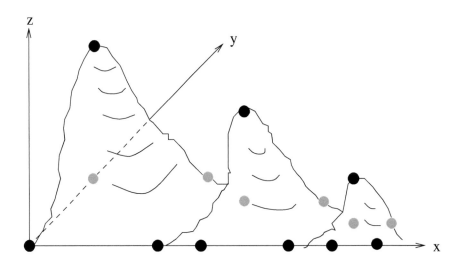

Figure 18.2: Sample points from the surface of a mountain range.

The selection of the sample points can be arbitrary. For example, it can be a random set of points or some regular pattern of points. Often the points are special points of the landscape, for example, mountain tops or the deepest points in valleys. The exact (x, y, z) coordinates of the sample points of Figure 18.2 are given in relation *Sample_Points*.

Sample_Points

ID	X	Y	Z
1	0	0	0
2	0	6	0
3	3	3	9
4	6	0	0
5	6	6	0
6	8	0	0
7	8	4	0
8	10	2	6
9	12	0	0
10	12	4	0
11	14	0	0
12	14	2	0
13	15	1	3
14	16	0	0
15	16	2	0

We construct now a triangulated irregular network (or TIN) interpolation of the surface using the sample points. First, we project the sample points to the (x, y) plane, as shown in Figure 18.2.

Next we find a *triangulation* of the sample points, that is, we add a set of edges to the sample points until the whole set of sample points is within a polygon and each inside region is a triangle. One triangulation is shown in Figure 18.2. There are many different possible triangulations of the given set of sample points. The *Delaunay triangulation* algorithm from computational geometry is a commonly used triangulation method.

While the resulting triangulation is a two-dimensional structure, the triangulated irregular network is a three-dimensional structure. It is found by raising, in the two-dimensional triangulation, each sample point to its proper elevation, that is, its z-coordinate value, as shown in Figure 18.2.

The mountain range is now interpolated by a TIN that contains three adjacent pyramids. The sample points were used to interpolate the elevation data of the whole space, by taking, for each triangle, the surface above the triangle that is a flat plane going through the corner vertices. For example, the east side surface of the large pyramid, shown shaded in Figure 18.2,

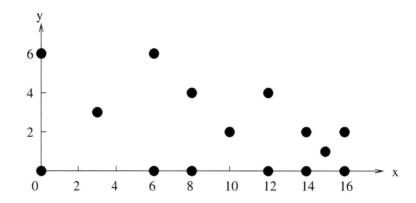

Figure 18.3: The spatial points.

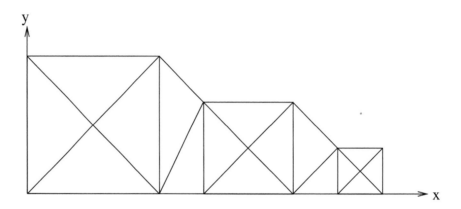

Figure 18.4: The triangulation.

is a part of the TIN that corresponds to the triangle with corner vertices $(3,3)$, $(6,0)$, and $(6,6)$. The TIN surface can be naturally represented in a constraint database, using the following lemma.

Lemma 18.2.1 Let (x_1, y_1, z_1), $x_2, y_2, z_2)$, and (x_3, y_3, z_3) be three corner nodes of a triangle in 3-dimensional space. Let

$$\Delta x = x_1 - x_3 \quad \Delta y = y_1 - y_3 \quad \Delta z = z_1 - z_3$$

$$\Theta x = x_2 - x_3 \quad \Theta y = y_2 - y_3 \quad \Theta z = z_2 - z_3$$

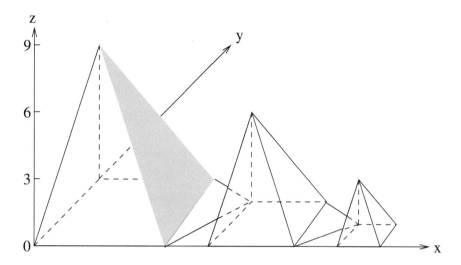

Figure 18.5: The triangulated irregular network corresponding to the mountain range.

The equation of the plane through the nodes is $ax + by + cz = d$ where:

$$
\begin{aligned}
a &= \Delta y \,\Theta z \;-\; \Delta z \,\Theta y \\
b &= \Delta z \,\Theta x \;-\; \Delta x \,\Theta z \\
c &= \Delta x \,\Theta y \;-\; \Delta y \,\Theta x \\
d &= ax_1 + by_1 + cz_1
\end{aligned}
\tag{18.2}
$$

■

For example, let us find the equation of the plane which contains the shaded east side surface of the large pyramid, which has corner vertices $(3,3,9)$, $(6,6,0)$, and $(6,0,0)$. First we find:

$$
\Delta x = -3 \quad \Delta y = 3 \quad \Delta z = 9
$$

$$
\Theta x = 0 \quad \Theta y = 6 \quad \Theta z = 0
$$

Second, we compute the coeffients:

$$
\begin{aligned}
a &= (3 \times 0) \;-\; (9 \times 6) = -54 \\
b &= (9 \times 0) \;-\; (-3 \times 0) = 0 \\
c &= (-3 \times 6) \;-\; (3 \times 0) = -18 \\
d &= (-54 \times 3) + (0 \times 3) + (-18 \times 9) = -324
\end{aligned}
$$

Hence we obtained $-54x + 0y - 18z = -324$. Finally, simplifying by dividing by -18, we get $3x + z = 18$. From this 3-dimensional plane we only need the area directly above the 2-dimensional triangle with corner vertices $(3,3)$, $(6,6)$, and $(6,0)$. The 2-dimensional triangle is represented by the conjunction of the three inequality constraints $x \leq 6$, $y \leq x$, and $x + y \geq 6$. Hence the east side surface of the large pyramid can be represented as shown in the last tuple in relation *Pyramid*.

Pyramid

X	Y	Z				
x	y	z	$y \geq 0$,	$y \leq x$,	$x + y \leq 6$,	$3y - z = 0$
x	y	z	$x \geq 0$,	$y \geq x$,	$x + y \leq 6$,	$3x - z = 0$
x	y	z	$y \leq 6$,	$y \geq x$,	$x + y \geq 6$,	$3y + z = 18$
x	y	z	$x \leq 6$,	$y \leq x$,	$x + y \geq 6$,	$3x + z = 18$

18.2.1 Parametric Triangulated Irregular Network

To represent approximately some spatio-temporal objects, for example, a changing landscape, we can combine the TIN representation for spatial data and the piecewise linear representation for time series data. The combined representation is called a *parametric triangulated irregular network* (PTIN).

A PTIN is created by fixing on the surface of the landscape a set of (x, y) locations. Unlike in a TIN, in a PTIN the z value of each (x, y) location changes over time, that is, it is associated with a time series, which we approximate by a piecewise linear function $z(t)$.

Example 18.2.1 Suppose that the mountain in Figure 18.2 is gradually eroding over a long period of time. In particular, suppose that the speed of erosion is one unit height per thousand years. This can be represented by the *Pyramid_Erode* constraint relation shown here:

Pyramid_Erode

X	Y	Z	T	
x	y	z	t	$y \geq 0$, $y \leq x$, $x + y \leq 6$, $3z = (9-t)y$, $t \geq 0$, $z \geq 0$
x	y	z	t	$x \geq 0$, $y \geq x$, $x + y \leq 6$, $3z = (9-t)x$, $t \geq 0$, $z \geq 0$
x	y	z	t	$y \leq 6$, $y \geq x$, $x + y \geq 6$, $3z = (9-t)(6-y)$, $t \geq 0$, $z \geq 0$
x	y	z	t	$x \leq 6$, $y \leq x$, $x + y \geq 6$, $3z = (9-t)(6-x)$, $t \geq 0$, $z \geq 0$

The PTIN can be used in other situations too where the third variable is different from elevation.

Example 18.2.2 Suppose we know the (x, y) locations of the four weather stations in relation *Temperature*. Then we can use a PTIN to approximate the temperature at each location around the four weather stations at each time. The PTIN can be represented as a constraint relation *Temperature3(x,y,temp,t)*, where *temp* is the approximate temperature at location (x, y) at time t. This approximation can be used within spatio-temporal queries. The following SQL query finds the locations where the temperature rises above 75 degrees between days 180 and 230:

> **select** x, y
> **from** *Temperature3*
> **where** $temp > 75$ **and** $t \geq 180$ **and** $t \leq 230$

18.3 Shape Functions

Shape functions are popular spatial interpolation methods in engineering applications, for example, in Finite Element algorithms. Section 18.3.1 reviews 2-dimensional shape functions for triangles, and Section 18.3.2 reviews 3-dimensional shape functions for tetrahedra. Both of these spatial interpolations methods yield simple linear equations.

18.3.1 Shape Functions for Triangles

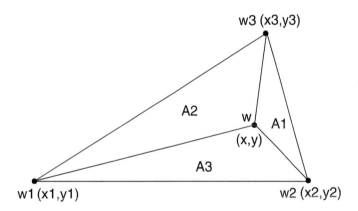

Figure 18.6: Computing shape functions by area divisions.

A linear interpolation function for a triangular area can be written in terms of three shape functions N_1, N_2, N_3, and the corner values w_1, w_2, w_3 as:

$$w(x, y) = N_1(x, y)\, w_1 + N_2(x, y)\, w_2 + N_3(x, y)\, w_3 \qquad (18.3)$$

where N_1, N_2 and N_3 are the following shape functions:

$$N_1(x,y) = \frac{\mathcal{A}_1}{\mathcal{A}}, \quad N_2(x,y) = \frac{\mathcal{A}_2}{\mathcal{A}}, \quad N_3(x,y) = \frac{\mathcal{A}_3}{\mathcal{A}} \tag{18.4}$$

where $\mathcal{A}_1$, $\mathcal{A}_2$ and $\mathcal{A}_3$ are the three small triangle areas shown in Figure 18.6, and $\mathcal{A}$ is the area of the outside triangle $w_1 w_2 w_3$.

The area $\mathcal{A}$ can be computed using the corner coordinate values in the determinant of the following 3×3 matrix:

$$\mathcal{A} = \frac{1}{2} \, det \begin{bmatrix} 1 & x_1 & y_1 \\ 1 & x_2 & y_2 \\ 1 & x_3 & y_3 \end{bmatrix} \tag{18.5}$$

The areas $\mathcal{A}_1, \mathcal{A}_2$, and $\mathcal{A}_3$ can be computed similarly to equation (18.5) by using the appropriate coordinate values.

Example 18.3.1 Let $w_1 = 18$, $w_2 = 27$, and $w_3 = 25$ be the values measured, respectively, at the corner nodes $(x_1, y_1) = (2, 1)$, $(x_2, y_2) = (11, 4)$, and $(x_3, y_3) = (3, 8)$ of the triangle in Figure 18.6. Find an estimate for w at location $(6, 4)$.

First we find by Equation (18.5) that $\mathcal{A} = 30$, $\mathcal{A}_1 = 10$, $\mathcal{A}_2 = 12.5$, and $\mathcal{A}_3 = 7.5$. Then we find by Equation (18.3) that:

$$w(6,4) \;=\; \frac{10}{30} \times 18 \;+\; \frac{12.5}{30} \times 27 \;+\; \frac{7.5}{30} \times 25 = 23.5$$

Lemma 18.3.1 Equation (18.3) is an interpolation function that respects the known values.

Proof: It is easy to see that the area of a small triangle opposite to a corner node of the outside triangle in Figure 18.6 increases when the unknown point (x, y) moves closer to that corner node. For example, the area of $\mathcal{A}_1$ increases as (x, y) moves closer to (x_1, y_1). In addition, by (18.4) the weight given to w_1 increases too. In the limit when $(x, y) = (x_1, y_1)$ and $\mathcal{A} = \mathcal{A}_1$ and $\mathcal{A}_2 = \mathcal{A}_3 = 0$, then $w = w_1$. Similarly, when $(x, y) = (x_2, y_2)$, then $w = w_2$, and when $(x, y) = (x_3, y_3)$, then $w = w_3$. Hence (18.3) defines an interpolation function that respects the known values. ∎

Alternatively, we can also express the 2-dimensional shape functions as follows:

$$N_1(x,y) \;=\; \frac{x\,(y_2 - y_3) \;-\; y\,(x_2 - x_3) \;+\; (x_2\,y_3 - x_3\,y_2)}{2\mathcal{A}}$$

$$N_2(x,y) \;=\; \frac{x\,(y_3 - y_1) \;-\; y\,(x_3 - x_1) \;+\; (x_3\,y_1 - x_1\,y_3)}{2\mathcal{A}} \tag{18.6}$$

$$N_3(x,y) \;=\; \frac{x\,(y_1 - y_2) \;-\; y\,(x_1 - x_2) \;+\; (x_1\,y_2 - x_2\,y_1)}{2\mathcal{A}}$$

We can now show the following:

Theorem 18.3.1 The interpolations given by triangulated irregular networks and shape-functions for triangles are equivalent.

Proof: It is easy to see from (18.6) that all the 2-dimensional shape functions are linear equations. Hence the interpolation function in Equation (18.3) is also a linear equation, and by Lemma 18.3.1 the interpolation function passes through the corner vertices of the triangle. hence the shape-function-based interpolation function must be identical to the TIN triangle in 3-dimensional defined in Lemma 18.2.1.   ∎

Example 18.3.2 Let $w_1 = 10$, $w_2 = 20$, and $w_3 = 30$ be the values measured at locations $(x_1, y_1) = (0, 0)$, $(x_2, y_2) = (10, 0)$, and $(x_3, y_3) = (10, 5)$ in Figure 18.6, respectively. Find an estimate for all locations within the triangle with corner nodes $(0, 0)$, $(10, 0)$, and $(10, 5)$.

To solve this, first we find by Equation (18.5) that $\mathcal{A} = 25$. Then we find by Equation (18.6) that:

$$N_1(x, y) = \frac{x(0 - 5) - y(10 - 10) + (10 \times 5 - 10 \times 0)}{2 \times 25} = \frac{-x + 10}{10}$$

$$N_2(x, y) = \frac{x(5 - 0) - y(10 - 0) + (10 \times 0 - 0 \times 5)}{2 \times 25} = \frac{x - 2y}{10}$$

$$N_3(x, y) = \frac{x(0 - 0) - y(0 - 10) + (0 \times 0 - 10 \times 0)}{2 \times 25} = \frac{2y}{10}$$

Finally, by Equation (18.3) we estimate the value $w(x, y)$ as follows:

$$w(x, y) = \frac{-x + 10}{10} \times 10 + \frac{x - 2y}{10} \times 20 + \frac{2y}{10} \times 30 = x + 2y + 10$$

Hence the result of the interpolation can be expressed in the constraint relation *Triangle*.

Triangle

X	Y	W	
x	y	w	$y \geq 0$, $x \leq 10$, $y \leq 0.5x$, $w = x + 2y + 10$

Many engineering applications consider a network of triangles or even several networks of triangles similar to the triangulations in Section 18.2.

Filter

X	Y	R
2	1	0.9
2	14	0.5
25	14	0.3
25	1	0.8

Example 18.3.3 Suppose relation $Filter(x, y, r)$ records for some ground longitude and latitude locations (x, y) the measurement of the ratio r of the ultraviolet radiation that is usually filtered out by the atmosphere before reaching the ground of the earth. Further, suppose relation $Ultraviolet(y, t, u)$ records for some latitude degree y and day t pairs the amount of the ultraviolet radiation u that the atmosphere of the earth receives from the Sun.

Ultraviolet

Y	T	U
0	1	60
13	22	20
33	18	70
29	0	40

Suppose we want to find the amount of ultraviolet radiation that reaches each ground location (x, y) on day t. We first map separately as shown in the top row of Figure 18.7 the locations of the (x, y) and (y, t) pairs where the measurements for r and u, respectively, are recorded. The numbers indicate the record number in the input relations. Next we create a triangulation of the measurement locations as shown in the bottom row of Figure 18.7. Then we use 2-dimensional shape function interpolation to estimate u and r for each location within the triangles and store the interpolation data in two constraint relations. Finally, we write a query that uses the constraint relations to find an output relation $Ground(x,y,t,g)$ that gives at every ground location (x, y) on day t the amount of ground ultraviolet radiation g, where $g = u(1 - r)$.

18.3.2 Shape Functions for Tetrahedra

Three-dimensional domains can be divided into finite number of simple sub-domains. For example, we can use tetrahedral or hexahedral sub-domains. Tetrahedral meshing is of particular interest. With a large number of tetra-

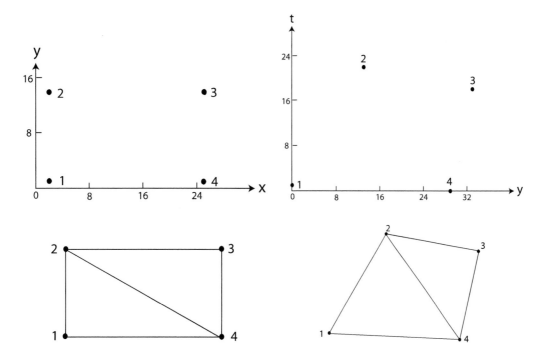

Figure 18.7: *Filter* (left) and *Ultraviolet* (right) samples (top) and triangulations (bottom).

hedral elements, we can also approximate complicated 3-dimensional objects. Figure 18.8 shows a tetrahedral mesh of a 3-dimensional object. This object has a cutout (one quarter of a cylinder) behind the boundary defined by the points $ABCD$.

A linear approximation function for a 3-dimensional tetrahedral element can be written in terms of four 3-dimensional shape functions N_1, N_2, N_3, N_4 and the corner values w_1, w_2, w_3, w_4 as follows:

$$w(x, y, z) = \sum_{i=1}^{4} N_i(x, y, z) w_i \tag{18.7}$$

where N_1, N_2 N_3 and N_4 are the following:

$$N_1(x, y, z) = \frac{\mathcal{V}_1}{\mathcal{V}}, \ N_2(x, y, z) = \frac{\mathcal{V}_2}{\mathcal{V}}, \ N_3(x, y, z) = \frac{\mathcal{V}_3}{\mathcal{V}}, \ N_4(x, y, z) = \frac{\mathcal{V}_4}{\mathcal{V}}$$

where $\mathcal{V}_1$, $\mathcal{V}_2$, $\mathcal{V}_3$, and $\mathcal{V}_4$ are the volumes of the four sub-tetrahedra $ww_2w_3w_4$, $w_1ww_3w_4$, $w_1w_2ww_4$, and $w_1w_2w_3w$, respectively, as shown in Figure 18.9; and $\mathcal{V}$ is the volume of the outside tetrahedron $w_1w_2w_3w_4$ which can be computed using the corner coordinates (x_i, y_i, z_i) $(i =$

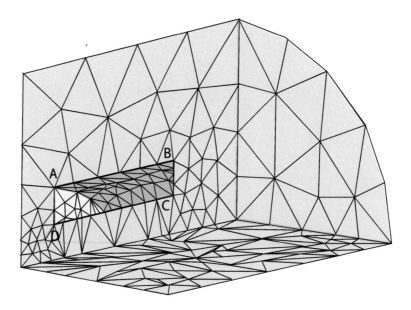

Figure 18.8: A Tetrahedral Mesh.

$1, 2, 3, 4$) in the determinant of the following 4×4 matrix:

$$\mathcal{V} = \frac{1}{6} \, det \begin{bmatrix} 1 & x_1 & y_1 & z_1 \\ 1 & x_2 & y_2 & z_2 \\ 1 & x_3 & y_3 & z_3 \\ 1 & x_4 & y_4 & z_4 \end{bmatrix} \tag{18.8}$$

All the $\mathcal{V}_i$'s $(1 \leq i \leq 4)$ can also be computed similarly to equation (18.8) by using the appropriate coordinate values.

Example 18.3.4 In Example 18.3.3 after applying 2-dimensional shape functions to the *Filter* and the *Ultraviolet* input relations we obtained interpolations that can be stored in linear constraint relations. In the constraint relations, r is a linear function of x and y, and u is a linear function of y and t. Hence $g = u(1 - r)$ is a polynomial function of x, y, and t. However, g can be interpolated by linear functions as follows.

First, take a join of the constraint relations for *Filter* and *Ultraviolet* and obtain a linear constraint relation *Ultraviolet-Filter*. Second, take any tetrahedral mesh that covers in the x, y and t dimensions the 3-dimensional volume in which g is to be interpolated. The nodes of the tetrahedral mesh

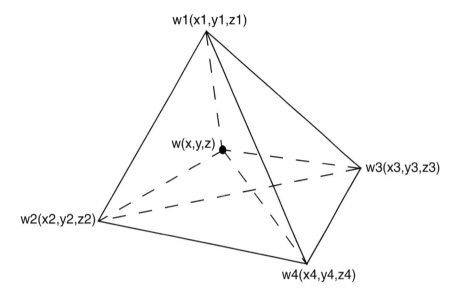

Figure 18.9: Computing shape functions by volume divisions.

can be placed in 3-dimensional space either regularly or irregularly. Third, calculate the g values for the nodes of the tetrahedral mesh using the *Ultraviolet-Filter* relation, which gives constant values for r and u for each node, and the equation $g = u(1 - r)$. Finally, interpolate the mesh using tetrahedral shape functions. The details are left as an exercise.

18.4   Spatiotemporal Interpolation

There are two fundamentally different approaches to spatiotemporal interpolation: reduction methods and extension methods. Reduction methods reduce a spatiotemporal interpolation problem to simpler spatial and temporal interpolation problems. Extension methods reduce a d-dimensional spatiotemporal interpolation problem to a $d + 1$ dimensional spatial interpolation problem. Section 18.4.1 describes reduction methods and Section 18.4.2 describes extension methods in more detail.

18.4.1   Reduction Methods

Reduction methods reduce a spatiotemporal interpolation problem to lower-dimensional temporal and spatial interpolation problems. There are several examples of reduction methods.

The Time-Slices Method

The *Time-Slices* spatiotemporal interpolation method is a simple method that can be used in problems with a finite number of discrete time instances. Consider a relation $R(x, y, t, w)$ to be interpolated. For a finite number of discrete time instances $t_1, \ldots, t_n$, the *Time-Slices* method uses for each c_i a separate 2-dimensional spatial interpolation using only the records in R with $t = t_i$.

The ST-Product Method

The *ST-product* method first interpolates using any 1-dimensional temporal interpolation the measured value over time at each sample point. Then by substituting the desired time instant into some spatial interpolation function, we can get a spatiotemporal interpolation function.

As an example, consider the ST-product method which combines linear interpolation in 1-dimensional time and spatial interpolation by shape functions in 2-dimensional space. This problem can be again illustrated as in Figure 18.6 but with the value of the three corner nodes changing in time. Assume the value at node i at time t_1 is w_{i1}, and at time t_2 the value is w_{i2}. The value at the node i at any time between t_1 and t_2 can be estimated using linear interpolation (18.1) as follows:

$$w_i(t) = \frac{t_2 - t}{t_2 - t_1} w_{i1} + \frac{t - t_1}{t_2 - t_1} w_{i2} \tag{18.9}$$

Combining the above with Equation (18.3), the spatiotemporal interpolation function for any point within the triangle in Figure 18.6 can be estimated as follows:

$$
\begin{aligned}
w(x, y, t) &= N_1(x, y) \left[\frac{t_2 - t}{t_2 - t_1} w_{11} + \frac{t - t_1}{t_2 - t_1} w_{12} \right] \\
&+ N_2(x, y) \left[\frac{t_2 - t}{t_2 - t_1} w_{21} + \frac{t - t_1}{t_2 - t_1} w_{22} \right] \\
&+ N_3(x, y) \left[\frac{t_2 - t}{t_2 - t_1} w_{31} + \frac{t - t_1}{t_2 - t_1} w_{32} \right] \\
&= \frac{t_2 - t}{t_2 - t_1} \left[N_1(x, y) w_{11} + N_2(x, y) w_{21} + N_3(x, y) w_{31} \right] \\
&+ \frac{t - t_1}{t_2 - t_1} \left[N_1(x, y) w_{12} + N_2(x, y) w_{22} + N_3(x, y) w_{32} \right]
\end{aligned}
\tag{18.10}
$$

Since the space shape functions N_1, N_2, and N_3 and the linear interpolation (18.9) are linear, the spatiotemporal interpolation function (18.10) is quadratic.

As a more complex example, the ST-product method can combine also linear interpolation in 1-dimensional time (18.9) and spatial interpolation by shape functions in 3-dimensional space (18.7) to estimate the value of any point within the tetrahedron in Figure 18.9, assuming that the values of the corner nodes of the tetrahedron change over time. For any time between t_1 and t_2 the estimation function is the following:

$$
\begin{aligned}
w(x,y,z,t) \;=\;\; & N_1(x,y,z)\left[\frac{t_2-t}{t_2-t_1}w_{11}+\frac{t-t_1}{t_2-t_1}w_{12}\right] \\
& + N_2(x,y,z)\left[\frac{t_2-t}{t_2-t_1}w_{21}+\frac{t-t_1}{t_2-t_1}w_{22}\right] \\
& + N_3(x,y,z)\left[\frac{t_2-t}{t_2-t_1}w_{31}+\frac{t-t_1}{t_2-t_1}w_{32}\right] \\
& + N_4(x,y,z)\left[\frac{t_2-t}{t_2-t_1}w_{41}+\frac{t-t_1}{t_2-t_1}w_{42}\right] \qquad (18.11) \\[2mm]
\;=\;\; & \frac{t_2-t}{t_2-t_1}\sum_{i=1}^{4}N_i(x,y,z)w_{i1}+\frac{t-t_1}{t_2-t_1}\sum_{i=1}^{4}N_i(x,y,z)w_{i2}
\end{aligned}
$$

Since the space shape functions N_1, N_2, N_3, and N_4 and the linear interpolation functions (18.9) are linear, the spatio-temporal interpolation function (18.11) is quadratic.

Comparison of the ST-product and the Time-Slices Methods: An obvious difference is that the ST-product method can deal with continuous time while the Time-Slices method is limited to discrete time. Now let us assume that time is discrete.

For problems with a finite number of discrete time instances, one can subsitute for t in the Equations (18.10) and (18.11) those time instances. Then one obtains a finite system of linear functions with the ST-product method that uses 2-dimensional shape-functions. The Time-Slices method can also use 2-dimensional shape-functions to get linear interpolation functions. Hence in this respect they are similar.

However, the ST-product method is better than the Time-Slices method because if there are only a few sample values for each time instance t_i, then for the Time-Slices method the separate 2-dimensional spatial interpolations can use only a small fraction of the total number of locations occurring in R. Hence the separate spatial interpolations cannot be accurate.

For example, suppose $R(x,y,t,w)$ contains some real estate data in a town and records for each house standing at location (x,y) and sold on day t the per square foot sale price w. Suppose someone inherited a house at location (x_1,y_1) and at time t_1. What was the value of the house at the time of inheritance? We cannot always do the estimation based only on the records from day t_1 because there may be no houses sold on day t_1. The ST-product method can handle this problem nicely because it estimates the entire price history of houses that are sold several times. Some of those houses can be expected to be in the neighborhood of the inherited house, making the estimation possible.

Furhermore, for the Time-Slices method usually a new triangulation needs to be computed for each c_i, while the ST-product method may need only one triangulation if all measurement locations have enough time measurements to do some temporal interpolation. If there are not enough data for some locations, then the ST-product method also may need to have a different triangulation. Alternatively, for the sake of achieving uniformity, the ST-product method may ignore those locations that have too few data. For example, when considering a climate data set, the ST-product method may ignore data from some defunct weather stations.

Example 18.4.1 The *Temperature-Location* relation below records at latitude X, longitude Y, and hour T, the measured temperature W in Fahrenheit degrees. Let us find using the SP-product method (with 1-dimensional linear interpolation and 2-dimensional shape functions) an estimate for the value of w at time $t = 10$.

Temperature_Location

X	Y	T	W
2	1	10	18
3	8	10	25
6	4	5	26
6	4	15	34
11	4	10	27

First, the ST-product method uses linear interpolation (18.1) to find an estimate for w at all (x, y) locations in *Temperature-Location* that do not have a record at time 10 but have records at other times. In particular, location $(6, 4)$ in *Temperature-Location* does not have a record at time 10 but has records at times 5 and 15. Hence by Equation 18.1:

$$w(6, 4, 10) = \frac{15 - 10}{15 - 5} 26 + \frac{10 - 5}{15 - 5} 34 = 30$$

Now we have for each of the four (x, y) locations in *Temperature-Location* either an original record or an estimate for w at time $t = 10$. Next, the ST-product method triangulates the space, which in this case is similar to Figure 18.6 with $(x_1, y_1, w_1) = (2, 1, 18)$, $(x_2, y_2, w_2) = (11, 4, 27)$, $(x_3, y_3, z_3) = (3, 8, 25)$, and $(x, y, w) = (6, 4, 30)$.

There are three separate triangles for which we can use either 2-dimensional shape functions or Lemma 18.2.1. The results are shown in relation *Temperature_Location_Interpolated*.

Temperature_Location_Interpolated

X	Y	W	
x	y	w	$4x + 3y \geq 36, \quad x + 2y \leq 19, \quad y \geq 4,$ $6x + 17y + 10w = 404$
x	y	w	$4x + 3y \leq 36, \quad -3x + 4y \geq -2, \quad 7x - y \geq 13,$ $-63x - 16y + 25w = 308$
x	y	w	$-x + 3y \geq 1, \quad 3x - 4y \geq 2, \quad y \leq 4,$ $3x - 24y + 5w = 72$

The Adaptive Method

The adaptive method treats the temporal dimension differently from the spatial dimensions in a way that allows it to surpass even the ST-product method in interpolation accuracy.

The first idea behind the adaptive method is that to interpolate a spatiotemporal relation $R(x, y, t, w)$ where (x, y) is the location, t is the time instance, and w is the measured value, there are two main choices:

Spatial Projection + 1-dimensional temporal interpolation: Select from R the records with $x = a$ and $y = b$. Then use any 1-dimensional temporal interpolation method on the selected records.

Temporal Projection + 2-dimensional spatial interpolation: Select from R the records with $t = c$. Then use any 2-dimensional spatial interpolation method on the selected records.

When the spatial and temporal projections of R both contain enough number of records to do an interpolation, one could choose either (1) or (2) as an option.

Example 18.4.2 Let us find an estimate for the value of w at location $(6, 4)$ and time 10 using the *Temperature-Location* relation using the two choices.

Spatial Projection: This was done in Example 18.4.1 using the ST-product method. The estimated value was 30.

Temporal Projection: This was done in Example 18.3.1, using only the original records at $t = 10$ and spatial interpolation with 2-dimensional shape functions. The estimated value was 23.5.

Which one of the results in Example 18.4.2 should we trust? The *choice-based adaptive interpolation method* decides that based on the *relationship strength measures* for space and time. Intuitively the larger the relationship strength measure for space (or time), the more reliable is the estimation using a spatial (or temporal) interpolation. These measures, which are defined precisely later, are denoted by the following symbols:

$\mathcal{S}(a, b, c)$ – the relationship strength measure for space at location (a, b) and time c.

$\mathcal{T}(a, b, c)$ – the relationship strength measure for time at location (a, b) and time c.

Both measures are localized, hence the spatial relationship strength can be larger than the temporal relationship strength at some locations and times, while the reverse may be true at a different location and time within the same problem. The choice-based adaptive method works as follows whenever there is a choice:

$$\begin{cases} \text{Spatial interpolation} & \text{if } \mathcal{S}(a, b, c) > \mathcal{T}(a, b, c) \\ \\ \text{Temporal interpolation} & \text{if } \mathcal{S}(a, b, c) \leq \mathcal{T}(a, b, c) \end{cases}$$

Both the ST-product and the choice-based adaptive methods first fill in the missing values for the (a, b) locations where some measurements are known. While the ST-product method always preferred to do a temporal interpolation, the adaptive method at some spatiotemporal locations will prefer to do a spatial interpolation. This is the only reason why the two interpolation results may disagree. Finally, for both methods the non-measurement locations, that is, the locations that do not appear in the original data set, need to be estimated using some 2-dimensional spatial interpolation.

Relationship Strength Measures

Suppose we want to calculate the relationship strength measures at location (a, b) and time c for relation $R(x, y, t, w)$. Let $w_1, \ldots, w_N$ be the w values of the records in the *spatial projection neighborhood*, that is those records in the spatial projection of R onto (a, b) that are also in the neighborhood of c. The neighborhood is a flexible concept that range in meaning from all the spatial projection of R onto (a, b) to only those that are immediately preceeding and succeeding in time. These different meanings of neighborhood lead to slightly different alternative strength measures. In any case, we calculate the standard deviation σ_T of the $w_1, \ldots, w_N$ values as follows:

$$\sigma_T(a,b,c) = \sqrt{\frac{\sum_{k=1}^{N}(w_i - \overline{w})^2}{N}} \qquad (18.12)$$

where $\overline{w} = \frac{1}{N}\sum_{k=1}^{N} w_i$.

Similarly, let $v_1, \ldots, v_M$ be the w values in the *temporal projection neighborhood*, that is, those records that are in the temporal projection of R onto c and are also in the neighborhood of (a, b). The neighborhood can be defined also in a variety of ways, from the entire temporal projection to only those locations that are within some constant d Euclidean distance from (a, b), or some constant k number of closest locations measured according to Euclidean distances. In all cases, we calculate the standard deviation σ_S of the $v_1, \ldots, v_M$ values as follows:

$$\sigma_S(a,b,c) = \sqrt{\frac{\sum_{k=1}^{M}(v_i - \overline{v})^2}{M}} \qquad (18.13)$$

where $\overline{v} = \frac{1}{M}\sum_{k=1}^{M} v_i$.

Since the $w_1, \ldots, w_N$ values vary only in time, intuitively the smaller their standard deviation, the stronger is the temporal relationship. Similarly the $v_1, \ldots, v_M$ values vary only in space. Hence the smaller their standard deviation, the stronger is the spatial relationship. Hence one may define the temporal and the spatial relationship strength measures as follows:

$$\mathcal{T}(a,b,c) = \frac{1}{\sigma_T(a,b,c)}$$

$$\mathcal{S}(a,b,c) = \frac{1}{\sigma_S(a,b,c)}$$

where $\sigma_T(a,b,c),\ \sigma_S(a,b,c) > 0$.

Example 18.4.3 The spatial projection of the *Temperature* relation onto the location $(6, 4)$ contains two records. These records have measured values $w_1 = 36$ and $w_2 = 40$. Both of these records are temporal neighbors of $t = 10$. Hence $\overline{w} = 40$ and

$$\sigma_T(6,4,10) = \sqrt{\frac{(26 - 30)^2 + (34 - 30)^2}{2}} = 4$$

Similarly, the temporal projection of the *Temperature* relation onto time 10 contains three records. These records have measured values $v_1 = 18$, $v_2 = 25$, and $v_3 = 27$. These records are equidistant from $(6, 4)$, hence they are all spatial neighbors. Here $\overline{v} = \frac{70}{3}$ and

$$\sigma_S(6, 4, 10) = \sqrt{\frac{(18 - \frac{70}{3})^2 + (25 - \frac{70}{3})^2 + (27 - \frac{70}{3})^2}{3}} = \frac{134}{9}$$

Hence $\mathcal{S}(6, 4, 10) = \frac{9}{134}$ and $\mathcal{T}(6, 4, 10) = \frac{1}{4}$. Since $\mathcal{S}(a, b, c) < \mathcal{T}(a, b, c)$ the choice-based adaptive interpolation method chooses in this case a temporal interpolation instead of a spatial interpolation.

Linear Combination Adaptive Method

Instead of choosing either a temporal or a spatial interpolation method when there is a choice between them, one can use a *linear combination adaptive method* as follows.

Let E_s be the interpolated value using a spatial interpolation method. Let E_t be the interpolated value using a temporal interpolation method. Then find a combined interpolated value E using the linear combination function:

$$E \;=\; \alpha\, E_s + \beta\, E_t \tag{18.14}$$

where α and β are some constants such that $\alpha + \beta = 1$ and $0 \leq \alpha,\ \beta \leq 1$.

What values of α and β should one use? Intuitively, the values of α and β depend on the *relationship strength measures*. For example, we can take:

$$\alpha = \frac{\mathcal{S}(a, b, c)^p}{\mathcal{S}(a, b, c)^p + \mathcal{T}(a, b, c)^p}$$

$$\beta = \frac{\mathcal{T}(a, b, c)^p}{\mathcal{S}(a, b, c)^p + \mathcal{T}(a, b, c)^p}$$

where $p > 0$ is any real number constant. These equations assign α and β proportionally to the power p of the relationship strength measures.

Example 18.4.4 Using the relationship strength measures from Example 18.4.3 and taking $p = 1$, we find that:

$$\alpha = \frac{\frac{9}{134}}{\frac{9}{134} + \frac{1}{4}} = \frac{18}{85}$$

$$\beta = \frac{\frac{1}{4}}{\frac{9}{134} + \frac{1}{4}} = \frac{67}{85}$$

As Example 18.4.2 shows, the spatial interpolation-based estimate is $E_s = 23.5$ and the temporal interpolation-based estimate is $E_t = 30$. Hence using Equation 18.14 the linear combination adaptive method finds the estimate for w at location $(6, 4)$ and time 10 to be:

$$E = \frac{18}{85} \times 23.5 + \frac{67}{85} \times 30 = 28\frac{53}{85} \approx 28.6$$

18.4.2 Extension Methods

Extension methods deal with time as another dimension in space and extend a spatiotemporal interpolation problem into a one-higher dimensional spatial interpolation problem.

For example, 3-dimensional extension method can be used to estimate the value of any 2-dimensional spatial point in 1-dimensional time. Treating time as one extra spatial dimension, the extension method in this case may use 3-dimensional shape functions for tetrahedra (Section 18.3.2). The only modification is to substitute variable z in Equation (18.7) by the time variable t.

Extension methods are attractive theoretically because they can deal with even continuous time problems in 2-dimensional space and 1-dimensional time by using only linear equations generated by Equation (18.7). In some experimental tests, that extension method achieved the best estimation accuracy among the interpolation methods tested. However, it is in general harder to find tetrahedral tesselations in 3-dimensional than to find triangulations in 2-dimensional. In addition, for an intepolation problem in 3-dimensional space and 1-dimensional time, the extension method requires 4-dimensional tesselations, whose definition requires nonlinear polynomial equations.

18.5 Inverse Distance Weighting

Inverse distance weighting or IDW is another spatial interpolation method. When estimating the value of a point $p_0 = (x_1, \ldots, x_k)$ in k-dimension IDW considers only the nearest N Euclidean distance neighbors $p_1, \ldots, p_N$. Let d_i be the Euclidean distance between p_0 and p_i. The weight λ_i of each p_i is assigned as follows:

$$\lambda_i \;=\; \frac{\left(\dfrac{1}{d_i}\right)^c}{\displaystyle\sum_{k=1}^{N}\left(\dfrac{1}{d_k}\right)^c} \tag{18.15}$$

where $c > 0$ is a fixed constant exponent. The sum of the weights is equal to 1, and the weights of the neighbors are assigned proportionally to the inverse of the power c of the distance between them and p_0. Then w_0 the interpolated value at point p_0 is found as follows:

$$w_0 \;=\; \sum_{i=1}^{N}\lambda_i \cdot w_i \tag{18.16}$$

where w_i is the observed value at p_i.

Example 18.5.1 Let us use the 3-dimensional IDW method to estimate the temperature at location $(6,4)$ and time 10 given the *Temperature* relation. First, the 3-dimensional IDW finds the Euclidean distance between $(6,4,10)$ and each (x,y,t) point in the *Temperature* relation. In this case all of the Euclidean distances are 5. Therefore, with any exponent c, each point has a weight of $\frac{1}{5}$, and the interpolation value will be 26.

An attractive feature of the IDW method is that it can be used in any dimension. However, there are several problems with the IDW method. Below is a list of some of the problems.

Non-Flat Triangle Surface The TIN method expresses the intuition that one can expect a flat surface inside a triangle formed by three nodes. In contrast, the IDW method often gives values which are above or below the expected flat surface.

Non-Invariance to Scaling The TIN and the shape function methods are invariant to coordinate scaling. In contrast, the IDW method is not invariant to coordinate scaling. If the unit of measurement changes in one dimension, for example in the time dimension, then the interpolation value may change.

Affected by Uneven Distribution of Neighbors If the neighbors are not evenly distributed in all directions, then the interpolation value is too heavily influenced by the denser region of the neighbors.

Affected by Changing Exponent It is not clear what the value of c should be in a problem. Changing the value only slightly could have a significant effect on the estimated value.

Non-Linear Interpolation Function The IDW method yields a non-linear interpolation function. Hence in general it is hard to use the result for further querying in constraint database systems.

Some of these problems may look surprising at first sight. The last two problems are probably easy to see, but the first three problems are explained below by a few examples.

Example 18.5.2 [Non-Flat Triangle] Consider again Example 18.3.1 where the estimated value was 23.5. By Theorem 18.3.1 this is on the plane spanned by the three corner nodes. Since each of the corner nodes are equidistant from $(6, 4)$, in the IDW method, they have the same weight of $\frac{1}{3}$. Hence IDW estimates the value to be $23\frac{1}{3}$, which is slightly below the flat surface.

Example 18.5.3 [Non-Invariance to Scaling] Many applications may require the time unit to be rescaled without rescaling the spatial units. Suppose the time units are rescaled from days to hours. Then the *Temperature_Location* relation becomes:

Temperature_Location_Rescaled

X	Y	T	W
2	1	240	18
3	8	240	25
6	4	120	26
6	4	360	34
11	4	240	27

Now we need to find an estimate at $(6, 4, 240)$. The Euclidean distances between $(6, 4, 240)$ and the five spatiotemporal points with measurements are $d_1 = 5$, $d_2 = 5$, $d_3 = 120$, $d_4 = 120$, and $d_5 = 5$, respectively. Hence calculating with exponent $c = 1$, we have:

$$\sum_{k=1}^{5} \left(\frac{1}{d_k} \right)^1 = \frac{37}{60}$$

and the weights are $\lambda_1 = \lambda_2 = \lambda_5 = \frac{12}{37}$ and $\lambda_3 = \lambda_4 = \frac{1}{74}$. Therefore, the interpolated value is $23\frac{19}{37} \approx 23.5$. Note that the interpolated value changed from Example 18.5.1, where the estimate was 26.

The scaling problem is especially problematic in spatiotemporal applications because there is no natural choice of time units for any given spatial unit. For pure spatial interpolations, the usual choice is to have each spatial dimension measured with the same units. If all spatial dimensions are rescaled simultaneously, then the IDW interpolation value does not change.

Example 18.5.4 [Affected by Uneven Distribution of Neighbors]
Imagine a flat circlular area with unit radius on a hillside with p_0, the point to be interpolated, in the center of the circle. Imagine also that the neighbors p_1, p_2, p_3, and p_4 are placed at 0, 90, 180, and 270 degrees and have values 0, 10, 0, and -10. Then the interpolation value by both TIN and IDW is 0. Now move p_1 to 45 degrees and change its value to 5. Now the interpolation value for the TIN is still 0 but for IDW it changes to 1.25.

The problems described above are only some of the cases when the IDW interpolation value may change in an unintuitive manner. These changes may be confusing for the unaware.

18.6   Piecewise Linear Approximation

A simple but often useful approximation of a time series data is called *piecewise linear approximation* or *piecewise linear interpolation*, which is a function composed of a set of line segments. For any time series S and error tolerance value Ψ we can find a piecewise linear function f with the following property:

$$|f(t_i) - y_i| \leq \Psi \quad \text{for each} \quad (t_i, y_i) \in S \tag{18.17}$$

The relation *Temperature* can be approximated with piecewise linear functions, and the approximation can be represented in a constraint database. For example, relation *Temperature2* gives one constraint database approximation when $\Psi = 5$.

Temperature2

SN	t	Temp	
1	t	y	$y = 0.5(t-1) + 68, \quad t \geq 1, \quad t \leq 15$
1	t	y	$y = -0.5(t-15) + 75, \quad t \geq 15, \quad t \leq 29$
2	t	y	...
⋮	⋮	⋮	⋮

Piecewise linear approximations have several advantages. They can be used for data compression because the number of pieces in an approximation is usually much fewer than the number of points in the time series. For example, relation *Temperature* has 9 tuples, while relation *Temperature2* has only 2 tuples corresponding to the first weather station. Second, querying can be done faster using the compressed data as will be shown in Examples 18.6.2 and 18.6.3. Third, the approximation gives an interpolation that allows us to find the temperature at *any* time instance. For example, we can get the daily high temperature for each station on the second Wednesday, i.e., day 10, with the following SQL query, which uses the constraint representation:

> **select**   *Temp*
> **from**   *Temperature2*
> **where** $t = 10$

We will describe a piecewise linear approximation algorithm that runs in linear time in the number of time series data points. First we give some definitions.

Definition 18.6.1 Given two points (t_b, y_b) and (t_e, y_e) where $(b < e)$, and the maximum approximation error threshold is Ψ, we denote by:

$L_{b,e}(t)$ the *lower line* passing through (t_b, y_b) and $(t_e, y_e - \Psi)$ and
$U_{b,e}(t)$ the *upper line* passing through (t_b, y_b) and $(t_e, y_e + \Psi)$.

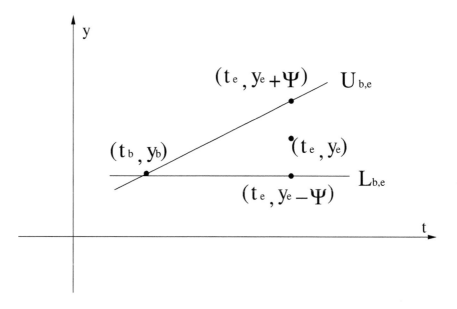

Figure 18.10: Lines $Y_{b,e}$, $U_{b,e}$, and $L_{b,e}$.

The lower and upper lines are shown in Figure 18.10. Note that any line that passes through (t_b, y_b) and has a slope between that of the lower and the upper lines is a line that at t_e must have a value between $y_e - \Psi$ and $y_e + \Psi$.

In the following algorithm, we assume that if A and B are points, then the function $slope(A, B)$ returns the slope of the line segment between those two points.

The idea behind the algorithm is that it tries to extend each piece until it cannot because the upper line becomes lower than the lower line. This idea will become clearer following Example 18.6.1 and the proof of correctness in Theorem 18.6.1.

Piecewise Linear Approximation(S,Ψ)

input: A time series S and a maximum error threshold Ψ.
output: A piecewise linear approximation function.
local vars Begin is start, S_L min and S_U max slope of a piece.

$Begin := (t_1, y_1)$
$S_L := -\infty$
$S_U := +\infty$

for $i = 1$ **to** $(n-1)$ **do**
    $S'_L := \max(S_L,\ slope(Begin, (t_{i+1}, y_{i+1} - \Psi))$
    $S'_U := \min(S_U,\ slope(Begin, (t_{i+1}, y_{i+1} + \Psi))$
    if $S'_L \leq S'_U$ **then**
        $S_L := S'_L$
        $S_U := S'_U$
    else
        Add line $f(t) = \frac{S_L+S_U}{2}(t - Begin.t) + Begin.y$
        $Begin := (t_i, f(t_i))$
        $S_L := slope(Begin, (t_{i+1}, y_{i+1} - \Psi))$
        $S_U := slope(Begin, (t_{i+1}, y_{i+1} + \Psi))$
    end-if
end-for

Add line $f(t) = \frac{S_L+S_U}{2}(t - Begin.t) + Begin.y$

Example 18.6.1 Let us find a piecewise linear approximation with $\Psi = 5$ for the time series that corresponds to the first weather station in relation

Temperature, that is, for:

$$(1, 68), (5, 71), (8, 76), (12, 73), (15, 71), (19, 68), (22, 70), (26, 74), (29, 73)$$

The algorithm works as follows. The initialization sets $Begin := (1, 68)$, $S_L := -\infty$ and $S_U := +\infty$. Next we see what happens in the *for loop* for successive values of i.

$i = 1$:

$$S_L' := \max(-\infty, \frac{(71 - 5) - 68}{5 - 1}) = -0.5$$

$$S_U' := \min(+\infty, \frac{(71 + 5) - 68}{5 - 1}) = 2$$

The *if* condition is true, hence $S_L := S_L'$ and $S_U := S_U'$.

$i = 2$:

$$S_L' := \max(-0.5, \frac{(76 - 5) - 68}{8 - 1}) = \max(-0.5, 3/7) = 3/7$$

$$S_U' := \min(2, \frac{(76 + 5) - 68}{8 - 1}) = \min(2, 13/7) = 13/7$$

The *if* condition is true, hence $S_L := S_L'$ and $S_U := S_U'$.

$i = 3$:

$$S_L' := \max(3/7, \frac{(73 - 5) - 68}{12 - 1}) = \max(3/7, 0) = 3/7$$

$$S_U' := \min(13/7, \frac{(73 + 5) - 68}{12 - 1}) = \min(13/7, 10/11) = 10/11$$

The *if* condition is true, hence $S_L := S_L'$ and $S_U := S_U'$.

$i = 4$:

$$S_L' := \max(3/7, \frac{(71 - 5) - 68}{15 - 1}) = \max(3/7, -1/7) = 3/7$$

$$S_U' := \min(10/11, \frac{(71 + 5) - 68}{15 - 1}) = \min(10/11, 4/7) = 4/7$$

The *if* condition is true, hence $S_L := S'_L$ and $S_U := S'_U$.

$i = 5$:

$$S'_L \quad := \quad \max(3/7, \frac{(68-5)-68}{19-1}) = \max(3/7, -5/18) = 3/7$$

$$S'_U \quad := \quad \min(4/7, \frac{(68+5)-68}{19-1}) = \min(4/7, 5/18) = 5/18$$

Because $3/7 > 5/18$, the *if* condition is false and the following line will be added as the first piece:

$$f(t) = 0.5(t-1) + 68$$

We also set $Begin := (15, 75)$ and

$$S_L \quad := \quad \frac{(68-5)-75}{19-15} = -3$$

$$S_U \quad := \quad \frac{(68+5)-75}{19-15} = -0.5$$

$i = 6$:

$$S'_L \quad := \quad \max(-3, \frac{(70-5)-75}{22-15}) = \max(-3, -10/7) = -10/7$$

$$S'_U \quad := \quad \min(-0.5, \frac{(70+5)-75}{22-15}) = \min(-0.5, 0) = -0.5$$

The *if* condition is true, hence $S_L := S'_L$ and $S_U := S'_U$.

$i = 7$:

$$S'_L \quad := \quad \max(-10/7, \frac{(74-5)-75}{26-15}) = \max(-10/7, -6/11) = -6/11$$

$$S'_U \quad := \quad \min(-0.5, \frac{(74+5)-75}{26-15}) = \min(-0.5, 4/11) = -0.5$$

The *if* condition is true, hence $S_L := S'_L$ and $S_U := S'_U$.

$i = 8$:

$$S'_L \quad := \quad \max(-6/11, \frac{(73-5)-75}{29-15}) = \max(-6/11, -7/14) = -0.5$$

$$S'_U \quad := \quad \min(-0.5, \frac{(73+5)-75}{29-15}) = \min(-0.5, 3/14) = -0.5$$

The *if* condition is true, hence $S_L := S'_L$ and $S_U := S'_U$.

Now we exit the *for loop* and in the last line we create the piece:

$$f(t) = -0.5(t-15) + 75$$

Therefore, the algorithm returns the sequence of linear pieces $0.5(t-1)+68$ for $1 \leq t \leq 15$ and $-0.5(t-15) + 75$ for $15 \leq t \leq 29$. This is exactly the same piecewise linear function that is represented as the first two constraint tuples in relation *Temperature2*.

Next we show the correctness of the piecewise linear approximation algorithm.

Theorem 18.6.1 The piecewise linear approximation algorithm is correct for any time series S and error tolerance value Ψ and runs in $O(n)$ time where n is the number of points in S.

Proof: To prove correctness, it is enough to show the following:

Claim: If the algorithm creates a piece $f(t)$ between (t_b, y_b) and (t_e, c), then that piece satisfies Formula (18.17) for each (t_i, y_i) where $b \leq i \leq e$.

The piece has a slope that is greater than or equal to the slope of all the lower lines $L_{b,i}$ and less than or equal to the slope of all the upper lines $U_{b,i}$, because the values of S_L and S_U are updated by taking the maximum of the lower lines and the minimum of the upper lines from $b \leq i \leq e$.

Let S^e_L and U^e_L be the values of the S_L and S_U variables at time t_e. It is obvious that any line that has a slope s such that $S^e_L \leq s \leq S^e_U$ satisfies Formula (18.17) for each $b \leq i \leq e$. Because the slope of the piece $f(t)$ is $(S^e_L + U^e_L)/2$, it is between S^e_L and S^e_L.

For computational complexity, it is easy to see that the for loop is entered $n-1$ times, and within it each step takes a constant time. Therefore, the worst-case computational complexity of this algorithm is $O(n)$. ■

It is interesting to analyze the expected number of points spanned by a single piece of the piecewise linear approximation. In the following analysis we assume that the time series $(t_1, y_1), \ldots, (t_n, y_n)$ satisfies the following property, for some constant M and for each $1 < i \leq n$:

$$\begin{cases} y_1 = 0 \\ Prob(y_i - y_{i-1} = M) = 0.5 \\ Prob(y_i - y_{i-1} = -M) = 0.5 \end{cases} \qquad (18.18)$$

For example, consider the time series that starts with $(0, 0)$ and records (t, y) pairs where t is the time a coin is flipped and y is the number of heads minus the number of tails seen since the beginning. This time series satisfies Property (18.18) with $M = 1$ if heads and tails have the same probability.

As another example, the daily temperature could be described by a time series that satisfies Property (18.18), if we use a thermometer in which the adjacent scales are M Fahrenheit degrees apart instead of the usual single Fahrenheit degrees, where M is the largest daily change, and if we record only on those days when there is a change in temperature according to the rougher thermometer.

Let $E(\Psi, M)$ be the expected number of original points spanned by a single piece of the piecewise linear approximation, including the two endpoints, when the approximation uses the tolerance Ψ and the time series satisfies Property (18.18). We can prove the following.

Theorem 18.6.2 If a time series satisfies Property (18.18), then

$$E(\Psi, M) \geq \left(\left\lfloor \frac{\Psi}{2M} \right\rfloor + 1 \right)^2$$

■

For example, for the coin flipping time series, when $\Psi = 6$ each piece of the piecewise linear approximation function is expected to span at least 16 original time series points.

Experiments also show that the piecewise linear approximation algorithm provides good data compression. One experiment used two time series for weather station number 252820 in Nebraska. The first time series in relation $High\_Temperature(t, y)$ recorded the daily high temperature with a seven-day moving window, i.e., for each day t the y recorded the average temperature measured at days $t - 3$, $t - 2$, $t - 1$, t, $t + 1$, $t + 2$, and $t + 3$. Similarly, the second time series in relation $Low\_Temperature(t, y)$ recorded the daily low temperature with a seven-day moving window. Both time series recorded the moving averages for each day between $1/1/1987$ and $12/31/1996$. Since this period contained three leap years, the total number of data points was 3653 in each time series. Let us now consider some queries.

Example 18.6.2 Find all pairs of days such that for each the high temperature in the first day is greater than the high temperature in the second day. This can be expressed in SQL as follows:

> **select** $R1.t$, $R2.t$
> **from** $High\_Temperature$ **as** $R1$, $High\_Temperature$ **as** $R2$
> **where** $R1.y > R2.y$

The output of this query is a relation with $6,645,646$ tuples.

Example 18.6.3 Find all pairs of days such that for each pair the first day has a high temperature greater than the high temperature of the second day and the first day has a low temperature greater than the low temperature of the second day. This can be expressed in SQL as follows:

> **select** $R1.t$, $R2.t$
> **from** $High\_Temperature$ **as** $R1$, $High\_Temperature$ **as** $R2$
> $Low\_Temperature$ **as** $R3$, $Low\_Temperature$ **as** $R4$
> **where** $R1.t = R3.t$ **and** $R2.t = R4.t$ **and**
> $R1.y > R2.y$ **and** $R3.y > R4.y$

The output of this query is a relation with $6,091,441$ tuples.

Neither of the preceding SQL queries is easy to evaluate because the output relations are so large. This is another reason to use approximation. Let $High\_temperature2(t,y)$ and $Low\_Temperature2(t,y)$ be the output constraint relations of the piecewise linear approximation. The following table shows the number of pieces in the piecewise linear approximations that are obtained using various Ψ error tolerance values.

Ψ	$High\_Temperature2$	$Low\_Temperature2$
—	3653	3653
1.0	1426	1084
2.0	790	594
4.0	428	335
8.0	197	140

These relations can be used in the preceding queries. Because the input is approximate, the output relation will also be approximate. We measure how good the approximation is by the values of *precision* and *recall*. Note that the original SQL output relations are pairs of integers, with each integer between 1 and 3653.

Let N be the number of (t_1, t_2) integer pairs with $1 \leq t_1, t_2 \leq 3653$ that satisfy the output constraint relation. In our context, *precision* is the percentage of those N pairs that are also in the original SQL query output.

Similarly, let M be the number of (t_1, t_2) pairs that are the output of a SQL query. *Recall* is the percentage of those M that satisfy the output constraint relation.

Usually, it is easy to achieve high precision at the expense of low recall or vice versa. A good system will have both high precision and high recall. Using the constraint approximation *High_Temperature2* instead of *High_Temperature*, the output of the first SQL query is shown in the following table.

Ψ	Constraint Approx.	Precision	Recall
—	6,645,646	100.00%	100.00%
1.0	2,006,001	99.39%	99.49%
2.0	1,208,010	98.54%	98.67%
4.0	235,639	96.83%	96.97%
8.0	51,681	93.39%	93.53%

Using *High_Temperature2* instead of *High_Temperature* and using *Low_Temperature2* instead of *Low_Temperature*, the output of the second SQL query is shown in the following table.

Ψ	Constraint Approx.	Precision	Recall
—	6,091,441	100.00%	100.00%
1.0	1,836,631	99.30%	99.44%
2.0	639,797	98.40%	98.66%
4.0	215,649	96.45%	96.67%
8.0	46,449	92.72%	92.68%

In both cases the output constraint relation is much smaller than the output relation of the original SQL queries, while the precision and recall are both high. Because of the smaller number of tuples, the constraint query can be evaluated much faster. Hence there is a trade-off between speed of evaluation and precision and recall of the output. So when time is critical and absolute precision is not necessary, the constraint query evaluation can be advantageous.

18.6.1 Updating Piecewise Linear Approximations

Updates modify the database as the user requests either the insertion or deletion of tuples in a relation. For example, a user may request the insertion or deletion of tuple (i, t, y) into the *Temperature* relation, where i is a weather station number, t is the time measured in days, and y is the temperature at that time and location. While modifying the *Temperature* relation is a trivial task, the corresponding modification of *Temperature2* merits some consideration.

In general, assume that f_0 is a piecewise linear approximation of a time series S. If the user requests a deletion of a time series data point (t, y) from S, then the request can be ignored because f_0 still satisfies the error tolerance for the remaining points.

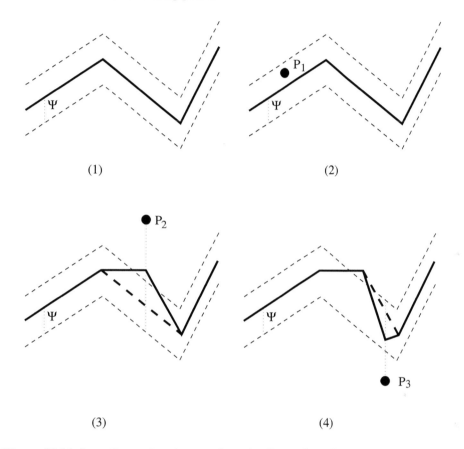

Figure 18.11: Inserting points into a piecewise linear function.

However, the insertion of points is more complex, because it requires updating the piecewise linear function. Consider Figure 18.6.1. There the original piecewise linear function is shown as a solid black line in (1). In (2) the point P_1 is to be inserted, but the piecewise linear function is not changed because P_1 is in the error tolerance Ψ. In (3) the point P_2 is to be inserted, and the piecewise linear function is updated by splitting the middle piece into two pieces. In (4) the point P_3 is to be inserted, and the piecewise linear function is updated by splitting the third piece into two pieces.

Based on these ideas, the insertion algorithm for a single data point (t_α, y_α) is shown next. We assume that f_0 is the original piecewise linear function into which we repeatedly insert data points. At any time, f is the current piecewise linear function after a number of insertions.

Insert$(f_0, f, \Psi, t_\alpha, y_\alpha)$

```
input: The piecewise linear function f_0 before insertions.
       The piecewise linear function f after some insertions.
       Ψ the maximum error threshold in the f_0 approximation.
       (t_α, y_α) the next point to be inserted.
output: An updated f with (t_α, y_α) inserted.
```

if there is a piece AB of f such that
    $A = (t_i, y_i)$ and $B = (t_{i+1}, y_{i+1})$ and $t_i < t_\alpha < t_{i+1}$ **then**
    if $f_o(t_\alpha) - \Psi > y_\alpha$ **then**
        $C := (t_\alpha, \quad 0.5 \ (f_o(t_\alpha) + \Psi + y_\alpha))$
        delete AB and insert AC and CB into f
    end-if
    if $f_o(t_\alpha) + \Psi < y_\alpha$ **then**
        $C := (t_\alpha, \quad 0.5 \ (f_o(t_\alpha) - \Psi + y_\alpha))$
        delete AB and insert AC and CB into f
    end-if
else
    let (t_b, y_b) be leftmost and (t_e, y_e) be rightmost point in f
    if $t_\alpha < t_b$ **then**
        insert piece between (t_α, y_α) and (t_b, y_b) into f
    else
        insert piece between (t_e, y_e) and (t_α, y_α) into f
    end-if
end-if

We can show the following theorem.

Theorem 18.6.3 Suppose that a time series S is approximated by a piecewise linear function f_o with n "pieces" and Ψ error tolerance. Then any set I of m insertions such that each insertion point is at most some constant $\delta \geq \Psi$ distance from f_o can be done by the insertion algorithm such that the updated piecewise linear function f has at most $n + m$ "pieces" and the following holds:

$$|f(t_i) - y_i| \leq \frac{\Psi + \delta}{2} \quad \text{for each } (t_i, y_i) \in S \cup I \tag{18.19}$$

Proof: There are four cases to insert one point (t_α, y_α), namely:

(1): $t_i < t_\alpha < t_{i+1}$ and $f_o(t_\alpha) - \Psi > y_\alpha$
(2): $t_i < t_\alpha < t_{i+1}$ and $f_o(t_\alpha) + \Psi < y_\alpha$
(3): $t_\alpha < t_b$
(4): $t_\alpha > t_e$

First we prove that the updated piecewise linear function f has at most $n + m$ pieces after m insertions. In each of the four cases, the algorithm adds one point to f. In other cases, the algorithm does not add any point to f. Therefore, for a sequence of m insertions, at most m points are added to f. Hence, f has at most $n + m$ points.

Next, we prove by induction that condition (18.19) holds. When $I = \emptyset$ the condition is obviously true. Let us assume that after a sequence of insertions the condition is true and we are inserting some new point (t_α, y_α). We prove that the condition also holds after the insertion.

Case (1): We have to prove that the condition is still true for the points of f that are between A and B. First let us consider the points on the piece AC.

Consider the original piecewise linear function f_0 between A and B shown by the bold line in Figure 18.12. Let D and E be points on the line $f_o(t) - \Psi$, and F and G be points on the line $f_o(t) + \Psi$ as shown in the figure. The coordinates of these four points can be calculated to be $D(t_i, f_o(t_i) - \Psi)$, $E(t_\alpha, f_o(t_\alpha) - \Psi)$, $F(t_i, f_o(t_i) + \Psi)$, and $G(t_\alpha, f_o(t_\alpha) + \Psi)$. For the point (t_α, y_α) to be inserted we calculate the following:

$$
\begin{aligned}
|f(t_\alpha) - y_\alpha| &= 0.5\,((f_o(t_\alpha) + \Psi) + y_\alpha) - y_\alpha \quad \text{by y-coordinate of } C \\
&= 0{,}5\,((f_o(t_\alpha) + \Psi) - y_\alpha) \\
&= 0.5\,(\Psi + (f_o(t_\alpha) - y_\alpha)) \\
&\leq \frac{\Psi + \delta}{2}
\end{aligned}
$$

The last inequality follows from the condition that each point inserted is at most δ distance from f_0. Hence (t_α, y_α) satisfies the condition.

Note that there cannot be any other I point H before (t_α, y_α) that is between A and C and has more than Ψ distance from f_o. If we had, then we would have to use either AH or HB instead of AB when we are inserting (t_α, y_α).

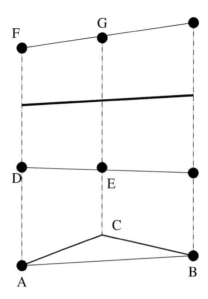

Figure 18.12: Insertion of a point.

Now we can assume that all S and I points before (t_α, y_α) and between A and C are at most Ψ distance from f_o. Therefore, these all fall into the trapezoid region $DEGF$, showing that any point within $DEGF$ satisfies the condition.

First we show the condition for the corner vertices. For D and F the condition is true by the induction hypothesis, that is, they are both at most $(\Psi + \delta)/2$ distance from A. Note that y_α is at most δ and both E and G are at most Ψ distance from f_o. Because the y-coordinate of C is at the midpoint of y_α and the y-coordinate of G, both G and E are at most $(\Psi + \delta)/2$ distance from C.

Let A' be the point exactly $(\Psi + \delta)/2$ below F, and let C' be the point exactly $(\Psi + \delta)/2$ below G. Suppose $M = (t, y)$ is any point within $DEGF$. Let M_1 be the point directly above M and intersecting the line segment FG and M_2 be the point directly below M and intersecting the line segment $A'C'$ as shown in Figure 18.13. Clearly, the distance between M and AC is less than the distance between M_1 and M_2, which is exactly $(\Psi + \delta)/2$. Hence M must satisfy the condition. Therefore, all points within $DEGF$ satisfy the condition.

This took care for points between A and C. We can prove similarly that all points in S and in I before (t_α, y_α) and between C and B also satisfy the condition.

Case (2): This is similar to case (1).

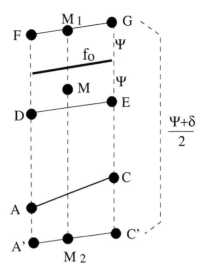

Figure 18.13: Proof condition for point M.

Case (3): The condition is clearly true in this case, because the point (t_α, y_α) is contained in the new piece and there are no other points between it and (t_b, y_b).

Case (4): This is similar to case (3).   ■

For example, if $\delta = 3\Psi$, then the error tolerance for the updated piecewise linear approximation will be 2Ψ for all original and newly inserted data points.

18.6.2 Parametric Rectangles Approximation of Raster Movies

Imagine that a movie shows on a white screen some moving black objects. The video can be represented as a raster image every $t/20$ second. However, that representation requires a huge amount of computer memory if the movie lasts several hours. In this section we describe a space-efficient parametric rectangles approximation of raster movies. The parametric rectangles representation can also be translated into a constraint representation by the interoperability results of Chapter 7.

The idea behind the parametric rectangles representation is the following. We can expect in a typical movie that the objects move slowly and with uniform speed and change directions infrequently. In addition, they may be moving away from us, which makes their images gradually shrink, or toward us, which makes their images gradually grow on the screen.

As a simple example, suppose the black object is a rectangle. If it does not change direction between times t_1 and t_2, and it is $[x_1, x_2] \times [y_1, y_2]$ at time t_1 and $[x'_1, x'_2] \times [y'_1, y'_2]$ at time t_2, then there is a parametric rectangle:

$$([at + b, \ ct + d], \ [et + f, \ gt + h], \ [t_1, \ t_2])$$

where a, b, c, d, e, f, g, h are constants that describe the black object. For example, we have that:

$$x_1 \ = \ a\,t_1 + b$$
$$x'_1 \ = \ a\,t_2 + b$$

Subtracting the second from the first equation and then simplifying gives for a and b the following:

$$a = \frac{x_1 - x'_1}{t_1 - t_2} \quad \text{and} \quad b = x_1 - \frac{x_1 - x'_1}{t_1 - t_2}t_1$$

Therefore,

$$at + b \ = \ (x_1 - x'_1)\frac{t - t_1}{t_1 - t_2} + x_1$$

By doing similar simplifications for the other parametric endpoints, we see that the parametric rectangle can be written as:

$$([x_1 - x'_1)T + x_1, \ (x_2 - x'_2)T + x_2],$$
$$[(y_1 - y'_1)T + y_1, \ (y_2 - y'_2)T + y_2], \ [t_1, \ t_2])$$

where

$$T = \frac{t - t_1}{t_1 - t_2}$$

If the shape of the black object is more complex than a rectangle, then we break it up into a set of rectangles at both time t_1 and time t_2, then we match the two sets of rectangles with each other. This can be done in a number of ways.

Let us assume that at time t_1 the object is within a rectangle that is ch_1 pixels in height and cw_1 pixels in width, and at time t_2 it is within another rectangle that is ch_2 pixels in height and cw_2 pixels in width.

Then we divide the first picture into $h_1 \times w_1$ size small rectangles and the second picture into $h_1 \times w_1$ size small rectangles. Note that this way we divide both big rectangles into the same c^2 number of smaller rectangles.

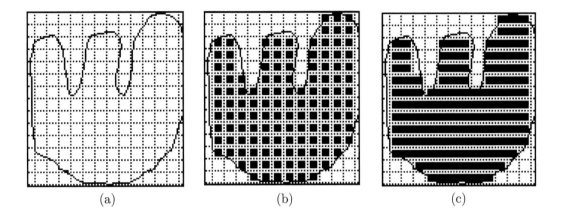

Figure 18.14: Dividing an image into rectangles.

For example, Figure 18.14 shows a glovelike image that fits into a square, which is subdivided into a set of small squares in part (a).

Next we mark each small rectangle as **on** if more than 50 percent of the pixels in it are black, otherwise we mark it as **off**. Part (b) of the figure shows as black squares those that are **on** and as white squares those that are **off**.

Next we merge in each row the adjacent black squares, yielding a set of rectangles in each row. This is shown as part (c) of the figure. We find these rectangles in each row in both pictures. Then for each row we pair the rectangles of the image at time t_1 with the rectangles of the image at time t_2. This can be done as follows. Let m and n be the number of rectangles in the two rows to be matched. There are three cases:

(1) If $m = n$ then we simply pair the ith rectangle of the first with the ith rectangle of the second row each for $1 \leq i \leq m$.

(2) If $m < n$ then, then let $d = \lfloor m/n \rfloor$. We pair the first rectangle at t_1 with the first d rectangles at t_2, the second rectangle with the second d rectangles, and so on until we come to the mth rectangle at t_1, which we pair with all the remaining unpaired rectangles at t_2.

(3) If $m > n$, we can do the pairing similarly to the preceding.

Finally, for each pair we compute a parametric rectangle that takes the first rectangle into the second as we did earlier when we considered only one moving rectangle.

The preceding is an informal description of an algorithm that approximates by parametric rectangles a raster movie with only black objects on a white screen. There are many possible extensions. For example, in the presence of colors, the rectangles may be assumed to change color gradually. It is also not necessary to always make the assumption of linear motion. For example, in the y direction when an object is moving downward, it may be assumed that the motion is a quadratic polynomial motion due to the acceleration caused by gravity, similarly to the motion in relation *Bomb* of Chapter 7.

Bibliographic Notes

Shape functions and other finite element algorithms are described in [440, 59]. Li and Revesz [263] describe the reduction and extension methods for spatio-temporal interpolation. Grumbach et al. [170] also consider the constraint database representation and management of interpolated spatial data.

There are several methods to generate automatic tetrahedral meshes, such as the 3-dimensional Delaunay tetrahedrilization and some tetrahedral mesh improvement methods to avoid poorly-shaped tetrahedra. For example, the tetrahedral mesh generation by Delaunay refinement [376] and tetrahedral mesh improvement using swapping and smoothing [141]. Inverse distance weighting is introduced in [375]. There are other spatial interpolation techniques that we did not cover in this chapter. Among these are kriging [244, 113], splines [159], trend surfaces [441], and Fourier series [190].

Triangulated irregular networks are used in several geographic information systems [5, 260, 432], including as an option by the ARC/INFO system [283]. Davis [104] is a book on approximation and interpolation.

The piecewise linear approximation problem for time series data has been studied by many researchers. The piecewise linear approximations can be divided into two main groups, namely (at least) time coordinate preserving approximations, in which the endpoints of the pieces have time coordinates that occur in the original time series data, or inventing approximations, in which the coordinate values can be any real numbers. The piecewise linear approximation algorithm in Section 18.6 is a preserving approximation. For example, in Example 18.6.1 the endpoints of the pieces are $(1, 68)$, $(15, 75)$, and $(29, 68)$ and 1, 15, and 29 all occur in the time series as time coordinates.

In 1991, Hakimi and Schmeichel [185] gave an $O(n^2)$ preserving piecewise linear approximation algorithm and an $O(n)$ inventing piecewise linear approximation algorithm that return approximations with a minimum number of possible pieces. Recently, Agarwal and Varadarajan [9] gave an improved preserving algorithm with complexity $O(n^{\frac{4}{3}+\epsilon})$, where ϵ is any arbitrarily small positive constant. The piecewise linear approximation and the update algorithms in Section 18.6 are improvements of algorithms by Chen et al. [77], and the weather data used in Section 18.6 was obtained from the Web site of the National Climatic Data Center at http://www.ncdc.noaa.gov. A recent extension of the piecewise linear approximation algorithm allows it to be applied to find the contour of two-dimensional objects, such as lakes and other natural landmarks [262].

In the preserving case, both [185] and [9] return fewer pieces but run slower than the $O(n)$ time piecewise linear algorithm presented in this section. It remains an open problem to find a preserving piecewise linear approximation algorithm that both returns the fewest number of pieces and runs in $O(n)$ time.

Update operators can be classified as proper updates, revision, and arbitration operators. Revision methods are axiomatized in Alchourrón et al. [11], update methods in Katsuno and Mendelzon [221, 222, 223, 224], and arbitration in Revesz [329]. The complexity of propositional updates and revision is studied in Eiter and Gottlob [123], and the complexity of first-order updates is studied in Grahne et al. [162]. An extension of the update and the revision operators with weights is presented in Benczur et al. [39]. Three types of operators are extended for constraint databases in Revesz [328]. The parametric rectangles approximation of raster movies is from Cai et al. [64].

Exercises

1. Find the piecewise linear approximation of the following time series data using the given error tolerance values:

   (a) The following time series S when $\Psi = 1$:
       (1,2), (2,4), (3,2), (4,4), (5,5), (6,4), (7,5), (8,5), (9,6), (10,4), (11,4), (12,6), (13,6), (14,6), (15,7), (16,7), (17,9), (18,10), (19,11), (20,13)

   (b) The time series S when the error tolerance $\Psi = 2$.

   (c) The following time series when $\Psi = 3$:
       (0,0), (1,1), (2,3), (3,4), (4,2), (5,3), (6,5), (7,6), (8,8), (9,11), (10,12), (11,10), (12,9), (13,11), (14,13), (15,14), (16,17), (17,16), (18,18), (19,15), (20,13), (21,12), (22,11), (23,9), (24,10), (25,12), (26,11), (27,9), (28,8), (29,6), (30,5)

   (d) The following time series when $\Psi = 4$:
       (1,1), (3,3), (6,4), (7,7), (10,6), (13,9), (15,7), (18,4), (20,5), (22,4), (23,7), (25,9), (26,10), (28,9), (29,12)

2. Consider the time series:

   (1,1), (3,3), (10,6), (13,9), (15,7), (18,4), (22,4), (23,6), (28,9), (29,12)

   (a) Find a piecewise linear approximation when $\Psi = 2$.

   (b) Update the piecewise linear approximation by inserting into it the following points in order: $(16, 5)$, $(26, 5)$, $(5, 12)$, and $(8, 2)$.

3. Suppose that four weather stations in relation *Temperature* in Section 18.6 are located at $(0,0)$, $(1,0)$, $(0,1)$, and $(1,1)$, respectively.

   (a) Find a triangulation of the stations.

   (b) Find a piecewise linear approximation for the first month for each weather station. (*Hint:* Extend the first and last pieces in each approximation to day 1 and 31, respectively.)

   (c) Find a parametric triangulated irregular network description of the temperature at each location.

   (d) Represent the parametric triangulated irregular network as a constraint relation.

4. Consider the following single triangle facet of a triangulated irregular network. Corner vertex A_1 is at location $(0,0)$ and at elevation 100. Corner vertex A_2 is at location $(5,2)$ and at elevation 60. Corner vertex A_3 is at location $(3,6)$ and at elevation 40. Find a constraint database representation of this TIN triangle.

5. Consider the following vertices. Vertex V_1 is at location $(2,1)$ and at elevation 18. Vertex V_2 is at location $(11,4)$ and at elevation 27. Vertex V_3 is at location $(3,8)$ and at elevation 25. Vertex V_4 is at location $(6,4)$ and at elevation 30. Find a triangulated irregular network and a constraint database representation.

6. The *Stocks* relation records in dollars the prices of the stocks of companies A and B at the beginning of each month. Assume that 1/1/2008 is month 0, 2/1/2008 is month 1, and so on until 1/1/2009, which is month 12.

Stocks

Id	Price	Month
A	100	0
A	110	1
A	120	2
A	130	3
A	140	4
A	150	5
A	160	6
A	170	7
A	180	8
A	160	9
A	140	10
A	120	11
A	100	12
B	100	0
B	115	1
B	130	2
B	145	3
B	160	4
B	175	5
B	175	6
B	175	7
B	175	8
B	175	9
B	175	10
B	175	11
B	175	12

Translate the *Stocks* relation into a constraint relation by using a piecewise linear interpolation of the share prices and then express in SQL the following queries:

(a) Find the stock price of company A at 6.5 month.

(b) Find the times when companies A and B have the same stock price.

(c) Find the maximum stock price for each company during the year.

(d) Find the time when the stock price of company A is maximum.

7. The *Employee* relation records in dollars the salary of some employees in a company. Assume that the salaries change always on January 1st of each year. Also assume that 0 is year 1995, 1 is 1996 and so on.

Employee

Name	Salary	Year
Paul	50,000	0
Paul	60,000	1
Paul	70,000	2
Paul	80,000	3
Paul	90,000	4
Paul	100,000	5
Paul	110,000	6
Paul	120,000	7
Paul	130,000	8
Paul	140,000	9
Paul	150,000	10
Paul	153,000	11
Paul	156,000	12
Paul	159,000	13
Paul	162,000	14
Paul	165,000	15
Peter	60,000	0
Peter	64,000	1
Peter	68,000	2
Peter	72,000	3
Peter	76,000	4
Peter	80,000	5
Peter	84,000	6
Peter	88,000	7
Peter	92,000	8
Peter	96,000	9
Peter	100,000	10
Peter	104,000	11
Peter	108,000	12
Peter	112,000	13
Peter	116,000	14
Peter	120,000	15

Translate the *Employee* relation into a constraint relation by using a piecewise linear interpolation of the salaries and then express in SQL the following queries:

(a) Find the salary of Paul in year 10.

(b) Find the times when Paul and Peter have the same salary.

(c) Find the maximum difference between the salaries of Paul and Peter in the same year.

(d) Find the year when the salary difference of Paul and Peter is maximum.

8. Mr. Brown owns two houses between January 2000 and January 2010. Relation *Houses* records their prices in dollars at certain points in time. The number of months is counted from January 2000, which is taken as month 0.

House

Id	Price	Time
1	80,000	0
1	110,000	30
1	140,000	60
1	260,000	120
2	280,000	40
2	240,000	80

Translate the *House* relation into a constraint relation by using a piecewise linear interpolation of the share prices and then express in SQL the following queries:

(a) Find the price of house 1 at 50 months.

(b) Mr. Brown always lives in the cheaper and rents the more expensive house. Find the time when Mr. Brown moves from one house to another.

(c) Find the maximum of the sum of the prices of the two houses at any point of time.

9. The triangulated irregular network shown in Figure 18.15 represents a mountaineous area with the measured elevation values in feet given for each corner vertex.

(a) Represent the TIN as a textfile shown below, where each row contains the description of one triangle facet. For example, the first row that represents the triangle facet with corner vertices $(0, 0, 9915)$, $(5, 0, 12915)$, and $(3, 6, 9870)$.

0	0	9915	5	0	12915	3	6	9870
5	0	12915	10	6	12600	3	6	9870
5	0	12915	20	0	13680	10	6	12600
0	0	9915	3	6	9870	0	10	10500
3	6	9870	10	6	12600	0	10	10500
10	6	12600	20	0	13680	16	12	12240
0	10	10500	10	6	12600	5	13	13650
5	13	13650	10	6	12600	12	20	11592
10	6	12600	16	12	12240	12	20	11592
0	10	10500	5	13	13650	0	20	11550
0	20	11550	5	13	13650	12	20	11592
16	12	12240	20	20	11640	12	20	11592
16	12	12240	20	0	13680	20	20	11640

(b) Write a program that takes as input textfiles of the above form representing triangulated irregular networks and gives as output a constraint relation. Apply your program for the above sample textfile.

(c) Using the constraint database relation write SQL queries that find the six regions that have the following elevations:

- Between 9,000 and 10,000 feet
- Between 10,000 and 11,000 feet
- Between 11,000 and 12,000 feet
- Between 12,000 and 13,000 feet
- Between 13,000 and 14,000 feet

10. Write a program that takes as input textfiles of the form of the previous exercise and calulates the surface area of the TIN within a rectangle specified by the user. For example, the user may ask to find the surface area of the TIN that falls within the rectangle with lower-left point $(0, 0)$ and upper-right point $(20, 20)$.

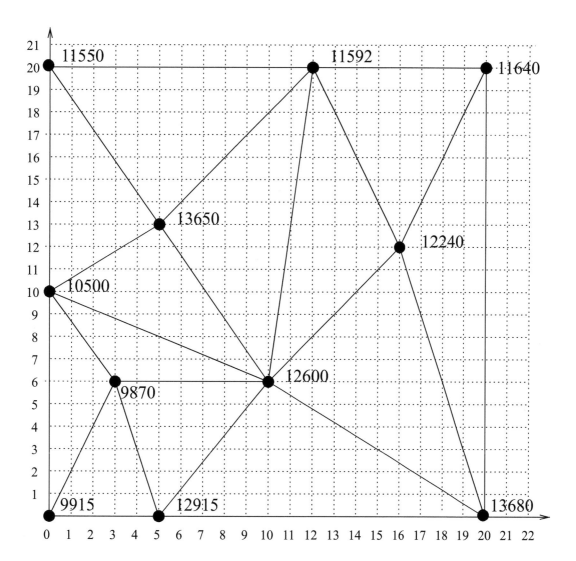

Figure 18.15: Measured elevations in feet.

19

Prediction and Data Mining

Queries often aim to discover what the data predict, that is, imply for the future, or what other precious patterns may be discovered from the data. This chapter considers these two types of queries. In particular, Section 19.1 considers predictions in the context of environmental modeling, where many important prediction problems from global warming to deforestation occur. Section 19.2 discusses data mining. Section 19.3 considers model-based diagnosis.

19.1   Prediction

Environmental modeling problems occur in many applications, for example, in flood, fire, and pollution control or drought, urban development, and wildlife habitat change monitoring. Environmental modeling systems are used by flood, fire, or pollution control emergency response teams, and in agriculture by farmers, insurance companies, crops market analysts, and various government agencies. Each environmental modeling system is specialized for the phenomena of interest and the local conditions and regulations. However, in general one can identify the following three common requirements of environmental modeling systems:

- **Predictive Spread Modeling:** Environmental modeling systems should predict over time intervals the spread of natural phenomena like a flood, a drought, or a forest fire or man-made phenomena like an oil spill or industrial smoke.

- **Visualization:** Environmental modeling systems should provide useful visualization of the modeled phenomena. The goal of the visual-

P. Revesz, *Introduction to Databases: From Biological to Spatio-Temporal*,
Texts in Computer Science, DOI 10.1007/978-1-84996-095-3_19,
© Springer-Verlag London Limited 2010

ization is not prettiness but usefulness to the users. Therefore, the visualization should be fast and safe. For example, the visualization should overpredict rather than underpredict the flooded area at any given time instance.

- **Decision Support:** The visualization may not be enough for users to make valid or fast decisions, especially in emergency situations. In these cases, environmental modeling systems should provide *decision support*, which means the ability to help evaluate the situation and possible responses to it.

It is possible to build, using the MLPQ/PReSTO constraint-relational database systems, environmental modeling systems that provide all three features. This chapter describes the process of building an environmental modeling system and illustrates the process by a sample environmental modeling system for monitoring and controlling forest fire spread.

Section 19.1.1 describes predictive spread modeling. Section 19.1.2 describes the visualization of the fire spread. Finally, Section 19.1.3 describes a decision support system for the fire control problem.

19.1.1   Predictive Spread Modeling

Technological advances in remote sensing, global positioning systems (GPS), and high-speed telecommunication make it possible to build a real-time system to track the spread of phenomena like flood, fire, desertification, and smoke. For example, suppose that an airborne or satellite-based sensor sends two successive snapshots of a forest fire at times $t = 1$ and $t = 5$ hours, as shown in Figure 19.1.

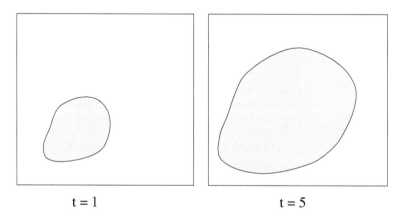

t = 1   t = 5

Figure 19.1: Raster snapshots of the fire.

We apply the approximation algorithm of Section 18.6.2 to interpolate between the two snapshots. The algorithm breaks both snapshots into the same number of rectangles and then matches the rectangles in order, as shown in Figure 19.2.

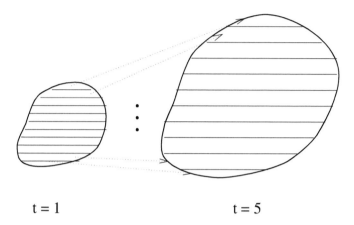

$$t = 1 \qquad\qquad t = 5$$

Figure 19.2: Interpolation between the snapshots.

Next, the approximation algorithm builds for each matching pair of rectangles a parametric rectangle. For each pair, the parametric rectangle changes from the rectangle at time $t = 1$ hour into the rectangle at time $t = 5$ hours. Therefore, the set of parametric rectangles gives an interpolation of the spread between times $t = 1$ and $t = 5$ hours.

This interpolation can be easily extended backward in time to estimate the origin of the fire and forward in time to estimate the state of the fire at any given time instance in the future, because it is reasonable to assume that the rate of the fire spread does not change much over a relatively short time. To do this *extrapolation*, we simply change in each parametric rectangle the *from* value to something less than 1 or increase the *to* value to something greater than 5. For example, suppose we change the time interval to $[0, 10]$. Then at any time between $t = 0$ and $t = 10$ we have an estimate for the fire spread. For example, the dashed line in Figure 19.3 shows the predicted fire front at $t = 8$ hours.

The prediction backward in time can be very useful to identify the possible source of the fire, essential information, for example, for insurance companies. The prediction forward in time is useful to enable emergency response to the spreading phenomena. For example, firefighters need to know, to identify the endangered locations, where the fire may spread by $t = 8$ hours.

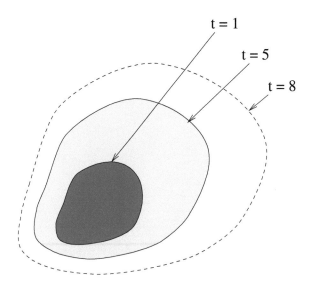

Figure 19.3: Predicted spread of the fire.

The preceding prediction may need some modification when the sensor sends some new information or when there are some blocks in the way of the spreading fire.

The forward prediction can be interactively modified when new data are received. Suppose that the sensor sends a new image every 4 hours. Then when the next image arrives at time $t = 9$ hours, the interpolation can be recomputed based on the latest pair of snapshots, that is, using only the snapshots for the times $t = 5$ and $t = 9$.

In addition, there may be some static blocks of the fire, for example, lakes, rivers, or some rocky or sandy land areas or dynamic blocks of the fire, for example, fire extinguishing foam or water spread by the firefighters. The interaction of the fire and these blocking objects can be modeled using the *Block* operator.

For example, suppose that, as shown in Figure 19.4, a fire starts in one portion of a forest and begins to spread but there is a lake, which acts as a natural block to the fire

Suppose further that the firefighters can choose, as shown in Figure 19.5, from the following three strategies that determine which way a number of helicopters fly and drop foam in the way of the fire:

1. All fly north.

2. All fly east.

3. Some fly east and some fly west.

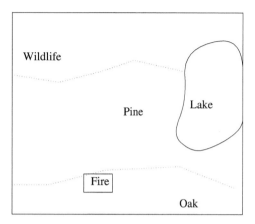

Figure 19.4: A fire starts in a forest.

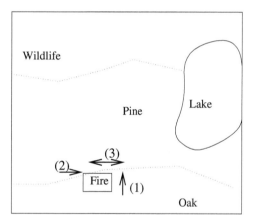

Figure 19.5: Three strategies for blocking the fire.

We model by a parametric rectangles relation $Strategy(x, y, t, s)$, where the attribute s indicates which strategy is used, the foam dropped by the helicopters. Let us assume that the current prediction for the spread of the fire is stored in relation *Fire* and the lake area in relation *Lake*. For example, in MLPQ/PReSTO, we can use the block operator to compute a more refined prediction for the spread of the fire at time 8 hours in case strategy (1) is used as follows:

$$Fire_{1,8} = Block((Lake \cup (\sigma_{s=1} \ Strategy)), Fire, 8)$$

Similarly, we can estimate the spread of the fire at any time and for any strategy.

19.1.2 Visualization

We can use the MLPQ/PReSTO animation operator to show the spread of the fire and the blocking agents. Figure 19.6 shows an example of using approximation by a set of parametric rectangles to predict the spread of a fire for time instances $t = 6$ and $t = 10$ based on the snapshots at times $t = 0$ and $t = 2$ hours. The images at $t = 0$ and $t = 2$ were simplified from actual satellite images. We see in pictures $t = 6$ and $t = 10$ that the fire spreads to the east and slightly to the north until the lake blocks its spread.

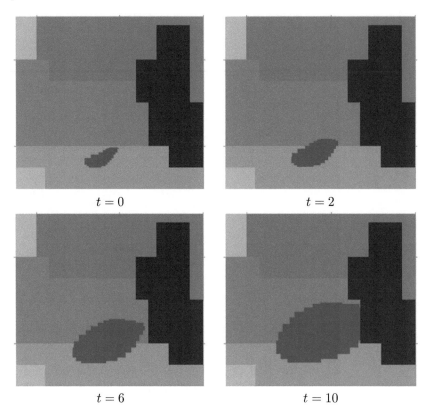

$t = 0$ $t = 2$

$t = 6$ $t = 10$

Figure 19.6: Predictions for the fire spread.

We also created in MLPQ/PReSTO a *Strategy* relation that contained descriptions of the three strategies using parametric rectangles. Figure 19.7 shows the result of the predictions at time instances $t = 6$ and $t = 10$ when both the lake and the foam spread by the firefighters blocks the spread of the fire.

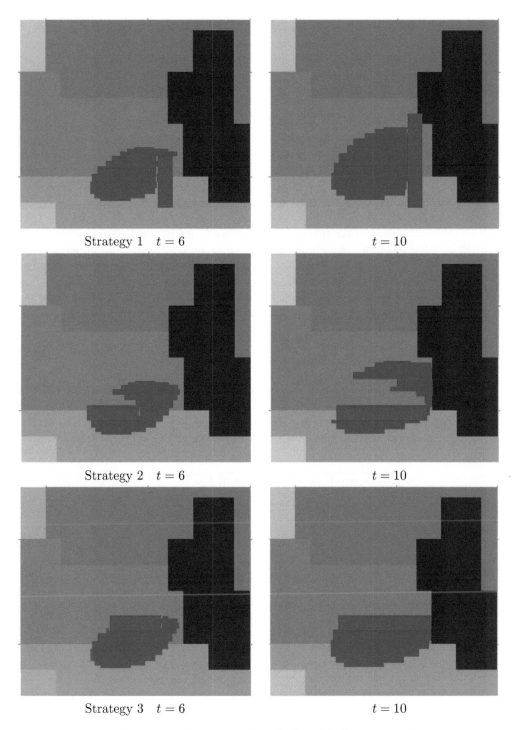

Figure 19.7: Fire spread with three blocking strategies.

The visualization allows some qualitative assessments. For example, by time $t = 10$ hours, strategy (1) blocks the fire completely in the east and strategy (3) in the north direction. On the other hand, strategy (2) is risky because it leaves a part of the fire escaping to the north of the foam block.

19.1.3   A Decision Support System

Now we describe a simple decision support system that allows firefighters to choose among the available strategies. Let B_W, B_P, and B_O be the total area burned of the wildlife reserve, the pine forest, and the oak forest, respectively. First for each strategy and any time instance of interest, we calculate using the area operator of MLPQ/PReSTO the values of B_W, B_P, and B_O.

Suppose that the three regions have different priorities for protection. For example, the wildlife preserve may be relatively more important than the pine forest per unit area. To reflect these priorities we associate with each region a different damage weight. Let α_W, α_P, and α_O be the damage weights associated with a unit area of wildlife reserve, pine, and oak, respectively. Then the total damage can be estimated by the following formula:

$$Damage = \alpha_W B_W + \alpha_P B_P + \alpha_O B_O$$

The decision support system can quickly compare the estimated damages for a set of possible strategies and find the one with the least damage. For example, assuming that $\alpha_W = 3$, $\alpha_P = 2$, and $\alpha_O = 1$, the decision support system would compute the values of the following table:

Strategy	Burned area at $t = 10$			Estimated total
	Wildlife	Pine	Oak	damage
1	0	11203.32	6048.95	28455.59
2	0	6902.92	3292.87	17098.76
3	0	4916.63	6875.0	16708.26

The computation shows that the best of the three strategies is strategy (3) because it leaves the least damage after ten hours.

19.2   Data Mining

Many data mining algorithms derive categories of objects. For example, Chapter 17 described support vector machines and decision trees. Our emphasis in this section is not on particular algorithms but on the general idea of representing and querying categories. The representation and querying of categories is often cumbersome with much software required outside of the database system. Hence several proposals suggest to represent categories by constraint relations, which can be easily queried.

In general, when we are considering n variables $x_1, \ldots, x_n$ that range over either the rational or the interger numbers, each category is a polyhedral space within $dom(x_1) \times \ldots \times dom(x_n)$. These polyhedral spaces are naturally represented by constraint databases.

Example 19.2.1 An art foundation is looking for a new director who is both artistic and reliable. The art foundation is flooded with applicants for the advertised position. The foundation is uncertain about how to make a wise selection and turns for help to an executive headhunting company.

Being methodological, the executive headhunting company gets from applicants resume and available credit reports the following information:

1. The number of exhibitions made by the applicant.

2. The current amount of personal debt of the applicant (measured in multiples of $1000).

Based on these data, the company creates the following database.

Applicant

Name	Exhibitions	Debt
Brown	70	15
Green	80	50
Red	10	40
⋮	⋮	⋮

For example, applicant Red had only ten exhibitions and has a $40,000.00 personal debt. The headhunting company conducted several previous personality studies which identified based on the above two variables the categories of artistic and reliable persons as regions in the plane shown in Figure 19.8. The company represents these regions using a constraint database as follows.

Personality

Type	Exhibitions	Debt	
t	x	y	$t = $ "Artistic", $x \geq 40, x \leq 90, y \geq 10, y \leq 60, y \geq -x + 80$
t	x	y	$t = $ "Reliable", $x \leq 80, y \geq -20, y \leq 20, y \leq x, y \geq -x$

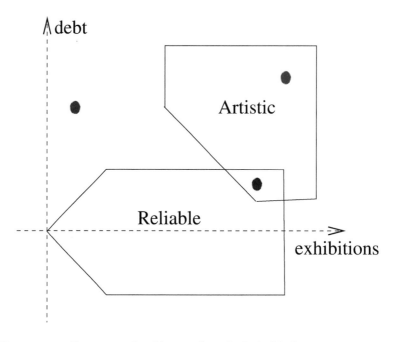

Figure 19.8: Categories for "Artistic" and "Reliable."

Given the above information, the company can find the applicants who are both artistic and reliable using the following SQL query.

```
CREATE VIEW    Promising_Candidate(Name)
SELECT         Name
FROM           Applicant AS A,  Personality AS P
WHERE          A.Exhibition = P.Exhibition  AND
               A.Debt = P.Debt  AND
               P.Type = "Artistic"
INTERSECT
SELECT         Name
FROM           Applicant AS A,  Personality AS P
WHERE          A.Exhibition = P.Exhibition  AND
               A.Debt = P.Debt  AND
               P.Type = "Reliable"
```

Hence the company reports to the art foundation that Brown is a promising candidate for the position of art foundation director because according to the personality type analysis Brown is both artistic and reliable.

The above simple example only hints at the possibilities that constraint databases provide for data mining applications. More complex categories using hundreds of variables can be also described, but they are beyond the scope of this textbook.

19.3 Model-Based Diagnosis

Model-based diagnosis is concerned with fault detection and the identification of faulty components in systems. Model-based diagnosis identifies which component of a system affect which observable variables, thereby localizing the testing of each component to those observable variables.

Although there are many proposals for model-based diagnosis, they often ignore the importance of the issue of storing and manipulating in a convenient way the model-based diagnosis data. Hence while the model-based diagnois theories are sound and well-established, they require in general much software implementation effort before they can be applied. In constrast, an innovative and practical proposal suggests constraint databases as a solution to the complex implementation requirements. Some of the ideas of that proposal are illustrated in the following example.

Example 19.3.1 Consider a system with a, b, c, d, e inputs and f, g outputs. Such a system can be illustrated as follows.

$$a, b, c, d, e \longrightarrow \boxed{\text{Circuit}} \longrightarrow f, g$$

Suppose we need to test whether the system is correct. If any fault is detected, then we need to find the faulty component. Hence let us take a look at the components of the system with their intended functions. This system consists of three multipliers and two adders as shown below.

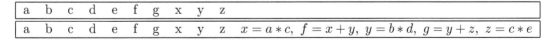

Let us label the components from left to right as M_1, A_1, M_2, A_2 and M_3. The first question is how to represent the system. We can represent the intended behavior of the system by the following constraint database.

Design

a	b	c	d	e	f	g	x	y	z	
a	b	c	d	e	f	g	x	y	z	$x = a*c,\ f = x+y,\ y = b*d,\ g = y+z,\ z = c*e$

Suppose that instead of the above low-level, component-by-component description of the system, one would like to know how the observable input and output variables are related to each other. Using constraint databases, this problem can be solved by the following simple SQL query.

CREATE VIEW	Intent(a, b, c, d, e, f, g)
SELECT	a, b, c, d, e, f, g
FROM	Design

The above simple query works because constraint database queries are evaluated by quantifier elimination. In particular, the existentially quantified variables x, y, z are eliminated. As a result, a constraint database system returns the following output relation.

Intent

a	b	c	d	e	f	g	
a	b	c	d	e	f	g	$f = a*c + b*d, \quad g = b*d + c*e$

The *Intent* relation is an example of a *context analytical redundancy constraint*, or *CARC*, which is a constraint on only the observable variables and derived from the system specifications.

A *context set* is any groups of system components. Some context sets are more meaningful or important than others because the components in those context sets work closer together than in a random group of the system components. Model-based diagnosis focuses on those more important context sets. In the above example, the following context sets may be identified as important.

1. $C_1 = \{M_1, M_2, A_1\}$

2. $C_2 = \{M_2, M_3, A_2\}$

3. $C_3 = \{M_1, M_3, A_1, A_2\}$

Similarly to the above SQL query, we can derive one or more *CARC*s for any context set. Each *CARC* tells us the intended effects of the context set on the observable variables. For example, one *CARC* for each of the above three contex sets would be the following.

1. $CARC_1 = \{f = a*c + b*d\}$

2. $CARC_2 = \{g = b*d + c*e\}$

3. $CARC_3 = \{f - g = a*c - c*e\}$

A hitting set of a collection of sets is a set that contains at least one element from each set. Model-based diagnosis identifies a hitting set of the above chosen context sets. That further enables the generation of testing examples that test simultaneously all the chosen context sets. The selection of the hitting sets is also based on constraint databases. The details can be found in the bibliographic references.

Now suppose that we are given a set of testing results. The following example explains how constraint databases can be used to find whether the test results conform to the design specifications.

Example 19.3.2 Suppose that the testing results are given in the following relation.

Behavior

a	b	c	d	e	f	g
5	4	2	3	0	22	12
1	7	0	9	2	63	63
⋮	⋮	⋮	⋮	⋮	⋮	⋮

The following SQL query checks whether any of the testing results indicates a fault in the system, that is, that some of the test results contradict the intent of the designer.

CREATE VIEW	Fault(a, b, c, d, e, f, g)
SELECT	a, b, c, d, e, f, g
FROM	Behavior
MINUS	
SELECT	a, b, c, d, e, f, g
FROM	Intent

Finally, suppose that somebody redesigned the system with a fewer number of components. Hence in principle it would be be beneficial for a company to use the more efficient system. How can the company verify that the new design is logically equivalent to the old design? This problem can be solved using constraint databases.

Example 19.3.3 Suppose that the new design is described in the $Design2(a, b, c, d, e, f, g, s, t, w)$ relation. Note that this design uses different internal components and variables. To test whether the second design is logically equivalent to the previous design, we can use the following SQL query.

CREATE VIEW	Difference(a, b, c, d, e, f, g)
(SELECT	a, b, c, d, e, f, g
FROM	Design
MINUS	
SELECT	a, b, c, d, e, f, g
FROM	Design2)
UNION	
(SELECT	a, b, c, d, e, f, g
FROM	Design2
MINUS	
SELECT	a, b, c, d, e, f, g
FROM	Design)

If the constraint database returns an empty relation, then the two designs are logically equivalent.

Bibliographic Notes

The forest fire prediction system described in Section 19.1 is based on Cai and Revesz [65]. Several earlier fire spread models, like BURN by M. Veach et al. [418] and FIREGIS by Goncalves and Diogo [158] use some kind of cellular automata [427], which divide the region into a finite grid of square cells and assume that the fuel, wind, and terrain parameters are uniform in each cell. The rule of how a fire propagates from cell to cell is based on Rothermel's model [357] in BURN and FIREGIS and also in related systems like BEHAVE [22]. These system focus on predicting the local behavior and characteristics of the fires, for example, the spread rate, the flame length, and the intensity.

Other fire spread models, like the FIRE! system [424], represent the fire front using a vector data model and use Huygen's principle [17] and elliptical growth model [355] to expand the fire fronts in two dimensions. Yuan [435, 436] represents time as an independent object linked to the objects in the spatial domain. None of these earlier models supports modeling the interaction between the fire and the firefighting agents and provides complete decision support for firefighting like [65] provides.

There are several general textbooks on data mining, for example, Fayyad et al. [126] and Han and Kamber [189]. Geist [147], Johnson et al. [212], and Trurmeaux and Vrain [407] apply constraint databases to data mining and knowledge discovery. Lakshmanan et al. [253] apply constraints for data mining in a different context.

Model-based diagnosis with constraint databases is proposed by Gómez-López et al. [157]. Example 19.3.1 is based on [157].

Exercises

1. Suppose that weeds at time $t = 0$ occupy the region $[8, 15] \times [10, 36]$ meters and first spread south with a speed of 2 meters per week until $t = 10$ weeks. Then they spread in all directions (east, west, south, and north) until $t = 30$ weeks with a speed of 3 meters per week.

   (a) Represent the weeds by a MLPQ/PReSTO relation and animate their unchecked growth on the computer screen.

   (b) Suppose that you are allowed to apply a weed killer only at the rate of 9 square meters per week. The weed killer is effective for 5 weeks after being sprayed and a 1-meter-wide band can block the spread of the weeds. How would you apply the weed killer? Express your plan in a MLPQ/PReSTO relation, and visualize it at several time instances on the computer screen.

2. Find remote sensing images of any spreading phenomenon at times $t_1, \ldots, t_n$ where $n \geq 5$. Then do the following:

   (a) Apply the approximation algorithm in Section 18.6.2 for each adjacent pair of images, that is, for each pair of images at times t_i and t_{i+1} for each $1 \leq i \leq n - 1$.

   (b) Use each (t_i, t_{i+1}) pair to estimate the value of the spread at t_{i+2} for each $1 \leq i \leq n - 2$.

   (c) Let A_i be the actual and E_i be the estimated area at time t_i. Find the percent difference in the two areas, that is, find:

   $$\Delta_i = \frac{area(A_i - E_i) + area(E_i - A_i)}{area(A_i)}$$

   How well does the approximation work? What is the average value of Δ_i? What factors may have contributed to the average being large or small?

3. Continuing the previous exercise use the MLPQ/PReSTO system to do the following:

   (a) Enter the approximation between every adjacent time image into a MLPQ/PReSTO relation.

   (b) Define at least two blocking agents that may control the spread. For example, a flood may be blocked by a mountain and water pollution sweeping into the soil may be blocked by rocks. Find the spread in the presence of the blocking agents.

(c) Visualize at several time instances the spread both with and without the blocking agents. How effective are they in controlling or stopping the spread?

20

Indexing

Applications such as air traffic control and weather forecasting require the monitoring of a large number of moving objects; hence they require large spatio-temporal databases. Efficient query processing for large spatio-temporal databases is an important challenge.

For example, when monitoring thousands of airplanes and clouds, even simple-looking queries like *"find all the airplanes that are currently traveling within some cloud"* become difficult to evaluate in a naive approach that tries to find for each pair of airplane and cloud whether they intersect. *Indexing* is a way to efficiently evaluate such queries.

In this chapter we assume that the moving objects are represented as linear parametric rectangles, and we describe an indexing method for *linear parametric rectangle* relations. For the rest of this chapter *parametric rectangle* will always mean linear parametric rectangle.

Section 20.1 describes *minimum bounding parametric rectangles*, which are parametric rectangles that enclose a set of other parametric rectangles. This section presents an algorithm to find a minimum bounding parametric rectangle.

Section 20.2 describes *parametric R-trees*, or PR-trees. This is a tree index structure in which each leaf node is a parametric rectangle and each internal node is a minimum bounding parametric rectangle for the leaves below it. This section describes algorithms for searching, insertion, and deletion of parametric rectangles from the PR-tree.

Section 20.3 describes an extension of the PR-trees from indexing moving objects that are linear parametric rectangles to indexing more general moving objects that are described by linear constraints.

P. Revesz, *Introduction to Databases: From Biological to Spatio-Temporal,*
Texts in Computer Science, DOI 10.1007/978-1-84996-095-3_20,
© Springer-Verlag London Limited 2010

20.1   Minimum Bounding Parametric Rectangles

The *minimum bounding parametric rectangle* (MBPR) of a set of parametric rectangles S is a parametric rectangle r such that:

1. r contains all the parametric rectangles in S.

2. The area of the project of r onto the (x_i, t) space is minimized for each $i = 1, \ldots, d$.

Let us consider how to compute the minimum bounding parametric rectangle. Suppose that S is a set of d-dimensional parametric rectangles. Let R be the MBPR of S. It is easy to see that the start time of R is the minimum of the start times of the parametric rectangles in S and the end time of R is the maximum of the end times of the parametric rectangles in S. Let $t_{\min}$ and $t_{\max}$ denote the start and end times of R, then

$$t_{\min} = \min_{r \in S}(r.t^{[}) \quad \text{and} \quad t_{\max} = \max_{r \in S}(r.t^{]})$$

Hence the main task of computing R is to compute the functions for the lower and upper bounds of R in each x_i dimension. For each $i = 1, \ldots, d$, the projection of each parametric rectangle in S onto the (x_i, t) space corresponds to a trapezium with four extreme points, as shown in Figure 20.1 (left). The projection of S onto the (x_i, t) space corresponds to a set P of $4|S|$ extreme points in the (x_i, t) space. Let H_i be the convex hull of P. We show that the lower and upper bounds of R for the x_i are extensions of some edges of the convex hull H_i, which can be computed efficiently. For example, the thin solid line polygon in Figure 20.1 is the convex hull of four parametric rectangles in the (x_i, t) space, and the bold line trapezium in Figure 20.1 (right) is their MBPR projected on the (x_i, t) space.

Lemma 20.1.1 For each x_i, let S_i be the projection of a set S of parametric rectangles onto the (x_i, t) space. Then the lower and upper bounds of the minimum bounding parametric rectangle R of S projected onto (x_i, t) overlaps some edge of the convex hull of S_i.

Proof: Let H_i be the convex hull of S_i. It is easy to see that the lower bound of R must touch at least one extreme point of the lower half of the convex hull. Otherwise, we can shift the lower bound upward until it touches one point. This shift only reduces the area of the trapezium, showing that R is not minimal as required in condition (2) for MBPRs.

Now let us prove that the lower bound of R overlaps one edge of H_i. Suppose the lower bound of R touches the convex hull H_i at the extreme

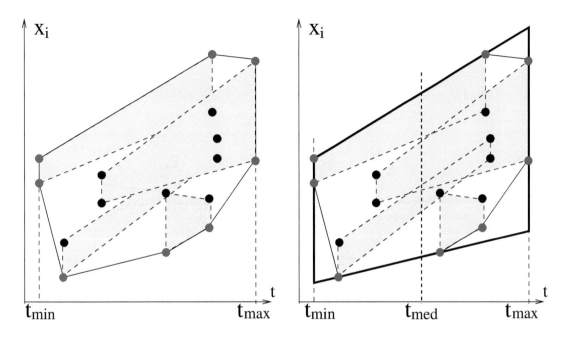

Figure 20.1: The convex hull and MBPR of parametric rectangles.

point P_j as shown in Figure 20.2. Let P_{j-1} be the adjacent extreme point to the left of P_j and P_{j+1} be the adjacent extreme point to the right of P_j. Suppose also that the extension of $P_{j-1}P_j$ intersects with the left bound $t = t_{\min}$ and the right bound $t = t_{\max}$ at points A and B. The extension of $P_j P_{j+1}$ intersects with the left and right bounds at points C and D. Then the lower bound should fall in the range between AB and CD. Assume that the lower bound is the bold line EF, as shown in Figure 20.2. Let $t_{\mathrm{med}} = (t_{\min} + t_{\max})/2$. If P_j is to the right of the line $t = t_{med}$ then the height of AP_jE is greater than the height of BP_jF. We substitute EF by AB and get a parametric rectangle R' that includes all the parametric rectangles in S. The area of R' is

$$area(R') = area(R) + area(BP_jF) - area(AP_jE)$$

Because the triangle AP_jE is similar to BP_jF and the height of AP_jE is greater than that of BP_jF, the area of AP_jE is greater than that of BP_jF. Hence $area(R') < area(R)$. Then R is not an MBPR, because that contradicts minimality condition (2) for MBPR. Hence the lower bound must overlap AB. If P_j is to the left of the line $t = t_{med}$, we similarly prove that the choice of CD is better than that of EF. Hence, EF cannot be an optimal choice; it is either AB or CD, and in each case the minimum bounding parametric rectangle overlaps one edge of the convex hull.   ■

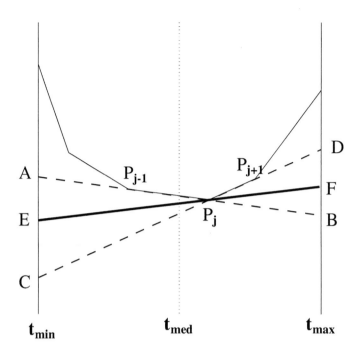

Figure 20.2: Lower hull and lower bound.

Lemma 20.1.2 The lower and upper bounds of the minimum bounding parametric rectangle R of S projected onto (x_i, t) are the extensions of the edges of H_i that intersect the median line $t = t_{med}$ where $t_{med} = 0.5(t_{\min} + t_{\max})$.

Proof: By Lemma 20.1.1, if $P_{j-1}P_j$ is the edge of H that overlaps the lower bound of R, then P_j must be to the right of the median line $t = t_{\mathrm{med}}$, otherwise, by substituting $P_j P_{j+1}$ for $P_{j-1}P_j$ we would get a bound parametric rectangle R' whose area is less than that of R, as shown in Figure 20.3. Similarly P_{j-1} must be to the left of the median line. Thus the lower bound of R overlaps the edge of the lower half of H_i that intersects with the median line $t = t_m$. Similarly, the upper bound of R overlaps the edge of the upper half of H_i that intersects with the median line. ∎

For example, Figure 20.1 shows that in the x_i dimension the lower and upper bounds of the MBPR of a set of parametric rectangles are extensions of those edges of the convex hull that intersect the line $t = t_{\mathrm{med}}$.

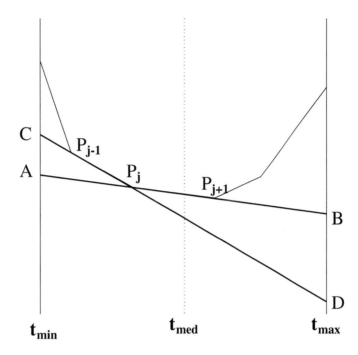

Figure 20.3: P_j is to the left of t_{med}; AB is a better bound than CD.

Theorem 20.1.1 The minimum bounding parametric rectangle R of a set S with n number of d-dimensional parametric rectangles can be computed in $O(d\, n \log n)$ time.

Proof: It is easy to see that $t_{\max}$ and $t_{\min}$ can be computed in $O(n)$ time. For each $i = 1, \ldots, d$, let S_i be the projection of S onto the $(x_i,\ t)$ space; we can compute the corresponding extreme points of S_i in $O(n)$ time by substituting the start and end times of each parametric rectangle in S into the parametric functions. The convex hull of S_i can be computed in $O(n \log n)$ time. We can also find the edges of H_i that intersect with t_{med} in $O(n)$ time. By Lemmas 20.1.1 and 20.1.2, the functions of the lower and upper bounds of R in x_i are the functions of the edges of H_i that intersect with t_{med}. Therefore the bounds of R in x_i can be computed in $O(n) + O(n \log n) + O(n) = O(n \log n)$ time. Hence, for d dimensions, the complete R can be computed in $O(d\, n \log n)$ time. ∎

The algorithm that finds minimum bounding parametric rectangles is outlined next.

FindMBPR(S)

input: S, a set of parametric rectangles
output: R_S, the minimum bounding parametric rectangle of S
$t_{min} = \min_{r \in S}(r.t^{[})$
$t_{max} = \max_{r \in S}(r.t^{]})$
$t_{med} = (t_{min} + t_{max})/2$
for each dimension x_i **do**
  Find S_i the set of extreme points of projection (x_i, t) of S
  Compute the convex hull H_i of S_i
  Find the edges of H_i that intersect with t_{med}
  Construct $x_i^{[}$ and $x_i^{]}$
end-for

Example 20.1.1 Let us calculate the MBPR of the following parametric rectangles:

ID	X	Y	T
r1	$[7t + 30,\ 7t + 90]$	$[5t + 50,\ 6t + 100]$	$[0,\ 10]$
r12	$[4t + 70,\ 3t + 90]$	$[6t + 45,\ 6t + 55]$	$[2,\ 10]$

Figure 20.4 (left) shows that the projection of r_1 in the (x, t) space already includes that of r_{12}. Hence the MBPR of the two is r_1 in the x dimension.

Figure 20.4 (right) shows the projection of r_1 and r_{12} in the (y, t) space. The dashed line segments AB and BC form the lower half of the convex hull of r_1 and r_{12} in (y, t) space, where A is $(0, 50)$, B is $(2, 57)$, and C is $(10, 100)$. Because the midline crosses BC, the lower bound of the MBPR of r_1 and r_{12} is the extension of BC and the upper bound is the same as the upper bound of r_1 in the y dimension. Note that the line extending BC is $5.375t + 46.25$. Hence the MBPR of r_1 and r_{12} is:

$$([7t + 30,\ 7t + 90], [5.375t + 46.25,\ 6t + 100], [0, 10])$$

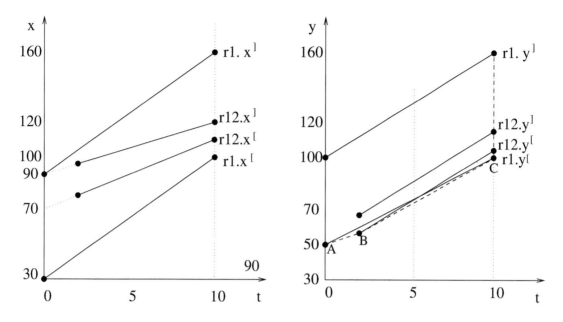

Figure 20.4: Find MBPR of r_1 and r_{12}.

Airplane

ID	X	Y	T
r4	$[7t + 30,\ 7t + 50]$	$[6t + 80,\ 6t + 100]$	$[0,\ 10]$
r5	$[12t + 30,\ 12t + 40]$	$[5t + 50,\ 5t + 65]$	$[0,\ 10]$
r6	$[6t + 75,\ 7t + 90]$	$[8t + 70,\ 8t + 80]$	$[2,\ 10]$
r7	$[0,\ 15]$	$[5t + 40,\ 5t + 55]$	$[0,\ 9]$
r8	$[0,\ 12]$	$[4t + 20,\ 4t + 40]$	$[1,\ 10]$
r9	$[30,\ 50]$	$[7t + 10,\ 7t + 20]$	$[0,\ 10]$
r10	$[-5t + 80,\ -5t + 100]$	$[2t,\ 3t + 20]$	$[0,\ 10]$
r11	$[-6t + 60,\ -6t + 70]$	$[-3t + 30,\ -2t + 40]$	$[0,\ 10]$

Example 20.1.2 Relation *Airplane* describes the movement of eight airplanes as parametric rectangles. We can compute using the preceding algorithm that the minimum bounding parametric rectangle for the airplanes r_4, r_5, r_6 is r_1, for the airplanes r_7, r_8, r_9 is r_2, and for the airplanes r_{10} and r_{11} is r_3, shown in relation *AirplaneMBPR*.

AirplaneMBPR

ID	X	Y	T
r1	$[7t+30,\ 7t+90]$	$[5t+50,\ 6t+100]$	$[0,\ 10]$
r2	$[0,\ 50]$	$[5t+10,\ 5t+55]$	$[0,\ 10]$
r3	$[-6t+60,\ -5t+100]$	$[0,\ t+40]$	$[0,\ 10]$

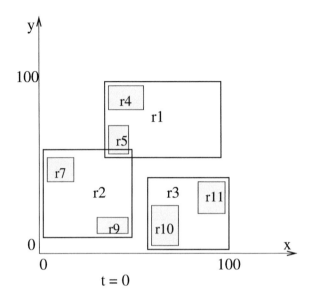

Figure 20.5: MBPRs for the airplanes at time $t = 0$.

Figure 20.5 shows the airplanes (shaded) and their MBPRs at $t = 0$ and Figure 20.6 shows those at $t = 10$. Note that r_6 and r_8 are not shown in Figure 20.5 because they do not exist at $t = 0$. Similarly, r_7 is not shown in Figure 20.6 because it does not exist at $t = 10$.

20.2 The Parametric R-Tree Index Structure

The parametric R-tree (PR-tree) is an index structure for parametric rectangles. It is a height-balanced tree in which each node has between $M/2$ and M children, where M is a constant depending on the page size. Each node of a PR-tree is associated with a minimum bounding parametric rectangle.

Example 20.2.1 A PR-tree with $M = 3$ for the Airplanes relation is shown in Figure 20.7.

PR-trees are useful for efficiently *searching* the databases in answering queries of the form *"find all objects that intersect a parametric rectangle*

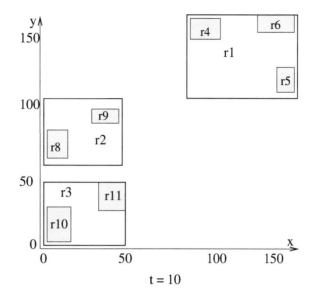

Figure 20.6: MBPRs for the airplanes at time $t = 10$.

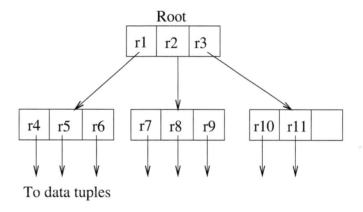

Figure 20.7: A PR-tree.

A." PR-trees are also dynamic index structures that allow *insertions* and *deletions* of moving objects. The next three sections describe these three operations on PR-trees.

20.2.1   Searching

Given a parametric rectangle R, *searching* a PR-tree returns all the parametric rectangles that intersect with R. The search starts from the root of

the PR-tree and moves down to those children that contain an MBPR or
parametric rectangle that intersects with R.

By Theorem 16.2.2 it can be checked in $O(d)$ time whether two d-
dimensional linear parametric rectangles intersect. If one child is always
chosen, then because the PR-tree is always kept balanced, the search can be
done in logarithmic time in the number of stored parametric rectangles. In
practice, like in several other spatial search structures, there are sometimes
several children that intersect R and need to be explored.

20.2.2   Insertion

During *insertion* of a parametric rectangle R into a *PR*-tree, we go down
from the root of the PR-tree to find an appropriate leaf node to insert R.
At each step we update the current MBPR of the chosen subtree by adding
R to it.

If there are any nodes that overflow, i.e., exceed the maximum size
bound, then we *split* them and then propagate upward the split while
changing accordingly the MBPRs of the affected nodes. The following defines more precisely the criteria for choosing the appropriate subtree and
splitting.

Appropriate Subtree: As we saw in the case of searching, a key performance issue is the number of children visited at each node during the
search. We would like to keep that number as low as possible. That implies that we should keep the MBPRs as small as possible. Therefore, when
inserting a new parametric rectangle, the *insertion* algorithm always tries
to add it to the subtree whose associated MBPR needs the least volume
enlargement to include it. The least volume enlargement can be defined as
follows.

If R is any d-dimensional parametric rectangle, then the *volume* of R,
denoted $Vol(R)$, is the volume of the polyhedron P that contains exactly
the $(x_1, \ldots, x_d, t)$ points defined by R.

Because for each time instance t' between $from$ and to, the intersection
of P with the plane $t = t'$ is a rectangle with area $\prod_{i=1}^{d}(X_i^] - X_i^[)(t')$, the
volume of R is the integral of the area function, that is:

$$Vol(R) \quad = \quad \int_{t^[}^{t^]} \prod_{i=1}^{d}(x_i^] - x_i^[) \, dt \qquad (20.1)$$

Example 20.2.2 The volume of r_1 is:

$$
\begin{aligned}
Vol(r_1) &= \int_0^{10} ((7t+90)-(7t+30))\,((6t+100)-(5t+50))dt \\
&= \int_0^{10} 60(t+50)dt \\
&= 60(t^2/2+50t)\big|_0^{10} \\
&= 60(50+500) = 33,000
\end{aligned}
$$

Let $V = Vol(FindMBPR(r_1, r_{12}))$, i.e., the MBPR of r_1 and r_{12} of Example 20.1.1. Similarly to the preceding we can calculate the following:

$$
\begin{aligned}
V &= \int_0^{10} ((7t+90)-(7t+30))\,((6t+100)-(5.375t+46.25))dt \\
&= \int_0^{10} 60(0.625t+53.75)dt \\
&= 60(0.625t^2/2+53.75t)\big|_0^{10} \\
&= 60(0.625t^2/2+53.75t)\big|_0^{10} \\
&= 60(568.75) = 34,125
\end{aligned}
$$

Suppose we would like to insert a new parametric rectangle R into one child of an internal node E with children $E_1, \ldots, E_p$. Let M_j be the MBPR of E_j for $1 \le j \le p$. Then we choose the child that needs the least enlargement to include R, that is:

$$
\min_j \; Enlarge(M_j, R) = \min_j \; (Vol(FindMBPR(M_j, R)) - Vol(M_j))
$$

Example 20.2.3 Suppose we would like to add tuple r_{12} of Example 20.1.1 to the *PR*-tree in Example 20.1.2.

We start at the root of the PR-tree and try to add r_{12} to r_1, r_2, or r_3. This requires computation of the enlargement of each of r_1, r_2, and r_3 with r_{12}. We compute, using the results of Example 20.2.2, that:

$$
Enlarge(r_1, \; r_{12}) = Vol(FindMBPR(r_1, r_{12})) - Vol(r_1) = 1125
$$

Similarly, we can compute $Enlarge(r_2, \; r_{12})$ and $Enlarge(r_3, \; r_{12})$ to find which one needs the least enlargement and is chosen. We leave the rest of the calculations as an exercise.

Node Splitting: When a new entry is added to a node E with M entries an overflow occurs. In this case, it is necessary to split the collection of $M + 1$ entries into two nodes. The splitting is done in a way that results in small MBPRs for the two split halves of the node.

First we find among the $M + 1$ entries the two entries that are most undesirable to keep within a node. For those two entries their MBPR has a volume that is large compared to the sum of their volumes. Therefore, we are looking for the pair with the *maximum volume increase*, that is:

$$\max_{r_i, r_j \in E} Vol(FindMBPR(r_i, r_j)) - (Vol(r_i) + Vol(r_j))$$

Once we find r_i and r_j, we know that they are not desirable to keep together. Therefore, we choose r_i and r_j as the first elements of two new groups. Each of the remaining parametric rectangles is inserted into either the group containing r_i or the group containing r_j, depending on which would cause a smaller increase in the current MBPR of the two groups.

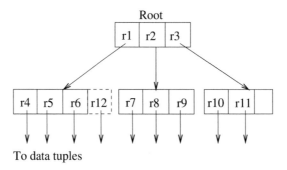

Figure 20.8: Inserting r_{12} into r_1.

Example 20.2.4 Let us continue Example 20.2.3. Suppose that the maximum allowed number of children of each node is 3 and the minimum required number of children is 2. In that case, as shown in Figure 20.8, an overflow occurs after the insertion of r_{12} into r_1. Therefore, we need to split r_1 into two new nodes r_{13} and r_{14}.

For each pair of children of r_1, we compute the volume increase of their minimum bounding parametric rectangles. (We leave the details as an exercise.) We find that r_4 and r_{12} are the least desirable to keep together. Therefore, we put r_4 into the new node r_{13} and r_{12} into the new node r_{14}. Next we add r_5 to r_{14}, because $Enlarge(r_{14}, r_5) < Enlarge(r_{13}, r_5)$. Then we add r_6 to r_{13}, because $Enlarge(r_{13}, r_6) < Enlarge(r_{14}, r_6)$.

Finally, we remove r_1 and insert r_{13} and r_{14} into the root as shown in Figure 20.9 (1). This causes the splitting of the root, and the height of the

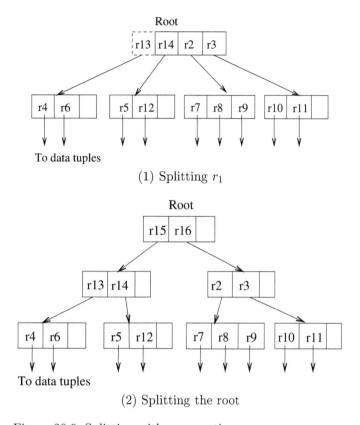

(1) Splitting r_1

(2) Splitting the root

Figure 20.9: Splitting with propagation.

tree increases by 1, as shown in Figure 20.9 (2). The process of the splitting of the root is similar to the splitting of r_1 and is also left as an exercise.

Theorem 20.2.1 The insertion of a parametric rectangle into a PR-tree can be done in $O(dM^2 \log_M n)$ time, where M is the maximum number of children per node, d is the dimension, and n is the number of parametric rectangles.

Proof: As we go down the tree we need at each level to find the appropriate subtree and update the MBPR of the chosen subtree. By Theorem 20.1.1 the computation of the MBPR of two parametric rectangles takes $O(d)$ time. The computation of the volume of a parametric rectangle depends on its dimension and takes $O(d)$ time. There are at most M entries in a node. Hence computing their enlargements and selecting the minimum out of those requires $O(dM)$ time at each level. The height of a PR-tree with n parametric rectangles is $\log_M n$. Therefore, going down the PR-tree to find an appropriate leaf node requires $O(dM \log_M n)$ time.

If we add the new entry to a node that has less than M entries, then splitting is not required and we are done. Otherwise, we need to split the last nonleaf node and then propagate the split upward. Each split requires finding the pair of nodes that are least desirable together. This requires M^2 computations of MBPRs of two parametric rectangles; hence this can be done by Theorem 20.1.1 in $O(dM^2)$ time. To add each of the $M - 2$ other entries to either of the two requires $O(dM)$ time. Because the height of a PR-tree with n parametric rectangles is $\log_M n$, the total time for splitting including propagation upward is $O(dM^2 \log_M n)$.

Finally, note that the PR-tree remains balanced after each insertion because the height of the PR-tree increases only when we split the root node, and that increases each path from the root to a leaf by one. ∎

Note that the value of M typically depends on the page size. We can minimize the number of page faults by letting M be the maximum number of entries that can be stored in a page.

20.2.3 Deletion

If we want to enable *deletion* of parametric rectangles, we do the following. We keep the IDs of the parametric rectangles in another search tree in which each entry has a pointer to the parametric rectangle record stored, just like the PR-tree has. After every insertion of a parametric rectangle R with ID i, we insert i and a pointer to R into the second search tree. (Instead of a second search tree we may also use a hashtable.)

To delete a parametric rectangle R with ID i, we first use the second search tree to look up a pointer to R, then delete i from the second search tree, which takes $O(\log_M n)$ time. We also delete R from the PR-tree. Let P be the parent of R. If P has at least $M/2$ children after the deletion, we simply recompute the MBPR of P and propagate this recomputation up to the root. In a PR-tree this takes $O(d \log_M n)$ time. Otherwise, that is, if P has fewer than $M/2$ children, then we delete P and reinsert the remaining children of P into the sub-PR-tree whose root is the parent of P. This takes $O(dM^3 \log_M n)$ time. If the parent of P has fewer than $M/2$ children, then the deletion is propagated upward in a similar manner. Therefore, we have the following.

Theorem 20.2.2 The deletion of a parametric rectangle from a PR-tree can be done in $O(dM^3 \log_M^2 n)$ time, where M is the maximum, $M/2$ is the minimum number of children per node, d is the dimension, and n is the number of parametric rectangles.

Example 20.2.5 Suppose that the current situation is the one shown in part (2) of Figure 20.9 and for some unexpected reason airplane r_{10} makes a forced landing. To reflect this change in the database, we need to delete the parametric rectangle with ID r_{10}. By searching for r_{10} in the second tree we find the pointer to the parametric rectangle whose ID is r_{10}. From there we search in the PR-tree for the parent of r_{10}. In this case it is r_3. Because r_3 contains only one other child, namely, r_{11}, it and r_{11} are deleted and r_{11} is reinserted in the sub-PR-tree with root r_{16}, which is the parent of r_3. We leave further details as an exercise.

20.3 Indexing Constraint Databases

So far we have assumed that moving objects are represented by parametric rectangles. However, PR-trees can be also used to index more general objects for which MBPRs can be found. For example, each linear constraint tuple T in d spatial and one temporal dimensions defines a moving object. We can find an MBPR that includes T by first taking the projection of T onto each (x_i, t) space. Then we find the extreme points of the projection and their convex hull in each (x_i, t) space, and from that we calculate as in Section 20.1 the lower and upper bounds of the MBPR in the x_i dimension.

The PR-tree for constraint objects would be like the PR-tree for parametric rectangles. For each constraint object we only store its MBPR and a pointer to the actual object.

Searching can be easily modified in the case of constraint objects. Suppose we want to find all objects that intersect a linear constraint object T. Then we find the MBPR of T; first we do the search as described in Section 20.2.1. The search returns all the intersections of MBPRs. Objects whose MBPRs intersect may not actually intersect. We call such cases *false hits*. Figure 20.10 shows an example of a false hit with one MBPR moving to the right containing an airplane and another MBPR moving upward containing a cloud. In the figure the objects do not intersect, even though their MBPRs intersect.

To eliminate false hits, for each returned MBPR we need to do a more refined check, that is, we have to check whether the conjunction of the constraints in T and the constraint of the object whose MBPR is returned is satisfiable. Then we only report those true hits where this more refined check also succeeds. The use of PR-trees greatly cuts down on the number of times the more refined check, which is computationally more expensive, needs to be performed.

The insertion and deletion operations can be similarly modified for constraint objects.

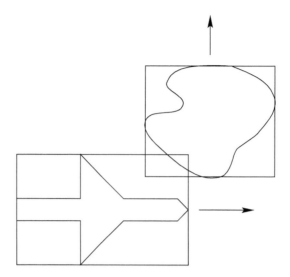

Figure 20.10: Example of a false hit.

20.4 The MaxCount Operator

Sometimes one needs to use an index not only to search for a particular item but to search for the total number of items with certain properties. That is still the case with spatiotemporal or moving objects indices. As a motivating example consider a set of airplanes, which are modeled as linearly moving objects with pre-established flight plans. Suppose, at any time, at most a constant number M of airplanes is allowed to be in the O'Hare airspace to avoid congestion. Suppose also a new airplane requests approval of its flight plan for entering the O'Hare airspace between times t_a and t_b. To avoid congestion, the air traffic controllers would need to test whether after adding the requested flight plan, the maximum number of airplanes in the O'Hare airspace at any time between t_a and t_b is still less than M. That congestion-testing problem can be abstracted as follows.

Definition 20.4.1 [MAXCOUNT] Let S be a set of moving points. Given a dynamic query space R defined by two moving points Q_1 and Q_2 as the lower-left and upper-right corners of R, and a time interval T, the MAXCOUNT operator finds the time $t_{\max}$ and the maximum number of points $M_{\max}$ in S that R can contain at any time instance within T.

We outline the following solution to the MAXCOUNT problem. First, we represent the moving points as static points in some representational space. Then we divide the representational space into small divisions called *buckets*. We create a bucket only if it contains at least one point. By having a small, fixed number of buckets and a potentially large database of varying number of moving points, each bucket will represent typically hundreds of moving points. Instead of representing each of these moving points individually, we establish a statistical approximation of the point distribution within each bucket. Therefore, a bucket will be able to estimate which subregion of it contains how many points. That is, we make each bucket *skew-aware* (see Section 20.4.1). Finally, we organize the buckets using an R-TREE structure. On each internal node of the R-TREE, we maintain the total count of the number of points of each of the buckets below it. Since the buckets do not overlap, insertion and deletion of moving points can be done in $O(\log B)$ time, where B is the number of buckets. Further, a moving point can be inserted into or deleted from a bucket in constant time (see Section 20.4.2).

20.4.1 Skew-Aware Buckets

Skew-aware buckets use a static representation of moving points. This static representation, called the *hex representation*, is defined as follows.

Definition 20.4.2 [Hex Representation] Given a linearly moving point in three dimensions

$$Q(t) = \begin{cases} q_x = v_x t + x_0 \\ q_y = v_y t + y_0 \\ q_z = v_z t + z_0 \end{cases}$$

the corresponding *hex representation* of $Q(t)$ is the tuple $(v_x, x_0, v_y, y_0, v_z, z_0)$.

If we divide the 6-dimensional space into axis-aligned hyper-rectangles, then each hyper-rectangle becomes a *bucket* B_i that contains the moving points whose hex representations fall inside the hyper-rectangle. For each such bucket B_i, we define the following.

Definition 20.4.3 [Bucket Dimension] Given a bucket B_i, its dimensions can be described by inequalities of the form:

$$\begin{aligned} v_{x,L_i} \le v_x < v_{x,U_i} &\quad \bigwedge \quad x_{0,L_i} \le x_0 < x_{0,U_i} \quad \bigwedge \\ v_{y,L_i} \le v_y < v_{y,U_i} &\quad \bigwedge \quad y_{0,L_i} \le y_0 < y_{0,U_i} \quad \bigwedge \\ v_{z,L_i} \le v_z < v_{z,U_i} &\quad \bigwedge \quad z_{0,L_i} \le z_0 < z_{0,U_i} \end{aligned}$$

where the subscripts with L indicate lower and the subscripts with U indicate upper bound constants. Similarly to the hex representation of Definition 20.4.2, we denote the bucket lower bound as:

$$(v_{x,L_i}, x_{0,L_i}, v_{y,L_i}, y_{0,L_i}, v_{z,L_i}, z_{0,L_i}) \tag{20.2}$$

and the bucket upper bound as:

$$(v_{x,U_i}, x_{0,U_i}, v_{y,U_i}, y_{0,U_i}, v_{z,U_i}, z_{0,U_i}). \tag{20.3}$$

A pair of lower and upper bounds is a concise description of the dimensions of B_i.

An important step in defining a skew aware bucket is *histogram*, which is a simple statistical analysis of the point distributions within it.

Definition 20.4.4 [Histogram] Given a bucket B_i and a constant s, we build *histograms* $h_{i,1},...,h_{i,6}$. Each histogram $h_{i,j}$ is built using the following three steps: (1) Project the points in bucket B_i onto the jth dimension. (2) Subdivide the projection into s equal-size intervals. (3) Record separately the number of points within each subdivision.

v_x	x_0	v_y	y_0	v_z	z_0
5.345	7.543	5.345	8.158	5.345	5.488
6.354	9.023	6.354	5.488	6.354	5.159
7.159	8.885	7.159	6.685	7.159	7.346
7.645	9.117	7.645	5.159	7.645	8.885
8.153	7.346	8.153	6.335	8.153	7.543
8.156	6.335	8.156	7.346	8.156	9.023
9.125	5.159	9.125	9.117	9.125	9.117
9.118	6.685	9.118	8.885	9.118	6.335
9.688	5.488	9.688	9.023	9.688	8.158
9.874	8.158	9.874	7.543	9.874	6.685

Table 20.1: The hex representation of a set of moving points.

Example 20.4.1 Supose bucket B_i has lower bound $(5, 5, 5, 5, 5, 5)$ and upper bound $(10, 10, 10, 10, 10, 10)$ and contains the points shown in Table 20.1. Also suppose the number of subdivisions is $s = 5$.

Figure 20.11 (a) shows $h_{i,1}$. It is built as follows. The projection onto velocity v_x is the first column of Table 20.1. Since in the v_x dimension bucket B_i ranges from 5 to 10, the five subdivisions are $5 < v_x \leq 6$, $6 < v_x \leq 7$, $7 < v_x \leq 8$, $8 < v_x \leq 9$, and $9 < v_x \leq 10$. The first bar of histogram $h_{i,1}$ rises to level 1 because the first subdivision $5 < v_x \leq 6$ contains one point. The second bar of histogram $h_{i,2}$ rises to level 1 because the second subdivision $6 < v_x \leq 7$ also contains one point. The other values of $h_{i,1}$ can be determined similarly.

Figure 20.11 (b) shows $h_{i,2}$. It is built using the projection onto position x_0, which is the second column of Table 20.1. Here we use the subdivision $5 < x_0 \leq 6, \ldots, 9 < x_0 \leq 10$. In this case the first bar of histogram $h_{i,2}$

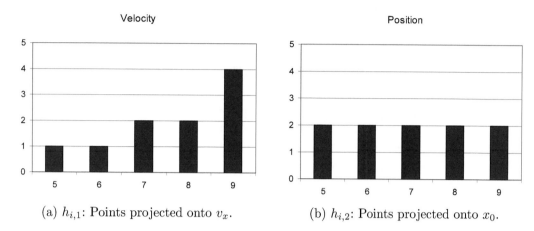

(a) $h_{i,1}$: Points projected onto v_x.   (b) $h_{i,2}$: Points projected onto x_0.

Figure 20.11: Two histograms of the points in B_i. The x-axis is the subdivision left-endpoint and the y-axis is the number of points.

rises to level 2 because the subdivision $5 < x_0 \leq 6$ contains two points. The other values of $h_{i,2}$ can be determined similarly.

Further, in this example $h_{i,1} = h_{i,3} = h_{i,5}$ because all the points listed in Table 20.1 have the same velocities in the x, y, and z directions. Also, $h_{i,2} = h_{i,4} = h_{i,6}$ because the columns for x_2, x_4, and x_6 all have the same values but in different orders.

Definition 20.4.5 [Trend Function] Given a bucket B_i and axis j, the *axis trend function* $f_{i,j}$ is some polynomial function such that the following hold:

1. $f_{i,j} \geq 0$ over the j-dimension of B_i.

2. $f'_{i,j}$, the derivative $f_{i,j}$, does not change sign over the j-dimension of B_i.

The *bucket trend function* f_i for bucket B_i is the product of the axis trend functions, that is:

$$f_i = \prod_{j=1}^{6} f_{i,j} \tag{20.4}$$

Condition 1 ensures that the bucket trend function, built from the axis trend functions, does not contain a negative probability region. Condition 2 requires that the bucket density increase, decrease, or remain constant when considering any single axis.

Example 20.4.2 Histograms $h_{i,1}$ and $h_{i,2}$ in Example 20.4.1 can be represented as the following set of points:

$$h_{i,1} = \{(5,1),(6,1),(7,2),(8,2),(9,4)\} \tag{20.5}$$
$$h_{i,2} = \{(5,2),(6,2),(7,2),(8,2),(9,2)\} \tag{20.6}$$

where the first coordinate is v_x in $h_{i,1}$ and x_0 in $h_{i,2}$, and the second coordinate is y, the number of points.

To find a trend function, we can choose a least squares method to fit each of these histograms to a line. The least square line for $h_{i,1}$ is:

$$y = 0.7v_x - 2.9$$

The least square line for $h_{i,2}$ is:

$$y = 0x_0 + 2$$

We need to ensure that Condition 1 in Definition 20.4.5 holds. A simple way to ensure that is to find the minimum of the line in the range of the histogram and if it is a negative value, then shift the line upward by that amount. For a line segment the minimum occurs always at one of the end points. Taking the minimum of the least square line equations at the histogram range end points 5 and 10 gives for $h_{i,1}$ the value $\min(y(5) = 1, y(10) = 4.3) = 4.3$, and for $h_{i,2}$ the value $\min(y(5) = 2, y(10) = 2) = 2$. Since in this case Condition 1 is satisfied by the least square lines, they do not need to be shifted upward. Condition 2 also is satisfied by line segments. Hence the least square lines can be taken as axis trend functions.

Further, since in Example 20.4.1 $h_{i,1} = h_{i,3} = h_{i,5}$ and $h_{i,2} = h_{i,4} = h_{i,6}$ the other axis trend functions can be found similarly to those of $h_{i,1}$ and $h_{i,2}$. Hence the trend function becomes:

$$
\begin{aligned}
f_i &= (0.7v_x - 2.9)(0x_0 + 2)(0.7v_y - 2.9)(0y_0 + 2)(0.7v_z - 2.9)(0z_0 + 2) \\
&= 8(0.7v_x - 2.9)(0.7v_y - 2.9)(0.7v_z - 2.9)
\end{aligned}
$$

The next lemma considers some properties of axis trend functions in general.

Lemma 20.4.1 Given a bucket B_i with axis trend functions $f_{i,j}$, let r_1 and r_2 be identically sized regions in bucket B_i. If the density in B_i along each axis monotonically increases from r_1 to r_2, then the following holds:

$$\int_{r_2} f_i \, d\phi \geq \int_{r_1} f_i \, d\phi$$

Proof: Increasing densities from r_1 to r_2 translates into histograms that also increase from r_1 in the direction of r_2 along each axis. The translation from histograms to the axis trend functions gives the following conditions:

$$f_{i,j}(x_{2,j}) \geq f_{i,j}(x_{1,j})$$

where $x_{1,j}$ and $x_{2,j}$ are the jth coordinates of the points in r_1 and r_2 respectively, and are located the same distance from the jth coordinates of the lower bounds of r_1 and r_2 respectively. Since this constraint holds for each j and $f_{i,j} \geq 0$ we have:

$$f_i(x_2) \geq f_i(x_1)$$

Hence by the properties of integration we conclude

$$\int_{r_2} f_i \, d\phi \geq \int_{r_1} f_i \, d\phi$$

■

In the following, we assume that the trend functions are polynomial functions derived from the product of linear functions, which are obtained by using the least squares method for each histogram as in Example 20.4.2.

Definition 20.4.6 [Normalized Trend Function] Let n be the number of points in the database, b_i the number of points in bucket B_i, and f_i be given by Equation (20.4). The *normalized trend function* F_i for bucket B_i is:

$$F_i = \frac{b_i f_i}{n \int\limits_{B_i} f_i \, d\phi} \tag{20.7}$$

and the *percentage of points* in bucket B_i is:

$$p = \int\limits_{B_i} F_i \, d\phi. \tag{20.8}$$

Example 20.4.3 Assume that bucket B_i in Example 20.4.1 is only a part of an index that contains $n = 100,000$ points. Then calculating F_i from Equation (20.7) requires integrating f_i over the bucket dimensions where $\int_{B_i} \equiv \int_5^{10} ... \int_5^{10}$ and where $d\phi \equiv dv_x dx_0 dv_y dy_0 dv_z dz_0$ rounded to the nearest integer gives:

$$\int_{B_i} f_i d\phi = 8 \int_{B_i} (0.7x_0 - 2.9)(0.7x_2 - 2.9)(0.7x_4 - 2.9) d\phi$$
$$\approx 1622234.$$

In this case the number of points in bucket B_i is $b_i = 10$. Hence we have:

$$\begin{aligned}
F_i &= \frac{b_i f_i}{n \int\limits_{B_i} f_i \, d\phi} \\
&\approx \frac{10 \times 8 (0.7v_x - 2.9)(0.7v_y - 2.9)(0.7v_z - 2.9)}{100000 \times 1622234} \\
&\approx 49.312 \times 10^{-11} (0.7v_x - 2.9)(0.7v_y - 2.9)(0.7v_z - 2.9)
\end{aligned}$$

Using Definition 20.4.6, we can calculate the number of points in a bucket in $O(1)$ time using the following lemma.

Lemma 20.4.2 Let B_i be a bucket, n the total number of points in the database, and p be given by Definition 20.4.6. Then np is the number of points in bucket B_i and np is calculated in $O(1)$ time.

Proof: By Equation (20.7) and (20.8) we have:

$$
\begin{aligned}
np &= n \int_{B_i} F_i \, d\phi \\
&= n \int_{B_i} \frac{b_i}{n} \frac{f_i}{\int_{B_i} f_i \, d\phi} \, d\phi \\
&= n \frac{b_i}{n} \cdot \frac{\int_{B_i} f_i \, d\phi}{\int_{B_i} f_i \, d\phi} \\
&= b_i.
\end{aligned}
$$

Clearly the above calculations take only $O(1)$ time. ∎

Using the above definitions we can now define the skew-aware bucket data structure.

Definition 20.4.7 [Skew Aware Buckets] A *skew aware bucket* is a hyper-rectangle with dimensions given by Definition 20.4.3 and that maintains histograms given by Definition 20.4.4, additional data for the least squares method, and the normalized trend function given by Definition 20.4.6.

In the following, we refer to skew aware buckets as simply buckets.

20.4.2 Inserts and Deletes

We maintain the bucket (and hence the index) while deleting or inserting a point for any bucket B_i by recalculating the trend function F_i for the bucket.

Lemma 20.4.3 Insertion and deletion of a moving point can be done in $O(1)$ time.

Proof: When we insert or delete a point, we need to update the histograms and the normalized trend function. Let the point to insert/delete be P_a represented using the hex representation as $(a_0, a_1, a_2, a_3, a_4, a_5)$, let d_j, for $0 \leq j \leq 5$ be the bucket width in the jth, and let s be the number of subdivisions in each histogram. The concatenation of $id_0, \ldots, id_5$ gives the ID_i of bucket i to insert (or delete) P_a into where each id_l and $0 \leq l \leq 5$ is defined by:

$$id_l = \left\lfloor \frac{a_l}{d_l} \right\rfloor.$$

The calculation of ID_i and retrieving bucket B_i takes $O(1)$ time using a HASHTABLE.

Let $hw_{i,j}$ be the histogram-division width for the jth calculated as $hw_{i,j} = \left\lceil \frac{d_j}{s} \right\rceil$. Then p is projected onto each dimension to determine which division of the histogram to update. For the jth dimension the kth division of histogram $h_{i,j}$ is given as follows:

$$k(j) = \left\lfloor \frac{a_j - id_j * d_j}{hw_k} \right\rfloor$$

Let $h_{i,j,k}$ be the histogram division to update for each histogram. Update $h_{i,j,k}$ and the sums $\sum y_i$, and $\sum x_i y_i$ from the normal equations in the least squares method. N, $\sum x_i$ and $\sum x_i^2$ from the normal equations do not need updating since the number of histogram divisions s is fixed within the database.

We can now recalculate each $f_{i,j}$ in constant time by solving the 2×3 matrix corresponding to the normal equations of the least squares method for each histogram. For each $f_{i,j}$ calculate the endpoints to determine the required shift amount (Definition 20.4.5, property 1) and calculate f_i from Equation (20.4). Now we calculate F_i using Equation (20.4.6). Each of these steps depends only on the dimension of the database. Hence for any fixed dimension we can rebuild the normalized trend function F_i in $O(1)$ time. ■

Point domination is an important concept that is defined as follows.

Definition 20.4.8 [Point Domination] Given two linearly moving points in three dimensions

$$Q(t) = \begin{cases} q_x = v_x t + x_0 \\ q_y = v_y t + y_0 \\ q_z = v_z t + z_0 \end{cases} \quad \text{and} \quad P(t) = \begin{cases} p_x = x_1 t + x_2 \\ p_y = x_3 t + x_4 \\ p_z = x_5 t + x_6 \end{cases}$$

$Q(t)$ dominates $P(t)$ at time t if and only if the following condition holds:

$$p_x < q_x \quad \bigwedge \quad p_y < q_y \quad \bigwedge \quad p_z < q_z \tag{20.9}$$

Further, the *dominating lines* of $Q(t)$ at time t are the following:
l_x is the line $x_2 = -x_1 t + (v_x t + x_0)$.
l_y is the line $x_4 = -x_3 t + (v_y t + y_0)$.
l_z is the line $x_6 = -x_5 t + (v_z t + z_0)$.

For convenience in visualizing the hex representations, we introduce the following definition.

Definition 20.4.9 [x-view, y-view and z-view] The projection of a 6-dimensional space of hex representations onto the first two dimensions is the *x-view*, onto the second two dimensions the *y-view*, and onto the third two dimensions the *z-view*.

It is now easy to prove the following lemma.

Lemma 20.4.4 Let $Q(t)$ and $P(t)$ be moving points, and let l_x, l_y, and l_z be the dominance lines of $Q(t)$ at time t as in Definition 20.4.8. Let x-view, y-view, and z-view be the projections of the hex representations of moving points as in Definition 20.4.9. Then $Q(t)$ dominates $P(t)$ at time t if and only if (x_1, x_2) lies below l_x in the x-view, (x_3, x_4) lies below l_y in the y-view, and (x_5, x_6) lies below l_z in the z-view.

Proof: We rewrite the condition (20.9) in Definition 20.4.8 as follows:

$$x_1 t + x_2 < v_x t + x_0 \bigwedge x_3 t + x_4 < v_y t + y_0 \bigwedge x_5 t + x_6 < v_z t + z_0 =$$

$$x_2 < -x_1 t + (v_x t + x_0) \bigwedge x_4 < -x_3 t + (v_y t + y_0) \bigwedge x_6 < -x_5 t + (v_z t + z_0)$$

Clearly, this condition is satisfied if (x_1, x_2) lies below l_x in the x-view, (x_3, x_4) lies below l_y in the y-view, and (x_5, x_6) lies below l_z in the z-view.
∎

Example 20.4.4 $Q(t) = (4, 6, 5, 6, 9, 10)$ dominates which points $P(t) = (x_1, x_2, x_3, x_4, x_5, x_6)$ at time $t = 1$?

Applying condition (20.9) in Definition 20.4.8 and substituting yields:

$$x_2 < -x_1 t + (v_x t + x_0) \bigwedge x_4 < -x_3 t + (v_y t + y_0) \bigwedge x_6 < -x_5 t + (v_z t + z_0)$$
$$= x_2 < -x_1 + 10 \bigwedge x_4 < -x_3 + 11 \bigwedge x_6 < -x_5 + 19$$

Hence at time $t = 1$, the point $Q(t)$ dominates those points $P(t)$ which satisfy the above condition.

Unlike in Example 20.4.4, in many applications we are interested in two moving points $Q_1(t)$ and $Q_2(t)$, which define the query space as follows.

Definition 20.4.10 [Query Space] Given two moving points $Q_1(t)$ and $Q_2(t)$ with respecting dominating lines l_{x1}, l_{y1}, l_{z1}, and l_{x2}, l_{y2}, l_{z2} at time t, the *query space* within the 6-dimensional space of hex representations is a hyper-tunnel formed by the cross product of the areas between l_{x1} and l_{x2} in the x-view, between l_{y1} and l_{y2} in the y-view, and between l_{z1} and l_{z2} in the z-view as shown in Figure 20.12.

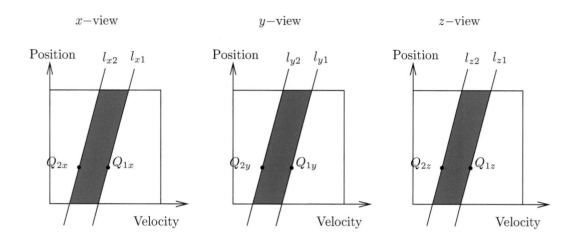

Figure 20.12: Views.

Two moving objects $Q_1(t)$ and $Q_2(t)$ define a query space at any time t. The query spaces are similar to each other. At any time t the projection of a query space onto each view is an area between two parallel lines with slopes $-t$ and passing through points $Q_1(t)$ and $Q_2(t)$. Hence we can visualize the query space as it changes over time as a moving region sweeping through space as the slopes of the lines change with time.

Intuitively, when at time t a moving point $P(t)$ is in the query space of moving points $Q_1(t)$ and $Q_2(t)$ as in Definition 20.4.10, then it dominates $Q_1(t)$ and is dominated by $Q_2(t)$ in the hex representation. Simultaneously, in the three dimensional space in which the objects move, $P(t)$ is in the box whose corner vertices are $Q_1(t)$ and $Q_2(t)$. In the following sections, like many other authors, we use the hex representation as a useful dual or alternative representation that is more amenable to efficient indexing.

20.4.3 Approximating the Number of Points in a Bucket

A basic query is to find the number of points that lie in the query space. To answer this basic query we need to look at each of the buckets separately. When the query space includes an entire bucket, then we need to count the every point in the bucket. That can be done using the normalized trend function of the bucket as defined in Definition 20.4.6. However, in many cases the query space includes only a part of a bucket. In that case we need to count only the points that are in the intersection of the bucket and the query space. In this section, we show how to do that using a *percentage function* that estimates the percentage of total points in the query space to be within the intersection of the bucket and the query space. This requires extending Definition 20.4.6 as follows.

Definition 20.4.11 [Percentage Function] If only one boundary line of the query space goes through a bucket, and r_1 is the region of the bucket in the query space and is above the boundary line, then the *percentage function* is:

$$p = \int_{r_1} F_i \, d\phi \tag{20.10}$$

If two boundary lines go through the same bucket as in Figure 20.12 and regions r_1 and r_2 correspond to regions above Q_1 and Q_2, respectively, then the *percentage function* is:

$$p = \int_{r_1} F_i \, d\phi - \int_{r_2} F_i \, d\phi. \tag{20.11}$$

The percentage function can be computed for each bucket as shown in the next lemma.

Lemma 20.4.5 For any time t and query space, the percentage function can be computed for each bucket that intersects the query space at time t.

Proof: The proof requires a case analysis. In each of the three views the query space intersects the plane giving the cases shown in Figure 20.13.

For each case shown in Figure 20.13, we describe the function that results from integration in one view. To extend the result to any number of views, we take the result from the last view and integrate it in the next view. If the region below the line were desired, $p_{lower} = \frac{b_i}{n} - p$ gives the percentage of points below the line.

Let $Q = (x_{1,q}, x_{2,q}, ..., x_{6,q})$. For the x-view, let the lower left corner vertex be $(x_{1,l}, x_{2,l})$ and the upper right corner vertex be $(x_{1,u}, x_{2,u})$. In addition each line denoted l is given by $x_2 = -t(x_1 - x_{i,q}) + x_{i+1,q}$ and corresponds to a line shown in the corresponding case in Figure 20.13.

Case (a): For this case l crosses the bucket at $x_{1,l}$ and $x_{2,u}$. The integral over the shaded region is:

$$p_a = \int_{x_{1,l}}^{\frac{x_{2,u} - x_{2,q}}{-t} + x_{1,q}} \int_{-t(x_1 - x_{1,q}) + x_{2,q}}^{x_{2,u}} F_i \, dx_2 dx_1 \tag{20.12}$$

Notice that the lower bound of the integral over dx_2 contains x_1. This dependence within each view does not affect the integration in the remaining

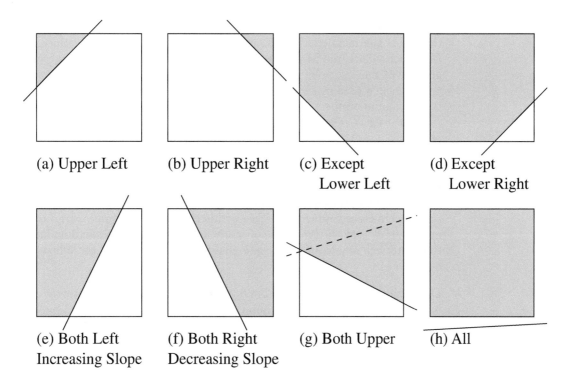

Figure 20.13: Eight cases of intersection of buckets and query space.

four dimensions. The solution to Equation (20.12) has the form:

$$at^2 + bt + c + \frac{d}{t} + \frac{e}{t^2}. \tag{20.13}$$

The other cases are similar, showing that all cases have solutions for each view in the form of Equation (20.13). Hence the percentage function for a single bucket as a function of t is of the form:

$$p = a_6 t^6 + a_5 t^5 + a_4 t^4 + a_3 t^3 + a_2 t^2 + a_1 t + c + \frac{d_1}{t} + \frac{d_2}{t^2} + \frac{d_3}{t^3} + \frac{d_4}{t^4} + \frac{d_5}{t^5} + \frac{d_6}{t^6} \tag{20.14}$$

where $t \neq 0$ when $d_i \neq 0$ for $1 \leq i \leq 6$. Since Equation (20.14) is closed under subtraction, p from Equation (20.11) will also have the same form.
■

As in Lemma 20.4.2, we can still find the number of points in the bucket by multiplying the percentage function by n, the total number of points in the database.

The MaxCount operator is more complex than just the basic operator that finds the number of points in the query space at a specific time. By Definition 20.4.1, the MaxCount operator needs to return the maximum number of moving points that are in a query space *at any time instance* $t_{\max}$ *during a time interval*, and it also needs to return the time $t_{\max}$ when the maximum occurs.

Hence for a time interval, we need to consider what happens to the query space as time changes. The query space changes as the dominance lines through the query points change, keeping always a slope of $-t$. As the dominance lines change their slopes, the query space sweeps across space and through the buckets that partition the space. As the query space sweeps through a bucket B_i, it may cross the bucket corner vertices. Each time such a cross happens, the case within the proof of Lemma 20.4.5 that applies to B_i may change in one or more of the views. Hence handling large time intervals requires further case analysis. This motivates the following definitions.

Definition 20.4.12 [Bucket Time-Interval] A *bucket time-interval* for bucket B_i is a maximal time interval during which no vertex of bucket B_i enters or leaves the query space.

Definition 20.4.13 [Index Time-Interval] An *index time-interval* for a set of buckets $\mathcal{B}$ of an index structure is a maximal time interval during which no vertex of *any* bucket in $\mathcal{B}$ enters or leaves the query space.

We follow the convention of denoting bucket and index time-intervals as half-open intervals $[l, u)$ where l is the lower bound and u is the upper bound time instance. This allows a partition of large time intervals.

Definition 20.4.14 [Time-Partition Order] Let $\mathcal{B}$ be the set of buckets in an index. Let $(t^[, t^])$ be a time interval. The *Time-Partition Order* is the set of ordered time instances $t_1, t_2, ..., t_i, ..., t_k$ such that $t_1 = t^[$ and $t_k = t^]$, and each $[t_i, t_{i+1})$ is an *index time-interval*.

Now we are ready to prove the following.

Lemma 20.4.6 For any time interval element of the Time-Partition Order, the MaxCount operator can be approximately computed in $O(1)$ time.

Proof: For any element of the time partition order we compute the sum of the percentage functions in each bucket as in Lemma 20.4.5. That gives a function of the form of Equation (20.14). We find the maximum of that function in the *temporal dimension* by first taking the derivative p' and then solving $p' = 0$. That requires finding an approximation of the roots of a polynomial function using a numerical method. ∎

Although Lemma 20.4.6 considers only one time interval element of the Time-Partition Order, it is easy to see that all the other elements can be found easily and handled similarly. At first we find the bucket time-intervals using the following lemma.

Lemma 20.4.7 Given B buckets, all the bucket time-intervals can be found in $O(B)$ time.

Proof: The bucket time-intervals can be found by finding for each bucket the slopes of the lines through its corner vertices and the query points. Any slope $-t$ means a crossing at time t. Since each bucket has only a constant number of corner vertices, and there are only two query points, finding the crossing times and bucket time-intervals requires only a constant number of calculations for each bucket. Since there are B buckets, this requires only $O(B)$ total time. ∎

We present below the complete MAXCOUNT algorithm.

MAXCOUNT$(H, Q_1, Q_2, t^[, t^])$
input: Set of buckets H built by the index structure,
         query points $Q_1(t)$ and $Q_2(t)$ and time interval $(t^[, t^])$.
output: The estimated MAXCOUNT value.

01. $TimeIntervals \leftarrow \emptyset$
02.   **for** $i \leftarrow 0$ **to** $|H| - 1$
03. $CrossTimes \leftarrow$ CALCULATECROSSTIMES$(Q_1, Q_2, t^[, t^], H_i)$
04.   **for** $j \leftarrow 1$ **to** $|CrossTimes| - 1$
05.   UNION$(TimeIntervals, TimeInterval(t_{j-1}, t_j))$
06.   **end for**
07.   **end for**

08. $TimeIntervals =$ BUCKETSORT$(TimeIntervals)$
09. $IndexTimeIntervals =$ MERGE$(TimeIntervals)$
10.   **for each** $IndexTimeInterval \in IndexTimeIntervals$
11.   CALCULATE$(MaxCount, MaxTime, IndexTimeInterval)$
12.   **end for**

13.   **return** $(MaxCount, MaxTime)$

In the algorithm, line 01 initiates a set of bucket time-interval objects to be empty. Line 03 returns a list of ordered times when a line through Q_1 or Q_2 crosses a bucket corner vertex. As in the proof of Lemma 20.4.7 this can be found in $O(1)$ time. Line 05 turns this list into a set of *TimeInterval* objects and adds them to the set of *TimeIntervals*. This "for each" loop requires $O(1)$ because it consists of a constant number of calculations bounded by the number of vertices in the bucket. Line 08 uses the linear time sorting algorithm BUCKETSORT to sort the bucket time intervals. Line 09 creates the time-partition order and index bucket time intervals from the bucket time intervals in $O(B)$. An additional pass adds the bucket time intervals to the appropriate index time-intervals in $O(B)$. Lines 10-12 perform the MAXCOUNT calculation discussed above.

In order to use the linear time BUCKETSORT algorithm, we need the following definition and lemmas.

Definition 20.4.15 [Time-Interval Ordering] The lexicographical ordering $\prec$ of *time intervals* A and B is:

$$A.l < B.l \quad \Rightarrow \quad A \prec B \tag{20.15}$$

$$A.l = B.l \quad \wedge \quad A.u < B.u \quad \Rightarrow \quad A \prec B \tag{20.16}$$

$$A.l = B.l \quad \wedge \quad A.u = B.u \quad \Rightarrow \quad A = B \tag{20.17}$$

The distribution of time interval objects created in Line 08 of the MAXCOUNT algorithm may not be uniform across the query time interval $T = [t^{[}, t^{]}]$. However, we can still prove the following.

Lemma 20.4.8 If the distribution of buckets is uniform, then the distribution of bucket time-interval objects can be uniformly distributed within the sorting buckets of the bucket sort.

Lemma 20.4.9 Insertion of any bucket time-interval object T_O into the proper sorting bucket can be done in $O(1)$ time.

Now we can prove the following.

Theorem 20.4.1 The running time of the MAXCOUNT algorithm is $O(B)$ where B is the number of buckets.

Proof: Let H be the set of buckets where each bucket B_i contains the normalized trend function F_i. Let Q_1 and Q_2 be the query points and $[t^{[}, t^{]}]$ be the query time interval. (Lines 01-07): Calculating the time intervals takes $O(B)$ time because the cross times for each bucket can be calculated in constant time. (Line 08): By Lemmas 20.4.8 and 20.4.9, we have an approximately even distribution of time interval objects within the sorting buckets where we can insert an object in constant time. This result fulfills the requirements of the BUCKETSORT, which allows the intervals to be sorted in $O(B)$ time. (Lines 09-12): Calculate the MAXCOUNT and time for each time interval in constant time using Lemma 20.4.6. These lines take $O(B)$ time because there are $O(B)$ time intervals. Finding the global MAXCOUNT and time requires retaining the maximum time and count at line 11. Returning the MAXCOUNT and time takes $O(1)$ time. Thus, the running time is given by $O(B) + O(B) + O(B) + O(1) = O(B)$. ∎

20.4.4 Approximating the Number of Points Below a Line

In this section we consider index data structures for a set of points S that allow efficiently finding the following values:

$\#Dom(P, S)$: – the number of points in S dominated by a point P.

$\#Below(\ell, S)$: – the number of points in S below a line ℓ.

$\#Dom(P, S)$ can be found in logarithmic time in the size of S using the well-known ECDF-tree data structure, which is described in many other books. Finding $\#Below(\ell, S)$ can be reduced to finding a sequence of $\#Dom(P, S)$ values as follows.

1. Find the rectangle that contains all the points in S.

2. Cut the part of ℓ within the rectangle into m number of equal pieces by horizontal and vertical line segments. Number the new points created by the cuts as $A_1, \ldots, A_{m+1}$, $B_1, \ldots, B_m$, and $C_1, \ldots, C_m$, as shown in Figure 20.14.

3. Approximate $\#Below(\ell, S)$ by the following:

$$\#Below(\ell, S) \approx \frac{\#Dom(A_1, S) + \#Dom(A_{m+1}, S) + \sum_{i=1}^{m} \#Dom(B_i, S) - \#Dom(C_i, S)}{2}$$

The above is the average of the points that are possibly below ℓ, based on the B points:

$$\#Below(\ell, S) \leq \#Dom(A_{m+1}, S) + \sum_{i=1}^{m} \#Dom(B_i, S) - \#Dom(A_{i+1}, S)$$

and the points that are surely below ℓ, based on the C points:

$$\#Below(\ell, S) \geq \#Dom(A_{m+1}, S) + \sum_{i=1}^{m} \#Dom(A_i, S) - \#Dom(C_i, S)$$

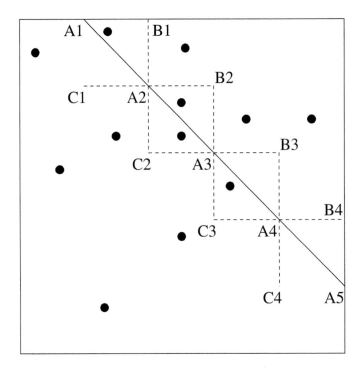

Figure 20.14: Approximating points below line ℓ with $m = 4$.

Example 20.4.5 Figure 20.14 shows a set of points within a rectangle and a line that crosses the rectangle. The crossing line is cut into $m = 4$ pieces horizontally by the line segments C_i and B_{i+1} for $1 \leq i \leq 3$ and vertically by the line segments B_j and C_{j+1} for $1 \leq j \leq 3$. In Figure 20.14 the lower bound is 5 and the upper bound is 9, and the average of these is 7, which is exactly the number of points below the line.

Since ECDF-trees work in logarithmic time in the size of S, we can show the following.

Theorem 20.4.2 An approximation of $\#Below(\ell, S)$ can be found in $O(n \log n)$ space and $O(m \log n)$ time where n is the number of points in S and m is the number of pieces the line is cut into by the above algorithm.

In general m can be considered to be a constant that affects the accuracy of the approximation. Since ECDF-trees are applicable in higher dimensions, the above approximation algorithm can be extended to higher dimensions too. For example, in three dimensions, the approximation would find the number of points below a plane by using a set point dominance queries using ECDF-trees. In this case the plane is cut using a grid parallel to the axes.

Theorem 20.4.2 can be applied to moving objects because moving objects can be represented by static points, as we saw above in the hex-representation for three-dimensional moving points. For simplicity, the following theorem considers only points moving along the x-axis.

Theorem 20.4.3 Let S be a set of points that move linearly along the x-axis. Construct an ECDF-tree that stores for each moving point $P_i(t) = a_i t + b_i$ in S the static point (a_i, b_i) in a *dual plane*. Then we can find the number of moving points in S that are to the left of a new moving point $Q(t) = at + b$ at time t by finding the number of points below the line ℓ that crosses (a, b) with slope $-t$ in the dual plane.

Bibliographic Notes

Günther [176], Overmars [294], and Samet [360, 361] are books on spatial data structures. R-trees [179], R*-trees [35], and R+-trees [369] are indexing methods for stationary spatial objects. Each of these spatial indexing methods models stationary objects as high-dimensional bounding boxes. It is possible to use these spatial indexing techniques with $(d + 1)$-dimensional bounding boxes to index d-dimensional moving objects. However, that naive approach requires much larger bounding boxes than the MBPRs. Hence that approach also leads to too many false hits.

PR-trees were proposed as an index structure for parametric rectangles in Cai and Revesz [66]. The computation of MBPRs relies on the computation of convex hulls. Efficient algorithms to compute convex hulls are described in Preparata and Shamos [309]. Most of the presentation in this chapter, including Theorems 20.1.1 and 20.2.1 and the examples, are adapted from Cai and Revesz [66].

Most current indexing approaches for moving objects are based on the moving points data model [125, 134, 378], which represents moving objects as a continuous function of time $f(t)$ and updates the database when the parameters of the motion like speed or direction change. Moving points do not represent the spatial extents of the moving objects. Several works including [8, 231, 359, 395] consider the indexing of moving objects.

Agarwal et al. [8] proposes index structures for two-dimensional moving points and shows that it can find all moving points lying in a static rectangle R in $O((N/B)^{1/2+\epsilon} + T/B)$ I/Os. However, it cannot be used to index moving objects with spatial extents and does not consider the queries where R is moving.

Kollios et al. [231] proposes to map the trajectories of a moving point represented by linear functions of the form $y = vt + a$ to a point (v, a) in the dual space and to index them by a regular spatial index structure such as a kd-trees [45]. Kollios et al. [231] also provides a theoretical lower bound on the number of I/Os needed to answer d-dimensional range searching problems. However, [231] assumes the trajectories of the moving objects extend to "infinity." It is not clear how to use this method to index objects with a finite duration.

Saltenis et al. [359] propose an R-tree-like index structure for moving points, which uses a time-parameterized "conservative" bounding rectangle to group moving points together. However, the "conservative" bounding rectangle, of which the lower and upper bounds are set to move with the minimum and maximum speeds of the enclosed points, respectively, is a less tight bound of moving points than MBPRs would be in the case of moving points.

Tayeb et al. [395] uses Quadtree [360] for indexing one-dimensional moving points as line segments in the (x, t) plane. It partitions the time dimension into time intervals of length H and indexes the part of the trajectory of each moving object that falls in the current time interval. This approach introduces substantial data replication in the index because a line segment is usually stored in several nodes.

In general, linear constraint databases cannot be efficiently indexed directly without the use of MBPRs. Some special cases are considered in Bertino et al. [48], Brodsky et al. [56], Goldstein et al. [156], Kanellakis et al. [216], Ramaswamy [315], Ramaswamy and Subramanian [316], and Zhu et al. [439]. Let N/B and T/N be the number of pages required to store N constraint tuples and T retrieved tuples, respectively. Bertino et al. [48] describe a method that can answer half-plane queries for nonmoving 2D linear constraint tuples in $O(log_B N/B + T/B)$ time, assuming that the angular coefficient of the line associated with the half-plane query belongs to a fixed finite set. For spatio-temporal constraint databases no such upper bound is known yet.

The algorithm in Section 20.4 is from [21], which differs from earlier MaxCount algorithms [18, 79, 350] by the integration of a skew-aware density function over the spatial dimensions of the bucket. Computer experiments show that this increases accuracy [21].

ECDF-trees were introduced by Bentley [46]. Although the ECDF-tree is a static data structure that does not allow updates, it can be extended to an ECDF-B-tree which can be updated by insertions and deletions of points in polylogarithmic amortized time, as described in Zhang et al. [437].

Theorem 20.4.2 and 20.4.3 are from Revesz [342]. Alternative solutions to estimating the number of points below a line using a type of buckets are described by Choi and Chung [81] and Tao et al. [390].

Exercises

1. Considering r_2, r_3, and r_{12} of Example 20.2.3, find the following:

   (a) $Vol(r_2)$

   (b) $Vol(r_3)$

   (c) $FindMBPR(r_2, \ r_{12})$

   (d) $FindMBPR(r_3, \ r_{12})$

   (e) $Enlarge(r_2, \ r_{12})$

   (f) $Enlarge(r_3, \ r_{12})$

2. Considering Example 20.2.4, find the following:

   (a) Find for each pair of r_4, r_5, r_6, and r_{12} the volume enlargement of their MBPRs.

   (b) Find the MBPRs of r_{13} and r_{14}.

   (c) Find for each pair of r_2, r_3, r_{13}, and r_{14} the volume enlargement of their MBPRs.

   (d) Find the MBPRs of r_{15} and r_{16}.

3. Delete in order the following from the PR-tree in Figure 20.9 (2):

   (a) r_{10}

   (b) r_{11}

4. Implement the algorithm that approximates the number of points below a line.

21

Data Visualization

In this chapter we consider visualization of constraint databases. The visualizations can be divided into static displays and *animations*, which are movielike displays of spatio-temporal objects that are represented implicitly by one of the spatio-temporal data models discussed in Chapter 7. Constraint databases are particularly well-suited for animation because they allow any granularity for the animation without requiring much data storage.

Section 21.1 describes *isometric color bands*, which are well-suited to visualize the triangulated irregular networks of Chapter 18. Isometric color bands are static displays, but a sequence of them can be used to animate parametric triangulated irregular networks.

Section 21.2 discusses value-by-area cartograms, which are different from regular maps in that in value-by-area cartograms the area of each cell corresponds to its value. For example, the area of a state is proportional to its population in a value-by-area cartogram. Value-by-area cartograms are static displays, but they can also be animated. For example, if the population values are not constants but functions of time, then value-by-area cartogram animation can be used to visualize the population changes over time. The functions of time that describe the value of a cell may be obtained in a number of ways. If we are given a time series, then we can use the piecewise linear approximations of Chapter 18.

Section 21.3 describes the animation of moving objects that are represented by either parametric extreme point databases or constraint databases that are equivalent to parametric 2-spaghetti databases.

P. Revesz, *Introduction to Databases: From Biological to Spatio-Temporal*,
Texts in Computer Science, DOI 10.1007/978-1-84996-095-3_21,
© Springer-Verlag London Limited 2010

21.1 Isometric Color Bands

Suppose a hill climber would like to know the landscape surface of the mountain range in Section 18.2 before planning a trip. A convenient way to indicate the elevation of a surface is by using colors. For example, we may color the surface areas that are below 2 black, the areas between 2 and 5 dark gray, and those areas that are above 5 units elevation gray. In this example, a unit may be a thousand feet. We summarize the elevation information in relation $Color\_Configuration$:

Color_Configuration

Color	Z	
Black	z	$z \leq 2$
Dark gray	z	$z \geq 2, z \leq 5$
Gray	z	$z \geq 5$

We can give the hill climber a view of the landscape or some part of it, for example, the large pyramid, as shown in Figure 21.1.

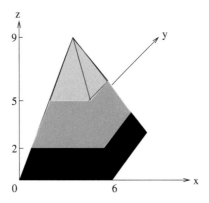

Figure 21.1: Side view of the pyramid.

The view given in Figure 21.1 is a natural side view of the large pyramid with color information added. However, it is not the most useful information for the hill climber, who would need to know, for example, the steepness on the other side of the mountain to plan for a trip. An alternative view of the mountain is called an *isometric color band map*. The isometric color band for the large pyramid is shown in Figure 21.2.

The isometric color band map is a two-dimensional map with color information added. It is the view of the mountain from the top as we would see it from an airplane. Even the color bands may sometimes be

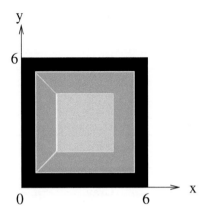

Figure 21.2: The view of the large pyramid from above.

visible from the airplane, as for example, when there are pine trees below 2, grass lands between 2 and 5, and only snow above 5 units of height. Clearly, the isometric color band map provides elevation information for each point of the surface, as is needed by the hill climber. The map shows, for example, that the steepness of the large pyramid, approximating the largest mountain, is about the same from each of the four major directions.

21.1.1 An Isometric Color Band Map Display Algorithm

In this subsection we sketch an algorithm that finds and displays the isometric color band map for any given triangulated irregular network and color configuration. We assume that the TIN and color configuration are already represented using constraint databases similar to relations *Pyramid* and *Color_Configuration* described in Section 21.1. Then we define relation *Isometric_Map* as follows:

$$Isometric\_Map = \Pi_{X,Y,Color}(Pyramid \bowtie Color\_Configuration)$$

This is a simple relational algebra query as described in Chapter 3. We also know that it can be evaluated in closed form. In fact, the result will be the constraint relation shown next.

Now the preceding relation can easily be displayed. For each constraint tuple, we find the corner points of the convex polygon that is defined by the conjunction of linear inequality constraints over the x and y variables. Then we color the area of the isometric map corresponding to the polygon with the specified color. It is easy to verify that this would indeed result in the isometric color band map shown in Figure 21.2.

Isometric_Map

X	Y	Color	
x	y	Black	$y \leq x,\ x + y \leq 6,\ y \geq 0,\ 3y \leq 2$
x	y	Dark gray	$y \leq x,\ x + y \leq 6,\ 3y \geq 2,\ 3y \leq 5$
x	y	Gray	$y \leq x,\ x + y \leq 6,\ 3y \geq 5$
x	y	Black	$y \geq x,\ x + y \leq 6,\ x \geq 0,\ 3x \leq 2$
x	y	Dark gray	$y \geq x,\ x + y \leq 6,\ 3x \geq 2,\ 3x \leq 5$
x	y	Gray	$y \geq x,\ x + y \leq 6,\ 3x \geq 5$
x	y	Black	$y \geq x,\ x + y \geq 6,\ y \leq 6,\ 3y \geq 16$
x	y	Dark gray	$y \geq x,\ x + y \geq 6,\ 3y \geq 13,\ 3y \leq 16$
x	y	Gray	$y \geq x,\ x + y \geq 6,\ 3y \leq 13$
x	y	Black	$y \leq x,\ x + y \geq 6,\ x \leq 6,\ 3x \geq 16$
x	y	Dark gray	$y \leq x,\ x + y \geq 6,\ 3x \geq 13,\ 3x \leq 16$
x	y	Gray	$y \leq x,\ x + y \geq 6,\ 3x \leq 13$

As a practical example, Figure 21.3 shows the isometric color band display for precipitation in the United States in the year 1997. The high precipitation areas are displayed by blue (darker gray) and the low precipitation areas by red (lighter gray). In this case the map contains more than eight thousand triangles.

Figure 21.3: Isometric color band map for U.S. precipitation in 1997.

21.1.2   Isometric Color Band Animation

Visualizing the eroding pyramid of Example 18.2.1 requires animation. The animation would display a sequence of snapshots of the pyramid at monotone increasing time instances. For each given t instance of time, we can generate a snapshot by substituting into the *Pyramid_Erode* relation the value of t, then eliminating the attribute T. The resulting relation is like the Pyramid relation discussed earlier and can be visualized using isometric color bands the same way.

Since the mountain is 9 units high initially, that is, at $t = 0$, it will be 8, 7, and 6 units high, respectively, at times $t = 1$, $t = 2$, and $t = 3$. Figure 21.4 shows the snapshots of the eroding mountain at four different times. If these pictures were displayed one after the other on the computer screen at a reasonable speed, we would actually see the animation.

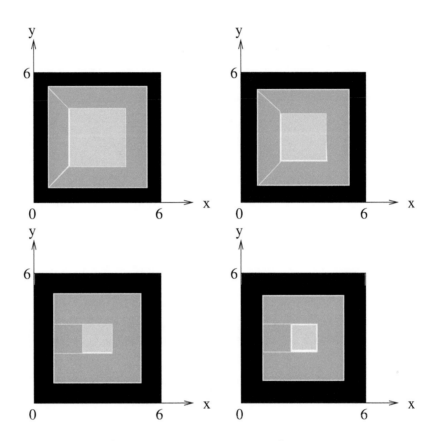

Figure 21.4: The mountain at $t = 0, 1, 2$, and 3.

For each time instance t, let $Isometric\_Map_t$ be the relation that describes the snapshot of the isometric color animation of the $Pyramid\_Erode$ relation. $Isometric\_Map_t$ can be calculated using the following relational algebra expression:

$$\Pi_{X,Y,\text{Color}}(\sigma_{T=t}Pyramid\_Erode \bowtie Color\_Configuration)$$

21.2   Value-by-Area Cartogram

Now we consider maps that divide the plane into a set of disjoint regions, or *cells*. For example, the map of the continental United States consists of 48 cells, that is, one cell for each state. Maps give information only about the location of the individual cells, not other information like their populations.

Suppose someone would like to know the relative population of each state. We could use a *value-by-area cartogram*. A value-by-area cartogram is a map in which each cell is inflated or deflated so that its area is proportional to its associated "value." For example, Figure 21.5 is a value-by-area cartogram where the value of each cell is its population in 1990.

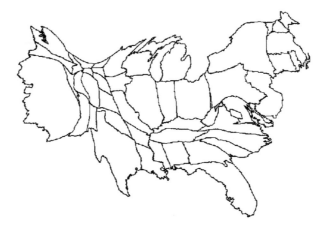

Figure 21.5: A value-by-area cartogram for the U.S. population in 1990.

Value-by-area cartograms provide easy-to-understand visualizations. For example, one can learn from Figure 21.5 that California has a high population density because its area is greatly enlarged, while Nebraska has a small population density because its area is reduced.

21.2.1   Value-by-Area Cartogram Display Algorithm

We describe an algorithm that finds the value-by-area cartogram for any given map and set of cell values. We assume that the cells are polygons and the cell values are positive real numbers.

Let n be the number of cells and D_{AVG} be the *average cell density* of the map. For each $1 \le i \le n$, let C_i be the ith cell, V_i its value, AC_i its actual area, AD_i its *desired area*, Δ_i its *distortion*, and ER_i its *effective range*. The desired area is the area we best represent as the value of the cell. The distortion is the percent increase or decrease from the desired area to the actual area. The effective range ER_i is the area of the map that contains all the corner vertices that could change while inflating or deflating C_i. More formally, let us use the following definitions:

$$D_{AVG} = \frac{\sum_{i=1}^{n} V_i}{\sum_{i=1}^{n} AC_i}$$

$$AD_i = \frac{V_i}{D_{AVG}}$$

$$\Delta_i = \frac{|AD_i - AC_i|}{AD_i}$$

The *centroid* (x_c, y_c) of a polygon with corner vertices (x_1, y_1), (x_2, y_2), ..., (x_k, y_k) is defined as follows:

$$x_c = \frac{1}{k} \left(\sum_{i=1}^{k} x_i \right) \tag{21.1}$$

$$y_c = \frac{1}{k} \left(\sum_{i=1}^{k} y_i \right) \tag{21.2}$$

The effective range of a cell is a circle around its *centroid*. The radius of the effective range r_{eff} is:

$$r_{eff} = \frac{100|AD_i - AC_i|}{\sqrt{\pi} AC_i}$$

The algorithm, which is shown next, will iteratively inflate or deflate in sequence each cell whose distortion is greater than some error tolerance value ϵ. A cell is inflated if its actual area is smaller than its desired area, and it is deflated if its actual area is larger than its desired area. When we inflate a cell C_i, all its neighbors within the effective range ER_i are also influenced. Hence a change made for the ith cell may inadvertently negate a change made previously for an earlier cell. To minimize the effect of such inadvertent interactions, in each iteration, we order the cells according to their distortions. Hence we first change those cells that need a big change and then those cells that need only a small change.

Value-by-Area Cartogram Animation
Input: A map with n cells, a value for each cell,
 and an error tolerance value ϵ.
Output: A value-by-area cartogram in which each
 Δ_i is less than or equal to ϵ.
begin
  For each cell, compute its AD_i and AC_i.
  repeat
   Sort the cells by their distortions Δ_i.
   for $i = 1$ to n **do**
     Compute AC_i.
     Inflate/deflate C_i by changing corner vertices in ER_i.
   end-for
  until $\forall i \ \Delta_i \leq \epsilon$.
end

We still did not specify precisely how the corner vertices change within an effective range. There are many good alternative definitions, but the main idea is that the further a corner vertex is from the centroid of the inflated or deflated cell the less its location should be changed. Let (x_i, y_i) be the centroid of the cell C_i to be inflated or deflated. Then for each corner vertex (x, y) in the effective range of the cell, the new coordinates (x', y') will be:

$$x' = x_i + (x - x_i)\sqrt{\frac{AD_i}{AC_i}}$$

$$y' = y_i + (y - y_i)\sqrt{\frac{AD_i}{AC_i}}$$

(21.3)

These definitions are intuitive in the following sense. Suppose a cell has a circular shape approximated by a high-degree polygon. Suppose further that the desired area of the cell is $\pi r'^2$, but the actual area is πr^2. Then by making the preceding changes, we change r to r', which is exactly as desired.

A refinement of this would be to change according to Equation (21.3) only those corner vertices that are within the circle with radius $\sqrt{AC_i/\pi}$. If they are outside that circle, then we change them a little less, because they are in danger of intruding too much into the neighboring cells. For those corner vertices we choose the new coordinates as follows:

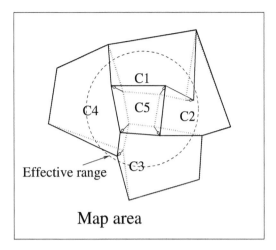

Figure 21.6: Effective range.

$$x' = x_i + (x - x_i)\frac{AD_i - AC_i}{2\pi d^2}$$

$$y' = y_i + (y - y_i)\frac{AD_i - AC_i}{2\pi d^2}$$

For example, in Figure 21.6 the dotted lines represent the original cell division and C_5 is inflated. Here the effective range is shown by the dashed cycle. The corner vertices within the effective range are changed resulting in the new cell division shown in solid lines.

21.2.2   Value-by-Area Cartogram Animation

If the value of each cell is changing over time, we can represent each cell value as a function $V_i(t)$. For example, the cell value of a state with a population that is one million at $t = 0$ and growing each year by 2 percent can be represented by the function $1.02^t \times 1,000,000$.

Value-by-area cartogram animation can be used to visualize maps where cell values are functions of t. The animation displays a sequence of value-by-area cartogram "snapshots." Each snapshot is a value-by-area cartogram that corresponds to the cell values at a given time instance. There are three basic methods for value-by-area cartogram animation.

Parallel Method: For each time instance t to be displayed, this method takes the original map with the cell values at time t and gives an output map or snapshot. This is called the parallel method because the snapshots

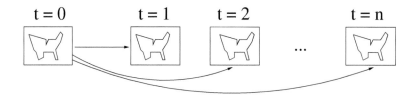

Figure 21.7: The parallel method for cartogram animation.

can be computed in parallel (see Figure 21.7).

Serial Method: In this method each cartogram snapshot is constructed from the previous cartogram snapshot (except for the first cartogram snapshot, which is constructed from the original map), as shown in Figure 21.8.

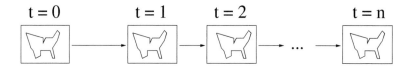

Figure 21.8: The serial method for cartogram animation.

Hybrid Method: This method combines the previous two methods. It generates each $kn + 1$st snapshot from the original map and all the other snapshots from the previous snapshots (see Figure 21.9).

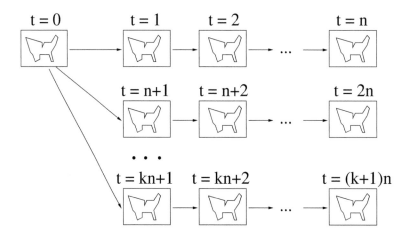

Figure 21.9: The hybrid method for cartogram animation.

The serial method is faster than the parallel method on a single-processor computer because there is usually a smaller difference between two consecutive snapshots than between the original map and a snapshot; hence calculating a snapshot from the previous snapshot requires generally fewer iterations of the value-by-area cartogram algorithm. However, in general, the cells are harder to recognize in the cartogram snapshots generated by the serial method, because in the serial method each snapshot will transmit to its successors some possible cell shape distortion, which may accumulate. The hybrid method is almost as fast as the serial method, but it avoids the accumulation of cell shape distortions.

21.2.3   Volume and Color Cartograms and Animations

A map may be displayed by a *volume cartogram*, which is a three-dimensional view in which each cell has a height that corresponds to its value. An example of this is shown in Figure 21.10, which shows for each continental U.S. state the daily mean temperature value in October 1990.

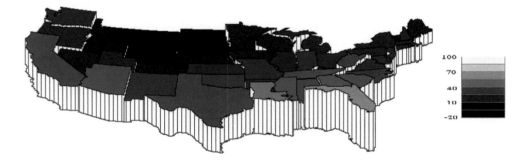

Figure 21.10: U.S. daily mean temperature in October 1990.

Besides using the height of the cells to represent the values, we may also use a *color cartogram* that colors the cells using some scale. For example, in Figure 21.10 lighter colors indicate greater cell values. This makes it clearer to see, for example, that the daily mean temperature in Texas is higher than in North Dakota.

When there is only one spatial variable to be displayed for each cell, then any of the three map visualizations we discussed could be used. Someone may prefer value-by-area cartograms because in them each cell is visible, while in volume cartograms some taller objects may obstruct the view of smaller objects in the background. Sometimes, a combination of the different visualizations could enhance each other as in Figure 21.10.

However, suppose we need to display a map with three different cell variables. In this case the three visualizations could be combined. For example, someone may wish to see the population, the per capita income, and the per capita energy consumption of the continental United States. This could be displayed by first computing a value-by-area cartogram using the population values then generating from that a volume cartogram using the gross income values, and finally coloring each state using the energy consumption values.

We may also animate volume and color cartograms similarly to the animation of value-by-area cartograms.

21.3 Animation of Moving Objects

Animation is the natural visualization of moving objects. As we saw in Chapter 7, moving objects may be described using several different data models. Each of these needs slightly different animation methods. We describe animation methods for periodic parametric databases in Section 21.3.1 and for linear constraint databases in Section 21.3.2.

21.3.1 Animation of Periodic Parametric Databases

Most computer systems provide in their graphics library as a primitive a display module for triangles and rectangles defined by their corner vertices. The animation algorithms we describe will assume that these primitives are available.

Periodic parametric 2-spaghetti and parametric rectangle databases can be easily animated. In order to display a relation at a time instant t_i, we first check each parametric rectangle tuple r whether it exists at time t_i, that is, whether $t_i \in T_r$, where T_r is the time interval of r.

If the tuple is a nonperiodic parametric rectangle ($period = +\infty$), it is easy to check whether $t_i \in T_r$.

If the tuple is a periodic parametric rectangle of form $T_r = [from, to]_{\text{period, end}}$, then we need to check the following:

$$from \ \leq \ t_i - \lfloor \frac{t_i - from}{period} \rfloor \cdot period \ \leq \ to \ AND \ t_i \ \leq \ end$$

If r exists at t_i, we substitute the variable t in the functions with t_i' and obtain the snapshot of r at t_i

Proceeding in this manner, we obtain a set of triangles or rectangles corresponding to the relation at time t_i. These can be displayed using the graphics primitives.

21.3.2 Animation of Constraint Databases

Constraint databases with two spatial and one temporal attributes, where for each instance of t the constraints are linear, the spatial variables can be animated by two different methods, called the *naive animation* and the *parametric animation* methods (see Figure 21.11).

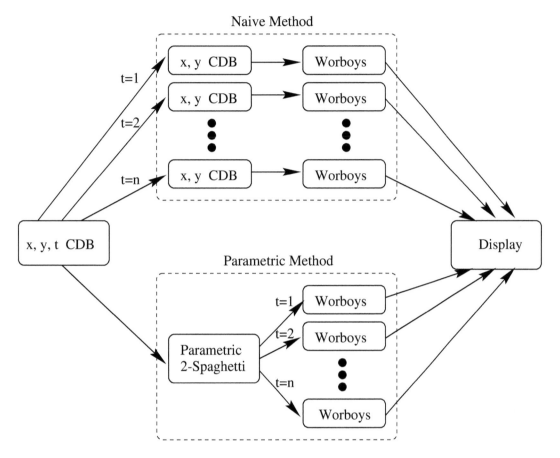

Figure 21.11: Animation of x, y, t linear constraint databases.

Naive Animation Method: This method works directly on constraint databases. It finds for each time instance t_i, by instantiating the variable t to t_i, a linear constraint relation that has only two spatial variables, namely, x and y. This linear constraint relation is translated into a Worboys relation where $from = to = t_i$. This translation uses Theorem 16.1.2. Finally, it displays as a set of triangles each Worboys relation.

Parametric Animation Method: This method has a *preprocessing* step and a *display* step. In the preprocessing step it constructs a parametric 2-spaghetti representation of the linear constraint relation using the algorithm outlined in Theorem 16.1.4. This construction needs to be done only once, before any user requests it. The construction also finds for each parametric triangle p a beginning time $t_{\text{p.from}}$ and an ending time $t_{\text{p.to}}$. Before $t_{\text{p.from}}$ or after $t_{\text{p.to}}$ the parametric triangle has no spatial extent and does not need to be displayed.

During the display step, which is done at the user's request, for each consecutive time instant t_i and for each parametric triangle it is checked first that t_i is between $t_{\text{p.from}}$ and $t_{\text{p.to}}$. Corresponding to the parametric triangles whose range includes t_i, the parametric method finds, by instantiating the variable t to t_i, a set of triangles defined by their corner vertices. Then it displays the set of triangles.

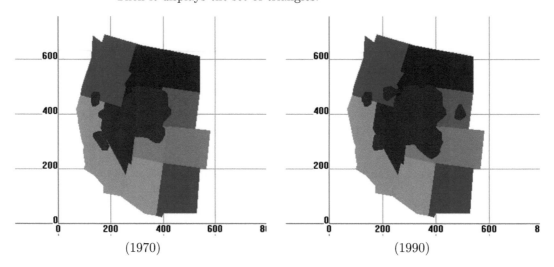

(1970)   (1990)

Figure 21.12: Two snapshots of a video on California gull ranges.

As an example, the habitat area of California gulls, a bird species usually found in the western United States, is a moving object described by a linear constraint database. It was first converted to a parametric 2-spaghetti representation before generating the two snapshots shown in Figure 21.12.

Example 21.3.1 A wilderness area is divided into grass land, pine forest, and oak forest. For various reasons these regions change over time. The left side of Figure 21.13 shows the three regions at time $t = 0$ and the right side at $t = 10$ after a gradual expansion of the pine and oak forests to the northeast.

The changing of the grass land and trees can be represented by the linear constraint relation *Wilderness*. We assume that each of the four boundary lines moves linearly. For example, both boundary lines between the oak and pine forests move to the east with speed two units and north with one unit per year. Similarly, the boundary lines between the pine forest

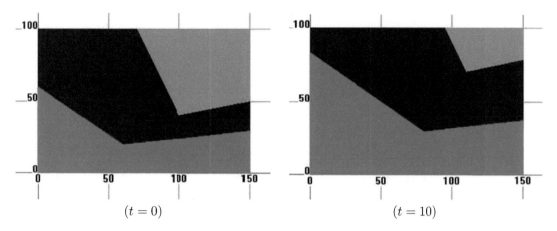

$(t = 0)$ $(t = 10)$

Figure 21.13: Grass (top right), pine (middle), and oak (bottom) areas.

and grass land move to the east with speed one unit and north three units per year.

The oak forest area can be divided into two parts. The first part is a triangular area whose upper boundary is the line $2x + 3y - 7t \leq 180$. The other area will be a quadrangle where this line is a lower bound and the line $x - 9y + 7t \geq -120$ is an upper bound. These lines can be obtained from the endpoints $(0, 60), (60, 20)$, and $(150, 30)$ at $t = 0$ and the endpoints $(0, 250/3), (80, 30)$, and $(150, 340/9)$. Considering the speed of the shifting lines, the entire relation can be represented as shown in relation *Wilderness*.

Wilderness

ID	X	Y	T	
G	x	y	t	$x \leq 150,\ y \leq 100,\ 2x + y - 5t \geq 240,$ $x - 5y + 14t \leq -100,\ t \geq 0,\ t \leq 10$
O	x	y	t	$x \leq 150,\ y \geq 0,\ 2x + 3y - 7t \geq 180,$ $x - 9y + 7t \geq -120,\ t \geq 0,\ t \leq 10$
O	x	y	t	$x \geq 0,\ y \geq 0,\ 2x + 3y - 7t \leq 180,\ t \geq 0,\ t \leq 10$
P	x	y	t	$x - 9y + 7t \leq -120,\ 2x + 3y - 7t \geq 180,$ $x \geq 0,\ y \leq 100,\ 2x + y - 5t \leq 240, t \geq 0,\ t \leq 10$
P	x	y	t	$x \leq 150,\ 2x + y - 5t \geq 240,\ x - 5y + 14t \geq -100,$ $x - 9y + 7t \leq -120,\ t \geq 0,\ t \leq 10$

Finally, it can be translated to the parametric 2-spaghetti relation *Wilderness2* shown next (except for the *From* and *To* attributes, which are always 0 and 10, respectively):

Wilderness2

ID	Ax	Ay	Bx	By	Cx	Cy
G	$2.5t + 70$	100	$t + 100$	$3t + 40$	150	100
G	150	100	$t + 100$	$3t + 40$	150	$2.8t + 50$
P	0	100	0	2.33t+60	$2.5t + 70$	100
P	0	2.33t+60	$2t + 60$	$t + 20$	$2.5t + 70$	100
P	$2t + 60$	$t + 20$	$t + 100$	$3t + 40$	$2.5t + 70$	100
P	$2t + 60$	$t + 20$	$t + 100$	$3t + 40$	150	$.77t + 30$
P	$t + 100$	$3t + 40$	150	$.77t + 30$	150	$2.8t + 50$
O	0	2.33t+60	0	0	$2t + 60$	$t + 20$
O	0	0	$2t + 60$	$t + 20$	150	0
O	$2t + 60$	$t + 20$	150	0	150	$.77t + 30$

Bibliographic Notes

Isometric color bands are part of the display options in the MLPQ constraint database system and were discussed briefly in Revesz at al. [349] and in more detail in Chen [76]. The animation of parametric triangulated irregular networks is new.

Value-by-area cartogram algorithms using rubber-sheet-based algorithms were given by Dougenik [116] et al. and Gusein-Zade and Tikunov [177]. The value-by-area cartogram algorithm in Section 21.2 is by Ouyang and Revesz [293]. Ouyang and Revesz [293] is an extension of the previous algorithms by the introduction of an effective range and by sorting

Value-by-area cartogram animations were considered by House and Kocmoud [199], which gives an animation for the U.S. population change from 1900 to 1996, and White et al. (geog.qmw.ac.uk/gbhgis/gisruk98), which gives an animation for the infant mortality in the United Kingdom from 1856 to 1925. In these animations, each value-by-area cartogram is precomputed and stored, and there are fewer than 20 of them in the animation. They use precomputation because they are based on the slower cartogram display algorithms. The value-by-area cartogram animation in Section 21.2 is also by Ouyang and Revesz [293].

The animation of parametric rectangles was considered in Cai et al. [64]. The animation of linear constraint databases was considered in Chomicki et al. [86]. The constraint database animation in Section 21.3 is based on [86] but extends it from linear constraint databases to any x, y, t variable constraint database in which the constraints are linear for each instance of t. This extension is possible because of Theorem 16.1.4.

Exercises

1. Show each step of the evaluation of the relational algebra query that defines the $Isometric\_Map$ relation.

2. Give the corresponding constraint representations of the three snapshots of the Pyramid_Erode relation at $t = 1$, $t = 2$, and $t = 3$ in the isometric color animation.

3. Suppose a city is expanding by acquiring some suburban areas, while the suburbs are expanding by taking over some farmlands, as described in the following three relations, where x, y are spatial variables, t is time, and p is population. The population of the three areas also changes linearly with time.

$$
\begin{aligned}
city(x, y, t, p) \quad :- \quad & x > 0, x < 50 + 20t \\
& y > 0, y < 35 + 15t, \\
& t > 0, t < 1, \\
& p = 9000t + 7000.
\end{aligned}
$$

$$
\begin{aligned}
suburb(x, y, t, p) \quad :- \quad & x > 0, x < 50 + 20t, \\
& y > 35 + 15t, y < 70, \\
& t > 0, t < 1, \\
& p = 2000t + 10000.
\end{aligned}
$$

$$
\begin{aligned}
suburb(x, y, t, p) \quad :- \quad & x > 50 + 20t, x < 100, \\
& y > 0, y < 35 + 15t, \\
& t > 0, t < 1, \\
& p = 2000t + 9000.
\end{aligned}
$$

$$
\begin{aligned}
farm\_land(x, y, t, p) \quad :- \quad & x > 50 + 20t, x < 100, \\
& y > 35 + 15t, y < 70, \\
& t > 0, t < 1, \\
& p = -3000t + 8000.
\end{aligned}
$$

(a) Draw how the three relations would look at times $t = 0$ and $t = 1$.

(b) Translate the x, y, t projection of the relations into a parametric 2-spaghetti representation.

(c) What animation method would you use to show both the area and population changes?

22

Safe Query Languages

Any programmer knows that programs may fall into infinite loops and never terminate. Datalog with constraint programs may have the same problem. When providing library programs for naive users, we need to guarantee that our programs terminate and give a meaningful answer each time they are called and for any possible valid database input. This guarantee is what we call *safety*.

In Section 22.1 we describe different degrees of safety. Sometimes the guarantee is conditioned on the type of database input. It is important that users be warned of what is guaranteed by the program, what is not, and on what condition. The simpler these are to explain the better. A user may still continue to use an unsafe program after receiving a warning from the system but without false expectations. That is the purpose of this chapter.

In this chapter we restrict the syntax of the query language. This is a simple approach to use and explain to a user. Therefore, it is the preferred approach whenever it is possible to use.

22.1 Safety Levels

We say that a program is *safe* if its semantics can be at least partially checked or computed on any valid database input. Obviously only safe programs are useful for applications. We distinguish five levels of safe programs, as shown in Figure 22.1.

1. **Closed-Form.** When the semantics of a program can be computed such that the output database contains the same type of constraints as the input database, then the program is said to be *closed-form safe*. Queries that

P. Revesz, *Introduction to Databases: From Biological to Spatio-Temporal*,
Texts in Computer Science, DOI 10.1007/978-1-84996-095-3_22,
© Springer-Verlag London Limited 2010

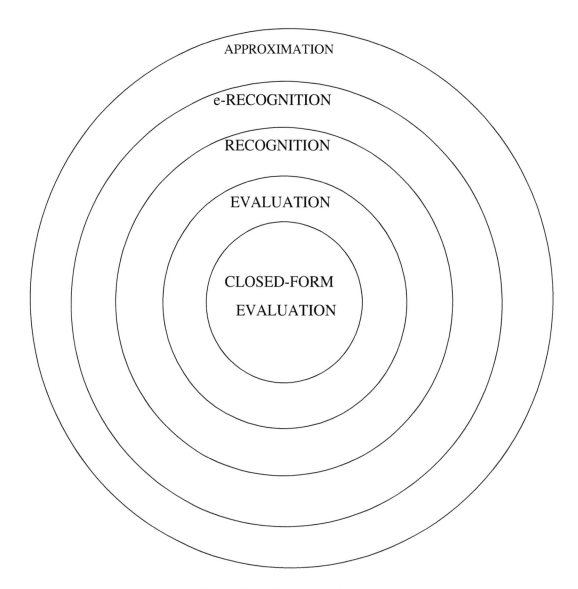

Figure 22.1: The safety hierarchy.

take databases without contraints to databases without constraints are also closed-form safe.

2. **Evaluation.** When the semantics of a program can be computed but the output could contain more complex constraints than the input, then the program is *evaluation safe*. For example, suppose an input relation

$Line(x, y)$ contains only the line $y = 2x$. Then the output of the following program:

$$Slope(x, y) \quad :— \quad Slope(x, z), \ Line(z, y).$$
$$Slope(x, y) \quad :— \quad Line(x, y).$$

is the relation $Slope(x, y)$ that contains all the lines $y = 2^k x$ for each integer $k > 0$. Although this program is evaluation safe, the output, which contains an exponentiation constraint, is more complex than the input, which contains only a multiplication constraint.

3. **Recognition.** When any tuple of constants can be tested to be in the semantics of a program, then the program is *recognition safe.*

4. ϵ-**Recognition.** When for any tuple of rational numbers $(a_1, \ldots, a_k)$ and small positive rational number ϵ, it can be tested whether there is a tuple $(b_1, \ldots, b_k)$ in the semantics of the program such that $\mid a_i - b_i \mid < \epsilon$; then the program is ϵ-*recognition safe.*

5. **Approximation.** When the semantics of a program can be approximated by a lower and an upper bound, many individual tuples can be said to be definitely in or not in the semantics of the program, but for some tuples we will not be able to get a definite answer.

It is obvious that these are increasingly broader classes of safe programs. For example, any closed-form safe program is also evaluation safe.

Nevertheless, there are many programs that do not meet any of the five safety conditions. We call these programs *unsafe.* Imagine you are given a library of unsafe programs. If you tried to execute a program from that library on your database, then the execution may never return any answer.

On the other hand, if your library contained only safe programs, then at least you could always get an answer to the question whether a particular tuple or some other tuple very close to it is in the semantics of the query.

If your library contained only closed-form safe programs, then you would be assured to get a database as output that uses the same type of constraints as your input database. Therefore, after creating the output database you could execute another query from the library and you would be still guaranteed an output database in the same form. In fact, you could execute any composition of programs on the input database and get an output database.

Obviously, it is important to provide for constraint database users only libraries of safe programs. But how can a programmer guarantee that a program is safe before adding it to the library? That is a difficult task in general, not only for Datalog programs but in any programming language.

Domain	Constraint	Datalog	Max Min (Q)	Area Vol (Q)	Negation
$\mathcal{Q}, \mathcal{Z}$	equality, inequality	any	any		any
$\mathcal{Q}$	order	any	any	any	any
$\mathcal{Q}, \mathcal{Z}$	lower bound, upper bound gap-order, positive linear	any	any	any	any^e unary
$\mathcal{Q}, \mathcal{Z}$	lower bound, upper bound gap-order, negative linear	any	any	any	any^e unary
$\mathcal{Q}, \mathcal{Z}$	lower bound, upper bound half-addition	any	any	any	any^e unary
$\mathcal{Q}, \mathcal{Z}$	difference	any^a	any	any	any
$\mathcal{Q}, \mathcal{Z}$	addition	any^a	any	any	any
$\mathcal{Q}, \mathcal{Z}$	linear	nonrecursive	any	any	any
$\mathcal{R}$	polynomial	nonrecursive			any
$\mathcal{B}$	equality	any			
$\mathcal{B}^{aless}$	equality, inequality	any			any
$\mathcal{B}$	order	any			

Figure 22.2: Restrictions that guarantee safety.

However, it is known that Datalog programs are always safe when executed on certain types of constraint databases.

22.2   Restriction

By restricting the allowed type of constraints we may obtain a query language in which every program is terminating on every input database. The advantage is that it is easy to check whether all the constraints used are of the allowed type. The disadvantage is that the expressiveness of the language is limited, hence it would be difficult to express many useful queries.

Figure 22.2 summarizes some restrictions that guarantee safety in evaluating Datalog, maximum, minimum, area, volume, and negation queries. In the figure superscript *aless* means atomless, *e* means evaluation safe, and superscript *a* means approximation safe. The negation of a gap-order constraint is not always a gap-order constraint because the bound may become negative by the negation. The negation of a positive linear constraint is a negative linear constraint and vice versa. We can use Figure 22.2 to show that the following queries are safe.

Example 12.1.3: This example used a half-addition constraint within each constraint tuple to record the possible travel times between a pair of cities.

Therefore, Q_{travel} must be a safe query by Figure 22.2.

Example 12.1.9: This Datalog program contains only a single addition constraint. Hence if the input relations *Fire* and *Forest* also contain only addition constraints, then the query is approximation safe by Figure 22.2.

Example 12.2.2: This query used only Boolean equality constraints. Therefore it is a safe query.

Example 12.2.6: Here we used the constraint $A \cap B \neq \emptyset$, which is a monotone Boolean inequality constraint. Because this is the only constraint used, it is a safe query by Figure 22.2.

Example 15.2.3: This Datalog query about the ferry system contains only positive linear constraints. Hence it is safe.

In the restriction approach we simply check what is the domain, the type of constraints, and the type of the query used. If library queries are labeled as being recursive or nonrecursive and both queries and input databases are labeled as the type of constraints used and their domains, then users can do this type of safety checking themselves.

Alternatively, one or more of the restricted constraint query languages can be provided within a system. That is similar to relational database systems that provide safe languages like SQL for users instead of the complete power of high-level programming languages. Users of these systems do not have to be concerned with safety issues, although they may find the expressiveness of the query languages too limited. There is always a trade-off between more safety and less flexibility.

22.3   Safe Aggregation and Negation Queries

Aggregation and negation are safe in the cases listed in Figure 22.2. Note that the negation of a half-addition constraint may not be a half-addition constraint, although it is always a linear constraint. Therefore, relations with only half-addition constraints are evaluation safe—the output of the negation will be a general linear constraint relation—but not closed-form evaluation safe.

There are techniques to test and certify that a stratified query in which Datalog with half-addition constraint queries and negation queries alternate is safe. Note that each half-addition constraint in which at least one of the variables becomes a constant, is equivalent to an order constraint. The certification method essentially verifies that in each half-addition constraint in the output relation at least one variable becomes constant. Because order constraint relations can be negated, the stratified Datalog query is therefore also evaluable. Chapter 22.5 describes several certification methods.

22.4 Safe Refinement and Projection Queries

Refinement queries are always safe because they can be evaluated only by adding constraints to the UCOR. Projection queries are also evaluable whenever the UCOR contains only addition, linear, or polynomial constraints.

However, we should not take for granted that projection queries are always evaluable. For example, when the UCOR contains integer polynomial constraints, the projection may not be safe and evaluable.

22.5 Certification

In Chapter 22 we saw one approach to guarantee the termination of queries. It placed various syntactic restrictions on the constraint query language used such that every query expressible in the restricted constraint query language was safe.

Certification is another approach to safety. The idea is to certify that a query is safe before adding it to a query library. Certification is not based on simple syntax checking but on more complicated tests. Certification either runs a special algorithm that verifies that a query is safe or uses some ad hoc arguments.

In both cases certification is better done by expert programmers. In the latter case an expert is needed because the ad hoc arguments require some knowledge about the evaluation of queries that cannot be expected from naive database users. In the former case, if certification fails an expert may rewrite the query to make it safe, something that again cannot be expected from naive database users.

Certification is important because it can sometimes yield guarantees when the first approach fails. There are many certification techniques. We describe and illustrate some of them in this chapter.

22.5.1 Constant Propagation

Constant propagation occurs when in a rule body some of the attributes of some relations are known to contain only constants. That information is passed to the other relations within the same rule. This may lead to a simplification of the constraints in the rules and restriction may become applicable to prove safety.

Example 22.5.1 In Example 12.1.4 about the *Travel* query we can assume that the third argument of *Go2* is a constant. Then at each rule application we have only a (half)-addition constraint. Hence the *Travel* query is safe, by Figure 22.2.

22.5.2   Variable Independence

Variable independence occurs when knowing the value of a variable does not improve our knowledge of the value of another variable. For example, consider gap-order constraint tuples over the variables $x_1, \ldots, x_k$. If there is no gap-order constraint between any two of the variables then they are independent. There could be other constraints between variables and constants, for example, we could have $x_1 - x_2 \geq 30$, but even if knowing the exact value of x_1 does not help us know more about x_2.

We say that the variables are independent in a relation if they are independent in each tuple of the relation. Negation is closed-form safe for gap-order relations in which the variables are independent. This is stronger than being simply evaluation safe. Therefore, if we have a stratified Datalog query with some alternation of Datalog queries and negations such that the variables are independent in the relations negated, then the stratified program is also closed-form evaluation safe. Based on this observation we can define very complex queries that are closed-form evaluation safe. Following is just a simple example.

Example 22.5.2 We computed relation $Travel(x, y, t)$ in Example 12.1.3. It is easy to see that the three variables are independent in this relation. Hence let us define the following query:

$$Not\_Fastest(x, y, t_2) \quad :\!\!- \quad Travel(x, y, t_1), Travel(x, y, t_2), t_1 < t_2.$$
$$Fastest(x, y, t) \quad :\!\!- \quad Travel(x, y, t), notNot\_Fastest(x, y, t).$$

Here the first rule computes for each pair of cities the set of time instances that are not fastest. The variables are independent in relation $Not\_Fastest$. Hence $\angle Fastest$ can be negated in the second rule to get a new gap-order constraint relation, which is then joined with the $Travel$ relation. Therefore relation $Fastest$ can be evaluated in gap-order closed form. Hence this is a closed-form evaluation safe query.

22.5.3   Monotonicity

Monotonicity occurs when a value is monotone increasing. Monotonicity conditions can be often used to prove termination.

Example 22.5.3 In the subset sum query of Example 12.1.10 the first argument of *Sum* is 0 in the very first tuple that can be derived. With all applications of the second and third rules, the value of the first attribute increases by one. Therefore, there are at most 2^n different tuples that can be derived when there are n items numbered 1 to n in the *Item* relation. This proves that $Q_{\mathrm{subsetsum}}$ is a safe query.

22.5.4 Acyclicity

Acyclicity means that the database input can be considered a directed acyclic graph. If the query is traversing the edges in a direction, then the query must terminate.

Example 22.5.4 The query in Example 12.1.6 about water flowing in a river contains only linear constraints in the second and third rules of the query. However, we can expect that the river is acyclic. Therefore, the first, second, and third rules need to be applied only as many times as source, dam, and merge tuples we have. Therefore, the query will have to terminate.

22.5.5 Tightening Bounds

Tightening bounds is another technique of proving termination. This occurs when we have a constraint that is almost like a negative linear constraint except that its bound is a variable that increases on each rule application while the other variables are bounded from below.

Example 22.5.5 A possible solution for Exercise 9.3.4 would be a constraint automaton that can be translated to the following Datalog program:

$$Money(500, 3000, -100, 0, 3300).$$
$$
\begin{aligned}
Money(x', y', z', i', b') \quad :- \quad & Money(x, y, z, i, b), \\
& -x' - y' - z' \geq -b, \\
& x' \geq 0, \ y' \geq 0, \ z' \geq -1000, \\
& i' = i + 1, \ b' = b - 100.
\end{aligned}
$$

Here the constraint $-x' - y' - z' \geq -b$ is a tightening negative linear constraint, where the bound $-b$ increases by one hundred on each rule application, and all the other variables are bounded from below. Therefore this second rule can be applied only a finite number of times to derive anything; thus it is a safe query. Note that this is a recursive query with linear constraints that cannot be shown to be safe by restriction.

22.5.6 Tightening Coefficients

Tightening coefficients is similar to the previous technique. This occurs when the domain is the nonnegative integers and we have a constraint that is like a negative linear constraint except that the bound and one or more coefficients are variables and on each rule application the coefficients are all growing with a faster rate than the bound.

Example 22.5.6 The annual purchase automaton in Figure 15.2.5 with only the left arc results in a Datalog program with polynomial constraints. However, the polynomial constraint $ax' + by' + cz' \leq d$ is like a linear constraint where a, b, and c are coefficients and d is the bound that takes on different values for each rule application. Namely a, b, and c grow by 5, 10, and 5 percent, respectively, while d grows by only 2 percent. Hence this rule can be applied only a finite number of times.

Note that the Datalog rule corresponding to the other arc of the automaton can also be applied only a finite number of times successively. That is because there the value of i decreases by one on each rule application but must stay above 0. Because the second rule cancels the effect of the other and restores the values of the variables, it can be seen that the Datalog query can derive only a finite number of different tuples, no matter what are the initial values of the variables.

22.5.7 Vector Addition System

Sometimes a Datalog program with addition constraints can be recognized to define a vector addition system. In a vector addition system there is a vector of variables to which we only add constant vectors to go to different states. Vector addition systems also correspond to constraint automata whose transitions contain only comparison constraints and only add or subtract from each state variable a constant.

Vector addition systems are recognition safe. A special case of vector addition systems is when they are *lossy*. In a lossy system if $(a_1, \ldots, a_n)$ is the state of the automaton at a time instance, then at any later time and state $(b_1, \ldots, b_n)$ it must be the case that for some $1 \leq i \leq n$ $b_i < a_i$. Lossy vector addition systems are evaluable in closed form.

Example 22.5.7 The Datalog query in Example 15.2.1 about the tourist is a vector addition system. Hence it is recognition safe. In fact, because some part of the tourist's money is used to pay commissions, it is not possible for the tourist to have more or equal amount of dollars, euros, and yen at a later state than at an earlier state due to the commission charges. Hence this is also a lossy vector addition system and is evaluable in closed form.

Recognition Safety

Suppose that the initial values for a vector addition system with n variables are $a = (a_1, \ldots, a_n)$. Is the configuration $b = (b_1, \ldots, b_n)$ possible? Let

$v_1, \ldots, v_m$ be the transition vectors, and let $M = (v_1, \ldots, v_m)$ be the $n \times m$ matrix of transitions.

For configuration b to be possible we have to have a vector $x \in \mathcal{N}^n$ such that:

$$a + Mx = b$$

But this is not enough, because there must exist a sequence of vectors $x_0, \ldots, x_k$ where x_0 is the zero vector, $x_k = x$, and each x_{i+1} is obtained from x_i by adding 1 to one of its elements, such that the following is true for each $0 \leq i \leq k$:

$$a + Mx_i \geq 0$$

In Example 15.2.1 the transition matrix is:

$$\begin{pmatrix} -100 & -100 & 99 & 0 & 99 & 0 \\ 198 & 0 & -200 & -200 & 0 & 198 \\ 0 & 29700 & 0 & 29700 & -30000 & -30000 \end{pmatrix}$$

Suppose that $a = (0, 600, 0)$ and $b = (98, 0, 59400)$. Then a solution for the equality is $x = (0, 1, 2, 1, 0, 0)$, which means that we need to exchange dollars into yen once, euros into dollars twice, and euros into yen once. There are 4! possible vector sequences from the zero vector to x. Out of these, the sequence $(0, 0, 1, 0, 0, 0)$, $(0, 0, 2, 0, 0, 0)$, $(0, 0, 2, 1, 0, 0)$, $(0, 1, 2, 1, 0, 0)$ is one that satisfies the inequality. This sequence corresponds to exchanging euros to dollars twice, then exchanging euros to yen, and then exchanging dollars to yen. There are other possible solutions, but this solution shows that the configuration is reachable.

This technique works well if there are only a few solutions of the equality. This may happen if the equality solved in the rationals is a hyperplane that intersects the all-positive quadrant in only a few integer solutions (this is true for Example 15.2.1) or when the rank of the matrix is m (i.e., it contains m linearly independent rows). For a vector addition system if there is only one way to reach from a to b and that requires n transitions, then we can find this solution in $O(n!)$ time. There are more general but also more complex techniques for solving the reachability problem in vector addition systems where the equality yields many solutions in nonnegative integers.

Now we will look at how we can certify that a vector addition system is evaluation safe by checking for the lossy property. We use the following theorem.

Theorem 22.5.1 A vector addition system with n variables is lossy if and only if there exist positive constants $c = (c_1, \ldots, c_n)$ such that for each transition v_i we have $\sum_j c_j v_{i,j} < 0$.

Proof: *(If)* If there exist such positive constants c, then on each transition from some configuration a to another configuration b the dot product of the cs and the configuration value decreases. Hence $ca > cb$. Now if each $b_i \geq a_i$, then $ca \leq cb$, which is a contradiction. Hence, there must be some i such that $b_i < a_i$. Therefore, the system must be lossy.

(Only if) If the vector addition system is not lossy then it is possible to go from a configuration a to a configuration b such that $b_i \geq a_i$ for each $1 \leq i \leq n$. Then for any set of positive constants c we have $ca \leq cb$. Hence at least for some transition v_i that was made when going from a to b, it must be the case that $\sum_j c_j v_{i,j} > 0$. Hence if the system is not lossy, then there cannot be positive constants as required.   ∎

Corollary 22.5.1 It can be tested whether a vector addition system is lossy.

Proof: By Theorem 22.5.1 it is enough to write a formula $\exists c \, \forall i (c v_i < 0)$. This formula is a linear Diophantine formula, which can be solved in general.   ∎

For the vector addition system in Example 15.2.1 a set of positive constants that satisfies the condition of Theorem 22.5.1 is $c = (300, 150, 1)$. This shows that it is a lossy vector addition system.

For lossy vector addition systems one can find all possible configurations by either breadth-first or depth-first search. Each branch of the search tree will be finite length because for some set of positive constants c, the dot product of c and the value of the state variables monotone decreases in discrete steps (because the values are integers) and only down to zero (because the value of each state variable must be always a nonnegative integer).

22.5.8   Positive Stochastic Matrix Multiplication

Sometimes it is possible to recognize that a Datalog program with linear constraints defines repeated multiplication of a vector by a *positive stochastic matrix*. A positive stochastic matrix is a square matrix that has only positive entries and in each column the sum of its elements is 1. It can be shown that during repeated positive stochastic matrix multiplication the values of the variables are monotone converging to some steady state with values $(s_1, \ldots, s_n)$. This steady state can be computed even though an infinite number of matrix multiplications may be needed to reach it.

Suppose we wish to test whether there is ever a derived tuple such that each of its values is ϵ close to the corresponding value in some tuple $(a_1, \ldots, a_n)$. We can do this test by first testing whether $(a_1, \ldots, a_n)$ is

ϵ close to $(s_1, \ldots, s_n)$. If it is, then the answer is yes. Otherwise, we just repeatedly perform the matrix multiplication and check that the current state is ϵ close to $(a_1, \ldots, a_n)$. We keep doing this until the last derived tuple is so close to the steady state that there is no chance for any derived tuple between the last derived tuple and the steady state to be ϵ close to $(a_1, \ldots, a_n)$. Hence Datalog programs that correspond to repeated positive stochastic matrix multiplication are ϵ-recognition safe.

Example 22.5.8 The query about the water cycle in Example 15.2.7 is safe for years $3n$ for each integer n. Suppose that we want to test whether vector w is a configuration that can occur after some $3n$ number of years. In Example 15.2.7 the matrix A is:

$$\begin{pmatrix} \frac{1}{2} & \frac{1}{3} & \frac{1}{6} & \frac{1}{60} \\ \frac{1}{2} & 0 & 0 & 0 \\ 0 & \frac{1}{3} & \frac{2}{3} & 0 \\ 0 & \frac{1}{3} & \frac{1}{6} & \frac{59}{60} \end{pmatrix}$$

Note that A is not positive stochastic because it has some zero entries, but $B = A^3$ is positive stochastic. To answer the question it is enough to consider whether for any n the vector $B^n u$ where u is the initial value of the state variables is ϵ-close to w.

ϵ-Recognition Safety

In this section we assume some familiarity with basic concepts in linear algebra. Positive stochastic matrix multiplication is also called *Markov chains*; we will use this term for simplicity. For Markov chains the most important theorem is the following.

Theorem 22.5.2 Let A be any positive stochastic matrix. Then there exists a unique distribution v such that $Av = v$. Further, let u be any vector different from v, and let $\sum u_i = c$. Then

$$\lim_{k \to \infty} A^k u = cv$$

Proof: One can show that any positive stochastic matrix has 1 as an eigenvalue and for any other eigenvalue λ it may have it must be true that its absolute value is less than 1.

Suppose that A has n distinct eigenvalues $\lambda_1 = 1, \lambda_2, \ldots, \lambda_n$, where $| \lambda_i | < 1$ for $i \geq 2$. (The proof is similar but has to be modified slightly if the eigenvalues are not distinct.) It has corresponding eigenvectors $v_1, \ldots, v_n$ where v_1 is a distribution and the vs are linearly independent. This implies that the matrix $V = (v_1, \ldots, v_n)$ is invertible. Let V^{-1} be the inverse of V and let Λ be the matrix where the eigenvalues appear on the main diagonal.

Then $A = V\Lambda V^{-1}$. Hence $A^k = V\Lambda^k V^{-1}$ for any k. Note that $\lim_{k\to\infty} \Lambda^k = D$, where D is the matrix that has all 0 entries except in its upper-left corner, which is 1. Therefore, $\lim_{k\to\infty} A^k = VDV^{-1} = V(DD)V^{-1} = (VD)(DV^{-1}) = (v_1, 0, \ldots, 0)(w_1, 0, \ldots, 0)^{-1}$, where w_1 is the first row of the matrix V^{-1}.

Hence we have $\lim_{k\to\infty} A^k u = v_1 c$ where c is the dot product of w_1 and u. Because multiplication of a positive stochastic matrix by any vector yields a vector in which the sum of the entries is the same, and v_1 is a distribution, $\sum u_i = c$. ∎

We can use Theorem 22.5.2 to evaluate ϵ-recognition safe queries.

Theorem 22.5.3 For any vectors w and u and matrix M we can find whether there exists a k such that $M^k \sim_\epsilon w$.

Proof: By Theorem 22.5.2 the value $A^k u$ converges to cv, where v and c are as defined there. We test first whether $w \sim_\epsilon cv$. If yes, then clearly w can be reached with ϵ-closeness. Otherwise, we calculate repeatedly $A^k u$ for $k = 1, 2, \ldots$ until either $(A^k u) \sim_\epsilon w$ or $(A^k u) \sim_\epsilon cv$. In the former case w can be still reached with ϵ-closeness, while in the latter case w cannot be reached with ϵ-closeness because for all larger k the vector $A^k u$ will just get closer and closer to cv, which we already know is not close to w. ∎

For example, consider Example 15.2.7 with A as given earlier, $B = A^3$, $u = (8, 16, 2, 8)$, $w = (2, 1.5, 1, 29.5)$, and $\epsilon = 0.5$. Because B is positive stochastic, by Theorem 22.5.2 there is a unique distribution v such that $Bv = v$. Solving this system of linear equations $Bv = v$ together with the distribution requirement $\sum v_i = 1$ we obtain the unique solution $v = (1/34)(2, 1, 1, 30)$. Here $c = 34$. Therefore by Theorem 22.5.2 the value of $B^k u$ converges to $cv = (2, 1, 1, 30)$. Because $w \sim_\epsilon cv$ is true, we know that the configuration w is ϵ-reachable.

Domain	Constraint	Property Verified
$\mathcal{N}$	Addition	Vector addition system^r
$\mathcal{N}$	Addition	Lossy vector addition system
$\mathcal{Q}$	Linear	Positive stochastic matrix multiplication$^\epsilon$
$\mathcal{Z}$	Linear	Tightening (pseudo-negative)
$\mathcal{N}$	Polynomial	Constricting (pseudo-linear)

Figure 22.3: Certifications that Guarantee Safety.

Figure 22.3 summarizes some conditions that can be verified to guarantee the safety of a constraint automaton. Superscripts r, ϵ mean recognition and ϵ-recognition safe, respectively.

Bibliographic Notes

The restrictions of Datalog with only inequality, rational order, or Boolean term equations was shown to be safe by Kanellakis, Kuper, and Revesz [214]. The restrictions of Datalog with integer or rational gap-order constraints was shown to be safe by Revesz [325]. This was extended to half-addition constraints in Revesz [334], which also showed that the restrictions with only positive and only negative linear inequality constraints are safe. Kreutzer [242, 243] is a recent work on the fixed-point evaluation of Datalog with linear constraints. The restriction with $\subseteq$ and monotone Boolean term inequation constraints is shown to be safe in Revesz [333].

That nonrecursive Datalog queries with rational linear inequality constraints are safe follows from the general evaluation strategy described in [214], which reduces the evaluation to existential quantifier elimination in the theory of rational linear inequality constraints. The first quantifier elimination algorithm for this case was given by Fourier [135]. Nonrecursive Datalog queries with real polynomial constraints are handled similarly by quantifier elimination in the theory of real polynomial inequality constraints. The first quantifier elimination algorithm for this case was given by Tarski [394]. In both cases, computationally more efficient quantifier elimination algorithms have been developed by other authors. For a review of these see Revesz [332].

Toman [398] shows that any type of restriction satisfying certain (sufficient but not necessary) conditions yields a closed-form evaluation safe Datalog query. Sufficient termination conditions under the assumption of top-down evaluation in constraint logic programs is studied in Aiken et al. [10], Colussi et al. [96], Giacobazzi et al. [150], and Heintze and Jaffar [194]. Safety of other constraint Datalog queries using a nonstandard semantics (i.e., different from the one described in Chapter 12) is studied by Grumbach and Kuper [166].

The approximate evaluation of Datalog with difference constraints was studied by Revesz [336].

That projection is safe in the cases shown in Figure 22.2 follows again from the quantifier elimination methods listed earlier. The result that quantifier elimination in the existential theory of integer polynomial constraints is unsafe follows from the undecidability result of the same theory by Matiyasevich [269], which improves an undecidability result for the whole theory by Gödel.

The minimum and maximum aggregate operators are safe for the case of linear inequality constraints and are used in several systems, including CCUBE [57] and MLPQ [351]. These operators are not generally evaluable for polynomial constraints. However, in many cases they are evaluable. For example, commercial systems like *Mathematica* or *Maple* can evaluate many queries involving polynomial constraints. The safety of aggregation operators is studied in Benedikt and Libkin [43], Chomicki et al. [82, 85], and Kuper and Su [252].

Vector addition systems were introduced in an equivalent but different notation by Petri; hence they are sometimes called Petri nets [304, 318]. The recognition problem in vector addition systems was shown to be decidable by Kosaraju [233] and Mayr [271]. A recognition algorithm that requires double exponential space in the size of the automaton was claimed recently by Bouziane [53]. However, Jancar [209] found a hole in the proof and argues that it cannot be filled.

Constraint automata with a single self-transition with positive stochastic matrix multiplication, are also called Markov chains, because they were studied by Markov, who showed that there is a steady-state vector to which the nth power of the matrix converges. More about steady states of matrix multiplication can be found in [285, 364, 386].

Certification using lossy constraint automata, tightening, and constricting transitions is new. Certification algorithms using constraint simplification by constant passing for stratified Datalog queries with gap-order and set-order constraints are described in Revesz [335].

Exercises

1. Prove that the following queries are safe:

    (a) Example 12.1.1 about the taxes due.

    (b) Example 12.1.8 about the broadcast areas of radio stations.

    (c) Example 15.2.2 about the elevator system.

    (d) Example 15.2.4 about the subway train control system.

    (e) Example 15.2.6 about the cafeteria.

2. Is the query that you wrote for the following exercises safe? Why or why not?

    (a) Exercise 15.6 about the thermostat.

    (b) Exercise 15.10 about employment.

    (c) Exercise 15.11 about the wealth of people.

3. Prove that the following queries in Chapter 12.4 are safe:

    (a) The Q_{profit} query.

    (b) The Q_{edge} query.

    (c) The $Q_{\text{not\_cover}}$ query.

    (d) The Q_{fastest} query.

    (e) The Q_{Alice} query.

4. Prove that the following queries are safe:

    (a) Example 12.1.1 about the taxes due.

    (b) Example 12.1.8 about the broadcast areas of radio stations.

    (c) Example 15.2.2 about the elevator system.

    (d) Example 15.2.4 about the subway train control system.

    (e) Example 15.2.6 about the cafeteria.

5. Is the query you wrote for the following exercises safe? Why or why not?

    (a) Exercise 15.6 about the thermostat.

    (b) Exercise 15.10 about employment.

    (c) Exercise 15.11 about the wealth of people.

6. Prove that the following queries in Chapter 12.4 are safe:

    (a) The Q_{profit} query.

    (b) The Q_{edge} query.

    (c) The $Q_{\text{not\_cover}}$ query.

    (d) The Q_{fastest} query.

    (e) The Q_{Alice} query.

7. Prove that lossy vector addition systems are evaluable in closed form. (*Hint:* Use Lemma 6 and König's Lemma, which says that any bounded-degree infinite tree must have an infinite path.

23

Evaluation of Queries

Our notion of queries is as abstract as our notion of databases. Therefore, we may talk about different levels of query abstraction, just as we talked about different levels of data abstraction. In the previous chapters we usually thought of queries as functions from (possibly) infinite relational databases to (possibly) infinite relational databases as shown in Figure 23.1. This is the logical level of query abstraction. This level was enough to write good queries. However, in this chapter we consider queries at the constraint level. At the constraint level, queries can be thought of as functions from finite constraint databases to finite constraint databases, as shown in Figure 23.2.

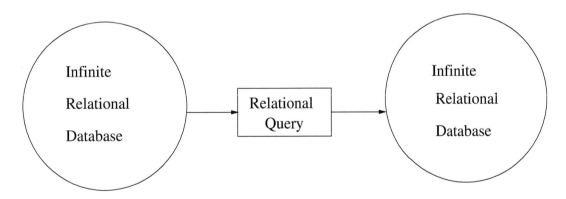

Figure 23.1: Queries in the relational data model.

P. Revesz, *Introduction to Databases: From Biological to Spatio-Temporal*,
Texts in Computer Science, DOI 10.1007/978-1-84996-095-3_23,
© Springer-Verlag London Limited 2010

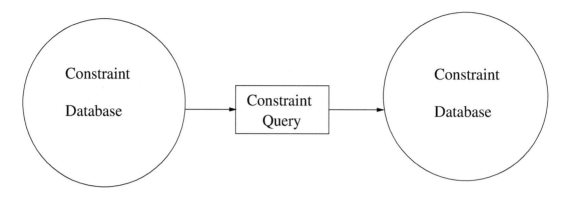

Figure 23.2: Queries in the constraint data model.

In Section 23.1 we describe quantifier elimination algorithms. In Sections 23.2, 23.3, and 23.4, we describe the evaluation of relational algebra, SQL, and Datalog queries, respectively.

23.1   Quantifier Elimination and Satisfiability

In Chapter 4 we defined constraint tuples as conjunctions of atomic constraints. Suppose now that S is a constraint tuple over the variables $x, y_1, \ldots, y_n$ ranging over some domain D. Then S defines an infinite relation r that is a subset of D^{n+1}. If we project out from r all the variables except x, that is, if we drop the x attribute column, then we get a new relation r'.

The goal of *existential quantifier elimination* is to find a finite constraint representation of r' that uses only the variables $y_1, \ldots, y_n$. If there is such a finite constraint representation S' then we write $S' = \exists x S$, where the $\exists$ symbol is read as "exists" and it is referred to as the "existential quantifier." The notation reminds us that for each tuple t' in r' there exists in r a tuple t that is the same as t' on the y attributes and has some x value in it.

If for any x and S over some type of constraints there is always an S' over the same type of constraints such that $S' = \exists x S$, then we say that existential quantifier elimination is closed for that type of constraint. The next few theorems give examples of closed quantifier elimination algorithms in various cases of constraints.

Theorem 23.1.1 Existential quantifier elimination is closed for conjunctions of any infinite domain equality and inequality constraints where each constant in the conjunction is an element of D that is a nonempty finite subset of the domain for any fixed D.

Proof: Let S be any conjunction of equality and inequality constraints over x and some other variables as required. Without loss of generality we can assume that each constraint that contains x has x on the left-hand side. We show that $S' = \exists x S$ can be written as required.

S' will be the conjunction of all the constraints in S that do not contain the variable x and all the constraints that can be derived from a pair of constraints in S using the following rule. If $x\theta_1 u$ and $x\theta_2 v$ are in S for any pair u, v of variables or constants and at least one of θ_1 and θ_2 is $=$ then add to S' the constraint $u\theta_3 v$ where if θ_1 and θ_2 are both $=$ then θ_3 is also $=$ else it is $\neq$. By this rule, we add to S' only equality and inequality constraints that use only constants from D. This proves syntactic closure.

Now we prove the soundness of the quantifier elimination. It can be seen that for any instantiation if the two constraints in S are both true, then the constraint added to S' is also true. Hence if S is true, then S' must be true for any instantiation of x and the other variables.

For the other direction, suppose that S' is true for some instantiation of all the variables except x. Then make the same instantiation into S. Suppose that S contains a list of equality constraints $x = u_1$, $x = u_2, \ldots$, and a list of inequality constraints $x \neq v_1$, $x \neq v_2, \ldots$ in which x occurs.

Because S' is true, after the instantiation of S all the u_is must be the same constant c. Otherwise we would have two different constants c_1 and c_2 equal to x and by our rule we would have derived $c_1 = c_2$, which is false and therefore a contradiction to S' being true. Further, no constant among the vs can be c. Therefore if there is any equality constraint, then we could let $x = c$, and that would make S true. Otherwise, we can choose any constant for x that is different from all the vs. Because the domain is infinite, we can do that. Then again, S must be true. ∎

Theorem 23.1.2 Existential quantifier elimination is closed for conjunctions of rational order constraints where each constant in the conjunction is an element of a nonempty set $D \subset \mathcal{R}$.

Proof: Let S be any conjunction of order constraints over x and some other variables as required. We show that $S' = \exists x S$ can be written as a conjunction of order constraints over only the other variables and using only constants from D.

S' will be the conjunction of all the constraints in S that do not contain the variable x and all the constraints that can be derived from a pair of constraints in S using transitivity. That is, if $u\theta_1 x$ and $x\theta_2 v$ are in S for any pair u, v of variables or constants, then add to S' the constraint $u\theta_3 v$ where if θ_1 and θ_2 are both $\geq$ then θ_3 is also $\geq$ else it is $>$. By using transitivity we add to S' only order constraints that use only constants from D. This proves syntactic closure.

Now we prove the soundness of the quantifier elimination. It can be seen that for any instantiation if the two constraints in S are both true, then the constraint added to S' is also true. Hence if S is true, then S' must be true for any instantiation of x and the other variables.

For the other direction, suppose that S' is true for some instantiation of all the variables except x. Then make the same instantiation into S. Suppose that S contains a list of upper bound constraints $u_1 \geq x$, $u_2 \geq x, \ldots$ and a list of lower bound constraints $x \geq v_1$, $x \geq v_2, \ldots$ in which x occurs.

Suppose that after the instantiation the largest lower bound of x is c and the smallest upper bound of x is d. Then by transitivity we must have added a constraint to S', which after instantiation is $d \geq c$. Because S' is true, we can find a value between c and d inclusively for x that will make S also true. ∎

Theorem 23.1.3 Existential quantifier elimination is closed for conjunctions of integer and rational gap-order, lower bound and upper bound constraints where each lower bound and upper bound constraint has a minimum bound of l, and all constants occurring in the conjunction are integers or rational numbers with denominator p for any fixed $l \leq 0$ and $p > 0$.

Proof: Let S be any conjunction of gap-order, lower bound, and upper bound constraints over x and some other variables such that each bound is $\geq l$. We show that $S' = \exists x S$ can be written as a conjunction of gap-order, lower bound, and upper bound constraints over only the other variables such that each bound is $\geq l$.

S' will be the conjunction of all the constraints in S that do not contain the variable x and all the constraints that can be derived by taking the sum of any pair of constraints in S with opposite signs for x. This can happen in three different ways:

Case I: There are two gap-order constraints of the form $x - y \geq a$ and $z - x \geq b$, respectively. Their sum will be $z - y \geq a + b$. Because a and b are nonnegative, their sum will be nonnegative; hence the new constraint is a gap-order constraint.

Case II: There is a gap-order constraint of the form $x - y \geq a$ and an upper bound constraint of the form $-x \geq b$. Their sum will be $-y \geq a + b$.

Case III: There is a gap-order constraint of the form $y - x \geq a$ and a lower bound constraint of the form $x \geq b$. Their sum will be $y \geq a + b$.

Note that $a + b$ is an integer if a and b are integers, and it is a rational with denominator p if a and b are rationals with denominator p. In addition, in each case, $a + b \geq b$ because $a \geq 0$. This proves that if all bounds were greater than l before the shortcut, then all bounds will still be greater than l after the shortcut. This shows that the quantifier elimination is closed for any fixed l.

Now we prove the soundness of the quantifier elimination. For any instantiation, if two constraints are both true, then their sum also must be a true constraint. Hence if S is true, then S' must be true for any instantiation of x and the other variables.

For the other direction, suppose that S' is true for some instantiation of all the variables except x. Then make the same instantiation into S. After the instantiation, x will be the only remaining variable in S. Wherever x occurs positively, the constraint implies a lower bound for x, and wherever x occurs negatively the constraint implies an upper bound for x.

Suppose that the largest lower bound c is implied by some constraint f and the smallest upper bound d is implied by some constraint g. Because the sum of f and g under the current instantiation is equivalent to $d \geq c$ and is in S', which is true, we can find a value between c and d inclusively for x that will make S also true. ∎

We can extend Theorem 23.1.3 in two different ways. The first extension replaces gap-order constraints with half-addition constraints.

Theorem 23.1.4 Existential quantifier elimination is closed for conjunctions of integer and rational half-addition, lower bound, and upper bound constraints where all bounds in the half-addition constraints are integers or rational numbers with denominator p and all bounds in the lower and upper bound constraints are integers or rationals with denominator $2p$ and greater than l for any fixed $l \leq 0$ and $p > 0$.

Proof: Let S be any conjunction of half-addition, lower bound, and upper bound constraints over x and some other variables. We show that $S' = \exists x S$ can be written as a similar conjunction of constraints over only the other variables.

S' will be the conjunction of all the constraints in S that do not contain the variable x and all the constraints that can be derived from any pair of constraints in S that have opposite signs for x. There are the following cases:

Cases I–III: Similar to Cases I–III of Theorem 23.1.3.

Case IV: There are two half-addition constraints of the form $x + y \geq a$ and $z - x \geq b$ where $z \neq y$. Their sum will be $y + z \geq a + b$. In this case, if a and b are nonnegative integers or rational numbers with denominator p then so is $a + b$.

Case V: There are two half-addition constraints of the form $x + y \geq a$ and $y - x \geq b$. Their sum will be $2y \geq a + b$.

We can write the new constraint as the lower bound constraint $y \geq (a+b)/2$ in the case of rational numbers and as $y \geq ceiling((a+b)/2)$ in the case of integers, where the ceiling function takes the smallest integer value that is greater than or equal to any given rational value. Because a and b are rational numbers with p as the denominator, the new bound $(a+b)/2$ can be written as a rational with denominator $2p$ as required.

Case VI: There are two half-addition constraints of the form $x - y \geq a$ and $-x - z \geq b$ where $z \neq y$. Their sum will be $-y - z \geq a + b$. In this case the proof is similar to Case IV.

Case VII: There are two half-addition constraints of the form $x - y \geq a$ and $-x - y \geq b$. Their sum will be $-2y \geq a + b$. In this case the proof is similar to Case V.

Case VIII: There are two constraints of the form $x + y \geq a$ and $-x \geq b$. Their sum will be $y \geq a + b$. In this case, if a and b are nonnegative integers or rational numbers with denominators p and $2p$, respectively, then $a + b$ is also an integer or a rational number with denominator $2p$.

Case IX: There are two constraints of the form $-x - y \geq a$ and $x \geq b$. Their sum will be $-y \geq a + b$. In this case, if a and b are nonnegative integers or rational numbers with denominators p and $2p$, respectively, then $a + b$ is also an integer or a rational number with denominator $2p$.

We can prove the logical equivalence of $\exists x S$ and S' similarly to the proof in Theorem 23.1.3. ∎

We say that the *arity* of a linear constraint is the number of variables with nonzero coefficients. We say that a linear constraint is in *normal form* if all of its coefficients are nonzero integers. Clearly, every linear constraint can be put into normal form. We call *positive* those linear constraints in which all coefficients are nonnegative.

Note that each lower bound constraint can be expressed as a 1-arity positive normal linear constraint. The second extension of Theorem 23.1.3 replaces lower bound constraints with positive linear constraints.

Theorem 23.1.5 Existential quantifier elimination is closed for conjunctions of integer or rational gap-order, upper bound and positive normal linear constraints where each upper bound constraint has a minimum bound of l, each positive normal linear constraint has a maximum arity m, a maximum sum of coefficients s, and a minimum bound $l + (m - k)sl$ where k

is its arity and all constants occurring in the conjunction are integers or rational numbers with denominator p for any fixed $l \le 0$ and $m, p, s > 0$.

Proof: Let S be any conjunction of gap-order, upper bound, and positive normal linear constraints over x and some other variables as required. We show that $S' = \exists x S$ can be written as a similar conjunction of constraints over only the other variables.

S' will be the conjunction of all the constraints in S that do not contain the variable x and all the constraints that can be derived from any pair of constraints in S with opposite signs for x. This can happen in five different ways:

Cases I–II: These are similar to Cases I–II of Theorem 23.1.3. These clearly preserve the required form.

For **Cases III–V**, assume that one of the constraints is a k-arity positive normal linear constraint of the form

$$c_0 x + c_1 y_1 + \ldots + c_{k-1} y_{k-1} \theta_2 a$$

Case III: The second constraint is an upper bound constraint of the form $-x \theta_1 b$. Multiplying the second constraint by c_0 and adding it to the first yields:

$$c_1 y_1 + \ldots + c_{k-1} y_{k-1} \theta_3 a + c_0 b$$

where θ_3 is $\ge$ if θ_1 and θ_2 are both $\ge$ and $>$ otherwise.

The new constraint is the same as the positive normal linear constraint except that the term $c_0 x$ is deleted and the bound changed from a to $a + c_0 b$. This decreases its arity by one and the sum of its coefficients by $c_0 > 0$. Hence its arity is $\le m$, and the sum of its coefficients is $\le s$.

We know that $b \ge l$. Multiplying by $c_0 > 0$ we get $c_0 b \ge c_0 l$. We also know that $c_0 \le s$. Multiplying by $l \le 0$ we get $c_0 l \ge sl$. Hence $c_0 b \ge sl$. Because $a \ge l + (m - k)sl$, we have $a + c_0 b \ge l + (m - k)sl + sl = l + (m - k + 1)sl = l + (m - (k - 1))sl = l + (m - k')sl$ where $k' = k - 1$ is the arity of the new constraint.

Case IV: The second constraint is a gap-order constraint of the form $z - x \theta_1 b$ where z is different from each y_i for $1 \le i \le k - 1$. Multiplying the second constraint by c_0 and adding it to the first yields:

$$c_0 z + c_1 y_1 + \ldots + c_{k-1} y_{k-1} \theta_3 a + c_0 b$$

where θ_3 is $\ge$ if θ_1 and θ_2 are both $\ge$ and $>$ otherwise.

The new constraint is the same as the positive normal linear constraint except the variable x is replaced by z and the bound changed from a to

$a + c_0 b$. Hence its arity and sum of coefficients are the same. Hence its arity is $\leq m$, and the sum of its coefficients is $\leq s$. Further, $a + c_0 b \geq a$ because $b \geq 0$ and $c_0 > 0$. Therefore its bound is also $\geq l + (m - k)sl$ as required.

Case V: The second constraint is a gap-order constraint of the form $y_i - x\theta_1 b$ where $1 \leq i \leq k - 1$. Multiplying the second constraint by c_0 and adding it to the first yields:

$$c_1 y_1 + \ldots + (c_0 + c_i)y_i + \ldots + c_{k-1}y_{k-1}\theta_3 a + c_0 b$$

where θ_3 is $\geq$ if θ_1 and θ_2 are both $\geq$ and $>$ otherwise.

The new constraint is still a positive normal linear constraint because the sum of c_0 and c_i is a positive integer and the other coefficients did not change. The arity decreased by one and the sum of the coefficients stayed the same. Hence its arity is $\leq m$, and the sum of its coefficients is $\leq s$. Further, $a + c_0 b \geq a$ because $b \geq 0$ and $c_0 > 0$. Also, $sl \leq 0$ because $s > 0$ and $l \leq 0$. Because $a \geq l + (m - k)sl$ we have $a + c_0 b \geq l + (m-k)sl \geq l + (m-k)sl + sl = l + (m-k')sl$ where $k' = k-1$ is the arity of the new constraint.

Finally, note that in Cases III–V if a, b are rationals with common denominator p then the new bound $a + c_0 b$ can be also expressed as a quotient of some integer and p because c_0 is an integer. Therefore the closed form is preserved.

We can prove the logical equivalence of $\exists x S$ and S' similarly to the proof in Theorem 23.1.3. ∎

The following is similar to Theorem 23.1.5.

Theorem 23.1.6 Existential quantifier elimination is closed for conjunctions of integer or rational gap-order, lower bound, and negative normal linear constraints where each lower bound constraint has a minimum bound of l, each negative normal linear constraint has a maximum arity m, a maximum sum of coefficients $-s$, and a minimum bound $l - (m - k)sl$ where k is its arity, and all constants occurring in the conjunction are integers or rational numbers with denominator p for any fixed $l \leq 0$, $s < 0$, and $m, p > 0$. ∎

The following theorem is about linear constraints. We only prove it for the case of the rationals; we omit the proof for the case of the integers.

Theorem 23.1.7 Existential quantifier elimination is closed for rational linear inequality constraints.

Proof: Without loss of generality assume that the conjunction S of linear inequality constraints is a set of linear inequalities that do not contain x

and a set of k linear inequalities of the form:

$$x + c_{1,1}y_1 + \ldots + c_{1,n}y_n \;\geq\; b_1$$
$$\vdots$$
$$x + c_{k,1}y_1 + \ldots + c_{k,n}y_n \;\geq\; b_k$$

that contain x with a coefficient of one, and a set of $m-k$ linear inequalities of the form:

$$-x + c_{k+1,1}y_1 + \ldots + c_{k+1,n}y_n \;\geq\; b_{k+1}$$
$$\vdots$$
$$-x + c_{m,1}y_1 + \ldots + c_{m,n}y_n \;\geq\; b_m$$

that contain x with a coefficient of minus one. Then $S' = \exists x S$ will be the conjunctions of all the constraints in S that do not contain x and the $k \times (m - k)$ constraints that we can obtain by adding one of the k constraints in the first displayed set to one of the $m - k$ constraints in the second displayed set. This preserves syntactical closed form.

We can prove the logical equivalence of $\exists x S$ and S' similarly to the proof in Theorem 23.1.3. ∎

The following theorem about polynomial constraints requires a more difficult proof, which we omit here.

Theorem 23.1.8 Existential quantifier elimination is closed for real polynomial inequality constraints. ∎

Next we consider free Boolean algebras. First we show the following.

Lemma 23.1.1 Conjunctions of Boolean minterm equality constraints are equivalent to conjunctions of Boolean equality constraints.

Proof: Because each minterm equality constraint is also an equality constraint, one direction of the lemma is obvious. We show that each conjunction of Boolean equality constraints can be expressed as a conjunction of Boolean minterm equality constraints as follows. Let the conjunction of Boolean equality constraints be of the form

$$f_1 =_B \emptyset \quad \text{and} \quad \ldots \quad \text{and} \quad f_l =_B \emptyset$$

where f_i is a Boolean term for each $1 \leq i \leq l$. For each i we can put f_i into disjunctive normal form, that is, in the form:

$$d_{i,1} \cup d_{i,2} \cup \ldots \cup d_{i,k_i} =_B \emptyset$$

where each $d_{i,j}$ is a minterm of the Boolean algebra B. This is equivalent to:

$$d_{i,1} =_B \emptyset \quad \text{and} \quad d_{i,2} =_B \emptyset \quad \text{and} \quad \ldots \quad \text{and} \quad d_{i,k_i} =_B \emptyset$$

This proves the lemma. ∎

Theorem 23.1.9 Existential quantifier elimination is closed for conjunctions of Boolean equality constraints.

Proof: By Lemma 23.1.1 we can rewrite the conjunction of equality constraints into a conjunction of minterm equality constraints.

Let S be any conjunction of Boolean minterm equality constraints over x and some other variables. We show that $S' = \exists x S$ can be written as a similar conjunction of constraints over only the other variables.

S' will be the conjunction of all the constraints in S that can be derived from any pair of constraints in S such that the first constraint has the form:

$$\overline{x} \cap y_1 \cap \ldots \cap y_n =_B \emptyset$$

and the second constraint has the form:

$$x \cap z_1 \cap \ldots \cap z_m =_B \emptyset$$

where the ys and zs are not necessarily distinct negated or unnegated Boolean algebra variables and constants. Here the first constraint is equivalent to $y_1 \cap \ldots \cap y_n \subseteq_B x$, and the second constraint is equivalent to:

$$x \subseteq_B \overline{(z_1 \cap \ldots \cap z_m)}.$$

Hence by transitivity, we can derive $y_1 \cap \ldots \cap y_n \subseteq_B \overline{(z_1 \cap \ldots \cap z_m)}$, which is equivalent to:

$$y_1 \cap \ldots y_n \cap z_1 \cap \ldots z_m =_B \emptyset$$

This is also a Boolean minterm equality constraint. Therefore this preserves syntactic closed form.

We can prove the logical equivalence of $\exists S$ and S' similarly to the proof in Theorem 23.1.3. ∎

The quantifier elimination method in Theorem 23.1.9 is only for equality constraints. In the case of *atomless* Boolean algebras, we can extend the quantifier elimination to both equality and inequality constraints.

Lemma 23.1.2 Each conjunction of Boolean minterm equality and inequality constraints is equivalent to a disjunction of conjunctions of Boolean equality and inequality constraints.

Proof: Take any conjunction of $C = E \cap I$, where E is a conjunction of Boolean equality and I is a conjunction of Boolean inequality constraints. We can use Lemma 23.1.1 to rewrite E into a conjunction of minterm equality constraints E_m. Let I be of the form

$$f_1 \neq_B \emptyset \quad \text{and} \quad \ldots \quad \text{and} \quad f_l \neq_B \emptyset \tag{23.1}$$

where f_i is a Boolean term for each $1 \leq i \leq l$. For each i we can put f_i into disjunctive normal form, that is, in the form:

$$d_{i,1} \cup d_{i,2} \cup \ldots \cup d_{i,k_i} \neq_B \emptyset$$

where each $d_{i,j}$ is a minterm of the Boolean algebra B. Because the disjunction of minterms is nonzero if only one of them is nonzero, the preceding is equivalent to:

$$d_{i,1} \neq_B \emptyset \ \text{ or } \ d_{i,2} \neq_B \emptyset \ \text{ or } \ \ldots \ \text{ or } \ d_{i,k_i} \neq_B \emptyset$$

When we substitute into (23.1) the preceding for each i, then we get a conjunction of disjunctions. We can rewrite the formula using the distributivity axioms into a disjunction of conjunctions of minterm inequality constraints. Finally, we can add to each disjunct E' to obtain a disjunction of conjunctions of minterm equality and inequality constraints that is equivalent to C. ∎

Now we consider quantifier elimination in atomless Boolean algebras.

Theorem 23.1.10 Existential quantifier elimination is closed for conjunctions of Boolean equality and inequality constraints in atomless Boolean algebras.

Proof: By Lemma 23.1.2 we may assume that we have only minterm equality and inequality constraints.

Let S be any conjunction of Boolean minterm equality and inequality constraints over x and some other variables. We show that $S' = \exists x S$ can be written as a similar conjunction of constraints over only the other variables.

First we derive constraints as in Theorem 23.1.9. Then we check whether there is any minterm such that $m \neq_B \emptyset$ and $m =_B \emptyset$ are both in the conjunction. If not, then we drop from each minterm x or $\overline{x}$. ∎

Next we consider Boolean order constraints.

Theorem 23.1.11 Existential quantifier elimination is closed for conjunctions of Boolean order constraints.

Proof: Let S be any conjunction of Boolean order constraints over x and some other variables. We show that $S' = \exists x S$ can be written as a similar conjunction of constraints over only the other variables.

S' will be the conjunction of all the constraints in S that do not contain the variable x and all the constraints that can be derived from any pair of constraints in S using the following cases:

Case I: We have two Boolean order constraints. The first is of the form $f \supseteq_B x$, which is equivalent to:

$$x \cap \overline{f} =_B \emptyset \tag{23.2}$$

and the second is of the form $g \supseteq_B y$, which is equivalent to $y \cap \overline{g} =_B \emptyset$. Using Lemma 23.1.1 and breaking up the disjunctions, the latter is also equivalent to:

$$x \cap y \cap \overline{g}_x(1) =_B \emptyset \quad \text{and} \quad \overline{x} \cap y \cap \overline{g}_x(\emptyset) =_B \emptyset \tag{23.3}$$

As in Theorem 23.1.9, from (23.2) and the second part of (23.3) we can derive $\overline{f} \cap \overline{g}_x(\emptyset) \cap y =_B \emptyset$, which is equivalent to:

$$f \cup g_x(\emptyset) \supseteq_B y \tag{23.4}$$

The closed form is preserved because (23.4) is a Boolean order constraint.

Case II: We have in the conjunction a constraint $g(x, v_1 \ldots, v_n) \supset_B \emptyset$ and a set of Boolean order constraints where the ith-order constraint has the form:

$$f_i \supseteq_B x \tag{23.5}$$

Let u be $\bigcap_i f_i$. Then the derived constraint will be $g(u, v_1, \ldots, v_n) \supset_B \emptyset$, i.e., x is replaced by u. Because all the f_i are monotone, u is monotone. Because g and u are monotone, the left-hand side of the derived constraint will also be monotone. This shows syntactical closed form.

Now we prove the soundness of the quantifier elimination. For Case I the soundness can be proven similarly to Theorem 23.1.9.

Case II First Direction: Suppose that S is true. Then by the merge of the formulas (23.5), $u \supseteq_B x$ is true. Further, for any $g(x, v_1, \ldots, v_n) \supset_B \emptyset$ constraint in S, the preceding and our observation in Remark 11.2.3 imply that the condition $g(u, v_1, \ldots, v_n) \supseteq_B g(x, v_1 \ldots, v_n)$ is true. Hence by transitivity $g(u, v_1 \ldots, v_n) \supset_B \emptyset$ is true. Therefore, all the constraints in S' derived by Case II must also be true using the same substitutions for the variables as in S.

Case II Second Direction: Suppose that S' is true for some substitution of the variables in it. Then S is true with the same substitutions of the variables as in S' and the substitution of x by u. This is because the augmentation rule implies for each i that $f_i \supseteq_B u$, which is equivalent to (23.5) with x replaced by u. In addition, with that substitution, each $g(x, v_1 \ldots, v_n) \supset_B \emptyset$ constraint in S becomes equivalent to the corresponding constraint in S'. Hence S must also be true. ∎

Example 23.1.1 We can represent the information in Exercise 9.9 as the following conjunction of constraints in the specific Boolean algebra B_W of Example 11.2.3, where capitalized strings are words in $\mathcal{W}$ and lower case letters are variables:

$$
\begin{array}{rcl}
\{Lilla\} & \subseteq & p \\
\{Bob, Peter\} & \subseteq & f \\
t & \subseteq & \{Bob, Jenny, Peter, Tom\} \\
o & \subseteq & p \\
t & \subseteq & f \\
p & \subseteq & d \\
v & \subseteq & g \\
v & \subseteq & p \\
f \cap g & \neq & \emptyset \\
d \cap p & \neq & \emptyset \\
t \cap (v \cup p) & \neq & \emptyset
\end{array}
$$

These constraints can be rewritten as the conjunction of eight simple upper bound constraints and three monotone inequality constraints as follows:

$$
\begin{array}{rcl}
\overline{p} & \subseteq & \overline{\{Lilla\}} \\
\overline{f} & \subseteq & \overline{\{Bob, Peter\}} \\
t & \subseteq & \{Bob, Jenny, Peter, Tom\} \\
o \cap \overline{p} & \subseteq & \emptyset \\
\overline{f} \cap t & \subseteq & \emptyset \\
\overline{d} \cap p & \subseteq & \emptyset \\
\overline{g} \cap v & \subseteq & \emptyset \\
\overline{p} \cap v & \subseteq & \emptyset \\
f \cap g & \neq & \emptyset \\
d \cap p & \neq & \emptyset \\
t \cap (v \cup p) & \neq & \emptyset
\end{array}
$$

Let us eliminate the variable p. Note that p occurs unnegated in only one upper bound constraint, which is equivalent to $p \subseteq d$. Hence we get:

$$
\begin{array}{rcl}
\overline{f} & \subseteq & \overline{\{Bob, Peter\}} \\
t & \subseteq & \{Bob, Jenny, Peter, Tom\} \\
\overline{f} \cap t & \subseteq & \emptyset \\
\overline{d} & \subseteq & \overline{\{Lilla\}} \\
\overline{d} \cap o & \subseteq & \emptyset \\
\overline{d} \cap v & \subseteq & \emptyset \\
\overline{g} \cap v & \subseteq & \emptyset \\
f \cap g & \neq & \emptyset \\
d & \neq & \emptyset \\
t \cap (v \cup d) & \neq & \emptyset
\end{array}
$$

The next theorem considers quantifier elimination for Boolean linear cardinality constraint formulas in atomic Boolean algebras of sets.

Theorem 23.1.12 [constant-free case] Existentially quantified variables can be eliminated from Boolean linear cardinality constraint formulas. The quantifier elimination is closed, that is, yields a quantifier-free Boolean linear cardinality constraint formula.

Proof: Let S be any conjunction of Boolean linear cardinality constraints over x and some other Boolean set variables $y_1, \ldots, y_n$. We show that $F = \exists x S$ can be written as a conjunction of Boolean cardinality constraints over only the other variables $y_1, \ldots, y_n$.

S has 2^{n+1} minterms. Let us order these minterms assuming that x is the first variable.

For each $1 \leq i \leq 2^n$ the pair of minterms m_i and m_{2^n+i} differ only on x. (The minterm m_i will have x positively and the minterm m_{2^n+i} will have x negatively occurring in it.) Now let us introduce a new symbol for the union of these pairs of minterms as follows.

$$n_i = m_i \cup m_{2^n+i} \tag{23.6}$$

for $1 \leq i \leq 2^n$. Then the following must hold:

$$|n_i| - |m_i| - |m_{2^n+i}| = 0 \tag{23.7}$$

Note that $|m_i|$ for $1 \leq i \leq 2^{n+1}$ and $|n_i|$ for $1 \leq i \leq 2^n$ are integer variables. Let S^* be the union of S in normal form (11.1) and the system (23.7). Let us eliminate from S^* the variables $|m_i|$ for $1 \leq i \leq 2^{n+1}$ using a quantifier elimination algorithm for integer linear equality and inequality constraints. That is, let us find:

$$F = \exists |m_1|, \ldots, |m_{2^{n+1}}| \quad S^*$$

The linear quantifier elimination clearly preserves the closed-form requirement. Hence we also get a closed-form for the Boolean linear cardinality constraint quantifier elimination. Next we show the soundness of the Boolean linear cardinality quantifier elimination.

S **implies** F: Take any assignment of the set variables $x, y_1, \ldots, y_n$ that satisfies S. This assignment must also satisfy the system (23.7), because of the definition (23.6). Hence the assignment satisfies S^*. By the correctness of the quantifier elimination algorithm for integer linear equality and inequality constraints, F is also satisfied.

F **implies** S: Take any assignment of the set variables $y_1, \ldots, y_n$ that satisfies F. We need to extend this assignment by an assignment for x that satisfies S.

The assignment for the set variables $y_1, \ldots, y_n$ determines the value of n_i and hence the value of $|n_i|$ for $1 \leq i \leq 2^n$. Since F is satisfied by the $|n_i|$ values, we can find for the integer variables $|m_i|$ also some values that satisfy S^*. The system (23.7) must be satisfied because S^* contains it. Hence it must be possible to arbitrarily partition the elements of n_i into two sets with the first set having $|m_i|$ and the second set having $|m_{2^n+i}|$ elements for each $1 \leq i \leq 2^n$. These partitions are independent of each other because the n_i for $1 \leq i \leq 2^n$ are disjoint.

The above partition yields an assignment to each m_i for $1 \leq i \leq 2^{n+1}$ that satisfies all the cardinality constraints in S^*. By definition:

$$x = \bigcup_{1 \leq i \leq 2^n} m_i$$

because x occurs positively in exactly the first 2^n minterms out of the total of 2^{n+1} minterms of S. This identity and the above assignment to each m_i for $1 \leq i \leq 2^{n+1}$ immediately gives a value for x that clearly satisfies S. ∎

Example 23.1.2 Let S be the Boolean cardinality formula in Example 11.2.8. A quantifier elimination problem would be to find a quantifier-free formula that is logically equivalent to the following:

$\exists x \, S$

First, we put S into a normal form as shown in Example 11.2.15. Then let S^* be the conjunction of the normal form and the following:

$$
\begin{aligned}
|y \cap z| - |x \cap y \cap z| - |\overline{x} \cap y \cap z| &= 0 \\
|y \cap \overline{z}| - |x \cap y \cap \overline{z}| - |\overline{x} \cap y \cap \overline{z}| &= 0 \\
|\overline{y} \cap z| - |x \cap \overline{y} \cap z| - |\overline{x} \cap \overline{y} \cap z| &= 0 \\
|\overline{y} \cap \overline{z}| - |x \cap \overline{y} \cap \overline{z}| - |\overline{x} \cap \overline{y} \cap \overline{z}| &= 0
\end{aligned}
$$

Second, we consider each expression that is the cardinality of a minterm (over x, y, z or over y, z) as an integer variable. Then by integer linear constraint variable elimination we get:

$$
\begin{aligned}
|y \cap z| + |y \cap \overline{z}| &\equiv_6 0 \\
|y \cap z| + |\overline{y} \cap z| &\equiv_9 0 \\
|y \cap z| &= 7
\end{aligned}
$$

By Theorem 23.1.12, the above is equivalent to $\exists x \, S$. For instance, the following is one solution for the above:

$$
\begin{aligned}
|y \cap z| &= 7 \\
|y \cap \overline{z}| &= 5 \\
|\overline{y} \cap z| &= 2 \\
|\overline{y} \cap \overline{z}| &= 0
\end{aligned}
$$

Corresponding to this we can find the solution:

$$|x \cap y \cap z| = 0 \qquad |\overline{x} \cap y \cap z| = 7$$
$$|x \cap y \cap \overline{z}| = 2 \qquad |\overline{x} \cap y \cap \overline{z}| = 3$$
$$|x \cap \overline{y} \cap z| = 1 \qquad |\overline{x} \cap \overline{y} \cap z| = 1$$
$$|x \cap \overline{y} \cap \overline{z}| = 0 \qquad |\overline{x} \cap \overline{y} \cap \overline{z}| = 0$$

Finally, given any assignment of sets to y and z such that the first group of equalities holds, then we can find an assignment to x such that the second set of equalities also holds. While this cannot be illustrated for all possible assignments, consider just one assignment shown in Figure 23.3 where each dot represents a distinct person. Given the sets y and z (shown with solid lines), we can find a set x (shown in Figure 23.3 with a dashed line) that satisfies the required constraints.

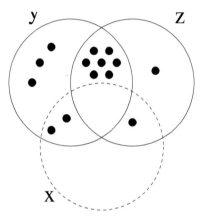

Figure 23.3: Venn diagram for the employee example.

In the constant-free case, once we know the cardinality of each minterm, any assignment of the required number of arbitrary distinct atoms to the minterms yields an assignment to the variables that satisfies the Boolean formula.

Of course, when the minterms contain atoms, we cannot assign arbitrary atoms. We have to assign to a minterm that contains an atom a positively either the atom that a denotes or the bottom element $\emptyset$. There is no other choice that can be allowed.

We handle atomic constants as follows. We consider them as additional Boolean algebra variables that have cardinality one and the cardinality of their intersection is zero. That is, if we have atomic constants $a_1, \ldots, a_c$ in a formula, then we add to S^* the following for each $1 \leq i \leq c$:

$$|a_i| = 1$$

and also for each $1 \leq i, j \leq c$ and $i \neq j$:

$$|a_i \cap a_j| = 0$$

Of course, both of the above conditions have to be put into a normal form before adding them to S^*. Then we solve these as in Theorem 23.1.12. Now we can prove the following.

Theorem 23.1.13 [with atomic constants] Existentially quantified variables can be eliminated from Boolean linear cardinality constraint formulas. The quantifier elimination is closed, that is, yields a quantifier-free Boolean linear cardinality constraint formula.

Proof: We described above the quantifier elimination method in the case when the Boolean linear cardinality formula contains both variables $x, y_1, \ldots, y_n$ and atomic constants $a_1, \ldots, a_c$. In this case there are 2^{n+1+c} minterms. We need to prove the soundness of the quantifier elimination.

S **implies** F: Take any assignment of the set variables $x, y_1, \ldots, y_n$ *and correct assignment of atoms to the atomic symbols* $a_1, \ldots, a_c$ that satisfies S. This assignment must also satisfy the system (23.7) *as augmented above*. Hence the assignment satisfies S^*. By the correctness of the quantifier elimination algorithm for integer linear equality and inequality constraints, F is also satisfied.

F **implies** S: Take any assignment of the set variables $y_1, \ldots, y_n$ *and correct assignment of atoms to the atomic symbols* $a_1, \ldots, a_c$ that satisfies F. We need to extend this assignment by an assignment for x that satisfies S.

The assignment for the set variables $y_1, \ldots, y_n$ *and atomic constant symbols* $a_1, \ldots, a_c$ determines the value of n_i and hence the value of $|n_i|$ for $1 \leq i \leq 2^{n+c}$. Since F is satisfied by the $|n_i|$ values, we can find for the integer variables $|m_i|$ also some values that satisfy S^*. The system (23.7) *as augmented above* must be satisfied because S^* contains it. Hence it must be possible to arbitrarily partition the elements of n_i into two sets with the first set having $|m_i|$ and the second set having $|m_{2^{n+c}+i}|$ elements for each $1 \leq i \leq 2^{n+c}$. These partitions are independent of each other because the n_i for $1 \leq i \leq 2^n$ are disjoint.

The above partition yields an assignment to each m_i for $1 \leq i \leq 2^{n+1+c}$ that satisfies all the cardinality constraints in S^*. By definition:

$$x = \bigcup_{1 \le i \le 2^{n+c}} m_i$$

because x occurs positively in exactly the first 2^{n+c} minterms out of the total of 2^{n+1+c} minterms of S. This identity and the above assignment to each m_i for $1 \le i \le 2^{n+1+c}$ immediately gives a value for x that clearly satisfies S. ∎

Example 23.1.3 Let S be the Boolean cardinality formula that is the conjunction of the formula in Example 11.2.8 and the constraint in Example 11.2.9. A quantifier elimination problem would be to find a quantifier-free formula that is logically equivalent to the following:

$$\exists x \, S$$

First we put S into a normal form. Then let S^* be the conjunction of the normal form and the following:

$$
\begin{aligned}
|y \cap z \cap a| - |x \cap y \cap z \cap a| - |\overline{x} \cap y \cap z \cap a| &= 0 \\
|y \cap z \cap \overline{a}| - |x \cap y \cap z \cap \overline{a}| - |\overline{x} \cap y \cap z \cap \overline{a}| &= 0 \\
|y \cap \overline{z} \cap a| - |x \cap y \cap \overline{z} \cap a| - |\overline{x} \cap y \cap \overline{z} \cap a| &= 0 \\
|y \cap \overline{z} \cap \overline{a}| - |x \cap y \cap \overline{z} \cap \overline{a}| - |\overline{x} \cap y \cap \overline{z} \cap \overline{a}| &= 0 \\
|\overline{y} \cap z \cap a| - |x \cap \overline{y} \cap z \cap a| - |\overline{x} \cap \overline{y} \cap z \cap a| &= 0 \\
|\overline{y} \cap z \cap \overline{a}| - |x \cap \overline{y} \cap z \cap \overline{a}| - |\overline{x} \cap \overline{y} \cap z \cap \overline{a}| &= 0 \\
|\overline{y} \cap \overline{z} \cap a| - |x \cap \overline{y} \cap \overline{z} \cap a| - |\overline{x} \cap \overline{y} \cap \overline{z} \cap a| &= 0 \\
|\overline{y} \cap \overline{z} \cap \overline{a}| - |x \cap \overline{y} \cap \overline{z} \cap \overline{a}| - |\overline{x} \cap \overline{y} \cap \overline{z} \cap \overline{a}| &= 0
\end{aligned}
$$

We also add the constraint $|a| = 1$ expressed using minterms as:

$$
\begin{aligned}
|x \cap y \cap z \cap a| &+ |x \cap y \cap \overline{z} \cap a| + |x \cap \overline{y} \cap z \cap a| + |x \cap \overline{y} \cap \overline{z} \cap a| \\
+ |\overline{x} \cap y \cap z \cap a| &+ |\overline{x} \cap y \cap \overline{z} \cap a| + |\overline{x} \cap \overline{y} \cap z \cap a| + |\overline{x} \cap \overline{y} \cap \overline{z} \cap a| = 1
\end{aligned}
$$

Second, we consider each expression that is the cardinality of a minterm (over x, y, z, a or over y, z, a) as an integer variable. Then by integer linear constraint variable elimination we get:

$$
\begin{aligned}
|y \cap z \cap a| + |y \cap z \cap \overline{a}| + |y \cap \overline{z} \cap a| + |y \cap \overline{z} \cap \overline{a}| &\equiv_6 0 \\
|y \cap z \cap a| + |y \cap z \cap \overline{a}| + |\overline{y} \cap z \cap a| + |\overline{y} \cap z \cap \overline{a}| &\equiv_9 0 \\
|y \cap z \cap a| + |y \cap z \cap \overline{a}| &= 7 \\
|\overline{y} \cap z \cap a| &= 1
\end{aligned}
$$

The last linear cardinality constraint comes from the constraint in Example 11.2.9 and the constraint that $|a| = 1$. By Theorem 23.1.13, the above is equivalent to $\exists x\ S$. For instance, the following is one solution for the above:

$$
\begin{aligned}
|y \cap z \cap a| &= 0 \\
|y \cap z \cap \overline{a}| &= 7 \\
|y \cap \overline{z} \cap a| &= 0 \\
|y \cap \overline{z} \cap \overline{a}| &= 5 \\
|\overline{y} \cap z \cap a| &= 1 \\
|\overline{y} \cap z \cap \overline{a}| &= 1 \\
|\overline{y} \cap \overline{z} \cap a| &= 0 \\
|\overline{y} \cap \overline{z} \cap \overline{a}| &= 0
\end{aligned}
$$

Corresponding to this we can find the solution:

$$
\begin{aligned}
|x \cap y \cap z \cap a| &= 0 & |\overline{x} \cap y \cap z \cap a| &= 0 \\
|x \cap y \cap z \cap \overline{a}| &= 0 & |\overline{x} \cap y \cap z \cap \overline{a}| &= 7 \\
|x \cap y \cap \overline{z} \cap a| &= 0 & |\overline{x} \cap y \cap \overline{z} \cap a| &= 0 \\
|x \cap y \cap \overline{z} \cap \overline{a}| &= 2 & |\overline{x} \cap y \cap \overline{z} \cap \overline{a}| &= 3 \\
|x \cap \overline{y} \cap z \cap a| &= 1 & |\overline{x} \cap \overline{y} \cap z \cap a| &= 0 \\
|x \cap \overline{y} \cap z \cap \overline{a}| &= 0 & |\overline{x} \cap \overline{y} \cap z \cap \overline{a}| &= 1 \\
|x \cap \overline{y} \cap \overline{z} \cap a| &= 0 & |\overline{x} \cap \overline{y} \cap \overline{z} \cap a| &= 0 \\
|x \cap \overline{y} \cap \overline{z} \cap \overline{a}| &= 0 & |\overline{x} \cap \overline{y} \cap \overline{z} \cap \overline{a}| &= 0
\end{aligned}
$$

Finally, given any assignment of sets to y, z, and a such that the first group of equalities holds and the correct atom is assigned to a, then we can find an assignment to x such that the second set of equalities also holds. Again, consider just one assignment shown in Figure 23.4 where each dot represents a distinct person. Given the sets y, z, and a (shown with solid lines), we can find a set x (shown in Figure 23.4 with a dashed line) that satisfies the required constraints.

It is interesting to compare the above with Example 23.1.2. There we could choose for x an arbitrary atom of the set $\overline{y} \cap z$, but here we must choose the atom a. More precisely, we can choose an arbitrary atom of the set $\overline{y} \cap z \cap a$, which, of course, is the same.   ∎

Theorem 23.1.14 Universally quantified variables can be eliminated from Boolean linear cardinality constraint formulas. The quantifier elimination is closed, that is, yields a quantifier-free Boolean linear cardinality constraint formula.

Proof: Eliminating universally quantified variables can be reduced to eliminating existentially quantified variables using the well-known identity:

$$\forall x\ F \equiv \overline{\exists x\ \overline{F}}$$

where F is a Boolean cardinality constraint formula. Therefore, this case reduces to Theorem 23.1.13.   ∎

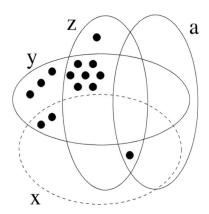

Figure 23.4: Venn diagram for Example 23.1.3.

Given any formula, it can be decided whether it is true by successively eliminating all variables from it. Then it becomes easy to test whether the variable-free formula is true or false. Hence, this also shows that:

Corollary 23.1.1 It can be decided whether a Boolean linear cardinality constraint formula is true or false. ∎

23.1.1 Satisfiability

We say that a conjunction of constraints S is true if there is an instantiation of the variables in the formula by constants in the allowed domain that makes the formula true.

Suppose that S is a conjunction of constraints with variables $x_1, \ldots, x_n$. Then it is satisfiable if and only if $S^* = \exists x_1 (\ldots (\exists x_n S) \ldots)$ is satisfiable. In other words, we can test the satisfiability of S by successively eliminating all variables from S and then testing whether the remaining variable-free formula is true. Usually this test is easy to do.

Theorem 23.1.15 In any constraint theory $\mathcal{C}$, it can be tested whether a conjunction of constraints is satisfiable if there is a closed form existential quantifier elimination algorithm in $\mathcal{C}$. ∎

23.2 Evaluation of Relational Algebra Queries

In the following we write $points(R)$ for the set of tuples that make R true. Hence $r = points(R)$ in this case. If there are several constraint relations in a database DB then $points(DB)$ is the set of infinite relations $points(R_i)$

such that $R_i \in DB$. If R contains k attributes and the domain of the attributes is D, then the *complement* of R is the set of all tuples in D^k that are not in r.

Before describing the relational algebra operators, note that we can find the complement of any constraint relation R by at first taking the formula that is the disjunction of all the constraint tuples of R and then taking its negation and putting the negated formula back into disjunctive normal form.

Suppose now that we have a relational algebra query Q. The definition of the relational algebra operators leads to a straightforward evaluation algorithm in the case of finite relational databases. However, we cannot use the straightforward algorithm to take as input an infinite relational database and evaluate a relational algebra query Q to give as output an infinite relation because that would take an infinite amount of time. Hence we have to use a finite constraint database representation of the input and output as shown in Figure 23.2. However, the relational algebra operators that we have within the query do not work on constraint relations. Therefore we replace them with their counterparts that perform on the constraint representation what is logically expected of the original operators.

We define the following relational algebra operators for constraint databases corresponding to the operators in Section 3.2.1. We refer to the original definitions and highlight only the differences. We also assume that each distinct attribute corresponds to the same distinct variable in each constraint relation in the database.

Intersection: The constraint intersection of two relations A and B, denoted $A \hat{\cap} B$, returns the same relation scheme as the intersection operator and all satisfiable conjunctions of S_i and T_j such that S_i is a constraint tuple of A and T_j is a constraint tuple of B.

Union: The constraint union of two relations A and B, denoted $A \hat{\cup} B$, returns the set of constraints tuples that belong to either A or B or both.

Difference: The constraint difference of two relations A and B, denoted $A \hat{\setminus} B$ takes first the complement B' of B and then the intersection of A and B'.

Product: The constraint product of two relations A and B, denoted $A \hat{\times} B$, returns the same relation scheme as the product operator and all conjunctions of S_i and T_j such that S_i is a constraint tuple of A and T_j is a constraint tuple of B. Note that S_i and T_j have no common variables because the product requires that A and B have no common attributes. Hence the conjunctions of S_i and T_j are always satisfiable if S_j and T_j are satisfiable.

Project: The constraint project operator $\hat{\pi}_L A$ eliminates from each constraint tuple of A all the variables that correspond to attributes that are not in L. Then it reorders the attribute columns in the order given in L.

Select: The constraint select operator $\hat{\sigma}_F A$ first expresses F as a conjunction of disjunctions of constraints, i.e., of the form $F_1 \vee \ldots \vee F_k$ where each F_i is a conjunction of constraints. Second, it returns all satisfiable conjunctions of S_i and F_j such that S_i is a constraint tuple of A.

Rename: The constraint rename operation $\hat{\rho}$ renames the attributes and the name of the constraint relation as ρ did for the infinite relations.

Natural Join: The constraint natural join operator $A \hat{\bowtie} B$ returns the same relation scheme as the natural join operator and all satisfiable conjunctions of S_i and T_j such that S_i is a constraint tuple of A and T_j is a constraint tuple of B.

In the following let us define for any constraint theory $\mathcal{C}$ that is closed under negation the following functions:

1. The function *elim* from pairs of variables and conjunction of constraints in $\mathcal{C}$ to conjunction of constraints in $\mathcal{C}$ such that $elim(x, S) = \exists S$.

2. The function *sat* from conjunction of constraints in $\mathcal{C}$ to $\{true, false\}$ such that $sat(S)$ is *true* if S is satisfiable and *false* otherwise.

3. The function *compl(R)* that returns the complement of the constraint relation R.

Theorem 23.2.1 Let DB be any constraint database over a constraint theory and let Q be any relational algebra query. Let $\hat{Q}$ be the query obtained by replacing each relational algebra operator with a corresponding constraint database operator. Then, do the following:

$$Q(points(DB)) = points(\hat{Q}(DB))$$

Proof: The theorem can be proven by induction on the operators in Q. This is done as follows. Let R, R_1, R_2 be constraint relations. Then:

Rename: $points(\hat{\rho}_C(R)) \equiv \rho_C(points(R))$ follows from the fact that substituting variables by other variables does not change the set of models of a constraint formula.

Select: $points(\hat{\sigma}_C(R)) \equiv \sigma_C(points(R))$ is true.

Project: We show that $points(\hat{\pi}_{X'}(R)) \equiv \pi_{X'}(points(R))$. Suppose that

$$t = a_1, \ldots, a_{j-1}, a_{j+1}, \ldots, a_k$$

is a tuple in $\pi_{X'}\, points(R)$. Then there must be a tuple $a_1, \ldots, a_k$ in $points(R)$. Also, $a_1, \ldots, a_k$ must be a model of some constraint tuple t_i of R. Then by definition of variable elimination t is a model of $elim(x_j, t_i)$. By the definition of $\hat{\pi}$ the tuple t must belong to $points(\hat{\pi}_{X'} R)$.

For the reverse direction, suppose that t is a tuple in $points(\hat{\pi}_{X'} R)$. Then there must be a constraint tuple t' in R such that t is a model of $elim(x_j, t')$. Therefore, there is some a_j value such that $a_1, \ldots, a_k$ is a model of t'. Then $a_1, \ldots, a_k$ must be in $points(R)$. Hence t must be in $\pi_{X'}\, points(R)$.

Natural Join: We show that $points(R_1 \bowtie R_2) \equiv points(R_1) \bowtie points(R_2)$. Suppose that $a_1, \ldots, a_{k1}$ is in $points(R_1)$ and $b_1, \ldots, b_{k2}$ is in $points(R_2)$, and $c_1, \ldots, c_k$ is the combination of $a_1, \ldots, a_{k1}$ and $b_1, \ldots, b_{k2}$ such that the same attributes are assigned the same values in $points(R_1) \bowtie points(R_2)$. Then $a_1, \ldots, a_{k1}$ is a model of some constraint tuple t_i in R_1 and $b_1, \ldots, b_{k2}$ is a model of some constraint tuple s_j in R_2. By the definition of $\hat{\bowtie}$ then (t_i, s_j) is a constraint tuple in $R_1 \hat{\bowtie} R_2$ and $c_1, \ldots, c_k$ is a model of $R_1 \hat{\bowtie} R_2$. Hence $c_1, \ldots, c_k$ must be in $points(R_1 \hat{\bowtie} R_2)$.

For the reverse direction, suppose that $c_1, \ldots, c_k$ is in $points(R_1 \hat{\bowtie} R_2)$. Then by the definition of $\hat{\bowtie}$ there must be a tuple of the form (t_i, s_j) in $R_1 \hat{\bowtie} R_2$ such that t_i is a constraint tuple in R_1 and s_j is a constraint tuple in R_2. That means that there must be projections of $c_1, \ldots, c_k$ onto the attributes of R_1 and R_2 that yield tuples $a_1, \ldots, a_{k1}$ and $b_1, \ldots, b_{k2}$, respectively, and that $a_1, \ldots, a_{k1}$ is a model of R_1 and $b_1, \ldots, b_{k2}$ is a model of R_2. Hence $a_1, \ldots, a_{k1}$ is in $points(R_1)$ and $b_1, \ldots, b_{k2}$ is in $points(R_2)$. Therefore $c_1, \ldots, c_k$ must be in $points(R_1) \bowtie points(R_2)$.

The intersection is proved similarly to natural join. Difference also follows from natural join and the definition of complement. Union is obvious, and set difference follows from union and intersection. This shows that the theorem is true. ∎

Example 23.2.1 Consider again the *Broadcast* relation of Example 6.4.2. The following relational algebra query finds which areas are reached by station 1 but not by station 3.

$$\pi_{X,Y}(\sigma_{\text{Radio}=1} Broadcast) - \pi_{X,Y}(\sigma_{\text{Radio}=3} Broadcast)$$

Here $\pi_{X,Y}(\sigma_{\text{Radio}=1}\, Broadcast)$ can be evaluated as:

$$(x - 8)^2 + (y - 9)^2 \le 25$$

Similarly, $\pi_{X,Y}(\sigma_{\text{Radio}=3} \; Broadcast)$ can be evaluated as:

$$(y - 1) \geq (x - 3)^2, \; y \leq 10$$

Set difference is implemented by taking first the complement of the second relation, which yields:

$$(y - 1) < (x - 3)^2 \;\; \text{or} \;\; y > 10$$

and then finally joining the first relation with the preceding. The final result, in disjunctive normal form, will be:

$$((x - 8)^2 + (y - 9)^2 \leq 25, \;\; (y - 1) < (x - 3)^2) \;\; \text{or}$$
$$((x - 8)^2 + (y - 9)^2 \leq 25, \;\; y > 10)$$

The output can be recognized to be a constraint relation with two constraint tuples.

23.3   Evaluation of SQL Queries

Evaluation of SQL queries without aggregate operators can be done by reduction to relational algebra, as we mentioned in Section 3.3. The evaluation of *Avg* and *Sum* operators is straightforward, because these are only applied to attributes that are constants and do not involve constraints.

The *Max* and *Min* aggregate operators can be applied to any linear constraint relation without any restriction. The evaluation of these operators is based on *linear programming*. Linear programming is the problem of finding the maximum or minimum of a linear function $f(x_1, \ldots, x_n)$ where the solution also must satisfy a conjunction of linear inequality constraints. The solution space of the conjunction of linear inequality constraints is called the *feasible region*.

To find the maximum value of a linear function on the attributes of a linear constraint relation R, we apply linear programming to each constraint tuple of R. Then we can take the maximum of all the linear programming solutions as the output of the aggregate query.

Example 23.3.1 Let us consider again the relation *Crops* of Chapter 3 and Example 12.4.1 where we expressed in Datalog with aggregation the query that finds the maximum profit for the farmer. In SQL the query can be expressed as follows:

SELECT Max(30 Corn + 25 Rye + 8 Sunflower + 15 Wheat)
FROM Crops

Because *Crops* contains only one constraint tuple, a single call to a linear programming subroutine can evaluate the query.

The evaluation of aggregate operators described in Chapter 12.4 is similar to the evaluation of the aggregate operators within SQL queries.

23.4 Evaluation of Datalog Queries

The constraint proof-based semantics of Datalog queries defines the set of constraint tuples that can be derived in the following way.

We call a *constraint instantiation* of a rule the substitution of each relation R_i in the body by a constraint tuple t_i that is in R_i. Note that the substitution renames the variables in t_i to those variables with which R_i occurs in the rule.

Let Q be a query, I an input constraint database, and $R_0(x_1, \ldots, x_k)$ a constraint relation scheme and let t be a constraint over the variables $x_1, \ldots, x_k$. We say that $t \in R_0$ has a constraint proof using Q and I, written as $\vdash^c_{Q,I} t \in R_0$, if and only if:

$R_0 \in \mathcal{I}$ and $t \in R_0$ or

$R_0 \in \mathcal{D}$ and for some rule of form (12.1) in Q there is a constraint instantiation

$$R_0(x_1, \ldots, x_k) :\!- t_1(x_{1,1}, \ldots, x_{1,k_1}), \ldots, t_n(x_{n,1}, \ldots, x_{n,k_n}).$$

where $\vdash^c_{Q,I} t_i \in R_i$ for each $1 \leq i \leq n$ and

$$t = \exists * \ t_1(x_{1,1}, \ldots, x_{1,k_1}), \ldots, t_n(x_{n,1}, \ldots, x_{n,k_n}).$$

where $*$ is the list of the variables in the body of the rule that do not occur in the head of the rule.

We call *constraint rule application* the constraint substitution of a rule and perform the implied existential quantifier elimination.

The *constraint proof-based* semantics of Datalog queries is the following. Each Datalog query Q is a function that on any input constraint database I returns for each relation name R the relation $\{t \ : \ \vdash^c_{Q,I} t \in R\}$.

When the query and the input constraint database are obvious, then we will write $\vdash^c$ without any subscript.

The following theorem shows that the proof-based semantics and the constraint proof-based semantics are equivalent.

Theorem 23.4.1 The following equality is true:

$$\{(a_1, \ldots, a_k) \ : \ \vdash_{Q,I} R(a_1, \ldots, a_k)\} = \{points(t) \ : \ \vdash^c_{Q,I} t \in R\} \quad \blacksquare$$

The *bottom-up constraint evaluation* of Datalog queries starts from an input constraint database and query and repeatedly applies some rule of the query until no new constraint tuples can be derived and added to the constraint database. We consider a constraint tuple of a relation new if there is some instantiation that makes it true but does not make any other constraint tuple of that relation true.

It is also possible to extend the least fixpoint semantics similarly. Then it can be shown that the constraint least fixpoint and the constraint proof-based semantics are equivalent. Hence in the following, we keep using $lfp(Q(D))$ to describe the semantics of a Datalog query Q on input constraint database D.

There are a few general techniques to prove the termination of the bottom-up evaluation in various cases of constraints. The first technique we consider is the following.

Theorem 23.4.2 Let $\mathcal{C}$ be any constraint theory with a closed form existential quantifier elimination. Let Q be any Datalog with $\mathcal{C}$ query and D be any $\mathcal{C}$ constraint input database D. Then $lfp(Q(D))$ is finitely computable if $\mathcal{C}$ can express only a finite number of atomic constraints using only a finite number of variables.

Proof: Consider any defined relation $R(x_1, \ldots, x_n)$ in Q. The constraint bottom-up evaluation can add to R only constraint tuples that are conjunctions of atomic constraints over the variables $x_1, \ldots, x_n$, which is a finite set. Hence if there is only a finite number of possible atomic constraints, then there is also a finite number of possible constraint tuples that can be added to R. Because the bottom-up evaluation never adds to R the same tuple twice, it must stop adding new tuples to R after a finite number of rule applications. The same happens to every other defined relation in Q. Hence the bottom-up evaluation must terminate after a finite number of rule applications. ∎

We give some examples where Theorem 23.4.2 can be applied.

Theorem 23.4.3 The least fixpoint of any Datalog query and input database with infinite domain equality and inequality constraints is closed-form evaluable.

Proof: Let D be the set of constants that occur in the Datalog program or the input database. Clearly D is a finite set. The constraint theory of infinite domain equality and inequality constraints and D set of constant symbols has a closed existential quantifier elimination (see Theorem 23.1.1) and can express only a finite number of atomic constraints using a finite set F of variables, i.e., the set $u\theta v$ where $u, v \in (D \cup F)$ and θ is either $=$ or $\neq$. Therefore, by Theorem 23.4.2 the least fixpoint is closed-form evaluable. ∎

Theorem 23.4.4 The least fixpoint of any Datalog query and input database with rational order constraints is closed-form evaluable.

Proof: Let D be the set of constants that occur in the Datalog program or the input database. Clearly D is a finite set. The constraint theory of rational order constraints and D set of constant symbols has a closed existential quantifier elimination (see Theorem 23.1.2) and can express only a finite number of atomic constraints using a finite set F of variables, i.e., the set $u\theta v$ where $u, v \in (D \cup F)$ and θ is either $\geq$ or $>$. Therefore, by Theorem 23.4.2 the least fixpoint is closed-form evaluable. ∎

Now we look at free Boolean algebras.

Theorem 23.4.5 The least fixpoint of any Datalog query and input database with free Boolean algebra constraints is closed-form evaluable if (1) there are only Boolean upper bound constraints, (2) there are only simple Boolean upper bound and monotone inequality constraints, or (3) the free algebra represents an atomless Boolean algebra.

Proof: Let $D = \{c_1, \ldots, c_m\}$ be the set of distinct constants that occur in the Datalog program or the input database. Clearly m is finite. The constraint theory of free Boolean algebras with m distinct constant symbols has a closed existential quantifier elimination in cases 1–3 (see Theorems 23.1.9, 23.1.11, and 23.1.10).

In case 1 with k variables, there are $3^k - 1$ different left-hand sides, because each variable appears unnegated, negated, or does not appear in the conjunction of the left-hand side. Also, only ground terms appear on the right-hand side. By Lemma 11.2.5 there can be only 2^{2^m} different right-hand sides. Constraints with the same left-hand sides can be combined into one upper bound constraint. Therefore, there could be only $(3^k - 1)2^{2^m}$ different atomic constraints.

In case 2 with k variables, because simple upper bound constraints are a subclass of upper bound constraints, the argument in case 1 also implies that there are $O((3^k - 1)2^{2^m})$ simple upper bound constraints. We can put each monotone inequality constraint with k variables into disjunctive normal form. By Lemma 11.2.5, there are $2^{2^{m+k}}$ different monotone inequality constraints in disjunctive normal form.

In case 3 we can argue similarly to case 2 that there are a finite number of different Boolean equality and inequality constraints formable from k variables and the constants in D.

In each case, because there is a finite number of atomic constraints, by Theorem 23.4.2 the least fixpoint is closed-form evaluable. ∎

Example 23.4.1 We can ask a number of questions about the musical group described in Exercise 9 of Chapter 9. For example, who could play the piano? We can find that out using the following query:

$$piano(p) \quad :\!- \quad plays(d, f, g, o, p, v, t).$$

Similarly, we can find out whether any person plays both the drum and the flute, by the following query:

$$drum\_and\_flute(d, f) \quad :\!- \quad plays(d, f, g, o, p, v, t).$$

We can evaluate these Datalog queries by successive existential quantifier elimination as described in Example 23.1.1. For example, the output of the second query is the constraint tuple $d \cap f \neq \emptyset$, which means that there is someone who can play both the drum and the flute.

The second technique to prove termination is based on geometry. We say that a point *dominates* another point if it has the same dimension and all of its coordinate values are greater than or equal to the corresponding coordinate values in the other point.

Lemma 23.4.1 In any fixed dimension, any sequence of distinct points with only natural number coordinates must be finite, if no point dominates any earlier point in the sequence.

Proof: We prove the lemma by induction on the dimension k of the space in which the points lie. For $k = 0$, the whole space is only a single point, hence the lemma holds. Now we assume that the theorem holds for k dimensions and show that it is true for $k + 1$ dimensions.

Let S be any arbitrary sequence of points in which no point dominates any earlier point. Let $x_1, \ldots, x_{k+1}$ be the coordinate axis of the $k+1$ dimensional space, and let $(a_1, \ldots, a_{k+1})$ be the first point in S. By the requirement of nondominating and distinctness, for any later point $(b_1, \ldots, b_{k+1})$ for some i, $0 < i \leq k + 1$ it must be true that $b_i < a_i$. That means that any point in the sequence after $(a_1, \ldots, a_{k+1})$ must be within one or more of the k-dimensional regions $x_1 = 0$, $x_1 = 1$, $\ldots$, $x_1 = a_1$, $\ldots$, $x_{k+1} = 0$, $x_{k+1} = 1$, $\ldots$, or $x_{k+1} = a_{k+1}$.

As we add points to each of these regions from S, no point can dominate any earlier one within these regions. Therefore, by the induction hypothesis, only a finite number of points from S can be placed into each of these k-dimensional regions. Because the number of these regions is finite, S must also be finite. ∎

Theorem 23.4.6 Let $\mathcal{C}$ be any constraint theory subset of linear inequality constraints. Let Q be any Datalog with $\mathcal{C}$ query and D be any $\mathcal{C}$ constraint input database D. Then $lfp(Q(D))$ is finitely computable over both integers and rational numbers as the domain of the variables if there exists an $l_{\min} \leq 0$ and a p such that $\mathcal{C}$ has a closed existential quantifier elimination that creates only conjunctions of atomic constraints such that the following two conditions hold.

1. There is a finite number N of different left-hand sides of the atomic constraints.

2. In each atomic constraint the bound is an integer or rational number with denominator p and is greater than or equal to $l_{\min}$.

Proof: Let us fix any ordering of the N possible left-hand sides of the atomic constraints. Using this fixed ordering, we can represent any conjunction S of $\mathcal{C}$ atomic constraints as an N-dimensional point in which the ith coordinate value will be $p(b - l_{\min}) + 1$ if S contains one or more atomic constraints with the ith left-hand side and b is the largest bound in them, and 0 otherwise.

Let $R(x_1, \ldots, x_n)$ be any defined relation in Q. Because quantifier elimination is closed in $\mathcal{C}$, the constraint bottom-up evaluation derives only new constraint tuples for R that are conjunctions of atomic constraints satisfying conditions 1 and 2. The sequence of derived constraint tuples can be represented as described earlier using a point sequence:

$$p_1, p_2, \ldots$$

It is easy to see that if point p_i dominates point p_j, then p_i and p_j represent conjunctions S_i and S_j of atomic constraints such that the set of solutions of S_i is included in the set of solutions of S_j. This shows that the constraint bottom-up evaluation adds only points that do not dominate any earlier point in the sequence. Note that each coordinate value of each point must be a natural number in the preceding representation. Therefore by Lemma 23.4.1 only a finite number of constraint tuples will be added to relation R. This shows that for each relation we can add only a finite number of constraint tuples. Hence the constraint bottom-up evaluation must terminate. ■

Next we see a few applications of Theorem 23.4.6.

Theorem 23.4.7 The least fixpoint of any Datalog query and input database with gap-order, lower bound, and upper bound constraints is closed-form evaluable when the domain of the variables is integers or rational numbers.

Proof: We can always find an $l < 0$ and a $p > 0$ for each query Q and input database D such that in each atomic constraint the bound is $\geq l$ and each constant is an integer or a rational number with denominator p. By Theorem 23.1.3 the existential quantifier elimination is closed for conjunctions of such atomic constraints.

Further, if a relation has n variables $x_1, \ldots, x_n$ in it, then it can easily be seen that each atomic constraint can have as its left-hand side only one of the following: $x_i - x_j$, x_i, or $-x_i$ where $1 \leq i, j \leq n$, and $i \neq j$. Hence there are only $n(n + 1)$ different left-hand sides. Therefore, by Theorem 23.4.6 the least fixpoint is closed-form evaluable.   ∎

Theorem 23.4.8 The least fixpoint of any Datalog query and input database with half-addition, lower bound, and upper bound constraints is closed-form evaluable when the domain of the variables is integers or rational numbers.

Proof: We can always find an $l < 0$ and a $p > 0$ for each query Q and input database D such that in each atomic constraint the bound is $\geq l$ and each constant is an integer or rational number with denominator p. By Theorem 23.1.4 existential quantifier elimination is closed in this theory.

If a relation has n variables $x_1, \ldots, x_n$ in it, then it can easily be seen that each half-addition, lower bound, and upper bound constraint with at least one variable can be written to have as its left-hand side only one of the following: x_i and $-x_i$ and $x_i - x_j$ where $i \neq j$, $x_i + x_j$, or $-x_i - x_j$ where $i < j$ and $1 \leq i, j \leq n$. Hence there are only $n(n+1)+n(n-1) = 2n^2$ different left-hand sides. Therefore, by Theorem 23.4.6 the least fixpoint is closed-form evaluable.   ∎

Theorem 23.4.9 The least fixpoint of any Datalog query and input database with gap-order, lower bound, upper bound, and positive linear constraints is closed-form evaluable when the domain of the variables is integers or rational numbers.

Proof: Put each positive linear constraint in the query and the input database into normal form. After that we can always find l, m, p, and s as required in the conditions of Theorem 23.1.5. By the same theorem the existential quantifier elimination is closed for conjunctions of such atomic constraints.

If a relation has n variables $x_1, \ldots, x_n$ in it, then it can easily be seen that each gap-order, lower bound, and upper bound atomic constraint can have as its left-hand side only one of the following: $x_i - x_j$, x_i, or $-x_i$ where $1 \leq i, j \leq m$, and $i \neq j$.

Further, in each positive normal linear constraint each coefficient is a positive integer and the sum of the coefficients is at most s. Therefore each coefficient is an integer between 1 and s. Because the maximum arity is m of any positive normal linear constraint, the number of possible left-hand sides is at most $s^m \binom{n}{m}$. Therefore, by Theorem 23.4.6 the least fixpoint is closed-form evaluable.   ∎

The following is similar to the preceding, but uses negative linear constraints and the quantifier elimination in Theorem 23.1.6.

Theorem 23.4.10 The least fixpoint of any Datalog query and input database with gap-order, lower bound, upper bound, and negative linear constraints is closed-form evaluable when the domain of the variables is integers or rational numbers. ∎

There is another type of application of Theorem 23.4.6. The main idea behind this is that in a linear constraint the value of the bound may be so small that we do not care too much about it. This leads to the idea of placing a limit l on the allowed smallest bound. To avoid smaller bounds than l, we may do two different modifications to a constraint tuple:

Modification 1: We change in the constraint tuple the value of any bound b to be $\max(b, l)$.

Modification 2: We delete from each constraint tuple any constraint with a bound that is less than l.

We can apply either of these modifications to each tuple in an input constraint database. During the constraint bottom-up evaluation we can also apply either of the modifications to the result of each rule application. In this way, we obtain modified bottom-up evaluations.

Given a query Q, input database D, and a fixed constant l, let $Q(D)_l$ and $Q(D)^l$ denote the output of the first and second modified evaluation algorithms, respectively. We can show the following.

Theorem 23.4.11 For any Datalog with integer or rational addition constraint program Q, input database D, and constant $l < 0$, the following is true:

$$Q(D)_l \subseteq lfp(Q(D)) \subseteq Q(D)^l$$

Further, $Q(D)_l$ and $Q(D)^l$ can be evaluated in finite time.

Proof: This is like the case in Theorem 23.4.8, except that half-addition is replaced with addition constraints. Therefore, the Datalog bottom-up evaluation can be done similarly, except that after each rule application some bounds may become less than l and have to be changed by one of the modifications.

In the case of the first modification, the modified tuple implies the original one. Therefore, after any number of rule applications the output relations obtained by the modified algorithm also imply the output relations obtained by the original algorithm. This shows that $Q(D)_l \subseteq lfp(Q(D))$.

In the case of the second modification, the original tuple implies the modified one. Therefore, after any number of rule applications the output relations obtained by the original algorithm also imply the output relations obtained by the modified algorithm. This shows that $lfp(Q(D)) \subseteq Q(D)^l$.

Clearly, there is a finite number of different left-hand sides of atomic addition constraints. That satisfies condition 1 of Theorem 23.4.6. Condition 2 we get free by choosing $l = l_{\min}$. Therefore, by that theorem both $Q(D)_l$ and $Q(D)^l$ can be evaluated in finite time. ∎

We can also get better and better approximations using smaller and smaller values as bounds. In particular, we have the following theorem.

Theorem 23.4.12 For any Datalog with addition constraints program Q, input database D, and constants l_1 and l_2 such that $l_1 \leq l_2 < 0$, the following hold:

$$Q(D)_{l_2} \subseteq Q(D)_{l_1} \quad \text{and} \quad Q(D)^{l_1} \subseteq Q(D)^{l_2}$$

∎

Theorem 23.4.13 For any Datalog with integer or rational difference, lower bound, upper bound, and positive linear constraints program Q, input database D, and constant $l < 0$, the following is true:

$$Q(D)_l \subseteq lfp(Q(D)) \subseteq Q(D)^l$$

Further, $Q(D)_l$ and $Q(D)^l$ can be evaluated in finite time.

Proof: We can argue similarly to Theorem 23.4.11 for the containment. We can argue similarly to Theorem 23.4.9 for the finite number of left-hand sides. Again we can choose $l = l_{\min}$ and apply Theorem 23.4.6 to show termination. ∎

Example 23.4.2 Consider the Datalog program in Example 12.1.7. This program contains only difference constraints. Therefore by Theorem 23.4.13 the lower and upper approximations of its least fixpoint model can be found in finite time. Before discussing the approximation, let us note that in this case the least fixpoint of the Datalog program can be expressed as the relation

$$\{(x, y, z) \; : \; \exists k \;\; x \geq z, \; z - x \geq -200k, \; z - y \geq 300k\}$$

This relation is not expressible as a finite set of gap-order constraint facts. However, we can express for each fixed $l < -200$ the relation

$$\{(x, y, z) \; : \; \exists k \;\; x \geq z, \; z - x \geq max(l, -200k), \; z - y \geq 300k\}$$

as a finite set of gap-order constraint facts. This would be a lower bound of the semantics of the *Balance* relation. We can also express the relation

$$\{(x, y, z) \; : \exists k \; \left\{ \begin{array}{ll} x \geq z, z - x \geq -200k, z - y \geq 300k & \text{if } -200k \geq l \\ x \geq z, \; z - y \geq 300k & \text{otherwise} \end{array} \right\}\}$$

as a finite set of difference constraint tuples. This would be an upper bound of the least fixpoint of the *Balance* relation.

The approximation could be used to decide whether some particular tuple of constants is in the least fixpoint. For example, is it possible that the account balances are at any time $x = 1500, y = 200$, and $z = 1000$? When we use an approximate evaluation with $l = -1000$, we see that it is not in the upper bound of the semantics of the *Balance* relation. Hence $(1500, 200, 1000)$ is not in the least fixpoint of the *Balance* relation.

23.4.1 The Ocean Crossing Example

From a practical point of view, we allow the variables in a constraint relation to range over different domains. Then the constraint tuple contains conjunctions of two or more types of atomic constraints. For example, some variables may be Boolean and other variables may be integers. In this case, the constraints over the Boolean variables can be separated from the constraints over the integer variables. When we have to eliminate a Boolean variable we do variable elimination using only the Boolean constraints and preserve intact all the constraints on the integer variables. Similarly, if we have to eliminate an integer variable, we use the variable elimination over the integer constraints and do not change the Boolean constraints within the constraint tuple.

Consider again the ocean crossing problem of Example 12.3.3, where the continents were strings but the other variables were integer numbers. The ocean crossing problem is an example of a recursive Datalog program with addition constraints, which is an unsafe class of Datalog programs. In fact, in the standard evaluation the Datalog program wold not terminate. However, we show that it terminates using the modified evaluation rules. First, let us rewrite the rules for the difference relation into the following equivalent form:

$$D(x, y, z) \quad :\!\!- \quad \begin{aligned} & x - y \geq 0, & y - x \geq 0, \\ & z \geq 0, & -z \geq 0. \end{aligned}$$

$$D(x, y, z) \quad :\!\!- \quad \begin{aligned} & D(x', y, z'), \\ & x - x' \geq 1, & x' - x \geq -1, \\ & z - z' \geq 1, & z' - z \geq -1. \end{aligned}$$

Taking the first rule and renaming x by x' and z by z', we get the following:

$$D(x', y, z') \quad :\!\!- \quad \begin{aligned} & x' - y \geq 0, & y - x' \geq 0, \\ & z' \geq 0, & -z' \geq 0. \end{aligned}$$

Now substitute the right hand side of the above into the second rule for D and get:

$$D(x,y,z) \quad :- \quad \begin{array}{ll} x'-y \geq 0, & y-x' \geq \quad 0, \\ z' \geq 0, & -z' \geq \quad 0, \\ x-x' \geq 1, & x'-x \geq \quad -1, \\ z-z' \geq 1, & z'-z \geq \quad -1. \end{array}$$

We eliminate the variables x' and z' by adding the first and third rows and adding the second and fourth rows. That yields:

$$D(x,y,z) \quad :- \quad \begin{array}{ll} x-y \geq 1, & y-x \geq -1, \\ z \geq 1, & -z \geq -1. \end{array}$$

This is the same as the first constraint tuple for D except that the right hand sides of the addition constraints have the bounds 1 and -1 instead of 0. We can continue similarly the constraint rule applications. For the ith application, we get:

$$D(x,y,z) \quad :- \quad \begin{array}{ll} x-y \geq i, & y-x \geq -i, \\ z \geq i, & -z \geq -i. \end{array} \tag{23.8}$$

The rule applications can continue similarly l times. Hence we get one copy of Equation (23.8) for each $0 \leq i \leq l$. In the $(l+1)$st rule application we get:

$$D(x,y,z) \quad :- \quad \begin{array}{ll} x-y \geq -l+1, & y-x \geq l-1, \\ z \geq -l+1, & -z \geq l-1. \end{array}$$

However, by Modification 1 we get:

$$D(x,y,z) \quad :- \quad \begin{array}{ll} x-y \geq -l+1, & y-x \geq l, \\ z \geq -l+1, & -z \geq l. \end{array}$$

because the bound $l-1$ is replaced with l as $\max(l-1,l) = l$. This conjunction of constraints is unsatisfiable. Hence we do not add anything to the D relation.

By Modification 2 we get:

$$D(x,y,z) \quad :- \quad \begin{array}{l} x-y \geq -l+1, \\ z \geq -l+1. \end{array} \tag{23.9}$$

because the bound $l-1$ is less than l and the addition constraints with $l-1$ bounds are deleted. The conjunction of the constraints on the right hand side is satisfiable.

Can we use this new constraint tuple in another rule application? If we substitute in it x by x' and z by z', then we get the following:

$$D(x',y,z') \quad :- \quad \begin{array}{l} x'-y \geq -l+1, \\ z' \geq -l+1. \end{array}$$

Now substitute the right hand side of the above into the second rule for D and get:

$$
\begin{aligned}
D(x,y,z) \;:-\quad & x' - y \geq \;-l+1, \\
& z' \geq \;-l+1, \\
& x - x' \geq \;\;1, \qquad x' - x \geq -1, \\
& z - z' \geq \;\;1, \qquad z' - z \geq -1.
\end{aligned}
$$

Eliminating variables x' and z', we get:

$$
\begin{aligned}
D(x,y,z) \;:-\quad & x - y \geq -l+2, \\
& z \geq -l+2.
\end{aligned}
$$

Since we got a set of constraints that is subsumed by the previously derived constraint tuple, we do not add this to the relation D. Therefore we can see that for any l, the under-approximation of $D(x,y,z)$ is the union of Equation (23.8) for $0 \leq i \leq -l$, and the over-approximation is the union of the under-approximation and Equation (23.9).

Now let us find the under-approximation of M. We claim that the under-approximation of $M(x,y,z)$ is:

$$
\begin{aligned}
M(x,y,z) \;:-\quad & x \geq j, \; -x \geq -j, \\
& y \geq i, \; -y \geq -i, \\
& z \geq ij, \; -z \geq -ij.
\end{aligned}
\tag{23.10}
$$

for each $0 \leq i, j \leq -l$ such that $l \leq -ij$.

First, we prove by induction on i and j that Equation (23.10) holds. The first rule of multiplication clearly implies the case for $i = j = 0$. Now let us assume for any $0 \leq i \leq -l$ and $0 \leq j < -l$ and prove for i and $j+1$. We use the second rule for multiplication. After the necessary substitutions we get:

$$
\begin{aligned}
M(x,y,z) \;:-\quad & x' \geq \;j, \qquad -x' \geq \;-j, \\
& y \geq \;i, \qquad -y \geq \;-i, \\
& z' \geq \;ij, \qquad -z' \geq \;-ij, \\
& z - z' \geq \;i, \qquad z' - z \geq \;-i, \\
& x - x' \geq \;1, \qquad x' - x \geq \;-1.
\end{aligned}
$$

The first three lines of constraints come from Equation (23.10) with the renaming of x by x' and z by z'. The fourth and the second line come from Equation (23.8) with the renaming of x by z, y by z', and z by y. The last line is a rewrite of $x = x' + 1$ in terms of addition constraints. After eliminating x' and z' we get:

$$
\begin{aligned}
M(x,y,z) \;:-\quad & x \geq j+1, \qquad -x \geq -(j+1), \\
& y \geq i, \qquad -y \geq -i, \\
& z \geq i(j+1), \; -z \geq -i(j+1).
\end{aligned}
\tag{23.11}
$$

If $l \leq -i(j+1)$, then the above is the same as Equation (23.10) with $j+1$ instead of j. Otherwise, if $l > -i(j+1)$, then Modification 1 changes the above to the unsatisfiable:

$$
\begin{aligned}
M(x,y,z) \quad :- \quad & x \geq j+1, \quad -x \geq -(j+1), \\
& y \geq i, \quad\quad\;\; -y \geq -i, \\
& z \geq i(j+1), \quad -z \geq l.
\end{aligned}
$$

hence nothing more is derived. The third rule can be used similarly to prove the condition for $i+1$ and j for any $0 \leq i < -l$ and $0 \leq j \leq -l$.

In each rule application either i or j is increased by one. If either of these increase to greater than $-l$, then again we get an unsatisfiable condition by Modification 1. Hence the lower bound in Equation (23.10) is exact.

Now let us find the over-approximation of M. Clearly it contains all the tuples of the under-approximation. However, if $l > -i(j+1)$ in Equation (23.11), and we use Modification 2 then we get:

$$
\begin{aligned}
M(x,y,z) \quad :- \quad & x \geq j+1, \quad -x \geq -(j+1), \\
& y \geq i, \quad\quad\;\; -y \geq -i, \\
& z \geq i(j+1).
\end{aligned}
$$

Since this is satisfiable, we have to see what other constraint tuples we can derive using it. It is easy to see that after applying the second rule and eliminating x and x' again, we get the following when $-(j+2) \leq l$:

$$
\begin{aligned}
M(x,y,z) \quad :- \quad & x \geq j+2, \quad -x \geq -(j+2), \\
& y \geq i, \quad\quad\;\; -y \geq -i, \\
& z \geq i(j+2).
\end{aligned}
$$

We can continue applying the second rule similarly until $-(j+2) = l-1$. Then by Modification 2 we get for any $0 \leq i \leq l$:

$$
\begin{aligned}
M(x,y,z) \quad :- \quad & x \geq -l+1, \\
& y \geq i, \quad -y \geq -i, \\
& z \geq i(-l+1). \quad\quad\quad\quad\quad\quad\quad\quad (23.12)
\end{aligned}
$$

By symmetry, by applying repeatedly the third rule until the lower bound of y will be $-l+1$ and using Modification 2 we get for any $0 \leq j \leq l$:

$$
\begin{aligned}
M(x,y,z) \quad :- \quad & x \geq j, \quad -x \geq -j, \\
& y \geq -l+1, \\
& z \geq (-l+1)j. \quad\quad\quad\quad\quad\quad\quad\quad (23.13)
\end{aligned}
$$

If the lower bound of both x and y reach $l+1$, then we get:

$$
\begin{aligned}
M(x,y,z) \quad :- \quad & x \geq -l+1, \\
& y \geq -l+1, \\
& z \geq (-l+1)^2. \quad\quad\quad\quad\quad\quad\quad\quad (23.14)
\end{aligned}
$$

The over-approximation of M will be the union of the under-approximation in Equation (23.10) and the constraint tuples in Equations (23.12-23.14).

As l decreases the under and over-approximations, which are always computable in finite time, get closer to the standard definitions of difference and multiplication, which are infinite relations.

Let us consider the other relations too. It is easy to find the closed form of AD. Further, if we choose $l < -100$, then both the under and the over-approximation of $Close$ is:

$$
\begin{aligned}
Close(x', y', x, y) \quad &:— \quad x - x' = 0, \ y - y' = 0. \\
Close(x', y', x, y) \quad &:— \quad x - x' = 0, \ y - y' = 1. \\
Close(x', y', x, y) \quad &:— \quad x - x' = 0, \ y - y' = 2. \\
Close(x', y', x, y) \quad &:— \quad x - x' = 0, \ y - y' = 3. \\
&\quad\ \ \vdots \quad \vdots \quad \vdots \\
Close(x', y', x, y) \quad &:— \quad x - x' = 6, \ y - y' = 8. \\
Close(x', y', x, y) \quad &:— \quad x - x' = 8, \ y - y' = 6.
\end{aligned}
\tag{23.15}
$$

Now let us use the input relations $Island$ and $Cont$ to find the defined relations $Ship$ and $Reach$. Applying the first rule yields:

$$
Ship(x, y) \quad :— \quad -x - y \geq 0.
$$

This simply means that we can be at any point of continent A. Now any application of the second rule for $Ship$ derives (x, y) values that are already in the $Ship$ relation. For example, let us consider the following application of the second rule using the above constraint tuple for $Ship$, the second constraint tuple for $Island$, and the second to the last constraint tuple for $Close$ in (23.15). We again expand each equality into a conjunction of inequalities.

$$
\begin{aligned}
Ship(x, y) \quad :— \quad &-x' - y' \geq 0, \\
&x \geq 6, \quad\ \ -x \geq -6, \\
&y \geq 8, \quad\ \ -y \geq -8, \\
&x - x' \geq 6, \quad x' - x \geq -6, \\
&y - y' \geq 8, \quad y' - y \geq -8.
\end{aligned}
$$

Eliminating x' and y' and simplifying the constraints by deleting those addition constraints that are implied by the others, we get:

$$
\begin{aligned}
Ship(x, y) \quad :— \quad &x \geq 6, \quad -x \ \geq \ -6, \\
&y \geq 8, \quad -y \ \geq \ -8.
\end{aligned}
$$

which is equivalent to the second constraint tuple for $Island$. This means that the ship can cruise to the second island. Similarly, we can prove that it can also cruise to the island at $(15, 12)$ and to the location $(22, 19)$ of continent B.

Although we used approximations for the difference, absolute difference, and multiplication relations, the output of the other relations were exactly calculated with matching lower and over-approximations. That is because for any particular instance of this problem where the absolute value of any island coordinate is at most some number n, we only need to find the difference and product of numbers that are at most $2n$. Hence we only need to use a finite subset of the difference and products relations on the integer numbers. The above approximation with $l = -2n$ returns the needed parts of the D and M relations.

23.4.2   Parametric Evaluation

For Boolean algebras there is a representation theorem, known as *Stone's theorem*: "Every Boolean algebra is isomorphic to Boolean algebra of sets (where $\cap, \cup, ^-$ are interpreted as intersection, union and set difference from 1, respectively) and every finite Boolean algebra is isomorphic to the power set of a finite set." Thus, there is a unique (up to isomorphism) finite Boolean algebra for every cardinality 2^m.

By Stone's representation theorem, if we know the interpretation ahead of time, then we can substitute the constants and functions of the Boolean algebra and obtain a set algebra, which we know how to evaluate. If we do not know the interpretation ahead of time, then we can evaluate the query using the free Boolean algebra. What we obtain is a *parametric evaluation* of the query.

Theorem 23.4.14 The least fixpoint of any Datalog query Q and input database D with free Boolean algebra constraints is closed-form evaluable under any specific interpretation $I = (B, \sigma)$ if (1) there are only Boolean equality constraints, (2) there are only simple Boolean upper bound and monotone inequality constraints, or (3) B is an atomless Boolean algebra. The evaluation can be done on the free Boolean algebra and then the result interpreted, or the input database and program can be interpreted and the evaluation can be done on the specific Boolean algebra. That is,

$$I(Q(D)) = Q(I(D)) \quad \blacksquare$$

Parametric tuples should not be confused with constraint tuples. A constraint tuple describes the set of all tuples that one gets by substituting values for its variables. A parametric tuple describes a single tuple, given a substitution for its parameters. Parametric constraint tuples do both.

Example 23.4.3 Consider the problem of finding the parity of n bits given in the relation $Input(i, c_i)$, where i is an integer and each c_i is a distinct constant symbol in the free Boolean algebra B_n. Assuming we also have the input relation $Last(n)$, the following Datalog query Q could be used:

$$Parity(1, x) \quad :\!- \quad Input(1, z).$$
$$Parity(i', x) \quad :\!- \quad Parity(i, y), \; Input(i', z), \; i' = i + 1, \; x =_{B_n} y \oplus z.$$
$$Paritybit(x) \quad :\!- \quad Parity(n, x), \; Last(n).$$

Under the parametric evaluation of the above Datalog program using the free Boolean algebra B_n, we would get:

$$Paritybit(x) :\!- x =_{B_n} c_1 \oplus c_2 \oplus \ldots \oplus c_n$$

Now suppose that we use the Boolean algebra B_0, which interprets each c_i as $false$, which is the zero element, for i odd and $true$, which is the identity element, for i even. Under this interpretation $Paritybit$ will be $false$ if n is odd and $true$ if n is even.

Alternatively, by making the interpretation of the parametric tuples in relation $Parity$ and then evaluating the query in B_0 instead of B_n, we would get the same result.

Example 23.4.4 Let us now consider the parametric evaluation of Example 12.2.3. Replacing the CS_Minor subgoal with its only constraint tuple yields:

$$Can\_Apply\_CS\_MS(y) \quad :\!- \quad x \subseteq_B \overline{c} \cap (d \cup s), \; \overline{x} \cap y \subseteq_B c.$$

Here we have to eliminate the variable y from a conjunction of Boolean upper bound constraints. Using the procedure described in the proof of Theorem 23.1.9 we get the following:

$$Can\_Apply\_CS\_MS(y) \quad :\!- \quad y \subseteq_B c \cup (\overline{c} \cap (d \cup s)).$$

Now let us assume the interpretation B for the Boolean algebra operators as in Example 11.2.11, and for the constants σ_4 as follows:

$$\sigma_4(a) \quad = \quad \{1, 2, 5, 6\}$$
$$\sigma_4(c) \quad = \quad \{5, 6, 7, 8\}$$
$$\sigma_4(d) \quad = \quad \{2, 4, 6, 8\}$$
$$\sigma_4(m) \quad = \quad \{1, 2, 3, 4\}$$
$$\sigma_4(s) \quad = \quad \{3, 6\}$$

Hence the last constraint tuple becomes $y \subseteq \{2, 3, 4, 5, 6, 7, 8\}$ after using substitution for the constants.

Alternatively, we can consider the evaluation of the Datalog query by first substituting. Then we obtain the following.

$$Math\_Minor(x) \quad\quad :\!\!- \quad x \subseteq \{5,6,7,8\} \cap \{1,2,5,6\}.$$

$$CS\_Minor(x) \quad\quad :\!\!- \quad x \subseteq \{1,2,3,4\} \cap (\{2,4,6,8\} \cup \{3,6\}).$$

$$Can\_Apply\_CS\_MS(y) \quad :\!\!- \quad CS\_Minor(x), \overline{x} \cap y \subseteq \{5,6,7,8\}.$$

It can be seen that when we evaluate this, we get the same result.

23.4.3   Evaluation with Parametric Rectangles

The evaluation of queries where the input database consists of parametric rectangles relations, like in MLPQ/PReSTO, in general follows the methods decribed in the previous sections. In this section we describe some details particular to the MLPQ/PReSTO implementation regarding (1) the block operator, (2) relational algebra, and (3) Datalog.

$\boxed{\text{B}}$ – The MLPQ/PReSTO **block operator** is a single time instant version of the block operator (see Chapter 7), which returns for each time t the points of the second relation that are not blocked by the first relation at any time before t.

In other words, if R_1 and R_2 are parametric rectangles relations and t_k is any time instance, then the MLPQ/PReSTO block operator, denoted by $Block(R_1, R_2, t_k)$, is the instantiation at t_k of the set of moving points in R_2 that did not intersect with R_1 any time before or at t_k. More precisely, $Block(R_1, R_2, t_k)$ returns the set of points:

$$\{ ((X(t_k), \; Y(t_k)) \quad : \quad \exists\, ([X^\lfloor, X^\rceil], [Y^\lfloor, Y^\rceil], I) \in R_2, \quad \alpha, \; \beta \in [0,1],$$
$$X = \alpha(X^\lfloor - X^\rceil) + X^\rceil,$$
$$Y = \beta(Y^\lfloor - Y^\rceil) + Y^\rceil,$$
$$\nexists\, t' \in I, \; t' \le t_k, \; (X(t'), Y(t'), t') \in sem(R_1)\}$$

In the preceding, X and Y are functions of time that always give the coordinates of the point that is at α and β fractions in the middle of the parametric rectangle. The point instance of these functions at time t_k is returned if its travel is not stopped by any point in R_1 before time t_k.

MLPQ/PReSTO computes an approximate result of a block operation by the following recursive algorithm, which assumes a constant threshold value max_depth to guarantee the termination of the recursion.

Block(R_1, R_2, t_k)
input: R_1 and R_2 parametric rectangles relations.
output: An approximate value of $Block(R_1, R_2, t_k)$.
local var: d is the current depth of recursion.

    for each tuple $r_2 \in R_2$ **do**
      $R' = R' \cup Blockrect(R_1, r_2, t_k, 0)$
    return R'

Blockrect(R_1, r_2, t_k, d)
    if $\{r_2\} \ \cap \ R_1 = \emptyset$ **then return** $\{r_2\}$ at t_k
    else if at t_k $\{r_2\} \subseteq R_1$ **then return** $\emptyset$.
    else if $d < max\_depth$ **then**
        partition r_2 into quadrants r_{21}, r_{22}, r_{23}, r_{24}
        return $\bigcup_{1 \leq i \leq 4}$ $Blockrect(R_1, r_{2i}, t_k, d+1)$

In the above algorithm, the function *Block* calls for each parametric rectangle of R_2 the auxiliary function *Blockrect*. Function *Blockrect* checks two cases when no further recursion is needed. In the first case, when r_2 and R_1 never intersect, *Blockrect* returns the value of r_2 with variable t instantiated with t_k because none of the points in r_2 are blocked by R_1. In the second case, when at time t_k the parametric rectangle is within R_1 completely, then *Blockrect* returns the empty set because all of the points in r_2 are blocked by R_1. Quite frequently one of the two cases will occur. However, if neither case occurs, then the algorithm breaks the parametric rectangle r_2 into four quadrants and calls *Blockrect* recursively. The union of the returned values will be passed back to the original function call. The depth of the recursion and the precision of the approximation are controlled by the value of max_depth.

Relational algebra – The following are some results concerning the evaluation of relational algebra queries.

Lemma 23.4.2 Given n different m-degree polynomial functions of time, $f_1(t), \ldots, f_n(t)$, we can find (precisely for $m < 5$, and approximately from $m \geq 5$) a partition of the time dimension into at most $N = O(mn^2)$ intervals $(-\infty, t_1), [t_1, t_2), \ldots, [t_{N-1}, \infty)$ such that within each interval for each time instance the order of the functions is the same.

Proof: The curves that correspond to distinct functions f_j and f_k intersect at most twice because the equation $f_j(t) = f_k(t)$ has at most m roots. Therefore, there are at most $m \times n(n-1)/2$ crossings between the n curves.

Let $t_1, \ldots, t_{N-1}$ be the time instances corresponding to the crossings sorted in increasing order. These time instances can be found precisely for $m < 5$ and approximately to any desired precision for larger m. Let $t_0 = -\infty$ and $t_N = \infty$.

Then the corresponding curves of the n functions can intersect in none of the $N \leq (m/2)(n^2 - n) = O(mn^2)$ open intervals (t_{i-1}, t_i) where $1 \leq i \leq N$. We also prove by contradiction that within these N intervals for each time instance the order of the functions is the same. Suppose that this claim is false. Then there must exist within some interval (t_{i-1}, t_i) two different time instances t', t'' such that $f_j(t') < f_k(t')$ and $f_j(t'') \geq f_k(t'')$ for some $1 \leq j, k \leq n$. Then there must be a time instance t''' such that $f_j(t''') = f_k(t''')$, which is a contradiction to the fact that there are no intersections within any interval. This proves the lemma. ■

Let f_1 and f_2 be two functions of time. We say "$f_1 << f_2$" in $[t1, t2]$ if for any time $t \in [t_1, t_2]$, $f_1(t) \leq f_2(t)$.

In the following, we will assume that if the degree $m > 5$, then we are talking about only approximate query evaluation as in the previous lemma.

Lemma 23.4.3 The intersection of two d-dimensional m-degree nonperiodic parametric rectangles relations is a parametric rectangles relation that can be evaluated in PTIME in the size of the relations.

Proof: In this proof, we assume for simplicity that tuples have only spatial and temporal attributes. Let

$$R1 = ([X_{1,1}^[, X_{1,1}^]], \ldots, [X_{1,d}^[, X_{1,d}^]], from1, to1)$$

and

$$R2 = ([X_{2,1}^[, X_{2,1}^]], \ldots, [X_{2,d}^[, X_{2,d}^]], from2, to2)$$

be two d-dimensional m-degree nonperiodic parametric rectangles. Let

$$from = \max(from1, from2) \quad \text{and} \quad to = \min(to1, to2)$$

For each spatial dimension x_i, by Lemma 23.4.2, there are $O(m) = O(1)$ crossings between bound functions of $R1$ and $R2$. Let S_i be the set of time instances that are between $from$ and to and that correspond to the crossings. This can be computed in $O(1)$ time.

Let $S = \bigcup_{i=1}^{d} S_i$. Let $t_1, \ldots, t_{N-1}$ be the time instances in S sorted in ascending order, and let $t_0 = from$ and $t_N = to$. We can partition the time dimension into $N = O(d)$ intervals using S. Then by Lemma 23.4.2, within each interval $(t_{j-1}, t_j]$ for any time instance the order of the functions of the lower and upper bounds of $R1$ and $R2$ in any dimension is the same. For each time interval $(t_{j-1}, t_j]$, let

$$X_i^[= \begin{cases} X_{1,i}^[& \text{if } X_{2,i}^[<< X_{1,i}^[\text{ in } [t_{j-1}, t_j] \\ \\ X_{2,i}^[& \text{otherwise} \end{cases}$$

$$X_i^] = \begin{cases} X_{1,i}^[& \text{if } X_{1,i}^] << X_{2,i}^] \text{ in } [t_{j-1}, t_j] \\ \\ X_{2,i}^[& \text{otherwise} \end{cases}$$

Then the intersection of $R1$ and $R2$ over $(t_{j-1}, t_j]$ is:

$$r_j' = \begin{cases} ([X_1^[, X_1^]], \ldots, [X_d^[, X_d^]], [t_{j-1}, t_j]) & \text{if } \forall i \ X_i^[<< X_i^] \text{ in } [t_{j-1}, t_j] \\ \\ \emptyset & \text{otherwise} \end{cases}$$

The intersection of $R1$ and $R2$ is:

$$R1 \cap R2 = \bigcup_{j=1}^{N} r_j'$$

Because S can be computed and sorted in $O(d + d \log d) = O(d \log d)$ time and computing each r_j' takes $O(d)$ time, thus $r1 \cap r2$ can be computed in $O(d \log(d)) + O(N \cdot d) = O(d^2)$ time. Let $R1$ and $R2$ be two parametric rectangle relations with at most n parametric rectangles in each relation, then:

$$R1 \cap R2 = \bigcup_{r1 \in R1, \ r2 \in R2} (r1 \cap r2)$$

which can be computed in $O(d^2 n^2)$. ∎

The union operator is easy to implement because it simply takes the set union of the parametric rectangles in the input relations. The project and selection operators are also easy to implement.

Lemma 23.4.4 The complement of a relation R of d-dimensional m-degree nonperiodic parametric rectangles can be evaluated in PTIME in the size of the relation. ∎

The difference operator can be expressed using the intersection and complement operators; hence it can also be evaluated. Recall that the definition of cross-product requires that the operand relations have no common attributes. Because each parametric rectangle relation is assumed to contain a T attribute, the cross-product does not apply as an operator. However, the join operator can be easily implemented, by taking for each of the common attributes, including T, the maximum of the lower bounds as the new lower bound and the minimum of the upper bounds as the new upper bound. Therefore, all the basic relational algebra operators that are applicable to parametric rectangles relations can be implemented.

Further, if we restrict the set of period values that may occur in the input database and queries to a fixed finite set, then the operators can also be evaluated in PTIME in the case of periodic parametric rectangles. Therefore, we have the following.

Theorem 23.4.15 For any fixed d dimension, any relational algebra expression (with rename, project, select, union, intersect, difference, complement, and join operators) can be evaluated in PTIME in the size of the input m-degree periodic parametric rectangle database. ∎

Datalog – The above result can be useful also for the evaluation of Datalog queries. In fact, we can note that any fixed database input has only a finite number of different constants. Using this finite number of constants, one can define only a finite number of different parametric rectangles. Therefore, it is also possible to prove the following.

Theorem 23.4.16 For any fixed d dimension, any Datalog query can be evaluated in closed form. ∎

23.5 Constraint Logic Programming

Constraint logic programming (CLP) is an extension of logic programming with constraints in which top-down evaluation style of Prolog is kept, but Prolog's term unification is replaced with constraint solving. For example, consider the following constraint logic program which describes the possible combinations of growing crops (c for corn, r for rye, s for sunflower, and w for wheat) and fertilizer f and irrigation i options for a farmer, as explained earlier in Example 13.7.1.

$$Grow(c, r, s, w) \qquad :— \qquad Fert(f, c, r, s, w), \ Water(i, c, r, s, w).$$

$$Fert(f, c, r, s, w) \quad :— \ f = 0, \qquad 15c + 8r + 10s + 15w <= 3000.$$

$$Fert(f, c, r, s, w) \quad :— \ f = 1, \quad 10c + 5.33r + 6.67s + 10w <= 2000.$$

$$Water(i, c, r, s, w) \ :— \ i = 0, \qquad 30c + 25r + 5s + 10w <= 8000.$$

$$Water(i, c, r, s, w) \ :— \ i = 1, \qquad 15c + 12.5r + 2.5s + 5w <= 4000.$$

Syntactically constraint logic programs and constraint deductive databases are similar. However, the evaluation styles are quite different. For instance, let us ask to evaluate the following goal.

$$? - Grow(0, r, s, 0)$$

Constraint logic programs find the first rule and subtitute into the body of the rule the known constants, yielding the following.

$$? - c = 0, w = 0, Fert(f, c, r, s, w), \ Water(i, c, r, s, w)$$

Next CLPs check that the constraints are satisfiable, which they are. Then CLPs substitute into the first *Fert* constraint tuple, which yields.

$$? - c = 0, w = 0, f = 0, 15c + 8r + 10s + 15w <= 3000, \ Water(i, c, r, s, w)$$

Then CLPs again check that the constraints are satisfiable, which they still are. Now CLPs substitute into the first *Water* constraint tuple, which yields.

$$? - c = 0, w = 0, f = 0, 15c + 8r + 10s + 15w <= 3000, i = 0, 30c + 25r + 5s + 10w <= 8000$$

Finally, CLPs check one last time that the constraints are satisfiable, which they are. Hence CLPs return the above constraint as the answer.

The above is a rare execution sequence without any backtracking. In general, if one of the satisfiability checks does not work, then CLPs need to backtrack and try a substitution into another contraint tuple for *Fert* or *Water*. Clearly, there are cases when CLPs will perform well and other cases when they do poorly and spend unnecessary time in backtracking. There are other cases when they fall into an infinite loop and never terminate the evaluation.

However, the biggest criticism of CLP is not that it does not work on truly hard programs, but that its result does not help the farmer. Apparently the farmer does not want to grow corn or wheat, but he would clearly want the best remaining option of growing the other two plants and fertilizing and irrigating those. In contrast to the farmer's desire, CLP returned only the choice of $f = 0$ and $i = 0$, which means one particular combination of fertilizer and irrigation options. Finding only this option is not satisfiable because the most profitable growing option for the farmer may be with the other choices. In fact, in this case another choice would be better.

In many applications, it is not enough to return one solution, but a query needs to return *all the solutions*. Constraint databases have evaluation methods that always return all the answers to a query. In fact, the MLPQ constraint-relational database system described in Chapter 13 incorporates linear programming as an aggregate operator. Hence it is possible to have in MLPQ the query:

$$G(MAX(300c + 250r + 100s + 150w - 10f - 5i)) :\!- Fert(f, c, r, s, w), Water(i, c, r, s, w).$$

which returns the maximum profit possible considering all the combinations of plants, fertilizers, and irrigation, or the query

$$G(MAX(250r + 100s - 10f - 5i)) :\!- c = 0, w = 0, Fert(f, c, r, s, w), Water(i, c, r, s, w).$$

which returns the best option without planting any corn or wheat.

The farmer example is a simple case of choice-based linear programming. Linear programming from operations research is only one area where a complete evaluation is a natural requirement. Most GIS applications (see Chapter 6) likewise require computing all the answers. Clearly, no user would be satisfied with a GIS system that returns always a small patch of a map as the answer. Similarly, no moving objects database (see Chapter 7) user would be satisfied with only a single instance of the trajectory of an airplane. As a final example out of numerous remaining ones, no software verification (see Chapter 26) would be possible if the verifier would analyze only one possible run of a computer program.

While constraint logic programming was one of the inspirations for the development of constraint databases, the contribution of constraint database researchers extended the use of constraints to areas where CLPs are not applicable. The differences between CLPs and constraint databases are not limited to "top-down" versus "bottom-up" evaluation styles, which sound superficial like two sides of an egg, but actually run deeper at the algorithmic level. The table below attempts to give a brief summary.

Comparison of CLP and CDB

Evaluation	Constraint Logic Programs	Constraint Databases
Style:	top-down tuple-at-a-time	bottom-up set-at-a-time
Algorithms:	constraint satisfiability Fourier's variable elimination	quantifier elimination Dantzig's simplex method indexing methods etc.

Bibliographic Notes

Quantifier elimination algorithms have a long history. One simple quantifier elimination method for conjunctions of Boolean equality constraints can be said to originate with George Boole. It was used in [215], but it is rather inefficient. Theorem 23.1.7 is another early quantifier elimination method for rational linear inequality constraints and is due to Fourier [135]. Theorem 23.1.8 on real polynomial constraints is by Tarski and is described in [394]. Both of the last two algorithms are computationally inefficient, but better algorithms were developed by several other authors for both linear constraints [258, 257, 259] and for polynomial constraints, including Basu [29], Ben-Or et al. [38], Caviness and Johnson [71], Collins [95], Renegar [322], and Van Den Dries [411]. Presburger [310] gave the first algorithm for quantifier elimination with linear constraints over the integers. The computational complexity of quantifier elimination for linear equality and inequality constraints is considered over the integers by Williams [426] and over the reals by Ferrante and Rackoff [129].

Theorems 23.1.1 and 23.1.2 on variable elimination, as well as Theorems 23.4.3, 23.4.4, and 23.4.5 on closed-form least fixpoint evaluations, are from Kanellakis et al. [214, 215]. An efficient quantifier elimination algorithm for rational order constraint formulas was also given by Ferrante and Geiser [128]. All of these closed-form evaluation results relied on the observation that only a finite number of atomic constraints are expressible in these cases. Theorem 23.4.2 is a generalization of that observation.

Some additional finite cases were discovered later. These include Boolean upper bound and monotone Boolean inequality constraints in free Boolean algebras as well as equality and inequality constraints in atomless Boolean algebras. Theorems 23.1.9, 23.1.11, and 23.4.5 are from Revesz [333]. The quantifier elimination method for atomless Boolean algebras in Theorem 23.1.10 is by Marriott and Odersky [266]. Further discussion on Boolean constraint solving can be found in Buttner and Simonis [61] and in Martin and Nipkow [268]. A least fixpoint evaluation for Datalog queries with Boolean algebra B_Z constraints is described in Revesz [326]. Quantifier elimination for the Boolean algebras of sets with linear cardinality constraints is presented in Kuncak et al. [249] and Revesz [341]. Revesz [341] is a more general result because it allows Boolean constant symbols as in Theorem 23.1.13. The expressivity of Boolean algebras of sets with linear cardinality constraints is investigated in [343].

Lemma 23.4.1 is variously known as Dickson's or Higman's lemma and is used in several different types of well-structured transition systems, which are reviewed by Finkel and Schnoebelen [130]. It has been rediscovered several times in the literature, including by the author, and its present form and proof is from Revesz [323, 325]. Several fixpoint evaluation termination results rely on that lemma, and Theorem 23.4.6 is a new summary of that fact. Kuijpers et al. [247] discusses termination of spatial Datalog queries.

In particular, gap-order constraints were considered and Theorems 23.1.3 and 23.4.7 were proven in Revesz [323, 325]. Half-addition, positive, and negative linear constraints were considered and Theorems 23.1.4, 23.1.5, and 23.1.6 on variable elimination and Theorems 23.4.8, 23.4.9, and 23.4.10 on least fixpoint evaluation were proven in Revesz [334]. The modified least fixpoint evaluation algorithms and Theorems 23.4.11, 23.4.12, and 23.4.13 are from Revesz [336].

Quantifier elimination for difference constraints over the rational numbers is studied in Koubarakis [235]. Efficient variable elimination algorithms for difference constraints, addition constraints, and their disjunctive extensions can be found in [238, 239, 240]. Constraint satisfaction and variable elimination for addition constraints and for two-variable-per-inequality linear constraints is studied in Dechter et al. [107, 106], Hochbaum and Naor [198], Goldin and Kanellakis [155], Jaffar et al. [206], and Harvey and Stuckey [192]. Geerts et al, [144, 146] consider terminating of recursive queries with polynomial constraints. The approximation of recursive queries with polynomial constraints in Example 12.3.3 is based on [340]. Toman et al. [403] describe an alternative evaluation method of constraint Datalog queries.

Parametric evaluation of Datalog queries was considered in [215]. Example 23.4.3 is from that paper, and Example 23.4.4 is from [333]. Stone's representation theorem and other general background on Boolean algebras is described in Burris and Sankappanavar [60] and Halmos [188].

The general relational algebra evaluation method in Theorem 23.2.1 is from [335]. Specific relational algebra evaluation methods will be discussed in Chapter 24, and more bibliography references can be found at the end of that chapter. The PTIME evaluation of relational algebra operators for nonperiodic parametric rectangles is from Cai et al. [64]. Theorem 23.4.15 on the PTIME evaluation of periodic parametric rectangles is from Revesz and Cai [347, 348] and Cai [63].

Evaluation of SQL with *Max* and *Min* aggregate operators based on linear programming was considered in Brodsky et al. [57] and Revesz and Li [351]. Dantzig [103], a classic book on linear programming, describes the simplex method. In the worst case the simplex algorithm requires an exponential number of steps in the size of the linear programming problem. Efficient polynomial time algorithms have been found for this problem by Khachiyan [227] and Karmarkar [219]. Chvatal [90] and Schrijver [366] are more recent books on linear programming that include newer methods. Megiddo [273] considers the computational complexity of linear programming when the dimension is fixed. Yannakakis [433] is a review of linear programming and its applications.

Exercises

1. Assume that x, y, z, and w are variables. Eliminate variable x from the following conjunctions of rational half-addition, lower bound, and upper bound constraints:

$$
\begin{aligned}
x - z &\geq 3 \\
y - z &\geq 8 \\
w - y &\geq 2 \\
w - x &\geq 4 \\
-w &\geq -40 \\
z &\geq 20
\end{aligned}
$$

2. Assume that x, y, z, and w are variables over the rational numbers. Eliminate variable x from the following conjunctions of linear constraints:

$$
\begin{aligned}
x + 3y - z &\geq 5 \\
-2x + 4y - 8z &\geq -8 \\
-x + 3z &\geq 4 \\
3x - 27y &\geq 3
\end{aligned}
$$

3. Assume that x, y, z, and w are variables over the rational numbers. Eliminate variable x from the following conjunctions of linear constraints:

$$
\begin{aligned}
7x + 5y - 13z &\geq 10 \\
-14x + 24y - 18z &\geq -20 \\
21x - 9y + 36z &\geq 15 \\
-3x - 6y + 3z &\geq 30
\end{aligned}
$$

4. Assume that x, y, and z are variables over the rational numbers. Eliminate variable x from the following conjunction of linear inequality constraints:

$$
\begin{aligned}
-26x + 50y + 40z &\geq -40 \\
-2x + 3y + 12z &\geq 0 \\
5x - 10y - 5 &\geq 10 \\
-7x + 15y + 16z &\geq 10
\end{aligned}
$$

5. Assume that x, y, and z are variables over the rational numbers.

   (a) Eliminate variable x from the following conjunction of linear constraints:

$$
\begin{aligned}
-2x - 34y + 46z &\geq 74 \\
3x + 69y - 87z &\geq -21 \\
x - 19y + 31z &\geq 5 \\
-6x + 42y - 66z &\geq -18
\end{aligned}
$$

   (b) Eliminate variable y from the result of the above.

   (c) What is the smallest rational number that z could be to satisfy the above conjunction?

6. Assume that x, y, z, and w are variables and a, b, c, d, and e are constant symbols of a free Boolean algebra. Eliminate variable x from the following conjunctions of constraints:

$$
\begin{aligned}
x \cap y &\subseteq (a \cup b) \cap \bar{c} \\
\bar{x} \cap \bar{y} \cap z &\subseteq (a \cap \bar{d}) \cup (a \cap e) \\
x \cap w &\subseteq (d \cup e) \\
\bar{x} \cap \bar{w} &\subseteq (a \cup c) \\
(x \cap y) \cup z &\neq \emptyset
\end{aligned}
$$

7. Which of the conjunction of constraints in the previous exercises are satisfiable? Prove your answer.

8. Are conjunctions of integer order constraints closed under existential quantifier elimination? Why or why not?

9. Are conjunctions of integer linear inequality constraints closed under existential quantifier elimination? Why or why not?

10. Prove the following: If in a sequence of k-dimensional rectangles $R_1, R_2, \ldots$ no rectangle contains any earlier rectangle, and every corner vertex of every rectangle has nonnegative integer coordinates, and the origin is a corner vertex of every rectangle, then the sequence of rectangles must be finite.

24

Implementation Methods

Chapter 23 discussed the evaluation of constraint query languages in general based on several assumptions, for example, that existential quantifier elimination and satisfiability can be implemented as functions. From a practical point of view there are many lower-level details that need to be considered for implementation of a constraint database system. In this chapter, we discuss two implementation approaches.

The first approach is a graph-based approach described in Section 24.1. This approach takes a step toward implementation by giving a graph data structure to the constraint data represented. Then it develops the algebraic operators in terms of this new data structure.

The second approach, described in Section 24.2, is a matrix-based approach that is even more concrete. In this, the graph data structure is replaced by matrices that lead to simple computer implementations. Throughout this chapter we will consider integer difference constraints as our main example. Similar graph-based or matrix-based implementation structures could be described for other types of constraints. We give just a brief outline for Boolean constraints in Section 24.3.1.

24.1 Evaluation with Gap-Graphs

In this section we assume that all atomic constraints in the input relations are difference constraints. Note that each lower bound constraint of the form $x \geq a$ and each upper bound constraint of the form $-x \geq b$ can be represented by the difference constraints $x - 0 \geq a$ and $0 - x \geq b$, respectively. Similarly, we can express equality constraint $x = y$ by the conjunction of $x - y \geq 0$ and $y - x \geq 0$.

P. Revesz, *Introduction to Databases: From Biological to Spatio-Temporal*,
Texts in Computer Science, DOI 10.1007/978-1-84996-095-3_24,
© Springer-Verlag London Limited 2010

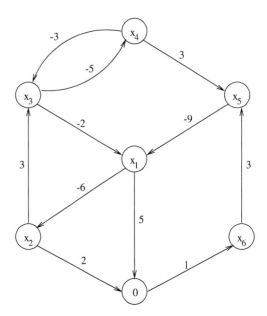

Figure 24.1: Gap-graph G_1.

Unlike gap-order constraints, which always have a nonnegative bound, difference constraints are closed under negation. More precisely, $not(x-y \geq b)$ is equivalent to $x - y < b$, which can be rewritten as the difference constraint $y - x > -b$. If the domain of the variables is the integers, then the latter can be further rewritten as $y - x \geq -b + 1$. Therefore, we will assume in the following that we have only integer difference constraints of the form $x - y \geq c$, where x and y are variables or 0 and c is some integer. We call this the normal form of integer difference constraints.

Conjunctions of integer difference constraints over the variables $x_1, \ldots, x_n$ can be represented as a *gap-graph* $G(V, E)$, where V is the set of vertices and E is the set of edges. V contains a vertex representing the constant 0 and one vertex for each variable. For each integer difference constraint of the form $x - y \geq c$, E contains a directed edge from y to x with label c. This edge is denoted as $y \xrightarrow{c} x$. We define the following operators.

Graph: This operator takes as input a set of constraint tuples and returns their gap-graph representations.

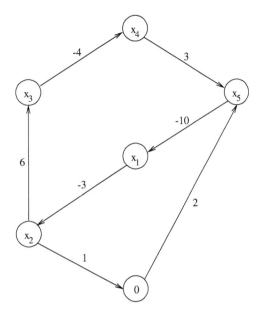

Figure 24.2: Gap-graph G_2.

Example 24.1.1 Consider the following conjunction of difference constraints:

$$
\begin{aligned}
0 - x_1 &\geq 5 \\
0 - x_2 &\geq 2 \\
x_1 - x_3 &\geq -2 \\
x_1 - x_5 &\geq -9 \\
x_2 - x_1 &\geq -6 \\
x_3 - x_2 &\geq 3 \\
x_3 - x_4 &\geq -3 \\
x_4 - x_3 &\geq -5 \\
x_5 - x_4 &\geq 3 \\
x_5 - x_6 &\geq 3 \\
x_6 - 0 &\geq 1
\end{aligned}
$$

This can be represented by gap-graph G_1, shown in Figure 24.1. Similarly, the conjunction

$$
\begin{aligned}
0 - x_2 &\geq 1 \\
x_1 - x_5 &\geq -10 \\
x_2 - x_1 &\geq -3 \\
x_3 - x_2 &\geq 6 \\
x_4 - x_3 &\geq -4 \\
x_5 - x_4 &\geq 3 \\
x_5 - 0 &\geq 2
\end{aligned}
$$

can be represented by G_2, shown in Figure 24.2.

Note that between any pair of vertices, at most two edges are enough because we need to keep in each direction only the highest labeled edges, as the others represent only weaker constraints. Therefore, each gap-graph with $k + 1$ vertices can be represented with at most $O(k^2)$ size.

Shortcut: This operator takes as input a variable x and a gap-graph $G(V, E)$ and returns a gap-graph $G'(V \setminus \{x\}, E')$, where E' is all the edges in E that are not incident on x and the edges

$$
u \xrightarrow{a+b} v \text{ if } u \xrightarrow{a} x \text{ and } x \xrightarrow{b} v \in E
$$

This operator implements existential quantifier elimination on gap-graphs.

Example 24.1.2 The shortcut of vertex x_1 from G_1 is shown in Figure 24.3. Because $x_5 \xrightarrow{-9} x_1$ and $x_1 \xrightarrow{5} 0$ are edges in Figure 24.1 we have the new edge $x_5 \xrightarrow{-4} 0$ in the shortcut graph because $-9 + 5 = -4$.

Merge: This operator takes as input two gap-graphs $G_1(V_1, E_1)$ and $G_2(V_2, E_2)$ and gives as output the gap-graph $G(V, E)$ where $V = V_1 \cup V_2$ and $E = E_1 \cup E_2$. This operator implements taking the conjunction of two constraint tuples.

Example 24.1.3 The merge of G_1 and G_2 is shown in Figure 24.4. Because $x_5 \xrightarrow{-9} x_1$ is an edge in Figure 24.1 and $x_5 \xrightarrow{-10} x_1$ is an edge in Figure 24.2 we have the first edge in the new gap-graph because $-9 > -10$.

Sat: This operator takes as input a gap-graph and returns it if the constraint tuple represented by the gap-graph is satisfiable. Otherwise the sat returns nothing.

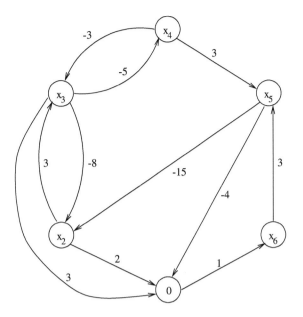

Figure 24.3: Shortcut of x_1 from G_1.

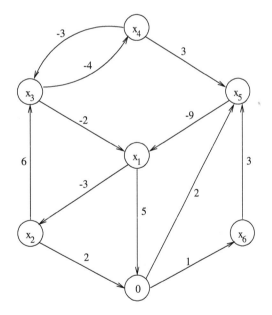

Figure 24.4: Merge of G_1 and G_2.

We call a chain of directed edges a *path*. If the path starts and ends at the same vertex, then we call it a *cycle*. We call the *length* of a path the sum of the gap values in the labels of its directed edges. For example, in G_2 the path $x_1 \xrightarrow{-3} x_2 \xrightarrow{6} x_3 \xrightarrow{-4} x_4$ has length -1.

Lemma 24.1.1 Let T be a difference constraint tuple. Then T is satisfiable if and only if in $graph(T)$ there is no cycle with length greater than 0.
∎

For example, suppose that in a gap-graph there is a directed edge from vertex x to vertex y with label 3, and there is another edge from y to x with label -2. Then there is a cycle in the gap-graph where the sum of the labels is 1. Hence the gap-graph is not satisfiable by Lemma 24.1.1.

Instead of using Lemma 24.1.1 we could reason as follows. The first edge represents the constraint $x + 3 \leq y$, while the second edge represents the constraint $y - 2 \leq x$, which is equivalent to $y \leq x + 2$. Hence the two constraints together would imply that $x + 3 \leq x + 2$, which is impossible.

The transitive closure G^* of a gap-graph G is the gap-graph with the same vertices as G and with a single directed edge $v_i - v_j \geq b$ between each pair of vertices v_i and v_j between which there is at least one directed path and the length of the longest directed path is b. Lemma 24.1.1 implies the following theorem.

Theorem 24.1.1 Let T be a difference constraint tuple. Then $G = graph(T)$ is satisfiable if and only if in G^* there is no vertex v with $v \xrightarrow{b} v$ and $b > 0$. ∎

Corollary 24.1.1 Let T be a difference constraint tuple with k variables and size $O(n)$. Then it can be decided in $O(n + k^3)$ time whether T is satisfiable.

Proof: We can build a gap-graph to represent T in $O(n)$ time such that there is at most one edge from each vertex to another vertex. Therefore, the size of the gap-graph will be $O(k^2)$. Then we can find the transitive closure of this gap-graph in $O(k^3)$ time. Finally, we can check that there is no edge from any vertex to itself with a bound greater than zero. ∎

Dnf: This operator takes as input a formula with difference constraints and puts it into disjunctive normal form.

Compl: This operator takes as input a formula with difference constraints, finds its complement, and puts it into disjunctive normal form.

Lemma 24.1.2 For any fixed k and variable n, the complement of any integer difference constraint relation R of arity k and size n can be found in $O(n^{k^2})$ time.

Proof: Without loss of generality let $R(x_1, \ldots, x_k)$ be the schema of R. The complement of R will be a relation with a set of integer difference constraint tuples. Each atomic constraint in these constraint tuples will have a left-hand side of the form $x_i - x_j$ where $1 \leq i, j \leq k$. Therefore, there are k^2 different left-hand sides. In each constraint tuple there need be at most one atomic constraint with each left-hand side. (This corresponds to having at most one edge from any vertex to another vertex in a gap-graph representation.)

Let B be the set of bound values that occur in R. Let also $\overline{B} = \{-b+1 : b \in B\}$. Clearly both B and $\overline{B}$ have size $O(n)$. It can be seen from De Morgan's laws that each constraint tuple in the complement of R can be represented as a conjunction of atomic constraints in which the bound is in $\overline{B}$.

We can build only at most $O(n^{k^2})$ different constraint tuples using atomic constraints with at most $O(k^2)$ distinct left-hand sides and $O(n)$ right-hand sides. (This corresponds to assigning to each directed edge in a gap-graph a value from $\overline{B}$.)

Each of these disjuncts can be tested to be in the relation in $O(n)$ time. We know that a constraint tuple t is in the complement of R if t and t_i is unsatisfiable for any constraint tuple t_i in R. Therefore, we can build and test each of the possible constraint tuples. Corollary 24.1.1 implies that satisfiability can be done in $O(k^3)$ time. Therefore, the complement can be found in at most $O(n^{k^2})$ time. ∎

Remark 24.1.1 For small k, there are special algorithms that can be used to take the complement of R. For example, when $k = 1$ then each constraint tuple of R represents an interval. Hence in this case the problem reduces to finding the complement of n intervals. The complement in this case can be represented by at most $n + 1$ intervals or constraint tuples, which can be found in $O(n \log n)$ time.

Based on these operators, we define the constraint relational algebra operators as follows:

$$A \hat{\cap} B = \{merge(G_1, G_2) : G_1 \in graph(A) \text{ and } G_2 \in graph(B)\}$$

$$A \hat{\cup} B = \{G : G \in graph(A) \text{ or } G \in graph(B)\}$$

$$A \hat{\setminus} B = A \hat{\cap} compl(B)$$

$$A \hat{\times} B = \{G(V_1 \cup V_2, E_1 \cup E_2) : G_1(V_1, E_1) \in graph(A) \text{ and } G_2(V_2, E_2) \in graph(B)\}$$

$$A \hat{\bowtie} B = \{merge(G_1, G_2) : G_1 \in graph(A) \text{ and } G_2 \in graph(B)\}$$

$$\hat{\pi}_L A = \{shortcut(x_i, G) : G \in graph(A)\}$$

$$\hat{\sigma}_F A = \{merge(G, graph(F)) : G \in graph(A) \text{ and } F_i \in dnf(F)\}$$

As a final step in each operation, we apply the sat operator to keep only the satisfiable gap-graphs in the output relation. The preceding list of relational algebra operators left out the rename operator, which just relabels the vertices of the gap-graph. Using the defined constraint relational algebra operators, it is possible to evaluate any relational algebra query.

24.2 Evaluation with Matrices

24.2.1 From Graphs to Matrices

We represent each gap-graph by a matrix M in which each entry $M[i,j] = b$ if there is an edge $x_i \xrightarrow{b} x_j$ and it is $-\infty$ otherwise. If there are several edges from x_i to x_j, then we take the maximum of the bounds.

Example 24.2.1 The following matrix represents G_1 in Figure 24.1:

	0	x_1	x_2	x_3	x_4	x_5	x_6
0	$-\infty$	$-\infty$	$-\infty$	$-\infty$	$-\infty$	$-\infty$	1
x_1	5	$-\infty$	-6	$-\infty$	$-\infty$	$-\infty$	$-\infty$
x_2	2	$-\infty$	$-\infty$	3	$-\infty$	$-\infty$	$-\infty$
x_3	$-\infty$	-2	$-\infty$	$-\infty$	-5	$-\infty$	$-\infty$
x_4	$-\infty$	$-\infty$	$-\infty$	-3	$-\infty$	3	$-\infty$
x_5	$-\infty$	-9	$-\infty$	$-\infty$	$-\infty$	$-\infty$	$-\infty$
x_6	$-\infty$	$-\infty$	$-\infty$	$-\infty$	$-\infty$	3	$-\infty$

Similarly, the following is the representation of G_2 in Figure 24.2:

	0	x_1	x_2	x_3	x_4	x_5
0	$-\infty$	$-\infty$	$-\infty$	$-\infty$	$-\infty$	2
x_1	$-\infty$	$-\infty$	-3	$-\infty$	$-\infty$	$-\infty$
x_2	1	$-\infty$	$-\infty$	6	$-\infty$	$-\infty$
x_3	$-\infty$	$-\infty$	$-\infty$	$-\infty$	-4	$-\infty$
x_4	$-\infty$	$-\infty$	$-\infty$	$-\infty$	$-\infty$	3
x_5	$-\infty$	-10	$-\infty$	$-\infty$	$-\infty$	$-\infty$

The satisfiability testing algorithm can be now given as follows:

Sat(M,n)
input: Matrix M representing a gap-graph over $n+1$ vertices.
output: True or False depending on whether M is satisfiable.

```
m := 0
repeat
        m := m + 1
        for i := 0 to n do
            for j := 0 to n do
                for k := 0 to n do
                    M[i,j] := max(M[i,j], M[i,k] + M[k,j])
                end-for
            end-for
        end-for
until  m = log(n + 1)

Flag := True

for i := 0 to n do
    if M[i,i] > 0 then
        Flag := False
end-for

return(Flag)
```

The repeat-until loop finds the transitive closure of M. For the body of the innermost for loop, note that $(-\infty)+(-\infty)=-\infty$ and $-\infty+b=-\infty$ for any integer b. The last for loop checks the condition in Theorem 24.1.1.

Example 24.2.2 The satisfiability algorithm for input G_1 will compute the transitive closure G_1^*, which is the following:

	0	x_1	x_2	x_3	x_4	x_5	x_6
0	0	−5	−11	−8	−13	4	1
x_1	5	0	−6	−3	−8	9	6
x_2	6	1	−5	3	−2	10	7
x_3	3	−2	−8	−5	−5	7	4
x_4	0	−5	−11	−3	−8	4	1
x_5	−4	−9	−15	−12	−17	0	−3
x_6	−1	−6	−12	−9	−14	3	0

Because in the main diagonal of this matrix there is no entry greater than 0, the gap-graph G_1 is satisfiable.

24.2.2   Shortcut and Project

Now we give an implementation of the shortcut function. We assume that there are already two functions available that can delete the kth row or column of a matrix.

Shortcut(k,M,n)
input: A matrix $M[0..n][0..n]$ and an integer k between 1 and n.
output: The submatrix M' with the kth vertex shortcut.

```
for i := 0 to n do
    for j := 0 to n do
        M[i, j] := max(M[i, j],  M[i, k] + M[k, j])
    end-for
end-for

M := delete_row(k,M)
M := delete_column(k,M)

return(M,n-1)
```

Example 24.2.3 Let us apply the shortcut algorithm for the input matrix for G_1. We obtain the following matrix, which represents the gap-graph shown in Figure 24.3:

	0	x_2	x_3	x_4	x_5	x_6
0	$-\infty$	$-\infty$	$-\infty$	$-\infty$	$-\infty$	1
x_2	2	$-\infty$	3	$-\infty$	$-\infty$	$-\infty$
x_3	3	-8	$-\infty$	-5	$-\infty$	$-\infty$
x_4	$-\infty$	$-\infty$	-3	$-\infty$	3	$-\infty$
x_5	-4	-15	$-\infty$	$-\infty$	$-\infty$	$-\infty$
x_6	$-\infty$	$-\infty$	$-\infty$	$-\infty$	3	$-\infty$

Based on the *shortcut* operation, we can now define projection. We assume that we have a function *insert* that inserts a matrix into the linked list, which represents a relation:

Project(X,R,n)
input: R is a linked list of matrices $[0..n]$ times $[0..n]$.

      A set X of indices of vertices to be projected out.
output: The project of R onto X.

$V := \{0, \ldots, n\}$
$S := V \setminus X$

```
T := empty-list

for each matrix M in R do
    for each x in S do
        M := shortcut(x,M)
    end-for
    T := insert(M,T)
end-for

return(T,n-1)
```

24.2.3 Merge and Join

Suppose we have two matrices T and M such that T includes all the variables of M. We would like to add M to T, that is, change T such that it will contain the merge of T and M.

The main problem is that the order of the variables in T and M may be different. For example, in T the columns may be in the order $0, x, y, t, z, t_2$ while in M they may be in the order $0, x, z, t_2$.

Although it is possible to implement an operator that reorders the columns and rows of M, it would be a time-consuming operation and would require extra storage space for an entire matrix. Instead we can just define an order vector $e[0,\ldots,6]$ such that $e[0] = 0$, and for $i > 0$ each $e[i]$ equals the order in M of the ith variable in T or blank if it does not occur in M. In this case, the vector would be the second row of the following matrix:

0	x	y	t	z	t_2
0	1		2	3	

Similar orderings can be found between any pair of T and M where the variables of T contain those of M. We assume that the order vector is known before calling merge. We pass the order vector e along with the matrices T and M and n the number of variables in T as parameters into the merge operator, which now can be implemented as follows:

Merge(T, M, e, n)
input: Matrices, order vector, and number of variables.
output: T will be updated to be the merge of T and M.

for i := 0 **to** n **do**
    for j := 0 **to** n **do**
        if $e[i] \neq blank$ **and** $e[j] \neq blank$ **then**
            $T[i,j] := max(T[i,j], M[e[i], e[j]])$
    end-for
end-for

return(T,n)

Example 24.2.4 Let's consider the matrix representations of G_1 and G_2 shown in Example 24.2.1. Here the variables of G_1 include those of G_2. Therefore, we have the order vector $e = [0, 1, 2, 3, 4, 5, blank]$. The result of the merge operation will be the following matrix:

	0	x_1	x_2	x_3	x_4	x_5	x_6
0	$-\infty$	$-\infty$	$-\infty$	$-\infty$	$-\infty$	2	1
x_1	5	$-\infty$	-3	$-\infty$	$-\infty$	$-\infty$	$-\infty$
x_2	2	$-\infty$	$-\infty$	6	$-\infty$	$-\infty$	$-\infty$
x_3	$-\infty$	-2	$-\infty$	$-\infty$	-4	$-\infty$	$-\infty$
x_4	$-\infty$	$-\infty$	$-\infty$	-3	$-\infty$	3	$-\infty$
x_5	$-\infty$	-9	$-\infty$	$-\infty$	$-\infty$	$-\infty$	$-\infty$
x_6	$-\infty$	$-\infty$	$-\infty$	$-\infty$	$-\infty$	3	$-\infty$

Now suppose that we would like to merge two matrices M_1 and M_2 in which neither contains all the variables of the other. We can do this by first taking the union of all the variables in the two matrices and creating a template matrix T that contains some ordering of all the variables. By a template matrix we mean a matrix in which all entries are $-\infty$. Next we find the order vectors of both M_1 and M_2 and then successively merge into T first M_1 and then M_2.

Similarly to the merge, we can implement the join of two relations represented by a linked list of matrices. Again we assume that the scheme of the first relation includes all the attributes in the scheme of the second relation. We also assume that the number of matrices in the linked lists can be found by the *size* function:

Join(T, R, e, n)
input: T and R, linked lists of matrices, e and n as in merge.
output: The join of T and M.

L := empty-list

for i := 1 to size(T) **do**
    for j := 1 to size(R) **do**
        Temp := T[i]
        Temp := merge$(Temp, R[j], e, n)$
        if sat(Temp) **then**
            $L := insert(Temp, L)$
    end-for
end-for

return(L)

24.2.4 Datalog Evaluation

It is easy to see that we can write each Datalog rule into a form where each subgoal contains only distinct variables. This is because we can always add some equality constraints to the end of the rule body and consider them as additional subgoals in the rule. We also assume that the same defined relation always contains the same list of variables in every rule. We say that Datalog programs in this form are in *rectified form*. From now on we assume that Datalog programs are in rectified form.

With each Datalog rule with n distinct variables and m subgoals we associate a matrix $M[0..m][0..n]$. The header of this matrix lists the constant 0 and the variables that occur in the rule in some fixed order, for example, the order of their occurrence as we read the rule from left to right. Then each ith row of the matrix corresponds to the ith subgoal in the rule and contains the order vector of the ith subgoal. More precisely, for each $1 \leq j \leq n$ the $M[i,j]$ entry is the rank of the jth variable within the ith relation. If a variable does not occur in the relation, then we will leave it blank. The $M[i,0]$ entry will always be 0 for any i. For example, let us consider the following rule of Example 12.1.3:

$$Travel(x,y,t) :- Travel(x,z,t_2), Go(z,t_2,y,t).$$

To this rule we assign the list: x,y,t,z,t_2 as the list of occurrence of the variables from left to right. For this rule, the order vectors of the two subgoals are shown as the second and third rows of the following *equality matrix*:

0	x	y	t	z	t_2
0	1			2	3
0		3	4	1	2

The equality matrix is an implicit representation of the renaming required of the variables in the subgoals. We will use this in the evaluation of Datalog queries.

To evaluate a Datalog rule, we have to do for each rule a join of the subgoals in the rule body and then a projection of the variables in the head of the rule. We have to do this repeatedly until there are no more matrices that can be added to the database. We only need to add to the database those matrices that do not dominate any earlier matrix. We assume that $dominates(M_1, M_2)$ is a function that returns true if M_1 dominates M_2. We also assume that each *bound* must have a value greater than or equal to $l_{\min}$ as explained in Chapter 23. The $Eval - Datalog$ program evaluates a Datalog query. The program assumes that we already defined the order matrices for each rule, and the function $subgoal(k,i)$ returns the ith subgoal of the kth rule and the function $order(k,i)$ returns its order vector.

Eval-Datalog(Q,D,$l_{\min}$)
input: Query Q, an input database D, and minimum bound $l_{\min}$.
output: Approximation of the least fixpoint model of $Q(D)$.

Rectify each rule of Q.

repeat
    MoreAdded := False
    for each rule r_k with n_k variables and m_k subgoals **do**

        Create a template matrix $Temp[0..n_k][0..n_k]$.
        Create a relation T containing only the $Temp$ matrix.

        for $i := 1$ to m_k **do**
            R := subgoal(k,i)
            e := order(k,i)
            T := join(T,R,e,n)
        end-for

        Suppose output relation R_0 has j number of variables
        X := $\{0,\ldots,j\}$
        P := project(X,T,n)

        for each matrix M_1 in P **do**
            In M_1 change each entry less than $l_{\min}$ to $-\infty$
            Need-to-Add := True
            for each matrix M_2 in R_0 **do**
                if dominates(M_1, M_2) **then**
                    Need-to-Add := False
            if Need-to-Add = True **then**
                $R_0 := insert(M_1, R_0)$
                MoreAdded := True
            end-if
        end-for
    end-for
until MoreAdded = False

Note that in the project it is enough to know the number of variables in the rule head because the rules are rectified and because of our assumption that variables in each rule are ordered according to their occurrence in the rule as it is read from left to right. An evaluation of a lower bound of the least fixpoint of a Datalog query can be done by changing in M_1 any bound that is less than $l_{\min}$ to $l_{\min}$ instead of to $-\infty$. This requires only changing one line in the preceding program.

24.2.5   Complement and Difference

At first we give an algorithm *Compl-Matrix* that takes the complement of a matrix M. Note that the complement of M is a linked list of matrices, where in each matrix we have one of the entries that is not $-\infty$ in M negated. Negation of an entry $[i, j]$ with value b is equivalent to a value of $-b + 1$ in the entry $[j, i]$. Hence we can implement the complement by at first defining a function *Compl-Matrix* as shown below.

Compl-Matrix(M,n)
input: A matrix $M[0..n][0..n]$.
output: The complement of M as a list of matrices and n.

```
L := emptyset

for i := 1 to n do
    for j := 1 to n do
        if M[i, j] ≠ −∞ then
            Create a template matrix Temp[0..n][0..n]
            Temp[j,i] := -M[i,j]+1
        end-if
        L := insert(Temp,L)
    end-for
end-for

return(T,L)
```

Using this function and another called *remove_duplicate*, which removes duplicate copies from a linked list of matrices, we describe the complement of a relation as follows:

Compl(R,n)
input: R is an array of $[0..n] \times [0..n]$ matrices.
output: The complement of R.

for i = 1 **to** n **do**
    $e[i] := i$
end-for

$T := compl\_matrix(R[1])$

for i := 2 **to** size(R) **do**
    $T := join(T, compl\_matrix(R[i]), e, n)$
    $T := remove\_duplicates(T)$
end-for
return(T)

The difference of relations R and P, written $R - P$ is equivalent to the join of R and the complement of P. Hence the difference operator can also be defined for integer difference constraint relations.

Remark 24.2.1 Using the difference operator it is possible to improve the Datalog evaluation slightly by replacing the dominance test (last two for loops of algorithm *Eval-Datalog*) with a test whether *Difference*(M_1, R_0) is nonempty. Nonemptiness of a relation can be tested by checking the satisfiability of each matrix in the relation. The relation is empty if each of the matrices in it is unsatisfiable.

24.3 Boolean Constraints

Suppose that $R(x_1, \ldots, x_k)$ is a relation where the domain of the variables is some Boolean algebra and each constraint tuple of R contains only Boolean algebra order constraints.

We saw in Theorem 23.4.5 that there can be only $3^k - 1$ possible left-hand sides in all the Boolean order constraints with variables $x_1, \ldots, x_k$. We can fix an ordering of these left-hand sides.

In a constraint tuple there is no need to have two different Boolean order constraints with the same left-hand sides because using the merge rule for precedence constraints we can show that

$$x \subseteq a \ \text{ and } \ x \subseteq b \ \text{ iff } \ x \subseteq (a \cap b) \tag{24.1}$$

Hence each constraint tuple can be represented by an array $A[0..3^k - 1]$ of Boolean constants, where the ith entry corresponds to the right-hand side of the ith upper bound constraint.

Example 24.3.1 The conjunction of upper bound constraints:

$$
\begin{aligned}
x \cap y \cap z &\subseteq_B a \cup b \\
x \cap \overline{y} &\subseteq_B (a \cap c) \cup d \\
\overline{x} \cap \overline{y} \cap \overline{z} &\subseteq_B \overline{b} \cap e
\end{aligned}
$$

can be represented by the array:

Lower Bound	Upper Bound
$x \cap y \cap z$	$a \cup b$
$\vdots$	1
$x \cap \overline{y}$	$(a \cap c) \cup d$
$\vdots$	1
$\overline{x} \cap \overline{y} \cap \overline{z}$	$\overline{b} \cap e$

which has all its entries 1 except for the three entries that show the right-hand sides of the Boolean order constraints.

The merge of two Boolean order constraint tuples represented by arrays A_1 and A_2 can be done by applying rule (24.1) for each corresponding pair of entries in A_1 and A_2 and then simplifying and putting the right-hand sides back to disjunctive normal form.

Existential quantifier elimination of a variable x can be done following Theorem 23.1.9 by taking each pair of left-hand sides such that one contains x and the other contains $\overline{x}$ and then finding their implication and merging that with the corresponding entry in the array.

24.3.1 Evaluation with Set-Graphs

Consider again the Boolean algebra $B_Z = \langle \mathcal{P}(\mathcal{Z}), \cap, \cup, ^-, \emptyset, \mathcal{Z} \rangle$, which we defined in Example 11.2.2, but this time allowing the use of set constants $\{c_1, \ldots, c_n\}$, where each c_i is an integer constant, and allowing the use of $\{\}$ as a substitute for $\emptyset$.

The left-hand sides are simpler in B_Z because we can have only 2^D possible sets or their complements on the right-hand side where D is the set of integer constants that occur in the input database or the query.

The following *set containment* constraints are possible to express using only variables ranging over B_Z, the precedence operator $\subseteq$, and set constants:

$$\{c\} \subseteq x \tag{24.2}$$

which means that c is in x, and

$$x \subseteq \overline{\{c\}} \tag{24.3}$$

which means that c is not in x.

If we use only constraints of the form (24.2) and (24.3), then we can express the constraint tuples in an even simpler structure called a *set-graph*. Set-graphs provide a visual representation of conjunctions of set containment constraints. For example, the conjunction of the constraints:

$$
\begin{array}{rcl}
\{3,6,9\} & \subseteq & X_1 \\
\{1,2,3,4\} & \subseteq & Y \\
Y & \subseteq & X_1 \\
Y & \subseteq & X_2 \\
X_3 & \subseteq & Y \\
X_3 & \subseteq & X_2 \\
X_1 & \subseteq & \{1,2,3,4,5,6,7,8,9\} \\
X_2 & \subseteq & \{1,2,3,4,5,6,7,8,9\}
\end{array}
$$

can be represented by the set-graph shown on the left in Figure 24.5. In the set-graph, each directed edge from a vertex labeled X to another vertex labeled Y represents the constraint $X \subseteq Y$.

Set-graphs with n variables can also be represented by a matrix of size $n \times n$ and an array of size $n \times 3$. In the first matrix the i,jth entry will be a 1 if the ith variable is a subset of the jth variable or 0 otherwise. For example, the set-graph on the left of Figure 24.5 can be represented by the matrix:

	x_1	x_2	x_3	y
x_1	0	0	0	0
x_2	0	0	0	0
x_3	0	1	0	1
y	1	1	0	0

In the second matrix there will be a row for each variable and two columns. The first column will list the lower bound and the second the upper bound for each set variable. In the example the second matrix would be:

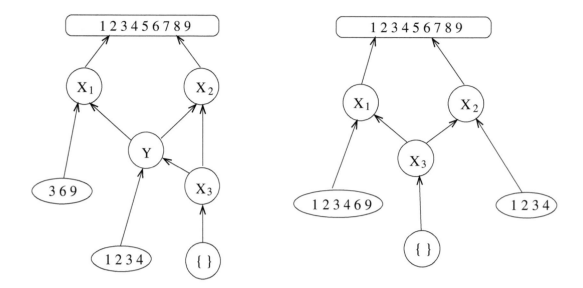

Figure 24.5: Example of variable elimination from a set-graph.

	L	U
x_1	$\{3,6,9\}$	$\{1,2,3,4,5,6,7,8,9\}$
x_2	$\{\}$	$\{1,2,3,4,5,6,7,8,9\}$
x_3	$\{\}$	$\mathcal{Z}$
y	$\{1,2,3,4\}$	$\mathcal{Z}$

In this matrix the upper bound of x_3 is the entire set of integers.

We define the transitive closure G^* of a set-graph G with vertices $v_1, \ldots, v_n$ as the set-graph that has an edge from v_i to v_j whenever there is a directed path from v_i to v_j in G. The satisfiability of set-graphs can be tested based on the following lemma.

Lemma 24.3.1 Let G be a set-graph with vertices $v_1, \ldots, v_n$. G is satisfiable if and only if in G^* for each pair of vertices v_i and v_j if there is a directed edge from v_i to v_j, then $L_i \subseteq U_j$ is true.   ∎

The variable elimination operation can be defined similarly to the one for gap-graphs. If we want to eliminate variable Y, then we have to add for each pair of vertices V_i and V_j with $V_i \subseteq Y$ and $Y \subseteq V_j$ the edge $V_i \subseteq V_j$. Further we have to make the lower bound of V_j the union of the lower bounds of V_i and V_j, and we have to make the upper bound of V_i the intersection of the upper bounds of V_i and V_j.

For example, if we want to eliminate variable Y from the set-graph on the left of Figure 24.5, then we get the set-graph on the right side of the figure.

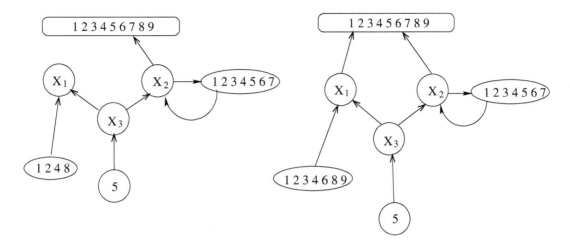

Figure 24.6: Example of merge of set-graphs.

The merge operation can be defined between set-graphs as well. The merge returns a set-graph that contains all the edges of the two input set-graphs plus the lower and upper bounds are also merged as in the variable elimination algorithm. For example, the merge operation on the inputs that is the right side of Figure 24.5 and the left side of Figure 24.6 will return the set-graph on the right side of Figure 24.6.

The relational algebra operators rename, select, and join can be defined similarly to the definitions for relations with gap-graphs. Finally, the evaluation of Datalog queries with B_Z set containment constraints can be defined similarly to Section 24.2.

24.4   Optimization of Relational Algebra

Because relational algebra is a procedural language, each relational algebra query can be evaluated simply by following the sequence of operations in the relational algebra expression. However, this simple evaluation method is not always the best possible.

Relational algebra query optimization algorithms rely on the fact that a relational algebra expression can be rewritten into other logically equivalent relational algebra expressions by using several rewriting rules. The rewritten relational algebra expression can often be evaluated much more simply than the original one, although they always yield the same output relation.

The following are some rewriting rules that can be used by query optimization algorithms:

1. *Commutative laws for join and products:*

$$R_1 \bowtie R_2 \equiv R_2 \bowtie R_1$$
$$R_1 \times R_2 \equiv R_2 \times R_1$$

2. *Associative law for joins and products:*

$$(R_1 \bowtie R_2) \bowtie R_3 \equiv R_1 \bowtie (R_2 \bowtie R_3)$$
$$(R_1 \times R_2) \times R_3 \equiv R_1 \times (R_2 \times R_3)$$

3. *Cascade of projections:*

$$\pi_{A_1,\ldots,A_k}\left(\pi_{B_1,\ldots,B_l}(R)\right) \equiv \pi_{A_1,\ldots,A_k}(R)$$

if $\{A_1, \ldots, A_k\} \subseteq \{B_1, \ldots, B_l\}$

4. *Cascade of selections:*

$$\sigma_{F_1}(\sigma_{F_2}(R)) \equiv \sigma_{F_1 \wedge F_2}(R) \equiv \sigma_{F_2}(\sigma_{F_1}(R))$$

5. *Commuting selections and projections:*
   If the set of attributes in condition F is the subset of $\{A_1, \ldots, A_k\}$:

$$\pi_{A_1,\ldots,A_k}(\sigma_F(R)) \equiv \sigma_F(\pi_{A_1,\ldots,A_k}(R))$$

   If the set of attributes in F is $\{A_{i_1}, \ldots, A_{i_m}\} \cup \{B_1, \ldots, B_l\}$:

$$\pi_{A_1,\ldots,A_k}(\sigma_F(R)) \equiv \pi_{A_1,\ldots,A_k}(\sigma_F(\pi_{A_1,\ldots,A_k,B_1,\ldots,B_l}(R)))$$

6. *Commuting selection with join:*
   If all the attributes of F are the attributes of R_1:

$$\sigma_F(R_1 \bowtie R_2) \equiv \sigma_F(R_1) \bowtie R_2$$

If $F = F_1 \wedge F_2$, the attributes of F_1 are only in R_1, and the attributes in F_2 are only in R_2, then:

$$\sigma_F(R_1 \bowtie R_2) \equiv \sigma_{F_1}(R_1) \bowtie \sigma_{F_2}(R_2)$$

If $F = F_1 \wedge F_2$ and the attributes of F_1 are only in R_1, but the attributes in F_2 are in both R_1 and R_2:

$$\sigma_F(R_1 \bowtie R_2) \equiv \sigma_{F_2}(\sigma_{F_1}(R_1) \bowtie R_2)$$

7. *Commuting a projection with a join:*

$\{A_1, \ldots, A_k\} = \{B_1, \ldots, B_l\} \cup \{C_1, \ldots, C_m\}$, where B_is are attributes of R_1, and C_is are attributes of R_2:

$$\pi_{A_1, \ldots, A_k}(R_1 \bowtie R_2) \equiv \pi_{B_1, \ldots, B_l}(R_1) \bowtie \pi_{C_1, \ldots, C_m}(R_2)$$

The following description of the optimization algorithm is clearer if we visualize each relational algebra expression as a tree in which each internal node is a relational algebra operator and its children are the operands. Then the general principles behind the query optimization algorithm can be stated as follows:

1. Perform selections as early as possible.

2. Perform projections as early as possible.

3. Combine sequences of selection operations.

These principles lead to a basic optimization algorithm that at first uses for each selection the identities 4–6 to move the selections down. Second, it uses the identities 3 or 7 to move the projections down, and if possible to delete some projections. Finally, it uses the identity 4 to combine cascades of selections into one selection.

Example 24.4.1 Consider the following relational algebra formula:

$$\pi_{x,y}\left(\sigma_{x \cap y \neq \emptyset}\left(\sigma_{y \cap \{4\} = \emptyset}\left(\sigma_{x \cap \{6,8\} = \emptyset}\left(\sigma_{x \cap \{2,4\} = \emptyset}(A(x,z) \bowtie B(v,y) \bowtie C(x) \bowtie D(v,y))\right)\right)\right)\right)$$

This formula can be visualized as the tree shown in Figure 24.7. We now briefly illustrate each of these steps of the optimization.

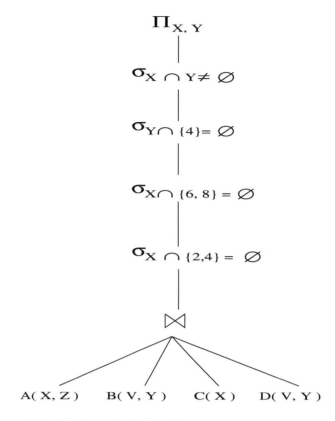

Figure 24.7: The formula before the optimization.

Perform Selections as Early as Possible: To apply this step, we find which relations and selections have common variables. Suppose that in a (sub)formula a set of selections $(S_1, S_2, \ldots ,S_k)$ follows the join of a set of relations $(R_1,R_2, \ldots ,R_l)$. Let V_i be the set of relations that have common variables with S_i, that is:

$$V_i = \{R_n \mid (variables\ in\ R_n) \cap (variables\ in\ S_i) \neq \emptyset\}$$

A selection (S_i) can be executed if the join of all the relations mentioned in V_i is already calculated. This gives an obvious limit for how far we can move down the selection S_i.

Whenever there are several selections to choose to move down, then we check whether there is any i such that $\forall j : V_i \subseteq V_j$. In this case S_i will be moved down before all the other selections. If there is no such i, then the algorithm chooses some index i with a minimal cardinality V_i. After a selection is moved down, the V_is are updated and the preceding is repeated.

In Figure 24.7 there are four selections to choose from to move down first. For the four selections $\sigma_{y \cap \{4\}=\emptyset}$, $\sigma_{x \cap \{6,8\}=\emptyset}$, $\sigma_{x \cap \{2,4\}=\emptyset}$, and $\sigma_{x \cap y \neq \emptyset}$, we calculate the values $V_1 = \{A, B, C, D\}$, $V_2 = \{B, D\}$, $V_3 = \{A, C\}$, and $V_4 = \{A, C\}$, respectively.

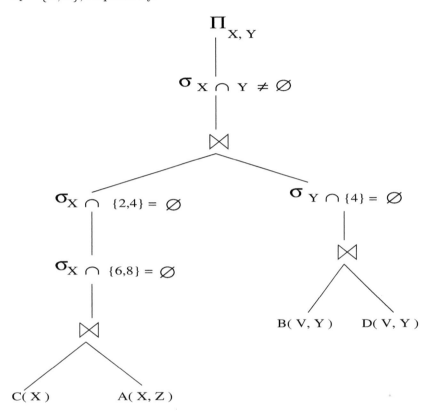

Figure 24.8: The formula after the first step of the optimization.

Because no V_i is the subset of all the other V_js, the algorithm chooses the minimal cardinality V_i with the smallest index, that is, V_2. When S_2 is moved down over the join of the relations B and D, the subformula $\sigma_{y \cap \{4\}=\emptyset}(B(v, y) \bowtie D(v, y))$ will be treated as a single relation S_2.

The process is repeated and the values $V_1 = \{A, C, S_2\}$, $V_3 = \{A, C\}$, and $V_4 = \{A, C\}$ are found. Because $V_3 \subseteq V_1$ and $V_3 \subseteq V_4$, we now choose S_3 to move down. From now on the subformula $\sigma_{x \cap \{6,8\}=\emptyset}(C(x) \bowtie A(x, z))$ will be treated as the single relation S_3. Then the process is repeated again and the values $V_1 = \{S_2, S_3\}$ and $V_4 = \{S_3\}$ are found. Because $V_4 \subseteq V_1$, we choose S_4 to move down. Now, let S_4 be the formula

$$\sigma_{x \cap \{2,4\}=\emptyset}(\sigma_{x \cap \{6,8\}=\emptyset}(C(x) \bowtie A(x, z)))$$

The process is repeated again and V_1 cannot be pushed down further. Hence we obtain the formula shown in Figure 24.8.

Perform Projections as Early as Possible: The optimization algorithm also moves down the projection operations. The set of variables used in each branch of the formula tree is calculated and the variables that are not needed higher up are eliminated. Moving down projections in Figure 24.8 results in the formula shown in Figure 24.9.

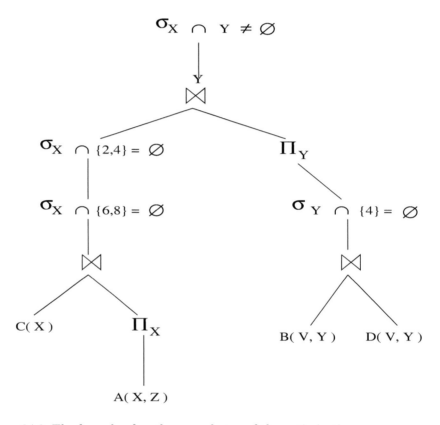

Figure 24.9: The formula after the second step of the optimization.

Combine Sequences of Selection Operations: The optimization algorithm combines cascades of selections into one selection. The optimization algorithm checks every edge in the tree, and if both vertices of an edge are selection operations, then combines them. In this example one pair of selections between the joins on the top and the left can be combined.

Bibliographic Notes

Although the quantifier elimination algorithms in Section 23.1 are only subcases of Fourier's method extended to the integers [426], the interesting point here is that these subcases are closed. Gap-graphs are considered as a representation in Revesz [324, 325]. Temporal constraint networks that are similar to gap-graphs are considered in the area of artificial intelligence by Dechter et al. [107]. Stone's representation theorem is described in Burris and Sankappanavar [60] and Halmos [188].

The Datalog evaluation in Section 24.2.4 is based on the naive evaluation described in Ullman [408]. The use of an equality matrix in the Datalog evaluation method is new. More details about the evaluation of Datalog queries within the DISCO system are described in Section 14.2.

Michaylov [275], Ramakrishnan and Srivastava [314, 381], and Stuckey and Sudarshan [388] consider the optimization of constraint logic programs pushing constraint selections and efficient subsumption testing.

The discussion about the relational algebra identities follows Ullman [408]. Example 24.4.1 about relational algebra optimization is from Salamon [358]. Another algebraic optimization technique based on an efficient parallel algorithm for hypergraph partitioning is described in Ouyang [292].

Pratt [308] gave efficient algorithms for testing the satisfiability and the implication problem for conjunctions of potential constraints. Harvey and Stuckey [192] gave a polynomial algorithm for the implication problem in the case of conjunctions of sum constraints with integer variables.

Exercises

1. We know about a certain class of students the following.

   - Al is at least 5 inches taller that Bob.

   - Al and Carl have the same height.

   - Ed is at least 8 inches taller than Fred.

   - Ed is at least 2 inches shorter that Greg.

   - Carl is at least 6 inches shorter than Ed.

   - Bob is at least 60 inches.

   - Greg is at most 75 inches.

   Let a, b, c, e, f, g describe the heights of Al, Bob, Carl, Ed, Fred and Greg, respectively. Given the above information, do the following.

(a) Represent *Heights(a,b,c,e,f,g)* by a constraint database.

(b) Draw the conjunction as a gap-graph.

(c) Draw the transitive closure of the gap-graph.

(d) Represent the transitive closure of the gap-graph as a matrix.

(e) Is the gap-graph satisfiable? Why or why not?

2. We know about a certain group of employees the following.

- Kevin's salary is at least $5,000 higher than Larry's salary.

- Kevin and Mary have the same salary.

- Nancy's salary is at least $8,000 higher than Olivia's salary and at least $2,000 less than Peter's salary.

- Mary's salary is at least $6,000 less than Nancy's salary.

- Larry's salary is at least $60,000.

- Peter's salary is at most $75,000.

Given the above information, do the following.

(a) Draw the conjunction as a gap-graph.

(b) Represent the gap-graph as a matrix.

(c) Is the gap-graph satisfiable? Why or why not?

3. Consider the following conjunction of half-addition constraints:

$$\begin{aligned}
x - z &\geq 3 \\
y - z &\geq 8 \\
w - y &\geq 2 \\
w - x &\geq 4 \\
-w &\geq -40 \\
z &\geq 20
\end{aligned}$$

(a) Draw the conjunction as a gap-graph.

(b) Draw the transitive closure of the gap-graph.

(c) Represent the transitive closure of the gap-graph as a matrix.

(d) Is the gap-graph satisfiable? Why or why not?

4. Consider the following conjunction of half-addition constraints:

$$
\begin{aligned}
x - z &\geq 7 \\
y - z &\geq 5 \\
y - x &\geq 0 \\
x - y &\geq 0 \\
-x &\geq -20 \\
z &\geq 10
\end{aligned}
$$

   (a) Draw the conjunction as a gap-graph.

   (b) Draw the transitive closure of the gap-graph.

   (c) Represent the transitive closure of the gap-graph as a matrix.

   (d) Is the gap-graph satisfiable? Why or why not?

5. A constraint database relation $R(x, y, z)$ consists of two constraint tuples t_1 and t_2, where t_1 is:

$$
\begin{aligned}
y - x &\geq 5 \\
z - y &\geq 4
\end{aligned}
$$

and t_2 is:

$$
\begin{aligned}
y - x &\geq 6 \\
z - y &\geq 3
\end{aligned}
$$

   (a) Find the complement of R.

   (b) Suppose that another relation $Q(x, y, z)$ consists of only one constraint tuple as follows:

$$
\begin{aligned}
y - x &\geq 5 \\
z - y &\geq 3 \\
z - x &\geq 9
\end{aligned}
$$

   Find the difference $Q - R$. (Simplify the relation $Q - R$ by deleting unsatisfiable constraint tuples.)

   (c) Is the relation $Q - R$ nonempty?

   (d) Suppose relation $S(x, y, z)$ consists of only the constraint tuple t_1. Is the relation $Q - S$ nonempty?

6. (a) Represent the following conjunction of half-addition constraints as a gap-graph:

$$u - x \geq 9$$
$$y - x \geq 4$$
$$z - y \geq 2$$
$$z - u \geq 3$$
$$z - x \geq 5$$

   (b) Find an assignment to the variables that satisfies the gap-graph.

   (c) Find the gap-graph obtained by shortcutting vertex u from the gap-graph.

   (d) Represent the following conjunction of half-addition constraints as a gap-graph:

$$y - x \geq 6$$
$$z - y \geq 3$$

   (e) Find the merge of the gap-graphs in parts (c) and (d).

7. The following hold about a group of people and a certain company.

   (a) Al and Bob are managers.

   (b) Al, Bob, and Carl are employees.

   (c) Ed and Fred are customers.

   (d) Only Al, Bob, Carl, and Dave could be employees.

   (e) Only Bob, Carl, Ed, Fred, Greg, Han, and Ken could be customers.

   (f) Only Bob, Ed, Fred, Greg, and Li could be customers.

   (g) All managers are employees.

   (h) All employees are persons.

   (i) All customers are persons.

   (j) Some employees are customers.

   Assume that we represent Al, Bob, Carl, Dave, Ed, Fred, Greg, Han, Li, and Ken by the numbers 1 to 10, respectively. Find a constraint database representation in B_Z for the relation $Company(C, E, M, P)$ where C, E, M, P are the set of customers, employees, managers, and persons, respectively.

8. We know about disciplines taught at a university the following, where the strings starting with capital letters are set variables, and those starting with lower case letters are constants. We assume the Boolean algebra of sets of English words W written with lower case letters.

$$
\begin{aligned}
Science &\subseteq Discipline \\
Engineering &\subseteq Discipline \\
Natural\_Science &\subseteq Science \\
Physical\_Science &\subseteq Science \\
\{biology, physics\} &\subseteq Natural\_Science \\
\{computer\_science, mathematics, physics\} &\subseteq Physical\_Science \\
\{computer\_science, electrical\_engineering\} &\subseteq Engineering
\end{aligned}
$$

(a) Draw the conjunction as a set-graph.

(b) Represent the set-graph by two matrices.

(c) Draw the transitive closure of the set-graph.

(d) Simplify the transitive closure set-graph by merging set-constant lower bounds and set-constant upper bounds whenever possible. Also drop edges between two set-constant vertices.

(e) Represent the transitive closure set-graph by two matrices.

9. Consider the following conjunction of $\subseteq$ constraints in B_Z:

$$
\begin{aligned}
S &\subseteq E \\
S &\subseteq T \\
E &\subseteq \{2, 4, 6, 8, 12\} \\
T &\subseteq \{3, 6, 9, 12\} \\
\{2, 4, 8\} &\subseteq E \\
\{6, 12\} &\subseteq S \\
\{3, 9\} &\subseteq T
\end{aligned}
$$

(a) Draw the conjunction as a set-graph.

(b) Represent the set-graph by two matrices.

(c) Draw the transitive closure of the set-graph.

(d) Represent the transitive closure set-graph by two matrices. (*Hint:* This needs merging of set-constant lower bounds and set-constant upper bounds.)

(e) Is the set-graph satisfiable? Why or why not?

10. Consider the following conjunction of $\subseteq$ constraints in B_Z that define relation $R(S, M, N)$:

$$
\begin{aligned}
S &\subseteq M \\
M &\subseteq N \\
N &\subseteq S \\
M &\subseteq \{1, 2, 4, 5, 6, 7, 8\} \\
S &\subseteq \{1, 2, 3, 4, 5, 6, 7, 8, 9\} \\
\{1, 4, 8, \} &\subseteq N \\
\{2, 5, 7\} &\subseteq M
\end{aligned}
$$

(a) Draw the conjunction as a set-graph.

(b) Represent the set-graph by two matrices.

(c) Draw the transitive closure of the set-graph.

(d) Is the set-graph satisfiable? Why or why not?

(e) Find the natural join of $R(M, N, S)$ and $Q(P, S, T)$, where $Q(S, P, T)$ is defined by the following conjunction of constraints:

$$
\begin{aligned}
S &\subseteq P \\
P &\subseteq T \\
T &\subseteq \{1, 2, 4, 5, 6, 7, 8\}
\end{aligned}
$$

(f) Eliminate the variables M and P from the natural join.

11. Implement the algebraic operators of project, join, union, and intersection for *integer half-addition* constraint databases.

You can assume that we are given the values of u and l. The input relations will be a number of files. Each file represents a relation. Each file will have in it a, the arity of the relation, followed by a list of matrices of size $1 + a$ by $1 + a$ each. Each matrix represents a gap-graph of the input relation. (The header and the first column of the matrices are not present, and you can use any large negative integer instead of $-\infty$.)

The program should prompt users with a menu that lists the available relational algebra operators, the print operator, and quit. If one of the relational algebra operators is entered, the system should prompt for the names of the files that contain the input relations (one or two) and will contain the output relation. In addition, the selection and the join operations should be followed by a prompt asking for the conditions.

For the selection operation the condition may look like this:

$$\$i = c$$

which means that the ith attribute variable should be replaced by the constant c.

For the join operation the condition may look like this:

$$i = j, \ldots, k = l$$

which means that the ith attribute of the first relation equals the jth attribute of the second relation ... and the kth attribute of the first relation equals the lth attribute of the second relation.

The print operator should be followed by a prompt for the name of the file to be displayed. (The relation may be displayed as a set of matrices or as a set of graphs.)

After each operation, except quit, display the menu again.

12. Implement similarly to Exercise 11 the algebraic operators of complement and difference for *integer half-addition* constraint databases.

13. Implement similarly to Exercise 11 the algebraic operators of project, join, union, and intersection for *rational linear* constraint databases.

14. Implement similarly to Exercise 11 the algebraic operators of complement and difference for *rational linear* constraint databases.

15. Implement similarly to Exercise 11 the algebraic operators of project, join, union, and intersection for B_Z constraint databases with only $\subseteq$ constraints.

Computational Complexity

This chapter considers the computational complexity of evaluating constraint queries. Section 25.1 describes Turing machines, which form a simple model of computation. Section 25.2 reviews the most important complexity classes and complexity measures. Section 25.3 discusses the computational complexity of Datalog. Section 25.4 discusses the computational complexity of relational algebra.

25.1 Turing Machines

Turing machines are a simple model of computation. Turing machines use as input and output a single tape. The leftmost tape cell is numbered 1, the tape cell to the right of it is numbered 2, and so on. The size of the tape is infinite to the right direction. Within each tape cell is written one of the characters of a fixed set of symbols, called the *alphabet* σ of the Turing machine. The tape can be described by a relation $T(i, c)$ where i is the tape cell number and $c \in \sigma$.

Example 25.1.1 Suppose the alphabet is $\sigma = \{a, b, \#\}$ and the tape contains the following string:

$$aba\#\#\#\#\#\#\#\#\#\#\# \cdots$$

P. Revesz, *Introduction to Databases: From Biological to Spatio-Temporal*,
Texts in Computer Science, DOI 10.1007/978-1-84996-095-3_25,
© Springer-Verlag London Limited 2010

This tape can be described as follows:

$T(1, a)$.
$T(2, b)$.
$T(3, a)$.
$T(i, \#)$:— $i \geq 4$.

Initially the Turing machine points to the leftmost tape cell and is in an initial state s_0. At each step the Turing machine reads the tape cell to which it points and does one of three actions (1) moves one tape cell to the left and switches to another state, (2) moves one tape cell to the right and switches to another state, or (3) replaces the tape cell symbol with another one and switches to another state. All the options of a Turing machine are listed in a transition function δ. The Turing machine chooses one of the available actions at each step until it reaches a special state, called the *halt state*, when it stops. If Turing machine has only one choice in each possible pair of state and input tape symbol, then it is called a *deterministic Turing machine*. Otherwise, it is called a *non-deterministic Turing machine*.

A Turing machine $\mathcal{T}$ can be defined as a tuple $\langle K, \sigma, \delta, s_0, h \rangle$ where K is the set of states of the machine, σ is the alphabet, δ is the transition function, s_0 is the initial state, and h is the halt state.

Example 25.1.2 A Turing machine $\mathcal{T}_1 = \langle K, \sigma, \delta, s_0, h \rangle$ where $K = \{s_a, s_b, h\}$, $\sigma = \{a, b, \#\}$, δ is

$Right(s_a, a, s_a)$.
$Right(s_a, b, s_a)$.
$Right(s_a, \#, s_b)$.

$Right(s_b, a, h)$.
$Right(s_b, b, s_b)$.
$Right(s_b, \#, s_a)$.

and the initial state is s_a and the halting state is h. In this example, $\mathcal{T}$ is a deterministic Turing machine that moves one tape cell to the right in each step until the halting state is reached.

The following theorem shows the connection between Turing machines and Datalog with addition constraints.

Theorem 25.1.1 The computation of a Turing machine $\mathcal{T} = \langle K, \sigma, \delta, s_0, h \rangle$ on a given input tape can be expressed by a Datalog with addition constraints program.

Proof: First, as in Example 25.1.1, we create a relation $T(i, c)$ to describe the input tape.

Second, as in Example 25.1.2, we create for each possible machine input state s, output state s', and tape symbols c and w, a fact $Left(s,c,s')$, $Right(s,c,s')$, or $Write(s,c,s',w)$ if according to the transition function δ when the machine is in state s and pointing to c, then the machine can go to state s' and move one tape cell to the left or to the right or stay and write w on the tape, respectively.

Third, we use a relation C to describe the configuration of the machine. The relation $C(t,i,s)$ describes that at time step t the machine is pointing to tape position i and is in state s. Since at time zero that the Turing machine is pointing to the first tape cell, we create a fact:

$$C(0,1,s_0).$$

Fourth, we express the sequence of transitions of the machine by a relation $R(t,j,c)$ that is true if and only if at time t the jth tape cell contains the tape symbol c. To initialize R we write the rule:

$$R(0,j,c) :\!- T(j,c).$$

Finally, we express the computation of the Turing machine as follows:

$$
\begin{aligned}
C(t',i',s') \quad &:\!- \quad C(t,i,s),\ R(t,i,c),\ Left(s,c,s'),\ t'-t=1,\ i-i'=1.\\
C(t',i',s') \quad &:\!- \quad C(t,i,s),\ R(t,i,c),\ Right(s,c,s'),\ t'-t=1,\ i'-i=1.\\
C(t',i,s') \quad &:\!- \quad C(t,i,s),\ R(t,i,c),\ Write(s,c,s',w),\ t'-t=1.
\end{aligned}
$$

$$
\begin{aligned}
R(t',i,c) \quad &:\!- \quad C(t,i,s),\ R(t,i,c),\ Left(s,c,s'),\ t'-t=1.\\
R(t',i,c) \quad &:\!- \quad C(t,i,s),\ R(t,i,c),\ Right(s,c,s'),\ t'-t=1.\\
R(t',i,w) \quad &:\!- \quad C(t,i,s),\ R(t,i,c),\ Write(s,c,s',w),\ t'-t=1.\\
R(t',i',c) \quad &:\!- \quad C(t,i,s),\ R(t,i',c),\ t'-t=1,\ i'>i.\\
R(t',i',c) \quad &:\!- \quad C(t,i,s),\ R(t,i',c),\ t'-t=1,\ i>i'.
\end{aligned}
$$

∎

Example 25.1.3 Using Theorem 25.1.1 the computation of the Turing machine of Example 25.1.2 on the input tape of Example 25.1.1 can be simulated as follows.

Because of the input values of the tape and the assumption that the Turing machine starts in state s_a pointing to the leftmost tape cell, we have initially the following:

$$
\begin{aligned}
&C(0,1,s_a).\\
&R(0,1,a).\\
&R(0,2,b).\\
&R(0,3,a).\\
&R(0,i,\#) \quad :\!- \quad i\geq 4.
\end{aligned}
$$

In the first step the Turing machine uses the transition $Right(s_a, a, s_a)$ and moves one cell to the right and keeps being in state s_a. The contents of the tape cells do not change.

$C(1, 2, s_a)$.
$R(1, 1, a)$.
$R(1, 2, b)$.
$R(1, 3, a)$.
$R(1, i, \#)$:— $i \geq 4$.

In the second step the Turing machine uses the transition $Right(s_a, b, s_a)$.

$C(2, 3, s_a)$.
$R(2, 1, a)$.
$R(2, 2, b)$.
$R(2, 3, a)$.
$R(2, i, \#)$:— $i \geq 4$.

In the third step the Turing machine uses the transition $Right(s_a, a, s_a)$.

$C(3, 4, s_a)$.
$R(3, 1, a)$.
$R(3, 2, b)$.
$R(3, 3, a)$.
$R(3, i, \#)$:— $i \geq 4$.

In the fourth step the Turing machine uses the transition $Right(s_a, \#, s_b)$.

$C(4, 5, s_b)$.
$R(4, 1, a)$.
$R(4, 2, b)$.
$R(4, 3, a)$.
$R(4, i, \#)$:— $i \geq 4$.

In the fifth step the Turing machine uses the transition $Right(s_b, \#, s_a)$.

$C(5, 6, s_a)$.
$R(5, 1, a)$.
$R(5, 2, b)$.
$R(5, 3, a)$.
$R(5, i, \#)$:— $i \geq 4$.

The last configuration is like the one after the third step, except the machine pointer is shifted two tape cells to the right. It is easy to see that the computation of the Turing machine never terminates because it just continues to move to the right forever without changing the tape and just alternates between states s_a and s_b.

As Example 25.1.3 shows, sometimes the computation of a Turing machine does not terminate because the halting state is never reached. The question whether the computation of a Turing machine on a particular input tape terminates is called the *halting problem*. The halting problem is *undecidable*, meaning that one cannot write an algorithm that in a finite number of steps can tell for any pair of Turing machine and input tape whether the computation of the Turing machine on the input tape will terminate.

To enforce the termination of a Turing machine we can place a *time bound n* on the maximum number of steps it may take in any computation. An *n time-bounded Turing machine* will stop either when it reaches the halt state or when the number of steps in the computation reaches n. The length of the tape used by an n time-bounded Turing machine is always assumed to be of size n.

25.2   Complexity Classes

Turing machines are divided into several classes according to their computational complexities. The computational complexity of a Turing machine is measured as a time or space function of the input tape size. Here the measure of the input tape size is only the number of cells that contain useful information. Hence we do not count the infinite number of # symbols at the end of the tape.

The most common computational complexity classes are the following:

- P—deterministic TM polynomial time

- PSPACE—deterministic TM polynomial space

- EXP—deterministic TM exponential time

- iEXP—deterministic TM i levels of exponential time

These complexity classes are increasingly powerful. Later ones include all the earlier ones.

Beside Turing machines, sometimes the *Parallel Random Access Machine* or PRAM model serves as a useful computational model. The PRAM model allows several processors to work concurrently on the same problem. For the PRAM model of computation, one can define additional complexity classes, such as the following:

- LOGSPACE— logarithmic memory space with one processor

- NC— logarithmic time with a polynomial number of processors

When analyzing the computational complexity of queries, the size of the query evaluation problem is divided into two parts: the program part and the data part. The complexity of the query evaluation complexity depends on the size of each part. Hence we may talk of three different measures of computational complexity.

- **Data Complexity:** This measures the computational complexity of a fixed program and a variable size database.

- **Expression Complexity:** This measures the computational complexity when the size of the program may change and the database is fixed.

- **Combined Complexity:** This measures the computational complexity when both the size of the program and the database may change.

Data complexity makes sense when we think about the library of programs that is provided to users. Because the set of programs in the library is fixed, the users may be interested in knowing the computational complexity of those programs on their variable size databases.

Another motivation for data complexity may be that the size of the database often dominates the size of the program. This certainly seems true for relational database systems in practice. However, it may be unwarranted to jump to the conclusion that it will also be true for constraint databases. In fact, because constraint tuples can describe an infinite number of constant tuples, we may expect that they could sometimes provide a very condensed description of the user's data. Therefore, the size of the constraint databases may be much smaller than the relational databases. Hence in the following we will consider both complexity measures. Also, whenever we use logarithms we assume that the base is two unless otherwise indicated.

When one can reduce all problems of size $O(n)$ in a computational complexity class A to size $O(n)$ problems in another class B and do so efficiently, which is typically assumed to be doable by a LOGSPACE algorithm, then B is said to be A-*hard*. When the reverse translation also can be carried out, then B is said to be A-*complete*. Hence hardness results are computational lower bound results, while completeness results are more precise because they are both lower and upper bound results.

25.3 Complexity of Datalog

Section 25.3.1 considers the problem of defining the successor relation in various cases of Datalog with constraints. It is shown that such a counting relation enables the simulation of n time-bounded Turing machines. That implies for Datalog queries with $\mathcal{C}$ constraints a number of computational complexity lower bounds, which are examined in Section 25.3.2.

25.3.1 Counting

The next theorem shows that if a successor relation $Succ(i, j)$ can be defined to count from 1 to n using a Datalog query with $\mathcal{C}$ constraints, then we can simulate n time-bounded Turing machines.

Theorem 25.3.1 Let $\mathcal{C}$ be any type of constraint. If in Datalog with $\mathcal{C}$ constraints we can define the relation $Succ$ that enables counting from 0 to n and the relations $First$ and $Last$ that contain a representation of 0 and n, respectively, then we can write a Datalog query with $\mathcal{C}$ constraints that can simulate an n time-bounded Turing machine.

Proof: We can simulate n time-bounded Turing machine in Datalog with $\mathcal{C}$ similarly as in Theorem 25.1.1 except instead of the addition constraints we use a successor relation $Succ$ that contains the tuples $(i, i+1)$ for $0 \le i \le n - 1$. The last two rules in Theorem 25.1.1 use the $<$ relation, which we can define using $Succ$ as follows:

$$Less(i, j) \quad :— \quad Succ(i, k),\ Less(k, j).$$
$$Less(i, j) \quad :— \quad Succ(i, j).$$

∎

Theorem 25.3.1 motivates the definition of successor relations in several cases of Datalog with constraints.

Lemma 25.3.1 There is a Datalog program with gap-order constraints, that given as inputs two relations containing the numbers s and 2^s and a relation that enables counting from 0 to s, defines a relation that enables counting from 0 to 2^s.

Proof: Let us assume that the input relations are $Next(0, 1), \ldots, Next(s - 1, s)$, $No\_Digits(s)$, and $Two\_to\_s(2^s)$. Using a Datalog query we define an output relation $Succ(0, 1), \ldots, Succ(2^s - 1, 2^s)$.

It helps to think of each number being written in binary notation. Because the number 2^s has s binary digits, what we really need is, given a counter on the digits and the value 2^s, to define a counter from 0 to 2^s.

We start by representing the value of each digit using a constraint interval, where the bound is the actual value. That is, for each $1 \le i \le s$, we want to represent the value of the ith digit from the right as: $Digit(i, x_1, x_2)$:— $x_2 - x_1 \ge 2^{(i-1)}$. The following rules define the desired constraint tuples:

$$Digit(j, x_1, x_2) \quad :— \quad Next(i, j),\ Digit(i, x_1, x_3),\ Digit(i, x_3, x_2).$$
$$Digit(1, x_1, x_2) \quad :— \quad x_2 - x_1 \ge 1.$$

Note that we can represent each number i by a pair of constraints: $i \leq x$ (which is equivalent to $x \geq i$) and $x \leq i$ (which is equivalent to $-x \geq -i$). Because each number can be expressed as the sum of a subset of the values of the n digits, if we start out from the constraint $1 \leq x$ and $x \leq 2^s$ and choose to either increase the first or decrease the second bound by the value of the ith digit for each $1 \leq i \leq s$, then we will get a single integer between 1 and 2^s as output.

This gives an idea about how to define any number we need. We can use a separate x_1 and x_2 to represent x to make it easy to tighten either the lower or upper bound on x while preserving the other bound.

We can define any integer n between 1 and 2^s if for each binary digit value we add it to the lower bound if the corresponding binary digit is 1 in $n-1$ or subtract it from the upper bound if the corresponding binary digit is 0 in $n-1$.

To express the successor function, we define pairs of integers. Let x_1 and x_2 represent the first and y_1 and y_2 represent the second integer. The following rules make sure that when we add a digit to the xs we also add the same digit to the ys the right way:

$$Succ(x, y) \quad :- \quad Succ2(x, x, y, y, s), No\_Digits(s).$$

$$Succ2(x_3, x_2, y_3, y_2, j) \quad :- \quad Succ2(x_1, x_2, y_1, y_2, i), \ Next(i, j),$$
$$Digit(j, x_1, x_3), \ Digit(j, y_1, y_3).$$

$$Succ2(x_1, x_3, y_1, y_3, j) \quad :- \quad Succ2(x_1, x_2, y_1, y_2, i), \ Next(i, j),$$
$$Digit(j, x_3, x_2), \ Digit(j, y_3, y_2).$$

$$Succ2(x_1, x_3, y_3, y_2, j) \quad :- \quad Succ3(x_1, x_2, y_1, y_2, i), \ Next(i, j),$$
$$Digit(j, x_3, x_2), \ Digit(j, y_1, y_3).$$

$$Succ3(x_3, x_2, y_1, y_3, j) \quad :- \quad Succ3(x_1, x_2, y_1, y_2, i), \ Next(i, j),$$
$$Digit(j, x_1, x_3), \ Digit(j, y_3, y_2).$$

$$Succ3(x_1, x_2, y_1, y_2, 0) \quad :- \quad 1 \leq x_1, \ x_2 \leq n, \ 1 \leq y_1, \ y_2 \leq n,$$
$$Two\_to\_s(n).$$

In this program, in each recursive step, x_1 will be bounded by higher and higher constants from below and x_2 will be bounded by lower and lower constants from above. In the second rule when j has reached the number of digits, the possible values of x_1 and x_2 overlap on exactly one integer. A similar note applies to y_1 and y_2. ∎

Example 25.3.1 Let $s = 3$. Then we can prove that $Succ(5, 6)$ is true. It helps to think that the numbers 4 and 5 are written in binary notation as 100 and 101. The sequence of derived constraint tuples leading to the conclusion is the following:

$$Succ3(x_1, x_2, y_1, y_2, 0) :\!-\, 1 \le x_1,\ x_2 \le 8,\ 1 \le y_1,\ y_2 \le 8. \qquad \text{by } 6^{th} \text{ rule}$$

$$Succ2(x_1, x_2, y_1, y_2, 1) :\!-\, 1 \le x_1,\ x_2 \le 7,\ 2 \le y_1,\ y_2 \le 8. \qquad \text{by } 5^{th} \text{ rule}$$

$$Succ2(x_1, x_2, y_1, y_2, 2) :\!-\, 1 \le x_1,\ x_2 \le 5,\ 2 \le y_1,\ y_2 \le 6. \qquad \text{by } 4^{th} \text{ rule}$$

$$Succ2(x_1, x_2, y_1, y_2, 3) :\!-\, 5 \le x_1,\ x_2 \le 5,\ 6 \le y_1,\ y_2 \le 6. \qquad \text{by } 3^{rd} \text{ rule}$$

$$Succ(x, y) :\!-\, 5 \le x,\ x \le 5,\ 6 \le y,\ y \le 6. \qquad \text{by } 1^{st} \text{ rule}$$

Lemma 25.3.2 There is a stratified Datalog program with gap-order constraints and a single negation of a one-arity relation that, given as inputs a relation containing the number s and a relation that enables counting from 0 to s, defines a relation containing the number 2^s.

Proof: Let us assume that $No\_Digits(s)$ and $Next(0,1), \ldots, Next(s-1, s)$ are the input relations. We define the relation $Two\_to\_s(2^s)$.

First we write a rule for exponentiation as follows:

$$Exp(j, x_1, x_2) \quad :\!-\quad Next(i,j),\ Exp(i, x_1, x_3),\ Exp(i, x_3, x_2).$$
$$Exp(1, x_1, x_2) \quad :\!-\quad x_2 - x_1 > 1.$$

This will define the constraint tuples $Exp(i, x_1, x_2) :\!-\, x_2 - x_1 \ge 2^i$ for each $1 \le i \le s$. Therefore, $Exp(s, 0, x) :\!-\, x \ge 2^s$ is one of the constraint tuples defined. We can find the value 2^s as follows. First we write the Datalog program Q_1:

$$Grt\_Two\_to\_s(x) \quad :\!-\quad x - y \ge 0,\ Geq\_Two\_to\_s(y).$$
$$Geq\_Two\_to\_s(x) \quad :\!-\quad No\_Digits(s),\ Exp(s, 0, x).$$

Then we finds its complement using negation query Q_2:

$$Not\_Grt\_Two\_to\_s(x) \quad :\!-\quad not\ Grt\_Two\_to\_s(x).$$

Note that we negated only a single attribute relation. Finally, we use the following Q_3:

$$Two\_to\_s(x) \quad :\!-\quad Geq\_Two\_to\_s(x),\ Not\_Grt\_Two\_to\_s(x).$$

Clearly, the stratified Datalog query $Q_3(Q_2(Q_1()))$ will find the number 2^s as required. ∎

Lemma 25.3.3 There is a stratified Datalog program with gap-order constraints and i negations of one-arity relations that given as inputs a relation containing the number s and a relation that enables counting from 0 to s defines a relation that enables counting from 0 to $2^{\cdot^{\cdot^s}}$ with i levels of exponentiations.

Proof: We can build a stratified Datalog program in which the stratum of Lemma 25.3.2 and the stratum of Lemma 25.3.1 alternate i times. ∎

Lemma 25.3.4 There is a Datalog program with B_Z Boolean algebra equality constraints that, given a database input of size $O(s \log s)$, can define a successor relation from 0 to $2^s - 1$.

Proof: We can encode any number n as the set N that contains the place numbers of the digits that are one in the binary notation of n where we count the digits from right to left. For example, 10 can be represented as the set $N = \{2, 4\}$ because the 9 is 1010 in in binary.

We define as an input relation $Next(\{1\}, \{2\}), \ldots, Next(\{s - 1\}, \{s\})$ and the relations $First(\{1\})$ and $Last(\{s\})$, where s is the number of binary digits we need to count to $2^s - 1$. This database input requires only size $O(s \log s)$ because we have s number of input database tuples each with one or two integer representations and the size of each integer representation is at most $O(\log s)$.

We can now express the successor relation $Succ(N, M)$, which is true if and only if N and M represent the integer numbers n, m, respectively, and $m = n + 1$ for any $0 \leq n, m < 2^s - 1$:

$$Succ(N, M) \quad :— \quad Succ2(N, M, S), \; Last(S).$$

$$Succ2(N, M, I) \quad :— \quad Succ2(N, M, J), \; Next(J, I), \\ Zero(N, I), \; Zero(M, I).$$

$$Succ2(N, M, I) \quad :— \quad Succ2(N, M, J), \; Next(J, I), \\ One(N, I), \; One(M, I).$$

$$Succ2(N, M, I) \quad :— \quad Zero(N, I), \; One(M, I), \; First(I).$$

$$Succ2(N, M, I) \quad :— \quad Succ3(N, M, J), \; Next(J, I), \\ Zero(N, I), \; One(M, I).$$

$$Succ3(N, M, I) \quad :— \quad Succ3(N, M, J), Next(J, I), \\ One(N, I), Zero(M, I).$$

$$Succ3(N, M, I) \quad :— \quad One(N, I), \; Zero(M, I), \; First(I).$$

$$Zero(N, I) \quad :— \quad N \cap I =_{B_Z} \emptyset.$$

$$One(N, I) \quad :— \quad \overline{N} \cap I =_{B_Z} \emptyset.$$

In the preceding, $Zero(N, I)$ is true if and only if the Ith digit of N is zero. Similarly, $One(N, I)$ is true if and only if the Ith digit of N is one. ∎

Lemma 25.3.5 There is a Datalog program with B_Z Boolean algebra order constraints that, given a database input of size $O(s \log s)$, can define a successor relation from 0 to $2^s - 1$.

Proof: The proof is similar to Lemma 25.3.4, but we replace in the definitions of $Zero$ and One the Boolean equality constraints with Boolean order constraints. That is easy to do because the constraint $N \cap I =_{B_Z} \emptyset$ is equivalent to $N \subseteq_{B_Z} \overline{I}$ and the constraint $\overline{N} \cap I =_{B_Z} \emptyset$ is equivalent to $I \subseteq_{B_Z} N$. ∎

The following lemma is similar to the previous one, and its proof is left as an exercise.

Lemma 25.3.6 There is a Datalog program with free B_s Boolean algebra simple upper bound constraints that, given a database input of size $s^2 \log s$, can define a function that enables counting from 0 to $2^{2^s} - 1$. ∎

25.3.2 Complexity Results

The evaluation of Datalog queries in general was discussed in Section 23.4. It follows from the discussion there that the constraint consequence operator can be implemented by repeatedly taking in each Datalog rule the join of the subgoal relations of the rule body and then projecting out the variables from the join relation that occur on the left-hand side and adding the result to the relation defined by the rule. We do this until there is no new tuple added to any defined relation.

Fortunately, for the constraints discussed in Section 25.4.1, we know the maximum number of normal form tuples that may be added to each defined relation. Let us define the following list of parameters:

- m—the number of constants that occur in either the input database or the Datalog program

- k—the maximum arity of any relation

- M—the maximum number of normal form constraint tuples in k-arity relations with m constants in use

- s—the maximum size of a constraint tuple

- d—the number of defined relations

- i—the number of input relations

- t_1—the time to evaluate each d relational algebra query on an input database with i normal form relations of size at most Ms

- t_2—the time to eliminate duplicates from a database with d normal form relations of size at most Ms

Using these parameters it is now possible to show the following.

Lemma 25.3.7 Let $\mathcal{C}$ be any type of constraint discussed in Section 25.4.1. Let Q be a Datalog program and I a normal form input constraint database with $\mathcal{C}$ constraints. Let the other parameters be as earlier. Then the least fixed point of the Datalog program Q on input I can be evaluated in $O(dM(t_1 + t_2))$ time.   ■

Domain	Constraint	Data complexity	Combined complexity
$\mathcal{Q}, \mathcal{Z}$	Equality	P-comp	EXP-comp
$\mathcal{Q}, \mathcal{Z}$	Equality, inequality	P-comp	EXP-comp
$\mathcal{Q}$	Order	P-comp	EXP-comp
$\mathcal{Q}, \mathcal{Z}$	Lower and upper bound, gap-order	EXP-hard	EXP-hard
$\mathcal{B}$	Binary order	EXP-comp	EXP-comp
$\mathcal{B}$	Equality	2EXP-comp	2EXP-comp
$\mathcal{B}^{aless}$	Equality, inequality	2EXP-comp	2EXP-comp
$\mathcal{B}$	Order	2EXP-comp	2EXP-comp

Figure 25.1: Datalog computational complexity.

The next theorem summarizes the implications of the above lemmas for the computational complexity of various cases of Datalog with constraints.

Theorem 25.3.2 Datalog queries with $\mathcal{C}$ constraints have data complexity and combined complexities as shown in Figure 25.1.

Proof: In each case the upper bounds follow from Lemma 25.3.7 and Theorem 25.4.3. For the first three cases the lower bound follows from the fact that we can define an input relation that can count from 0 to some number m. Using that relation we can define in Datalog a relation of arity k to count from 0 to $m^{k/2} - 1$, where the numbers are represented as $k/2$ digit base m numbers. Therefore, by Theorem 25.3.1 we can simulate any $m^{k/2} - 1$ time-bounded Turing machine.

For gap-order, upper bound, and lower bound constraints the complexity lower bound follows from Lemma 25.3.1 and Theorem 25.3.1. Hence the three cases all include the same computational lower bound.

For B_Z Boolean constraints the lower bound follows from Lemmas 25.3.4 and 25.3.5.

For B_{k+m} Boolean constraints the lower bounds follow from Lemma 25.3.6. Note that the query described there used only simple Boolean upper bound constraints, which are included in each of the three B_{k+m} constraint cases.   ■

The next theorem considers the computational complexity of stratified Datalog queries with $\mathcal{C}$ constraints. In each case considered in the theorem and in Figure 25.2 the $\mathcal{C}$ constraints are closed under negation or unary negation, in which case consideration is stratified Datalog with only unary negation.

Domain	Constraint	Data complexity	Combined complexity
$\mathcal{Q}, \mathcal{Z}$	Equality, inequality	P-comp	EXP-comp
$\mathcal{Q}$	Order	P-comp	EXP-comp
$\mathcal{B}^{aless}$	Equality, inequality	2EXP-comp	2EXP-comp
$\mathcal{Q}, \mathcal{Z}$	Lower bound, upper bound, gap-order	$(i+1)$EXP-hard with i unary neg.	$(i+1)$EXP-hard with i unary neg.

Figure 25.2: Stratified Datalog computational complexity.

Theorem 25.3.3 Stratified Datalog queries with $\mathcal{C}$ constraints have data and combined complexities as shown in Figure 25.2.

Proof: For the first three cases, for each strata we first find the complement of the negated relations and then repeat the evaluation of a Datalog program as in Theorem 25.3.2. For i unary negations and gap-order, upper bound, and lower bound constraints or theories that include these, the lower bound follows from Lemma 25.3.3.   ■

25.4 Complexity of Relational Algebra

Relational algebra can be easily rewritten into *relational calculus*. The rewriting is a simple mapping that replaces some symbols of relational algebra with other symbols in relational calculus. We also mentioned that constraint relations can be viewed as a disjunction of constraint tuples, that is, as a disjunctive normal form formulas of some type of atomic constraints. If we replace in the relational calculus expressions the relational symbols with the corresponding disjunctive normal form formula we get what is called a *first-order formula of constraints*.

Quantifier elimination from a first-order formula of constraints is similar to existential quantifier eliminations from conjunctions of constraints as described in Chapter 23, but it is more complex, because we also have to deal with disjunctions and negations in the formula. We do not give details of these more complex quantifier eliminations because they have been studied extensively by many researchers, and good descriptions can be found in many other books. We note, however, the following connection between quantifier eliminations from first-order formulas and relational algebra query evaluations.

Theorem 25.4.1 Let $\mathcal{C}$ be any type of constraint. If we can do closed-form quantifier elimination from $\mathcal{C}$ constraint formulas of size n in $f(n)$ time, then the output of each relational algebra query on $\mathcal{C}$ constraint relations can be evaluated in $O(f(n))$ time. ∎

This translation from relational algebra query evaluation to quantifier elimination from formulas does not yield a nicely structured algebraic evaluation like that described in Section 23.2.1. However, Theorem 25.4.1 is useful to prove several computational complexity results, by taking advantage of what is known about the complexity of various quantifier elimination from formulas. In particular, some of the relational algebra with constraints combined complexity results that can be shown using Theorem 25.4.1 are summarized in Figure 25.3. In Figure 25.3 and most of this section we are interested only in complexity class classifications.

Domain	Constraint	Data complexity	Combined complexity
$\mathcal{Q}, \mathcal{Z}$	Lower bound, upper bound, gap-order	LOGSPACE-comp	PSPACE-comp
$\mathcal{Q}, \mathcal{Z}$	Lower bound, upper bound, half-addition	LOGSPACE-comp	PSPACE-comp
$\mathcal{Q}, \mathcal{Z}$	Difference	LOGSPACE-comp	PSPACE-comp
$\mathcal{Q}, \mathcal{Z}$	Addition	in NC	PSPACE-comp
$\mathcal{Q}, \mathcal{Z}$	Linear	in NC	EXP-comp
$\mathcal{R}$	Polynomial	in NC	EXP-comp

Figure 25.3: Relational algebra computational complexity (I).

25.4.1 Normal Form Relations

The problem of relational algebra query evaluation is greatly simplified when we know that there can be only a finite number of different atomic constraints. In these cases it is also possible to describe the maximum size that any constraint relation can contain. Therefore, in these cases the complexity of the query evaluation can be analyzed in a simpler way than by using Theorem 25.4.1.

Query evaluation is more efficient when the constraint relations are in *normal form*. The main purpose of normal forms is to reduce the size of the representation of constraint tuples and to eliminate redundancies of representation.

Let $A = \{a_1, \ldots, a_l\}$ be the set of constant symbols that appear in the input database or the relational algebra program. Note that for each instance of query evaluation (input database and program) A is only a small finite part of a larger domain of possible constant symbols. We consider in this section only constraints for which the output relation can also be represented by using only constants in A.

The following lemma can be used to simplify the query evaluation in the case of Boolean constraints.

Lemma 25.4.1 Query evaluation in any free Boolean algebra with l constants can be translated to a query evaluation in a Boolean algebra with $m = 2^l$ constants where the conjunction of any pair of constant symbols is 0.

Proof: Let $D = \{c_1, \ldots, c_m\}$ for $m \leq 2^l$ be the distinct ground minterms of the Boolean algebra defined by $A = \{a_1, \ldots, a_l\}$. Then we have that $c_i \cap c_j = \emptyset$.

We can eliminate the constants in D by replacing each with some equivalent disjunction of the minterms. Therefore, the query evaluation in B_A can be translated to a query evaluation in B_D, which is a Boolean algebra where conjunction of any two constant symbols is the zero element. After the query evaluation, we can translate back from B_D to B_A by writing each c_i in terms of the constants in A. ∎

Example 25.4.1 If we have a query in B_Z such that the constants that appear in the query are $D = \{\{2\}, \{5\}, \{9\}\}$, then there will be four ground minterms in the transformed algebra, namely, $\{2\}, \{5\}, \{9\}$, and $Z - \{1, 2, 3\}$.

Hence in the rest of this section, we will assume that $D = \{c_1, \ldots, c_m\}$ is the set of constants that appear in the query and that for each pair $c_i \cap c_j = \emptyset$.

Before defining normal forms, we need some more definitions in the case of Boolean constraints. Recall that for any set of constant symbols D as earlier and set of variable symbols $\{x_1, \ldots, x_k\}$ we can define a free Boolean algebra B_{k+m}. We already defined minterms of B_{k+m}. We will refine that concept in the following definitions:

- We call *ground minterm* a minterm of the subalgebra B_m, i.e., conjunctions of unnegated or negated constants.

- We call *variable minterm* a minterm of the subalgebra B_k, i.e., conjunctions of unnegated or negated variables.

- We call *monotone minterm* any conjunction of one or more unnegated variables and a ground minterm. That is, in a monotone minterm each variable is either unnegated or absent and each constant appears either negated or unnegated.

- We call *minterm equality constraints* those equality constraints in which the left-hand side is a minterm. We call *(monotone) minterm inequality constraints* those inequality constraints in which the left-hand side is a (monotone) minterm.

- We call *minterm upper bound constraints* those upper bound constraints in which the left-hand side is a variable minterm and the right-hand side is a ground minterm.

Now we define for various types of constraints *normal form constraint tuples* with k variables as follows:

- We call *order constraints* those precedence constraints in which the left-hand side is an unnegated variable and the right-hand side is a monotone Boolean term.

- We call *order constraints* those precedence constraints in which the left-hand side is an unnegated variable and the right-hand side is a disjunction of variables and constants.

- We call *minterm order constraints* those precedence constraints in which the left-hand side is an unnegated variable and the right-hand side is a disjunction of variables.

Remark 25.4.1 Each order constraint is equivalent to a conjunction of minterm order constraints. Further, each minterm order constraint is equivalent to a minterm equality constraint in which on the left-hand side all but one variable is negated.

Equality: Each constraint tuple contains at most k equality constraints between variables. For each equivalence class with variables $x_1, \ldots, x_n$ and optionally some constant c we have a conjunction of constraints $x_1 = x_2, \ldots, x_{n-1} = x_n, x_n = c$. The constant must appear as the last element in the conjunction that represents the equivalence class.

Equality and Inequality: Each constraint tuple contains a conjunction of equality constraints as described earlier. In addition, for each pair of equality classes, including single variables, the tuple also contains an inequality constraint between their last elements, unless those are both constants. Finally, if the last element x of an equivalence class is a variable, then there is also an inequality constraint $x \neq c_i$ for each $1 \leq i \leq m$.

Rational Order: We may assume that $c_i < c_j$ whenever $i < j$. Each constraint tuple contains for each variable x one of the following: $x < c_1$, $c_m < x$, $c_i < x, x < c_{i+1}$, or $x \geq c_i, x \leq c_i$ for some $1 \leq i \leq m$. In addition, the tuple contains for some permutation $x_1, \ldots, x_k$ of the variables either $x_i < x_{i+1}$ or $x_i \leq x_{i+1}, x_{i+1} \leq x_i$ for each $1 \leq i < m$.

Boolean Equality: Each constraint tuple contains only constraint of the form $m_i \cap c_j = \emptyset$, where m_i is a variable minterm and c_j is a constant.

Atomless Boolean Equality and Inequality: Each constraint tuple contains for each variable minterm m_i and constant c_j either $m_i \cap c_j = \emptyset$ or $m_i \cap c_j \neq \emptyset$.

Boolean Order: Each constraint tuple contains for each variable and one element on one side at most one order constraint with the monotone function in monotone disjunctive normal form. In addition, the tuple contains minterm monotone inequality constraints of the form $m_i c_j \neq \emptyset$, where m_i is a monotone variable minterm.

Boolean Binary Order: Each constraint tuple contains at most k^2 binary order constraints between pairs of variables and $2k$ binary order constraints between a variable on one side and disjunctions of constants on the other side.

We say that a $\mathcal{C}$ constraint relation is in normal form if each constraint tuple in it is in normal form, and there are no duplicate tuples. We say that a $\mathcal{C}$ constraint database is in normal form if each constraint relation in it is in normal form.

Remark 25.4.2 Some details are skipped here about orderings of the constraints and specific forms of the constraints. These details are important to efficiently check for duplicate tuples, because otherwise the same constraint could be in different forms and the atomic constraints may appear in any permutations if we do not fix some standard forms and orderings. We give one example. In B_{k+m} we can fix an order of the variables and the constant symbols. Then we keep in each minterm the variables and constants in increasing order, and we keep an ordering of the minterms similar to that in

Lemma 11.2.5. We also keep the constraint tuples in sorted order. Having these fixed orderings enables us to check for duplicates in linear time in the size of the constraint relations.

Remark 25.4.3 In this section we take the size of the representation of each constant and variable to be a constant.

The following theorem shows that in the normal forms, the maximum number of atomic constraints in each tuple and the maximum number of constraint tuples in each relation depends only on k and m.

Domain	Constraint	Number of tuples in relation
$\mathcal{Q}, \mathcal{Z}$	Equality	$(m+k)^k$
$\mathcal{Q}, \mathcal{Z}$	Equality, inequality	$(m+k)^k$
$\mathcal{Q}$	Order	$k!\,(4m)^k$
$\mathcal{B}$	Equality	$2^{2^{k+\log m}}$
$\mathcal{B}^{aless}$	Equality, inequality	$2^{2^{k+\log m}}$
$\mathcal{B}$	Order	$2^{2^{k+\log k+\log m}}$
$\mathcal{B}$	Binary order	2^{k^2+2km}

Figure 25.4: Normal form sizes: O(number of tuples).

Theorem 25.4.2 Let $\mathcal{C}$ be any type of constraint listed earlier. Let m be the number of different constants in use. Then each k-arity normal form $\mathcal{C}$ constraint tuple contains at most as many atomic constraints and has size, and each k-arity normal form $\mathcal{C}$ constraint relation contains at most as many tuples as shown in Figure 25.4.

Proof: For each type of constraint we analyze the maximum number of atomic constraints in a normal form tuple, the maximum number of tuples in a normal form relation, and the maximum size of a normal form relation.

Equality
Number of Atomic Constraints: Each equivalence class with n elements is represented using $n-1$ equality constraints. Hence we need at most k equality constraints in each normal form tuple.

Number of Constraint Tuples: We can assign to the first variable any of the m constants or some new unspecified constant. We can assign to the second variable any of the m constants or the previously assigned unspecified constant or some new unspecified constant. We can continue in this way untill the last variable. Each assignment clearly describes a unique constraint tuple. Therefore, there are $O((m+1)(m+2)\ldots(m+k)) = O((m+k)!/m!) \leq$

$O((m + k)^k)$ different normal form constraint tuples.

Size: By Remark 25.4.3, the size of each normal form relation is a constant factor of the number of tuples.

Equality and Inequality

Number of Atomic Constraints: We have $O(k)$ equality and $O(k^2 + km)$ inequality constraints in each normal form tuple.

Number of Constraint Tuples: We have the same number of tuples as in the case of only equality constraints because each constraint tuple describes a partition into equivalence classes as in the case of only equality constraints. We only add inequality constraints to each partition to make sure that elements of different equivalence classes are different for each instantiation of the constraint tuple.

Size: By Remark 25.4.3, the size of each normal form relation is a constant factor of the number of tuples.

Order

Number of Atomic Constraints: We have at most $2k$ constraints between variables. We also have at most $2k$ constraints between variables and constants.

Number of Constraint Tuples: We have $k!$ possible permutations of k variables. Each permutation can be extended to a total ordering by adding between adjacent elements either $>$ or two $\leq$ to denote equality. Hence there are $k!2^k$ total orderings of the variables. Each variable must belong to one of the $m + 1$ intervals between constants or to one of the m constants. Hence for each variable there are $2m + 1$ choices. Therefore, there are $O(k! \, 2^k (2m + 1)^k) = O(k! \, (4m)^k)$ choices.

Size: By Remark 25.4.3, the size of each normal form relation is a constant factor of the number of tuples.

Boolean Equality

Number of Atomic Constraints: There are 2^k different left variable minterms and m different constants, therefore $2^k m = 2^{k+\log m}$ different atomic constraints.

Number of Constraint Tuples: Each atomic constraint may or may not be present in a constraint tuple. Hence there are at most $2^{2^{k+\log m}}$ different constraint tuples.

Size: The size of each minterm equality constraint is k, therefore, the size of each constraint tuple is $O(k2^{k+\log m}) \leq O(2^{k+\log k+\log m})$.

Atomless Boolean Equality and Inequality

Number of Atomic Constraints: There are $2^k m$ different left-hand sides in the minterm equality and inequality constraints. Therefore, there are that many atomic constraints in each constraint tuple.

Number of Constraint Tuples: There are $2^{2^{k+\log m}}$ possible constraint tuples.

Size: The size of each minterm equality and inequality constraint is $O(k)$. Therefore the total size of each constraint tuple is at most $O(k2^{2^{k+\log m}})$.

Boolean Order

Number of Atomic Constraints: There are at most $k+1$ monotone upper bound constraints because there are k variables and the one element. Also, there are at most $2^{k+\log m}$ monotone minterm inequality constraints in each tuple because there are that many different monotone minterms.

Number of Constraint Tuples: There are at most $2^{k-1} m$ different monotone minterms with $k-1$ variables. Therefore, for each of the variables there are $2^{2^{k-1}m} = O(2^{2^{k+\log m-1}})$ different monotone disjunctive normal form upper bounds. Hence there can only be $O((2^{2^{k+\log m-1}})^k) = O(2^{2^{k+\log k+\log m-1}})$ combinations. In addition, there are $2^{2^{k+\log m}}$ different monotone disjunctive normal form upper bounds for the one element and the monotone inequality constraints. Hence the number of different constraint tuples is at most

$$O(2^{2^{k+\log k+\log m-1}}(2^{2^{k+\log m}})^2) \leq O(2^{2^{k+\log k+\log m}})$$

Size: The size of each order constraint is $O(2^k m)$. The size of each monotone-minterm inequality constraint is $O(k)$. Therefore the size of each constraint tuple is at most $O(2^k m(k+1) + 2^k mk) \leq O(2^{k+\log k+\log m})$.

Boolean Binary Order

Number of Atomic Constraints: There are k^2 different binary order constraints between pairs of variables. There are $2k2^m$ different binary order constraints between variables and constants. In each constraint tuple by the merge rule, each variable needs at most two binary order constraints with constants, one lower bound and one upper bound.

Number of Constraint Tuples: There are 2^{k^2} combinations of binary order constraints between variables. Also, there are 2^m possible right-hand sides in the binary order constraints between variables and constants. Hence there are at most $(2^{k^2})(2^m)^2 k \leq 2^{k^2+2km}$ different constraint tuples.

Size: The size of each var-var set containment constraint is a constant, and the size of each var-constant set containment constraint is $O(m)$. Therefore the size of each constraint tuple is $O(k^2 + 2km) = O(k^2 + km)$. ∎

We call a normal form constraint tuple C a *cell* if either all the models or none of the models of C satisfy each relational algebra query.

Lemma 25.4.2 The normal form constraint tuples for infinite domain equations and inequations, rational order, and atomless Boolean equality and inequality constraints are cells. ∎

It is easy to take the complement of the difference of relations that are composed of cells.

Next we look at algebraic evaluations assuming that the input constraint relations are in normal form. We will show for each case of constraints that the relational algebra operators can be evaluated efficiently such that the normal forms are preserved.

Domain	Constraint	Project (Elim x)	Join	Difference
$\mathcal{Q}, \mathcal{Z}$	Equality	$(m+k)^k$	$(m+k)^k$	
$\mathcal{Q}, \mathcal{Z}$	Equality, inequality	$(m+k)^k$	$(m+k)^{2k}$	$(m+k)^k$
$\mathcal{Q}$	Order	$k!\,(4m)^k$	$(k!)^2\,(4m)^k$	$k!\,(4m)^k$
$\mathcal{B}$	Equality	$2^{2^{k+\log m}}$	$2^{2^{k+\log m}}$	
$\mathcal{B}^{aless}$	Equality, inequality	$2^{2^{k+\log m}}$	$2^{2^{k+\log m}}$	$2^{2^{k+\log m}}$
$\mathcal{B}$	Order	$2^{2^{k+\log k+\log m+1}}$	$2^{2k+2\log m+\log k}$	
$\mathcal{B}$	Binary order	$2^{k^2+2mk}\,km$	$2^{k^2+2mk}\,km$	

Figure 25.5: Relational algebra operator complexity $O(\ )$.

Lemma 25.4.3 For normal form relations, the project, join, and difference operators can be evaluated in the times shown in Figure 25.5.

Proof: We show the theorem for each case as follows.

Equality

Project: Because this is a subcase of equality and inequality where only equality constraints appear, we may use Theorem 23.1.1 to eliminate variable x. We show that this preserves normal form as follows.

If x appears in the equality constraint tuple, then it must belong to some equivalence class with at least two members. If x appears at the beginning or end of the conjunction of equality constraints that represent the equivalence class x, then just drop the equality constraint in which x appears. Otherwise, if x appears somewhere in the middle of a conjunction of the form $\ldots, y = x, x = z, \ldots$ Then replace the constraints $y = x$ and $x = z$ with $y = z$. Clearly, this preserves the normal form.

Join: Let us consider the join of two tuples. For each pair of equivalence classes, check that they have any element in common, i.e., that they need to be merged. If we have two equivalence classes that need to be merged of the form $u_1 = u_2, \ldots, u_{n-1} = u_n$ and $v_1 = v_2, \ldots, v_{m-1} = v_m$, where u_n and v_m are the same constants, then replace them with $u_1 = u_2, \ldots, u_{n-1} = v_1, v_1 = v_2, \ldots, v_{m-1} = v_m$. If only u_n is a constant or there are no constants, then replace them with $v_1 = v_2, \ldots, v_{m-1} = v_m, v_m = u_1, u_1 = u_2, \ldots, u_{n-1} = u_n$. If only v_m is a constant replace them with $u_1 = u_2, \ldots, u_{n-1} = u_n, u_n = v_1, v_1 = v_2, \ldots, v_{m-1} = v_m$. Delete tuple if it is unsatisfiable. Also delete duplicate tuples.

Equality and Inequality

Project: Use Theorem 23.1.1 to eliminate equality and inequality constraints. Clearly this preserves normal form.

Join: For each pair of tuples, do the join similarly to the earlier equality case. Note that it may occur that some pair of equivalence classes that do not have a common element do not have an inequality constraint between them. To make the constraint tuple a cell, we can do two things: either add a new inequality constraint between the last elements of these equivalence classes or merge the two equivalence classes. These options create different cells that are all added to the output relation. The number of options is clearly fewer than the total number of possible tuples. Hence we get the result shown in Figure 25.5. Finally, we delete duplicate tuples.

Difference: The output will be those cells that are in the first but not the second argument. This is correct because of the disjointness of cells and Lemma 25.4.2. If we store the cells in each relation in some sorted order, then the difference can be done in linear time in the size of the input relations.

Rational Order

Project: Use Theorem 23.1.2 to eliminate equality and inequality constraints. Eliminate all but the highest lower bound and all but the smallest upper bound constraint for each variable. Clearly this preserves normal form.

Join: For each pair of tuples, if the conjunction of their constraints is satisfiable, then we create several cells by extending the order of the variables in the two arguments into a total order. We add all of the cells to the output relation. The number of options is clearly fewer than $k!$. Hence we get the result shown in Figure 25.5. Finally, we delete duplicate tuples.

Difference: This is similar to the case of infinite domain equality and inequality constraints.

Boolean Equality

Project: We may use Theorem 23.1.9 to eliminate variable x. Let m_x be the minterm m with variable x deleted from it.

Let $xm_{1_x}c_1 = \emptyset$ and $\overline{x}m_{2_x}c_2 = \emptyset$ be equality constraints. Then Theorem 23.1.9 will create the equality constraint $m_{1_x}m_{2_x}c_1c_2 = \emptyset$. Note that the left hand side is zero if $c_1 \neq c_2$ or $m_{1_x} \neq m_{2_x}$, hence the constraint can be deleted. Otherwise, we create the constraint $m_{1_x}c_1 = \emptyset$, which is equivalent to $m_{2_x}c_2 = \emptyset$. Therefore, the created constraints are simply the original ones with x or $\overline{x}$ deleted from them. Clearly this preserves normal form and can be done in linear time.

Join: If the conjunction of constraints is satisfiable, then we create several normal form tuples by extending all possible combinations in each argument the minterms with the variables that occur only in the other argument. We add all of the normal form tuples to the output relation.

Atomless Boolean Equality and Inequality

Project: We can use Theorem 23.1.10. However, we can note a simplification in this case because of the normal form. The elimination of a variable x from a satisfiable normal form atomless Boolean equality and inequality constraint tuple, i.e., cell, can be done by simply deleting x and $\overline{x}$ in each minterm within the Boolean equality and inequality constraints. Note that each cell is satisfiable except the one that contains only inequality constraints. That cell can be deleted from any relation. This preserves normal form and can be done in linear time.

Join: This is similar to the case of Boolean equality constraints.

Difference: This is similar to the case of infinite domain equality and inequality constraint.

Boolean Order
Project: We can use Theorem 23.1.11 to eliminate variable x. In this case, u will be the order of x, which we already have in disjunctive normal form, i.e., of the form

$$v_{1,1}c_1 \cup \ldots \cup v_{1,n_1}c_1 \cup \ldots \cup v_{m,1}c_m \cup \ldots \cup v_{m,n_m}c_m$$

where each $v_{i,j}$ is a variable monotone minterm and each c_i is a ground minterm, for $1 \leq i \leq m$ and each $j \leq n_i \leq 2^k$.

In the monotone minterm inequalities, each monotone minterm has the form vc_i where v is a variable monotone minterm and c_i is a ground minterm.

After the substitution of x by u and rewriting using distributivity the left-hand side of the monotone minterm of the preceding form, we get a formula of the form

$$v_{i,1}v\,c_i \cup \ldots \cup v_{i,n_1}v\,c_i \neq \emptyset \tag{25.1}$$

Note that all terms of u that did not have c_i in them dropped out because the conjunction of two constants is zero. Formula (25.1) has at most 2^k disjuncts. We simplify the formula by eliminating in each $v_{i,j}v$ the duplicate variables and then deleting duplicate disjuncts.

We can do the preceding substitution and simplification for each monotone minterm inequality constraint of the form (25.1). Note that each of the results is equivalent to a disjunction of at most 2^k inequality constraints. Because there are at most $2^k m$ monotone inequality constraints, we have the conjunction of at most that many disjunctions. We can rewrite this conjunctive normal form formula into a disjunctive normal form formula.

The process of rewriting can be done by first taking the conjunction of the first two disjuncts and then eliminating duplicates. Then we take the conjunction of the result with the third disjunct. Then we again eliminate duplicates, and so on until the last disjunct. The elimination of duplicates guarantees that in each disjunct of the temporary relation obtained after each conjunction, we have only $2^k m$ different monotone inequality constraints. Hence the size of the temporary relation is at most $2^{2^{k+\log m}}$ tuples.

We can do the preceding for each constraint tuple. Because originally there are at most $2^{2^{k+\log k+\log m}}$ different tuples, we will get a temporary relation that has at most $2^{2^{k+\log k+\log m+1}}$ tuples before we eliminate duplicate tuples in the output relation.

Note that the conjunction of the order constraints and each disjunct of the formula is a normal form constraint tuple. We add all of these to the database.

Join: We merge the order constraints with the same variable on the right-hand side.

For each variable, there is at most one order constraint in each argument of the join. Because in each of these there are at most $2^k m$ disjuncts on the left-hand side. Merge takes the conjunction of the left-hand sides. When we put that conjunction back into monotone disjunctive normal form, we obtain at most $(2^k m)^2 = 2^{2k+2\log m}$ disjuncts. Then we eliminate duplicates. Doing this for each of the k variables requires at most $O(k 2^{2k+2\log m}) = O(2^{2k+2\log m + \log k})$ time.

We also eliminate duplicate monotone inequality constraints, which can be done within the same time.

Boolean Binary Order

Project: Because each Boolean binary order constraint is also an upper bound constraint, we can use Theorem 23.1.9 to eliminate variable x. Then we merge those binary order constraints that have the same variable in them on the same side. We show that this preserves normal form.

The application of Theorem 23.1.9 can be shown to create a binary order constraint $y \subseteq z$ for each pair of binary order constraints $y \subseteq x$ and $x \subseteq z$. Before normalization, x had only one upper bound u and one lower bound v. We take the conjunction (or disjunction) of u (or v) and the upper bound (or the lower bound) of each y for which we have the constraint $y \subseteq x$ (or $x \subseteq y$).

Because the constant sides of binary order constraints are disjunctions of minterms, the conjunction of constants will be a disjunction of those minterms that are in each of the constants, and the disjunction of constants will be a disjunction of those minterms that are in at least one of the constants. Therefore, this preserves closed form. For each constraint tuple, the projection of of x requires merging two sets of at most m minterms, each at most $2k$ times. Hence this takes $O(km)$ time for each constraint tuple.

Join: We again merge binary order constraints with the same variable in them in the same side as in the preceding project. Then we eliminate duplicate constraints. ∎

It is now obvious that any relational algebra query can be evaluated using normal form relations. However, to improve the space efficiency of the query evaluation, it is better to test one at a time for each normal form tuple C whether it satisfies the query (or more precisely, whether all the models of C satisfy the query). We do that by going recursively down the structure of the relational algebra expression. If the top level operator is:

- *Project:* Recall that the project means the elimination of some variables. We find all possible extensions of C with the eliminated variables and test whether any of those satisfies the argument.

- *Join:* We find the projections of C onto the variables of the first and second arguments. Then we test whether the projections satisfy the corresponding arguments.

- *Difference:* This is applicable for cells only. We test whether the cell satisfies the first and not the second argument.

The cases for the other operators are similar to these three.

What we do in each case is to implement the reverse of each of the three operators. Note that in the case of project, there are at most as many extensions as there are number of normal form tuples. In the case of join, the two projections are unique. In the case of difference we do not change the cell. This shows that the inverse operations take the same time as the original operators.

Example 25.4.2 Suppose that $A = \{2, 5, 9\}$ and we have the normal form tuple C with the following equality constraints $y = z = 2, u = v = 9$. Suppose that the top-level operator is a project that eliminates the variable x.

While extending C with x we have to make a decision as to which equivalence class to add x and if the equivalence class does not include a constant whether to make it equal to one of the constants in A. Therefore there are the following cases:

$x = y = z = 2,\ u = v = 9$ add to first equivalence class

$y = z = 2,\ x = u = v = 9$ add to second equivalence class

$y = z = 2,\ u = v = 9,\ x$ make it a new equivalence class

$y = z = 2,\ u = v = 9,\ x = 5$ make it a new equivalence class with 5

Note that there are no more cases because there are only three constants in A, and if x is neither unspecified nor 5 then it must be either 2, in which case x belongs to the first equivalence class, or 9, in which case x belongs to the second equivalence class.

Note that the four normal form tuples are the only normal form tuples whose projection onto u, v, y, z is C.

Domain	Constraint	Difference okay?	Data complexity	Combined complexity
$\mathcal{Q}, \mathcal{Z}$	Equality	No	in LOGSPACE	PSPACE-comp
$\mathcal{Q}, \mathcal{Z}$	Equality, inequality	Yes	in LOGSPACE	PSPACE-comp
$\mathcal{Q}$	Order	Yes	in LOGSPACE	PSPACE-comp
$\mathcal{B}$	Equality	No	in PSPACE	2EXP-comp
$\mathcal{B}^{aless}$	Equality, inequality	Yes	in PSPACE	2EXP-comp
$\mathcal{B}$	Order	No	in PSPACE	2EXP-comp
$\mathcal{B}$	Binary order	No	in PSPACE	EXP-comp

Figure 25.6: Relational algebra computational complexity (II).

We can now show the following theorem.

Theorem 25.4.3 Let $\mathcal{C}$ be any of the constraints listed in Figure 25.4. Then any relational algebra query on $\mathcal{C}$ constraint relations can be evaluated in the combined complexity shown in Figure 25.6.

Proof: *Upper bounds:* When we evaluate the relational algebra query using the reverse operators as described earlier, we need to repeatedly read the relational algebra query and the input database. Also, we have to use space to store our current positions in the query and the input database. We use space to store the normal form tuples in use and their order number, so that we can always get the next normal form tuple. As we noted earlier, the reverse operators can be done in at most as much time as the number of possible tuples in a normal form relation, because there are at most that many possible extensions of each normal form tuple.

Therefore, when there are a polynomial (exponential) number of normal form tuples, we need to use some logarithmic (polynomial) size counter to do the query evaluation. Finally, for data complexity we can take k to be fixed, hence the first four cases can contain at most some polynomial and the last three cases at most some exponential number of normal form tuples.

Lower bounds: The lower bounds in the non-Boolean cases follow from the P-hardness combined complexity of relational algebra queries without constraints. For the lower bound proofs note that each fixed Datalog program restricted to a number n of iterations can be expressed by a relational algebra query of $O(n)$ size. Hence if there is a fixed Datalog program that has with n iterations some $\mathcal{C}$-hard data complexity then there is also a (positive) relational algebra query that has $\mathcal{C}$-hard combined complexity where $\mathcal{C}$ is any complexity class used in this chapter. We will analyze the computational complexity of Datalog queries in Section 25.3, hence we skip further details here. ∎

In the space-efficient evaluation described earlier, we did not have to assume that the input database is normalized. However, the following is convenient to know in case of bottom-up evaluation.

Lemma 25.4.4 Let $\mathcal{C}$ be any of the constraints for which we defined normal forms. Then any $\mathcal{C}$ constraint relation of size n can be put into normal form in $O(nT)$ where T is the number of tuples shown in Figure 25.4. ∎

Bibliographic Notes

We gave an extensive bibliographic reference at the end of Chapter 23 for Datalog with constraints. Here we concentrate on the computational complexity references.

Papadimitriou [297] is a book on computational complexity in general. The definition of data complexity is from Vardi [417] and Immerman [204]. The data complexity of Datalog with inequality and rational order constraints as well as the data complexity of relational algebra with real polynomial constraints was studied by Kanellakis et al. [214, 215]. For Datalog with gap-order the data complexity is studied in [323, 324, 325] and the combined complexity in those, in Cerans [72], and in Cox and McAloon [101]. Stolboushkin and Taitslin [384] show that no query language can express precisely those Datalog with gap-order constraints that are safe.

The expressive power of first-order queries with linear and polynomial constraints is considered in Afrati et al. [7, 6], Benedikt et al. [40, 41, 42, 43], Grumbach and Su [171, 172, 173, 174], Ibarra and Su [201], Kuper [250], Otto and Van den Bussche [291], and Paredaens et al. [300].

Gyssens et al. [180] studied constraint-based geometric query languages that are complete. Dumortier et al. [117, 118] consider the problem of deciding whether a constraint relation with real polynomial constraints can be simplified and expressed with only linear constraints. Jeavons et al. [210] studied the tractability of constraint queries in general. Koubarakis [238] studied the complexity of query evaluation in indefinite temporal constraint databases; and van der Meyden [412, 413] studied indefinite order databases. Kozen [241] and Kanellakis and Revesz [217] study the complexity of Boolean algebras.

Baudinet et al. [31] study constraint-generating dependencies and Zhang and Ozsoyoglu [438] study implication constraints. Kolaitis and Vardi [230] study the complexity of conjunctive query containment. Lemma 25.3.6 and the Boolean case of Theorem 25.3.2 are from Revesz [333]. Lemma 25.3.4 is from Revesz [326, 335]. Lemmas 25.3.1, 25.3.2, and 25.3.3 and the set order and gap-order constraint cases of Theorems 25.3.2 and 25.3.3 are from Revesz [327, 335]. A recent paper on the complexity of linear programming is Grimson and Kuijpers [165].

Exercise

1. Find any NP-complete problem not seen before in the text and express it in:

   (a) Datalog with Boolean binary constraints.
   (b) Datalog with Boolean equality constraints.
   (c) Stratified Datalog with lower bound, upper bound, and gap-order constraints.

26

Software Verification

Software verification is the task of checking that computer programs work correctly on any valid input. Software verification is a basic concern of computer science and has been around since the first software was written. This chapter shows that constraint databases can be useful for software verification.

Section 26.1 describes *addition bound matrices*, which are useful as a constraint representation in software verification.

Section 26.2 presents the *abstract interpretation* approach to software verification. The *octogonal abstract domain* is used as an example of abstract interpretation methods.

Section 26.3 describes the constraint database approach to software verification and compares it to the abstract interpretation approach.

26.1 Addition-Bound Matrices

A conjunction of lower bound, upper bound, and addition constraints over variables $V = \{x_1, \ldots, x_n\}$ can be represented by a conjunction of difference constraints over variables $V^+ = \{x_1^+, x_1^-, \ldots, x_n^+, x_n^-\}$, that is, every variable has a positive form x_i^+ equivalent to x_i and a negative form x_i^- equivalent to $-x_i$. This fact can be shown by the following logical

P. Revesz, *Introduction to Databases: From Biological to Spatio-Temporal*,
Texts in Computer Science, DOI 10.1007/978-1-84996-095-3_26,
© Springer-Verlag London Limited 2010

equivalences.

$$
\begin{aligned}
x \geq b &\equiv x^+ - x^- \geq 2b \\
-x \geq b &\equiv x^- - x^+ \geq 2b \\
x + y \geq b &\equiv x^+ - y^- \geq b \\
x - y \geq b &\equiv x^+ - y^+ \geq b \\
-x + y \geq b &\equiv x^- - y^- \geq b \\
-x - y \geq b &\equiv x^- - y^+ \geq b
\end{aligned}
$$

If the conjunction contains two difference constraints of the form $x - y \geq b$ and $x - y \geq c$ where $b > c$, then we can delete $x - y \geq c$ because it is already implied by $x - y \geq b$. By this simplification, there is at most one constraint with the left hand side $x - y$, for any pair of variables x and y.

As a result of this simplification, any conjunction C of lower bound, upper bound, and addition constraints over variables $\{x_1, \ldots, x_n\}$ can be represented by a $2n \times 2n$ *Addition-Bound Matrix* M in which each row and column is labeled by one of the variables in V^+, and each entry in $M[i, j]$ is the bound of the difference constraint between the variable in the ith row and the variable in the jth column.

Example 26.1.1 Consider the following conjunction of lower bound, upper bound, and addition constraints over the variables x and y:

$$-x \geq -25, \quad y \geq 3, \quad x - y \geq 4, \quad x + y \geq 10, \quad -x - y \geq -40$$

These can be translated into the following difference constraints over the variables x^+, x^-, y^+, y^-:

$$x^- - x^+ \geq -50, \quad y^+ - y^- \geq 6, \quad x^+ - y^+ \geq 4, \quad x^+ - y^- \geq 10, \quad x^- - y^+ \geq -40$$

This set of difference constraints can be represented by the following ABM:

	x^+	x^-	y^+	y^-
x^+	$-\infty$	$-\infty$	4	10
x^-	-50	$-\infty$	-40	$-\infty$
y^+	$-\infty$	$-\infty$	$-\infty$	6
y^-	$-\infty$	$-\infty$	$-\infty$	$-\infty$

26.1.1 Operations on ABMs

Next we define some basic operators on ABMs.

Definition 26.1.1 [minimum ∨:] Let M and N be two ABMs. Then the minimum of M and N, written as $M \vee N$, is defined as follows.

$$
[M \vee N][i, j] = \left\{ \begin{array}{ll} M[i, j] & \text{if } M[i, j] \leq N[i, j] \\ N[i, j] & \text{if } N[i, j] < M[i, j] \end{array} \right\}
$$

Definition 26.1.2 [widening $\triangledown$:] Let M and N be two ABMs. Then the *widening* of M by N, written as $M \triangledown N$, is defined as follows.

$$[M \triangledown N][i,j] = \left\{ \begin{array}{ll} M[i,j] & \text{if } M[i,j] \leq N[i,j] \\ -\infty & \text{if } N[i,j] < M[i,j] \end{array} \right\}$$

We say matrix M has domain D if all entries of M are in D. If all entries of M are $\geq l$ and $\leq u$ or $-\infty$, where l and u are some integer constants, then the domain of M is $\{-\infty\} \cup \{l, l+1, \ldots, u-1, u\}$.

Definition 26.1.3 [l-u-widening $\Diamond_{l,u}$:] Let $l < 0$ and $u > 0$ be two integer numbers. Let M and N be two ABMs such that the domain of M is $\{-\infty\} \cup \{l, l+1, \ldots, u-1, u\}$. Then the *l-u-widening* of M by N, written as $M\Diamond_{l,u}N$, is defined as follows.

$$[M\Diamond_{l,u}N][i,j] = \left\{ \begin{array}{ll} M[i,j] & \text{if } M[i,j] \leq N[i,j] \\ N[i,j] & \text{if } l \leq N[i,j] < M[i,j] \\ -\infty & \text{if } N[i,j] < l \leq M[i,j] \end{array} \right\}$$

Example 26.1.2 Let M be as in Example 26.1.1, and let N be the following ABM:

	x^+	x^-	y^+	y^-
x^+	$-\infty$	$-\infty$	15	10
x^-	-60	$-\infty$	$-\infty$	$-\infty$
y^+	$-\infty$	7	$-\infty$	2
y^-	$-\infty$	$-\infty$	$-\infty$	$-\infty$

In this case $M \vee N$ is:

	x^+	x^-	y^+	y^-
x^+	$-\infty$	$-\infty$	4	10
x^-	-60	$-\infty$	$-\infty$	$-\infty$
y^+	$-\infty$	$-\infty$	$-\infty$	2
y^-	$-\infty$	$-\infty$	$-\infty$	$-\infty$

while $M \triangledown N$ is:

	x^+	x^-	y^+	y^-
x^+	$-\infty$	$-\infty$	4	10
x^-	$-\infty$	$-\infty$	$-\infty$	$-\infty$
y^+	$-\infty$	$-\infty$	$-\infty$	$-\infty$
y^-	$-\infty$	$-\infty$	$-\infty$	$-\infty$

When $l = -50$ and $u = 50$, then $M \Diamond_{-50,50} N$ is:

	x^+	x^-	y^+	y^-
x^+	$-\infty$	$-\infty$	4	10
x^-	$-\infty$	$-\infty$	$-\infty$	$-\infty$
y^+	$-\infty$	$-\infty$	$-\infty$	2
y^-	$-\infty$	$-\infty$	$-\infty$	$-\infty$

The following theorem compares the precision of the above operators.

Theorem 26.1.1 Let $\mathcal{S}$ be the solution space of an ABM or union of ABMs. For any $l < 0$ and $u > 0$, the following holds:

$$\mathcal{S}(M \cup N) \subseteq \mathcal{S}(M \vee N) \subseteq \mathcal{S}(M \Diamond_{l,u} N) \subseteq \mathcal{S}(M \triangledown N).$$

Proof: Each entry of $M \vee N$ is smaller than or equal to the corresponding entries in M and N. Hence $\mathcal{S}(M) \subseteq \mathcal{S}(M \vee N)$ and $\mathcal{S}(N) \subseteq \mathcal{S}(M \vee N)$ hold. Therefore, $\mathcal{S}(M \cup N) \subseteq \mathcal{S}(M \vee N)$ also must hold.

The *minimum*, *widening*, and *l-u-widening* operators behave the same when $M[i,j] \leq N[i,j]$. When $N[i,j] < M[i,j]$ then there are two cases. In the first case, when $l \leq N[i,j]$, then the l-u-widening operator behaves like the *minimum* operator and returns $N[i,j]$. When $N[i,j] < l$, then the *l-u-widening* operator behaves like the *widening* operator and returns $-\infty$. Therefore, $\mathcal{S}(M \vee N) \subseteq \mathcal{S}(M \Diamond_{l,u} N) \subseteq \mathcal{S}(M \triangledown N)$ must hold. ∎

26.1.2 An Efficient Representation of ABMs

Without loss of generality we can fix an order of the variables and assume that in all addition constraints of the form $x - y \geq b$ or $-x + y \geq b$, x is earlier than y, and in all addition constraints of the form $x + y \geq b$ and $-x - y \geq b$ x is earlier than y or $x = y$. We can represent lower bound constraints of the form $x \geq b$ by $x + x \geq 2b$ and and upper bound constraints of the form $-x \geq b$ by $-x - x \geq 2b$.

Then we can represent $x - y \geq b$ and $x + y \geq b$ constraints by a matrix L as follows:

$$L[i,j] = \begin{cases} b & \text{if } (x_i - x_j \geq b) \in C \text{ and } i < j \\ b & \text{if } (x_j + x_i \geq b) \in C \text{ and } j \leq i \\ -\infty & \text{otherwise} \end{cases}$$

Similarly, we can represent $-x + y \geq b$ and $-x - y \geq b$ constraints by a matrix U as follows:

$$U[i,j] = \begin{cases} b & \text{if } (-x_i + x_j \geq b) \in C \text{ and } i < j \\ b & \text{if } (-x_j - x_i \geq b) \in C \text{ and } j \leq i \\ -\infty & \text{otherwise} \end{cases}$$

Note that the above is equivalent to the following:

$$U[i,j] = \left\{ \begin{array}{ll} b & \text{if } (x_i - x_j \leq -b) \in C \text{ and } i < j \\ b & \text{if } (x_j + x_i \leq -b) \in C \text{ and } j \leq i \\ -\infty & \text{otherwise} \end{array} \right\}$$

For example, the ABM in Example 26.1.1 can be represented by the following matrices. L is:

	x	y
x	$-\infty$	4
y	10	6

and U is:

	x	y
x	-50	$-\infty$
y	-40	$-\infty$

The above representation with matrices L and U requires only $2n^2$ matrix entries, while the previous ABM representation requires $4n^2$ matrix entries. Moreover, since the corresponding entries in L and U are lower and upper bounds of the same $x_i - x_j$ or $x_j + x_i$, they can be put together as follows:

	x	y
x	$[-\infty, 50]$	$[4, +\infty]$
y	$[10, 40]$	$[6, +\infty]$

Therefore, each ABM can be represented using a matrix with only n^2 interval entries.

26.2 Abstract Interpretation

The *collecting semantics* of a procedural program means that we find for each line of the program an *invariant*, which is a constraint that gives for each variable the set of possible values that may occur at that line. Software verification would be easy if we could compute the precise semantics of programs. While in general the program semantics cannot be computed precisely, it is possible to give for it an over-approximation or an under-approximation.

Abstract interpretation is a method that finds an over-approximation. Abstract interpretation evaluates the program using an abstraction of the input data. This is called an *abstract execution*. For recursive programs, the abstract execution repeatedly generalizes the invariants using a *widening operator* until the invariants cannot be further widened.

A widening operator generalizes at a program location an invariant constraint M with a new constraint N that describes an additional set of possible values of the program variables at that location.

The widening operator cannot just take $M \cup N$ as the new value of the invariant because it may cause the invariant to grow without bound causing a non-terminating abstract execution. Instead, the widening operator uses the following clever idea: *preserve those constraints of M that are satisfied by N*. That is attractive because if M contains k linear inequalities, then at most k widening operators can be performed on M. Hence the abstract execution must terminate in k iterations.

The widening operator defined in Definition 26.1.2 is such an operator, except that instead of more general linear constraints, we allow only addition constraints. Widening general linear constraints always return a *convex* region, that is, a conjunction of linear inequality constraints that includes both M and N. In the case of addition constraints, widening always returns a convex region, which is called the *octagonal abstract domain* because it has at most eight sides.

Example 26.2.1 Consider the following simple program fragment.

```
1   a = 0
2   a = a + 1
3   if a > 2 then   goto 6
4   if a = 2 then   goto 7
5   goto 2
6
7
```

Let $L_{i,j}$ be the invariant at the beginning of line i at the jth entry of that line. The widening operator works on the program as follows.

$L_{1,1} = \emptyset$ because there are no constraints on a yet.

$L_{2,1} = \{a = 0\}$ because line 1 set a to zero.

$L_{3,1} = \{a = 1\}$ because line 2 incremented a by one.

$L_{4,1} = \{a = 1\}$ because line 3 if condition is false and a does not change.

$L_{5,1} = \{a = 1\}$ because line 4 if condition is false and a does not change.

The execution of line 5 takes us back to the beginning of line 2 with no change in a. Since this is the second entry to line 2 and there is a previous invariant, we widen it as follows:

$$L_{2,2} = L_{2,1} \triangledown \{a = 1\} = \{0 \le a, a \le 0\} \triangledown \{1 \le a, a \le 1\} = \{0 \le a\}.$$

Line 2 executes $a = a + 1$ on the invariant $\{0 \le a\}$, yielding $1 \le a$. Hence when we enter line 3 for the second time, we get by widening the following:

$$L_{3,2} = L_{3,1} \triangledown \{1 \le a\} = \{1 \le a, a \le 1\} \triangledown \{1 \le a\} = \{1 \le a\}.$$

We enter the if statement of line 3 and find that $(1 \le a) \wedge (a > 2)$ is satisfiable when $a > 2$, causing us to go to line 6, and is unsatisfiable when $1 \le a \le 2$, causing us to go to line 4. Hence we have:

$$L_{6,1} = \{a > 2\}.$$

$$L_{4,2} = L_{4,1} \triangledown \{1 \le a \le 2\} = \{1 \le a\}.$$

In the latter case, we enter line 4 and find that $(1 \le a) \wedge (a = 2)$ is satisfiable when $a = 2$, causing us to go to line 7, and not satisfiable when $1 \le a, a \ne 2$, causing us to go to line 5. Hence we have:

$$L_{7,1} = \{a = 2\}.$$

$$L_{5,2} = L_{5,1} \triangledown \{1 \le a, a \ne 2\} = \{1 \le a \le 1\} \triangledown \{1 \le a, a \ne 2\} = \{1 \le a\}.$$

From line 5, we go to line 2, where we apply again the widening operator.

$$L_{2,3} = L_{2,2} \triangledown \{1 \le a\} = \{0 \le a\} \triangledown \{1 \le a\} = \{0 \le a\}.$$

Since there are no more changes in the invariants, the fixed point of the abstract execution is reached, and we terminate the execution. The following table summarizes the obtained invariants.

Invariants Obtained by Widening

Line	1st Entry	2nd Entry
1	$\emptyset$	
2	$0 \leq a \leq 0$	$0 \leq a$
3	$1 \leq a \leq 1$	$1 \leq a$
4	$1 \leq a \leq 1$	$1 \leq a$
5	$1 \leq a \leq 1$	$1 \leq a$
6	$2 < a$	
7	$2 \leq a \leq 2$	

Software verification problem: Suppose that a simple software verification problem asks to check whether it is possible to enter line 6 during some execution of the program. The abstract interpretation using widening returns an over-approximation which suggests that it may be possible to enter line 6 with a value of a that is greater than 2.

However, the program can never actually enter line 6. When we first get to line 5, then $a = 1$. Hence when we get back to line 2 and execute $a = a + 1$, then $a = 2$. Therefore, the if condition of line 3 will fail, and the program goes on to line 4. The if condition of line 4 will be true, hence we go to line 7 and never enter line 6. Clearly, the abstract interpretation has a too loose over-approximation that prevents finding the bug of never entering line 6.

The l-u-widening operator in Definition 26.1.3 can give a more precise over-appoximation.

Theorem 26.2.1 Let P be a program with m lines and n variables. Let $l < 0$ and $u > 0$ be integer constants and $W^{l,u}$ be the result of evaluating the least fixed point of P using l-u-widening. Then the following holds.

$$lfp(P) \subseteq W^{l,u}$$

where $lfp(P)$ is the least fixed point of P. Further, $W^{l,u}$ can be computed using $O(|u - l|mn^2)$ time.

Proof: We start evaluating P. For each new line L_i of P, when we find the first ABM for it, we change all entries greater than u to u and call the resulting ABM M_i. Then whenever a new ABM N is found for line L_i, we update M_i to be the result of $M_i \Diamond_{l,u} N$. This ensures that the domain of each M_i is $\{-\infty\} \cup \{l, l+1, \ldots, u-1, u\}$ throughout the approximate evaluation. In each iteration at least one entry in at least one of the M_is must decrease. Moreover, each entry can decrease at most $|u - l|$ times and each M_i has n^2 entries. Since there are m number of M_is, the total number of iterations is at most $|u - l|mn^2$. It is also clear that the approximate evaluation is always computing an upper approximation of the actual least fixed point. ∎

If the values of u and l are fixed constants, then the l-u-widening operator has an $O(mn^2)$ time complexity. Using increasingly smaller values of l or larger values of u leads to tighter approximations of the least fixed point.

Theorem 26.2.2 For each program P and constants l_1, l_2, u_1, and u_2 such that $l_1 \leq l_2 < 0 < u_2 \leq u_1$, the following conditions hold:

$$lfp(P) \subseteq W^{l_1, u_1} \subseteq W^{l_2, u_2}$$

Example 26.2.2 Let us apply to the program of the previous example *l-u-widening* with $l = -5$ and $u = 5$. The abstract execution starts similarly to the previous abstract execution, hence again we have:

$L_{1,1} = \emptyset$.

$L_{2,1} = \{a = 0\}$.

$L_{3,1} = \{a = 1\}$.

$L_{4,1} = \{a = 1\}$.

$L_{5,1} = \{a = 1\}$.

The execution of line 5 takes us back to the beginning of line 2 with no change in a. On the second entry to line 2, the execution diverges because we use l-u-widening:

$$L_{2,2} = L_{2,1} \Diamond_{-5,5} L_{5,1} = \{a = 0\} \Diamond_{-5,5} \{a = 1\} = \{0 \leq a \leq 1\}.$$

Line 2 executes $a = a + 1$ on the invariant $0 \leq a \leq 1$, yielding $1 \leq a \leq 2$. We enter line 3 for the second time and get:

$$L_{3,2} = L_{3,1} \Diamond_{-5,5} \{1 \leq a \leq 2\} = \{1 \leq a \leq 2\}.$$

We enter the if statement of line 3 but find $L_{3,2} \wedge (a > 2)$ unsatisfiable. Therefore, we continue to line 4 and find that:

$$L_{4,2} = L_{4,1} \Diamond_{-5,5} \{1 \leq a \leq 2\} = \{1 \leq a \leq 2\}.$$

We enter the if statement of line 4 with $L_{4,2}$. The if condition $L_{4,2} \wedge (a = 2)$ is satisfiable when $a = 2$, causing us to go to line 7, and is unsatisfiable when $1 \leq a < 2$, causing us to go to line 5. Hence we have:

$$L_{7,1} = \{a = 2\}$$

$$L_{5,2} = L_{5,1} \Diamond_{-5,5} \{1 \leq a < 2\} = \{1 \leq a < 2\}.$$

In the latter case, we also enter a third time line 2 and get:

$$L_{2,3} = L_{2,2} \Diamond_{-5,5} \{1 \leq a < 2\} = \{0 \leq a \leq 1\} \Diamond_{-5,5} \{1 \leq a < 2\} = \{0 \leq a < 2\}.$$

After adding one to a, we get $1 \leq a < 3$ and enter with it line 3 for the third time. That yields:

$$L_{3,3} = L_{3,2} \Diamond_{-5,5} \{1 \leq a < 3\} = \{1 \leq a \leq 2\} \Diamond_{-5,5} \{1 \leq a < 3\} = \{1 \leq a < 3\}.$$

We enter the if statement of line 3 with $L_{3,3}$. The if condition $L_{3,3} \wedge (a > 2)$ is satisfiable when $2 < a < 3$, causing us to go to line 6, and is unsatisfiable when $1 \leq a \leq 2$, causing us to go to line 4. Hence we have:

$$L_{6,1} = \{2 < a < 3\}.$$

$$L_{4,2} = L_{4,1} \Diamond_{-5,5} \{1 \leq a \leq 2\} = \{1 \leq a \leq 1\} \Diamond_{-5,5} \{1 \leq a \leq 2\} = \{1 \leq a \leq 2\}.$$

In the latter case, we also enter a second time line 7 when $a = 2$, which does not change the invariant at line 7, and enter line 5 when $1 \leq a < 2$, which does not change the invariant at line 5. Hence we get:

$$L_{7,2} = L_{7,1} = \{2 \leq a \leq 2\}.$$

$$L_{5,3} = L_{5,2} = \{1 \leq a < 2\}.$$

Since there are no more changes to the invariants, the abstract evaluation has reached a fixed point and terminates. The invariants found by the l-u-widening are summarized in the following table.

Invariants Obtained by l-u Widening

Line	1st Entry	2nd Entry	3rd Entry
1	$\emptyset$		
2	$0 \leq a \leq 0$	$0 \leq a \leq 1$	$0 \leq a < 2$
3	$1 \leq a \leq 1$	$1 \leq a \leq 2$	$1 \leq a < 3$
4	$1 \leq a \leq 1$	$1 \leq a \leq 2$	
5	$1 \leq a \leq 1$	$1 \leq a < 2$	$1 \leq a < 2$
6	$2 < a < 3$		
7	$2 \leq a \leq 2$	$2 \leq a \leq 2$	

Note that for line 6 the l-u-widening result is $2 < a < 3$, which is tighter than the previous widening result of $2 < a$, but it still misleadingly suggests that the program may enter line 6 during some execution if the domain of the variables is the rational numbers.

26.3 Software Verification using MLPQ

We now describe the constraint database approach to software verification. Suppose that we need to check that certain *error states* never occur during any execution of a program. The error states are expressed as a quantifier-free formula of the variables used in the program. Each satisfying assignment of values to the variables is an error that needs to be avoided. The outline of the constraint database approach to software verification consists of the following steps.

1. Translate the procedural program into a Datalog program that always derives conjunctions of addition constraints.

2. Find an under-approximation and an over-approximation of the least fixed point semantics of the Datalog program.

3. If the under-approximation and the error state intersect, then return *"Unsafe"*, else if the over-approximation and the error states do not intersect, then return *"Safe,"* else return *"Test was inconclusive. Rerun with a smaller l parameter to tighten the approximations."*

Step (1) can be accomplished by translating first to a constraint automaton, which is also called a *transition system* in software verification, and then using the method described in Chapter 15 to translate the constraint automata to Datalog with constraints program. However, it is also possible to directly translate a procedural program into a Datalog with constraints program such that the collecting semantics of the procedural program is equivalent to the least fixed point semantics of the Datalog with constraints program. The translation requires creating a new Datalog relation $Line\_i(v_1 \ldots, v_n)$ for each line i of the procedural program with variables $v_1, \ldots, v_n$.

Example 26.3.1 The procedural program of Section 26.2 can be translated into Datalog with addition constraints as follows.

$$Line2(a) \quad :\!— \quad 0 \leq a \leq 0. \tag{26.1}$$

$$Line3(a) \quad :\!— \quad Line2(a1),\ a = a1 + 1. \tag{26.2}$$

$$Line6(a) \quad :\!— \quad Line3(a),\ 2 < a. \tag{26.3}$$

$$Line4(a) \quad :\!— \quad Line3(a),\ a \leq 2. \tag{26.4}$$

$$Line7(a) \quad :\!— \quad Line4(a),\ 2 \leq a \leq 2. \tag{26.5}$$

$$Line5(a) \quad :\!— \quad Line4(a),\ a < 2. \tag{26.6}$$

$$Line5(a) \quad :\!— \quad Line4(a),\ 2 < a. \tag{26.7}$$

$$Line2(a) \quad :\!— \quad Line5(a). \tag{26.8}$$

Step (2) follows from Theorem 23.4.11, which proves that the underapproximation and the over-approximation can be found in finite time for Datalog with integer or rational addition constraints. The approximations are implemented within the MLPQ constraint database system described in Chapter 13. The MLPQ system returns as under-approximation or over-approximation for each relation a disjunction of conjunctions of addition constraints. In this sense the approximation is different from any of the widening operators that always yield a conjunction of addition constraints. The constraint database approximation can be more precise that the abstract interpretations based on the widening operators.

Example 26.3.2 Let us find the over-approximation of the least fixed point of the Datalog program in Example 26.3.1 using $l = 5$.

$$
\begin{array}{llll}
Line2(a) & :\!— & 0 \leq a \leq 0. & \text{by rule 1} \\
Line3(a) & :\!— & 1 \leq a \leq 1. & \text{by rule 2} \\
Line4(a) & :\!— & 1 \leq a \leq 1. & \text{by rule 4} \\
Line5(a) & :\!— & 1 \leq a \leq 1. & \text{by rule 6} \\
Line2(a) & :\!— & 1 \leq a \leq 1. & \text{by rule 8} \\
Line3(a) & :\!— & 2 \leq a \leq 2. & \text{by rule 2} \\
Line4(a) & :\!— & 2 \leq a \leq 2. & \text{by rule 4} \\
Line7(a) & :\!— & 2 \leq a \leq 2. & \text{by rule 5}
\end{array}
$$

Since there are no more constraint tuples that can be derived, the fixed point is reached and the evaluation terminates. Note that this over-approximation is precise, that is, it happens to be the same as the actual least fixed point. Since the over-approximation does not contain any constraint tuple for relation $Line6$, the program can never enter line 6. That conclusion solves the original software verification problem for this program.

Step (3) requires to test the satisfiability of the conjunction of the under-approximation or the over-approximation with the error state. Many of these satisfiability testing algorithms were described in Chapter 24. Finally, the idea of rerunning the under- and over-approximations if the tests are inconclusive follows from Theorem 23.4.12, which proves that the under-approximation and the over-approximation can be tightened by choosing a smaller l parameter. In the MLPQ system the user can specify any negative l value.

Bibliographic Notes

There are many different approaches to software verification, including abstract interpretation [99, 100, 98, 186, 226], model checking in [14, 92, 108, 272], predicate abstraction in [152], data flow analysis and mathematical induction. Today there are many examples of successful applications of these approaches to the verification of digital circuits and programs. Common abstract interpretation widening operators use the domains of intervals [99] or polyhedra [100, 226]. The octagonal domain, which is composed of lower bound, upper bound, and addition constraints is from Miné [276, 277].

The idea of translating from procedural programs to constraint query languages or constraint logic programs for the purpose of software verification occurs first in Delzanno and Podelski [108], Fribourg and Richardson [143], and Fribourg and Olson [142]. However, these papers did not use the latest approximation results. For example, [143] relied on the least fixpoint semantics of Datalog with integer gap-order constraints, which can be precisely evaluated [325]. Therefore, [143, 142] advocate the rewriting of more complex constraints into gap-order constraints. Delzanno and Podelski [108] only point out the potential of using constraint query languages and constraint logic programs for software verification if the translation has a terminating evaluation. Therefore, none of these papers take advantage of the approximation theorems that we described in [336] and Chapter 23. As we saw, the use of those approximation theorems makes the constraint database approach practical and competitive with the abstract interpretation techniques. The constraint database approach as a general idea is presented in [344], extending earlier work in [19, 338]. A software verifier based on these ideas is presented in [20].

Exercises

1. Redo Example 26.2.1 using addition-bound matrices instead of an interval representation.

2. Redo Example 26.2.2 using addition-bound matrices instead of an interval representation.

3. The following program implements the subway train regulation system of Chapter 15 using parallel case statements. In a parallel case statement one of the cases is selected randomly. If the condition of the selected case statement is false, then another is selected and executed. This repeats until one of the cases succeeds.

Train(b,s,d)

```
1 ONTIME
  begin parallel
2       if b − s > −9 then s = s + 1 goto ONTIME
3       if b − s = −9 then s = s + 1 goto LATE
4       if b − s < 9   then b = b + 1 goto ONTIME
5       if b − s = 9   then b = b + 1 goto BRAKE
  end parallel
6 LATE
  begin parallel
7       if b − s < −1 then b = b + 1 goto LATE
8       if b − s = −1 then b = b + 1 goto ONTIME
  end parallel
9 STOPPED
  begin parallel
10      if b − s > 1 then s = s + 1 goto STOPPED
11      if b − s = 1 then s = s + 1 goto ONTIME
  end parallel
12 BRAKE
  begin parallel
13      if b − s > 1 then s = s + 1 goto BRAKE
14      if b − s = 1 then s = s + 1, d = 0 goto ONTIME
15      if d < 9    then b = b + 1, d = d + 1 goto BRAKE
16      if d ≤ 9    then b = b + 1, d = 0 goto STOPPED
  end parallel
```

Suppose we know that the subroutine $Train$ can be called with any values where $b = s$ and $d = 0$. Find the invariants of the program using abstract interpretation with the widening operator.

Note: In the above program, the variable d is changed only in the parallel case statement after BRAKE. When we exit the BRAKE region and go to either ONTIME or STOPPED, then d is reset to 0. Hence d always remains 0 outside of the BRAKE region.

4. Write a Datalog query with addition constraints that is equivalent to the subway train control program of Chapter 15.

5. Let $\mathcal{E}_{subway}$, the error states for the subway train control system, be the following:

$$\mathcal{E}_{subway} = \{b, s \; : \; |b - s| > 20\}.$$

Check the safety of the subway train system using the over-approximation found in the previous exercise.

6. Consider the following program.

```
1 x = 1,  y = 1
2 x = x + 1,  y = y + 2x - 1
3 goto 2
```

(a) Translate this program into constraint Datalog.

(b) Find the over-approximation of this program using constraint databases and $l = -10$.

(c) Let the error state $\mathcal{E}$ be as follows:

$$\mathcal{E} = \{y \; : \; y \geq 10, \; -y \geq -15\}.$$

Check the safety of the program.

7. Consider the following program, where a, b, and c are arbitrary constants.

```
1 x = 1,  y = c
2 x = x + 1,  y = y + ax + b
3 goto 2
```

(a) Translate this program into constraint Datalog.

(b) Find the over-approximation of this program using constraint databases and $l = -10$.

(c) Using mathematical induction prove that the least fixed point of the program contains the following:

$$Line2(y, x) \; : - \; y = \frac{a}{2}x^2 + (\frac{a}{2} + b)x + (b + c), \quad x \geq 1.$$

(d) Compare the constraint database over-approximation and the mathematical induction results. Give an example error state that intersects the constraint database over-approximation but does not intersect the mathematical induction result. Would decreasing the value of the l parameter allow the over-approximation to tighten to the point of no longer intersecting the error state? If yes, how small should l be to avoid intersection between the constraint database over-approximation and the error state?

Bibliography

[1] S. Abbasi, F. Mokhtarian, and J. Kittler. Curvature scale space image in shape similarity retrieval. *Multimedia Systems*, 7(6):467–476, 1999.

[2] S. Abiteboul, R. Hull, and V. Vianu. *Foundations of Databases*. Addison-Wesley, 1995.

[3] S. Abiteboul, P. Kanellakis, and G. Grahne. On the representation and querying of sets of possible worlds. *Theoretical Computer Science*, 78(1):159–87, 1991.

[4] S. Abiteboul, D. Quass, J. McHugh, J. Widom, and J. L. Wiener. The Lorel query language for semistructured data. *International Journal on Digital Libraries*, 1(1):68–88, 1997.

[5] N. R. Adam and A. Gangopadhyay. *Database Issues in Geographic Information Systems*. Kluwer, 1997.

[6] F. Afrati, T. Andronikos, and T. Kavalieros. On the expressiveness of first-order constraint languages. In G. Kuper and M. Wallace, editors, *Proc. Workshop on Constraint Databases and Applications*, volume 1034 of *Lecture Notes in Computer Science*, pages 22–39. Springer, 1995.

[7] F. Afrati, S. Cosmadakis, S. Grumbach, and G. Kuper. Linear versus polynomial constraints in database query languages. In A. Borning, editor, *Proc. 2nd International Workshop on Principles and Practice of Constraint Programming*, volume 874 of *Lecture Notes in Computer Science*, pages 181–92. Springer, 1994.

[8] P. K. Agarwal, L. Arge, and J. Erickson. Indexing moving points. *Journal of Computer and System Sciences*, 66(1):207–243, 2003.

[9] P. K. Agarwal and K. R. Varadarajan. Efficient algorithms for approximating polygonal chains. *Journal of Discrete & Computational Geometry*, 23:273–91, 2000.

[10] A. Aiken, D. Kozen, and E. Wimmers. Decidability of systems of set constraints with negative constraints. *Information and Computation*, 122(1):30–44, 1995.

[11] C. E. Alchourrón, P. Gärdenfors, and D. Makinson. On the logic of theory change: Partial meet contraction and revision functions. *Journal of Symbolic Logic*, 50:510–30, 1985.

[12] J. F. Allen. Maintaining knowledge about temporal intervals. *Communications of the ACM*, 26(11):832–843, 1983.

[13] R. Alur, C. Courcoubetis, and D. L. Dill. Model-checking in dense real-time. *Information and Computation*, 104(1):2–34, 1993.

[14] R. Alur, C. Courcoubetis, N. Halbwachs, T. Henzinger, P.-H. Ho, X. Nicollin, A. Olivero, J. Sifakis, and S. Yovine. The algorithmic analysis of hybrid systems. *Theoretical Computer Science*, 138(1): 3–34, 1995.

[15] R. Alur and D. L. Dill. A theory of timed automata. *Theoretical Computer Science*, 126(2):183–235, 1994.

[16] R. Alur and T. A. Henzinger. A really temporal logic. *Journal of the ACM*, 41(1):181–204, 1994.

[17] D. G. Anderson, E. A. Catchpole, N. J. DeMestre, and T. Parkes. Modeling the spread of grass fires. *Journal of Australian Mathematical Society (Ser.B)*, 23:451–66, 1982.

[18] S. Anderson. Aggregation estimation for 2D moving points. In J. Pustejovsky and P. Revesz, editors, *13th International Symposium on Temporal Representation and Reasoning*, pages 137–144. IEEE Press, 2006.

[19] S. Anderson and P. Revesz. Verifying the incorrectness of programs and automata. In *Proc. 6th International Symposium on Abstraction, Reformulation, and Approximation*, volume 3607 of *Lecture Notes in Computer Science*, pages 1–13. Springer, 2005.

[20] S. Anderson and P. Revesz. CDB-PV: A constraint database-based program verifier. In I. Miguel and W. Ruml, editors, *Proc. 7th International Symposium on Abstraction, Reformulation, and Approximation*, volume 4612 of *Lecture Notes in Computer Science*, pages 35–49. Springer, 2007.

[21] S. Anderson and P. Revesz. Efficient maxcount and threshold operators of moving objects. *Geoinformatica*, 13(4):355–96, 2009.

[22] P. Andrews and C. Chase. BEHAVE: Fire behavior prediction and fuel modeling system. In *USDA PMS-439-2, NFES 0277*, 1989.

[23] K. Arbter, W. E. Snyder, H. Burkhardt, and G. Hirzinger. Application of affine-invariant Fourier descriptors to recognition of 3D objects. *IEEE Transactions on Pattern Analysis and Machine Intelligence*, 12(7):640–47, 1990.

[24] M. P. Armstrong. Temporality in spatial databases. In *Proc. URISA Conference on Geographic and Land Information Systems*, volume 2, pages 880–89, 1988.

[25] T. Aschenbrenner, A. Brodsky, and Y. Kornatzky. Constraint database approach to spatio-temporal data fusion and sensor management. In *Proc. ILPS95 Workshop on Constraints, Databases and Logic Programming*, Portland, OR, December 1995.

[26] M. M. Astrahan, D. D. Chamberlin, W. F. King III, and I. L. Traiger. System R: A relational data base management system. In H. F. Hasselmeier and W. G. Spruth, editors, *Data Base Systems*, volume 39 of *Lecture Notes in Computer Science*, pages 139–148. Springer, 1976.

[27] C. W. Bachman. Data structure diagrams. *Data Base*, 1(2):4–10, 1969.

[28] C. W. Bachman. The programmer as navigator. *Commun. ACM*, 16(11):635–658, 1973.

[29] S. Basu. New results on quantifier elimination over real closed fields and applications to constraint databases. *Journal of the ACM*, 46(4):537–55, 1999.

[30] C. Batini, S. Ceri, and S. B. Navathe. *Conceptual Database Design: An Entity-Relationship Approach*. Benjamin/Cummings, 1992.

[31] M. Baudinet, J. Chomicki, and P. Wolper. Constraint-generating dependencies. *Journal of Computer and System Sciences*, 59(1): 94–115, 1999.

[32] M. Baudinet, M. Niézette, and P. Wolper. On the representation of infinite temporal data and queries. In *Proc. ACM Symposium on Principles of Database Systems*. ACM Press, 1991.

[33] M. Y. Becker and P. Sewell. Cassandra: Distributed access control policies with tunable expressiveness. In *5th IEEE International Workshop on Policies for Distributed Systems and Networks*, pages 159–168, 2004.

[34] M. Y. Becker and P. Sewell. Cassandra: Flexible trust management, applied to electronic health records. In *CSFW*, pages 139–154, 2004.

[35] N. Beckmann, H.-P. Kriegel, R. Schneider, and B. Seeger. The R*-tree: An efficient and robust access method for points and rectangles. In *Proc. ACM SIGMOD International Conference on Management of Data*, 1990.

[36] A. Beller, T. Giblin, K. V. Le, S. Litz, T. Kittel, and D. Schimel. A temporal GIS prototype for global change research. In *Proc. URISA Conference on Geographic and Land Information Systems*, volume 2, pages 752–65, 1991.

[37] J. Ben-Arie and Z. Wang. Pictorial recognition of objects employing affine invariance in the frequency domain. *IEEE Transactions on Pattern Analysis and Machine Intelligence*, 20(6):604–18, 1998.

[38] M. Ben-Or, D. Kozen, and J. Reif. The complexity of elementary algebra and geometry. *Journal of Computer and System Sciences*, 32(2):251–64, 1986.

[39] A. Benczur, A. Novak, and P. Revesz. Classical and weighted knowledgebase transformations. *Computers and Mathematics*, 32(5):85–98, 1996.

[40] M. Benedikt, G. Dong, L. Libkin, and L. Wong. Relational expressive power of constraint query languages. *Journal of the ACM*, 45(1):1–34, 1998.

[41] M. Benedikt, M. Grohe, L. Libkin, and L. Segoufin. Reachability and connectivity queries in constraint databases. *Journal of Computer and System Sciences*, 66(1):169–206, 2003.

[42] M. Benedikt and L. Libkin. Relational queries over interpreted structures. *Journal of the ACM*, 47(4):644–80, 2000.

[43] M. Benedikt and L. Libkin. Safe constraint queries. *SIAM Journal of Computing*, 29(5):1652–82, 2000.

[44] F. Benhamou and A. Colmerauer, editors. *Constraint Logic Programming: Selected Research.* MIT Press, 1993.

[45] J. L. Bentley. Multidimensional binary search trees used for associative searching. *Communications of the ACM*, 18(9):509–17, 1975.

[46] J. L. Bentley. Multidimensional divide-and-conquer. *Communications of the ACM*, 23(4), 1980.

[47] E. Bertino, C. Bettini, E. Ferrari, and P. Samarati. An access control model supporting periodicity constraints and temporal reasoning. *ACM Transactions on Database Systems*, 23(3):231–85, 1998.

[48] E. Bertino, B. Catania, and B. Shidlovsky. Towards optimal two-dimensional indexing for constraint databases. *Information Processing Letters*, 64:1–8, 1997.

[49] C. Bettini, X. S. Wang, E. Bertino, and S. Jajodia. Temporal semantic assumptions and their use in databases. *IEEE Transactions on Knowledge and Data Engineering*, 10(2):277–96, 1998.

[50] T. Bittner and A. Frank. On the design of formal theories of geographic space. *Geographical Systems*, 1(3):237–75, 1999.

[51] B. Boigelot, S. Rassart, and P. Wolper. On the expressiveness of real and integer arithmetic automata. In *International Colloquium on Automata, Languages and Programming*, volume 1443 of *Lecture Notes in Computer Science*, pages 152–63. Springer, 1998.

[52] B. Boigelot and P. Wolper. Symbolic verification with periodic sets. In D. L. Dill, editor, *Proc. 6th International Conference on Computer-Aided Verification*, volume 818 of *Lecture Notes in Computer Science*, pages 55–67. Springer, 1994.

[53] Z. Bouziane. A primitive recursive algorithm for the general Petri net reachability problem. In *Proc. IEEE Symposium on Foundations of Computer Science*, pages 130–6. IEEE Press, 1998.

[54] A. Brodsky, J. Jaffar, and M. Maher. Towards practical query evaluation for constraint databases. *Constraints*, 2(3–4):279–304, 1997.

[55] A. Brodsky and Y. Kornatzky. The LyriC language: Querying constraint objects. In M. Carey and M. Schneider, editors, *Proc. ACM SIGMOD International Conference on Management of Data*, pages 35–46. ACM Press, 1995.

[56] A. Brodsky, C. Lassez, J. L. Lassez, and M. J. Maher. Separability of polyhedra for optimal filtering of spatial and constraint data. *Journal of Automated Reasoning*, 23(1):83–104, 1999.

[57] A. Brodsky, V. Segal, J. Chen, and P. Exarkhopoulo. The CCUBE constraint object-oriented database system. *Constraints*, 2(3–4): 245–77, 1997.

[58] A. Brodsky, V. Segal, J. Chen, and P. Exarkhopoulo. The CCUBE constraint object-oriented database system. In *Proc. ACM SIGMOD International Conference on Management of Data*, pages 577–9, 1999.

[59] G. R. Buchanan. *Finite Element Analysis*. McGraw-Hill, New York, 1995.

[60] S. Burris and H. P. Sankappanavar. *A Course in Universal Algebra*. Springer, 1981.

[61] W. Buttner and H. Simonis. Embedding Boolean expressions into logic programming. *Journal of Symbolic Computation*, 4(2):191–205, 1987.

[62] J.-H. Byon and P. Revesz. DISCO: A constraint database system with sets. In *Proc. Workshop on Constraint Databases and Applications*, volume 1034 of *Lecture Notes in Computer Science*, pages 68–83. Springer, 1995.

[63] M. Cai. *Parametric Rectangles: A Model for Spatiotemporal Databases*. PhD thesis, University of Nebraska-Lincoln, 2000.

[64] M. Cai, D. Keshwani, and P. Revesz. Parametric rectangles: A model for querying and animating spatiotemporal databases. In *Proc. 7th International Conference on Extending Database Technology*, volume 1777 of *Lecture Notes in Computer Science*, pages 430–44. Springer, 2000.

[65] M. Cai and P. Revesz. Forest fire modeling in a spatio-temporal database. In *Proc. 4th International Conference on Integrating GIS and Environmental Modeling*, 2000.

[66] M. Cai and P. Revesz. Parametric R-tree: An index structure for moving objects. In *Proc. 10th COMAD International Conference on Management of Data*, pages 57–64. McGraw-Hill, 2000.

[67] A. Calì, D. Calvanese, G. De Giacomo, and M. Lenzerini. Data integration under integrity constraints. *Information Systems*, 29(2): 147–163, 2004.

[68] D. Calvanese and M. Lenzerini. On the interaction between ISA and cardinality constraints. In *Proceedings of the Tenth International Conference on Data Engineering*, pages 204–213. IEEE Computer Society Press, 1994.

[69] D. Calvanese, M. Lenzerini, and D. Nardi. A unified framework for class based representation formalisms. In *Proceedings of the Fourth International Conference on Principles of Knowledge Representation and Reasoning*, pages 109–120. Morgan Kaufmann, 1994.

[70] M. J. Carey, D. Florescu, Z. G. Ives, Y. Lu, J. Shanmugasundaram, E. J. Shekita, and S. N. Subramanian. XPERANTO: Publishing object-relational data as XML. In *WebDB (Informal Proceedings)*, pages 105–110, 2000.

[71] B. F. Caviness and J. R. Johnson, editors. *Quantifier Elimination and Cylindrical Algebraic Decomposition*. Springer, 1998.

[72] K. Cerans. Deciding properties of integral relational automata. In *International Colloquium on Automata, Languages and Programming*, volume 820 of *Lecture Notes in Computer Science*, pages 35–46. Springer, 1994.

[73] D. D. Chamberlin. XQuery: An XML query language. *IBM Systems Journal*, 41(4):597–615, 2002.

[74] D. D. Chamberlin and R. F. Boyce. SEQUEL: A structured English query language. In R. Rustin, editor, *Proc. ACM-SIGMOD Workshop on Data Description, Access and Control*, pages 249–264. ACM Press, 1974.

[75] D. D. Chamberlin, J. Robie, and D. Florescu. Quilt: An XML query language for heterogeneous data sources. In D. Suciu and G. Vossen, editors, *Proc. 3rd International Workshop on the World Wide Web and Databases*, volume 1997 of *Lecture Notes in Computer Science*, pages 1–25. Springer, 2001.

[76] R. Chen. *Temporal and Video Constraint Databases*. PhD thesis, University of Nebraska-Lincoln, 2000.

[77] R. Chen, M. Ouyang, and P. Revesz. Approximating data in constraint databases. In *Proc. Symposium on Abstraction, Reformulation and Approximation*, volume 1864 of *Lecture Notes in Computer Science*, pages 124–43. Springer, 2000.

[78] Y. Chen and P. Revesz. Querying spatiotemporal XML using DataFox. In *Proc. IEEE International Conference on Web Intelligence*, pages 301–9. IEEE Press, 2003.

[79] Y. Chen and P. Revesz. Max-count aggregation estimation for moving points. In *Proc. Eleventh International Symposium on Temporal Representation and Reasoning*, pages 103–8. IEEE Press, 2004.

[80] X. Cheng, G. Dong, T. Lau, and J. Su. Data integration by describing sources with constraint databases. In *IEEE International Conference on Data Engineering*, pages 374–381. IEEE Press, 1999.

[81] Y.-J. Choi and C.-W. Chung. Selectivity estimation for spatio-temporal queries to moving objects. In *Proc. ACM SIGMOD International Conference on Management of Data*. ACM Press, 2002.

[82] J. Chomicki, D. Q. Goldin, G. M. Kuper, and D. Toman. Variable independence in constraint databases. *IEEE Transactions on Knowledge and Data Engineering*, 15(6):1422–36, 2003.

[83] J. Chomicki, S. Haesevoets, B. Kuijpers, and P. Revesz. Classes of spatiotemporal objects and their closure properties. *Annals of Mathematics and Artificial Intelligence*, 39(4):431–461, 2003.

[84] J. Chomicki and T. Imielinski. Finite representation of infinite query answers. *ACM Transactions on Database Systems*, 18(2):181–223, 1993.

[85] J. Chomicki and G. Kuper. Measuring infinite relations. In *Proc. ACM Symposium on Principles of Database Systems*, pages 78–85. ACM Press, 1995.

[86] J. Chomicki, Y. Liu, and P. Revesz. Animating spatiotemporal constraint databases. In *Proc. Workshop on Spatio-Temporal Database Management*, volume 1678 of *Lecture Notes in Computer Science*, pages 224–41. Springer, 1999.

[87] J. Chomicki and P. Revesz. Constraint-based interoperability of spatiotemporal databases. In *Proc. 5th International Symposium on Spatial Databases*, volume 1262 of *Lecture Notes in Computer Science*, pages 142–61. Springer, 1997.

[88] J. Chomicki and P. Revesz. Constraint-based interoperability of spatiotemporal databases. *Geoinformatica*, 3(3):211–43, 1999.

[89] J. Chomicki and P. Revesz. A geometric framework for specifying spatiotemporal objects. In *Proc. International Symposium on Temporal Representation and Reasoning*, pages 41–6. IEEE Press, 1999.

[90] V. Chvatal. *Linear Programming*. W. H. Freeman, 1983.

[91] A. Cimatti, F. Giunchiglia, and M. Roveri. Abstraction in planning via model checking. In *Proc. Symposium on Abstraction, Reformulation and Approximation*, pages 37–41, 1998.

[92] E. M. Clarke, O. Grumberg, and D. A. Peled. *Model Checking*. MIT Press, 1999.

[93] A. Cobham. On the base-dependence of sets of numbers recognizable by finite automata. *Mathematical Systems Theory*, 3:186–92, 1969.

[94] E. F. Codd. A relational model for large shared data banks. *Communications of the ACM*, 13(6):377–87, 1970.

[95] G. E. Collins. Quantifier elimination for real closed fields by cylindrical algebraic decomposition. In H. Brakhage, editor, *Automata Theory and Formal Languages*, volume 33 of *Lecture Notes in Computer Science*, pages 134–83. Springer, 1975.

[96] L. Colussi, E. Marchiori, and M. Marchiori. On termination of constraint logic programs. In U. Montanari and F. Rossi, editors, *Proc. 1st International Conference on Principles and Practice of Constraint Programming*, volume 976 of *Lecture Notes in Computer Science*, pages 431–48. Springer, 1995.

[97] J. J. Comuzzi and J. M. Hart. Program slicing using weakest precondition. In *Proc. Industrial Benefit and Advances in Formal Methods*, volume 1051 of *Lecture Notes in Computer Science*. Springer, 1996.

[98] P. Cousot. Proving program invariance and termination by parametric abstraction, Langrangian relaxation and semidefinite programming. In *Proc. 6th International Conference on Verification, Model Checking, and Abstract Interpretation*, volume 3385 of *Lecture Notes in Computer Science*, pages 1–24. Springer, 2005.

[99] P. Cousot and R. Cousot. Abstract interpretation: A unified lattice model for static analysis of programs by construction or aproximation of fixpoints. In *Proc. ACM Principles on Programming Languages*, pages 238–252. ACM Press, 1977.

[100] P. Cousot and N. Halbwachs. Automatic discovery of linear restraints among variables of a program. In *Proc. ACM Principles on Programming Languages*, pages 84–97. ACM Press, 1978.

[101] J. Cox and K. McAloon. Decision procedures for constraint based extensions of datalog. In *Constraint Logic Programming*, pages 17–32. MIT Press, 1993.

[102] D. Cyganski and R. F. Vaz. A linear signal decomposition approach to affine invariant contour identification. *Pattern Recognition*, 28(12):1845–53, 1995.

[103] G. B. Dantzig. *Linear Programming and Extensions.* Princeton University Press, 1963.

[104] P. J. Davis. *Interpolation and Approximation.* Dover Publications, 1975.

[105] T. Dean and M. Boddy. Reasoning about partially ordered events. *Artificial Intelligence*, 36(3):375–99, 1988.

[106] R. Dechter. *Constraint Processing.* Morgan Kaufmann, 2003.

[107] R. Dechter, I. Meiri, and J. Pearl. Temporal constraint networks. *Artificial Intelligence*, 49(1–3):61–95, 1991.

[108] G. Delzanno and A. Podelski. Constraint-based deductive model checking. *International Journal on Software Tools for Technology Transfer*, 3(3):250–70, 2001.

[109] Y. Deng. *Similarity Queries for Linear Constraint Databases.* PhD thesis, University of Nebraska-Lincoln, 1999.

[110] B. Dent. *Cartography Thematic Map Design.* McGraw-Hill, 1999.

[111] A. Deutsch, M. Fernández, D. Florescu, A. Y. Levy, and D. Suciu. A query language for XML. *Computer Networks*, 31(11-16):1155–1169, 1999.

[112] A. Deutsch, M. Fernández, and D. Suciu. Storing semistructured data with STORED. In *Proc. ACM SIGMOD International Conference on Management of Data*, pages 431–442. ACM Press, 1999.

[113] C. V. Deutsch and A. G. Journel. *GSLIB: Geostatistical Software Library and User's Guide.* Oxford University Press, New York, 2nd edition, 1998.

[114] A. Di Deo and D. Boulanger. A formal background to build constraint objects. In *Proc. 4th International Database Engineering and Applications Symposium*, pages 7–15. IEEE Press, 2000.

[115] T. I. Dix and C. N. Yee. A restriction mapping engine using constraint logic programming. In *Proc. 2nd International Conference on Intelligent Systems for Molecular Biology*, pages 112–20. AAAI Press, 1994.

[116] J. A. Dougenik, N. R. Chrisman, and D. R. Niemeyer. An algorithm to construct continuous area cartograms. *Professional Geographer*, 37(1):75–81, 1985.

[117] F. Dumortier, M. Gyssens, L. Vandeurzen, and D. Van Gucht. On the decidability of semi-linearity for semi-algebraic sets and its implications for spatial databases. *Journal of Computer and System Sciences*, 58(3):535–71, 1999.

[118] F. Dumortier, M. Gyssens, L. Vandeurzen, and D. Van Gucht. On the decidability of semi-linearity for semi-algebraic sets and its implications for spatial databases—Corrigendum. *Journal of Computer and System Sciences*, 59(3):557–62, 1999.

[119] M. Egenhofer. Spatial SQL: A query and presentation language. *IEEE Transactions on Knowledge and Data Engineering*, 6(1):86–95, 1994.

[120] M. Egenhofer and R. Franzosa. Point-set topological spatial relations. *International Journal of Geographical Information Systems*, 5(2):161–74, 1991.

[121] M. Egenhofer and R. Franzosa. On the equivalence of topological relations. *International Journal of Geographical Information Systems*, 9(2):133–52, 1995.

[122] M. Egenhofer and D. Mark. Modeling conceptual neighborhoods of topological line-region relations. *International Journal of Geographical Information Systems*, 9(5):555–65, 1995.

[123] T. Eiter and G. Gottlob. On the complexity of propositional knowledge base revision, updates, and counterfactuals. *Artificial Intelligence*, 57(2–3):227–70, 1992.

[124] T. Eiter and H. Mannila. Distance measures for point sets and their computation. *Acta Informatica*, 34, 1997.

[125] M. Erwig, R. H. Güting, M. M. Schneider, and M. Vazirgiannis. Abstract and discrete modeling of spatio-temporal data types. *Geoinformatica*, 3(3):269–96, 1999.

[126] U. M. Fayyad, G. G. Grinstein, and A. Wierse, editors. *Information Visualization in Data Mining and Knowledge Discovery*. Morgan Kaufmann, 2001.

[127] M. Fernández, Y. Kadiyska, D. Suciu, A. Morishima, and W. C. Tan. SilkRoute: A framework for publishing relational data in xml. *ACM Transactions on Database Systems*, 27(4):438–493, 2002.

[128] J. Ferrante and J. R. Geiser. An efficient decision procedure for the theory of rational order. *Theoretical Computer Science*, 4:227–33, 1977.

[129] J. Ferrante and C. Rackoff. A decision procedure for the first order theory of real addition with order. *SIAM Journal of Computing*, 4(1):69–76, 1975.

[130] A. Finkel and Ph. Schnoebelen. Well-structured transition systems everywhere. *Theoretical Computer Science*, 256(1–2):63–92, 2001.

[131] T. R. Fleming and D. P. Harrington. *Counting Processes and Survival Analysis*. Wiley, New York, 1991.

[132] M. Flickner, H. Sawhney, W. Niblack, J. Ashley, Q. Huang, and B. Dom. Query by image and video content: The QBIC system. *IEEE Computer*, 28(9):23–32, 1995.

[133] R. B. Floyd and R. Beigel. *The Language of Machines: An Introduction to Computability and Formal Languages*. Computer Science Press, 1994.

[134] L. Forlizzi, R.H. Güting, E. Nardelli, and M. Schneider. A data model and data structure for moving object databases. In *Proc. ACM SIGMOD International Conference on Management of Data*, pages 319–30. ACM Press, 2000.

[135] J. B. J. Fourier. Solution d'une question particuliére du calcul des inégalités. *Nouveau Bulletin des Sciences par la Société philomathique de Paris*, pages 99–100, 1826.

[136] A. Fournier and D. Y. Montuno. Triangulating simple polygons and equivalent problems. *ACM Transactions on Graphics*, 3:153–74, 1984.

[137] A. Frank, S. Grumbach, and R. Guting et al. Chorochronos: A research network for spatiotemporal database systems. *SIGMOD Record*, 28(3):12–21, 1999.

[138] A. Frank and W. Kuhn. Specifying open GIS with functional languages. *Geomatica*, 49(3):411–36, 1995.

[139] A. U. Frank and M. Wallace. Constraint based modeling in a GIS: Road design as a case study. In *Proc. 12th Auto Carto Conference*, volume 4, pages 177–86, 1995.

[140] U. Frank, I. Campari, and U. Formentini. *Theories and Methods of Spatio-Temporal Reasoning in Geographic Space*. Springer, 1992.

[141] L. A. Freitag and C. O. Gooch. Tetrahedral mesh improvement using swapping and smoothing. *International Journal for Numerical Methods in Engineering*, 40:3979–4002, 1997.

[142] L. Fribourg and H. Olsén. A decompositional approach for computing least fixed-points of Datalog programs with Z-counters. *Constraints*, 2(3–4):305–36, 1997.

[143] L. Fribourg and J. D. C. Richardson. Symbolic verification with gap-order constraints. In *Proc. Logic Program Synthesis and Transformation*, volume 1207 of *Lecture Notes in Computer Science*, pages 20–37. Springer, 1996.

[144] F. Geerts and B. Kuijpers. On the decidability of termination of query evaluation in transitive-closure logics for polynomial constraint databases. *Theoretical Computer Science*, 336(1):125–151, 2005.

[145] F. Geerts, B. Kuijpers, and J. Van den Bussche. Topological canonization of planar spatial data and its incremental maintenance. In K.-D. Schewe, editor, *Proc. 7th International Workshop on Foundations of Models and Languages for Data and Objects*. Kluwer, 1998.

[146] F. Geerts, B. Kuijpers, and J. Van den Bussche. Linearization and completeness results for terminating transitive closure queries on spatial databases. *SIAM Journal of Computing*, 35(6):1386–1439, 2006.

[147] I. Geist. A framework for data mining and KDD. In H. Haddad and G. Papadopoulos, editors, *Proc. ACM Symposium on Applied Computing*, pages 508–13, New York, 2002. ACM Press.

[148] A. Van Gelder. The well-founded semantics of aggregation. In *Proc. ACM Symposium on Principles of Database Systems*, pages 127–38. ACM Press, 1992.

[149] C. Gervet. Interval propagation to reason about sets: Definition and implementation of a practical language. *Constraints*, 1(3):191–244, 1997.

[150] R. Giacobazzi, S. K. Debray, and G. Levi. Generalized semantics and abstract interpretation for constraint logic programs. *Journal of Logic Programming*, 25(3):191–247, 1995.

[151] W. Gillett, L. Hanks, G. K-S. Wong, J. Yu, R. Lim, and M. V. Olson. Assembly of high-resolution restriction maps based on multiple complete digests of a redundant set of overlapping clones. *Genomics*, 33:389–408, 1996.

[152] P. Godefroid, M. Huth, and R. Jagadeesan. Abstraction-based model checking using modal transition systems. In *12th International Conference on Concurrency Theory*, pages 426–440, 2001.

[153] C. H. Goh, S. Bressan, S. E. Madnick, and M. Siegel. Context interchange: New features and formalisms for the intelligent integration of information. *Transactions on Information Systems*, 17(3):270–293, 1999.

[154] D. Goldin and P. C. Kanellakis. On similarity queries for time-series data: Constraint specification and implementation. In U. Montanari and F. Rossi, editors, *Proc. 1st International Conference on Principles and Practice of Constraint Programming*, volume 976 of *Lecture Notes in Computer Science*, pages 137–53. Springer, 1995.

[155] D. Goldin and P. C. Kanellakis. Constraint query algebras. *Constraints*, 1:45–83, 1996.

[156] J. Goldstein, R. Ramakrishnan, U. Shaft, and J-B. Yu. Processing queries by linear constraints. In *Proc. ACM Symposium on Principles of Database Systems*, pages 257–67, 1997.

[157] M. T. Gómez-López, R. Ceballos, R. M. Gasca, and C. Del Valle. Developing a labelled object-relational constraint database architecture for the projection operator. *Data and Knowledge Engineering*, 68(1):146–172, 2009.

[158] P. P. Goncalves and P. M. Diogo. Geographic information systems and cellular automata: A new approach to forest fire simulation. In *Proc. 5th European Conference and Exhibition on Geographic Information Systems*, pages 702–12, 1994.

[159] J. E. Goodman and J. O'Rourke, editors. *Handbook of Discrete and Computational Geometry*. CRC Press, Boca Raton, New York, 1997.

[160] S. Graf and H. Saidi. Constructing abstract graphs using PVS. In *Proc. Computer-Aided Verification*, volume 1102 of *Lecture Notes in Computer Science*. Springer, 1996.

[161] G. Grahne. *The Problem of Incomplete Information in Relational Databases*, volume 554 of *Lecture Notes in Computer Science*. Springer, 1991.

[162] G. Grahne, A. O. Mendelzon, and P. Revesz. Knowledgebase transformations. *Journal of Computer and System Sciences*, 54(1):98–112, 1997.

[163] E. D. Green and P. Green. Sequence-tagged site (STS) content mapping of human chromosomes: Theoretical considerations and early experiences. *PCR Methods and Applications*, 1:77–90, 1991.

[164] M. Grigni, D. Papadias, and C. H. Papadimitriou. Topological inference. In *International Joint Conference on Artificial Intelligence*, pages 901–6, 1995.

[165] R. Grimson and B. Kuijpers. Some lower bounds for the complexity of the linear programming feasibility problem over the reals. *J. Complexity*, 25(1):25–37, 2009.

[166] S. Grumbach and G. Kuper. Tractable recursion over geometric data. In *International Conference on Constraint Programming*, volume 1330 of *Lecture Notes in Computer Science*, pages 450–62. Springer, 1997.

[167] S. Grumbach and Z. Lacroix. Computing queries on linear constraint databases. In *5th International Workshop on Database Programming Languages*, Electronic Workshops in Computing. Springer, 1995.

[168] S. Grumbach, P. Rigaux, and L. Segoufin. The DEDALE system for complex spatial queries. In *Proc. ACM SIGMOD International Conference on Management of Data*, pages 213–24, 1998.

[169] S. Grumbach, P. Rigaux, and L. Segoufin. Spatio-temporal data handling with constraints. In *ACM Symposium on Geographic Information Systems*, pages 106–11, 1998.

[170] S. Grumbach, P. Rigaux, and L. Segoufin. Manipulating interpolated data is easier than you thought. In *Proc. IEEE International Conference on Very Large Databases*, pages 156–65, 2000.

[171] S. Grumbach and J. Su. First-order definability over constraint databases. In U. Montanari and F. Rossi, editors, *Proc. 1st International Conference on Principles and Practice of Constraint Programming*, volume 976 of *Lecture Notes in Computer Science*, pages 121–36. Springer, 1995.

[172] S. Grumbach and J. Su. Finitely representable databases. *Journal of Computer and System Sciences*, 55(2):273–98, 1997.

[173] S. Grumbach and J. Su. Queries with arithmetical constraints. *Theoretical Computer Science*, 173(1):151–81, 1997.

[174] S. Grumbach, J. Su, and C. Tollu. Linear constraint query languages: Expressive power and complexity. In D. Leivant, editor, *Logic and Computational Complexity*, volume 960 of *Lecture Notes in Computer Science*, pages 426–46. Springer, 1995.

[175] P. Gundavarapu. Implementation of a refinement query system. Master's thesis, University of Nebraska-Lincoln, August 1998.

[176] O. Günther. *Efficient Structures for Geometric Data Management*, volume 337 of *Lecture Notes in Computer Science*. Springer, Berlin, 1988.

[177] S. M. Gusein-Zade and V. S. Tikunov. A new technique for constructing continuous cartograms. *Geography and Geographic Information Systems*, 20(3):167–73, 1993.

[178] R. Güting and M. Schneider. *Moving Objects Databases*. Morgan Kaufmann, 2005.

[179] A. Guttman. R-trees: A dynamic index structure for spatial searching. In *Proc. ACM-SIGMOD Conference on Management of Data*, pages 47–57, 1984.

[180] M. Gyssens, J. Van den Bussche, and D. Van Gucht. Complete geometric query languages. *Journal of Computer and System Sciences*, 58(3):483–511, 1999.

[181] S. Haesevoets and B. Kuijpers. Closure properties of classes of spatio-temporal objects under Boolean set operations. In *Proc. International Workshop on Time Representation and Reasoning*, pages 79–86, 2000.

[182] S. Haesevoets and B. Kuijpers. Time-dependent affine triangulation of spatio-temporal data. In D. Pfoser, I. F. Cruz, and M. Ronthaler, editors, *ACM Symposium on Geographic Information Systems*, pages 57–66. ACM Press, 2004.

[183] S. Haesevoets, B. Kuijpers, and P. Revesz. Efficient affine-invariant similarity retrieval. In *Proc. Second International Conference on Geometric Modeling and Imaging*, pages 99–108. IEEE Press, 2007.

[184] M. Hagedoorn and R. C. Veltkamp. Reliable and efficient pattern matching using an affine invariant metric. *International Journal of Computer Vision*, 31:203–25, 1999.

[185] S. L. Hakimi and E. F. Schmeichel. Fitting polygonal functions to a set of points in the plane. *Computer Vision, Graphics, and Image Processing*, 52(2):132–6, 1991.

[186] N. Halbwachs. Delay analysis in synchronous programs. In *Proc. International Conference on Computer-Aided Verification*, volume 697 of *Lecture Notes in Computer Science*, pages 333–46. Springer, 1993.

[187] A. Y. Halevy, N. Ashish, D. Bitton, M. J. Carey, D. Draper, J. Pollock, A. Rosenthal, and V. Sikka. Enterprise information integration: Successes, challenges and controversies. In *ACM SIGMOD International Conference on Management of Data*, pages 778–787, 2005.

[188] P. Halmos. *Lectures on Boolean Algebras*. Springer, 1974.

[189] J. Han and M. Kamber. *Data Mining: Concepts and Techniques*. Morgan Kaufmann, 2nd edition, 2006.

[190] J. W. Harbaugh and F. W. Preston. *Fourier Analysis in Geology*, pages 218–238. Prentice-Hall, Englewood Cliffs, 1968.

[191] E. Harley, A. J. Bonner, and N. Goodman. Uniform integration of genome mapping data using intersection graphs. *Bioinformatics*, 17(6):487–494, 2001.

[192] W. Harvey and P. Stuckey. A unit two variable per inequality integer constraint solver for constraint logic programming. In *Proc. Australian Computer Science Conference*, pages 102–11. Australian Computer Science Communications, 1997.

[193] K. Havelund, M. R. Lowry, and J. Penix. Formal analysis of a spacecraft controller using spin. *IEEE Transactions on Software Engineering*, 27(8):749–765, 2001.

[194] N. Heintze and J. Jaffar. Set constraints and set-based analysis. In A. Borning, editor, *Proc. 2nd International Workshop on Principles and Practice of Constraint Programming*, volume 874 of *Lecture Notes in Computer Science*, pages 1–17. Springer, 1994.

[195] R. Helm, K. Marriott, and M. Odersky. Spatial query optimization: From Boolean constraints to range queries. *Journal of Computer and System Sciences*, 51(2):197–201, 1995.

[196] T. A. Henzinger, P.-H. Ho, and H. Wong-Toi. HyTech: A model checker for hybrid systems. In *Proc. Conference Computer-Aided Verification*, number 1254 in Lecture Notes in Computer Science, pages 460–63. Springer, 1997.

[197] M. J. Hernandez. *Database Design for Mere Mortals*. Addison-Wesley, 2nd edition, 2003.

[198] D. S. Hochbaum and J. Naor. Simple and fast algorithms for linear and integer programs with two variables per inequality. *SIAM Journal of Computing*, 23(6):1179–92, 1994.

[199] D. H. House and C. J. Kocmoud. Continuous cartogram construction. In D. Ebert, H. Hagen, and H. Rushmeier, editors, *Proc. IEEE Visualization Conference*, pages 197–204. IEEE Press, 1998.

[200] D. P. Huttenlocher, G. A. Klauderman, and W. J. Rucklidge. Comparing images using the Hausdorff-distance. *IEEE Transactions on Pattern Analysis and Machine Intelligence*, 15:850–63, 1993.

[201] O. H. Ibarra and J. Su. A technique for proving decidability of containment and equivalence of linear constraint queries. *Journal of Computer and System Sciences*, 59(1):1–28, 1999.

[202] T. Imielinski. Incomplete information in logical databases. *Data Engineering*, 12(2):29–39, 1989.

[203] T. Imielinski and W. Lipski. Incomplete information in relational databases. *Journal of the ACM*, 31(4):761–91, 1984.

[204] N. Immerman. Relational queries computable in polynomial time. *Information and Control*, 68:86–104, 1986.

[205] J. Jaffar and J. L. Lassez. Constraint logic programming. In *Proc. 14th ACM Symposium on Principles of Programming Languages*, pages 111–9. ACM Press, 1987.

[206] J. Jaffar, M. J. Maher, P. Stuckey, and R. H. Yap. Beyond finite domains. In A. Borning, editor, *Proc. 2nd International Workshop on Principles and Practice of Constraint Programming*, volume 874 of *Lecture Notes in Computer Science*, pages 86–94. Springer, 1994.

[207] J. Jaffar, S. Michaylov, P. J. Stuckey, and R. H. Yap. The CLP(R) language and system. *ACM Transactions on Programming Languages and Systems*, 14(3):339–95, 1992.

[208] H. V. Jagadish. A retrieval technique for similar shapes. In *Proc. ACM SIGMOD International Conference on Management of Data*, pages 208–17. ACM Press, 1991.

[209] P. Jancar. Bouziane's transformation of the Petri net reachability problem and incorrectness of the related algorithm. *Information and Computation*, 206(11):1259–1263, 2008.

[210] P. Jeavons, D. Cohen, and M. Gyssens. How to determine the expressive power of constraints. *Constraints*, 4(2):113–31, 1999.

[211] C. S. Jensen, M. D. Soo, and R. T. Snodgrass. Unifying temporal data models via a conceptual model. *Information Systems*, 19(7):513–547, 1994.

[212] T. Johnson, L. V. S. Lakshmanan, and R. T. Ng. The 3W model and algebra for unified data mining. In *Proc. IEEE International Conference on Very Large Databases*, pages 21–32. Morgan Kaufmann, 2000.

[213] F. Kabanza, J.-M. Stevenne, and P. Wolper. Handling infinite temporal data. *Journal of Computer and System Sciences*, 51(1):1–25, 1995.

[214] P. C. Kanellakis, G. M. Kuper, and P. Revesz. Constraint query languages. In *Proc. ACM Symposium on Principles of Database Systems*, pages 299–313. ACM Press, 1990.

[215] P. C. Kanellakis, G. M. Kuper, and P. Revesz. Constraint query languages. *Journal of Computer and System Sciences*, 51(1):26–52, 1995.

[216] P. C. Kanellakis, S. Ramaswamy, D. E. Vengroff, and J. S. Vitter. Indexing for data models with constraints and classes. *Journal of Computer and System Sciences*, 52(3):589–612, 1996.

[217] P. C. Kanellakis and P. Revesz. On the relationship of congruence closure and unification. *Journal of Symbolic Computation*, 7(3-4): 427–44, 1989.

[218] P. Kanjamala, P. Revesz, and Y. Wang. MLPQ/GIS: A GIS using linear constraint databases. In C. S. R. Prabhu, editor, *Proc. 9th COMAD International Conference on Management of Data*, pages 389–93. McGraw Hill, 1998.

[219] N. K. Karmarkar. A new polynomial-time algorithm for linear programming. *Combinatorica*, 4:373–95, 1984.

[220] R. M. Karp. Mapping the genome: Some combinatorial problems arising in molecular biology. In *Proc. 25th ACM Symposium on Theory of Computing*, pages 278–85. ACM Press, 1993.

[221] H. Katsuno and A. O. Mendelzon. A unified view of propositional knowledge base updates. In *Proc. 11th International Joint Conference on Artificial Intelligence*, pages 1413–19. Morgan Kaufmann, 1989.

[222] H. Katsuno and A. O. Mendelzon. On the difference between updating a knowledge base and revising it. In *Proc. 2nd International Conference on Principles of Knowledge Representation and Reasoning*, pages 387–94. Morgan Kaufmann, 1991.

[223] H. Katsuno and A. O. Mendelzon. Propositional knowledge base revision and minimal change. *Artificial Intelligence*, 52:263–94, 1991.

[224] H. Katsuno and A. O. Mendelzon. On the difference between updating a knowledge base and revising it. In *Belief Revision*, pages 183–203. Cambridge University Press, 1992.

[225] A. Kemper and M. Wallrath. An analysis of geometric modeling in database systems. *ACM Computing Surveys*, 19(1):47–91, 1987.

[226] A. Kerbrat. Reachable state space analysis of lotos specifications. In *Proc. 7th International Conference on For Description Techniques*, pages 161–76. Chapman & Hall, 1994.

[227] L. G. Khachiyan. A polynomial algorithm in linear programming. *Doklady Akademii Nauk SSR*, 20:191–4, 1979.

[228] W. Kim, I. Choi, S. Gala, and M. Scheevel. On resolving semantic heterogeneity in multidatabase systems. In W. Kim, editor, *Modern Database Systems: The Object Model, Interoperability, and Beyond*, pages 521–50. ACM Press, 1995.

[229] P. Kolaitis and C. H. Papadimitriou. Why not negation by fixpoint? *Journal of Computer and System Sciences*, 43(1):125–44, 1991.

[230] P. Kolaitis and M. Vardi. Conjunctive-query containment and constraint satisfaction. *Journal of Computer and System Sciences*, 61(2):302–32, 2000.

[231] G. Kollios, D. Gunopulos, and V. J. Tsotras. On indexing mobile objects. In *Proc. ACM Symposium on Principles of Database Systems*, pages 261–72. ACM Press, 1999.

[232] C. P. Kolovson, M-A. Neimat, and S. Potamianos. Interoperability of spatial and attribute data managers: A case study. In *International Symposium on Large Spatial Databases*, volume 692 of *Lecture Notes in Computer Science*, pages 239–64. Springer, 1993.

[233] R. Kosaraju. Decidability of reachability in vector addition systems. In *Proc. 14th Annual ACM Symposium on Theory of Computing*, pages 267–80. ACM Press, 1982.

[234] M. Koubarakis. Representation and querying in temporal databases: The power of temporal constraints. In *Proc. 9th International Conference on Data Engineering*, pages 327–34. IEEE Computer Society, 1993.

[235] M. Koubarakis. Complexity results for first-order theories of temporal constraints. In *Principles of Knowledge Representation and Reasoning: Proc. 4th International Conference*, pages 379–90. Morgan Kaufmann, 1994.

[236] M. Koubarakis. Database models for infinite and indefinite temporal information. *Information Systems*, 19(2):141–73, 1994.

[237] M. Koubarakis. Foundations of indefinite constraint databases. In A. Borning, editor, *Proc. 2nd International Workshop on the Principles and Practice of Constraint Programming*, volume 874 of *Lecture Notes in Computer Science*, pages 266–80. Springer, 1994.

[238] M. Koubarakis. The complexity of query evaluation in indefinite temporal constraint databases. *Theoretical Computer Science*, 171(1–2):25–60, 1997.

[239] M. Koubarakis. From local to global consistency in temporal constraint networks. *Theoretical Computer Science*, 173:89–112, February 1997.

[240] M. Koubarakis and S. Skiadopoulos. Querying temporal and spatial constraint networks in PTIME. *Artificial Intelligence*, 123(1–2): 223–63, 2000.

[241] D. Kozen. Complexity of Boolean algebras. *Theoretical Computer Science*, 10:221–47, 1980.

[242] S. Kreutzer. Fixed-point query languages for linear constraint database. In *Proc. ACM Symposium on Principles of Database Systems*, pages 116–25. ACM Press, 2000.

[243] S. Kreutzer. Query languages for constraint databases: First-order logic, fixed-points, and convex hulls. In *International Conference on Database Theory*, volume 1973 of *Lecture Notes in Computer Science*, pages 248–62. Springer, 2001.

[244] D. G. Krige. A statistical approach to some mine valuations and allied problems at the witwatersrand. Master's thesis, University of Witwatersrand, South Africa, 1951.

[245] B. Kuijpers. *Topological Properties of Spatial Databases in the Polynomial Constraint Model*. PhD thesis, University of Antwerp, 1998.

[246] B. Kuijpers and J. Van den Bussche. On capturing first-order topological properties of planar spatial databases. In C. Beeri and P. Buneman, editors, *International Conference on Database Theory*, volume 1540 of *Lecture Notes in Computer Science*, pages 187–98. Springer, 1999.

[247] B. Kuijpers, J. Paredaens, M. Smits, and J. Van den Bussche. Termination properties of spatial datalog programs. In D. Pedreschi and C. Zaniolo, editors, *Proc. Logic in Databases*, volume 1154 of *Lecture Notes in Computer Science*, pages 101–16. Springer, 1996.

[248] B. Kuijpers and M. Smits. On expressing topological connectivity in spatial datalog. In V. Gaede, A. Brodsky, O. Gunter, D. Srivastava, V. Vianu, and M. Wallace, editors, *Proc. Workshop on Constraint Databases and Their Applications*, volume 1191 of *Lecture Notes in Computer Science*, pages 116–33. Springer, 1997.

[249] V. Kuncak, H. H. Nguyen, and M. C. Rinard. An algorithm for deciding bapa: Boolean algebra with presburger arithmetic. In *Proc. 20th International Conference on Automated Deduction*, volume 3632 of *Lecture Notes in Computer Science*, pages 260–277. Springer, 2005.

[250] G. M. Kuper. On the expressive power of the relational calculus with arithmetic constraints. In *International Conference on Database Theory*, volume 470 of *Lecture Notes in Computer Science*, pages 202–14. Springer, 1990.

[251] G. M. Kuper, L. Libkin, and J. Paredaens, editors. *Constraint Databases*. Springer, 2000.

[252] G. M. Kuper and J. Su. A representation independent language for planar spatial databases with Euclidean distance. *Journal of Computer and System Sciences*, 73(6):845–874, 2007.

[253] L. V. S. Lakshmanan, C. K. S. Leung, and R. T. Ng. Efficient dynamic mining of constrained frequent sets. *ACM Transactions on Database Systems*, 28(4):337–389, 2003.

[254] Y. Lamdan, J. T. Schwartz, and H. J. Wolfson. Affine invariant model-based object recognition. *IEEE Journal of Robotics and Automation*, 6:578–89, 1990.

[255] E. S. Lander and M. S. Waterman. Genomic mapping by fingerprinting random clones: A mathematical analysis. *Genomics*, 2:231–9, 1988.

[256] G. Langran and R. N Chrisman. A framework for temporal geographic information. *Cartographica*, 25(3):1–14, 1988.

[257] C. Lassez and J-L. Lassez. Quantifier elimination for conjunctions of linear constraints via a convex hull algorithm. In *Symbolic and Numerical Computation for Artificial Intelligence*, pages 103–19. Academic Press, 1992.

[258] J-L. Lassez, T. Huynh, and K. McAloon. Simplification and elimination of redundant linear arithmetic constraints. In E. L. Lusk and R. A. Overbeek, editors, *Proc. North American Conference on Logic Programming*, pages 35–51. MIT Press, 1989.

[259] J-L. Lassez and M. Maher. On Fourier's algorithm for linear constraints. *Journal of Automated Reasoning*, 9(3):373–9, 1992.

[260] R. Laurini and D. Thompson. *Fundamentals of Spatial Information Systems*. Academic Press, 1992.

[261] H. J. Levesque. Foundations of a functional approach to knowledge representation. *Artificial Intelligence*, 23:155–212, 1984.

[262] J. Li, R. M. Narayanan, and P. Revesz. A shape-based approach to shape detection. In C. H. Chen, editor, *Frontiers of Remote Sensing Information Processing*, pages 63–86. World Scientific Publishing, 2003.

[263] L. Li and P. Revesz. Interpolation methods for spatiotemporal geographic data. *Journal of Computers, Environment, and Urban Systems*, 28(3):201–27, 2004.

[264] N. Li and J. C. Mitchell. Datalog with constraints: A foundation for trust management languages. volume 2562 of *Lecture Notes in Computer Science*, pages 58–73. Springer, 2003.

[265] B. Louie, P. Mork, F. Martín-Sánchez, A. Y. Halevy, and P. Tarczy-Hornoch. Data integration and genomic medicine. *Journal of Biomedical Informatics*, 40(1):5–16, 2007.

[266] K. Marriott and M. Odersky. Negative Boolean constraints. *Theoretical Computer Science*, 160(1–2):365–80, 1996.

[267] K. Marriott and P. J. Stuckey. *Programming with Constraints: An Introduction*. MIT Press, 1998.

[268] U. Martin and T. Nipkow. Boolean unification—The story so far. *Journal of Symbolic Computation*, 7:275–93, 1989.

[269] Y. Matiyasevich. Enumerable sets are diophantine. *Doklady Akademii Nauk SSR*, 191:279–82, 1970.

[270] W. May. Xpath-logic and xpathlog: A logic-programming-style XML data manipulation language. *Theory and Practice of Logic Programming*, 4(3):239–287, 2004.

[271] E. Mayr. An algorithm for the general Petri net reachability problem. *SIAM Journal of Computing*, 13(3):441–60, 1984.

[272] K. McMillan. *Symbolic Model Checking*. Kluwer, 1993.

[273] N. Megiddo. Linear programming in linear time when the dimension is fixed. *Journal of the ACM*, 31(1):114–27, 1984.

[274] R. Mehrotra and W. I. Grosky. Shape matching utilizing indexed hypotheses generation and testing. *IEEE Transactions on Robotics and Automation*, 5(1):70–7, 1989.

[275] S. Michaylov. *Design and Implementation of Practical Constraint Programming Systems*. PhD thesis, Carnegie-Mellon University, 1992.

[276] A. Miné. The octagon abstract domain. In *Proc. Analysis, Slicing and Transformation*, pages 310–319. IEEE Press, 2001.

[277] A. Miné. The octagon abstract domain. *Higher-Order and Symbolic Computation*, 19(1):31–100, 2006.

[278] M. L. Minsky. Recursive unsolvability of Post's problem of "tag" and other topics in the theory of Turing machines. *Annals of Mathematics*, 74(3):437–55, 1961.

[279] M. L. Minsky. *Computation: Finite and Infinite Machines*. Prentice Hall, 1967.

[280] F. Mokhtarian and S. Abbasi. Affine curvature scale space with affine length parametrisation. *Pattern Analysis and Applications*, 4(1):1–8, 2001.

[281] F. Mokhtarian and S. Abbasi. Shape similarity retrieval under affine transforms. *Pattern Recognition*, 35(1):31–41, 2002.

[282] B. Momjian. *PostgreSQL: Introduction and Concepts*. Addison-Wesley, 2000.

[283] S. Morehouse. ARC/INFO: A geo-relational model for spatial information. In *Proc. International Symposium on Computer Assisted Cartography*, pages 388–97, 1985.

[284] S. Morehouse. The architecture of ARC/INFO. In *Proc. 9th Auto Carto Conference*, pages 266–77, 1989.

[285] J. R. Norris. *Markov Chains*. Cambridge University Press, 1997.

[286] H. J. Ohlbach and J. Koehler. *How to extend a formal system with a Boolean algebra operator*, pages 57–75. Kluwer Academic Publisher, 1998.

[287] H. J. Ohlbach and J. Koehler. Modal logics, description logics, and arithmetic reasoning. *Journal of Artificial Intelligence*, 109(1-2):1–31, 1999.

[288] M. V. Olson, J. E. Dutchik, M. Y. Graham, G. M. Brodeur, C. Helms, M. Frank, M. MacCollin, R. Scheinman, and T. Frank. Random-clone strategy for genomic restriction mapping in yeast. *Genomics*, 83:7826–30, 1986.

[289] P. E. O'Neil and E. J. O'Neil. *Database: Principles, Programming, and Performance*. Morgan Kaufmann, 2nd edition, 2000.

[290] B. C. Ooi. *Efficient Query Processing in a Geographic Information System*, volume 471 of *Lecture Notes in Computer Science*. Springer, 1990.

[291] M. Otto and J. Van den Bussche. First-order queries on databases embedded in an infinite structure. *Information Processing Letters*, 60:37–41, 1996.

[292] M. Ouyang. *Efficient Visualization and Querying of Geographic Databases*. PhD thesis, University of Nebraska-Lincoln, 2000.

[293] M. Ouyang and P. Revesz. Algorithms for cartogram animation. In *Proc. 4th International Database Engineering and Applications Symposium*, pages 231–5. IEEE Press, 2000.

[294] Mark H. Overmars. *The Design of Dynamic Data Structures*, volume 156 of *Lecture Notes in Computer Science*. Springer, 1983.

[295] M. T. Özsu and L. Liu, editors. *Encyclopedia of Database Systems*. Springer, 2009.

[296] A. Paoluzzi, F. Bernardini, C. Cattani, and V. Ferrucci. Dimension-independent modeling with simplicial complexes. *ACM Transactions on Graphics*, 12:56–102, 1993.

[297] C. H. Papadimitriou. *Computational Complexity*. Addison-Wesley, 1994.

[298] C. H. Papadimitriou, D. Suciu, and V. Vianu. Topological queries in spatial databases. *Journal of Computer and System Sciences*, 58(1):29–53, 1999.

[299] J. Paredaens, J. Van den Bussche, and D. Van Gucht. Towards a theory of spatial database queries. In *Proc. ACM Symposium on Principles of Database Systems*, pages 279–88. ACM Press, 1994.

[300] J. Paredaens, J. Van den Bussche, and D. Van Gucht. First-order queries on finite structures over the reals. *SIAM Journal of Computing*, 27(6):1747–63, 1998.

[301] J. Paredaens, B. Kuijpers, and J. Van den Bussche. On topological elementary equivalence of spatial databases. In *International Conference on Database Theory*, volume 1186 of *Lecture Notes in Computer Science*, pages 432–46. Springer, 1997.

[302] J. Paredaens, B. Kuijpers, G. Kuper, and L. Vandeurzen. Euclid, Tarski and Engeler encompassed. In S. Cluet and R. Hull, editors, *Proc. 6th International Workshop on Database Programming Languages*, volume 1369 of *Lecture Notes in Computer Science*, pages 1–24. Springer, 1998.

[303] A. Pentland, R. Picard, and S. Sclaroff. Photobook: Content-based manipulation of image databases. *International Journal of Computer Vision*, 18(3):233–54, 1996.

[304] J. Peterson. *Petri Net Theory and Modeling of Systems*. Prentice-Hall, 1981.

[305] E. G. M. Petrakis and C. Faloutsos. Similarity searching in large image databases. *IEEE Transactions on Knowledge and Data Engineering*, 9(3):435–47, 1997.

[306] D. J. Peuquet and N. Duan. An event-based spatiotemporal data model (ESTDM) for temporal analysis of geographical data. *International Journal of Geographical Information Systems*, 9(1):7–24, 1995.

[307] D. J. Peuquet and D. F. Marble. ARC/INFO: An example of a contemporary geographic information system. In D. J. Peuquet and D. F. Marble, editors, *Introductory Readings in Geographic Information Systems*. Taylor & Francis, 1990.

[308] V. Pratt. Two easy theories whose combination is hard. *MIT Technical Report*, 1977.

[309] F. P. Preparata and M. I. Shamos. *Computational Geometry: An Introduction*. Springer, 1985.

[310] M. Presburger. Über die vollständigkeit eines gewissen systems der arithmetik ganzer zahlen, in welchem die addition als einzige operation hervortritt. In *Comptes Rendus, I. Congrès des Math. des Pays Slaves*, pages 192–201, 1929.

[311] X. Qian and T. F. Lunt. A semantic framework of the multilevel secure relational model. *IEEE Transactions on Knowledge and Data Engineering*, 9(2):292–301, 1997.

[312] J.R. Quinlan. Induction of decision trees. *Machine Learning*, 1(1): 81–106, 1986.

[313] R. Ramakrishnan. *Database Management Systems*. McGraw-Hill, 1998.

[314] R. Ramakrishnan and D. Srivastava. Pushing constraint selections. *Journal of Logic Programming*, 16(3&4):361–414, 1993.

[315] S. Ramaswamy. Efficient indexing for constraint and temporal databases. In *International Conference on Database Theory*, volume 1186 of *Lecture Notes in Computer Science*, pages 419–31. Springer, 1997.

[316] S. Ramaswamy and S. Subramanian. Path caching: A technique for optimal external searching. In *Proc. ACM Symposium on Principles of Database Systems*, pages 25–35. ACM Press, 1994.

[317] S. Ravela. Shaping receptive fields for affine invariance. In *Proc. Conference on Computer Vision and Pattern Recognition*, pages 725–730. IEEE Press, 2004.

[318] W. Reisig. *Petri Nets: An Introduction*. Springer, 1985.

[319] R. Reiter. Towards a logical reconstruction of relational database theory. In M. Brodie, J. Mylopoulos, and J. Schmidt, editors, *On Conceptual Modelling: Perspectives from Artificial Intelligence, Databases and Programming Languages*, pages 191–233. Springer, 1984.

[320] R. Reiter. A sound and sometimes complete query evaluation algorithm for relational databases with null values. *Journal of the ACM*, 33(2):349–70, 1986.

[321] R. Reiter. On specifying database updates. *Journal of Logic Programming*, 25(1):53–91, 1995.

[322] J. Renegar. On the computational complexity and geometry of the first-order theory of the reals. *Journal of Symbolic Computation*, 13(3):255–352, 1992.

[323] P. Revesz. A closed form for Datalog queries with integer order. In *International Conference on Database Theory*, volume 470 of *Lecture Notes in Computer Science*, pages 187–201. Springer, 1990.

[324] P. Revesz. *Constraint Query Languages*. PhD thesis, Brown University, 1991.

[325] P. Revesz. A closed-form evaluation for Datalog queries with integer (gap)-order constraints. *Theoretical Computer Science*, 116(1): 117–49, 1993.

[326] P. Revesz. Datalog queries of set constraint databases. In G. Gottlob and M. Y. Vardi, editors, *International Conference on Database Theory*, volume 893 of *Lecture Notes in Computer Science*, pages 425–38. Springer, 1995.

[327] P. Revesz. Safe stratified Datalog with integer order programs. In *Proc. 1st International Conference on Principles and Practice of Constraint Programming*, volume 976 of *Lecture Notes in Computer Science*, pages 154–69. Springer, 1995.

[328] P. Revesz. Model-theoretic minimal change operators for constraint databases. In *International Conference on Database Theory*, volume 1186 of *Lecture Notes in Computer Science*, pages 447–60. Springer, 1997.

[329] P. Revesz. On the semantics of arbitration. *International Journal of Algebra and Computation*, 7(2):133–60, 1997.

[330] P. Revesz. Problem solving in the DISCO constraint database system. In *Proc. Constraint Databases and Applications*, volume 1191 of *Lecture Notes in Computer Science*, pages 302–15. Springer, 1997.

[331] P. Revesz. Refining restriction enzyme genome maps. *Constraints*, 2(3–4):361–75, 1997.

[332] P. Revesz. Constraint databases: A survey. In L. Libkin and B. Thalheim, editors, *Semantics in Databases*, volume 1358 of *Lecture Notes in Computer Science*, pages 209–46. Springer, 1998.

[333] P. Revesz. The evaluation and the computational complexity of Datalog queries of Boolean constraint databases. *International Journal of Algebra and Computation*, 8(5):472–98, 1998.

[334] P. Revesz. Safe Datalog queries with linear constraints. In *Proc. 4th International Conference on Principles and Practice of Constraint Programming*, volume 1520 of *Lecture Notes in Computer Science*, pages 355–69. Springer, 1998.

[335] P. Revesz. Safe query languages for constraint databases. *ACM Transactions on Database Systems*, 23(1):58–99, 1998.

[336] P. Revesz. Datalog programs with difference constraints. In *Proc. 12th International Conference on Applications of Prolog*, pages 69–76. Japanese Computer Society Press, 1999.

[337] P. Revesz. The dominating cycle problem in 2-connected graphs and the matching problem for bag of bags are NP-complete. In *Proc. International Conference on Paul Erdős and His Mathematics*, pages 221–5. DICO Publishing, 1999.

[338] P. Revesz. Reformulation and approximation in model checking. In *Proc. 4th International Symposium on Abstraction, Reformulation, and Approximation*, volume 1864 of *Lecture Notes in Computer Science*, pages 124–43. Springer, 2000.

[339] P. Revesz. *Introduction to Constraint Databases.* Springer, 2002.

[340] P. Revesz. A retrospective on constraint databases. In D. Q. Goldin, A. A. Shvartsman, S. A. Smolka, J. S. Vitter, and S. B. Zdonik, editors, *Principles of Computing & Knowledge: Paris C. Kanellakis Memorial Workshop*, pages 12–27, 2003.

[341] P. Revesz. Quantifier-elimination for the first-order theory of Boolean algebras with linear cardinality constraints. In *Proc. 8th Conference on Advances in Databases and Information Systems*, volume 3255 of *Lecture Notes in Computer Science*, pages 1–21. Springer, 2004.

[342] P. Revesz. Efficient rectangle indexing algorithms based on point dominance. In *Proc. 12th International Symposium on Temporal Representation and Reasoning*, pages 210–12. IEEE Press, 2005.

[343] P. Revesz. The expressivity of constraint query languages with Boolean algebra linear cardinality constraints. In *Proc. 9th Conference on Advances in Databases and Information Systems*, volume 3631 of *Lecture Notes in Computer Science*, pages 167–182. Springer, 2005.

[344] P. Revesz. The constraint database approach to software verification. In *Proc. 8th International Conference on Verification, Model Checking, and Abstract Interpretation*, volume 4349 of *Lecture Notes in Computer Science*, pages 329–345. Springer, 2007.

[345] P. Revesz. Constraint databases, spatial. In S. Shekhar and H. Xiong, editors, *Encyclopedia of GIS*, pages 157–160. Springer, 2008.

[346] P. Revesz. Robust affine-invariant similarity measures for patterned triangles. In *Proc. 10th IASTED International Conference on Computer Graphics and Imaging*, pages 292–297. ACTA Press, 2008.

[347] P. Revesz and M. Cai. Efficient querying of periodic spatiotemporal objects. In *Proc. 6th International Conference on Principles and Practice of Constraint Programming*, volume 1894 of *Lecture Notes in Computer Science*, pages 396–410. Springer, 2000.

[348] P. Revesz and M. Cai. Efficient querying of periodic spatio-temporal databases. *Annals of Mathematics and Artificial Intelligence*, 36(4):437–457, 2002.

[349] P. Revesz, R. Chen, P. Kanjamala, Y. Li, Y. Liu, and Y. Wang. The MLPQ/GIS constraint database system. In *Proc. ACM SIGMOD International Conference on Management of Data*. ACM Press, 2000.

[350] P. Revesz and Y. Chen. Efficient aggregation over moving objects. In *Proc. 10th International Symposium on Temporal Representation and Reasoning*, pages 118–127. IEEE Press, 2003.

[351] P. Revesz and Y. Li. MLPQ: A linear constraint database system with aggregate operators. In *Proc. 1st International Database Engineering and Applications Symposium*, pages 132–7. IEEE Press, 1997.

[352] P. Revesz and T. Triplet. Reclassification of linearly classified data using constraint databases. In P. Atzeni, A. Caplinskas, and H. Jaakkola, editors, *Proc. 12th Conference on Advances in Databases and Information Systems*, volume 5207 of *Lecture Notes in Computer Science*, pages 231–245. Springer, 2008.

[353] P. Revesz and T. Triplet. Classification integration and reclassification using constraint databases. *Artificial Intelligence in Medicine*, 42(3), 2010.

[354] P. Revesz and S. Wu. Spatiotemporal reasoning about epidemiological data. *Artificial Intelligence in Medicine*, 38(2):157–70, 2006.

[355] G. D. Richards. An elliptical growth model of forest fire fronts and its numerical solution. *International Journal of Numerical Methods Engineering*, 30:1163–79, 1990.

[356] P. Rigaux, M. Scholl, and V. Agnés. *Introduction to Spatial Databases: Applications to GIS*. Morgan Kaufmann, 2002.

[357] R. Rothermel. Modelling fire behavior. In *Proc. International Conference on Forest Fire Research*, pages 1–19. Coimbra, 1990.

[358] A. Salamon. Implementation of a database system with Boolean algebra constraints. Master's thesis, University of Nebraska-Lincoln, May 1998.

[359] S. Saltenis, C.S. Jensen, S.T. Leutenegger, and M.A. Lopez. Indexing the positions of continuously moving objects. In *Proc. ACM SIGMOD International Conference on Management of Data*, pages 331–42. ACM Press, 2000.

[360] H. Samet. *The Design and Analysis of Spatial Data Structures*. Addison-Wesley, 1990.

[361] H. Samet. *Foundations of Multidimensional and Metric Data Structures*. Morgan Kaufmann, Francisco, CA, 2005.

[362] V. Saraswat. *Concurrent Programming Languages*. PhD thesis, Carnegie-Mellon University, 1989.

[363] H. J. Schek and A. Wolf. From extensible databases to interoperability between multiple databases and GIS applications. In D. J. Abel and B. C. Ooi, editors, *International Symposium on Large Spatial Databases*, volume 692 of *Lecture Notes in Computer Science*, pages 207–38. Springer, 1993.

[364] H. Schneider and G. P. Barker. *Matrices and Linear Algebra*. Dover Publications, 2nd edition, 1973.

[365] M. Scholl and A. Voisard. Object-oriented database systems for geographic applications: An experiment with O2. In F. Bancilhon, C. Delobel, and P. C. Kanellakis, editors, *The O2 Book*, pages 585–618. Morgan Kaufmann, 1992.

[366] A. Schrijver. *Theory of Linear and Integer Programming*. John Wiley and Sons, 1986.

[367] L. Segoufin and V. Vianu. Querying spatial databases via topological invariants. *Journal of Computer and System Sciences*, 61(2):270–301, 2000.

[368] D. Seipel and U. Geske. Solving cardinality constraints in (constraint) logic programming. In *Proceedings of the International Workshop on Functional and Logic Programming*, 2001.

[369] T. Sellis, N. Roussopoulos, and C. Faloutsos. The R^+-tree: A dynamic index for multi-dimensional objects. In *Proc. IEEE International Conference on Very Large Databases*, pages 507–18, 1987.

[370] J. Setubal and J Meidanis. *Introduction to Computational Molecular Biology*. PWS Publishing, Boston, 1997.

[371] J. Shanmugasundaram, E. Shekita, J. Kiernan, R. Krishnamurthy, E. Viglas, J. Naughton, and I. T. Rinov. A general technique for querying XML documents using a relational d atabase system. In *SIGMOD Record*, pages 20–26, 2001.

[372] J. Shanmugasundaram, K. Tufte, C. Zhang, G. He, D. J. DeWitt, and J. F. Naughton. Relational databases for querying XML documents: Limitations and opportunities. In *Proc. IEEE International Conference on Very Large Databases*, pages 302–314. Morgan Kaufmann, 1999.

[373] J. Sharma. Oracle8i spatial: Experiences with extensible databases. In *An Oracle Technical White Paper*, May 1999.

[374] S. Shekhar and H. Xiong, editors. *Encyclopedia of GIS*. Springer, 2008.

[375] D. Shepard. A two-dimensional interpolation function for irregularly-spaced data. In *Proceedings of the ACM National Conference*, pages 517–524. ACM Press, 1968.

[376] J. R. Shewchuk. Tetrahedral mesh generation by delaunay refinement. In *Proc. 14th Annual ACM Symposium on Computational Geometry*, pages 86–95. ACM Press, 1998.

[377] A. Silberschatz, H. Korth, and S. Sudarshan. *Database System Concepts*. McGraw-Hill, 6th edition, 2010.

[378] A. P. Sistla, O. Wolfson, S. Chamberlain, and S. Dao. Modeling and querying moving objects. In *Proc. 13th IEEE International Conference on Data Engineering*, pages 422–32. IEEE Press, 1997.

[379] S. Smoliar and H. Zhang. Content-based video indexing and retrieval. *IEEE Multimedia Magazine*, 1(2):62–72, 1994.

[380] R. T. Snodgrass, editor. *The TSQL2 Temporal Query Language*. Kluwer, 1995.

[381] D. Srivastava. Subsumption and indexing in constraint query languages with linear arithmetic constraints. *Annals of Mathematics and Artificial Intelligence*, 8(3–4):315–43, 1993.

[382] D. Srivastava, R. Ramakrishnan, and P. Revesz. Constraint objects. In *Proc. 2nd International Workshop on Principles and Practice of Constraint Programming*, volume 874 of *Lecture Notes in Computer Science*, pages 218–28. Springer, 1994.

[383] J. Star and J. Estes. *Geographic Information Systems: An Introduction*. Prentice-Hall, 1989.

[384] A. P. Stolboushkin and M. A. Taitslin. Safe stratified Datalog with integer order does not have syntax. *ACM Transactions on Database Systems*, 23(1):100–9, 1998.

[385] M. H. Stone. The theory of representations of boolean algebras. *Transactions of the American Mathematical Society*, 40(1):37–111, 1936.

[386] G. Strang. *Linear Algebra and Its Applications*. Academic Press, 1976.

[387] M. Stricker and M. Orengo. Similarity of color images. In *Proc. SPIE Conference on Storage and Retrieval for Image and Video Databases III*, volume 2420, pages 381–92, 1995.

[388] P. J. Stuckey and S. Sudarshan. Compiling query constraints. In *Proc. ACM Symposium on Principles of Database Systems*, pages 56–68. ACM Press, 1994.

[389] S. Sudarshan, D. Srivastava, R. Ramakrishnan, and C. Beeri. Extending the well-founded and valid model semantics for aggregation. In *International Logic Programming Symposium*, pages 114–26, 1993.

[390] J. Sun, Y. Tao, D. Papadias, and G. Kollios. Spatio-temporal join selectivity. *Information Systems*, 31(8):793–813, 2006.

[391] P. Svensson and H. Zhexue. Geo-sal: a query language for spatial data analysis. In *Proc. Advances in Spatial Databases*, volume 525 of *Lecture Notes in Computer Science*, pages 119–40. Springer, 1991.

[392] M. Swain and D. Ballard. Color indexing. *International Journal of Computer Vision*, 7(1):11–32, 1991.

[393] A. Tansel, J. Clifford, S. Gadia, S. Jajodia, A. Segev, and R. T. Snodgrass, editors. *Temporal Databases: Theory, Design, and Implementation*. Benjamin/Cummings, 1993.

[394] A. Tarski. *A Decision Method for Elementary Algebra and Geometry*. University of California Press, Berkeley, 1951.

[395] J. Tayeb, O. Ulusoy, and O. Wolfson. A quadtree-based dynamic attribute indexing method. *The Computer Journal*, 41(3):185–200, 1998.

[396] T. J. Teorey. *Database Modeling and Design*. Morgan Kaufmann, 3rd edition, 1999.

[397] B. Thalheim. *Entity-Relationship Modeling: Foundations of Database Technology*. Springer, 2000.

[398] D. Toman. *Foundations of Temporal Query Languages*. PhD thesis, Kansas State University, 1995.

[399] D. Toman. Point vs. Interval-based Query Languages for Temporal Databases. In *Proc. ACM Symposium on Principles of Database Systems*, pages 58–67, 1996.

[400] D. Toman. Point-based Temporal Extensions of SQL. In *International Conference on Deductive and Object-Oriented Databases*, 1997.

[401] D. Toman. Point-Based Temporal Extensions of SQL and Their Efficient Implementation. In O. Etzion, S. Jajodia, and S. Sripada, editors, *Temporal Databases: Research and Practice*, Lecture Notes in Computer Science, pages 211–237. Springer, 1998.

[402] D. Toman and J. Chomicki. Datalog with integer periodicity constraints. *Journal of Logic Programming*, 35(3):263–90, 1998.

[403] D. Toman, R. Ramakrishnan, and P. Stuckey. Memoing evaluation for constraint extensions of Datalog. *Constraints*, 2:337–359, 1997.

[404] F. C. D. Tsai. Robust affine invariant matching with application to line features. In *Proc. Conference on Computer Vision and Pattern Recognition*, pages 393–9. IEEE Press, 1993.

[405] S. Tsur, F. Olken, and D. Naor. Deductive databases for genome mapping. In *Proc. NACLP Workshop on Deductive Databases*, 1993.

[406] S. Tsur and C. Zaniolo. LDL: A logic-based data-language. In *Proc. IEEE International Conference on Very Large Databases*, pages 33–41. IEEE Press, 1986.

[407] T. Turmeaux and C. Vrain. Learning in constraint databases. volume 1721 of *Lecture Notes in Computer Science*, pages 196–207. Springer, 1999.

[408] J. D. Ullman. *Principles of Database and Knowledge-Base Systems*. Computer Science Press, 1989.

[409] J. D. Ullman. Information integration using logical views. In F. N. Afrati and P. G. Kolaitis, editors, *International Conference on Database Theory*, volume 1186 of *Lecture Notes in Computer Science*, pages 19–40. Springer, 1997.

[410] K. Vadaparty. On the power of rule-based query languages for nested data models. *Journal of Logic Programming*, 21(3):155–75, 1994.

[411] L. Van Den Dries. Alfred Tarski's elimination theory for real closed fields. *Journal of Symbolic Logic*, 53:7–19, 1988.

[412] R. van der Meyden. Recursively indefinite databases. *Theoretical Computer Science*, 116(1):151–94, 1993.

[413] R. van der Meyden. The complexity of querying indefinite data about linearly ordered domains. *Journal of Computer and System Sciences*, 54(1):113–35, 1997.

[414] A. Van Gelder, K. A. Ross, and J. S. Schlipf. The well-founded semantics for general logic programs. *Journal of the ACM*, 38(3):620–50, 1991.

[415] P. Van Hentenryck. *Constraint Satisfaction in Logic Programming*. MIT Press, 1989.

[416] V. Vapnik. *The Nature of Statistical Learning Theory*. Springer, 1995.

[417] M. Vardi. The complexity of relational query languages. In *Proc. 14th ACM Symposium on the Theory of Computing*, pages 137–45. ACM Press, 1982.

[418] M. Veach, P. Coddington, and G. C. Cox. BURN: A simulation of forest fire propagation. In *Project Report for the Northeast Parallel Architectures Center*, 1994.

[419] M. B. Vilain and H. Kautz. Constraint propagation algorithms for temporal reasoning. In *Proc. National Conference on Artificial Intelligence*, 1986.

[420] K. Wang. *Affine-Invariant Moment Method of Three-Dimensional Object Identification*. PhD thesis, Syracuse University, 1977.

[421] X. S. Wang, S. Jajodia, and V. S. Subrahmanian. Temporal modules: An approach toward federated temporal databases. In *Proc. ACM SIGMOD International Conference on Management of Data*, pages 227–36, 1993.

[422] J. Warmer and A. Kleppe. *The Object Constraint Language: Precise Modeling with UML*. ACM Press, 1998.

[423] T. C. Waugh and R. G. Healey. The GEOVIEW design: A relational database approach to geographical data handling. *International Journal of Geographic Information Systems*, 1(2):101–18, 1987.

[424] D. Weinstein, K. Green, J. Campbell, and M. Finney. Fire growth modeling in an integrated GIS environment. In *Proc. Environmental System Research Institute User Conference*, 1995.

[425] M. Werman and D. Weinshall. Similarity and affine invariant distances between 2D point sets. *IEEE Transactions on Pattern Analysis and Machine Intelligence*, 17:810–14, 1995.

[426] H. P. Williams. Fourier-Motzkin elimination extension to integer programming problems. *Journal of Combinatorial Theory (A)*, 21:118–23, 1976.

[427] S. Wolfram. Cellular automata as models of complexity. *Nature*, 311:419–24, 1984.

[428] O. Wolfson, A. Sistla, B. Xu, J. Zhou, and S. Chamberlain. DOMINO: Databases for moving objects tracking. In *Proc. ACM SIGMOD International Conference on Management of Data*, pages 547–9, 1999.

[429] P. Wolper and B. Boigelot. An automata-theoretic approach to Presburger arithmetic constraints. In *Proc. Static Analysis Symposium*, volume 983 of *Lecture Notes in Computer Science*, pages 21–32. Springer, 1995.

[430] G. K-S. Wong, J. Yu, E. C. Thayer, and M. V. Olson. Multiple-complete-digest restriction fragment mapping: Generating sequence-ready maps for large-scale DNA sequencing. *Proceedings of the National Academy of Sciences, USA*, 94(10):5225–30, 1997.

[431] M. F. Worboys. A unified model for spatial and temporal information. *Computer Journal*, 37(1):26–34, 1994.

[432] M. F. Worboys. *GIS: A Computing Perspective*. Taylor & Francis, 1995.

[433] M. Yannakakis. Expressing combinatorial optimization problems by linear programs. In *Proc. ACM Symposium on Theory of Computation*, pages 223–8. ACM Press, 1988.

[434] R. H. C. Yap. A constraint logic programming framework for constructing DNA restriction maps. *Artificial Intelligence in Medicine*, 5:447–64, 1993.

[435] M. Yuan. Wildfire conceptual modeling for building GIS space-time models. In *Proc. URISA Conference on Geographic and Land Information Systems*, pages 859–68, 1994.

[436] M. Yuan. Modeling semantical, temporal and spatial information in geographic information systems. In *Geographic Information Research: Bridging the Atlantic*, pages 334–7. Taylor & Francis, 1996.

[437] D. Zhang, V. J. Tsotras, and D. Gunopulos. Efficient aggregation over objects with extent. In *ACM Symposium on Principles of Database Systems*, pages 121–132. ACM Press, 2002.

[438] X. Zhang and M. Ozsoyoglu. On efficient reasoning with implication constraints. In *International Conference on Deductive and Object-Oriented Databases*, volume 760 of *Lecture Notes in Computer Science*, pages 236–52. Springer, 1993.

[439] H. Zhu, J. Su, and O. H. Ibarra. An index structure for spatial joins in linear constraint databases. In *IEEE International Conference on Data Engineering*, pages 636–43. IEEE Press, 1999.

[440] O. C. Zienkiewics and R. L. Taylor. *Finite Element Method, Vol. 1, The Basis*. Butterworth Heinemann, London, 2000.

[441] E. G. Zurflueh. Applications of two-dimensional linear wavelength filtering. *Geophysics*, 32:1015–1035, 1967.

Index

ε-recognition safe, 557

abstract interpretation, 689
addition-bound matrix, 685
affine transformation, 112, 137, 138
affine-invariant, 137, 140
aggregate operator
    Avg, 29
    Count, 29
    Max, 29
    Min, 29
    Sum, 29
Allen's relation, 67, 68
animation, 287, 548
    color cartogram, 548
    constraint database, 549
    isometric color band, 540
    MLPQ, 287
    naive method, 549
    parametric method, 549
    parametric rectangles, 548
    volume cartogram, 548
antisymmetry, 222
approximation, 435
    piecewise linear, 436, 460
approximation module, 264
area, 255
atomic constraint, 56, 57
    arithmetic atomic constraint, 56
    boolean atomic constraint, 224

atomless, 580, 677
augment, 222

before operation, 67
bioinformatics, 179
block, 301, 610
Boolean algebra, 219
    atomless, 677
    constant, 223, 609
    disjunctive normal form, 226
    free, 227
    ground term, 223
    interpretation, 220
    interpretation function, 227
    minterm normal form, 226
    monotone term, 223
    sets, 220
    Stone's representation theorem, 220
    term, 223
bottom-up constraint evaluation, 596
bound, 56

cadastral, 327
certification, 560
    acyclicity, 562
    constant propagation, 560
    monotonicity, 561
    tightening bound, 562

tightening coefficient, 562
    variable independence, 561
    vector addition system, 563
closed form, 257
closed world assumption, 154
closed-form safe, 555
coefficient, 56, 576
collide, 301
color cartogram, 547
combined complexity, 660
common basis, 385, 402, 406–408, 411
complement, 591, 626
complexity class, 655, 659
    EXP, 659
    iEXP, 659
    LOGSPACE, 659
    NC, 659
    P, 659
    PSPACE, 659
complexity of Datalog, 660
computational complexity, 655, 672,
        675, 681
computer security
    trust management, 430
configuration, 375
constraint automata, 361
constraint data model, 43, 58, 61
constraint deductive database, 258
constraint instantiation, 595
constraint logic programming, 258
constraint proof-based, 595
constraint relation, 58
constraint rule application, 595
constraint tuple, 58, 105
contains operation, 67
contour map, 284
counting, 661

data abstraction, 3, 60, 61, 571
    constraint level, 61
    logical level, 61
    physical level, 61
    view level, 60
data complexity, 660
data compression, 460
data fusion
    constraint database, 430

data integration, 417
    constraint database, 427
data interpolation, 461
data model, 3
data warehouse, 432
database scheme, 16
Datalog, 235, 240
    aggregation, 254
    Boolean algebra of sets, 242
    evaluation, 633
    instantiation, 246
    least fixpoint, 252
    least fixpoint semantics, 253
    naive evaluation, 339, 341, 647
    negation, 254
    proof tree, 249, 250
    proof-based semantics, 246
    recursive query, 254, 257
    rule, 235
        body, 235
        head, 235
    semi-naive evaluation, 339, 341
    stratified, 254
    stratified query, 257
De Morgan's law, 58, 627
decision support system, 486, 492
Delauney refinement, 476
deoxyribonucleic acid, 179
depends_on relation, 254
difference, 300
DISCO, 335
disjunctive normal form, 626

entity relationship diagram, 351
environmental modeling, 485
equality matrix, 634
equals operation, 67
error state, 695
error tolerance, 460, 469
Euclidean distance, 251
evaluation, 161, 168
evaluation safe, 556
existential quantifier elimination, 573
existentially quantified variable, 361
export conversion module, 264
expression complexity, 660

false hit, 515
feasible region, 594
federated database, 432
finite element methods, 476
first-order formula, 667
Fourier series, 476

gap-graph, 621
gap-order, 56–58, 558, 568, 574
geographic data, 171
graph
    undirected, 242
graph-based implementation, 621

half-addition constraint, 56, 57, 559,
    575
halting problem, 659
Hamiltonia cycle, 242
hierarchical databases, 356

immediate consequence operator, 252
incomplete information, 153
indefinite temporal database, 71
index structure, 533
indexing, 137, 501
infinite relational database, 571, 591
instance, 16, 43
interoperability, 385
    data interoperability, 385, 411
    query interoperability, 402
interpolation, 435, 439, 487
    spatio-temporal, 476
interval-based queries, 73
inverse distance weighting, 476
isometric color band, 537–539

kriging, 476

least fixpoint, 596, 597, 599–601
linear interpolation, 436
linear programming
    choice-based, 315
linear repeating point, 70
linear transformation, 112
logical level, 61, 571

map overlay, 238, 278
marked null value, 71

matrix-based implementation, 621
maximum, 256
MBPR, 502
mediator system, 432
meets operation, 67
merge, 222, 624
metric interval relation, 68
minimum, 256
minimum bounding parametric
    rectangle, 502
minterm, 226, 228, 669
    ground minterm, 670
    minterm equality constraint, 670
    minterm upper bound constraint,
        670
    monotone minterm, 670
    order constraint, 670
    variable minterm, 670
MLPQ, 61
    area, 280
    block, 301
    buffer, 281
    collide, 301
    complement, 280
    difference, 300
    draw polygon, 281
    intersection, 279
    linear programming, 261, 315
    moving objects, 262
    similarity, 281
    union, 280
moving objects, 171
moving point, 533
multiset, 186

negation, 257
nested queries, 32, 54
network data model, 37
network databases, 356
normal form, 576, 668, 669
null value, 173

object-oriented databases, 356
open world assumption, 154
over-approximation, 689
overlap operation, 67

parametric affine transformation, 120, 412
parametric evaluation, 608
parametric linear transformation, 120
parametric rectangle, 296, 487, 501
parametric rectangles, 171, 296, 610
parametric scaling, 120
parametric translation, 120
parametric triangulated irregular network, 442
piecewise linear function, 460, 462
piecewise linear interpolation, 460
point-based queries, 77
pointizable interval relations, 69
polynomial constraint, 560, 568
positive linear, 576
positive stochastic matrix, 565
possible world assumption, 155
powerset, 221
PR-tree, 501, 511, 513, 514
    deletion, 514
    insertion, 510
    node splitting, 512
precision, 436
predictive modeling, 485
proof-based semantics, 595
propositional databases, 7

qualitative interval relation, 68
quantifier elimination, 572, 668
query evaluation module, 263
query optimization, 641

reachable configuration, 361
recall, 436
recognition safe, 557
reduction rule, 361, 373
refinement query, 153, 156, 167, 168
reflexivity, 222
relational algebra, 18, 23, 46, 611, 641
    difference, 21
    intersection, 20
    natural join, 22
    optimization, 641
    product, 21
    project, 18
    rename, 20
    select, 19
    union, 20

relational algebra operator, 591
relational calculus, 667
relational data model, 15, 34, 37, 43, 44, 55
relational database, 15
relational databases, 356
representation module, 262
restriction enzyme, 181
rule body, 156
rule head, 156

safe query language, 555
safety
    restriction, 558
safety level, 555
    ϵ-recognition, 557
    approximation, 557
    closed-form, 555
    evaluation, 556
    recognition, 557
satisfiability, 624
satisfiable, 57, 590, 592
scaling, 112
search, 509
set grouping, 254, 255
set logic databases, 205
set-graph, 638–640, 651
shape function, 476
shortcut, 624
simplification, 372
singleton set, 242
spatial attribute, 255
spatio-temporal, 2
splines, 476
stratified Datalog query, 257
subset sum, 239
successor relation, 661, 662
syllogism, 205

temporal database, 67
temporal intervals, 67
tetrahedral mesh, 476
topological data, 274
TQuel, 70
transitivity, 222
translation, 112
trend surface, 476

triangulated irregular network, 283, 331, 436
    parametric, 537
tuple, 58
Turing machine, 655
    time-bounded, 659

undecidability, 659
universal constraint object, 153
unsafe, 557
update module, 264
upper bound constraint, 574, 599
urban sprawl, 129

valid, 57
valid time, 70
value-by-area cartogram, 545
    hybrid method, 546

parallel method, 545
    serial method, 546
verification, 685
visualization, 485
visualization module, 263
VML, 171
volume, 255
volume cartogram, 547
Voronoi diagram, 107

WeNiVIS, 311
widening operator, 687
    l-u-widening, 687
wrapper, 426

XML, 168, 171

zero element, 222

Colour Plate Section

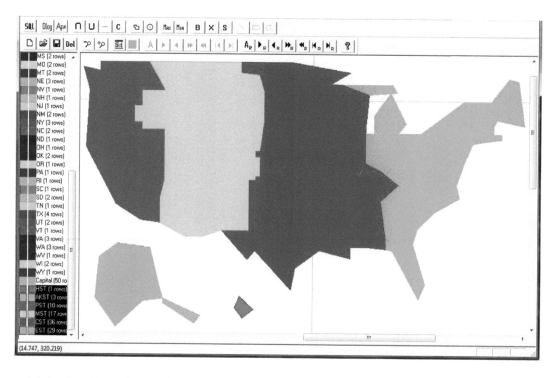

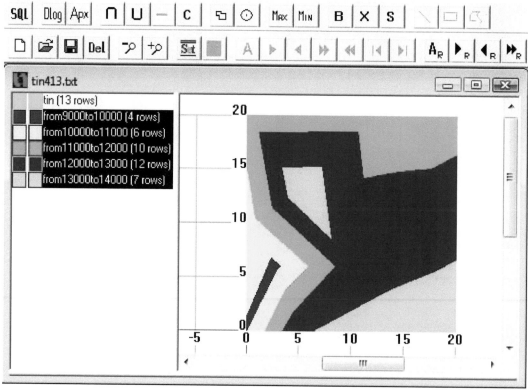

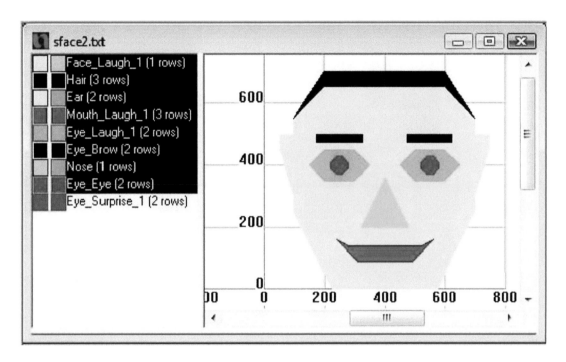

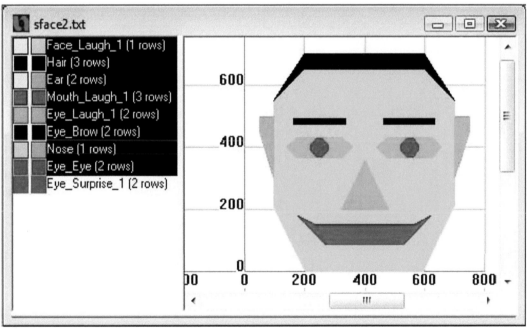

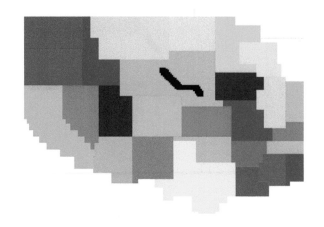

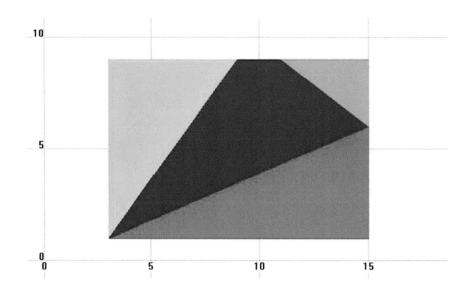

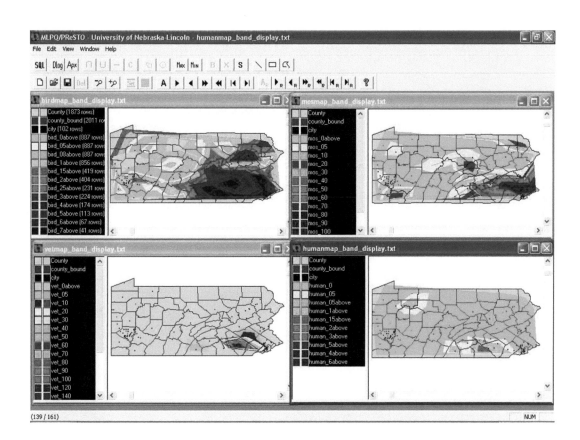

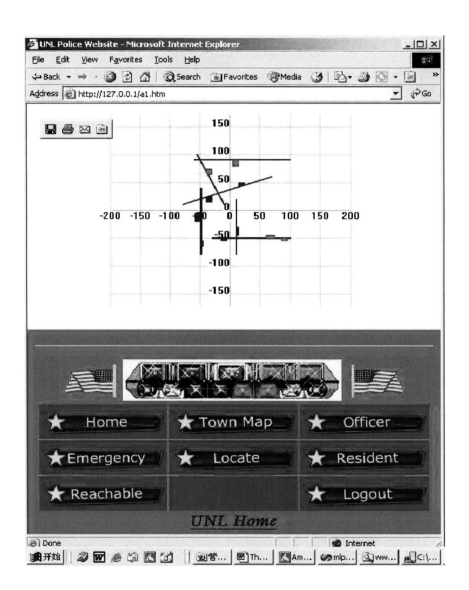

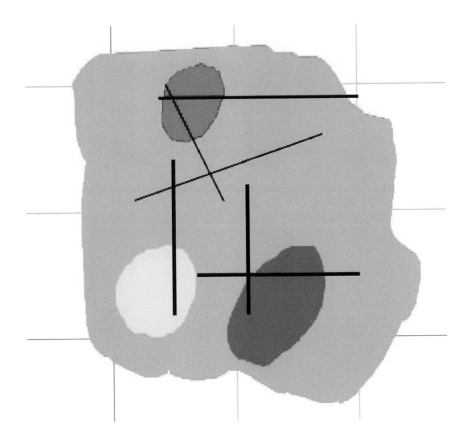

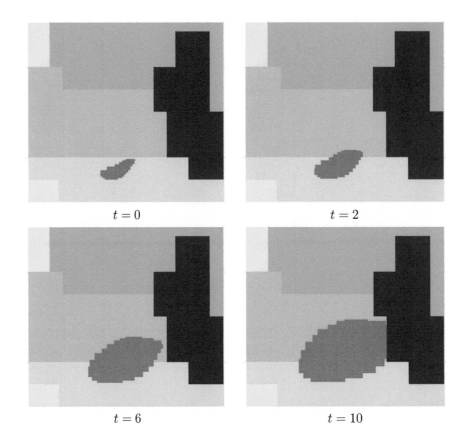

$t = 0$ $t = 2$

$t = 6$ $t = 10$

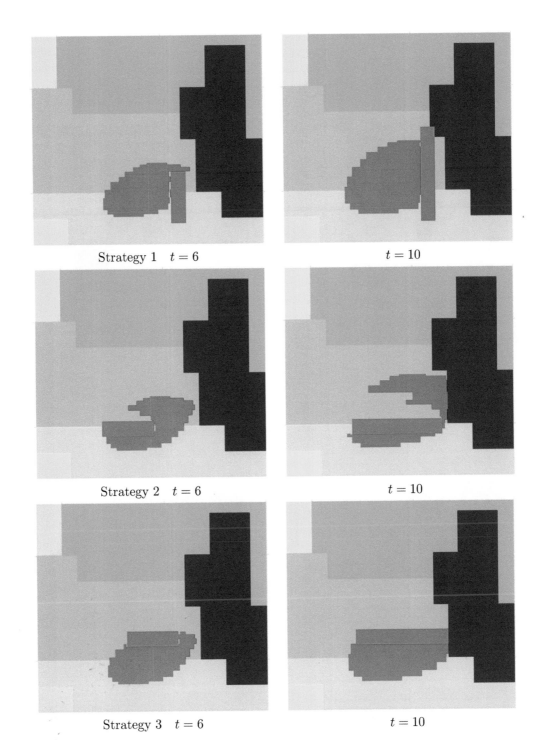

Strategy 1 $t = 6$ $t = 10$

Strategy 2 $t = 6$ $t = 10$

Strategy 3 $t = 6$ $t = 10$

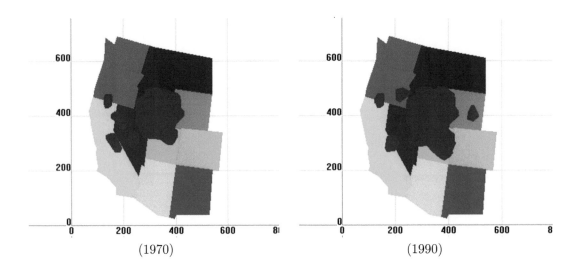

(1970)   (1990)

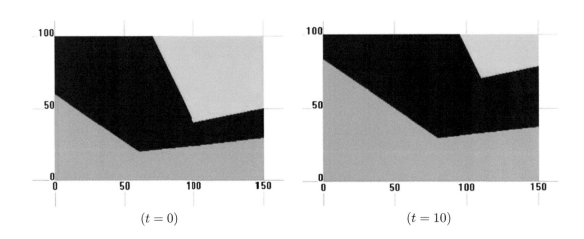

$(t = 0)$ $(t = 10)$